Agnolo Bronzino:
The Muse of Florence

Also by New Academia Publishing:

SELF-PORTRAITS BY WOMEN PAINTERS,
Liana De Girolami Cheney, Alicia Craig Faxon and Kathleen Russo

VASARI'S LIFE AND LIVES: The First Art Historian, by Einar Rud.
Editor and Preface by Liana De Girolami Cheney

GIORGIO VASARI: Artistic and Emblematic Manifestations,
by Liana De Girolami Cheney

*BREAKING NEW GROUND IN ART HISTORY: A Festschrift in Honor of
Alicia Craig Faxon.* Margaret A. Hanni, ed.

Read an excerpt at www.newacademia.com

Agnolo Bronzino: The Muse of Florence

Edited by
Liana De Girolami Cheney

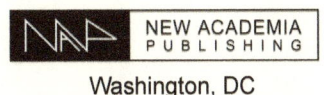

NEW ACADEMIA
PUBLISHING

Washington, DC

Library of Congress Control Number: 2014940349
ISBN 978-0-9915047-7-0 paperback (alk. paper)

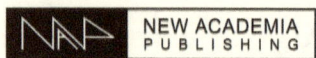 NEW ACADEMIA PUBLISHING

New Academia Publishing
PO Box 27420, Washington, DC 20038-7420
info@newacademia.com - www.newacademia.com

In Honor of Professor Craig Hugh Smyth

Contents

Illustrations

Front Cover
Agnolo Bronzino, *Head of a Woman* (det.), *Crossing of the Red Sea*

Preface
Fig. 1. Craig Hugh Smyth (1915–2006), photograph (2000)

PART ONE: INTRODUCTION
Fig. 1. Agnolo Bronzino, *Self-Portrait* (det.), *Descent from the Cross*

PART TWO: RELIGIOUS AND DEVOTIONAL PAINTINGS
Lynette M.F. Bosch, Orthodoxy and Heterodoxy in Agnolo Bronzino's
  Paintings for Bartolomeo and Lucrezia Panciatichi
Fig. 1. Agnolo Bronzino, *Portrait of Bartolomeo Panciatichi*
Fig. 2. Agnolo Bronzino, *Portrait of Lucrezia Panciatichi*
Fig. 3. Agnolo Bronzino, *Portrait of Lucrezia Panciatichi* (det.)
Fig. 4. Agnolo Bronzino, *Panciatichi Holy Family*
Fig. 5. Agnolo Bronzino, *Crucified Christ*
Fig. 6. Agnolo Bronzino, *The Madonna and Child with Saint John the Baptist
  and Elizabeth (or Saint Anne) (Madonna Hertford)*
Fig. 7. Agnolo Bronzino, *Holy Family with Saint Anne and Young John the
  Baptist*
Fig. 8. Agnolo Bronzino, *Saint Sebastian*

Elena Aloia, Culture, Faith, and Love: Bartolomeo Panciatichi
Fig. 1. Agnolo Bronzino, *Portrait of Bartolomeo Panciatichi*
Fig. 2. Agnolo Bronzino, *Portrait of Lucrezia Panciatichi*
Fig. 3. Agnolo Bronzino, *Panciatichi Holy Family*
Fig. 4. Panciatichi Family Gravestone
Fig. 5. Panciatichi Family Coat of Arms
Fig. 6. Ceramelli Papiani's Genealogy of the Panciatichi Family (Table IV)
Fig. 7. Agnolo Bronzino, *The Madonna and Child with Saint John the Baptist
  and Elizabeth (or Saint Anne) (Madonna Hertford)*
Fig. 8. Agnolo Bronzino, *Holy Family with Saint Anne and Young John the
  Baptist*
Fig. 9. Agnolo Bronzino, *Holy Family* (Stroganoff)
Fig. 10. Villa Corsini, *Mezzamonte*, Florence
Fig. 11. Villa Corsini, Mezzamonte, Florence, aerial photo

Foreword

Jan L. de Jong, Associate Professor of Art History
Institute for the History of Art and Architecture
University of Groningen, The Netherlands

The year that sees the release of George Clooney's film *The Monuments Men* is also witness to the publication of this present book, in honor of Craig Hugh Smyth. Smyth did active service during the Second World War as an officer of MFAA (Monuments, Fine Arts, and Archives program), whose members were known as Monuments Men. After the surrender of Germany, he was named director of the U.S. Army's Central Art Collecting Point in Munich, where he was tasked with gathering, saving, and redistributing many well- and less well-known works of art. He personally described his experiences in the Gerson lecture that he delivered at the University of Groningen in the Netherlands, in 1986.[1]

Smyth was not only responsible for the survival of many works of art that had disappeared during the war. He was also crucial for the "rediscovery" and revival of the work and reputation of the Italian artist Agnolo Bronzino (1503–72). Once a prominent painter at the Medici court in Florence, Bronzino was soon forgotten, and his fame was quickly eclipsed after his death. When Smyth wrote his first article on this artist, in 1949, he had to deal with publications that were, with one exception, more than fifteen years old, while the total number of publications dealing with Bronzino that had appeared since 1800 was less than fifty.[2] Smyth's article was followed by two books on Bronzino: one his dissertation in 1955, and the other on Bronzino as a draughtsman, in 1971. It is largely thanks to these books that Bronzino's work became better known and was extensively studied by a new generation of art historians, resulting in more than 200 publications since the year 2000 alone and a large exhibition in 2010–11, visited by more than 140,000 visitors.[3]

This intensified study of Bronzino's work has resulted in a picture of the artist that is at once more complete and more complex.

Attention is no longer focused on questions of dates, influences, and attributions but also takes into account such aspects as his poetry, his patrons, his position at the Medici court, and his religious leanings. In the current book, Liana De Girolami Cheney has brought together a number of studies by experts on the life and works of Bronzino, which build on observations and analyses from the last decades. They critically review recent interpretations and offer new insights and information. Sixty-five years after Smyth's first publication, they testify to the importance of Agnolo Bronzino, who is now largely recognized as a major artist of the sixteenth century in Italy.

NOTES

1. Repatriation of art from the collecting point in Munich after World War II. Background and beginnings, with reference especially to the Netherlands (Maarssen/The Hague: Schwartz/SDU, 1988).

2. Smyth lists the "principal modern accounts of Bronzino's career" in n. 2 of his article "The Earliest Works of Bronzino," *The Art Bulletin* 31, no. 3 (1949), 184–209. The number of fewer than fifty publications on Pontormo between 1800 and 1949 is based on a count of the publications listed in the Kubikat-catalogue, the collective catalogue of four of the leading German scholarly research institutes in the field of art history (http://aleph.mpg.de/F?func=file&file_name=find-b&local_base=kub01).

3. The count of publications on Bronzino since 2000 is based on the Kubikat-catalogue (see above, n. 2). The 2010–11 exhibition on Bronzino took place in Palazzo Strozzi, Florence.

Preface

Liana De Girolami Cheney

Agnolo Bronzino: The Muse of Florence is a collection of essays on Bronzino in honor of Professor Craig Hugh Smyth (1915–2006), who was a pioneer art historian in the field of art conservation, art historical education, and Mannerism. His seminal research on Agnolo Bronzino's art, particularly portraiture, contributed to the understanding of Manieroso portraiture in art as a subject of its own merit.

These studies investigate several art historical issues in the paintings and writings of Bronzino: the importance of his achievements and artistic status in the sixteenth century; his literary expression in poems, sonnets, and rhymes, appropriating the ancient *ut pictura poesis*; his role in the establishment of a decorative cycles convention; and his ability to connect courtly patronage and Florentine culture as a humanistic pursuit. With these artistic accomplishments, Bronzino is the embodiment of a Florentine muse.

The essays introduce the reader to Bronzino's religious and secular paintings, which reveal the development of the Maniera style throughout the Cinquecento and so enhanced artistic beauty in the court of Tuscany. Iconographically, he invents a visual imagery with poetic conceits whose *clavis interpretandi* denotes the cultural milieu of his patronage.

The book is composed of an introduction containing a general biography and bibliography of Professor Craig Hugh Smyth, followed by three parts. Part one includes a brief biography on Agnolo Bronzino, focusing on the historical placement of the commissions discussed in the essays of this volume, followed by a historical biography and interpretation of Bronzino's career by his biographer, artistic colleague, and friend Giorgio Vasari. Part two focuses on Bronzino's devotional and religious paintings, in particular, on the patronage of the Medici and Panciatichi families, noting the ability of Bronzino to capture the spirituality of the time as well as project his own religiosity. And part three analyzes Bronzino's secular paintings, including some portraits as well as allegorical paintings, crystallizing his artistic, emblematic, and poetical versatility.

Bronzino's theory of art (nature, classical, and beauty) and criteria for creating art (imitation, invention, and judgment) are articulated in his imagery, especially in his artistic commentary on the mastery of painting over sculpture at the *Accademia del Disegno*. In Florence, the culture of humanism and the demands of courtly and humanistic patrons imbued Bronzino with an intellectual and philosophical approach to his art. His achievement in making of pictures and poetry an instrument of beauty and thought personifies him as a Florentine virtuoso.

The purpose of this book, as Professor Craig Hugh Smyth visualizes in his scholarship, is to provide for students of fine arts, art history, and the humanities, as well as interested readers of European cultural history and decorative arts, an insight and understanding of sixteenth-century Italian art through the eyes and mind of an accomplished artist and writer of the time, *Il Bronzino*.

Acknowledgments

The essays developed in this book first took shape in a session in Honor of Professor Craig Hugh Smyth at the annual Renaissance Society Conference in New York City in 2004. The innovative presentations of my colleagues Donna Bilak, Lynette Bosch, Michael Giordano, and Leatrice Mendelsohn along with the collaboration of Elena Aloia, Thomas MacPherson, and Massimiliano Rossi contributed to the formation of this tome. I am humbly in their debt. I am also grateful for the comments of Elizabeth Cropper, Robert Gaston, and Janet Cox-Rearick, and especially of Jan L. de Jong.

My appreciation is also extended to all photographic companies, art collectors, galleries, and museums that permitted the reproductions of images included in this book, in particular, to Villa I Tatti, Harvard University Center for Italian Renaissance Studies, Florence, for providing the photograph of Professor Craig Hugh Smyth and giving permission for its reproduction. Gratitude is extended to Geneseo Foundation, SUNY at Geneseo, Faculty Publications Support, for granting assistance in the reproduction of the color cover image as well as many of Bronzino's pictures here reproduced.

My deepest intellectual debt, however, is to Professor Craig Hugh Smyth, who, like Angolo Bronzino, was a *musa inspiratrice* for understanding *Mannerism and Maniera*.

L'ingengo intanto mi si raccomanda,
Che senza aiuto a cose sì soprano
Teme il qualche erbaccia una grillanda.
Il Bronzino, *In Lode della Galea*, Capitolo Secondo

Liana De Girolami Cheney
January 2014

General Biography and Bibliography on Professor Craig Hugh Smyth

Liana De Girolami Cheney

Biography

> A Socratic teacher, a humanist scholar, a diplomatic genius,
> and a virtuoso musician[1]

Craig Hugh Smyth (1915–2006) was a pioneer in the field of Mannerism, Classical and Renaissance scholarship, an illustrious professor at New York University (NYU) and Harvard University, Director of the Institute of Fine Arts at New York University (1951–73),[2] and Director of Villa I Tatti in Florence of Harvard University (1973–85) (Fig. 1). He held significant art historical appointments all through his professional career, such as the Samuel H. Kress professorship at the Center for Advanced Study in the Visual Arts (CASVA) at the National Gallery of Art in Washington, D.C. (1983–84 and 1987–88), Trustee of the Institute of Fine Arts of New York University,[3] Honorary Trustee of the Metropolitan Museum of Art in New York, Chairman and Advisor of the J. Paul Getty Research Institute for the History of Art and Humanities (1982–84), and Trustee of *The Burlington Magazine* (1988–2006).

Professor Smyth received all his degrees from Princeton University, beginning with his A.B. in classics in 1938.[4] At Princeton, under Charles Rufus Morey, Smyth obtained a Master's degree in art history (M.F.A.) in 1941. In the same year, he joined the National Gallery of Art as a senior research assistant.[5] Here, he participated in protecting the National Gallery of Art's art collection by transferring the most important works to the Biltmore Estate in Asheville, North Carolina, and Randolph-Macon Women's College in Lynchburg, Virginia, during WWII.

In 1942, he was called up for duty in the U.S. Naval Reserve and became a naval lieutenant officer for the U.S. Naval Reserve in 1945. Under unforeseen circumstances, with the surrender of Germany, Smyth received a post as director of the U.S. Army's Central Art Collecting Point in Munich and was put in charge of misplaced cultural artifacts. Under the American Commission for the Protection and Salvage of Artistic and Historic Monuments in War Areas, implemented by President Roosevelt and known as the Robert Commission, he assisted the Allies in retrieving works of art that had been stolen by the Nazis. He also was responsible for converting the former National Socialist Democratic Party (NSDP; Nazi) headquarters into what is now known as the Zentralinstitut für Kunstgeschichte.[6] With masterful diplomatic and organization abilities, he formed an international committee of art historians, including German partners,[7] to oversee "the restitution of many of the greatest works of European art, including the Ghent altarpiece and Michelangelo's Bruges Madonna"[8] and art works from the Neapolitan museums. He received a U.S. Army Commendation medal for his outstanding and patriotic service.

In 1946–49, Smyth accepted a lecturer position at the Frick Collection in New York. During his time there he received a Fulbright Research fellowship from 1948 to 1950, which permitted him to travel to Florence. During this stay, he focused on the study of Mannerism. In the process of rescuing from Goering Bronzino's *Pygmalion and Galatea* during his Munich sojourn,[9] Smyth developed a love for Bronzino's drawings and paintings, in particular, his portraits.[10]

In 1950, Smyth was appointed assistant professor at New York University. In 1951, he became acting director of the Institute of Fine Arts, and in 1953, he was promoted to associate professor as well as appointed to be the second permanent director of the Institute, a position which he held until 1973. His Ph.D. on *Bronzino Studies* was granted by Princeton University in 1955, and he was promoted to full professor at NYU in 1957. The following year, he purchased the James B. Duke House on Fifth Avenue in New York, arranged to have it restored by the architect Robert Venturi, and then donated it to New York University. The Duke House, located a few blocks from the Metropolitan Museum of Art, became known as the Institute of Fine Arts for graduate studies in Art History. With his background in preserving works of art, he developed the first university curriculum in conservation in the country, administrated by the Fine Arts Institute. He also encouraged German scholars to engage in research at the Institute, for example, Erwin Panofsky from Hamburg, Max Friedlander from Freiburg, Richard Krautheimer from Marburg, and Jonathan Weinberg from Munich.[11]

In 1961, after returning from Rome as a fellow in residence at the American Academy in Rome (1959–60), Smyth participated in the re-evaluation of Mannerism at the Twentieth International Congress at Princeton University. His research demonstrated the visual and historical impact of Hellenistic art on Mannerism. His further observations of Mannerist and Maniera artists established the normative classification of the style (Early Mannerism 1520–40, Maniera 1540–65, and Late Mannerism 1565–85) as well as its merit as a new artistic style, void of decadence or decline that followed the High Renaissance. His lectures and studies resulted in the publication of *Mannerism and Maniera* in 1963.[12]

While a visiting scholar at the Institute for Advanced Study in Princeton, he published a seminal book on Bronzino's drawings, *Bronzino as Draughtsman* in 1971.[13] His fascination with the relationship of art in the High Renaissance to Venice's influence on Florence and Florence's on Milan culminated with the publication of *Florence and Venice: Comparison and Relations* and *Florence and Milan: Comparisons and Relations: Acts of Two Conferences at Villa I Tatti in 1982–1984.*[14]

With his friend and architectural art historian Henry Millon, Smyth published a series of articles on Michelangelo's architecture between 1969 and 1983, re-evaluating Michelangelo's contributions to the design of St. Peter's.[15] Once appointed Samuel Kress Professor at the Center for Advanced Study in Visual Arts (CASVA), National Gallery Art in Washington, in 1987–88, Smyth continued his interests in Michelangelo by planning a symposium on *Michelangelo Drawings.*

Before retiring as emeritus professor from Harvard University and Director of the Villa I Tatti in 1985, he established the prestigious periodical *I Tatti Studies: Essays in the Renaissance.* In turn, a *Craig Hugh Smyth Research Grant* scholarship was instituted in his honor at Villa I Tatti, and in 1999 another honorific recognition was established by the Institute of Fine Arts: a Craig Hugh Smyth Professorship, in appreciation for his dedication to teaching and research. In 2004, the Renaissance Society of America honored him with a special session on Bronzino Studies.[16]

Smyth's dedication to the preservation and conservation of European art and monuments as well as American historic buildings, his meticulous and pioneering scholarship on the style of Mannerism with his studies on Bronzino's art and Michelangelo's architecture, and his creative approach to the formation of programs in visual culture are legendary. His legacy continues in those of us who study Mannerism. However, his contributions as a scholar, teacher, and professional academician, although notable, are far more exceeded by his *humanitas*—his gentle nature, charismatic presence, sense of humor, and *bella figura*. His love for life was expressed not only in his engagement with visual art but also in his participation in the performing arts—as an admirer of jazz and player of clarinet, saxophone, and trombone. Craig Hugh Smyth epitomized the philosopher and physician Marsilio Ficino's motto: "Venus significant humanitatem" ("It is love which makes us human").

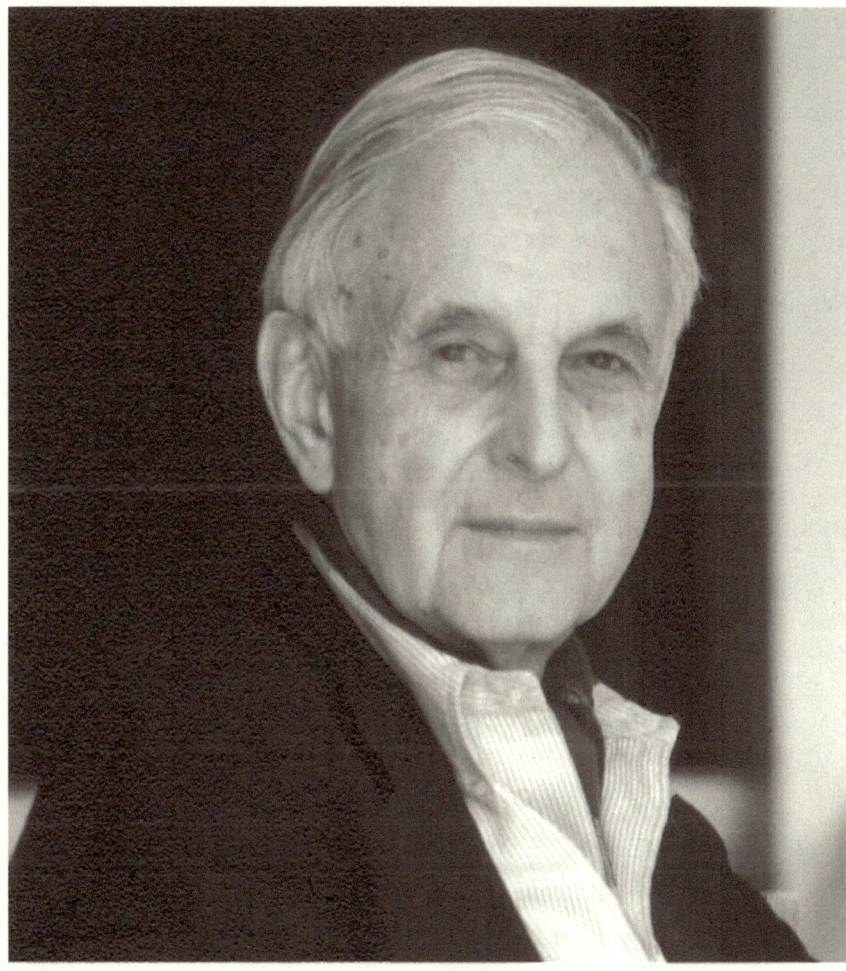

Fig. 1. Craig Hugh Smyth at Villa I Tatti. Photo credit: Courtesy of Villa I Tatti, Harvard University Center for Italian Renaissance Studies, Florence. A special acknowledgment to Susan Bates, Executive Assistant to the Director, for providing the photograph.

BIBLIOGRAPHY OF WORKS BY AND ON CRAIG HUGH SMYTH (NEW YORK 1915-NEW JERSEY 2006)

Smyth Craig Hugh. "The Earliest Words of Bronzino." *Art Bulletin* 31 (1949), 196–207.

Smyth, Craig Hugh. *Bronzino Studies (with a Book of) Illustrations*. Ph.D. diss., Princeton University, 1955.

Smyth, Craig Hugh. *Mannerism and Maniera*. Locust Valley, NY: J.J. Augustin, 1963, reissued in *Artibus et Historiae*, IRSA, 1992.

Smyth, Craig Hugh. *Bronzino as Draughtsman: an Introduction*. Locust Valley, NY: J.J. Augustin, 1971.

Smyth, Craig Hugh. "Venice and the Emergency of the High Renaissance: Observations and Questions." In *Florence and Venice: Comparisons and Relations*, vol. 1, *The Quattrocento*, eds. Sergio Berteli, Nicolai Rubenstein, and Craig Hugh Smyth. Florence: La Nuova Italia, 1979. 209–49.

Morrough, Andrew, Fiorella Superbi Gioffredi, Piero Morselli, and Eve Borsook, eds. *Renaissance Studies in Honor of Craig Hugh Smyth*. 2 vols. Florence: Giunti Baèra, 1985.

Smyth, Craig Hugh. *Repatriation of Art from the Collecting Point in Munich after World War II: Background and Beginnings, with Reference Especially to the Netherlands*. The Hague: Gary Schwartz/SDU, 1988.

Smyth, Craig Hugh, and Henry A. Millon. *Michelangelo architetto: la facciata di San Lorenzo e la cupola di San Pietro*. Milan: Olivetti, 1988. English: *Michelangelo Architect: The Facade of San Lorenzo and the Drum and Dome of St. Peter's*. Milan: Olivetti, 1988.

Smyth, Craig, Hugh, and Gian Carlo Garfagnini. *Florence and Milan: Comparisons and Relations: Acts of Two Conferences at Villa I Tatti in 1982–1984*. 2 vols. Florence: La Nuova Italia editrice, 1989.

Smyth, Craig Hugh, and Peter M. Lukehart, eds. *The Early Years of Art History in the United States: Notes and Essays on Departments, Teaching, and Scholars*. Princeton, NJ: Dept. of Art and Archaeology, Princeton University, 1993.

NOTES

1. See Andrew Morrough, Fiorella Superbi Gioffredi, Piero Morselli, and Eve Borsook, eds., *Renaissance Studies in Honor of Craig Hugh Smyth*, 2 vols. (Florence: Giunti Baèra, 1985), Introduction by Rensselaer W. Lee, 1:vii–vi; Elizabeth Cropper, "Biographical Memoirs of Craig Hugh Smyth," in *Proceedings of the American Philosophical Society* 153, no. 4 (December 2009), 495–500; and [obituaries] Judy Mariëtt Westerman and

Michael Steinhardt, Director, Institute of Fine Arts, NYU, "Craig Hugh Smyth: 1915–2006," <http://www.nyu.edu/gsas/dept/fineart/pdfs/press/ Smyth_memoriam.pdf>; Roja Heydarpour, "Craig Hugh Smyth, 91, Dies, Renaissance Art Historian," *New York Times*, 1 January 2007, 7; Willibald Sauerländer, "Art at Zero Hour: On the Death of the Art Historian Craig Hugh Smyth, Responsible for Pioneering Work after World War II," *Süddeutsche Zeitung*, no. 4, Friday–Sunday, 5–7 January 2007, 14; entry in *Dictionary of Art Historians*, <http://www.dictionaryofarthistorians.org>; and Helmut Wohl, "Obituaries: Craig Hugh Smyth (1915–2006)," *The Burlington Magazine* 149 (August 2007), 554.

2. See Westerman, "Craig Hugh Smyth," 1, noting how in 1958, Smyth, as Director of the Institute of Fine Arts, expanded the graduate program in Art History as well as its lodging by purchasing the James B. Duke House, restored by Robert Venturi.

3. With his advice, the Institute of Fine Arts acquired several historic buildings, including the James B. Duke House on Fifth Avenue in New York and Harold Acton's Villa La Pietra in Florence.

4. See Cropper, "Biographical Memoirs," 495, for her comment on Smyth's love for the classics, in reading Latin poetry out loud, and meditating on Seneca's letters.

5. At this time, he researched and wrote entries on the then-on-loan Chester Dale Collection.

6. See Craig H. Smyth, *Repatriation of Art from the Collecting Point in Munich after World War II* (The Hague: Gary Schwartz/SDU, 1988). Cropper, "Biographical Memoirs," 497, notes that in the Gerson Lecture at the University of Groningen, Smyth credited George Stout, Head of the Conservation Laboratory of the Fogg Museum of Art at Harvard University, for the establishment of the Robert Commission.

7. Among the German art historians were Dieter Sattler and Theodor Müller, who later became Director of the Bavarian National Museums. See Sauerländer, "Art at Zero," 14.

8. See Cropper, "Biographical Memoirs," 497.

9. See Cropper, "Biographical Memoirs," 497.

10. See Craig H. Smyth, "The Earliest Words of Bronzino," *Art Bulletin* 31 (1949), 196–207; and Craig H. Smyth, *Bronzino as Draughtsman: an Introduction* (Locust Valley, NY: J.J. Augustin, 1971).

11. See Sauerländer, "Art at Zero," 14.

12. See Craig H. Smyth, *Mannerism and Maniera* (Locust Valley, NY: J.J. Augustin, 1963), reissued in *Bibliotheca Artibus et Historiae* in 1992 with a foreword by Elizabeth Cropper. See Liana De Girolami Cheney, "Review of *Mannerism and Maniera*, by C.H. Smyth," *Sixteenth Century Studies Journal* 25, no. 4 (Winter 1994), 968–69.

13. See Smyth, *Bronzino as Draughtsman*.

14. See Craig Hugh Smyth, "Venice and the Emergency of the High Renaissance: Observations and Questions," in *Florence and Venice: Comparisons and Relations*, vol. 1, *The Quattrocento*, eds. Sergio Berteli, Nicolai Rubenstein, and Craig Hugh Smyth (Florence: La Nuova Italia, 1979), 209–49; and Craig, H. Smyth and Gian Carlo Garfagnini, *Florence and Milan: Comparisons and Relations: Acts of Two Conferences at Villa I Tatti in 1982–1984*, 2 vols. (Florence: La Nuova Italia editrice, 1989).

15. See Craig H. Smyth and Henry A. Millon, *Michelangelo architetto: la facciata di San Lorenzo e la cupola di San Pietro* (Milan: Olivetti, 1988), in English: *Michelangelo Architect: The Facade of San Lorenzo and the Drum and Dome of St. Peter's* (Milan: Olivetti, 1988).

16. In 1991, Professor Smyth presented an essay on "Maniera" at Liana De Girolami Cheney's session on "Mannerism: Historiography, Art and Art Theories," Sixteenth Century Studies Conference, Penn State University, Philadelphia, 7–10 October 1991. In 2004, Liana De Girolami Cheney organized two sessions on "Bronzino Studies" in honor of Professor Craig H. Smyth. Although too ill at this time to attend, Professor Smyth was delighted in hearing of this event. Some of the presentations are included in this volume.

PART ONE

INTRODUCTION TO AGNOLO BRONZINO

Il Bronzino (1530-72): A Short Biography

Liana De Girolami Cheney

Il Bronzino or *Bronzino*, Agnolo di Cosimo Mariano di Agnolo di Antonio di Agnolo di Toro, was born 17 November 1503, in the town of Monticello, near San Frediano, outside Florence, and died on 23 November 1572 in Florence (Fig. 1). His surname, *Il Bronzino* or *Bronzino* (little bronze), refers to the color of his hair or skin tone.[1] There is limited information on his family, none on his mother, Felice, or his siblings, although it is known that his father was a butcher. A commentary notes that Bronzino came from an "honest, humble and poor family."[2]

Bronzino commences his artistic education at the age of eleven as a pupil of the Florentine painter Raffaellino del Garbo (1466–1527), learning the art of drawing and color.[3] In 1514, he becomes an apprentice in the workshop of Jacopo Carucci or Jacopo da Pontormo (1494–1557). Their tutorial relationship through the years transforms into a close friendship and artistic symbiosis.[4] Bronzino begins to assimilate Pontormo's Mannerist style, developing lucidity of form rendered with a polished finish.[5]

In 1523, Pontormo and Bronzino, escaping the plague in Florence, move to Certosa di Galuzzo, a Carthusian monastery, to decorate *al fresco* stories on the Passion of Christ in the Chiostro Grande. During this soujourn, which lasted until 1525, Bronzino assists Pontormo in the completion of the Passion cycle, paints two lunettes in the Chiostro Grande—the *Dead Christ Supported by Angels* and the *Martyrdom of St. Lawrence*—and a small *Crucifixion*, and illustrates some liturgical books (*libri di culto*) for the monks.[6] At the Charterhouse at Galuzzo, he meets for the first time Giorgio Vasari (1511–74), who was admiring and studying Pontormo's Passion cycle. The two men forged a close friendship that spanned more than forty years.[7]

After the Certosa cycle, in 1525, Bronzino paints *al fresco* the *Temptation* of *Saint Benedict* in a lunette of the cloister of the Badia Fiorentina (now in the church of San Salvi in Florence). Between 1525 and 1527, he further assists Pontormo in decorating the Ludovico Capponi Chapel in Santa Felicita in Florence: the vault fresco (now destroyed), and the pendentive with tondi of the Four Evangelists. Bronzino paints two Evangelists: Saint Mark (now in the Musée des Beaux Arts at Bensançon in France) and Saint Luke (*in situ*).[8]

During the years 1527 and 1528, Bronzino again flees from the plague in Florence, this time to the villa of Ugo della Stufa in Bivigliano, near Florence. Here, he meets the classical humanist, historian, and poet Benedetto Varchi (1503–65) and his Latinist pupil Lorenzo Lenzi (1516–70?).[9] In 1528, Bronzino begins work on what will come to be considered a Manieroso portrait: The *Portrait of Lorenzo Lenzi* (now at the Civiche Raccolte d'Arte del Castello Sforzesco in Milan). The *Portrait of Lorenzo Lenzi* is an innovative fusion of imagery combined with an intellectual flair that emphasizes the noble social status of the sitter. By projecting Lenzi's inner psyche through gesture, costume, and facial expression, Bronzino renders an artistic portrait that is natural yet abstract.[10]

In 1529, Lorenzo Cambi, at the bequest of his father Antonio, commissions Bronzino to create a *Pietà with Mary Magdalene* for their private chapel in the church of Saint Trinity in Florence.[11] In this painting, Bronzino develops his artistic and poetic approaches, demonstrates his concern with artistic theories, and combines the acts of "evoking plasticity of sculpture and recreating nature."[12] He reveals a paragone that recurs in his devotional and historical religious paintings as well as in his poetic creations.

In 1530, as the War of the League of Cognac progressed, Florence came under siege. Yet, Bronzino's career continues to flourish, and he paints *Pygmalion and Galatea* (now in the Galleria degli Uffizi). During WWII, Craig Hugh Smyth rescued this picture from Goering and restored it to Florence, as noted in his biography in this volume. *Pygmalion and Galatea* was intended as the cover (*coperchio*) for Pontormo's *Portrait of Francesco Guardi* (*The Halderbier*, now at the J. Paul Getty Museum in Los Angeles, California).[13]

After the Florentine blockade, Bronzino is invited by Francesco Maria and Eleonora delle Rovere to their ducal court at Urbino in Pesaro, on the Adriatic coast of the Marches. He completes a *Portrait of Guidobaldo delle Rovere* (now at the Palatine Gallery in the Pitti Palace in Florence) and, for a harpsichord's music case (*cassa d'arpicordo*), an allegorical scene of *Apollo and Marsyas* (now at The Hermitage, Saint Petersburg, Russia).[14] Between 1530 and 1532, he assists local artists, for example, Girolamo Genga (1476–1551) and Raffaellino delle Colle (1490–1566), in painting for the chambers of the Duke of Urbino's Villa Imperiale at Pesaro decorating cycles with mythological and seasonal themes in the new Maniera style.[15]

In 1533, Bronzino returns to Florence to compose theatrical designs for a comedy of the Compagnia dei Negromanti. He requests Vasari's collaboration in the completion of these settings.[16] This early interest in theater accompanied his poetic endeavors. Throughout his career, Bronzino retains a fascination with the theater, as he develops his poetic expression.[17] In his theatrical decorations and poetic output, he creates interplays between the conceits of the hidden and the revealed—the masked and the unmasked—that tease the viewer and the reader in a manifestation of what can be identified as his Maniera style.[18] Still collaborating with Pontormo as late as 1536, Bronzino works with the older artist in the now-lost decoration of the Medici villas at Poggio a Caiano and Carreggi.[19]

In 1537, Bronzino becomes member of the prestigious academy *La Compagnia di San Luca*.[20] His artistic career begins to bloom, and his activities as a portrait painter expand. For the home of Florentine banker Bartolomeo Bettini, he completes a series of portraits of famous Tuscan writers.[21] In these portraits, which I would label as *Manieroso portraits*, Bronzino manifests a new approach to artistic expression and intellectual display that facilitates his entry into the savant circles of aristocratic humanists, poets, and merchants who form a circle of patrons who commission works of art denoted as Mannerist. Inspired by his artistic and intellectual surroundings, he collaborates with a group of poets, including Giovanni della Casa (1503–56), to publish a burlesque poem in terza rima: *Il pennello* in 1538 in Venice.[22]

The following year, 1539, together with other Florentine artists, he is engaged in the scenography of the entry and nuptial decorations for Eleonora de Toledo and Cosimo I de' Medici.[23] Impressed by Bronzino's artistic inventiveness and imagery, Cosimo I commissions him in 1542 to decorate a new religious chapel in Palazzo Vecchio: the Chapel of Eleonora de Toledo.[24] Bronzino becomes the court painter for the Medici family, composing tapestry design, settings for carnivals, and comical plays.[25]

As his career unfolds, Bronzino's circle of patrons increases, to include Medici associates such as Bartolomeo and Lucrezia Panciatichi, lords of Pistoia. For this family in the early 1540s, Bronzino paints their portraits, two *Holy Families*, and a *Crucifixion*.[26] These portraits, composed with preciously cultivated effects of design, convey the "precise elegance and complex expression of the Maniera style."[27]

In 1541, several significant events occur in Bronzino's life. His close friend Cristofano Allori dies. Bronzino transfers his lodging to the Allori household in order to assist Allori's mother, his niece, his widow Dianora Sofferoni, and his four children, among them Alessandro, who will later become his most devoted protegé.[28] Bronzino will pattern the tutor-son relationship with Allori on the paternal friendship he had with his master Pontormo.

When in 1541 Duke Cosimo I reforms the *Accademia degli Umidi* into the *Accademia Fiorentina*, Bronzino, along with other artists, is invited to join this prestigious new art society.[29] However, in 1547, again with other artists, Bronzino is expelled from the *Accademia Fiorentina*.[30] The reason for this action is still unclear.

Between 1544 and 1545, Vasari asserts that for Francis I, King of France, and at the request of Duke Cosimo I, Bronzino creates the ingenious and salacious *Venus and Cupid* (*Allegory of Love* or *Allegory of Lust*), now at the National Gallery of London.[31] Perhaps this painting constitutes the best expression of Bronzino's Maniera style in its combination of sensuality and capriciousness. With exquisite *disegno* (design) and *bella maniera* (refined style), Bronzino reveals the "passions of love with figures that turn into equivocations between nature and a [classical] statuary and improbable perfection, posturing in attitudes that are meant to tell [the viewer] primarily about their beauty and not about their meaning of the scene."[32]

During 1546 and 1547, Bronzino travels to Rome. The events of this sojourn are nebulous.[33] Upon his return to Florence, between

1547 and 1548, he participates in a debate on the paragone, initiated by Varchi in order to encourage contemporary humanists and
artists to consider the merits of painting over sculpture and the essential questions that concern him about the meaning and function
of art.[34]

During the 1550s, Bronzino's career as an artist of devotional
and portrait paintings continues to prosper. In 1552, he completes
two large religious paintings: for the Guadagni Chapel in the
church of Santissima Annunziata, the altarpiece of the *Resurrection of Christ*; and for the Zanchini Chapel in the Church of Santa
Croce, the *Descent of Christ in Limbo*.[35] When composing devotional
and religious scenes, Bronzino visualizes the holiness of the imagery by manipulating light and color, creating a luminous tonality,
and employing cool colors, thus achieving a celestial realm. When
viewing these paintings, the faithful are not moved by the religious
narrative or *istoria* but, instead, are transported aesthetically and
spiritually by perceiving the physical refinement of the design, the
beauty of the figures, and the ethereal tonality.[36] Bronzino creates
an elegant art form that transforms corporeal sensations into mystical vision.

Pleased with her earlier portrait of 1539,[37] Eleonora de Toledo
summons Bronzino to Pisa in 1550 to depict a portrait of her son,
Giovanni, who will become a future Medici cardinal. Throughout
this decade, Bronzino will continue to create his renowned series
of ducal portraits of the duke, duchess, and their children as "an
assertion of dynastic Medici continuity.[38]

From 1555 or 1556, Bronzino sustains an active dual career as a
poet and as a painter. As a poet, he composes numerous burlesque
rimes, satirical verses, and sonnets.[39] He befriends the poetess Laura
Battiferri (1523–69), married to the Mannerist architect and sculptor
Bartolomeo Ammanati (1511–92), and paints her with an open book
pointing to a passage of Petrarch's sonnet to Laura in his *Portrait of
Laura Battiferri* of 1555–60 (now in the Galleria degli Uffizi in Florence).[40] Inspired by the completion of the tapestries illustrating the
story of Joseph for the Salone dei Dugento in the Palazzo Vecchio,
Bronzino composes sonnets from these scenes.[41]

As a painter, he is very prolific with the invention of complex
allegorical portraits, whose *clavis interpretandi* is ambiguous and tit-

illating—for example, the *Portrait of Andrea Doria as Neptune* (now at the Pinacoeca Brera in Milan), *Portrait of Cosimo I de' Medici as Orpheus* (now at the Philadelphia Museum of Art), and the double portrait of *Il Nano Morgante* (now at the Galleria degli Uffizi in Florence).[42]

Bronzino collaborates with Pontormo again, in the 1550s, on the frescoes for the choir at San Lorenzo. He also assists his master with the diary he initiates in 1554.[43] When his master Pontormo dies in 1557, Bronzino completes Pontormo's lost cycle in 1558. Unfortunately, these frescoes were destroyed when the choir of the church was rebuilt in 1732.[44]

In 1563, Vasari establishes the Academy of the Arts of Drawing (*Accademia delle Arte del Disegno* or *Accademia del Disegno*) and includes his admired colleague Bronzino as a participating member.[45] Two years later, Bronzino completes three paintings: for the marriage of Francesco de' Medici and Joanna of Austria, as well as *The Nativity* for the church of San Stefano in Pisa and *The Martyrdom of Saint Lawrence*, which is unveiled in 1569 in the Medicean church of San Lorenzo in Florence.

Shortly after this successful unveiling event, Bronzino develops an unknown illness, and on 23 November 1572, at the age of 69, he dies in the house of Allori.[46] He is buried in the funeral chapel of the Allori family in San Cristoforo degli Adimari. Alessandro Allori composes a honorific eulogy, which he reads at the prestigious *Accademia del Disegno*.[47]

Bronzino's place in the history of art as an exponent of the Maniera style is revealed through satirical and lyrical poetic output, the meticulous rendition of nature in his drawings, his complex allegorical paintings that contain astonishing and puzzling conceits, enigmatic and mesmerizing portraits of aristocrats and humanists, and visionary devotional and religious paintings.

In honor of Craig Hugh Smyth, the essays included in this book explore different aspects of Bronzino's artistic expression, forming part of the ongoing historiography of this remarkable artist.

APPENDIX I. BRONZINO'S LETTER AND TRANSLATION

Al Molto Dotto M. Benedetto Varchi[48]

Mio onorando

Il proponimento mio, M, Benedetto vertuosissimo, è di scriver-
vi, in quel modo ch'io saprò più chiaro e breve, quale delle due più
eccellenti arti che con le mani si facciano tenga il grado principale,
e queste saranno la pittura e la scultura; e prima ponendo le ragioni
dell'una e poi quelle dell'altra, le verrò comparando insieme, e cosi
si potrà vedere a quale di loro al debba l'altra preporre. E perché
io intendo d'accostarmi dall'una delle due, come in verità mi pare
accostarmi alla più vera parte, cioè dalla parte della pittura, piglia-
rò per ora la sua difesa. ponendo nondimeno le ragioni della parte
opposita fedelmente, e con quanta verità più per me si potrà; materia in vero molto difficile e che arebbe bisogno di lunga e diligente
considerazione: né io prometto però parlarne a pieno, ma, come io
dissi, più chiaro e più breve che io potrò.

Sogliono adunque quegli che delle sculture sono o artefici o
partigiani, addurre fra l'altre loro ragioni che la scultura par essere
più perpetua che la pittura, e per questo volere che ella sia molto
più bella e più nobile, perché dicono che, quando dopo lunga fatica si conduce a somma perfezzione qualche opera, durando lungo
tempo tanto più si viene a godere, e così viene più lungamente a
rifrescare la memoria di quelli tempi ne' quali o per quali ella fu fatta; adunque è più utile che la pittura. Dicono ancora che con molto
maggior fatica si fa una statua che una figura dipinta, per rispetto
del subbietto durissimo, come sarebbe marmo o porfido o altra pietra; et ancora aggiungano che, non si potendo porre onde si leva,
talché, avendo storpiato una figura, non si può più racconciare, e la
pittura potendosi infinitamente e cancellare e rifare, essere di molta
più industria et aver bisogno di molto più giudizio e diligenza che
la pittura, e per questo essere e più nobile e più degna. Aggiungano
che, dovendo ambedue le dette arti immitare et assomigliarsi alla
natura lor maestra, e la natura faccendo le sue operagioni di rilievo
e che si possano toccare con mano; e così, dove la pittura solo è ob-
bietto del vedere e non d'altri sensi, la scultura, per essere cosa di
rilievo altresì, in che modo somiglia la natura, non solo del viso, ma
è ancora subbietto del toccamento, e per questo, essendo conosciuta
da più sensi, sarà più universale e migliore.

Dicono appresso che, dovendo farsi dagli scultori quasi sempre le statue tonde e spiccate intorno, o vestite o gnude che siano, bisogna aver sommo riguardo che stiano bene per tutte le vedute, e se ad una veduta la loro figura arà grazia, che non manchi nell'altre vedute, le quali, rivolgendosi l'occhio intorno a detta statua, sono infinite per essere la forma circolare di tal natura; dove cosi non avviene al pittore, il quale non fa mai in una figura altro che una sola veduta, la quale sceglie a suo modo e, bastandogli che per quel verso che la mostra abbia grazia, non si cura di quello che arebbe nell'altre vedute, che non appariscono; e per questo esser di nuovo più dificile. E seguitando alla sopradetta ragione, dicono che molto è più bello e dilettevole trovare in una sola figura tutte le parti che sono in uno uomo o donna o altro animale, come il viso, il petto e l'altre parti dinanzi, e volgendosi trovare il fianco e le braccia e quello che l'accompagna, e così di dietro le schiene, e vedere corrispondere le parti dinansi a quelle dallato e di dietro, e vedere come i muscoli cominciano e come finiscano, e godersi molte belle concordanzie, et insomma girandosi intorno ad una figura avere intero contento di vederla per tutto; e per questo essere di più diletto che la pittura.

Vogliono ancora innalzarla con dire la scultura esser molto magnifica e di grandissimo ornamento nelle cittadi, perché con quella si fanno colossi e statue, si di bronzo e sì di marmo e d'altro, che fanno onore agli uomini illustri et adornano le terre e pongon voglia, negli uomini che le veggano, di seguitare l'opere virtuose per avere simili onori, onde ne segue grandissima fama e giovamento. Né mancano di dire che bisogna essere molto avvertito nelle sculture d'osservare tutte le misure, come di teste e braccia e gambe e di tutte l'altre membra, per esservi la riprova sempre in pronto né si potere difraudare misura alcuna, come se può nelle pitture, dove non è tanta riprova, né essere di manco contento che difficultà trovarle in essere reale e da poterle misurare a sua voglia, il che della pittura non avvien sempre; e per questo la scoltura esser cosa manco fallace e più vera. Mostrano ancora che la scultura, oltre alla grandezza dell'artifizio, sia di non piccolo utile, potendosi servire di sue figure per reggere, in cambio di colonna o di mensole, o sopra fontane per gittar acqua, o per sepolture, o per infinite altre cose che si veggiono tutto il giorno, dove della pittura non può farsi altro che cose finte e di niuna utilitade, altro che di piacere; e per questo essere più utile la scultura.

Dell'altra parte, cioè dal canto della pittura, non mancano le risposte a tutte le ragioni addotte dalla scultura, anzi pare, a quegli che la pittura favoriscano, averne molte più; e dicono, rispondendo quanto alla prima ragione, dove si dice la scultura essere più durevole per essere in più saldo subbietto, che questo non si debbe attribuire all'arte, perché non è stato in poter dell'arte il fare il marmo o 'l porfido o l'altre pietre, ma della natura, né in questo si conviene a l'arte lode alcuna di più, se non come se il suo subbietto fosse terra o cera o stucco o legname, o altra materia manco durabile, esercitandosi, come ognuno sa, solo l'arte nella superficie. Rispondono ancora alla seconda ragione in questo modo, dove gli scultori adducano la difficultà tanto divolgata, cioè di non potere porre, ma solo levare, et essere gran fatica a far tale arte per avere le pietre dure per subbietto; rispondono — dico — che, se vogliono dire della fatica del corpo circa lo scarpellare, che questo non fa l'arte più nobile, anzi più presto gli toglie dignità, perché quanto l'arti si fanno con più esercizio di braccia o di corpo, tanto più hanno del meccanico, e per conseguente sono manco nobili; ché, se ciò non fosse, sarebbero da lodarsi per arti belle infinite che sono tenute a vile, come gli scarpellini che lavorano alle cave o che scarpellano le strade, o quegli che zappano, o scamatini o maniscalchi o simili; ma se vorranno dire della fatica dell'animo, dicono che non solo la pittura gli è eguale, ma la trapassa di gran lunga, come si dirà più di sotto. E dove dicono non si poter porre quando si sia troppo levato, dicono che, quando si dice scultore o pittore, s'intende eccellentissimo maestro o in pittura o in scultura, perché non si deve ragionare di quegli che solamente son nati per vituperare o l'una o l'altra arte; onde non si dee credere che uno scultore eccellente levi dove non bisogna, perché altramente non farebbe quello che ricerca l'arte, ma farà il suo modello tanto fornito, dove potrà aggiugnere e levare molto più facilmente che il dipintore, e di poi, trasportandolo all'opera con fedeli misure, non arà di bisogno di porre per aver levato troppo. Ma quando pure volessi o gli bisognassi porvi, chi non sa che acconciamente possano? Or non si fanno i colossi di molti pezzi? Et a quante figure si rifanno i busti e le braccia e quello che manca loro! Senza i tasselli, che si veggiano in dimolte figure, che sono uscite nuove con simili toppe di mano del loro artefice, sì che né in questo consiste l'arte, perché quando una figura sia d'infiniti pezzi, pur che stia bene, non dà noia alla bontà dell'arte.

Dicano, rispondendo alla terza ragione, che bene è vero che ambedue le dette arti si fanno per imitare la natura, ma quale delle due più conseguiscano l'intento loro, risponderanno più di sotto; solo dicono che, per questo, non imitano più la natura per far di rilievo che altrimenti, anzi tolgono la cosa che già era di rilievo fatta dalla natura, onde tutto quello che vi si truova di tondo o di largo o l'altro non è dell'arte, perché prima vi erano e larghezza et altezza e tutte le parti che si danno a' corpi solidi, ma solo è dell'arte le linee che cercondano detto corpo, le quali sono in superficie; onde, com'è detto, non è dell'arte l'essere di rilievo, ma della natura, e questa medesima risposta serve ancora dove dicano del senso del tatto, perché il trovare la cosa di rilievo di già è detto non essere dell'arte.

Non fornita
Il Bronzino

Bronzino: Answer to Benedetto Varchi[49]

My intention, most able Messer Benedetto, is to be as clear and as short as I can in writing you about which of the two most excellent manual arts, i.e., painting and sculpture, holds the first rank. Stating the arguments first in favor of one and then of the other, I shall compare them so that it will be possible to see which of the two should be preferred. And since I intend to take sides, and indeed believe myself to lie on the right side, i.e., on the side of painting, I shall now present its defense, stating, nevertheless, the opposite arguments as faithfully as I can. The subject, however, is really very difficult and would need long and careful consideration; therefore, I do not promise to discuss it fully, but, as I said, only as clearly and as briefly as I can.

Those who practice sculpture, or who take its part, are wont to put forth, among other arguments, that sculpture seems to be more permanent than painting, and for that reason they insist that it is much more beautiful and noble; they argue that, when a work is brought to ultimate perfection after long effort, it is enjoyable for a longer time, and, therefore, it will for a longer time bring back the memory of those times when or for which it was made; thus, it is more useful than painting. They also say that a statue requires much more effort than a painted figure, because of the very hard material used, such as marble, porphyry, or other stones. They also add that since [in sculpture] you cannot put back something where you have taken something away, so that when you have maimed a figure it cannot be mended, while in painting one can remove and rework indefinitely. Sculpture requires much greater skill and needs much more judgment and care than painting; it is, therefore, both nobler and worthier. They add this: both arts must imitate and resemble Nature, which is their master, and Nature's works are three-dimensional and can be touched with the hand; painting is only an object of vision and of no other sense, while sculpture exists also in three dimensions in which it resembles Nature, and is an object not only of vision but of touch, too. For that reason, sculpture, being known through more senses than painting, would be the more universal and superior.

Then they go on to say that, since sculptors must almost always make their statues, whether nude or clothed, in the round, and free on all sides, they must take great care that the work looks well from all views, and if their figure has grace from one view, they must make sure that it is not deficient from the other views, which, when the eye goes around the statue, are infinite in number, because such is the nature of the circular form. But this problem does not present itself to the painter, who, in each figure, never gives more than one view, which he chooses the way he wants; since he is satisfied if it is beautiful on the side he shows, he does not care what it would look like from the other view-points which cannot be seen. For this reason, also, sculpture would be the more difficult. And following their reasoning, they say that it is far more beautiful and gives greater delight to find in a single figure all the physical attributes of a man, of a woman, or of an animal, such as the face, the chest, and the other parts, and when turning around to find the side and the arm, and what goes with them, and then from the back the spine, and to see how the front parts correspond to the side and the back, and to see how the muscles start and how they end; and to appreciate many beautiful harmonies, and, in sum, moving around a statue, to be totally satisfied with seeing it entirely; for this reason, sculpture would be more enjoyable than painting.

They want, furthermore, to elevate sculpture by saying that it is magnificently effective and a great ornament for cities, because it serves to make colossi and statues, either in bronze, or marble, or other material, that honor illustrious men, and adorn the land, and give those that see them the will to emulate such virtuous actions in order to be honored in the same fashion, whence follows the greatest glory and advantage. And they do not forget to mention that, in sculpture, one has to be very skillful to respect all the measurements (e.g., of the heads and arms and legs, and all the other parts of the body), because verification is always at hand, and one cannot cheat on any of the measurements, as one can in paintings, where there is less possibility of verification; and it is a source of satisfaction no less than of difficulty to find sculptures to be material and measurable at will, which does not always happen with painting. For this reason, sculpture would be less deceptive and more real. They also show that sculpture, besides the greatness of the skill, is of no small utility, since one can use its figures for architectural support instead of columns or corbels, or for water spouts on fountains, for tombs, or for an infinite number of other things that one comes across all the time, while with painting, one can only make fictitious things of no utility other than giving pleasure. For this reason, sculpture would be the more useful.

On the other hand, on the side of painting, there is no lack of answers to all the arguments brought forth in favor of sculpture; on the contrary, it seems to those who favor painting that there is more to be said for it than for sculpture. Answering the first argument—that sculpture is more durable because it uses a more solid material—they deny that this is not to the credit of the art, because it is not in its power, but in that of Nature, to make marble, porphyry, or any other stone, and that the art of sculpture is not to be praised for its durable materials any more than it would be if executed in clay, wax, stucco, wood, or any other less durable material, since, as everyone knows, art works only on the surface. To the second argument they answer this way: while sculptors put forward their so much publicized difficulty of not being able to add to the work but only to take away, and what a great effort it is to apply their art because they have hard stone for material, the painters answer that if the sculptors mean the physical effort of chiseling, this does not make their art nobler, but that it rather diminishes its dignity, because the more the arts are exercised with manual and physical exertion, the closer they are to the technical crafts and, consequently, the less noble they are. If it were not so, one would have to praise as beautiful a great many arts that are considered inferior, such as ditch-digging or cleaning cloth or farrier work, or others of the same kind. But if one means mental effort, the painters say that painting is not only equal but also surpasses sculpture by far, as will be explained below. And as to not being able to put back anything when too much has been taken off, they say that when one speaks of the sculptor or the painter, one implies an accomplished master in either painting or sculpture, because one must not discuss those who were born only to disgrace either art; therefore, we ought not to believe that an outstanding sculptor claps oft when he should not, because otherwise he would not do what his art requires, but he will make a complete model, where he can add and take off more easily than the painter, and then, transferring this model to the final work with exact measurements, he will not have to add anything for having taken too much away. But if, however, he should desire or need to add something, who is not aware how easily he can do it? Are not colossal statues made of many pieces? And how many statues have their busts, their arms, or whatever is missing remade? Not to mention the plugs that one sees in many statues that come out brand new from the hands of the artists with such patches. The art of sculpture does not consist in avoiding repairs, because when a statue should be made up of an infinite number of pieces, if it is still good, it does not mar the quality of the art.

Answering the third argument, painters say that it is quite true that the purpose of both arts is the imitation of Nature, but which of the two comes closer to this end will be discussed later. Here we shall only say that sculptors do not imitate Nature more because they work in three dimensions, but that in fact they rather take over the object that was already made three-dimensional by Nature; so that rotundity, thickness, or anything else of that kind does not belong to art, because height and breadth and all the qualities of solids already existed in the material, but all that belongs to the art are the lines that outline such a body, which are on the surface; therefore, as we said, the three-dimensional existence does not appertain to art but to Nature, and the same objection also applies when they speak of touch, because, as it has already been said, to find that an object is three-dimensional is not a result of art.

Unfinished

Il Bronzino

NOTES

1. Agnolo's nickname "Bronzino" first appears in 1529 payment records for the *Pietà with Mary Magdalene* for the Church of Holy Trinity in Florence, now at the Galleria degli Uffizi, Florence. See Claudio Strinati, *Bronzino* (Florence: Viviani Editore, 2010), 15, and in his last will as "Angelus quondam Cosmi Mariani, vulgariter noncupatus Bronzino pictor." See Edi Baccheschi, ed., *L'Opera completa del Bronzino. Introdotta da scritti del pittore e coordinata* (Milan: Rizzoli, 1973), 83, citing Albertina Furno, *La vita e le rime di Agniolo Bronzino* (Pistoia: Lito-tipografia G. Flori, 1902, reissued 2009); and Elizabeth Pilliod, "The Life of Bronzino," in Carmen C. Bambach, Janet Cox-Rearick, and George R. Goldner, eds. *The Drawings of Bronzino* (New Haven, CT, and London: Yale University Press, 2010), 3–10.

2. See Raffaello Borghini, *Il Riposo* (Florence: Giorgio Marescotti, 1584), 113.

3. See Sydney Freedberg, *Painting in Italy, 1500–1600* (Baltimore, MD: Penguin Books, Pelican History of Art, 1971), 295; and Bambach, Cox-Rearick, and Goldner, *The Drawings of Bronzino*, passim, for a recent study on Bronzino's drawings.

4. Pontormo depicts Bronzino as a young boy seated in the entrance steps of a house in *Joseph with Jacob in Egypt* of 1518 (now at the National Gallery of London), a painting for a decorative cycle in one of the chambers of Pier Francesco Borgherini's palace in Florence.

5. See Freedberg, *Painting in Italy*, 296, and for an analysis of Bronzino's Maniera style, see 295–99; and Craig Hugh Smyth, *Mannerism and Maniera* (Locust Valley, NJ: J.J. Augustin Inc, 1962, reissued in *Artibus et Historiae*, IRSA, 1992), 35–41.

6. See Baccheschi, *L'Opera completa del Bronzino*, 83, citing Frederick Mortimer Clapp, *Les dessins de Pontormo: catalogue raisonné précédé d'une étude critique* (Paris: Universitè de Paris, 1914/16), passim.

7. This Passion cycle influenced by Albrech Dürer's prints will have a great impact on Vasari's art in subsequent years. See Kristina Hermann-Fiore, "Sui Rapporti Fra L'Opera Artistica del Vasari e del Dürer," in *Il*

Vasari Storiografo e Artista (Florence: Istituto Nazionale di Studi sul Rinascimento, 1974), 701–15; Graham Smith, "Bronzino and Dürer," *The Burlington Magazine* 119, no. 895 (October 1977), 709–10; and Maurizia Tazartes, *Il "ghiribizzoso" Pontormo* (Florence: Polistampa, 2008), 153–60.

8. See Strinati, *Bronzino*, 51–53.

9. See Alessandro Cecchi, "Famose Frondi di cui santi honori ..." Un sonetto del Varchi e il tritratto dal Bronzino," *Artista: Critica dell'arte in Toscana* (1990), 8–19, for the relationship between Varchi and Lenzi.

10. See Craig Hugh Smyth, "The Earliest Work of Bronzino," *The Art Bulletin* 32, no. 3 (September 1949), 194–210; idem, *Bronzino as Draughtsman: An Introduction, with Notes on His Portraiture and Tapestries* (Locust Valley, NY: J.J. Augustin, Inc, 1971). 80–86 and 94–101; and idem, *Mannerism and Maniera*, 41–42.

11. See Louis Alexander Waldman, "Bronzino's 'Uffizi Pietà' and the Cambi Chapel in S. Trinità, Florence," *The Burlington Magazine* 139, no. 1127 (February 1997), 94–102.

12. See Freedberg, *Painting in Italy*, 296.

13. See Liana De Girolami Cheney, "Agnolo Bronzino's *Pygmalion and Galatea*: The Metamorphoses of a Muse," in this volume; and Elizabeth Cropper, "Biographical Memoirs of Craig Hugh Smyth," *Proceedings of the American Philosophical Society* 153, no. 4 (December 2009), 495–500.

14. This oil on panel was transferred to canvas. See John T. Spike, "Rediscovery: *Apollo and Marsyas* by Bronzino," *FMR* 73 (April 1995), 14–24, and idem, *La Favola di Apollo e Marsia di Agnolo Bronzino* (Florence: Edizione Polistampa, 2000), passim.

15. See Luciana Miotto, *Villa Imperiale di Pesaro*: Girolami Genga (Venice: Marsilio, 2008), passim; Baccheschi, *L'Opera completa del Bronzino*, 87–88; Smyth, "The Earliest Work of Bronzino," 194–210; and Smyth, *Bronzino as Draughtsman*, 34–35.

16. See Alessandro del Vita, ed., *Il Libro delle Ricordanze di Giorgio Vasari* (Arezzo: Tipografia Zelli, 1938), Ricordo 20 di marzo 1533, 20.

17. See Franca Petrucci Nardelli, ed., *Agnolo Bronzino. Rime di burla* (Rome: Istituto della Enciclopedia Italiana, 1988), passim; Furno, *La vita e le rime di Agniolo Bronzino*, passim; and Deborah Parker, *Bronzino: Renaissance Painter as Poet* (Cambridge: Cambridge University Press, 2000), passim.

18. See Freedberg, *Painting in Italy*, 285–95; Smyth, *Mannerism and Maniera*, 39 and 86; and Cheney, *Readings in Italian Mannerism*, 9–34.

19. See Baccheschi, *L'Opera completa del Bronzino*, 89, where he cites Vasari: "Bronzino completes allegorical figures of Fortune, Fame, Peace, Justice and Prudence or Victory," now lost. See also Charles McCorquodale, *Bronzino* (London: Chaucer Press, 2005), 158.

20. See Strinati, *Bronzino*, 16.

21. See Strinati, *Bronzino*, 16.

22. See Petrucci Nardelli, *Agnolo Bronzino. Rime in burla*, 23–26, for the poem, and 475, for information on the Venetian press of Navo et fratelli in 1538.

23. See McCorquodale, *Bronzino*, 159.

24. See Janet Cox-Rearick, *Bronzino's Chapel of Eleonora in the Palazzo Vecchio* (Berkeley: University of California Press, 1993), passim; Lynette M.F. Bosch, "'A Room With Many Views': Eleonora de Toledo's Chapel by Agnolo Bronzino in The Palazzo Vecchio"; Massimiliano Rossi, "The Bystander" in the Chapel of Eleonora: A Lucretian Image in Bronzino's Work"; and Thomas MacPherson, "A Color Inventory of Selected Paintings by Agnolo Bronzino from 1540 to 1546: The Panciatichi Paintings and the Chapel of Eleonora de Toledo," all in this volume.

25. A newly founded Medici tapestry factory prompts Bronzino to design religious and secular cartoons illustrating the Story of Joseph and allegorical subjects of *Time, Abundance, Justice* and *Primavera*. See Lynette Bosch, "Bronzino's *Primavera* and the *Vindication of Innocence*," *Mitteilungen des Kunsthistorischen Institutes in Florenz* (June 1993), 74–82; Carmen C. Bambach, "Entries for Bronzino's Drawings on the Story of Joseph Tapestries," in Bambach, Cox-Rearick, and Goldner, *Drawings of Bronzino*, 150–86; Lucia Meoni, "Entries for Bronzino's The Story of Joseph Tapestries," in Carlo Falciani and Antonio Natali, *Bronzino: Artist and Poet at the Court of the Medici* (Florence: Mandragora, 2010), 124–31; Robert G. La France, "Bronzino and His Friends: The Medici-Toledo Tapestries," in Andrea M. Gáldy, ed., *Agnolo Bronzino: Medici Court Artist in Context* (Cambridge: Cambridge Scholars Publishing, 2013), 67–80; and Smyth, *Bronzino as Draughtsman*, 94–100.

26. See Elena Aloia, "Culture, Faith, and Love: Bartolomeo Panciatichi," Lynette M. F. Bosch, "Orthodoxy and Heterodoxy in Agnolo Bronzino's Paintings for Bartolomeo and Lucrezia Panciatichi," and MacPherson, "A Color Inventory of Selected Paintings by Agnolo Bronzino," all in this volume.

27. See Freedberg, *Painting in Italy*, 298. Another similar example is the *Portrait of Eleonora di Toledo* of 1539, in the Národní Galerie in Prague, see Donna A. Bilak, "Decoding Bronzino's *Portrait of Eleonora di Toledo* (c. 1539): An Iconography of Jewels and Dress," in this volume.

28. See Elizabeth Pilliod, *Pontormo, Bronzino, Allori: A Genealogy of Florentine Art* (New Haven, CT: Yale University Press, 2001), 81–83.

29. See Zygmunt Wazbinski, *L'Accademia Medicea del Disegno a Firenze Nel Cinquecento: Idea e Istituzione*, 2 vols. (Florence: Olschki, 1987), 159; and Tazartes, *Il "ghiribizzoso" Pontormo*, 153–60.

30. See Baccheschi, *L'Opera completa del Bronzino*, 83; Wazbinski, *L'Accademia Medicea*, 1:49, 59, 70, and 201–13; and Pilliod, *Pontormo, Bronzino, Allori*, 81–96.

31. See Leatrice Mendelsohn, "L'Allegoria di Londra del Bronzino e la retorica di carnevale," in *Kunst des Cinquecento in der Toskana*, ed. Monika Cämmerer (Munich: Bruckmann, 1992), 152–67; and Maurice Brock, *Bronzino* (Paris: Flammarion, 2002), 213–37, for a recent summary of the interpretation of this painting as well as *Venus and Cupid with Satyr* in the Galleria Colonna in Rome, *Venus and Cupid with Two Amoretti and Jealousy* at the Szépmüvészeti Múzeum in Budapest, and *Allegory of Felicity* at the Galleria degli Uffizi in Florence. See also Liana De Girolami Cheney, "Bronzino's *Triumph of Felicity:* A Wheel of Good Fortune," in this volume.

32. See Freedberg, *Painting in Italy*, 298, where he notes that the London *Venus and Cupid* (*Venus, Cupid, Folly, and Time*) is an "allegory on the passions of love, a reverse in moral content from the religious passion of the *Pietà* (now Besançon Museum in France)." Both secular and religious pictures were painted at the same time, revealing stylistic similarities of elegant artificiality and glacial beauty as well as complex and opposite allusions of love.

33. See Baccheschi, *L'Opera completa del Bronzino*, 83, quoting a letter that Bronzino writes to Cosimo I on his return from Rome in Smyth, *Bronzino as Draughtsman*, 47.

34. See Benedetto Varchi, "Lezzioni della maggioranza delle arti," in Paola Barocchi, *Trattati d'Arte del Cinquecento, fra manierismo e contrariforma*, 3 vols. (Bari: Laterza, 1960–62), 1:3–82, in particular, 63–67, for a reprinted and annotated comment on Bronzino's unfinished letter as a response to Varchi's question on the *paragone* of the arts. See also Robert Klein and Henri Zerner, *Italian Art: 1500–1600: Sources and Documents in the History of Art Series* (Englewood Cliffs, NJ: Prentice Hall, 1966), 10–13, for an English translation of Bronzino's letter. In this present volume, Bronzino's letter and its translation are reproduced as Appendix I.

See also Leatrice Mendelsohn, *Paragoni: Benedetto Varchi and Cinquecento Art Theory* (Ann Arbor, MI: UMI Research Press, 1982), 150–52, for a discussion on the urgency for Bronzino to finish the letter in honor of Michelangelo's funeral in 1564; see also 147–48, for a discussion on the letter of 5 August 1564, from the Florentine historian, classical scholar, and philologist Vincenzo Borghini (1515–80) to Vasari, commenting that he has encouraged Bronzino to finish the letter ("Ho scritto al Bronzino che dovrebbe finir la sua lettera"), citing Karl Frey, *Der literarische Nachlass Giorgio Vasaris*, 2 vols. (Munich: Georg Müller, 1930), 2:93.

35. See Brock, *Bronzino*, 268–94.

36. See Brock, *Bronzino*, 240–302, a chapter on "La Forza dell'Arte in the Service of Devotion."

37. See Bilak, "Decoding Bronzino's *Portrait of Eleonora di Toledo*," in this volume.

38. See Brock, *Bronzino*, 159. In addition, Bronzino continues to create portraits of important dignitaries with complex symbolism; see Leatrice Mendelsohn's lecture on Bronzino's Portraits in Honor of Craig Hugh Smyth, presented at the Renaissance Society of America in 2004; and eadem, "The Devil in the Details," in this volume.

39. See Petrucci Nardelli, *Rime in burla*, 23–398, for the inclusion of these poems; Stefania Pasti, "Le rime in burla," in Strinati, *Bronzino*, 203–24; and Stefania Pasti, "I sonnetti," in Strinati, *Bronzino*, 225–37.

40. See Graham Smith, "Bronzino's Portrait of Laura Battiferri," *Source: Notes in the History of Art* 15, no. 4 (Summer 1996), 30–38; Brock, *Bronzino*, 93–103; and Michael Giordano, "Bronzino's Art of Emblazoning: *The Young Man with a Book, Lucrezia Panciatichi, Saint Bartholomew*, and *Laura Battiferri*," in this volume.

41. See Baccheschi, *L'Opera completa del Bronzino*, 96–99.

42. See Brock, *Bronzino*, 162–81.

43. See Frederick Mortimer Clapp, *Jacoppo Carucci da Pontormo, His Life and Work* (New Haven, CT: Yale University Press, 1916), including his diary; and Elizabeth Pilliod, "Pontormo's Diary," *Cabinet* 18 (Summer 2005), 7–9.

44. See Freedberg, *Painting in Italy*, 317; and Tazartes, *Il "ghiribizzoso" Pontormo*, 1742.

45. See Wazbinski, *L'Accademia Medicea*, 2:235–66 and 421–45.

46. See Strinati, *Bronzino*, 17.

47. See Strinati, *Bronzino*, 17; and McCorquodale, *Bronzino*, 155.

48. Reprinted letter from Paola Barocchi, *Trattati d'Arte del Cinquecento, fra manierismo e contrariforma*, 3 vols. (Bari: Laterza, 1960–62), 1:63–67.

49. My English translation, in consultation with Klein and Zerner, *Italian Art: 1500–1600*, 10–13.

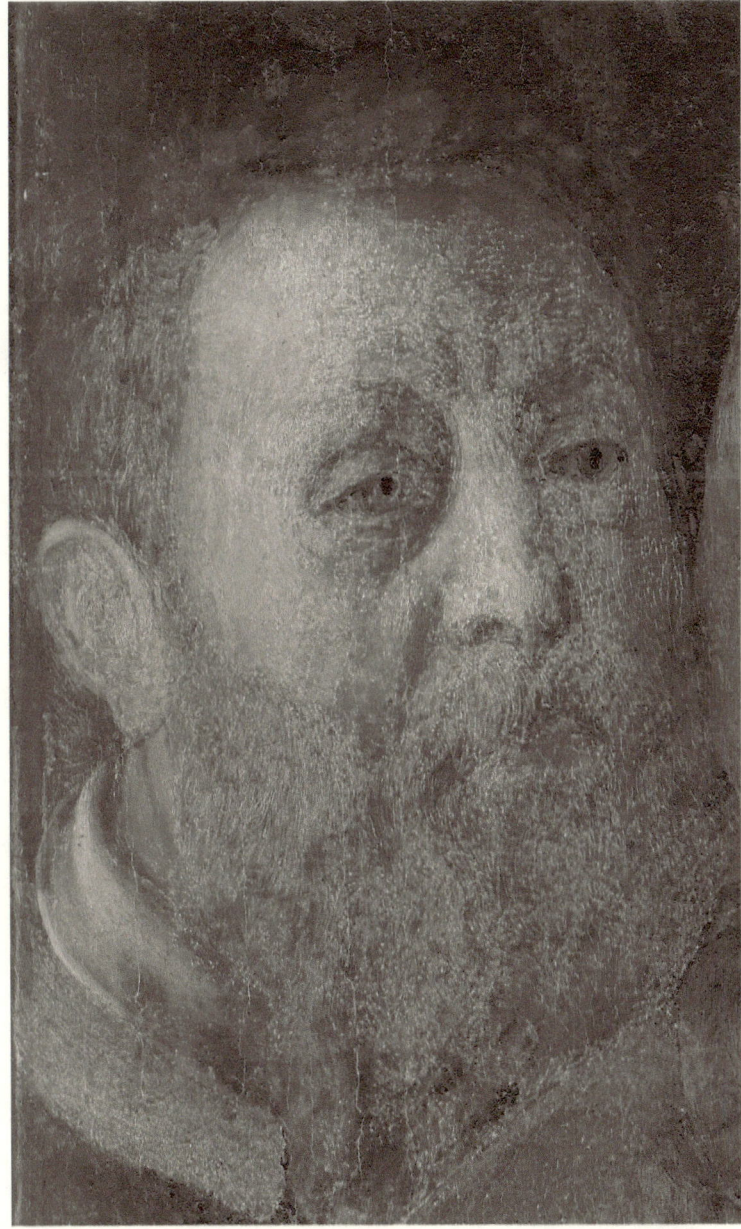

Fig. 1. Agnolo Bronzino, *Self-Portrait* (det.), *Descent from the Cross*, 1561. Accademia Gallery, Florence. Photo credit: Scala/Ministero per i Beni e le Attività culturali/Art Resource, NY.

Vita of Agnolo Bronzino (1568)[1]

Giorgio Vasari

Having written hitherto of the lives and works of the most excellent painters, sculptors, and architects, from Cimabue down to the present day, who have passed to a better life, and having spoken with the opportunities that came to me of many still living, it now remains that I say something of the craftsmen of our Academy of Florence, of whom up to this point I have not had occasion to speak at sufficient length. And beginning with the oldest and most important, I shall speak first of Agnolo, called Bronzino, a Florentine painter truly most rare and worthy of all praise.

Agnolo, then, having been many years with Pontormo, as has been told, caught his manner so well, and so imitated his works, that their pictures have been taken very often one for the other, so similar they were for a time. And certainly it is a marvel how Bronzino learned the manner of Pontormo so well, for the reason that Jacopo was rather strange and shy than otherwise even with his dearest disciples, being such that he would never let anyone see his works save when completely finished. But notwithstanding this, so great were the patience and lovingness of Agnolo towards Pontormo, that he was forced always to look kindly upon him, and to live with him as a son. The first works of account that Bronzino executed, while still a young man, were in the Certosa of Florence, over a door that leads from the great cloister into the chapter-house, on two arches, one within and the other without. On that without is a Pietà, with two Angels, in fresco, and on that within is a nude S. Lawrence upon the gridiron, painted in oil-colors on the wall; which works were a good earnest of the excellence that has been seen since in the works of this painter in his mature years. In the

Chapel of Lodovico Capponi, in S. Felicita at Florence, Bronzino, as has been said in another place, painted two Evangelists in two round pictures in oils, and on the vaulting he executed some figures in color. In the Abbey of the Black Friars at Florence, in the upper cloister, he painted in fresco a story from the life of S. Benedict, when he throws himself naked on the thorns, which is a very good picture. In the garden of the Sisters called the Poverine, he painted in fresco a most beautiful tabernacle, wherein is Christ appearing to the Magdalene in the form of a gardener. And in S. Trinita, likewise in Florence, may be seen a picture in oils by the same hand, on the first pilaster at the right hand, of the Dead Christ, Our Lady, S. John, and S. Mary Magdalene, executed with much diligence in a beautiful manner. And during that time when he executed these works, he also painted many portraits of various persons, and other pictures, which gave him a great name.

Then, the siege of Florence being ended and the settlement made, he went, as has been told elsewhere, to Pesaro, where under the protection of Guidobaldo, Duke of Urbino, besides the above-mentioned harpsichord case full of figures, which was a rare thing, he executed the portrait of that lord and one of a daughter of Matteo Sofferoni, which was a truly beautiful picture and much extolled. He also executed at the Imperiale, a villa of the said duke, some figures in oils on the spandrels of a vault; and more of these he would have done if he had not been recalled to Florence by his master, Jacopo Pontormo, that he might assist him to finish the Hall of Poggio a Caiano. And having arrived in Florence, he painted as it were by way of pastime, for Messer Giovanni de Statis, Auditor to Duke Alessandro, a little picture of Our Lady which was a much extolled work, and shortly afterwards, for Monsignor Giovio, his friend, the portrait of Andrea Doria; and for Bartolommeo Bettini, to fill certain lunettes in a chamber, the portraits of Dante, Petrarca, and Boccaccio, half-length figures of great beauty, which pictures finished. He made portraits of Bonaccorso Pinadori, Ugolino Martelli, Messer Lorenzo Lenzi, now Bishop of Fermo, and Pier Antonio Bandini and his wife, with so many others, that it would be a long work to seek to make mention of them all; let it suffice that they were all very natural, executed with incredible diligence, and finished so well, that nothing more could be desired. For Bartolommeo Panciatichi he painted two large pictures of Our Lady, with other figures, beautiful to a marvel and executed with infinite diligence, and besides these, portraits of him and his wife, so natural that they seem truly alive, and nothing is wanting in them save breath. For the same man he has painted a picture of Christ on the Cross, which is executed with much study and pains, insomuch that it is clearly evident that he copied it from a real dead body fixed on a cross, such is the supreme excellence and perfection of every part. For Matteo Strozzi he painted in fresco, in a tabernacle at his villa of S. Casciano, a Pietà with some Angels, which was a very beautiful work. For Filippo d'Averardo Salviati, he executed a Nativity of Christ in a small picture with little figures, of such beauty that it has no equal, as everyone knows, that work being now in engraving; and for Maestro Francesco Montevarchi, a most excellent physicist, he painted a very beautiful picture of Our Lady and some other little pictures full of grace. And he assisted his master Pontormo, as was said above, to execute the work of Careggi, where on the spandrels of the vaults he painted with his own hand five figures, Fortune, Fame, Peace, Justice, and Prudence, with some children, all wrought excellently well.

Duke Alessandro being then dead and Cosimo elected, Bronzino assisted the same Pontormo in the work of the Loggia of Castello. For the nuptials of the most illustrious Lady, Leonora di Toledo, the wife of Duke Cosimo, he painted two scenes in chiaroscuro in the court of the Medici Palace, and on the base that supported the horse made by Tribolo, as was related, some stories of the actions of Signor Giovanni de' Medici, in imitation of bronze; all which were the best pictures that were executed in those festive preparations. Wherefore the duke, having recognized the ability of this man, caused him to set his hand to adorning a chapel of no great size in the man was, and for her infinite merits worthy of eternal praise. In that chapel Bronzino made on the vault some compartments with very beautiful children and four figures, each of which has the feet turned towards the walls—S. Francis, S. Jerome, S. Michelangelo, and S. John; all executed with the greatest diligence and lovingness. And on the three walls, two of which are broken by the door and the window, he painted three stories of Moses, one of each wall. Where the door is, he painted the story of the snakes or serpents raining down upon the people, with many beautiful considerations in figures bitten by them, some of whom are dying, some are dead, and others, gazing on the Brazen Serpent, are being healed. On another wall, that of the window is the Rain of Manna; and on the unbroken wall of the Passing of the Red Sea, and the Submersion of Pharaoh; which scene has been printed in engraving at Antwerp. In a word, this work, executed as it is in fresco, has no equal, and is painted with the greatest possible diligence and study. In the altar-picture of this chapel, painted in oils, which was placed over the altar, was Christ taken down from the Cross, in the lap of His Mother; but it was removed from there by Duke Cosimo for sending as a present, as a very rare work, to Granville, who was once the greatest man about the person of the Emperor Charles V. In place of that altar-piece the same master has painted another like it, which was set over the altar between two pictures not less beautiful than the altar-piece, in which pictures are the Angel Gabriel and the Virgin receiving from him the Annunciation; but instead of these, when the first altar-picture was removed, there were a S. John the Baptist and a S. Cosimo, which were placed in the guardaroba when the Lady Duchess, having changed her mind, caused the other two to be painted.

The Lord Duke, having seen from these and other works the excellence of this painter, and that it was his particular and peculiar field to portray from life with the greatest diligence that could be imagined, caused him to paint a portrait of himself, at that time a young man, fully clad in bright armor, and with one hand upon his helmet; in another picture the Lady Duchess, his consort, and in yet another picture the Lord Don Francesco, their son and Prince of Florence. And no long time passed before he portrayed the same Lady Duchess once again, to do her pleasure, in a different manner from the first, with the Lord Don Giovanni, her son, beside her. He also made a portrait of La Bia, a young girl, the natural daughter of the duke; and afterwards all the duke's children, some for the first time and others for the second—the Lady Donna Maria, a very tall and truly beautiful girl, the Prince Don Francesco, the Lord Don Giovanni, Don Garzia, and Don Ernando, in a number of pictures which are all in the guardaroba of His Excellency, together with the portraits of Don Francesco di Toledo, Signora Maria, mother of the duke, and Ercole II Duke of Ferrara, with many others. About the same time, also, he executed in the Palace for the Carnival, two years in succession, two scenic settings and prospect views for comedies, which were held to be very beautiful. And he painted a picture of singular beauty that was sent to King Francis in France, wherein was a nude Venus, with a Cupid who was kissing her, and Pleasure on one side with Play and other Loves, and on the other side Fraud and Jealousy and other passions of love. The Lord Duke had caused to be begun by Pontormo the cartoons of the tapestries in silk and gold for the Sala del Consiglio de'Dugento; and, having had two stories of the Hebrew Joseph executed by the said Pontormo, and one by Salviati, he gave orders that Bronzino should do the rest. Whereupon he executed fourteen pieces with the excellence and perfection which everyone knows who has seen them; but since this was an excessive labor for Bronzino, who was losing too much time thereby, he availed himself in the greater part of these cartoons, himself making the designs of Raffaello del Colle, the painter of Borgo a San Sepolcro, who acquitted himself excellently well.

Now Giovanni Zanchini had built a chapel very rich in carved stone, with his family tombs in marble, opposite to the Chapel of the Dini in S. Croce at Florence, on the front wall, on the left hand as one enters the church by the central door; and he allotted the altar-piece to Bronzino, to the end that he might paint in it Christ descended into the Limbo of Hell in order to deliver the Holy Fathers. Agnolo, then, having set his hand to it, executed that work with the utmost possible diligence that one can use who desires to acquire glory by such a labor; wherefore there are in it most beautiful nudes, men, women, and children, young and old, with different features and attitudes, and portraits of men that are very natural, among which are Jacopo da Pontormo, Giovan Battista Gello, a passing famous Academician of Florence, and the painter Bacchiacca, of whom we have spoken above. And among the women he portrayed there, two noble and truly most beautiful young women of Florence, worthy of eternal praise and memory for their incredible beauty and virtue, Madonna Costanza da Sommaia, wife of Giovan Battista Doni, who is still living, and Madonna Camilla Tebaldi del Corno, who has now passed to a better life. Not long afterwards he executed another large and very beautiful altar-picture of the Resurrection of Jesus Christ, which was placed in the Chapel of Jacopo and Filippo Guadagni beside the choir in the Church of the Servites—that is, the Nunziata. And at this same time he painted the altar-piece that was placed in the chapel of the palace, whence there had been removed that which was sent to Granvella; which altar-piece is certainly a most beautiful picture, and worthy of that place. Bronzino then painted for Signor Alamanno Salviati a Venus with a Satyr beside her, so beautiful as to appear in truth Venus Goddess of Beauty.

Having then gone to Pisa, whither he was summoned by the duke, he executed some portraits for his Excellency; and for Luca Martini, who was very much his friend, and not of him only, but also attached with true affection to all men of talent, he painted a very beautiful picture of Our Lady, in which he portrayed that Luca with a basket of fruits, from his having been the minister and proveditor for the said Lord Duke in the draining of the Marshes and other waters that rendered unhealthy the country round Pisa and for having made it in consequence fertile and abundant in fruits. Nor did Bronzino depart from Pisa before there was allotted to him at the insistance of Martini, by Raffaello del Setaiulo, the Warden of Works of the Duomo, the altar-picture for one of the chapels in that Duomo, wherein he painted a nude Christ with the Cross, and about Him many saints, among whom is a S. Bartholomew flayed, which has the appearance of a true anatomical subject and of a man flayed in reality, so natural it is and imitated with such diligence from an anatomical subject. That altar-picture, which is beautiful in every part, was placed, as I have said, in a chapel from which they removed another by the hand of Benedetto da Pescia, a disciple of Giulio Romano. Bronzino then made for Duke Cosimo a full-length portrait of the dwarf Morgante, nude, and in two ways—namely, on one side of the picture the front, and on the other the back, with the bizarre and monstrous members which that dwarf has; which picture, of its kind, is beautiful and marvelous. For Ser Carlo Gherardi of Pistoia, who from his youth was a friend of Bronzino, he executed at various times, besides the portrait of Ser Carlo himself, a very beautiful Judith placing the head of Holofernes in a basket, and on the cover that protects that picture, in the manner of a mirror, a Prudence looking at herself; and for the same man a picture of

Our Lady, which is one of the most beautiful things that he has ever done, because it has extraordinary design and relief. And the same Bronzino executed the portrait of the duke when his Excellency was come to the age of forty, and also that of the lady duchess, both of which are as good likenesses as could be. After Giovan Battista Cavalcanti had caused a chapel to be built in S. Spirito, at Florence, with most beautiful variegated marbles conveyed from beyond the sea at very great cost, and had laid there the remains of his father Tommaso, he had the head and bust of the father executed by Fra Giovanni Agnolo Montorsoli, and the altar-piece Bronzino painted, depicting in it Christ appearing to Mary Magdalene in the form of a gardener, and more distant two other Maries, all figures executed with incredible diligence.

Jacopo da Pontormo having left unfinished at his death the chapel in S. Lorenzo, and the Lord Duke having ordained that Bronzino should complete it, he finished in the part where the Deluge is many nudes that were wanting at the foot, and gave perfection to that part, and in the other, where at the foot of the Resurrection of the Dead many figures were wanting over a space about one braccio in height and as wide as the whole wall, he painted them all in the manner wherein they are to be seen, very beautiful; and between the windows, at the foot, in a space that remained there unpainted, he depicted a nude S. Laurence upon a gridiron, with some little Angels about him. In that whole work he demonstrated that he had executed his painting in that place with much better judgment than his master Pontormo had shown in his pictures in the work; the portrait of which Pontormo Bronzino painted with his own hand in a corner of that chapel, on the right hand of the S. Laurence. The duke then gave orders to Bronzino that he should execute two large altar-pieces, one containing a Deposition of Christ from the Cross with a good number of figures, for sending to Porto Ferraio in the Island of Elba, for the Convent of the Frati Zoccolanti, built by his Excellency in the city of Cosmopolis; and another altar-piece, in which Bronzino painted the Nativity of Our Lord Jesus Christ, for the new Church of the Knights of S. Stephen, which has since been built in Pisa, together with their palace and hospital, after the designs and directions of Giorgio Vasari. Both these pictures have been finished with such art, diligence, design, invention, and supreme loveliness of coloring, that it would not be possible to go further; and no less, indeed, was required in a church erected by so great a Prince, who has founded and endowed the Order of Knights.

On some little panels made of sheet tin, and all of one same size, the same Bronzino has painted all the great men of the House of Medici, beginning with Giovanni di Bicci and the elder Cosimo down to the Queen of France, in that line, and in the other from Lorenzo, the brother of the elder Cosimo, down to Duke Cosimo and his children; all which portraits are set in order behind the door of a little study that Vasari has caused to be made in the apartment of new rooms in the ducal palace, wherein is a great number of antique statues of marble and bronzes and little modern pictures, the rarest miniatures, and an infinity of medals in gold, silver, and bronze, arranged in very beautiful order. These portraits of the illustrious men of the House of Medici are all natural and vivacious, and most faithful likenesses.

It is a notable thing that whereas many are wont in their last years to do less well than they have done in the past, Bronzino does as well and even better now than when he was in the flower of his manhood, as the works demonstrate that he is executing every day. Not long ago he painted for Don Silvano Razzi, a Camaldolite monk in the Monastery of the Angeli at Florence, who is much his friend, a picture about one braccio and a half high of a S. Catharine, so beautiful and well executed, that it is not inferior to any other picture by the hand of this noble craftsman; insomuch that nothing seems to be wanting in her save the spirit and that voice which confounded the tyrant and confessed Christ her well-beloved spouse even to the last breath; and that father, like the truly gentle spirit that he is, has nothing that he esteems and hold in price more than that picture. Agnolo made a portrait of the Cardinal, Don Giovanni de' Medici, the son of Duke Cosimo, which was sent to the Court of the Emperor for Queen Joanna; and afterwards that of the Lord Don Francesco, Prince of Florence, which was a picture very like the reality, and executed with such diligence that it has the appearance of a miniature. For the nuptials of Queen Joanna of Austria, wife of that Prince, he painted in three large canvases which were placed at the Ponte alla Carraia, as will be described at the end, some scenes of the Nuptials of Hymen, of such beauty that they appeared not things for a festival, but worthy to be set in some honorable place for ever, so finished they were and executed with such diligence. For the same Lord Prince he painted a few months ago a small picture with little figures, which has no equal, and it may be said that it is truly a miniature. And since at this his present age of sixty-five, he is no less enamoured of the matters of art than he was as a young man, he has undertaken recently, according to the wishes of the duke, to execute two scenes in fresco on the wall beside the organ in the Church of S. Lorenzo, in which there is not a doubt that he will prove the excellent Bronzino that he has always been.

This master has delighted much, and still delights, in poetry; wherefore he has written many capitol and sonnets, part of which have been printed. But above all, with regard to poetry, he is marvelous in the style of his capitoli after the manner of Berni, in so much that at the present day there is no one who writes better in that kind of verse, nor things more fanciful and bizarre, as will be seen one day if all his works, as is believed and hoped, come to be printed. Bronzino has been and still is most gentle and a very courteous friend, agreeable in his conversation and in all his affairs, and much honored; and as loving and liberal with his possessions as a noble craftsman such as he is could well be. He has been peaceful by nature, has never done an injury to any man, and he has always loved all able men in his profession, as I know, who have maintained a straight friendship with him for three and forty years, that is, from 1524 down to the present year, ever since I began to know and to love him in that year of 1524, when he was working at the Certosa with Pontorno, whose works I used as a youth to go to draw in that place.

NOTE

1. Excerpt from the section on The Academicians of Design, Painters, Sculptors and Architects, and of Their Works in Giorgio Vasari's *Le vite de' più eccellenti pittori, scultori e architetti* (Florence: Giuntina, 1568), ed. and trans. Gaston C. DeVere, 1912/1915 <http://members.efn.org/~acd/vite/VasariLives.html>.

PART TWO

RELIGIOUS AND DEVOTIONAL
PAINTINGS

Orthodoxy and Heterodoxy in Agnolo Bronzino's Paintings for Bartolomeo and Lucrezia Panciatichi

Lynette M.F. Bosch

"The Reformation of Luther cast a
shadow similar to that cast by
Bolshevism four centuries later."
—Aubrey G. Bell

"God has favored us in His beloved
Son. In Him we have redemption
through His Blood. The remission of sins,
according to the riches of His
grace has abounded beyond measure
in us."
—Ephesians 1:6–8

After 1539, the year in which Bartolomeo and Lucrezia Panciatichi returned to Florence from France, the couple commissioned a series of paintings from Agnolo Bronzino that can be considered remarkable for his *oeuvre* and for the history of Florentine painting. In 1568, in Bronzino's *vita*, Giorgio Vasari recorded the Panciatichi commissions as consisting of five paintings: their portraits; a Crucifixion; and two *Holy Families*:

A Bartolomeo Panciatichi fece due quadri grandi di Nostre Donne con altre figure, belli a maraviglia, e condotti con infinita diligenza; ed oltre ciò, I ritratti di lui e della moglie tanto naturali, che paiono vivi veramente, e che non manchi loro se non lo spirito. Al medesimo ha fatto in un quadro un Cristo crucifisso, che è condotto con molto studio e fatica, onde ben si conosce che lo ritrasse da un vero corpo morto confitto in croce; cotanto è in tutte le sue parti di somma perfezione e bontà.[1]

Of the works Vasari described—two large paintings of the Virgin with saints; portraits of Bartolomeo and Lucrezia; and a crucified Christ—three have always been easily identified as the paintings in the Uffizi's collection, these being: the *Portrait of Bartolomeo Panciatichi* (Fig. 1); the *Portrait of Lucrezia Panciatichi* (Figs. 2 and 3); and the *Holy Family*, in the Uffizi, in which the Panciatichi arms are visible on a flag that flies from a building in the upper left of the painting (Fig. 4). Recently, a candidate for the *Crucified Christ*, assumed to have been lost, has surfaced in the collection of the Musée des Beaux-Arts, in Nice (Fig. 5).[2]

Identifying the second painting of the Virgin and some figures mentioned by Vasari has proved somewhat problematic. In the literature on Bronzino's paintings for the Panciatichi, two very different paintings have been proposed as being the second painting of the Virgin: the *Holy Family* in London's National Gallery (Fig. 6),[3] or the *Holy Family* in Vienna's Kunsthistorisches Museum (Fig. 7).[4] The London *Holy Family* includes John the Baptist and Elizabeth, as does the Vienna *Holy Family*, and it has the figures pressed to the foreground, with a distant hill town in the landscape, as do the Uffizi and Vienna *Holy Families*. However, the Vienna *Holy Family*, as Graham Smith has indicated, is a more likely candidate for identification as the second *Holy Family*.[5] Smith identified, in the Vienna painting, what may be an allusion to the Panciatichi arms in the emblematic form created by St. John the Baptist's cross, which rests on his dish, creating a shadow that resembles the design of the Panciatichi arms. The Vienna painting is also closer in its detailed compositional structure to the Uffizi *Holy Family*, whereas the London *Holy Family*'s composition suggests a generic reworking of the format employed for the Uffizi painting. Currently, it is the Vienna *Holy Family* which is accepted as being the second painting of this subject that Bronzino painted for the Panciatichi. Thus, the five paintings on which this study focuses are: the *Portrait of Bartolomeo Panciatichi*; the *Portrait of Lucrezia Panciatichi*; *Holy Family with St. John the Baptist* in the Uffizi; the Vienna *Holy Family with Saints Elizabeth and St. John the Baptist*; and the Nice *Crucified Christ*.

The Panciatichi belonged to the wealthy, upper classes of Florentine society during the formation of Duke Cosimo I's principate; Bartolomeo served in a variety of ambassadorial and administrative positions, in Florence and in France.[6] As part of their courtly behavior, the Panciatichi commissioned this group of paintings from Bronzino, who had become part of the group of court artists in the aftermath of his participation in the decorations for Cosimo's marriage to Eleonora de Toledo, the daughter of the Viceroy of Naples, Don Pedro de Toledo.[7] The wedding took place in 1539, the same year in which the Panciatichi returned to Florence. Thus, the Panciatichi were among the first courtiers to commission works from the newly recognized, young artist.[8] It is the purpose of this chapter to explore the contextual religious and spiritual meanings of the Panciatichi commissions, painted by Bronzino during the years when confessional issues were foremost as topics for discussion among all classes of European society.[9]

In a manner of speaking, this consideration of the Panciatichi and Bronzino has been a long time coming, as the arguments presented below were first put forward, in 2001 and 2004, respectively, at the Sixteenth Century Studies Conference and at the Renaissance Society of America's Annual Meeting.[10] The 2001 and 2004 papers contained a discussion of the role that reformist ideas, such as those of Erasmus and Juan de Valdés, played in the formation of sixteenth-century art in relation to the articulation of the visual experiments that are identified with Mannerism. Consideration of the role played by members of the *Accademia Fiorentina* in this process was addressed in both papers, and, in the 2004 paper, the Panciatichi paintings were considered from the perspective of how their content reflected orthodoxy and heterodoxy. This essay argues that the Panciatichi paintings are more orthodox than heterodox, based on internal evidence found in the paintings that links them explicitly and implicitly to the dogma, liturgy, and devotional practices of the Catholic Church. Consideration is also given to recent heterodox interpretations for Bronzino's paintings, while correcting some errors in data found in earlier literature on the Panciatichi paintings.

The contextual background for the Panciatichi paintings is defined by the religious debates that ensued in Western Europe in the aftermath of Lateran V (1512–17).[11] Lateran V was the Council meant to initiate the Church's internal, reformist agendas, but it failed when attention was deflected from reform to other political debates focused on the temporal power of the Church. With the failure of Lateran V, the Roman Church's inability to lead a reformist agenda created the spiritual void that was filled by the Protestant Reformation. The challenge issued by Martin Luther, at Castle Church in Wittenberg, ended the Church's monolithic hegemony over European Christianity, on 30 August 1517, initiating the open rebellion against the Church that affected all social classes. Simultaneously, reformers within the Church, such as Erasmus, attempted to rebuild and reunite Christianity within a reformed Church.

While other reformers soon followed, it was Luther who became the label employed by the Church when it feared that orthodoxy was being eroded by heterodoxy leading to heresy.[12] After 1517, Christians in Europe found themselves caught between loyalty to tradition and the familiar and a spirit of experimentation and excitement engendered by sometimes dangerous reformist ideas. Throughout Europe, Catholics and Protestants alike preached reform, as the old devotional patterns changed into transformed versions of traditional dogmas and devotional practices.[13] In the confusion created by these changes, the Church and the Inquisition became increasingly intolerant, while secular rulers tried to gain political advantage for themselves by criticizing ecclesiastical authority. The Inquisition treated anyone, including their own, who called for reform with suspicion, as the Church divided into ultraconservatives and more moderate reformist groups. These internal reformers, such as Erasmus of Rotterdam, were often compared to Protestant reformers such as Luther, John Calvin, or Ulrich Zwingli because their call for reform was also perceived as a threat to the Church's hegemony over its members.

In the first half of the sixteenth century, the divisions between what was Catholic and Protestant became permeable and mutable, as reformers multiplied within and outside of the Church.[14] Even among the Protestants, positions changed on dogma and practice as the Reformation developed, and the reformers frequently disagreed with each other. For Catholics, the Council of Trent (1545–63) ended doctrinal confusion and forced Catholics to fall in line.[15]

However, before Trent ended spiritual experimentation among Catholics,[16] the Inquisition became more active in persecuting individuals accused of deviating from orthodoxy, frequently accusing them of Lutheranism—even when the accused were not Lutheran.[17]

With the end of the era of fluid religious identities, repressed by the opening sessions of Trent, came moments of choice, which forced individuals to abandon the spiritual experimentation they might have practiced between 1517 and 1545. Some of these free thinkers remained Catholic, despite their eclectic spirituality; others eventually transferred their allegiance to Protestant churches. Among those who experimented, some went back and forth between Catholic and Protestant, eventually returning to the Church. Throughout this process of redefinition of religious identity, there were individuals who found their spiritual identity defined for them by others, whose agendas were sometimes hostile for political or personal reasons. There were some who were accused of heresy when they were ignorant of having wanted to disavow the Church; and others who became crypto-Protestants (Nicodemists) to avoid persecution and prosecution or execution, yet were found out.

Specific examples of spiritual fluidity abound, and one example pertinent to Bartolomeo Panciatichi is that of Pietro Manelfi, the self-avowed Anabaptist who gave Bartolomeo's name to the Inquisition in 1551, accusing him of being "Lutherano et ha libri Lutherani."[18] Manelfi began life as a good Catholic, as he told Leandro degli Alberti, the Bolognese Inquisitorial representative, and Manelfi later recounted the same narrative to the Roman notary, Gerolamo Lippomani.[19] At some point in the 1540s, when he heard Bernardino Occhino preaching in Prato, Manelfi was influenced to change his religious allegiance and became a Lutheran. He read Luther's *"sopra la epistola di Paolo ad Galatas,"* the *"Annotationi del Melantone sopra s. Matheo,"* and Luther's *"De Papatu invento Sathanae."*[20] Then, as he traveled within Italy meeting with groups of Lutherans in Venice, Treviso, Acquileggia, Istria, Rovigo, Ferrara, Consandolo, Ravenna, Bagnacavallo, Immola, Florence, Pisa, Lucca, Asola, and Cittadella, he was persuaded by Giuseppe da Asola, Lorenzo da Modana, one "Titiano" (from Florence), and Giuseppe da Vicenza to become an Anabaptist, whereupon he began again to travel among Anabaptist groups and attended the Council of Anabaptists in Venice in 1550.[21] At the time of his confession to the Bolognese Inquisitor, in October 1551, Manelfi had come full circle back to the Roman Church, which accepted his return after his full confession and the list of names he gave them of Italian heretics.[22] During his confession, Manelfi mentioned that among the available books being read by many dissenters were: Calvin's *Excuse à Messieurs les Nicodémites*; Fra Benedetto da Mantova's *Beneficio di Cristo*; Fra Giorgio Siculo's *Epistola ai cittadini di Riva di Trento*; and Juan de Valdés' *Le cento et dieci divine considerationi*—all of which circulated in Italy after the mid-1540s.[23]

Equally eclectic is the spiritual path traveled by one of Manelfi's mentors, the mysterious "Tiziano."[24] Tiziano began in the bosom of the Church with friendships with Camillo Renato, Francesco Neri, and Pietro Bresciani da Casalmaggiore. At some point, "Tiziano" converted to Anabaptism. Imprisoned by the Inquisition in June 1554, Tiziano retracted his heresy and then disappeared from the historical record. Tiziano's Anabaptist converts declared, when questioned by the Inquisitors, that Tiziano had learned his Anabaptist faith in Germany. While Manelfi appears to have had a profound and actual change of faith, when he returned to the Church, Tiziano's retraction of Anabaptism seems to have been more a way to save his skin than a true return to the Church. Thus, in the spiritual crossings that marked the sixteenth century, any number of possibilities existed, including individual and eclectic blends of ideas and beliefs from different spiritual streams, without total abandonment of religious affiliation with any group, including the Roman Church.

Determining the actual status of the conscience of individuals across a gap of five hundred years is impossible, unless a clear, documented trail of thought and action exists that chronicles these changes, as there exists for Pietro Manelfi and "Tiziano." In times of changing and fluid allegiances, five years could make a tremendous difference in this process of spiritual self-definition and reinvention. Hence, scholars studying the circumstances of changing religious identity in the early sixteenth century need an analytical flexibility commensurate with the complexity of such studies. As the Catholic mainstream was shaken and before the Church recovered control of its members, among those who were caught in the

complex world of changing spiritual thought, expression and practice were the Florentines, Bartolomeo and Lucrezia Panciatichi.[25]
Bartolomeo survived the Inquisition unscathed in 1552, and he
was able to negotiate between his "heresy" and his orthodoxy so
successfully that immediately upon his release he returned to his
normal and illustrious life. He could not have accomplished such a
transition without being convincing and without there being good
reason for the Inquisition to think that his return to the Church was
real enough that they released him. Possibly, Bronzino's paintings
may hold a clue about how it was that Bartolomeo successfully
navigated those troubled waters.

BIOGRAPHICAL INFORMATION ABOUT THE PANCIATICHI

Information on the Panciatichi is not plentiful, but it is possible to
develop a chronology for their lives and for Bartolomeo's accomplishments that is indicative of the social position they enjoyed.
Bartolomeo Panciatichi was born wealthy but illegitimate, and
Lucrezia was born into a branch of the Pucci family that was respectable but modest in financial prospects.[26] Bartolomeo's father,
also named Bartolomeo (died 1463), married Annalena di Lorenzo
Lensi, but she died without issue; hence the elder Bartolomeo considered the younger Bartolomeo his heir.[27] The Panciatichi wealth
came from a family business, which had branches in Florence and
Lyon. The name of the younger Bartolomeo's mother is unknown,
but it is recorded that he was born in Lyon, in either June or February 1507.[28] The younger Bartolomeo was given the baptismal name
Giovanni, perhaps to establish a link between him and the city the
Panciatichi considered home, as John the Baptist was Florence's patron saint, which accounts for the presence of the saint in the Panciatichi paintings.

　　Pomponeo Litta recorded that the Panciatichi originated in Pistoia and then became Florentine citizens.[29] Litta also identified the
family as being of mixed French and Lombard ancestry and having
achieved Florentine citizenship long before the fifteenth century. In
effect, as Elena Aloia has traced, the Panciatichi became Florentine
in 1376.[30] By the early sixteenth century, the Panciatichi had risen to
prominence, and the elder Bartolomeo (1468–1533) participated in

Leo X's 1515 *ingresso* into the city and was subsequently awarded the title of *Conte Palatino* and *Cavaliere di San Pietro*, with the right to have his family arms displayed on his palace. He was also awarded the privilege of being allowed to place one of the Medici *palle* between the letters L.X., as a sign of special papal regard.[31] This device is visible on the arms that appear on the façade of the palace in Bronzino's portrait of Bartolomeo, where a single white *palla* is visible in the black field of the shield, thereby carefully identifying Bartolomeo as a supporter of Duke Cosimo. The Panciatichi palace represented in Bartolomeo's portrait is not the current building identified as the Palazzo Panciatichi, purchased by the Panciatichi in 1621, which is near the Medici Palace on Via Cavour.

As Aloia has discussed, the palace where Bartolomeo is depicted was located in the neighborhood near the Church of Sta. Maria Maggiore, close to the Palazzo Antinori but on the other side of the Via Tornabuoni.[32] This area was destroyed in the nineteenth century to make way for a "modern" Florence, when the city was briefly the capital of Italy. Aloia located the site of the sixteenth-century Panciatichi palace, using the map that was made by Guido Carocci, of this part of the city prior to the reconstruction. Carocci used the 1427 *catasto* entries to identify family ownership of specific palaces. On the map, the neighborhood's houses and palaces are clearly labeled with the names of the families, with the two Panciatichi *case* clearly identified.

There were two Panciatichi buildings, visible in the Carocci map, standing across the street from each other. This could explain why Bartolomeo is seen, in Bronzino's portrait, standing on the balcony of one building while a separate building behind him is decorated with the Panciatichi arms. Additionally, the elaborate and distinctive arch in Bartolomeo's portrait may have been a feature of either of the two Panciatichi buildings, which could have been linked by such an overpass bridge connector, or such a connector may have been part of other buildings in the neighborhood. For instance, the Carocci map shows that there were multiple domiciles in the area for the Agli family, which would have included the lost Agli loggia. Possibly, one of these buildings had a distinctive arch connecting two of the Agli homes, and Bronzino included it in the portrait as a marker of place; or the arch is a reference to the destroyed Agli loggia's arches and columns.

The sixteenth-century Panciatichi palace, depicted in Bronzino's portrait of Bartolomeo, had, as Vasari described, a *sgraffito* façade painted by Andrea di Cosimo Feltrini—"… a Bartolomeo Panciatichi un'altra della casa che e' muró su la piazza degli Agli, oggi di Ruberto de' Ricci, bellissima …"[33] The palace described in the *Vite* was, as Vasari states, near the Piazza degli Agli and the Palazzo Ricci-Altoviti (Via de' Vecchietti, 6), built in 1528, by the Altoviti, which has kneeling windows comparable to those seen in Bartolomeo's portrait.[34] The Ricci-Altoviti Palace is close to the Church of San Michele Berteldi or Bertelli, in the area of Sta. Maria Novella, near which was the original Piazza degli Agli, and the old Panciatichi palace was just down the block from San Michele Berteldi (moving away from the Via Tornabuoni) on the side that faces in the direction of Sta. Maria Maggiore. Thus, the Panciatichi palace was located near the Ricci-Altoviti Palace, with its distinctive windows, echoed in Bronzino's portrait, as a marker of Bartolomeo's neighborhood.

In Bartolomeo's portrait, Bronzino reworked the architectural identifiers of place for the palace into a sixteenth-century version of Cubism, where parts of the palace and its surrounding area are juxtaposed in an *assemblage* conceptualization that is an evocative reworking of the old Panciatichi palace's Florentine district. The elements in Bartolomeo's portrait include the tower, seen in the distance, evocative of that of Sta. Maria Novella, as a locator of the area where the Panciatichi lived. The vaulted crossover arch, whether it was a bridge between buildings or a reference to the Loggia degli Agli, assisted in identifying the neighborhood, as did the distinctive windows (similar to those of the Ricci-Altoviti Palace). Thus, Bartolomeo is depicted on a high balcony that would have been on one palace, with the other palace visible behind him, indicating that the Panciatichi owned two palaces. As these elements suggest identifiable segments of a neighborhood, they would have been recognizable to Bartolomeo's contemporaries as the *locus* of the Panciatichi palace.

The portrait's Bartolomeo, in his youth, served as a page at the court of Francis I, a connection that he renewed throughout his life, as he returned repeatedly to France for family business and as part of Cosimo I's ambassadorial appointments.[35] It would appear that Bartolomeo exhibited an early disposition for writing and scholarship, as he was sent to study at the University of Padua, where he is listed as a student in April 1529.[36] On 20 August, he was elected *Consigliere* of the "natio Tuscha," an honorable position of leadership for a student.[37] On 14 December 1530, Bartolomeo received a *dottorato in arte*, and on 6 February 1531, he was elected, along with five other students "ad procurandum quod tripudia que fiunt in carnis privio debeant fieri servato honore Universitatis."[38] At the age of twenty-four, shortly after he received his University degree, Bartolomeo was legitimized by Alessandro Campeggi and soon thereafter married Lucrezia di Gismondo Pucci.[39]

The date of Bartolomeo's marriage to Lucrezia varies in the early literature and ranges from 1528 (Litta) to 1532 (Piovan) to 1534. The likeliest date is 1534, two years after the death of Bartolomeo senior and the year in which the younger Bartolomeo took full possession of his inheritance.[40] Lucrezia Pucci was the daughter of Gismondo Pucci (1469–1543) and Francesca di Guido Mannelli (d. 1564). [41] The family was not wealthy, but it was thoroughly Florentine, and Gismondo had been one of the *Dodici Buonomini* in 1526 and *Potestà di Prato* in 1533.[42] The family, however, had a cloud in the form of the suicide of Puccio Pucci (1442–1507), who threw himself into the Tiber when the family finances collapsed under his guidance.[43] Thus, both Bartolomeo and Lucrezia had less than pristine family credentials, yet by marrying they provided for the other that which each lacked — wealth for her and a solid and legitimate Florentine family connection for him.

While Bartolomeo had an international, cosmopolitan, and upper-class upbringing and education, Lucrezia was through and through a *Fiorentina* from a conventional family. Yet, Bronzino represented her as a woman of education, able to pray from a Book of Hours written in Latin. She is also represented in luxurious clothing and an expensive hairstyle, which distinguish her as a woman aware of the height of 1530s Florentine fashion, who was meticulous about her appearance and careful to have her clothing, coiffure, jewelry, prayer book, and surroundings presented in accurate detail.[44] Lucrezia's family finances may have been modest, but she adapted quickly to the luxurious standard of the Panciatichi, and her evident intelligence and character, emphasized in Bronzino's portrait, must have been an asset to her as the couple advanced socially at home and abroad. Elizabeth Cropper attributed only one child to the couple, but they actually had four—Margherita (d. 16 October 1599), who married Altobianco di Buondelmondi (no issue); Carlo (17 August 1545–1620), who married Eleonora di Luigi degli Albizzi (d. 19 March 1634) and founded a branch of the family that continued until 1665; Francesco (d. 26 February 1614); and Maria, who married Francesco di Pierfilippo Gianfigliazzi (no issue).[45]

Starting with Pompeo Litta, the early sources on Bartolomeo note his literary activities as an author and poet as well as his friendship with leading Humanists and ecclesiastics in France and Italy.[46] Among the intellectuals with whom Bartolomeo established contact and friendship were Pietro Aretino, whom he assisted in publishing French translations of his *L'Umanità di Cristo* and his *Passione di Cristo*. Bartolomeo and Aretino were working with Jean de Vauzelles, the Abbot of Montrottier, whose press specialized in the production of religious books.[47] The result of the project was the Lyonese publication of Aretino's *Umanità di Cristo* and his Life of the Virgin Mary, as well as his Life of St. Catherine. The letters exchanged document Bartolomeo's friendship with both men and his involvement in the publication of religious treatises of diverse types.[48]

Bartolomeo was also friends with Jean de Vauzelles, Abbot of Montrottier (appointed by Marguerite d'Angoulême, Queen of Navarre), the reformist Bishop Jean di Meaux, Louis de Berquin, Guillaume Briçonnet, Clément Marot, Jacque Lefèvre d'Étaples, Antonio Paleario, Niccolò and Vincezio Martelli, Bastiano Sanleonini, Benedetto Varchi, and other members of the *Accademia Fiorentina*.[49] Bartolomeo's literary accomplishments were extensive and indicated a range of interests and abilities. While at the Accademia, he gave lectures on Dante and composed treatises on literary and philological debates of interest to the Academicians.[50] Bartolomeo's contact with the *Accademia Fiorentina* began, prior to its formation, with his membership in the *Accademia degli Umidi*, which he joined on 20 January 1541. After Duke Cosimo transformed the Umidi into the *Accademia Fiorentina* (1542), Bartolomeo joined the reformed organization on 25 March 1542 and became its *console* in 1545 when Benedetto Varchi stepped down.[51] As such, he was responsible for the establishment of new regulations that increased the quality and quantity of intellectual exchange, and for this accomplishment he was highly praised by his peers.

In his description of Bartolomeo's intellectual activities, Litta noted that it would have been in France where Bartolomeo would have come across the ideas of Protestant reformers, as Francis I and his sister, Marguerite de Navarre d'Angoulême, encouraged and befriended reformist intellectuals, such as Erasmus of Rotterdam and Jacques Lèfrevre d' Étaples, and encouraged reading the works of Luther and Calvin.[52] Doubtless it was this interest, known in Florence, which caused problems for Bartolomeo with the Inquisition from 1550 to 1552. More recently, Francesco Piovan has suggested that contact between Bartolomeo and the developing confessional issues of his time occurred also when he was a student at Padua, where there were Germans who would have been familiar with the development of the Protestant churches in Northern Europe.[53] When Bartolomeo was appointed as the duke's ambassador to the French Court, from 3 February 1549 to October 1550 (he was replaced by Luigi Capponi), he had opportunities to renew his contacts in France and learn about recent developments in the confessional debates proliferating in Northern Europe.[54] Carlo Falciani and Salvatore Caponetto have stated that Bartolomeo's trips to France can be documented to 1539, 1547, 1549, and 1552, but they do not specifically identify which trips were made for family business and which trips were part of Bartolomeo's ambassadorial efforts for Cosimo; and it should be noted that, in 1547, the official Florentine ambassador to the French Court was Giovanni Battista Ricasoli.[55] Ricasoli replaced Cosimo's previous ambassador, Bernardo de' Medici, who was the Florentine ambassador from 1544 to 1545, when Cosimo first established formal diplomatic relations with the French Court. Bartolomeo's stay in Lyon, begun soon after his marriage, had ended by 14 February 1539, when he was back in Florence, as is documented by a letter of that date written by Bartolomeo to Aretino from Florence.[56] The letter discussed details of their project to publish Aretino's work in France.

Bartolomeo's intellectual interests in literature, language, and history enabled him to successfully lead the *Accademia Fiorentina* during his directorship in 1545.[57] During Bartolomeo's consulate, the *Accademia* flourished and gathered together scholars interested

in studying a range of topics, including languages, history, literature, and theology in an ambitious agenda, which created the nexus
of intellectual exchange grounded in the past but aware of current
intellectual and religious debates.[58] Among Florentines interested in
confessional issues were several members of the *Accademia*.[59] Benedetto Varchi, for instance, gave a Sermon on the Cross on Good Friday in 1549, explicating Christ's Crucifixion as the path to salvation
in a manner that was characterized as Lutheran.[60] It is impossible to
discern the full extent or nature of Bartolomeo's engagement in discussions, with other members of the *Accademia*, about confessional
debates or his personal, spiritual position, but his contact with Jean
de Vauzelles would have brought a wide range of literature to his
attention, ranging from orthodox Catholic books to the most problematic of Lutheran or Calvinist treatises, suggesting that he would
have been well informed on such topics. That he was influenced
enough by his reading to be suspected of heresy and Lutheranism
may indicate that Bartolomeo talked freely about his ideas on religious issues.

Bartolomeo had two brushes with the Inquisition, the first occurring in 1550, when Lorenzo Davidico gave Bartolomeo's name
to the Inquisition.[61] Bartolomeo and the others whom Davidico accused escaped unscathed when Cosimo vouched for their status
as Catholics in good standing. However, in 1552, Bartolomeo was
not as fortunate, and the charges brought against him caused him
to be arrested by the Inquisition.[62] His arrest followed an accusation made against him by Pietro Manelfi, the fallen priest who was
repenting his own involvement with the Anabaptists and Lutherans of Italy.[63] Manelfi identified Bartolomeo and many others as
Lutherans masquerading among Catholics. The charge against Bartolomeo was made to the Bolognese Dominican Inquisitor, Leandro
Alberti, and the documents recording the events were published
and analyzed by Gustavo Bertoli.[64] Bertoli did not find Lucrezia's
name in the surviving documents, which do record the names of
other women who were arrested and prosecuted with their hus-
bands.[65]

The three women forced to recant at San Simone were: Giovanna, wife of Ser Lorenzo Niccolucci; Antonia, wife of Francesco
Gabelliere; and Lisabetta, wife of Bartolomeo Ducci. This Bartolo-

meo Ducci may be Ser Bartolomeo Notaro, who was the son of Ser Sebastiano Ducci of Monte Vettolini, who was imprisoned with his wife.[66] It appears that later readings of these documents have confused the Panciatichi with the Ducci couple. The implication of the absence of Lucrezia's name from the documents is that the charge of suspicion of heresy brought against Bartolomeo did not apply to her.

The heterodox/heretical sympathies of which Manelfi accused Bartolomeo were much later echoed by Pietro Carnesecchi during his Inquisitorial trial (1566–67). When questioned, Carnesecchi stated that Bartolomeo was

> imbuto di molte … opinione non cattoliche, se non è mutate da quell tempo in qua che io mi rovai seco alla corte di Francia … non saprei dire da che tempo cominciasse a claudicare ne anche mi ricordo d'haverli sentito dire in quello che lui dissentisse dalla Chiesa cattolica, se non in quanto faceva professione generalmente di assentire alle opinion delli heretici moderni. Et questo fu alla corte di Francia, dove si trovava essendo stato mandato dal duca a fare no so che complement con la regina: et fu del anno 1550 incita.[67]

Carnesecchi connected Bartolomeo's heterodox views to his stay in France, c. 1550, at the court of Henry II and Catherine de' Medici. Subsequently, Carnesecchi was tried and executed as a heretic. During the trial, his path to heresy was traced from his involvement with the Neapolitan circle of intimates who clustered around Giulia Gonzaga and her legal/spiritual adviser, the Spaniard, Juan de Valdés.[68] It would be difficult, however, to characterize Bartolomeo simply as a Valdesian, given his extensive and complex exposure in France to direct contact with a range of reformist ideas. To Bartolomeo, Valdés would have been one more Italian reformist, comparable to the Italian *Evangelisti* or the Spanish *Alumbrados* and, likely, not as important to him as Erasmus, Luther, or Calvin. Despite Carnesecchi's renewed accusation against Bartolomeo, it is clear from the data on Bartolomeo's life after 1552 that Carenesecchi's remarks did not renew Inquisitorial interest in Bartolomeo. He therefore lived out his life as a member of the Church that the Council of Trent reformed.

Bartolomeo's knowledge and friendship with reformers and heterodox thinkers dated from his early and continuing life in France and from his contact with the French Court. In Florence, after his return and into the late 1540s, Bartolomeo would have found similar associates at the *Accademia Fiorentina*,[69] where the members discussed the work of Dante and Boccaccio and knew the literary history of Hebrew Scripture, the Gospels, and Patristic literature and would have been familiar with the works of their contemporaries, such as Erasmus and Valdés, as well as those of Luther and other reformers. These texts were made available by a European printing industry that published treatises and books by contemporary and traditional authors, which circulated widely and sometimes anonymously (in order to hide the identity of individuals deliberately propagating reformist tracts).[70] As a member of the *Accademia*, Bartolomeo likely bought books frequently and was possibly given a wide range of books by his associates, which were found in his house by the Inquisition and which he was forced to burn. His Humanistic interest in *explication de texte* and his study of classical, medieval, and contemporary literature would have drawn him to the Lutheran idea that the interpretation of Scripture was a natural right of educated Christians. Hence, Bartolomeo's education, background, and life were all conducive to a path that would bring him to a collision with the Inquisition.

Orazio da Sangallo's *Cronica* notes that Bartolomeo was found guilty of wanting to interpret Scripture on his own, something that Luther encouraged and the Church banned; and he did burn his problematic books.[71] Yet, the Inquisition released Bartolomeo, who returned to a life of high regard and accomplishment.[72] This outcome of Bartolomeo's trial suggests that he was found to be more heterodox than heretic and able to return to orthodoxy upon recantation. No question the abjuration was the price of his freedom—and perhaps his life—but that the Inquisition accepted his abjuration indicates that he was able to make a convincing case for his return to the Church. Before, during, and after his recantation, only Bartolomeo really knew his true religious affiliation, and it is more likely that his reformist sympathies were more Erasmian than Valdesian and more in keeping with the spiritual thought of France than of Naples.

Based on Bertoli's reading of the documents, those Florentines who were judged to be guilty of unremitting heresy during the 1552 process were permanently imprisoned or worse. Yet, as Bertoli noted, Bartolomeo was not among those who were forced to wear the yellow and black *bigallo* adorned with a cross in the recantation process, as did those who were judged to be guilty of true heresy. Bertoli's summary of the documents clarified that those who did wear the yellow and black *bigallo* were taken back to jail, but Bartolomeo was free to go.[73] Thus, according to Bertoli, Bartolomeo was in the group of six men who were only made to carry torches, pay a fine, and burn problematic books, after which they were released under their own recognizance.[74] Relatively unscathed by this experience with the Inquisition, Bartolomeo continued his life with Lucrezia as the founder of a family line that lasted until 1665.[75]

Lucrezia's absence from the Inquisitorial records, according to Bertoli's reading of the documents, seems to suggest that she was not mentioned because she was not accused, arrested, or made to recant since nobody questioned her allegiance to the Church. Thus, the documentary record appears to indicate that Bartolomeo and Lucrezia Panciatichi perhaps were not necessarily of the same mind about religion or confessional issues. Because three of Bronzino's paintings for the Panciatichi are religious in subject and Lucrezia's portrait shows her holding a Book of Hours of the Virgin Mary, assessing the meaning of these paintings in relation to the orthodoxy and heterodoxy of the Panciatichi is important. Possibly, Bronzino's paintings may contain clues that can clarify why and how the Panciatichi escaped Carnesecchi's fate. However, such a consideration of the Panciatichi paintings requires a determination of their chronology so that they can be contextualized specifically in the changing religious atmosphere of the early sixteenth century.

CHRONOLOGY AND HETERODOXY: THE PORTRAITS, HOLY FAMILIES, AND THE *CRUCIFIED CHRIST*

An earlier, as opposed to a later, date for the Panciatichi paintings is suggested by their placement in Bronzino's *Vita*, which puts Vasari's description of the Panciatichi commissions after Bronzino's trip to Pesaro (1530–32/33) and before Bronzino began to work for the duke and duchess in the early 1540s.[76] The placement of the discussion of the Panciatichi paintings suggests that Vasari knew that at least some of these paintings were dated relatively early in Bronzino's career. Five large paintings, which these are, represent a significant amount of work. The style of the Panciatichi paintings is not uniform and indicates that time passed from the first to the last painting before all five works were completed.

Craig Hugh Smyth summarized the arguments for dating the Panciatichi portraits to the late 1530s when he argued their date on the basis of the development of Bronzino's style; and other scholars have also dated the portraits relatively early in Bronzino's *oeuvre* to c. 1540.[77] Maurice Brock and Elizabeth Cropper have both remarked on the similarity of Lucrezia's portrait to that of Bronzino's *Lady with a Little Dog* (Florence, Uffizi), traditionally accepted as dating from the mid-1530s, a similarity that implies that Lucrezia's portrait belongs within this time frame.[78] Both Lucrezia and the *Lady with a Little Dog* wear similar brilliant red dresses and comparably elaborate hair styles, belts, and jewelry; and both are represented seated in front of an architectural niche, framed by columns. Both sit on elaborate chairs decorated with grotesque masks. In effect, Lucrezia's portrait is a more refined and elaborate version of the portrait formula Bronzino used in the *Lady with a Little Dog*.

Bronzino depicted Lucrezia as a pious woman, and the *Lady* is also religious, as is emphasized by the rosary that she holds in her right hand and by the books that rest on a shelf behind her chair, the tassels of which suggest that they are prayer books. Cropper has identified Lucrezia's belt as being a rosary, but this is not evident, although in the sixteenth century rosaries were worn attached to belts.[79] Lucrezia's beaded belt, however, is similar to the belt of the *Lady*, indicating that they belong to a shared world of fashionable accessories. These correspondences argue for a close date between the two portraits, and it is possible that Lucrezia, having seen the portrait of the *Lady*, asked for a similar portrait or that Bronzino simply refined and adapted a portrait type that he knew was successful.

Red was very fashionable as a color for women's clothing in the sixteenth century. The color was also evocative of the Virgin's robe, as depicted by Bronzino. Red is the color of Mary's robe in Bronzino's *Holy Family*, now in the Kress Collection,[80] dated c. 1526–28; in the Virgin of the *Holy Family* in a private collection in Milan, dated c. 1530;[81] worn by the Magdalen and Christ in the *Noli me Tangere*, dated c. 1532;[82] and by Lucrezia and by the Virgin of the Uffizi and Vienna *Holy Families*, painted for the Panciatichi. The association of red with the robe of the Virgin provides an additional symbolic link between Lucrezia and the Virgin that emphasizes Lucrezia's Marian devotion, indicated by her Book of Hours. The use of this color to link the sitter to the Virgin occurs also in Bronzino's *Lady with a Little Dog*, wherein the woman holds a rosary in her left hand in a manner that evokes the book Lucrezia holds in *her* left hand. In both portraits, the women wear red and hold Marian symbols, which identify them as followers of the Church's cult of the Virgin. As such, these portraits make overt statements about the Catholic spirituality of the depicted women, through the inclusion of these identifiable and specific attributes. Although the Virgin Mary was not entirely cast out by Protestants, as Luther considered the Virgin as deserving honor as the mother of Christ, marked and overt Marian devotions, such as those exhibited in these two paintings, were essentially Roman.[83] Thus, the emphatic devotion to the Virgin represented in Lucrezia's portrait indicates that this painting should be understood in a Roman context, as an explicit statement of Lucrezia's spiritual practice and religious preference.

As Falciani noted, Bartolomeo's portrait is comparable to that of Bronzino's *Portrait of Guidobaldo della Rovere*, which dates from Bronzino's stay in Pesaro (1530–32).[84] This correspondence argues for an early date, c. 1539–41, for Bartolomeo's portrait, which is where Smyth placed it. Although the backgrounds of Bartolomeo and Guidobaldo's portraits are very different, Bartolomeo's portrait is a reworking into a Florentine, gentlemanly context of the pose of the portrait of Guidobaldo, who is depicted as a military man. Both men are posed, facing the spectator, with their left hand resting on or near the head of their dogs, while the right hand holds the attribute that identifies their occupation. In the case of Guidobaldo, a helmet, and for Bartolomeo—who was a statesman, intellectual, and author—a book. The concurrences evident between Bartolomeo and Guidobaldo and Lucrezia and the *Lady* indicate that the Panciatichi portraits correspond to Bronzino's work in the mid to late 1530s, and they likely were commissioned soon after the couple returned from France, in 1539. At that point, Bronzino had not yet developed the portrait style that would result from his work for the ducal family in the mid-1540s, where there is less emphasis placed on the background setting and attributes and more on the characterization of the sitter conveyed through gesture and expression, with a more condensed use of symbolic objects. Thus, the compositional structure of the Panciatichi portraits suggests that they should be dated before 1541–42.

The underdrawing of Lucrezia's portrait presents evidence that indicates the order in which Bronzino painted the Panciatichi. As Falciani discussed, Bronzino's initial design for the Panciatichi portraits demonstrates that their backgrounds were meant to match and that Lucrezia's portrait originally had an architectural background similar to that seen in Bartolomeo's portrait.[85] Although Cropper identified the column as Ionic, the column in Lucrezia's portrait is composite Tuscan/Corinthian and is a match for that found in Bartolomeo's portrait.[86] The exaggerated corners of the capital and the acanthus stems of the Tuscan/Corinthian order, employed by Filippo Brunelleschi in his Florentine buildings, are visible in the columns in Lucrezia's and in Bartolomeo's portrait. After Bronzino sketched in the architecture for Lucrezia's portrait, he painted over it and replaced it with the niche that frames her. The niche framing Lucrezia is not exactly like that of the recently identified *Crucified Christ*, but it is similar, which suggests that the *Christ* was also completed before Lucrezia's portrait was finished.

The *Christ* is similar in style to Bronzino's *St. Sebastian* (Madrid, Thyssen Bornemisza Collection), which has been dated to the early 1530s on the basis of its style, which reflects strong influence from Pontormo (Fig. 8).[87] The *Christ* is also very Pontormesque, as was noted by Philippe Costamagna and Falciani, who dated the painting to no later than 1540, when they published their attribution of the work to Bronzino.[88] The painting of faces and bodies in the *Christ* and the *St. Sebastian* are similar, and both have a level of physical idealization accompanied by an attention to detail that simultaneously renders them as spirit and body. Of the two, the more mature work is the *Christ*, which is more fully realized in its physicality than is the *St. Sebastian*. Despite a heightened realism that indicates a more accomplished technique, the *Christ* does belongs to Bronzino's early period and is an example of a large altarpiece, as the *Christ* is approximately 5' x 3'.

The portraits of Lucrezia and Bartolomeo represent the sitters as being of different ages, and cues about their respective stages of life exist within the controlled expressions that Bronzino gave his subjects. The initial impression derived from looking at Bartolomeo's portrait is that he is old, but this effect is created not by the detailing of his facial features but by the long, scraggly beard. Scrutiny of his face, however, belies the aging beard, as Bartolomeo's cheeks are firm, unlined, and pinkish and his jaw line can be clearly discerned, through the obscuring beard, as being tight, as it can only be in someone still in their early thirties. There is little sagging around Bartolomeo's eyes, which have slight pouches under them, again as would conform to someone of younger middle age. In 1539, the year in which the Panciatichi returned to Florence, Bartolomeo was thirty-two or thirty-three years old, just about right for the state of his facial skin and muscle tone represented in the portrait. Hence, while Bartolomeo is not a youth, Bronzino painted him as the relatively young man that he was c. 1540.

In his portrait, Bartolomeo is dressed in the latest fashion, with his beard done in the French, swallow-tail style.[89] Bartolomeo is wearing a *cioppettella*, a garment that originated at the Spanish court and came into vogue in Florence but with a softer, looser form than the garment had in Spain.[90] The *cioppettella* was fashionable for men from the 1530s into the late 1550s, thus it does not assist in dating the portrait. Bartolomeo wears the *cioppettella* over a shirt that is lined in contrasting color within the open vents of its sleeves. He wears a belt with a silver buckle, as was customarily worn with a *cioppettella*, and he sports an elegant and decorated beret, of a type worn in cities.[91] In his right hand, Bartolomeo holds a book, indicative of his poetic and authorial literary production, and his left hand hovers above the head of his dog, which jumps up on the balcony's sill, which runs parallel to the picture plane. Although Bartolomeo is meant to be standing in Florence, Carlo Falciani noted that the architecture in the background, while predominantly Mannerist in tone, combines Italian and Northern elements.[92] Thus, Bronzino's characterization of Bartolomeo renders him as a Florentine of the global *polis*, equally comfortable at home and abroad.

Lucrezia's birth date is unknown, so her age is not a determinant for dating the portrait, but she appears to be younger than her husband by some years. Her smooth cheeks, slim waist, fresh color, unlined face, and abundant, bright hair indicate that she is perhaps in her early to mid-twenties. Lucrezia is dressed in clothing and a hairstyle that was very fashionable in the mid to later 1530s and acceptable as not completely frumpy only until about 1541–42.[93] The elaborate sleeves of her costume and the plain cloth of her dress, while very fashionable in the 1530s, became outdated when Eleonora introduced a new style of clothing to Florence in the early 1540s. Hairstyles also changed under Duchess Eleonora's influence, when she introduced simpler, pulled-back hair and snoods. Lucrezia's hair is elaborately dressed and piled up on top of her head in the style of the 1530s, suggesting a date of no later than 1541–42.

By 1542, Lucrezia's hair and dress would not have been selected for an important portrait intended to convey the sitter's status. As a member of the Florentine court, Lucrezia would not likely have continued wearing clothing that was out of date and not in keeping with the taste of the duchess, as this would have been a sartorial and diplomatic *faux-pas*. Thus, Lucrezia's clothes and hair indicate a time for the portrait prior to 1541–42, when the style of her dress and hair would still have been fashionable. Bartolomeo's portrait would also pre-date the change of Florentine fashion, because his portrait preceded hers, as did the *Christ*.[94] Because Lucrezia's portrait can be dated prior to 1542, on the evidence of her clothing, Lucrezia's portrait provides a *terminus ante quem* for these three works. Thus, the order of commission and execution seems to have been the *Christ*, then Bartolomeo's portrait, followed by Lucrezia's portrait, with the *Holy Families* coming after these more important works were completed, suggesting that the Uffizi *Holy Family* and the Vienna *Holy Family* should be dated after 1542.

An additional *terminus ante quem* for the portraits is provided by Lucrezia's second pregnancy, which began in December of 1544, when she was pregnant with Carlo, who was born in August 1545.[95] Lucrezia could not have been painted as she is during the pregnancy, nor immediately after the pregnancy. The soonest Lucrezia could have been painted after the pregnancy and before Carlo was old enough to be included would have been 1546, but by then

Lucrezia's clothing would have been hopelessly dowdy, and the mother of two children (Margherita and Carlo) would not have been depicted as such a young woman.

Possibly, the couple's first child, Margherita, was born prior to their return to Florence in 1539. However, if Margherita was born after their return and before Carlo, this would further narrow the date for Lucrezia's portrait. In order for Lucrezia to have been pregnant in December 1544, the earliest Margherita could have been born was eleven months prior, making 1542/43 as the likely birth years for Margherita, if she was born in Florence after the couple's return. These are the years to which Lucrezia's costume and hair date the portrait. Had Margherita been born in France, Lucrezia's characterization would perhaps not have been as youthful, as her pregnancy would have changed her almost virginal appearance into a more matronly presentation.

An element in the portrait which suggests that Margherita was not born before 1539 is the Book of Hours Lucrezia holds. Petitions to the Virgin Mary for a child were and are part of Catholic devotional practices, for those who practice devotion to the cult of the Virgin. Perhaps Lucrezia's Hours is an indication of a petition to the Virgin for a child because she had not yet become a mother. As Cropper pointed out, Lucrezia's gaze, as she looks up from her Hours, evokes the manner in which the Virgin looks up from her book in representations of the Annunciation.[96] This contextual association is another argument for thinking that Lucrezia is indeed praying for a child and this detail could indicate that Margherita was born after 1541/42, closely followed by Carlo in 1545.

Recently, Massimo Firpo, Falciani, and Cropper have put forward a date as late as 1544–45 for the Panciatichi portraits, in an attempt to interpret them within a Protestant and/or Valdesian current of spiritual thought represented by Benedetto da Mantova's *Beneficio di Cristo* (Venice, 1543). This is precisely the time during which the portrait could not have been painted, because Lucrezia was pregnant with Carlo and, possibly, in 1542–43 with Margherita. Salvatore Caponetto proposed a date of c. 1540 for Lucrezia's portrait, arguing that the portrait is evidence for the diffusion of Valdesianism in Florence by that date.[97] However, Caponetto does not establish a chronology for this diffusion of "simpatie protes-

tante" in a specific manner, nor does he reconcile the late dates for
the publication of the *Beneficio* (1543) and for Valdés' own treatises (1545) with the assignation of a date of c. 1540 for Lucrezia's
portrait. While Caponetto places Lucrezia's portrait as postdating
Bartolomeo's portrait and the *Christ*, Firpo, Falciani, and Cropper
place the Panciatichi portraits and Holy Families after 1543, the
date of the *Beneficio*'s publication, while ignoring that they date the
Christ before 1540, even though they assign it influence from the
Beneficio. There are two problems with the line of reasoning taken
by Caponetto, Firpo, Falciani, and Cropper: one is the discrepancy
between the internal evidence and the historical data that exists
about Lucrezia and the proposed late dates for it; and the second
problem is the overemphatic focus on Valdesianism as being the
dominant interpretive filter for the Panciatichi paintings, given Lucrezia's Catholic Hours.

In analyzing the Panciatichi paintings from the predominant
perspective of the *Beneficio*, the problem of relative chronology
must have become clear to Falciani, who sought to resolve this conundrum by employing the *Alfabeto Cristiano* of Juan de Valdés to
prove that the Panciatichi paintings are Valdesian.[98] Falciani emphasized the *Alfabeto* because Valdés composed it in 1536, which
does allow enough time for influence for the early *Christ*. However, Falciani's interpretive attempt is not definitively convincing,
because the *Alfabeto* was not published until 1546, and there is no
evidence to prove that it was known in Florence or to Bartolomeo,
in manuscript form, before its publication.[99] Thus, it is unlikely that
the *Alfabeto* was available or important enough for the Panciatichi
to have used it as the source text for Bronzino's *Christ*. Nor is the
work of Valdés or the *Beneficio* necessary to argue that Bartolomeo's
heterodoxy might have been accommodated by Bronzino's rendition of the *Christ*, because Bartolomeo had a wide range of access to
reformist literature. Thus, the *Christ* should be studied as an image
remarkable for its ability to incorporate orthodox and heterodox
aspects that accommodated Lucrezia's Romanity and Bartolomeo's
eclectic spirituality.

The Valdesian approach taken for the Panciatichi paintings
ignores the graphically overt indicators of Catholicism in Lucrezia's portrait and Bartolomeo's wide experience with reform move-

ments, which was much more diverse than Juan de Valdés. Thus, it would be more appropriate to consider that Bronzino's paintings for the Panciatichi include explicit Catholic references along with a possibility for enabling Bartolomeo's more diverse spirituality to respond to Bronzino's rendition of the commissioned subjects. It should also be kept in mind that Protestant and reformist spirituality was grounded in the traditions of the Church; hence, the idea of a "pure" and Protestant Valdesianism cannot be supported by history.[100] Even interpreting Valdesianism through the filter of the *Beneficio* is problematic, as is interpreting Catholic and Protestant reform movements through the filter of Valdesianism, when the European, confessional situation was much more complex and in flux than this approach conveys.

The *Beneficio di Cristo* was important and was widely read, but it was not read in isolation. Its author, Fra Benedetto da Mantova, and its main editor, Marcantonio Flaminio, were widely read and familiar with the teachings of the Church, as well as with the thought of Erasmus, Luther, and Calvin.[101] Caponetto argued that the title of the work was intended to align its content with Philipp Melanchton and Desiderius Erasmus' identification of Christ's death on the Cross as a "beneficio" to humanity.[102] As such, the title would reference reformist concepts, with the title functioning as a unifying hinge for disrupted Christianity.[103] Prior to its publication, the *Beneficio* had limited circulation in manuscript form, and Pier Francesco Riccio, Cosimo's *majordomo*, owned one manuscript, but too late to have been very influential, although Riccio would not have been the only point of contact in Florence for this work as time passed.[104]

Caponetto's study of the manuscript in Riccio's possession, now in the Biblioteca Riccardiana, indicates that perhaps Riccio did not acquire the manuscript until after 1550, because there is a note on folio 1r which states: "Petri Francisci Riccii praepositi Pratensis mancipium Cosimo Medicis Florentiae et Senarum totiusque fere Thusciae regni Ducis optimi principis." Gigliola Fragnito discussed this note in her article on Riccio's life, noting that in it Riccio self-identifies as "praepositi," which implies that he did not own the manuscript until after he had been awarded the "praepositura" of Santo Stefano di Prato, conferred on him on February 1550.[105] On the manuscript's fols. 1r– 9v there is written: "Del Cardinale Contareno" (incipit: "Acccepti literas tuas…explicit: … Ratisponae. Die XXV May M.D.XLI"). On fols. 9v–13v is written: "Del Cardinale Sadoletto" (incipit: "Quod in minore schedula …"). On fols. 13v–55r we fnd: "Prima parte di una predica fatta il 2 dì di Pasqua de Frate Benedetto da Lucarno in Santa Croce di Firenze."[106] Thus, the manuscript also included Cardinal Gasparo Contarini's address to the Conference of Regensburg, dated 25 May 1541, indicating that the manuscript is dated later. Caponetto observed that the manuscript's text is very like the printed version, published in 1543, which argues for a date of 1542–43 for the compilation of the text of this manuscript, which was not available in Florence prior to c. 1540, the date currently proposed for the *Christ*.[107]

Reconciliation, Orthodoxy, and Heterodoxy

As a devotional treatise, the *Beneficio* was a combination of Valdesian spirituality, reformist ideas, Catholic tradition, and individualized devotional mysticism. Its text does not take sides in confessional debates; it is neither overtly Catholic nor overtly Lutheran or anything else—it is simply "Christian."[108] In short, the *Beneficio* was everything that the Catholic Church did not want to see circulating in contexts where Catholics, unaware of the text's problematic nature, could think that the *Beneficio* reflected orthodox teachings. It should be noted that Valdés never declared himself a Lutheran and never explicitly denied Catholicism in his pan-Christian writings, unlike Luther and the other Protestant reformers, who immediately disavowed allegiance to the Church. Nonetheless, by 1549, the *Beneficio* and Valdés' published works were placed on the index of prohibited books, along with the works of Luther, Calvin, and Zwingli.

Yet, the *Beneficio* is as much a text of reconciliation of confessional debates as it is a text of ambiguous allegiance, and in this it may be a parallel to Bartolomeo's heterodoxy. It must be noted that until Regensburg (1541) failed to effect reconciliation between Catholics and Lutherans, hope of reuniting the Church remained. Even after the Council of Trent began, some retained hope of reconciling.[109] Perhaps Bartolomeo belonged to this group, which sought until very late to reunite the Church and the Protestant reformers and which searched especially for a way in which Luther's theol-

ogy and that of the Church could be reconciled. As such, Bartolomeo, who was accused of being a "luterato," might have belonged
to the group that attempted to find a conciliatory approach to the
Church's dogma and Luther's challenge. Or, Bartolomeo may have
been denounced because he was an Erasmian, mistaken for a Lutheran.

The Council of Trent banned Valdesian treatises because Valdés
was early identified as an Erasmian reformer and later was perceived as another heretical Nicodemist of undefined allegiances.
As the Church had considered Erasmus problematic, they identified Valdés as an Erasmian of Lutheran sympathies.[110] Erasmus'
later repudiation of Luther was to no avail, and individuals labeled
Erasmian were automatically considered to be crypto-Lutherans.[111]
It is possible that Bartolomeo was an Erasmian, rather than a Lutheran, and perhaps belonged to the group which sought to bring
about a reconciliation of Luther and the Church. The Inquisitorial
documents record that Bartolomeo was forced to burn books, likely
books found by the Inquisitors in his palace library and in the libraries of the others who were accused by the Inquisitors. These
books may well have been combinations of Erasmian, Lutheran,
and Calvinist texts and possibly Valdesian, but there is no reason to
privilege the Valdesian texts over the others in either Bartolomeo's
religious thought or in interpreting Bronzino's paintings.

Thus, other productive interpretive strategies could be followed for the Panciatichi paintings that consider the significance
of Lucrezia's Roman Hours. Here, the perspective taken is based
on Roman orthodoxy, while allowing for heterodoxy, as the content of Books of Hours, the liturgy of the Church, and Catholic and
Lutheran theology on the Eucharist are considered to achieve an
understanding of the context for the Panciatichi paintings. As the
Holy Families feature Mary prominently and include Saints John the
Baptist and Elizabeth, these are paintings that reflect adherence to
the Church's cult of the Virgin and its cult of the saints. Additionally, the Vienna *Holy Family* can be demonstrated to reflect the liturgy
of the Feast of the Nativity of St. John the Baptist. Thus, the overt
Catholic content and context for the *Holy Families* and Lucrezia's
portrait enables a Catholic interpretation for the *Christ* as being part
of a group of works that can be demonstrated to be more orthodox

than heterodox.

The religious thought of Valdés, Benedetto, Flaminio, and Luther placed great emphasis on meditation on the Crucifixion as the path to salvation, which is why Firpo, Falciani, and Cropper employed Valdesianism as their interpretive strategy. Yet, Valdés and the *Beneficio* did not develop either from a vacuum or from Protestant reformist thought, which itself was informed by the theology and practices of the Church.[112] Valdesian and Protestant treatises on Christ's life and death developed from the extensive Catholic tradition of mystical devotion that began with the Patristic era, continued in the Middle Ages, and had recently been expressed in Northern Europe in the *Imitatio Christi* of Thomas à Kempis and, in Florence, by Girolamo Savonarola. It was Philippe Costamagna who suggested a Florentine context for the Bronzino *Christ* when he pointed out that its visionary configuration could be linked to Savonarola's sermons on the Crucifixion.[113] Thus, Bronzino's *Christ* fits within a continuum of Florentine and Catholic text and imagery that was an accepted part of Catholic devotional practices, recently manifested in Florence in Savonarolan reformist efforts. But Savonarola's was not the only text emphasizing the Crucifixion that was available in early sixteenth-century Florence.[114] Bronzino's *Christ* must then be considered first within primarily Florentine and Catholic contexts, which correspond to earlier and contemporary meditations on the Body of Christ, and then within the charge of Lutheranism that was brought against Bartolomeo.

In considering Bronzino's *Crucified Christ*, it should be noted that, after Savonarola, there was an increase in demand for copies of earlier texts that placed emphasis on Christ's passion and on his death on the Cross. Edoardo Barbieri's study of sixteenth-century popular devotional literature provides a compilation of the books that were generally known and used by the laity in their devotional practices and personal meditations on the life and death of Christ.[115] Barbieri's study of the titles published by Gabriele Giolito's press in Ferrara indicates that there was a market for the vernacular works of Cornelio Musso, Luís de Granada, and Antonio de Guevara and for the various versions of the *Imitation of Christ*.[116] Additionally, *The Golden Legend* of the pseudo-Bonaventure and the *Specchio di croce* along with the *Vite de santi padri* continued to sell.[112] Among the best sellers were versions of the *Vitae Christi* and the *Meditationes Vitae Christi*, which placed special emphasis on the Passion and the Crucifixion.[118] The *Passione* attributed to Niccolò di Mino Cicerchia, from Siena, was another best-seller, as was the *Vita Christi* by Ludolphe of Saxony, translated into Italian by Francesco Sansovino.[119] After 1471, the vernacular version of the Bible published by Nicolò Malermi continued to sell well into the sixteenth century.[120] What these diverse texts shared was a devotional emphasis on the Passion of Christ and on the salvation of the faithful. Bronzino's *Christ* cannot be analyzed without taking these contemporary, devotional texts into consideration, as well as the Roman liturgy from which they were derived.

This older, traditional and contemporary, sixteenth-century emphasis on the Crucifixion and on the Body and Blood of Christ found its roots in the texts of the Canon of the Mass (the oldest part of the service), where the devout are directed to focus their attention on the salvific sacrifice of Christ and on the Body and Blood that saved them.[121] Likely, Bartolomeo was among those who understood the orthodox and heterodox context of contemporary devotional literature and its more subtle dogmatic implications, which he could discuss with other like-minded, Florentine intellectuals who were similarly interested in the reform of the Church and in reformist ideas.

Possibly, Bartolomeo was familiar with attempts on the part of men such as Cardinal Reginald Pole and Cardinal Gasparo Contarini to reconcile and unite Christianity, and he may have been sympathetic with those attempts.[122] Therefore, it is important to situate the Panciatichi *Christ* within the continuum of popular devotional literature that was available before 1540 and within the moment of potential reconciliation that existed until 1541, when the failure of the Conference at Regensburg made it clear that the separation between Catholics and Lutherans would remain. As such, Bronzino's image becomes an image that stands at the threshold of the Reformation and the Counter-Reformation, with its foundation in orthodox Catholic liturgical, theological, textual, and devotional traditions and its intentionality within the attempt, at Regensburg, that failed to reunite the Church in 1541. After 1542, when the Inquisition was revived, the moment that created Bronzino's *Christ* passed, and the image could not have been formulated in the same way in the years that followed because reconciliation between Catholics and Protestants ended with Trent. The genius Bronzino displayed in his configuration of the *Christ* is found in the manner whereby the painting expressed the contextual fluidity of reconciliation in a painterly manner, which could accommodate Bartolomeo's interest in reformist principles, even as it hewed to the Roman orthodox allegiance so clearly expressed in Lucrezia's Book of Hours and its Latin text honoring the Virgin.

Bartolomeo was accused of having Lutheran books and of being a Lutheran; he was not accused of being a Valdesian. Hence, it would be appropriate to consider Bronzino's *Christ* from the perspective of Luther's beliefs about topics and issues related to Christ's Crucifixion. Such an interpretation does not require either Valdés or the *Beneficio*, because Bartolomeo was able to read Luther's teaching on salvation, the Eucharist, and Transubstantiation directly, without intermediary texts. And, as an intellectual who was in France when Luther and Erasmus began their work of reform, Bartolomeo would have understood the sources of the reform movements better than many Florentines, who were at a distance as key events unfolded. Thus, even though Bartolomeo very much identified himself as a Florentine, his international experience meant that he knew the larger context for reformist developments—not through a Valdesian filter but through his own experience of the events which became history. Likely, Bronzino was also familiar with Luther's ideas and the significance of Erasmus, as the artist was an educated and attuned member of the intelligentsia, even before he joined the *Accademia*.[123] Thus, patron and artist had a varied and diverse series of possibilities within which to frame the content of the Panciatichi *Christ*. These possibilities must not be overlooked in interpreting the Panciatichi paintings, which are simultaneously orthodox and heterodox.

INTERPRETING THE PANCIATICHI PAINTINGS: ORTHODOXY AND

HETERODOXY

The Portraits

While Firpo and Falciani emphasized Valdesian spirituality as the interpretive filter for the Panciatichi paintings, Cropper's interpretive strategy, which recalls Litta's assertion that Bartolomeo learned his problematic religious ideas in France, brought attention to Bartolomeo's French roots.[124] Paradoxically, Cropper's interpretation of Lucrezia's portrait contextualized it within Marian imagery, while interpreting the painting from a Protestant perspective, overlooking the significance of the overt orthodox and Catholic statement Lucrezia makes in her Hours about her adherence to the Church's cult of the Virgin (Fig. 3).[125] Lucrezia's Marian portrait is an explicit indication that points to the Catholic context within which the Panciatichi paintings should be primarily understood.

Lucrezia's Hours is open to Lauds (*Laudes*), the first service of morning, which honors the Virgin as the light of the sun illuminates the world at dawn, and the service conforms to that of the Roman Church in its format and language.[126] The place of Lauds in the day and its association with the illuminating light of faith and the sonorous evocation of the Alleluia recited in the celebration of the Roman Mass are reflected in the glowing light that bathes Lucrezia in a visual evocation of Lauds. Thus, Lucrezia is depicted as a pious Catholic woman engaged in praying to and honoring the female role model for all Catholic women—the Virgin Mary—at the hour indicated by her Hours—the first light of day, linked to the spiritual enlightenment and orthodox piety reflected in the Mass and its praise of God. This characterization, so carefully delineated by Bronzino in her portrait, distances Lucrezia and her portrait from a Lutheran or heterodox context.[127]

Luther honored the Virgin, as the mother of Christ, as a model of patience and virtue, and as an exemplar of someone deserving salvation. However, Luther did not allow the consideration of Mary as intercessor and co-redemptrix, nor did he admit the continuation of the Catholic cult of the Virgin.[128] Luther believed that the cult of the Virgin and the saints detracted from the focus on Christ as Savior, when too much emphasis was given to their ability to assist with the process of salvation. By 1539, it was clear that this divide existed between Catholics and Lutherans (and other Protestant denominations). It can even be suggested that the depiction of Lucrezia's Book of Hours is a conscious resistance to Bartolomeo's free-thinking.

Cropper's analysis of the Panciatichi portraits identified the format of Bartolomeo's portrait as an *Imago Christi*, which she interpreted as an example of reformist sympathies.[129] Leaving aside that the *Imago Christi* is a Catholic image based on the relic of Veronica's Veil, kept at the Vatican since the Middle Ages, it is difficult to reconcile the face of the Christ of the Passion with the evident secular urbanity of Bartolomeo's delineation as an urban sophisticate.[130] However, if Bartolomeo intended to reference the *Volto Santo*, the awareness of its source in Veronica's Veil would have resonated with Rome and not with Luther.

The only overt and identifiable religious element in Bartolomeo's portrait is the aforementioned evocation of the tower of Sta. Maria Novella, which situates Bartolomeo within the Church's neighborhood and near to where members of the family had been buried, as the Panciatichi had an "arca" in Sta. Maria Novella and their arms were displayed on the building, as Aloia has discussed.[131] The older chapel and tomb in Sta. Maria Novella was echoed in the sixteenth-century chapel and tomb in Sta. Maria Maggiore, which was the Panciatichi's personal church, where they are buried, along with a daughter and a nephew. Thus, the portrait affirms Bartolomeo as a *Fiorentino*, with a place in the Florentine, Catholic, ecclesiastical topography of the city, where his lost family tomb and chapel were located in Sta. Maria Novella.

The accent on Bartolomeo's *fiorentinità* made by the tower of Sta. Maria Novella is emphasized by the content of the Uffizi *Holy Family*, to which Bartolomeo's portrait is linked through the inclusion of the Panciatichi arms in both works. The presence of John the Baptist in this painting links its content to Bartolomeo's baptismal name, Giovanni, and to the patronage of the saint, which he shares with Florence. In the Catholic context of the cult of the saints, an individual's patron saint protected them from harm and this special protection was extended to cities dedicated to individual saints. Together, the presence of John the Baptist in the *Holy Families* and the bell tower of Sta. Maria Novella, found in Bartolomeo's portrait create Catholic associations that cannot be ignored in the interpretation of the Panciatichi paintings. The dominant presence of the Virgin Mary in the Uffizi and Vienna *Holy Families* is additional evidence of Catholic devotional practices reflected in the content and context of Bronzino's paintings. With the strong references to the Roman cult of the Virgin evident in Lucrezia's portrait, it is clear that the Panciatichi shared an affiliation to these Catholic devotional practices, which coexisted with Bartolomeo's interest in heterodox, confessional issues.

The Holy Families

Catholic and Florentine traditions are strongly evident in the Vienna *Holy Family*, which includes St. John the Baptist and St. Elizabeth, his mother, along with the Holy Family. In the Vienna *Holy Family*, the Virgin holds a book inscribed with Hebrew letters, which Elizabeth Pilliod discussed and Anthony Grafton identified as the name Isaiah, although earlier literature on the painting had read the letters as Jesus.[132] Rabbi Zachary Silver and Deborah Huacuja, a professional translator, concur that in the Vienna painting, the Hebrew letters do spell Isaiah, but they spell it not in Hebrew but in Italian as—Isaia—because the number of letters in the painting's Isaiah, and their diacritical marks, do not correspond to the actual spelling of Isaiah, which should be either ישעי or וישעי.[133] The Vienna *Holy Family*'s Isaiah is spelled עישי, whereas it should be וישעי. The third and fourth letters (read from right to left) in the painting's inscription are also flipped in a way that evokes the Hebrew spelling of the name Jesus (ישו). Rabbi Silver pointed out that the writer of the Hebrew letters did not use, or perhaps did not even know, Hebrew. However, it is also possible that he was making an allusion to the Messianic content of the book of Isaiah, an allusion accomplished in the flipped letters. As Rabbi Silver pointed out, the transliteration of the word on the Virgin's book would be "Yay-sha-yi-ah." As Isaiah's name means "Salvation of Yah," this being the beginning of the Tetragrammaton (God's name), as Pilliod discussed. Based on Rabbi Silver's information, it should be noted that this Christocentric use of Hebrew for the inscription, which is placed directly next to Christ, is a graphic indication that indeed the promise of Salvation of the Word was made Flesh in Christ.

In a Florentine context, the use of Hebrew corresponded to the linguistic interests of the *Accademia Fiorentina*, which included a study of ancient languages. There was also a group of intellectuals in Florence who identified themselves as the *Aramei* and who were especially interested in Hebrew.[134] Thus, the use of the Hebrew letters in the Vienna painting may indicate that Bartolomeo also had an interest in the language, which he shared with the *Aramei*. The Hebrew letters would have been able to be read by very few people in Florence, although identifying them as Hebrew would have been done easily by anyone seeing the painting. Possibly, the *Aramei* may have given Hebrew letters hermetic significance. However, from a Jewish perspective, this would be an incorrect application of such an interpretive strategy, because the Isaiah on the Virgin's book is not a correctly spelled Hebrew word. Nonetheless, for Bartolomeo, the employment of the Hebrew may have served to identify him as a member or an interested colleague of the *Aramei*.

Altogether, Lucrezia's Marian portrait, the emphasis in the *Holy Families* on Roman traditions, and the liturgy create a Catholic context for these works within which the *Christ* must be considered. Additionally, the book the Virgin holds in the Vienna *Holy Family* corresponds in motif to Lucrezia's Hours; hence, there is a formalistic link between the two paintings, even as the inclusion of John the Baptist in both connects them to Bartolomeo and Florence. Yet, the chronology of the five paintings must be developed prior to a consideration of their content towards providing a tighter focus for the interpretation of the paintings' contents.

There is agreement among scholars that the *Christ* came first, c. 1540, with the portraits following, between 1540 and 1546, although here the date of the portraits is given as before 1542. The Uffizi *Holy Family*, which includes the Panciatichi arms depicted in Bartolomeo's portrait, is close in style to the portrait and also to Bronzino's frescoes and to the first altarpiece Bronzino painted for Eleonora's chapel, dated to 1541–46. Hence, a chronological context for the Uffizi *Holy Family* is provided by its style, which would date it between 1541 and 1546. The Vienna *Holy Family* differs stylistically from the other four works, its colors, its forms, and the painterly execution of its surface argue for a later date, possibly into the 1550s and even after Bartolomeo's release from the Inquisitorial inquest. If so, then the Vienna *Holy Family* may be a painting commissioned after 1552, as a celebration of deliverance through the intercession of Bartolomeo's patron saint, John the Baptist (Bartolomeo was christened Giovanni), and linked to the liturgy of the Feast of the Nativity of St. John the Baptist as an explicit indication that the Panciatichi were now completely devoted Catholics.

The Crucified Christ

In Florentine art, there are a series of celebrated *Crucifixes*, which, by the third decade of the sixteenth century, would have been iconic reference points for Bronzino.[135] These other works include: the hanging *Crucifixes* of Cimabue, Giotto, Brunelleschi, Donatello, Masaccio, and Fra Bartolomeo, as well as the *Crucified Christ* in the Church of Santo Spirito, attributed to Michelangelo.[136] Later, Alessandro Allori continued the tradition in his *Crucifixion with the Virgin and John the Evangelist* (1550–1555), now in the Church of the Santissima Concezione, in Florence.[137] This representational history provides the context within which Bronzino's *Christ* should be primarily understood: as a painting that functioned as a meditative focus for prayer.

The placement of Christ in front of an architectural background also resonates with Northern traditions of placing religious figures against architectural niches, seen in the work of Rogier van der Weyden, Jan Van Eyck, and Hans Memling. In Florence, this Northern European tradition is best represented in Hugo Van der Goes's Portinari altarpiece, where the *Annunciation*, in *grisaille*, appears in front of a backdrop architectural niche. Masaccio's *Trinity* is set against an architectural recess, and the *Christ*s of Brunelleschi, Donatello, and Michelangelo would all have been seen against architectural backgrounds configured with niches and columns. As with the hybrid content of the Panciatichi portraits, the *Christ* blends models of *fiorentinità* and Northern European art into a hybrid of Italio/Northern visual presentation evocative of Bartolomeo's mixed French and Lombard heritage and resonant of his time spent abroad. Nonetheless, in its setting in the Panciatichi palace, Bronzino's *Christ* would have been predominantly considered within a Florentine context.

Florentines would have recognized the *pietra serena* stone of Christ's niche as being evocative of Brunelleschi's architecture, as found in the Church of San Lorenzo, in the Pazzi chapel of Santa Croce, and in the Church of Santo Spirito, as well as in the Old Sacristy of San Lorenzo. In a manner similar to that in which the figure of Christ evoked an earlier century of *Crucifixions*, the architectural backdrop of this image grounds the spectator in the architectural style introduced by Brunelleschi and Leone Battista Alberti and expanded by Michelangelo, which linked Florence in the fifteenth century to Rome in the early Christian Era of the Holy Roman Empire. Both the rendition of Christ and the configuration of the architecture in Bronzino's *Christ*, which are Brunelleschian and Donatellian and Massachesque, situate the Christ in a Florentine artistic continuum that symbolically references Rome and the cultural history of the Roman Church.

The Panciatichi *Christ* is a Florentine *Christ*, linked to Rome through the visual associations established by the carefully depicted architecture against which the Christ is seen. The Classical style of this architecture indicates a connection between the image and the history of the Roman Church, referenced by Brunelleschi and Alberti's employment of their interpretation of Classical style in ecclesiastical architecture. In Florence, this adapted Tuscan Classicism was associated with the celebration of the rituals of the Church, primarily with the celebration of the Mass, which focuses attention on the significance of Christ's sacrifice. Given this interaction between the Crucifixion and the performance of the Mass and the participation of the Panciatichi in this liturgical celebration, either in a palace chapel or in the family chapel in Sta. Maria Maggiore, Bronzino's *Christ* has to be understood primarily in the context from which and for which it was intended: a Roman/Florentine artistic and devotional context. Therefore, the primary meaning of the Panciatichi *Christ* should be sought in the content of the sixteenth-century Roman liturgy that was celebrated in private chapels in Florentine palaces and likely in the Panciatichi palace chapel.

The representation of Christ on the Cross, as an iconic image of Roman and Florentine veneration, traditionally resonates with the ritual and feasts of the Church's Canon of the Mass and with the feasts of *Corpus Christi*, the *Inventione Sanctae Crucis*, and the *Exaltatione Sancte Crucis*.[138] The Canon of the Mass focuses attention on the salvific properties of the Body and Blood of Christ, present in the Eucharist through the miracle and mystery of Transubstantiation. The devotion to the crucified Christ, central to Roman traditions of meditation on the life of Christ, his Passion and Crucifixion is an important part of the history of the Church that is grounded in its liturgy and in the imagery of the Canon of the Mass. The liturgical content of the feasts of the Cross brings additional attention to the Crucifixion and the finding of the True Cross by St. Helena. Bronzino's *Christ* is inextricably part of this continuum of word and image linked to the art of the Church, and its rendition is in keeping with the emphasis on salvation through Christ that is central to the Roman liturgy. That it might have had significance or meaning beyond the Roman tradition to which it can be contextualized is possible, but Bronzino's *Christ* was not created in a Lutheran or a Valdesian context separate or isolated from the painting's Roman origins or from the Church's visual culture or from the history of Florentine art or Panciatichi patronage of Catholic churches.

The body of Christ Bronzino depicted presents to the spectator a vision of Christ on the Cross. In this vision, Christ's pale body is simultaneously materially real, yet mystically present; and it is iconic, although it indicates the past narrative of his Passion and death. The Classical articulation of the wall into Doric pilasters implicitly identifies the vision with historic Rome as well as with Brunelleschian *Fiorentinità*, and it recalls the architectural style of early Christian churches, such as Santa Sabina, Santa Maria in Cosmedin, and Old St. Peter's—buildings wherein the Roman Mass was first celebrated.

Bronzino's *Christ* is curiously bloodless. The wound in His side is a small slit from which blood does not flow, and Christ's hands do not drip blood. The small rivulets of blood that tint the bottom of the Cross, with a central, but narrow, stream of red, is a detail that could almost be overlooked. The lack of blood of this Christ is significant, because it indicates that the spectator does not witnesses the mortal crucifixion of Christ's human body but, instead, sees his transfigured body in a manner that visually evokes Christ's return to the Church at the elevation of the Eucharist and the moment of Transubstantiation. The pale tint of Christ's skin is set off by the rose color of his loincloth, creating the illusion that Christ's body glows with a mystical and internal light, which evokes blood without graphically depicting it. The source of light for the painting is placed at the upper left of the image, the traditional position of God and the Holy Spirit in paintings of the Annunciation. In Bronzino's rendition, the geographic reality of Calvary is denied, as it is denied by Rogier Van der Weyden's *Seven Sacraments* altarpiece and, similarly, in his representation of the *Crucifixion* (Madrid, Philadelphia, and El Escorial). Thus, Bronzino's image of Christ evokes Northern and Italian earlier traditions.

Bronzino's *Christ* is not on the hill of his death but is instead vividly present in a Church, where the spectator encounters him hanging from a cross that is itself spiritualized, in its disproportionately small size, in relation to the body of Christ. Thus, the abbreviated height of the Cross suggests a displacement from the material to the spiritual, even as its lower height makes Christ more accessible, as he is brought to the level of the spectator's gaze. Because Christ is here, he is available to the spectator. Yet, in Bronzino's representation, Christ is not subject to the material laws of earthly existence. This is Christ as ethereal presence—available but distinct from his earthly life and death. Bronzino's portrayal of Christ is idealized, mystical, iconic, and detached from the narrative of the actual Crucifixion because it directly brings attention to the sacrifice of Christ as the subject of the image. As such, it is Eucharistic and linked, by association, to the Canon of the Mass, celebrated every day of the Roman liturgical year except on Holy Saturday.

The implications of the configuration of Bronzino's *Christ* indicate that the Panciatichi were interested in having an altarpiece that represented the significance of Christ after his death and not his actual death on the Cross. Thus, the result is an image that evokes the Christ of the Canon of the Mass, as Christ returns to earth at the moment of Eucharistic Transubstantiation. As such, the image delineates its context within the confessional debates of the 1530s, which continued into the 1540s, about the significance of the Cross, the Mass, and the Eucharist.[139] The Panciatichi Christ depicts the Crucifixion as an iconic sacrifice removed from time, place, and material existence on earth. Hence, this Christ is an imperishable and immanent presence, seen in the ecclesiastical context, indicated by the architectural niche. Thusly configured, this is the Christ of the Canon of the Roman Mass, as celebrated in Florentine churches, evoked by the Classical style of the niche and columns that Bronzino painted, as signifying identifiers of connection to the churches of Rome and Florence. Timely and timeless, historical and beyond history, Bronzino's *Christ* is a visual evocation of the climactic moment of the Canon of the Mass, reached at the elevation of the Eucharist, when the Eucharist becomes the Body and Blood of Christ.

In the Canon of the Mass, the oldest and most consistent part of the Mass, the image of the crucified Christ and the significance of his sacrifice for the personal salvation of the faithful, is emphasized during the Eucharistic part of the service.[140] At the Elevation of the Host, the priest recited (and recites) the words:

> On the day before he was to suffer, he took bread in his holy and venerable hands, and with eyes raised to heaven to you, O God, his almighty Father, giving you thanks, he said the blessing, broke the bread, and gave it to his disciples, saying: Take this, all of you, and eat of it: for this is my Body, which will be given up for you.
>
> (*Qui, pridie quam pateretur, accepit panem in sanctas ac venerabiles manus suas, et elevatis oculis in caelum ad te Deum Patrem suum omnipotentem, tibi gratias agens benedixit, fregit, deditque discipulis suis, dicens: Accipite et manducate ex hoc omnes: hoc est enim Corpus meum, quod pro vobis tradetur.*)

The key phrase in the Canon of the Mass is "hoc est enim Corpus meum" ("For this is my Body"), which precedes the elevation of the chalice and is accompanied by the words:

> In like manner, when the supper was done, taking also this goodly chalice into His holy and venerable hands, again giving thanks to You, He blessed it, and gave it to His disciples, saying: All of you take and drink of this: For this is the Chalice of My Blood of the new and eternal covenant:

the mystery of faith: which shall be shed for you and for many unto the forgiveness of sins.

(Simili modo postquam cenatum est accipiens et hunc pre-clarum calicem in sanctas ac venerabiles manus suas. Item tibi/ gratias agens, bene dixit dedique discipulis suis dicens. Accipite et bibite ex eo omnes: hic est enim calix Sanguinis mei novi et aeterni testamenti, qui pro vobis et pro multis effundetur in remissionem peccatorum.)

The Canon of the Mass focuses attention on the Crucifixion and on Christ's presence in the Eucharist, the "mystery of faith" exclaimed in the Canon, which provides "the forgiveness of sins." Thus, the Eucharistic moment in the Canon of the Mass explicitly brings attention to Christ as the path to salvation attained through his Body and Blood, as participants follow his instruction "As often as you shall do these things, in memory of Me shall you do them" (HEC QUOTIENSCUNQUE FECERITIS IN MEI MEMORIAM FACIETIS). Christ's gift of salvation was explicitly stated with the words:

Mindful, therefore, O Lord, not only of the blessed passion of the same Christ, You Son, our Lord, but also of His resurrection from the dead, and finally His glorious ascension into heaven, we, Your ministers, as also Your holy people, offer to Your supreme Majesty, of the gifts bestowed upon us, the pure Victim, the holy Victim, the all-perfect Victim: the holy Bread of life eternal and the Chalice of unending salvation.

(Unde et memores, Domine, nos servi tui, sed et plebs tua sancta, eiusdem Christi, Filii tui, Domini nostri, tam beatae passionis, necnon et ab inferis resurrectionis, sed et in caelos gloriosae ascensionis: offerimus praeclarae maiestati tuae de tuis donis ac datis hostiam puram, hostiam sanctam, hostiam immaculatam, Panem sanctum vitae aeternae et Calicem salutis perpetuae.)

As the Eucharistic part of the Mass was recited or recalled in front of the Panciatichi *Christ*, Bronzino's image would have functioned as the visible manifestation of the words being spoken by the priest, which bring the transformed Christ back to earth in Transubstantiation. As such, Bronzino's Christ is a unique *tour de force* that reifies into visual form the dogma represented by the Canon of the Mass with its "mystery of faith" through the explicit denial of the narrative of the Crucifixion. Every time a Mass was performed or remembered in front of the Panciatichi *Christ*, the connection between Christ's luminous body on the Cross and Eucharistic Transubstantiation was made explicit. This connection would have been made even more emphatically during feasts of the Cross.

Among the feasts of the Church's liturgical year, associated with the Cross and the Crucifixion, none is more important or more pertinent for interpreting Bronzino's *Christ* than is the Feast of *Corpus Christi*.[141] *Corpus Christi* was celebrated in Florence with a procession that culminated in Santa Maria Novella, the Church where Brunelleschi's *Crucifix* and Masaccio's *Trinity* were located.[142] To Florentines, the resonance between Bronzino's *Christ*, Brunelleschi's *Crucifix*, and Masaccio's *Trinity* would have been clear, as the Panciatichi *Christ* synchronically and diachronically evoked those and other Florentine images of the crucified Christ in stone, wood, and paint.

The liturgy of *Corpus Christi* has remained consistent, and the contemporary liturgy of this feast closely matches the sixteenth-century celebration. Throughout *Corpus Christi*, connections between Christ's Body, His Blood, salvation, and Eucharistic Transubstantiation are made explicit.[143] This set of associations begins with the opening of the liturgy of this day, in the *Introit*, which is Psalm 80:17: "He fed them with the best of wheat, alleluia; and filled them with honey from the rock, alleluia, alleluia, alleluia. Ps. 80:2. Sing joyfully to God our strength; acclaim the God of Jacob. Glory Be." The *Oratio* that follows is:

> O God, under a marvelous sacrament You have left us the memorial of Your Passion; grant us, we beseech you, so to venerate the sacred mysteries of Your Body and Blood, that we may ever perceive within us the fruit of Your Redemption. Who live, etc. S. Amen.

The Last Supper is commemorated in the Epistle, with the reading of 1 Corinthians 11:23–29: Brethren:
I myself have received from the Lord (what I also delivered

to you), that the Lord Jesus, on the night in which He was betrayed, took bread, and giving thanks broke, and said, "Take and eat. This is My Body which shall be given up for you; do this in remembrance of Me." In like manner also the cup, after He had supped, saying, "This cup is the new covenant in My Blood; do this as often as you drink it, in remembrance of Me. For as often as you shall eat this Bread and drink the cup, you proclaim the death of the Lord, until He comes. Therefore whoever eats this Bread or drinks the cup of the Lord unworthily, will be guilty of the Body and the Blood of the Lord. But let a man prove himself, and so let him eat of that Bread and drink of the cup; for he who eats and drinks unworthily, without distinguishing the Body, eats and drinks judgment to himself. Thanks be to God."

These are words that would have been heard by the Panciatichi, wherever they would have participated in the Mass of *Corpus Christi* and which they could connect directly to the image of Bronzino's *Christ*. Similar themes to those found above repeated in the Gradual, Psalm 144:15–16: "The eyes of all look hopefully to You, O Lord; and You give them their food in due season. You open Your hands; and satisfy the desire of every living thing." The closing reading, John 6:56–57, is: "My Flesh is food indeed, and My Blood is drink indeed. He who eats My Flesh, and drinks My Blood, abides in Me and I in him."

The iteration in this liturgy of the connection between the Body and Blood of Christ and salvation through participation in the Sacrament is clear and repetitive, and the repetition found in this service was originally intended to induce a meditative state focused on the significance of the Eucharist. The liturgy of *Corpus Christi* included the Hymn "Lauda Sion Salvatorem," which extols the significance for the faithful of Christ's sacrifice, its Eucharistic manifestation, and the manner in which his Body and Blood enable their salvation through His return to earth in the miracle of Transubstantiation.[144]

Lauda Sion Salvatórem
Lauda ducem et pastórem
In hymnis et cánticis.
Quantum potes, tantum aude:
Quia major omni laude,
Nec laudáre súfficis.
Laudis thema speciális,
Panis vivus et vitális,
Hódie propónitur.
Quem in sacræ mensa cœnæ,
Turbæ fratrum duodénæ
Datum non ambígitur.
Sit laus plena, sit sonóra,
Sit jucúnda, sit decóra
Mentis jubilátio.
Dies enim solémnis ágitur,
In qua mensæ prima recólitur
Hujus institútio.
In hac mensa novi Regis,
Novum Pascha novæ legis,
Phase vetus términat.
Vetustátem nóvitas,
Umbram fugat véritas,
Noctem lux elíminat.
Quod in cœna Christus gessit,
Faciéndum hoc expréssit
In sui memóriam.
Docti sacris institútis,
Panem, vinum, in salútis
Consecrámus hóstiam.
Dogma datur Christiánis,
Quod in carnem transit panis,
Et vinum in sánguinem.
Quod non capis, quod non vides,
Animósa firmat fides,
Præter rerum ordinem.
Sub divérsis speciébus,
Signis tantum, et non rebus,
Latent res exímiæ.
Caro cibus, sanguis potus:
Manet tamen Christus totus,
Sub utráque spécie.

Sion, lift up thy voice and sing:
Praise thy Savior and thy King,
Praise with hymns thy shepherd true.
All thou canst, do thou endeavour:
Yet thy praise can equal never
Such as merits thy great King.
See today before us laid
The living and life-giving Bread,
Theme for praise and joy profound.
The same which at the sacred board
Was, by our incarnate Lord,
Giv'n to His Apostles round.
Let the praise be loud and high:
Sweet and tranquil be the joy
Felt today in every breast.
On this festival divine
Which records the origin
Of the glorious Eucharist.
On this table of the King,
Our new Paschal offering
Brings to end the olden rite.
Here, for empty shadows fled,
Is reality instead,
Here, instead of darkness, light.
His own act, at supper seated
Christ ordain'd to be repeated
In His memory divine;
Wherefore now, with adoration,
We, the host of our salvation,
Consecrate from bread and wine.
Hear, what holy Church maintaineth,
That the bread its substance changeth
Into Flesh, the wine to Blood.
Doth it pass thy comprehending?
Faith, the law of sight transcending
Leaps to things not understood.
Here beneath these signs are hidden
Priceless things, to sense forbidden,
Signs, not things, are all we see.
Flesh from bread, and Blood from wine,
Yet is Christ in either sign,
All entire, confessed to be.

A suménte non concísus,
Non confráctus, non divísus:
Integer accípitur.
Sumit unus, sumunt mille:
Quantum isti, tantum ille:
Nec sumptus consúmitur.
Sumunt boni, sumunt mali:
Sorte tamen inæquáli,
Vitæ vel intéritus.
Mors est malis, vita bonis:
Vide paris sumptiónis
Quam sit dispar éxitus.
Fracto demum Sacraménto,
Ne vacílles, sed memento,
Tantum esse sub fragménto,
Quantum toto tégitur.
Nulla rei fit scissúra:
Signi tantum fit fractúra:
Qua nec status nec statúra
Signáti minúitur.
Ecce panis Angelórum,
Factus cibus viatórum:
Vere panis fíliórum,
Non mittendus cánibus.
In figúris præsignátur,
Cum Isaac immolátur:
Agnus paschæ deputátur
Datur manna pátribus.
Bone pastor, panis vere,
Jesu, nostri miserére:
Tu nos pasce, nos tuére:
Tu nos bona fac vidére
In terra vivéntium.
Tu, qui cuncta scis et vales:
Qui nos pascis hic mortales:
Tuos ibi commensáles,
Cohærédes et sodales,
Fac sanctórum cívium.
Amen. Allelúja.

They, who of Him here partake,
Sever not, nor rend, nor break:
But, entire, their Lord receive.
Whether one or thousands eat:
All receive the self-same meat:
Nor the less for others leave.
Both the wicked and the good
Eat of this celestial Food:
But with ends how opposite!
Here 't is life: and there 't is death:
The same, yet issuing to each
In a difference infinite.
Nor a single doubt retain,
When they break the Host in twain,
But that in each part remains
What was in the whole before.
Since the simple sign alone
Suffers change in state or form:
The signified remaining one
And the same for evermore.
Lo! bread of the Angels broken,
For us pilgrims food, and token
Of the promise by Christ spoken,
Children's meat, to dogs denied.
Shewn in Isaac's dedication,
In the manna's preparation:
In the Paschal immolation,
In old types pre-signified.
Jesu, shepherd of the sheep:
Thou thy flock in safety keep,
Living bread, thy life supply:
Strengthen us, or else we die,
Fill us with celestial grace.
Thou, who feedest us below:
Source of all we have or know:
Grant that with Thy Saints above,
Sitting at the feast of love,
We may see Thee face to face.
Amen. Alleluia.

The hymn's imagery dovetails with the spirit of Bronzino's *Christ* in every aspect, in the luminous quality of the flesh that illuminates the darkness and in the palpable transformative interaction between physicality and mysticism that is at the heart of the Eucharistic celebration in the Canon of the Mass. The content of "Lauda Sion Salvatorem" conforms closely to Bronzino's rendition of the body of Christ and to the mystical quality of the Eucharistic apparition he reified through his rendition. As the hymn states, praise is to be given to: Christ as the life-giving bread and wine; the triumph of light over darkness; the Eucharistic transformation where bread and wine become Flesh and Blood in the mystery of Transubstantiation; the connection between faith and the "law of light transcending;" and how the virtue of "Charity" attends those who are saved by their participation in "the feast of love." The Catholic dogma expressed in "Lauda Sion Salvatore" is expressed throughout the *Corpus Christi* liturgy and is especially found in Christ's words, recorded in John 6:56–59:

> My Flesh is food indeed, and My Blood is drink indeed. He who eats My Flesh and drinks My Blood, abides in Me and I in him. As the living Father, so he who eats Me, he also shall live because of Me. This is the Bread that has come down from heaven; not as your fathers ate the manna, and died. He who eats this Bread shall live forever.

Similar concepts are expressed in the Offertory, Secret, Prefatio, Communion, and Post-Communion.[145]

Bronzino and the Panciatichi and anyone who would have known the content of the Mass and the Feasts of the Cross would have connected their knowledge of the texts appropriate to these specific liturgical feasts with the imagery of Bronzino's *Christ*. This knowledge would have enabled them to connect Bronzino's painting to the words of the Church, forming a series of connections that would have grounded the image in the liturgy of the Church. Two other feasts of the Cross and the Crucifixion would have provided additional emphatic resonance for the Roman liturgy and Bronzino's *Christ*, these being: the Feast of the *Inventio Sanctae Crucis* (3 May), celebrated in pre-Trent, Roman Missals; and the Feast of the

Exaltatio Sanctae Crucis (14 September).[146] These two feasts commemorate the discovery of the True Cross by St. Helena in Jerusalem, as they pay special veneration to the Crucifixion.[147]

The sixteenth-century liturgy of the Feast of the *Inventio Sanctae Crucis* began with Galatians 6:14: "Jesus Christ: in whom our salvation, life, and resurrection: by whom we are saved and delivered." Light as a metaphor for salvation is expressed in the initial psalm, Psalm 66:2: "... may He cause the light of His countenance to shine upon us..." The direct connection between the image of the Crucified Christ and the Cross as the path to salvation was expressed by the *Oratio*: "O God, who in the glorious finding of the Cross of salvation didst renew the wonders of Thy passion; grant us by the price of the wood of life to win the palm of eternal life." The Gospel was John 3:1–15, where Christ tells Nicodemus that salvation can only be had by one who is born again in Christ, as he advises Nicodemus to lift his eyes in the manner in which the Israelites had lifted them to the Brazen Serpent for salvation from the poisonous snakes that were the result of their heresy. Thus, the Gospel of this Feast makes it clear that salvation is found only in the Church. The post-Communion recitation closes the circle with the words "Filled with the cup of heavenly nourishment and refreshed by spiritual drink, we beg you Almighty God that through the Holy Cross of your Son you defend us from the malignant enemy for the salvation of the world with the weapons of justice."

The liturgy of the *Exaltatio Sanctae Crucis* repeats concepts similar to those found in the Canon of the Mass, which is recited every time a Mass is celebrated, in *Corpus Christi*, in the *Inventio Sanctae Crucis*, and to which Bronzino's *Christ* also corresponds.[148] The liturgy of the *Exaltatio* also begins with Galatians 6:14 and Psalm 66:2. The Gradual was Philippians 2:8–9:

> Christ became obedient for us unto death: even the death on the cross: Wherefore God also hath exalted Him, and hath given a name which is above every name. Alleluia. Sweet the wood, sweet the nails, sweet the load that hangs on thee: though only was worthy to bear up the King and Lord of Heaven. Alleluia.

The characterization of the Instruments of the Passion, especially the Cross, as "sweet"/*dulcia* corresponds directly to the idealization evident in Bronzino's Christ, which renders the act of the Crucifixion as *dulcis* in the delineation of the body, the Cross, the nails, and the peaceful expression on Christ's face as Bronzino depicted it.

The Gospel for the Feast of the *Exaltatio* is John 12: 31–35, which emphasizes light as metaphor of salvation:

> Yet a little while, the light is among you. Walk whilst you have the light, that the darkness overtake you not. And he that walketh in darkness knoweth not whither he goeth. Whilst you have the light, believe in the light: that you may be the children of light.

The light is achieved through the Cross, and the Secret for the Exaltatio emphasized the connection between the Crucified Christ, the Eucharist, and Salvation:

> We who are about to feed on the Body and Blood of Jesus Christ our Lord, by whom the banner of the holy Cross was sanctified, beseech Thee, O Lord our God, that since we have been found worthy to venerate that same holy sign, it may be ours to enjoy forevermore the salvation secured for us by its triumph. Though the same Jesus Christ, Thy Son, who liveth and reigneth …

For the feasts of the Cross, the Church designates red vestments in commemoration of the blood shed by Christ on the Cross. And, as was pointed out by Firpo, Falciani, and Cropper, Lucrezia's red dress can be linked to reference to the blood of Christ.[149] Lucrezia's dress can also be linked to the liturgical red, which has been traditionally used by the Church for Lent, the feasts of the Cross, and the Feast of Pentecost, because red is the color of Christ's blood and of Charity and Love. These aspects of Lucrezia's dress enable a correlation between her portrait and the *Christ* that is indicated by the niches that form their background for these images, and the connection so created is a Roman connection intended to evoke the liturgy of the Roman Church and its history. This Roman connection was explicitly stated in the inclusion of Lucrezia's Book of Hours, wherein the service for Lauds is written in accordance with the use of Rome in the Latin of the Church.

LUCREZIA'S PORTRAIT, THE *CRUCIFIED CHRIST*, PENTECOST, AND THE HOURS OF THE VIRGIN

An explicit evocation of the Roman Church is manifested directly and specifically in Lucrezia's portrait in the text of the Book of Hours that she holds. The legible text in Lucrezia's Hours has been partially discussed by Firpo, Falciani, Cropper, and Aloia.[150] This discussion has been focused on the Psalm at the top of the left-hand page, which begins with "Laudate," has been identified by Falciani as Psalm 148, but has been identified correctly by Aloia as Psalm 150 because this Psalm is shorter and better fits the length of the Psalm in Lucrezia's Hours. It is also the Psalm that is recited during Lauds, in Rome Use Books of Hours.

Lucrezia's text specifically indicates that she is reading from Lauds, the service of first light in the Book of Hours, and the text of Lauds in Lucrezia's book conforms exactly and specifically to the use of the Roman Church.[151] Lutherans and other reformers did not use Books of Hours, written in accordance with Rome use or written in Latin; instead, they composed their own daily prayer books, in keeping with their respective dogmatic positions on the Virgin, which were all uniformly against the Catholic cult of the Virgin.[152] Lucrezia's portrait, therefore, specifically and emphatically aligns her with a Roman devotional practice that began in the early Middle Ages and continues today in the contemporary Catholic Church.[153]

In her Marian analysis of Lucrezia's portrait, Cropper emphasized the necklace worn by Lucrezia and decorated with the words "Amour Dure Sans Fin."[154] The necklace's French alludes directly to the Panciatichi's life in France, but it can also be interpreted in diverse ways. Most obviously, the necklace would seem to be a gift from Bartolomeo to Lucrezia, expressive of his love, and as such it was interpreted by Silvia Malaguzzi, who analyzed the meaning of the stones and words in this context.[155] Cropper's interpretation moved away from possible marital connotations for the necklace in an attempt to contextualize it within confessional controversies. In so doing, Cropper attempted to force a coincidence between a translation by Lefèvre d'Étaples and Clément Marot of Psalm 135, 136 (135), and 118 and the words of Lucrezia's necklace.

However, neither d'Étaples nor Marot's translations come close to "Amour Dure San Fin." The Étaples/Marot versions contemporary with Lucrezia's necklace translate the Psalms with the words "sa bontè notoire dure perpetuellemente" or "vraye amour pleine de purité n'avoir ne fin ne terme limité." There is no exact match in the sixteenth-century translations of the Psalms with the words of Lucrezia's necklace that clearly demonstrate that it can be linked to reformist heterodoxy. The closest Cropper can find to these words is a modern translation which states that "car son amour n'a pas de fin." Despite the problematic inexactitude of the sixteenth-century translations of the pertinent texts and "Amour Dure Sans Fin," Cropper's interpretation of the necklace demonstrates that these words, which can apply to the love between a husband and wife, can also apply to the love that the Virgin and Christ have for those who honor and worship them.

Christ and the Virgin are symbolically the Bridegroom and the Bride in the Song of Songs, and Bartolomeo and Lucrezia are Bridegroom and Bride in Bronzino's paintings. Thus, the necklace brings them together with the religious context of their union as members of the faithful, who honor Christ and the Virgin. Additionally emphasizing Lucrezia's devotion to the Virgin and Christ is the arrangement of Lucrezia's hand, with its fingers delicately poised above the words *Pulchra* and *Regis*, specifically indicating that it is the Virgin (*Pulchra*) and Christ (*Regis*), whom she honors and who love her without end. In connection with the necklace's "Amour Dure Sans Fin," Lucrezia's gesture links her devotional life and her marriage to the endless love that Christ and the Virgin Mary, in her role as intercessor, have for humanity. As the Bride, Lucrezia looks out of her portrait and across to that of her Bridegroom, Bartolomeo, because it is to Bartolomeo that the message of Lucrezia's portrait is primarily addressed, as he would have been the spectator who would most have looked at her representation in their home. To Bartolomeo, Lucrezia was "Pulchra," like the Virgin and she was the wife he loved and who loved him without end, as they were both loved by the Virgin and Christ, a connection emphasized by Lucrezia's gesture.

An additional reference to Catholic devotional and pictorial traditions is found in Lucrezia's pose, which, as Cropper pointed out, evokes the pose of the Annunciate Virgin, who looks up from her book when Gabriel enters her presence.[156] This clear reference to the Virgin, along with the Marian red of Lucrezia's dress, propagated in Catholic art, aligns Lucrezia with a Catholic visual culture that provides a context for the interpretation of Lucrezia's portrait. However, Lucrezia's pose and the position of her hands have additional significance in the context of the portrait.

As depicted, Lucrezia rests her right hand, the hand of honor, on her Hours, and her left (*sinistra*) arm rests on the arm of her chair, which is decorated with Italianate grotesque masks that are also reminiscent of the gargoyles found on Gothic Cathedrals. While sometimes gargoyles were functional, they also symbolized sin, and in her portrait, Lucrezia represses sin with her left hand and arm, even as the arrangement of her portrait recalls the placement of Heaven and Hell in Last Judgments. Thus Lucrezia's pose presents the spectator with a clear juxtaposition of good and evil—the Rome Use Book of Hours against demonic influences—the Church against Satanic manifestations or heresy. As Lucrezia's glowing skin and hair emerges from the dark background, her image recalls the words of St. Paul in 2 Corinthians 4:6: "Let light shine out of darkness ..." Thus, Lucrezia employs her Book of Hours and her devotion to the Virgin Mary to defeat the darkness of sin, as represented by the masks on her chair and the shadows behind her and, in so doing, emerges triumphantly bathed in the light of salvation and grace, dressed in red—the color of the Virgin's robe—the color of Charity, of the Roman liturgical colors of the feasts of the Cross, and of Love.

In choosing to be represented looking up from her Book of Hours, with her Marian attributes, Lucrezia was fully aware of the significance of the message given to the spectator by her portrait, and she understood that her contemporaries would also be aware of its Catholic connotations. For those who prayed regularly from the Book of Hours, the visible text would have provided them with Lucrezia's place in its services—Lauds—the service of first light, when morning comes after darkness. Hence, the selected time of prayer, evident in Lucrezia's portrait, is a key for understanding the choices made by patroness and artist in the design of this painting. As darkness recedes before light, Lucrezia is transformed into a reification of the technique of *chiaroscuro* that Bronzino used, here given a spiritual dimension by being juxtaposed with the Hours of the Virgin and with the concepts that are explicitly part of the significance of Lauds as the service that breaks the darkness with light.

The representation of Lucrezia's Book of Hours was an intentional link to Roman tradition and devotional practice. Practicing and devout Catholics who read the text of Lucrezia's Hours would have immediately recognized Lauds and understood the portrait's devotional message, grounded in the history of the Book of Hours, linked to the cult of the Virgin, originally part of the Benedictine monastic liturgy founded in the sixth century and incorporated into the Breviary, the priest's handbook for celebrating the rites of the Church. [157] In the late Middle Ages, the Book of Hours became detached from the Breviary and acquired the status of being the preferred devotional text for the laity, especially for members of the privileged aristocracy who could read its prayers in Latin or who had enough knowledge of the content of Books of Hours that they could follow the text with some measure of competency. Depictions of aristocratic women (and men) reading from their Books of Hours became ubiquitous in the fifteenth and sixteenth centuries, and the reading of the Hours of the Virgin (Matins, Lauds, Prime, Terce, Sext, Nones, Vespers, and Compline) was a standard devotional practice for Catholics.[158] Lucrezia's portrait conforms to the tradition of representing aristocrats with Books of Hours as a sign of their fidelity to the Church.

The liturgical format for Books of Hours followed the local use, with most Books of Hours written to accord with the Roman liturgy, although variations in the text, conforming to local liturgies, could alter the content of individual books. Additionally, because the Book of Hours was a book that was custom-made for individual patrons, the content of individual books could include in diverse combinations: the Hours of the Virgin, the Seven Penitential Psalms, the Hours of the Cross, the Hours of the Holy Spirit, the prayers "Obsecro Te" or "O Intermerata," Liturgies of Saints, Petitions, or various other prayers that were special to the owner of the book.[159] Hence, the Book of Hours was a devotional text that, while conforming to the liturgy of the Church, could also be an expressive instrument of individualized and independent devotion because it could be altered to reflect the special devotions of individuals. It was even possible to commission or incorporate unusual prayers or personalized prayers into a Book of Hours, without violating the orthodoxy of its identity and nature, as long as these prayers were in keeping with the Church's dogma.

It should be noted, however, that the Church, prior to the Council of Trent, did not examine individual Books of Hours to search out heterodoxy, as the assumption was that the owners of such books would hew to the Church's dogma. After Trent, all devotional and liturgical manuscripts and books were subjected to Inquisitorial approval. Thus, the Book of Hours was a flexible vehicle for direct prayer to the Virgin and to her Divine Son on the part of individuals who wished to extend their devotional life beyond participation in the celebration of the Mass. As such, it provided the patron of such a devotional text the opportunity to express control over their devotional life, within the traditions of the Church.

That Lucrezia chose to be portrayed holding a Book of Hours with visible text is a very direct message to the spectator about her aristocratic rank, her awareness of traditional representations of aristocratic women holding such books, her desire to represent herself as a pious woman engaged in daily (even hourly) prayer, and as a possible indication that she was also establishing individualized control over her devotional practices. However, the evident use of Rome seen in the text of her Hours establishes her as someone whose religious affiliation overtly conformed to orthodoxy. By requesting that Bronzino depict her Hours with the words of Lauds made legible, Lucrezia ensured that she could assert her spiritual independence, within the traditions and practices of the Church's Marian cult, without offending against orthodoxy. There is, however, even more information that can be gleaned from the text of Lucrezia's Hours which can be used to interpret other choices made for Lucrezia's portrait.

The format for Lauds found in Lucrezia's Hours is that which conforms to the Ordinary Time"—the time that begins after the Feast of the Pentecost and continues until the first day of Advent.[160] The two pages of Lucrezia's Hours contain Psalm 150:[161]

> Praise ye the Lord. Praise God in his sanctuary: praise Him in the firmament of His power.
> Praise Him for his mighty acts: praise Him according to his excellent greatness.
> Praise Him with the sound of the trumpet: praise Him with the psaltery and harp.
> Praise Him with the timbrel and dance: praise Him with stringed instruments and organs.
> Praise Him upon the loud cymbals: praise Him upon the high sounding cymbals.
> Let every thing that hath breath praise the Lord. Praise ye the Lord.

In Lauds, Psalm 150 is followed by the Versicle "Sicut erat," which is a doxology, beginning with the *Gloria*: "Glory be to the Father and to the Son and to the Holy Ghost. As it was in the beginning—"Sicut erat …"—both now and always, and to the ages of ages. Amen."[162] The next section of the text of Lauds is the Antiphon "Pulchra est et decora …" from the Song of Solomon (7:7): "Quam pulchra est et quam decora carissima in deliciis …" (How fair and how pleasant art thou, O love, for delights!). Incidentally, Falciani misidentified the source for "Pulchra est" as Song of Songs (6:4), but that text reads "Averte oculos tuos a me … (Avert your eyes from me …), not "Pulchra est."[163] Next comes the *Capitulum*—"Viderunt eam filiae Sion …"—from the Song of Songs (6:9): "Viderunt eam filiae Sion, et beatissimam predicaverunt, et reginae laudaverunt eam" (The maidens of Sion, having seen her, have called her blessed, and the queens have praised her). The *Capitulum* is followed by the Response *Deo Gratias* and the Hymn *O Gloriosa Domina*.[164] The text of this hymn is:

> O Heaven's glorious mistress, enthroned above the starry sky! Thou feedest with thy sacred breast thy own Creator, Lord most high.

What man had lost in hapless Eve, Thy sacred womb to man restores, Thou to the wretched here beneath hast opened Heaven's eternal doors.

Hail. O refulgent Hall of light! Hail Gate august of Heaven's high King! Through Thee redeemed to endless life, Thy praise let all the nations sing.

To the Father and the Spirit and to thy Son all glory be, who with a wondrous garment of graces encircled Thee. Amen.

This Catholic hymn reinforces the theme of light, which pushes back the darkness, found in Lucrezia's portrait in the phrase "O refulgent Hall of light!" The last phrase of Psalm 150—Let everything that hath breath praise the Lord—evokes Vasari's comment about the Panciatichi portraits that only "lo spirito" was required to make them even more alive than they seemed. Thus, the configuration of Lucrezia's portrait and the rendition of her form iterated the *Gloria* and emphasized her belief in the Trinity—"*Sicut erat* (As it had always been)—stated in the Church's liturgy and dogma. And the passages that refer to the beauty and grace of the Virgin Mary, praised by maidens and queens, is metonymically transferred to Lucrezia, whose beauty and decorous appearance was equally deserving of praise. Possibly, Lucrezia had been recently praised by aristocrats in France and by the Duchess Eleonora in Florence. Hence, the text of the Hours also had a potential autobiographical reference.

The manner in which Lucrezia's hand rests on the book was very specifically devised to ensure that as her thumb comes to rest on the word *Pulchra*, her little finger rests directly under the words *Tu regis*. Thus, Lucrezia's hand rests on the words which indicate the beauty of the Virgin Mary and the redemptive power of her son, *Christus Rex*, in a clear evocation of Marian devotion on her part and an affirmation of the important role the Virgin played, alongside her Son, in the process of redemption. The relationship between the Virgin and Christ, emphasized by the placement of Lucrezia's hand, conforms with the passages from the Song of Songs, which, in a Catholic context, was interpreted to indicate the relationship between Christ and the Church as the Bridegroom and Bride, with the Virgin being the Church.[165] The Panciatichi portraits are meant to be a pair—a Bridegroom and a Bride—in a parallel to the imagery of the Song of Songs. Thus, Lucrezia's Hours resonates with the Catholic significance for a husband and wife found in the Song of Songs and with the Catholic cult of the Virgin as co-redemptrix. Lucrezia's splendid gown also references the hymn, which includes the words "To the Father and the Spirit and to thy Son all glory be, who with a "wondrous garment of grace encircled Thee" (*Patri sit Paraclito tuoque Nato Gloria, qui veste te mirabili circumdederunt gratiae*). Thus, Bronzino presents Lucrezia magnificently dressed in the "wondrous garment of grace" mentioned in the hymn as the gift the Trinity gives to the Virgin, appropriately red in color, in keeping with the traditional representation of the Virgin's robe and the liturgical colors of the feasts of the Cross.

In her portrait, Lucrezia appears as a woman of Catholic virtue, resplendent in her "wondrous garment" of grace and embodying the qualities of a virtuous and chaste wife who is occupied with the recitation of the prayers to the Virgin. As Bronzino painted her, Lucrezia embodies the "Hall of light" described in *O Gloriosa Domina* and is as beautiful as a follower of the Virgin could and should be. Lauds, the service of light, emphasizes the theme of light and splendor that is basic to the *O Gloriosa Domina*. Thus, Bronzino's rendition of Lucrezia combines these motifs into a powerful individualized statement that reflects Lucrezia's spiritual life and religious preferences. In her fixed gaze, Lucrezia's personality is communicated to the spectator in a look of steady determination to hold the Roman faith upon which she places her hand. This assertion of Catholic identity concurs with the Classical and Brunelleschian architectural elements of Lucrezia's portrait, which resonate with her *fiorentinità* and with the historical time of the life of Christ, with the Canon of the Mass, the feasts of the Cross, and Bronzino's *Christ*.

Resonance between Lucrezia's portrait and the liturgy of the feasts of the Cross indicated by Bronzino's *Christ* is also found in the alliteration that exists between Lauds, the service to which Lucrezia's book is open, and the Hymn *Lauda Sion Salvatore*, with which the *Christ* resonates. The opening "Lauda," "Lauda," and "Laudis" of the hymn resonates with Lauds and the repetitive "Laudate" of Psalm 150's opening phrases. The employment of light and darkness as a metaphor for salvation surfaces in the *Lauda Sion Redemptore*, the hymn sung during *Corpus Christi*. Thus, Lucrezia's depiction as a beacon of light emerging from the dark background of her portrait evokes the imagery of the *Lauda Sion Salvatore* and additionally links her to the configuration of Bronzino's *Christ*.[166]

Lucrezia's red dress also resonates with the liturgical color for the Feast of Pentecost, for which red vestments were also traditionally worn.[167] Pentecost celebrates the descent of the Holy Spirit among those who were gathered in the upper room, as the source of grace that will enable the Apostles to be universally understood as they preach the Gospel. The Feast of Pentecost coincides with the Jewish Feast of Weeks (First Fruits) and is celebrated fifty days after the beginning of Lent.[168] The descent was in the form of tongues of fire, and the use of red as the liturgical color for Pentecost is symbolic of the flames of love and charity that were the gifts of the Holy Spirit to the assembled faithful. The use of red for liturgical vestments at Pentecost links its celebration to that of the Feast of *Corpus Christi*, which, in the Roman calendar, is celebrated on the Thursday after Pentecost.[169] Both Pentecost and *Corpus Christi* occur after Lent in the liturgical season identified as "Ordinary Time" (the liturgical season of Lucrezia's Hours), yet both feasts are linked to Lent through the symbolic red vestments and through the content of their liturgy, which relates these feasts to Lent.

Pentecost was also the day on which the last of the catechumens, who had not been baptized on Holy Saturday, were baptized, thus the ritual ceremonies of Pentecost and Lent were traditionally linked. The Paschal candle which was lit at Easter was lit again at Pentecost because the feast is marked by the fire and light of the Holy Spirit. Those gathered in the upper room are understood as being the first fruits of the Church, thus linking Pentecost to the Jewish Feast of Weeks.[170] Because Pentecost and Lent are linked, through baptism, texts that had been read during Lent were read again, among them the text of Exodus, which recounted the crossing of the Red Sea as a *figura* of baptism and salvation.[171] On Pentecost, Heavenly fire came down on the assembled, as the flames that signified the presence of the Holy Spirit manifested on the gathered, which included the Virgin Mary. Thus red, the color of Lucrezia's dress, is a color that indicates the robe of the Virgin and the feasts of the Cross, as well as Pentecost, during which the Virgin Mary received the gifts of love, light, and fire of the Holy Spirit. In choosing red for the color of her dress, Lucrezia identified herself with these liturgical traditions and their symbolic associations.

For the Roman Church, the color red is also the color of Charity, the virtue that represents good works, as well as the Blood and love of Christ for humanity.[172] Charity implies good works; thus, the selection of red for Lucrezia's dress is also an affirmation of her belief in charity and in the salvific benefit of good works. Pentecost is a feast of light, and Lucrezia's book is open to Lauds, the service of morning light, thus indicating a relationship between her Hours and Pentecost being made through the color of her dress, the "wondrous garment" evoked in the *O Gloriosa*. The hymn sung on *Corpus Christi—Lauda Sion Salvatore*—also emphasizes light as the manifestation of salvation, and the light that illuminates Lucrezia indicates that she is among the saved. The glowing light of Lucrezia's face and hands juxtaposed against the brilliant red, which stands out against the darkness, evokes the liturgy and the light of salvation and is a transformative and direct link to the Church's liturgy as celebrated and recited for the feasts of the Cross and Pentecost and the Canon of the Mass.

The Feast of the Pentecost is considered a Marian feast, and it is traditionally represented with an image wherein the Virgin is seated in the middle of the scene framed by the Apostles; often she holds a book in her hand or lap.[173] Thus, Lucrezia's portrait subtly evokes the compositional structure of the Pentecost and the Virgin Mary's depiction in that scene. As Lucrezia's Hours link her to the Virgin of the Pentecost, the Pentecostal color of her "wondrous" red dress evokes a series of associations that link Lucrezia to the Virgin and Christ, which represents the love of Christ and salvation through good works, which is what defines the virtue of Charity.

The Roman liturgy of the Church is the same now as it was in the Renaissance, and it begins with a reading from Wisdom 1:7: "The Spirit of the Lord fills the world, alleluia, is all-embracing, and knows man's utterance, alleluia, alleluia, alleluia."[174] The Epistle is Acts 2:1–11, which recounts how, when "the disciples were all together in one place," a violent wind blew and "filled the house" and then "there appeared to them parted tongues as of fire, which settled upon each of them. And they were filled with the Holy Spirit."[174] This text finds a poetic parallel in Lucrezia's red dress, which clothes her in a fiery simile of the text of Acts 2:1–11. The second Versicle which follows the reading of the Epistle is "Come, O Holy Spirit, fill the hearts of Your faithful; and kindle in them the fire of Your love." Thus does Lucrezia's red dress evoke not just the feasts of the Cross, but also the "fire" of "love" of the Pentecost's descent of the Holy Spirit, which enabled the disciples to preach in tongues.

The hymn that follows the epistle "Come, O Holy Spirit" speaks of "rays of healing light," the "source of gifts that will endure Light of every human heart." As it continues, the words of the hymn evoke Lucrezia's appearance in Bronzino's portrait: "O most blessed Light divine, Let Your radiance in us shine, And our inmost being fill... Melt the frozen, warm the chill, Guide the steps that go astray..." The Gospel that follows this hymn is John 14:23–31, wherein Jesus speaks to the Apostles about love and the Holy Spirit, the one who will come once Christ has ascended into Heaven. The correspondences between Lucrezia's appearance and her dress and the liturgy of Pentecost, as well as that of the feasts of the Cross and the Canon of the Mass, are not a coincidence. Bronzino and Lucrezia, born and raised in the Florentine traditions of the Roman Church, would have been familiar with these basic concepts of the Church's dogma and with the celebration of these feasts, with their content, and with the color of the vestments used by the celebrant priests on these Holy Days. Contemporary spectators visiting the Panciatichi palace, who would have seen Bronzino's paintings, shared this knowledge and these associations, which would have enabled them to make the connections that can be made now between Lucrezia's portrait and the liturgies of the Pentecost and the feasts of the Cross.

Within a Panciatichi context, there is another Marian feast that could also be indicated by Lucrezia's Hours, as was argued by Elena Aloia, this being the Feast of the Assumption of the Virgin. The Panciatichi had a special veneration for this feast, as Aloia pointed out in her analysis of Lucrezia's portrait.[175] Thus, the Marian aspects of Lucrezia's portrait might also include an association with this feast, which occurs during "Ordinary Time," the liturgical season of the format for Lauds displayed in Lucrezia's book.

Bronzino portrayed Lucrezia as belonging to the spiritual world inhabited by virtuous women who see the Virgin Mary as their role model. Additionally, placing her in a niche similar to that of the *Christ* created a connection between Lucrezia's portrait and Christ that linked the two paintings through their devotional and liturgical resonance. Thus, by situating Lucrezia within a liturgical and ecclesiastical setting and clothing her in red, the final version of her portrait establishes her as someone who can be identified with the liturgy and symbolism of the Roman Church, which emphasizes salvation through Christ and the role played by the Virgin Mary in the salvation of the individual. It is in the strong Marian elements of Lucrezia's portrait that her allegiance to the Roman Church can be detected, since the Catholic Church was the only institution that allowed a strong cult of the Virgin.

These are powerful statements for a woman to make, especially because by making them she separated and differentiated herself markedly from her husband, whose heterodox interests eventually led to his Inquisitorial trial. Such statements also indicate that Lucrezia was not a blank slate, molded by her husband's vision of himself, and that in her portrait she exercised a significant degree of control in fashioning her own image. Lucrezia Panciatichi was not an empty vessel waiting to be filled by her husband's dictated image of who she was or defined by her husband's intellectual and confessional heterodoxy. She was an individual woman, aware of her position in the world of Florentine and European hierarchy, who used her portrait to make statements about what was important to her; and what was most important to her was her devotional practice of reading the Hours of the Virgin, and especially the service of Lauds that opened the light of day and that aligned her with the traditions of the Church in which she was raised.

Lucrezia's Hours: Florence and France

The format for Lauds evident in Lucrezia's Hours matches that found in other Florentine Books of Hours, including the one written for Eleonora of Toledo, which is now in the Victoria & Albert Museum, where the text of Lauds is the same as that of Lucrezia's book.[177] The scribe "Aloysius" signed and dated Eleonora's Book of Hours to February 1541.[178] The same workshop that made the Hours of Eleonora also made a Book of Hours for Margaret of Austria, the illegitimate daughter of Charles V and the bride of Duke Alessandro de' Medici.[179] Lucrezia's Hours are Roman, and they are also Florentine and function in her portrait as another example of her *fiorentinità*. Additionally, the Hours place her within the matrix of aristocrats at the court of Duke Cosimo, who would have been able to afford such luxury books. As such, the Hours is also a statement of material wealth that matches Lucrezia's elaborate dress, expensive jewelry, and complex hair style. Status and spirituality are thus linked in Lucrezia's portrait, which reflects her influence and her self-definition as a Roman Catholic, aristocratic Florentine.

The script of Lucrezia's Hours does not match that of Eleonora's Hours, but it does match that of a French workshop, identified in the scholarly literature on this group as the 1520s Hours workshop, studied by Myra Orth.[180] One of the Orth's study of this group discussed its devotional context, as she identified the scattered members of the group for this workshop, which was associated with the Humanist, engraver, manuscript illuminator, author, poet, and book printer Geoffroy Tory.[181] Tory, who was based in Paris and who published his first Book of Hours in print, in 1524, was born in Bourges and educated at the *Sapienza* in Rome and in Bologna, where he studied with Philip Beroaldus. In 1530, Tory became printer to King Francis I and, in 1532, became a librarian at the University of Paris. The style of Tory's printed Hours was linked, by Orth and other scholars, to the style of the 1520s Hours Workshop, which made Books of Hours, as well as other types of manuscripts and documents.

The style of the script and the filigree decoration visible in Lucrezia's Hours conforms to that of the 1520s Hours Workshop and to Tory's manuscripts and printed Hours. This perceived correspondence seems to indicate that Lucrezia commissioned the manuscript in France, although it was written in accordance with Florentine use, something that could have been easily accomplished by copying a Florentine Hours, as such a process was a standard practice for making manuscripts. The 1520s Hours workshop employed a style that was a diverse admixture of Northern European and Italian influence, with traces of stylistic borrowing from the group known as the Antwerp Mannerists, Dürer, and Marcantonio Raimondi. International in style, yet French in context, the 1520s Hours Workshop was in its most productive phase at about the time that Bartolomeo would have been living in France, possibly still at the French Court. Perhaps Lucrezia's Hours was commissioned from this workshop because Bartolomeo also bought manuscripts there, as well as books printed by Tory. Primarily, Lucrezia's Hours would then indicate, along with the necklace, that she had been in France, where she had acquired these religious commodities.

Influence from the 1520s Hours Workshop may also be present in Bartolomeo's portrait. The buildings in the background of Bartolomeo's portrait are similar to those which appear in the background of the 1520s Hours Workshop manuscripts. Perhaps, Bronzino was shown such manuscripts so that he could include a visual reference to their international context, alongside the overt *fiorentinità* of the architecture. Possibly, Bronzino saw one or more of these manuscripts and was inspired by their style. If the text of Lucrezia's Hours and the buildings of Bartolomeo's background indicate a link to the 1520s Hours Workshop, then they also provide an indicator for where Bartolomeo would have purchased some of his heterodox books. Such an indicator would also resonate with the stylistic choice made for the architecture in the background of Bartolomeo's portrait, which, like the 1520s Hours Workshop, combined diverse elements into a cohesive whole. Hybridity in national and family identity marked Bartolomeo and was reflected in the Panciatichi portraits. Spiritual eclecticism denoted Bartolomeo's religiosity; hence, the plurality evident in the portrait's background could be indicative of the homogenous heterodoxy that eventually caused Bartolomeo's arrest and Inquisitorial process. While plurality of different kinds emerges in the portraits and the Christ, orthodoxy dominates and similar ideological foundations can be detected in the Uffizi and Vienna *Holy Families*.

THE PANCIATICHI *HOLY FAMILIES* AND THE ROMAN LITURGY

The clear ties to Catholicism evident in Lucrezia's portrait and in the configuration of the *Christ* as an evocation of Canon of the Mass and the feasts of the Cross can also be detected in the Uffizi *Holy*

Family and in the Vienna *Holy Family*.[182] In keeping with their heterodox interpretation of the Panciatichi paintings, Firpo, Cropper,
and Falciani have identified these paintings as being influenced by
Valdesianism and by Protestant concepts.[183] However, it is difficult
to reconcile two such strongly Marian paintings with heterodoxy
or heresy, as both works have their roots in the lengthy tradition
of representations of the Holy Family found in Catholic and Florentine art. The inclusion of saints in both paintings aligns them
with the Catholic cult of the saints, banned by Protestant churches. Furthermore, the impetus for their commission, emphatically
indicated by Graham Smith, is likely to be found in Bartolomeo's
baptismal name—Giovanni—which is reflected in the presence of
St. John the Baptist in both paintings.[184] Thus, the *Holy Families* belong to Catholic visual traditions of commissioning images of patron saints alongside representations of the Virgin and Christ. Both
paintings are also an affirmation of the couple's *fiorentinità*, as John
is the patron Saint of Florence, which makes his inclusion here doubly significant because it resonates with the Florentine celebration
of his feast days. The two paintings, however, similar in content
and in their incorporation of Lucrezia's devotion to the Virgin and
the reference to Bartolomeo's name saint, are markedly different in
context and meaning.

The Panciatichi *Holy Family* is an evocative representation of the
meeting of Christ and John in the wilderness, as the Holy Family is
fleeing Herod's persecution and is traveling to Egypt. This encounter is described in the Apocrypha, and it prefigures the meeting of
the adult Christ and John prior to the Baptism of Christ.[185] Christ's
head resting on the bundle of clothing carried by Joseph is the key
object that places the scene within the Apocryphal tradition. The
setting for the scene is the wild area outside the city, which is visible in the distant landscape and over which stormy clouds gather.
Again, the metaphor of light and darkness that recurs in Lucrezia's
portrait, in the *Christ*, in the content of Lucrezia's Hours and of the
feasts of the Cross appears in the *Holy Families*. The darkness of the
upper landscape presages the deaths of both Christ and John, who
will triumph over darkness but who must face the trials that await
them. John's loving kiss of Christ resonates with the kiss of Judas,
as the kiss of love indicates the kiss of betrayal.

The Vienna *Holy Family*'s context, however, is thematically very different from that of the Uffizi painting, even though the only difference in content is the addition of John's mother, Elizabeth. As with the Uffizi painting, the Vienna work commemorates Lucrezia's devotion to the Virgin, while indicating devotion to Bartolomeo's patron saint. However, the addition of Elizabeth and the employment of Hebrew letters to write "Isaiah" on the book the Virgin holds brings the Vienna *Holy Family* into close correspondence with the liturgy of the Feast of the Nativity of St. John the Baptist.[186] The liturgical readings for this day begin with the Introit for the Mass of this day, which is Isaiah 49:1–2: "The Lord has called me by my name from the womb of my mother, and He has made my mouth like a sharp sword; in the shadow of His hand He has protected me, and has made me as a chosen arrow."[187] The Gospel text for the Nativity of John the Baptist was Luke 1:57–68, which describes Elizabeth's prophesied delivery of John. By adding Elizabeth to the assembled group and by writing "Isaiah" on the book held by the Virgin, the Panciatichi directly aligned the image with the liturgy of the John's nativity. In so doing, the Panciatichi made an emphatic statement about their Catholic identity that would have been immediately understood by their contemporaries, as all Florentines would have been familiar enough with the liturgy of the Nativity of the city's patron saint to have recognized that the painting's content alluded to it.

Studied within the context of the Roman liturgy of the Nativity of St. John, the Vienna *Holy Family* presents an image that coincides with the themes of that day. In the painting, John holds an apple as Christ holds a bird, both symbols of the Passion. John's Cross and the words "Agnus Dei" written on the scroll indicate Christ as the sacrificial lamb. In the painting, Christ sits enthroned on a rock on which a white cloth has been laid, representative of both altar and tomb. Christ's pose draws attention to the motif of Christ as the rock of salvation on which his left foot rests and on which Bronzino signed the work. Hence, the placement of Bronzino's signature is a sign of his devotion to Christ and to the Eucharistic context of the child's depiction, as he appears seated on the altar cloth holding the bird as the symbol of his salvific sacrifice. The Virgin, dressed in red, holds Christ with her left hand and the book with the word

"Isaia" in her right, juxtaposing them in the traditional pairing indicative of the Word made Flesh. All focus their eyes on the child as Elizabeth, placed next to him, looks down; the Virgin, Joseph, and John all look at the Savior, as he is proclaimed in the liturgy of the Feast of John's nativity.

The relationship between John and Christ is made explicit in the liturgy of the Nativity of John at the Secret with the words "We heap Your altars with gifts, O Lord, as we celebrate with due honor the nativity of him who both proclaimed the coming of the Savior of the world and pointed Him out when He had come, our Lord Jesus Christ, Your Son."[188] This theme is rephrased in the Post Communion "Let Your Church O God rejoice at the birth of Blessed John the Baptist, through whom she came to know the Author of her regeneration, our Lord Jesus Christ, Your Son."[189] While the relationship between Christ and John is clear, whenever they are both included in representations of the *Holy Family*, as in the Uffizi *Holy Family*, the addition of Elizabeth in the Vienna painting indicates that the Panciatichi wished this painting to allude not just to Bartolomeo's patron saint but also to the liturgy of his saint's nativity. In so doing, attention was drawn to the painting's connection to the liturgy of the Roman Church in a manner similar to that explicitly evident in Lucrezia's portrait's depiction of her Book of Hours and in the *Christ*'s reification of the liturgical themes of the feasts of *Corpus Christi*, the *Inventione Sanctae Crucis*, and the *Exaltatio Crucis*. In effect, when the liturgy of the Church is employed as the interpretive medium for the Panciatichi paintings, the connections between it and the form and content of these paintings clarifies the patronage intention for these works, so aligned with the words known to the faithful familiar with the Masses, prayers, and hymns of the Roman liturgical year.

LUCREZIA AND THE PANCIATICHI PAINTINGS

Considered as a group, the Panciatichi paintings indicate that there was a deliberate intention to link these images to the liturgical and devotional texts of the Church and to its cult of the Virgin and saints. This alignment is most explicit in Lucrezia's portrait and in the Vienna *Holy Family*. Because alignment with the Roman Church is so explicit in Lucrezia's Hours, it can be suggested that it was perhaps Lucrezia who controlled the content of these images. Thus, if a dogmatic difference separated how Bartolomeo and Lucrezia responded to the Eucharistic message of Bronzino's *Christ*, the difference was contained in their private communion with Bronzino's depiction of the image of the crucified *Christ*.

The clear references to the liturgy of the Church found in Lucrezia's portrait, the *Christ*, and the Vienna *Holy Family* and the traditional context for the Uffizi *Holy Family* situate the Panciatichi paintings within a specific Roman context. Bartolomeo's portrait, while ambiguous in its confessional identification, nonetheless includes a topographical reference to Florentine ecclesiastical landmarks in the inclusion of the tower evocative of Sta. Maria Novella. If, as Cropper argued, the representation of Bartolomeo's face was intended as an allusion to the *Volto Santo* recalling the relic of the Veronica's veil, then this reference would have brought Bartolomeo's portrait within the referential system of the Roman Church.[190] Thus, even in Bartolomeo's portrait, indexical indicators of Romanity can be found. It should be noted that San Giovanni Laterano, in Rome, had a *Volto Santo* in the *Sancta Sanctorum*, providing perhaps a resonance between Bartolomeo's patron saint's name and the Roman relic.

The *Christ* may have been the altarpiece for the Panciatichi palace's chapel. Its size, content, and form do not suggest that the portraits were intended as lateral panels, nor would the *Holy Families* have been so used. However, the relationship between Lucrezia's portrait and the *Christ* indicates that the portrait was displayed near enough to the *Christ* that a visual connection could be made for the portrait with the Christ through the similar niches evident in both works. The portraits and the Uffizi and Vienna *Holy Families* are approximately the same size and could have been hung as a set, in proximity to the chapel, with Bartolomeo's portrait being linked to the Uffizi *Holy Family* through the employment of the Panciatichi arms. It is possible to envision an arrangement that would have aligned Bartolomeo's portrait with the Uffizi *Holy Family* on one wall with Lucrezia's portrait and the Vienna *Holy Family* on another wall.

However, Elena Aloia has a theory that the commission of two paintings of the same subject and of approximately the same size for one venue raises questions about the purpose of the second painting.[191] Therefore, she thinks that it is possible that the Vienna *Holy Family* was commissioned for the Panciatichi chapel in the church of Sta. Maria Maggiore, in front of which the Panciatichi are buried.[192] The liturgical associations that exist in the Vienna *Holy Family* support Aloia's suggestion, which would make the Vienna painting a more suitable painting for a public chapel in a church than the Uffizi *Holy Family*. Both paintings, as Aloia has pointed out, contain references to properties owned by the Panciatichi — the Uffizi painting references the Panciatichi holdings in Volterra, and the Vienna painting the Panciatichi palace at Mezzomonte.[193] Hence, as Aloia noted, these paintings are also about Bartolomeo's identity as a Panciatichi, a landowner, and a Florentine with holdings that extend beyond the city and which are linked to Bartolomeo's personal history. That history included his international life in France, his intellectual and personal interest in confessional issues, and his marriage to Lucrezia, who, in turn, expressed her devotional preferences in her portrait, indicating her identity as a *Fiorentina* and a Catholic. Bartolomeo's spiritual definition and his religious allegiance may be difficult to ascertain completely, but it seems clear, from the content of the Panciatichi paintings, that these paintings are predominantly orthodox and in keeping with the Church's liturgy and devotional practices. Lucrezia's portrait and the Vienna *Holy Family* explicitly reference the texts of the Church and its liturgy, while the *Christ* manifests resonance with the liturgies of the Church's feasts of the Cross. Yet, although Bartolomeo's portrait has some elements that could be codified as Catholic (Sta. M. N. and the possible *Volto Santo*), it remains a work that does not declare the religious identity of the sitter as does Lucrezia's portrait. Thus, it is important to examine the *Christ* from what might have been Bartolomeo's heterodox interests to understand how Bronzino's image could accommodate Luther's teachings on the Eucharist and disagreements with Roman dogma on Transubstantiation.

Bronzino's Christ: Orthodoxy and Heterodoxy

In Florence, it was the Catholic Mass that would have been primarily related to the Panciatichi *Christ*, evoking the Church's affirmation of Transubstantiation and the Pauline tradition of justification by faith that was part of the Church's dogma of salvation. If Bartolomeo was more *luterano* than Catholic, he would not have perceived the Eucharistic context of the *Crucified Christ* all that differently from Lucrezia, because Luther affirmed Christ's presence in the Eucharist, although he did not agree with the Church's definition of Transubstantiation.[194] Hence, any assertion that Bronzino's *Christ* is only or even predominantly "Lutheran," because the image somehow denies the presence of Christ in the Eucharist, ignores the history of Luther's position on the subject, as well as the Florentine and Roman context for Bronzino's image.

The lines that have been drawn in the recent scholarly literature on the Panciatichi paintings between the Church and Luther were there, but they were not as they have been expressed by Anne D'Evroye-Stiltz's analysis of the *Crucified Christ*: "Pour les réformistes, l'hostie n'est alors que le symbole du crops du Christ ..." (For the reformers, the host was no more than the symbol of the body of Christ).[195] This was not Luther's position on the Eucharist, as he accepted the manifestation of Christ in the Eucharist, although he differed in details from the Church's position. As Jari Jolkkonen summarized, Luther

> ... adhered to the traditional sacramental realism of the church, according to which, by the power of the Word of God and his promise, Christ's body and blood are really present in the bread and the wine, when the priest pronounces the words of consecration. In receiving Holy Communion the Christian is forgiven of his or her sins, is united with Christ, and receives, for the strengthening of faith, a concrete sign of his participation in the communion of saints and eternal life. The real presence is a consistent outcome of the Incarnation. By the work of the Holy Spirit and by the power of the Word of God, Christ's presence continues in the sacraments.[196]

The prevalent misunderstanding about Luther's position on the Eucharist can be blamed on William Dilthey, Friedrich

Schliermacher, and Adolf von Harnack, who could not accept that Luther accepted Christ's presence in the Host.[197] Because they wanted to bring modern Lutheranism more in line with other Protestant denominations, this group and others with similar intentions denied the clear implications of Luther's writings and substituted interpretations more in keeping with Calvin and Zwingli. Recent study of Luther's dogma on the Eucharist has rectified the disinformation on this subject. If Bartolomeo was "luterato" and looking at Bronzino's *Christ*, he would have understood it as an expression of proximity between Catholics and Luther. As an image that existed on the threshold between Catholics and Lutherans, Bronzino's *Christ* enabled spectators to bring their own interpretation to the work and provide their own context for its resonance. As such, the Panciatichi *Christ* is a chameleon, able to transmute its visual presentation into a conceptual metaphor, simultaneously satisfying orthodox (Catholic) and heterodox (Lutheran) interpretations of the Eucharistic dogmas.

Although there is nothing specifically Lutheran about Bronzino's *Christ*, and there is much that is Catholic, the Panciatichi *Christ* is not didactically exclusive of Luther's definition of the Eucharistic miracle, as something occurring within but not displacing the essential substance of the actual bread and wine.[198] Luther did not deny Eucharistic transformation, but he differed from the Church in the details of the miracle. Luther's position on the Eucharist was not that of Calvin or Zwingli or Johannes Oecolampadius and Andreas Karlstadt, who considered the Eucharistic part of the service commemorative and "symbolistic or spiritualist."[199] Luther considered that the bread and wine did transform into the Body and Blood of Christ, but, unlike the Church, he believed that the bread and wine remained as bread and wine and not as accidents of appearance. Thus, Luther admitted Christ's presence but with a significant difference from Rome, because he considered that the bread and wine became Christ's Body and Blood without ceasing to be bread and wine.

If Bartolomeo was a Lutheran sympathizer, then he would have known that Luther accepted Christ's presence in the Eucharist. He should not have been eager to make his differences with Luther known in Florence, but perhaps he did, leading to his problems with the Inquisition. Bronzino's *Christ* is not a denial of Eucharistic Transubstantiation; it is instead an affirmation of the Church's dogma, as expressed in the Canon of the Mass, depicted in such a way that it can extend to accommodate Luther's understanding of Christ's presence in the Eucharist.

In effect, the mystical and visionary aspect of Bronzino's *Christ* brings it closer to the Roman Church's emphasis on the transformative miracle that renders the bread and wine as "supernatural food" that is no longer earthly bread and wine. In considering the religious and dogmatic context of the Panciatichi Christ, it should be noted that the more mystical the Christ and the more spiritualized his representation, the more closely it conforms to the Roman Church's idea of Transubstantiation as a miracle that displaces earthly substance.

As depicted by Bronzino, the body of this Christ is an elegantly refined rendition of a body that was once fully human but is now divine, a concept conveyed by the realistic physicality of Christ's body juxtaposed with the idealized and glowing light that illuminates his presence. Essentially formed from the Church's teachings on salvation expressed in the Canon of the Mass and the feasts of the Cross, Bronzino's image is the visualization of Christ's return to earth during the Elevation of the Host. As it was for the Church, it almost was for Luther. The argument over *species* that separated Luther from the Church gave hope of reconciliation because resolution seemed possible. As with the debate over good works, there was hope, until Trent, that wording could resolve the conceptual differences that developed between Luther and the Church about Transubstantiation and the Eucharist. Hence, as the Panciatichi *Christ* was being commissioned, the gap that grew larger between Catholics and Lutherans, when Trent formulated its Eucharistic doctrine in 1547, had not yet opened too wide.[200] Before 1541, when reconciliation failed at Regensburg, it was still possible for Bartolomeo and Lucrezia to consider Bronzino's *Christ* from different perspectives, in a spirit of reconciliation. Thus, Bronzino's *Christ* is an image that embodies the changes in Eucharistic doctrine that began when Luther questioned the Church's Eucharistic dogma, even though it is an image grounded in the teachings of the Church. Bronzino's *Christ* succeeds as an image of transition not because it is exclusively Catholic or Lutheran or Valdesian but because it enables inclusion of heterodoxy; thus, it is an image that accommodated Bartolomeo's heterodoxy and Lucrezia's orthodoxy.

When the Inquisition searched Bartolomeo's palace, looking for incriminating evidence, its representatives would not have overlooked the religious paintings on its walls or Bronzino's portraits of the Panciatichi. Had Bronzino's *Christ* and the other Panciatichi paintings been seen as heretical because they overtly denied orthodox dogma, they would have likely been thrown into the fire that consumed Bartolomeo's problematic books and manuscripts. Bronzino's *Christ* and the other Panciatichi paintings survived because they exemplified Roman dogma and liturgical themes familiar to Inquisitors, who might have seen them and understood their Roman message. Thus, although Bronzino's *Christ* may have been designed as Nicodemist, to accommodate Barolomeo's heterodoxy, it is clear that it passed inspection as being Roman and orthodox, along with the other paintings.

Bartolomeo was raised in France, educated at the French court and at the University of Padua, where he was exposed to reformist ideas. Lucrezia's conventionally Florentine upbringing would have been free of the intellectual and international heterodoxy that characterized Bartolomeo's intellectual and spiritual interests. Hence, her portrait presents her fealty to the Church's teachings and its devotional practices.

There is little doubt that Bartolomeo was immersed in the confessional debates of his day and no doubt that he talked too much in favor of ideas considered to be Lutheran or that he wanted the right to interpret Scripture as he wished. Whether Bartolomeo looked at Bronzino's *Christ* and thought of Luther's Eucharistic teachings, even as Lucrezia adhered to Roman Transubstantiation, is something that we cannot know for certain. That Bronzino's *Christ* functions as a visual representation of the Church's doctrine on the Eucharist, aligned with orthodoxy, is attested to by its survival. That its orthodoxy was the result more of Lucrezia than Bartolomeo is tenable, given her clear allegiance to Rome manifested in her Hours.

Perhaps it was Bronzino's great triumph that his accommodation of slightly different patronage interests created images that can accommodate different audiences. In the *Christ*, the orthodox would have seen an image that reified the Canon of the Mass and the Church's dogma of Eucharistic Transubstantiation. In Bartolomeo's portrait, the far-away tower of Sta. Maria Novella placed him as a member of a family that had an "arca" in the cemetery, where the bones of his ancestors rested. In Lucrezia's portrait, Bronzino painted a woman of decorous behavior, dressed in the red liturgical color of the feasts of the Cross and Pentecost and the robe of the Virgin; reading her Book of Hours, in Latin, open to Lauds—the service of the morning light that would have identified her as a devout member of the Roman Church's cult of the Virgin. It was Bronzino's triumph that he painted, for the Panciatichi, paintings which subtly and delicately reveal their orthodoxy and heterodoxy, indicative of spiritual and dogmatic flexibility and reconciliation.

The approach employed here is based on an analysis of the Panciatichi paintings that addresses the overt significance of their content, which indicates that the Panciatichi retained a veneration for the Catholic cult of the Virgin Mary and the cult of the saints. This approach has also indicated that the Roman liturgy resonates specifically with the *Crucified Christ*, when the texts of the liturgies of the feasts of the Cross are read, while meditating on the image. Any interpretation of this painting that sets aside its Catholic content can only proceed by ignoring the contextual data so carefully included in its configuration. Such interpretations also deny the ongoing Roman devotional traditions exemplified in Lucrezia's Hours, with its visible Latin text. For individuals who had spent their lives worshipping in Catholic churches and hearing the repetition of its liturgy at major feasts, the Panciatichi paintings signified within this familiar and traditional context. While Bartolomeo and others who experimented with heterodoxy could have brought alternative texts to their reception of these paintings, those meanings would have coexisted with those provided by the Church.

Taken as a group, the *Portrait of Lucrezia* and the *Holy Families* are unquestionable affirmations of fealty to the cult of the Virgin and the cult of the saints rejected by Luther and other Protestants.[201] *The Portrait of Bartolomeo* remains ambiguous, with its secular urbanity, infused with its diffused references to Sta. Maria Novella and its allusion to the *Volto Santo*, evocative of Veronica's Veil in St. Peter's and the *Volto Santo* in the *Sanctum Sanctorum* of San Giovanni Laterano. It is, however, in the *Crucified Christ* that the imagery of the Panciatichi paintings becomes most accommodating, as its roots in the liturgy of the Church is able to expand to accommodate Roman Transubstantiation and Luther's teaching on the presence of Christ in the Eucharist. As an image of slippage between two religious cultures, the *Christ* is an image of reconciliation and an evocation of the time before Regensburg (1541), when Christian intellectuals still hoped that Christianity could once again become united. But, in the aftermath of Regensburg, the need to assert orthodoxy may have provided the impulse towards that assertion found in Lucrezia's portrait and in the *Holy Families*. In art as in life, in the end, the Panciatichi preferred the comforts of orthodoxy to the perils of spiritual experimentation.

NOTES

I thank Liana De Girolami Cheney for her encouragement of the work that led to this chapter and for providing me with the opportunity for its publication. I am especially grateful to my husband, Charles Burroughs, for his thought-provoking questions about the issues I considered while researching the Panciatichi and Bronzino. Special thanks are owed to Rabbi Zachary Silver and Deborah Huacuja for their assistance with the Hebrew letters of the Vienna *Holy Family*. For comments about the manuscript, I thank Paul Barolsky and Larry Silver. Gregory Clark was a valuable sounding board for things liturgical and for the ins and outs of "use" in liturgical and extra-liturgical, devotional books. For personal support, I thank Dorothy Limouze, Paul Barolsky, Maureen Pelta, Tina Waldeier Bizzarro, and Tom MacPherson. A Small Senate Grant and a Research Grant from the Geneseo Foundation, SUNY Geneseo supported the publication, preparation and research for this article.

1. Giorgio Vasari, *Le Opere di Giorgio Vasari*, ed. Gaetano Milanesi, 8 vols. (Florence: Sansoni, 1906, repr. Florence: Sansoni, 1973), 8:505. Hereafter Vasari-Milanesi.

2. Philippe Costamagna and Carlo Falciani, "Le Christ en Croix d'Agnolo Bronzino peint pour Bartolomeo Panciatichi," *Revue de l'art* 168, no. 2 (2010), 45–52; Maurice Brock, *Bronzino* (Paris: Flammarion, 2010); Carlo Falciani and Antonio Natali, eds., *Bronzino: Pittore e poeta alla corte dei Medici* (Florence: Mandragora, 2010) [henceforth cited as Falciani and Natali, *Bronzino*], 170–72; *Musée des Beaux-Arts. Nice. Le Bronzino. La Crucifixion*, Exhibition Catalogue, Curator, Anne D'Evroye-Stiltz, 2011.

3. Brock, *Bronzino*, 253–54.

4. Falciani and Natali, *Bronzino*; Elizabeth Pilliod, "*Holy Family with Sts. John and Elizabeth*," in Falciani and Natali, *Bronzino*, 300.

5. Graham Smith, "Bronzino's Holy Family in Vienna: A Note on the Identity of Its Patron," *Source: Notes in the History of Art* 2, no. 1 (1982), 21–25.

6. For a discussion of the career and life of Bartolomeo, see Carlo Falciani, "Il Bronzino e I Panciatichi," in Falciani and Natali, *Bronzino*, 153–65, 153, who states that Bartolomeo was Cosimo I's ambassador twice, once for Francis I and again for Henry II, and cites Massimo Firpo, *Gli affreschi di Pontormo a San Lorenzo: Eresia politica e cultura nella Firenze di Cosimo I* (Turin: G. Einaudi, 1997), 359–70. For a detailed summary of Bartolomeo's life, see Elena Aloia, *I Panciatichi degli Uffizi* (Tesi di Laurea, Perugia, Università degli Studi di Perugia, 2008–2009).

7. For a discussion of Cosimo I and Eleonora's court art, see Konrad Eisenbichler, ed., *The Cultural Politics of Duke Cosimo I de' Medici* (Aldershot: Ashgate, 2001); and idem, ed., *The Cultural World of Eleonora da Toledo: Duchess of Florence and Siena* (Aldershot: Ashgate, 2004), for essays discussing the significance of art at the Medici court.)

8. For an overview of Bronzino's paintings, see Brock, *Bronzino*; and Falciani and Natali, *Bronzino*, both with bibliographies.

9. On the *Accademia*'s history, see Iacopo Rilli, *Notizie letterarie ed istoriche intorno agli uomini illustri dell'Accademia Fiorentina* (Florence: Piero Matini, 1700); Salvino Salvini, *Fasti Consolari dell'Accademia Fiorentine* (Florence: Tartini, 1717); and for a modern summary of the *Accademia*'s history, see Karen-edis Barzman, *The Florentine Academy and the Early Modern State: The Discipline of Disegno* (Cambridge: Cambridge University Press, 2000). On the intellectual climate of the Florence and the *Accademia*, see Detlef Heikamp, "Rapporti fra accademici ed artisti nella Firenze del '500," *Il Vasari* 1 (1957), 139–63; A.L. De Gaetano, *Giambattista Gelli and the Florentine Academy: The Rebellion Against Latin* (Florence: Olsckhi, 1976); S.J. Batomsky, "Noah, Italy, and the Sea-Peoples: The Problem," *The Jewish Quarterly Review*, n.s. 67 (1977), 146–53; Cesare Vasoli, "Considerazione sull'Accademia Fiorentina," *Revue des etudes italiennes* 25 (1979), 41–72; G. Cipriani, *Il mito etrusco nel rinascimento fiorentino* (Florence: Olschki, 1980); Alessandro Cecchi, "Il Bronzino, Benedetto Varchi e l'Accademia Fiorentina: ritratti di poeti, letterati e personaggi illustri della corte medicea," *Antichità Viva* 30 (1991), 17–28; and M. Sherberg, "The Accademia Fiorentina and the Question of Language: The Politics of Theory in Ducal Florence," *Renaissance Quarterly* 56 (2003), 26–55.

10. In 2001, I presented a paper at The Sixteenth Century Studies Conference entitled "Mannerism and Spirituality at the Medici Court,"

in a session chaired by Liana De Girolami Cheney. In 2004, I presented a paper at the Renaissance Society of America's Annual Meeting, entitled, "Bronzino's Portraits of Lucrezia and Bartolomeo Panciatichi," in a session organized by Liana De Girolami Cheney.

11. On reform before and after Trent, see Nelson H. Minnich, *The Fifth Lateran Council: Studies on Its Membership, Diplomacy and Proposals for Reform* (London: Variorum, 1993); Lewis William Spitz, *The Protestant Reformation: Major Documents* (St. Louis, MO: Concordia Publishing House, 1997); Steven Ozment, *Protestants: The Birth of a Revolution* (New York: Image Books, 1993).

12. On Luther's theology, see Olli-Pekka Vainio, *Engaging Luther: A (New) Theological Assessment* (Eugene, OR: Cascade, 2010); and Robert C. Croken, S.J., *Luther's First Front: The Eucharist as Sacrifice* (Toronto: University of Ottawa Press, 1990).

13. For brief descriptions of Lutheran reformers and their doctrines, see Michael A. Mullett, *Historical Dictionary of the Reformation and Counter-Reformation* (Lanham, MD: Scarecrow Press, 2010); and David Bagchi and David C. Steinmetz, eds., *The Cambridge Companion to Reformation Theology* (Cambridge: Cambridge University Press, 2004).

14. For the changes in Protestant dogma and practice, see Salvatore Caponetto, *The Protestant Reformation in Sixteenth-Century Italy* (Kirksville, MO: Truman State University Press, 1999); Salvatore Caponetto, *Aonio Paleario (1503–1570) e la riforma protestante in Toscana* (Turin: Claudiana Editrice, 1979); and David M. Luebke, *The Counter-Reformation: The Essential Readings* (Oxford: Blackwell, 1999).

15. On the Council, see John W. O'Malley, *Trent and All That: Renaming Catholicism in the Early Modern Era* (Cambridge, MA, and London: Harvard University Press, 2000); John O'Malley, *What Happened at the Council of Trent* (Cambridge, MA: Harvard University Press, 2013); David Pietrusza, *Sursum Corda: Documents and Readings on the Traditional Latin Mass* (Seattle, WA: Createspace, 2008); Reverend H.J. Schroeder, *The Canons and Decrees of the Council of Trent* (Charlotte, NC: Tan Books, 1978); Outram H. Evennett, *The Spirit of the Counter-Reformation* (Notre Dame, IN: University of Notre Dame Press, 1970); Johann Peter Kirsch, *The Council of Trent* (San Diego, CA: Shamrock Eden Publishing, 2011); John A. McHugh, *The Catechism of the Council of Trent* (Charlotte, NC: Tan Books, 1982); and Hubert Jedin, *A History of the Council of Trent*, 2 vols. (vol. 1: *The Struggle for the Council*; vol. 2: *The First Sessions (1545–1547)*) (Humanities E-Book, 2008).

16. For a description of the Church's attempts to control and repress, see Giorgio Carnevale, *Forbidden Prayer: Church Censorship and Devotional Literature in Renaissance Italy* (Burlington, VT: Ashgate, 2011); Dermot Fenlon, *Heresy and Obedience in Tridentine Italy Cardinal Pole and the Counter*

Reformation (Cambridge: Cambridge University Press, 1973); and Gigliola Fragnito, ed., and Adrian Belton, trans., *Church, Censorship and Culture in Early Modern Italy* (Cambridge: Cambridge University Press, 2001).

17. For cases where the Inquisition persecuted for Lutheranism, where those persecuted considered themselves to be good Catholics, see John E. Longhurst, *Luther and the Spanish Inquisition: The Case of Diego de Uceda 1528–1529* (Albuquerque: University of New Mexico Press, 1953), 7–9. Erasmus, although a Catholic throughout his life, became a lightning rod for the Inquisition because the Protestants adapted his reformist ideas. On the use of Erasmus as a label to condemn other Catholics who sought reform within the Church, see Marçel Bataillón, *Érasme et l'Espagne: recherches sur l'histoire spirituelle du XVIe siècle* (Paris: Librairie Droz, 1937); and idem, *Erasmo y España: estudios sobre la historia espiritual del siglo XVI*, 2 vols. (Madrid: Fondo de Cultura Económica, 1950). John E. Longhurst, *Erasmus and the Spanish Inquisition: The Case of Juan de Valdés* (Albuquerque: University of New Mexico Press, 1950), 9–11, traces how Erasmus was initially favored in Spain, especially by Emperor Charles V and by the Inquisitor General of Spain, Alonso Manrique, who convoked the Council at Valladolid (1527) to approve Erasmus' reformist ideas. At about the same time, Alfonso de Valdés, Juan de Valdés' brother, wrote two popular dialogues attacking clerical abuses and praising Erasmian proposals for Church reforms. In 1529, Juan de Valdés published his *Diálogo de Doctrina Cristiana*, where he praised Erasmus. Until 1529, Spain had been favorably disposed to Erasmus because the emperor supported Erasmian reform agendas as a way to curb the power of the pope. However, in June 1529, the atmosphere changed when Charles V left for Italy, taking the pro-Erasmian courtiers with him. In December, the Inquisitor General, Manrique was banished by the Empress Isabella of Portugal, who did not like him, and the anti-Erasmians took power; when the emperor returned, in 1533, the Spanish Inquisition equated Erasmus with Luther, and Juan de Valdés had to flee Spain because he was identified as an Erasmian and any reformer so termed became associated with Luther because Erasmus early praised Luther's initial reformist work. For an example of personal spite leading to an Inquisitorial tribunal, see op. cit., 10–11, where Juan de Vergara was accused of Lutheranism by his half-brother's jilted lover. See also Aubrey G. Bell, "Liberty in Sixteenth Century Spain," *Bulletin of Spanish Studies* 10 (1933), 164–79, who writes that "The Reformation of Luther had cast a shadow similar to that cast by Bolshevism four centuries later." See also Peter G. Bietenholz, *Encounters with a Radical Erasmus* (Toronto: University of Toronto Press, 2009); and Gregory D. Dodds, *Exploiting Erasmus: The Erasmian Legacy and Religious Change in Early Modern England* (Toronto: University of Toronto Press, 2009). On Juan de Valdés, see Jose

C. Nieto, *Juan de Valdés and the Origins of the Spanish and Italian Reformation* (Geneva: Droz, 1970).

18. Carlo Ginzburg, *I costituti di don Pietro Manelfi* (DeKalb: Northern Illinois University Press, 1970), 39.

19. Ginzburg, *I costituti di don Pietro Manelfi*, 10–11.

20. Ginzburg, *I costituti di don Pietro Manelfi*, 32.

21. Ginzburg, *I costituti di don Pietro Manelfi*, 32–34.

22. Note Ginzburg, *I costituti di don Pietro Manelfi*, 11.

23. Ginzburg, *I costituti di don Pietro Manelfi*, 22–27.

24. Ginzburg, *I costituti di don Pietro Manelfi*, 18–21.

25. Among the sources for the lives of the Panciatichi are Pomponeo Litta, *Famiglie celebri di Italia* (1819–83), vol. 9, fasc. CLIV–CLV, "Panciatichi di Pistoia"; Francesco Piovan, "Gli studi padovani di Bartolomeo Panciatichi," *Quaderni per la storia dell'Università di Padova* 20, no. 11 (1987), 119–22; Luigi Passerini, *Genealogia e storia della famiglia Panciatichi* (Florence: Cellini, 1858), 68–75; Salvatore Caponetto, *La riforma protestante nell'Italia del Cinquecento* (Turin: Claudiana, 1977), 353–56 and passim; Gigliola Fragnito, "Un pratese alla corte di Cosimo I," *Archivio storico pratese* 62 (1986), 31–83; Gustavo Bertoli, "Luterani e anabattisti processati a Firenze nel 1552," *Archivio Storico Italiano* 154, no. 3 (1996), 59–122; and Elena Aloia, *I Panciatichi degli Uffizi* (Tesi di Laurea, Perugia, Università degli Studi di Perugia, 2008–2009).

26. Pomponeo Litta, *Famiglie celebri di Italia (1819–83)*, 16 vols., Guide Assembled by Princeton University Rare Books Room (Princeton: Princeton University Library, 2003),"Panciatichi di Pistoia," Tavola IV and "Pucci," Tavola XV.

27. Passerini, *Genealogia e storia della famiglia Panciatichi*, 68. The elder Bartolomeo's wife, Annalena di Lorenzo Lenzi, died without issue, on 9 March 1567. See Passerini, *Genealogia e storia della famiglia Panciatichi*, Tavola IV; and Émile Picot, *Les Italiens en France au XVIe siècle* (Paris: Editore Vecchiarelli, 1928), 83, where Bartolomeo's birth date is given as 21 June 1507.

28. Piovan, "Gli studi padovani di Bartolomeo Panciatichi," 119; and Passerini, *Genealogia e storia della famiglia Panciatichi*.

29. Litta, loc. cit., and Aloia, *I Panciatichi degli Uffizi*, 20–21, traced the documentation on the Panciatichi in Pistoia from 10 April 1208.

30. Litta, loc. cit., and Aloia, *I Panciatichi degli Uffizi*, 20–21, traced the documentation on the Panciatichi in Florence to 1375. The Panciatichi became citizens in 1376.

31. Passerini, *Genealogia e storia della famiglia Panciatichi*, 66.

32. The currently identified Palazzo Panciatichi on the corner of Via Cavour and Via Pucci is not the palace owned by Bartolomeo. The current

palace was built by Agnolo di Ghezzo della Casa, starting in 1445–46, and was acquired by Clarice Capponi, a member of the Pistoia branch of the Panciatichi, in 1621. On this palace, see Sandra Carlini, Lara Mercanti, and Giovanni Straffi, *I Palazzi parte prima: Arte e storia degli edifice civili di Firenze* (Florence: Alinea, 2001); Claudio Paolini and Vincenzo Vaccaro, *Via Cavour. Una strada per Firenze Capitale* (Florence: Edizioni Polistampa, 2011); and Anna Floridia, *Palazzo Panciatichi in Firenze* (Rome: Istituto della Enciclopledia Italiana, 1993). Aloia, *I Panciatichi degli Uffizi*, 2, identified the site of the original Panciatichi palace by using the map assembled by Guido Carocci, based on the 1427 *catasto* records, which documents how the area between Sta. Maria Maggiore and the Palazzo Ricci-Altoviti looked before the nineteenth-century reconstruction of the area. The map, as Aloia noted, is on view at the Archivio di Stato di Firenze. It is also published in Giovanni Fanelli, *Firenze: archetettura e città* (Florence: Vallechi, 1973), 168. The palace of Gabriello and Giovanni di Messer Bartolomeo Panciatichi is visible on the map, clearly marked near the then Piazza degli Agli (not today's Piazza degli Agli) and the then Chiasso dai Buoi.

33. Vasari-Milanesi, 5:209.

34. The Piazza degli Agli is by the Via de' Vecchietti, past the Church of San Michele Berteldi (Bertelli), by the Palazzo Ricci-Altoviti. On this palazzo, see Marcello Vannucci, *Splendidi palazzi di Firenze* (Florence: Le Lettere, 1995). The Ricci acquired the palace in 1528, whereupon they rebuilt it, incorporating the medieval Agli tower into the structure and adding a loggia, on the corner of the Piazza degli Agli. It was in this area that Vasari located Bartolomeo's palace. See R. Burr Lichtfield, "The Buonsignori Map (1584)," dedicated to the Grand Duke Francesco de' Medici, at the Online Gazetteer of Sixteenth Century Florence for the placement of this area in the parish of Santa Maria Novella <http://www.stg.brown.edu/projects/florentine_gazetteer/>.

35. Passerini, *Genealogia e storia della famiglia Panciatichi*, 74–75, gives the list of posts to which Cosimo appointed Bartolomeo: Senator (1567), Commissary to Pisa (1568), Commissary to Pistoia (1578).

36. Piovan, "Gli studi padovani di Bartolomeo Panciatichi," 120: ... April/August 1529—in Padova—record from the Lyonese cleric, Leonardo Dei—"actu studens in Universitate dominos et magistros Franciscum Colllucium de Piscia…nobilis et eruditus atrium scholaris dominus Bartholomeus filius alterius domini Bartholomei Panciatichi civis Florentini, habitator Paduae gratia studii in contrata Burgi Zuchi." Dei also was a Florentine who lived in Lyon.

37. Piovan, "Gli studi padovani di Bartolomeo Panciatichi," 121.

38. Piovan, "Gli studi padovani di Bartolomeo Panciatichi," 121, A.A.U. MS 675, fol. 38r.

39. Piovan, "Gli studi padovani di Bartolomeo Panciatichi," 119; and A. Prosperi, Campeggi, "Alessandro," in *Dizionario biografico degli Italiani*, vol. 17 (Rome: Treccani, 1974), 432–35.

40. The marriage dates can be found in Litta (1528), loc. cit.; and Piovan (1534), 119. Passerini, *Genealogia e storia della famiglia Panciatichi*, 70, noted that in 1538, while in Lyon, Bartolomeo wrote to Pietro Aretino, and in 1539, he wrote from Florence.

41. Litta, "Pucci," Tavola XV.

42. Litta, loc. cit.

43. Litta. loc. cit.

44. For the dating of Lucrezia's dress and hair, see Roberta Orsi Landini and Bruna Niccoli, *Moda a Firenze 1540–1580: Lo stile di Eleonora di Toledo e la sua influenza* (Florence: Pagliai Polistampa, 2005), 30: "Lucrezia è vestita secondo la moda degli anni '30 del secolo, con la vestre priva di decorazioni e caraterizzata da gonfi spallini, chiamati 'baragoni,' da cui fuoriescono maniche di colore contrastante con tagli decorative. Questa moda, che Eleonora trova giungendo Firenze, sarà da lei mutate per renderla più vicina ai canoni internazionali, senza però stravolgerne le caratteritiche fondamentali." Lucrezia's clothing would have been dowdy soon after 1540–42, when Eleonora's new style swept through Florence, after her arrival in 1539. For a comparison of the development before and after Eleonora, see 106, 128, 141 (for hairstyles).

45. Passerini, *Genealogia e storia della famiglia Panciatichi*, Tavola IV and 72–75.

46. Litta, loc. cit.; Passerini, *Genealogia e storia della famiglia Panciatichi*, 68–70; Émile Picot, *Les Français Italianisants au XVI siècle*, 2 vols. (Paris: Champion, 1906), 1:117–59; Natalie Zemon Davis, *Le culture del popolo: Sapere, rituali e resistenze nella Francia del Cinquecento* (Turin: Einaudi, 1980), 23–90; Piovan, "Gli studi padovani di Bartolomeo Panciatichi," 119–20.

47. For a description of the process, see Picot, *Les Français italianisants au XVI siècle*, 135–59; and Caponetto, *La riforma protestante nell'Italia del Cinquecento*, 354–55.

48. Karl-Heinz zur Mühlen, "Die Reichsreligionsgespräche von Hagenau, Worms und Regensburg 1540/41, Chancen und Grenzen des kontroverstheologischen Dialogs in der Mitte des 16. Jahrhunderts," in *Blätter für pfälzische Kirchengeschichte und religiöse Volkskunde (BPfKG)* 72 (2005), 319–34.

49. On the members of the *Accademia* and their activities, see Eric Cochrane, "Le Accademia," *Firenze e la Toscana dei Medici nell'Europa del '500. I: Strumenti e veicoli della cultura Relazioni politiche ed economiche* (Florence: Olschki, 1933); Alessandro Cecchi, "Il Bronzino, Benedetto Varchi e l'Accademia Fiorentine: Ritratti di Poeti, Letterati e Personaggi Illustri della Corte Medicea," *Antichità Viva*, 20, nos. 1–2 (1991), 17–28.

50. Passerini, *Genealogia e storia della famiglia Panciatichi*, 69, for a list of Bartolomeo's literary works; and Carlo Falciani, "Il Bronzino e I Panciatichi," in Falciani and Natali, *Bronzino*, 153–65, for an account of Bartolomeo's intellectual activities and literary accomplishments. See also Passerini, *Genealogia e storia della famiglia Panciatichi*, 69–70, who noted that Bartolomeo composed two epigrams for the wedding of Francesco de' Medici with Joanna of Austria (Florence: Giunti: 1565); contributed three epigrams to the collected works that were published, in 1566, gathering the tributes to Michelangelo (additional epigrams were found in the publication of similar material by Giovanni Tarsia); two epigrams praising Vincenzio Baonanni in Pasquati's *Il Tempio della Divina Signora, donna Girolama Colonna d'Aragona*; and verses in Latin composed for Varchi's funeral. Francesco Marcolini da Forlì, who printed the collected letters of Aretino, published two letters by Bartolomeo (1538/Lyon and 1539/Florence); and in Baccio Baldini's *Vita di Cosimo I* there is a Latin epigram by Bartolomeo: *Sette Canzoni* (similar to the Seven Penitential Psalms, which he presented to Joanna of Austria in 1576 (Biblioteca Magliabechiana, Codice 263, Classe VII) and other poems in Codice 357, Classe VII, and a short poem composed on the death of the Archbishop Bindo Altoviti (Magliabecchiano Carte 139, Codice 104, Classe XXVII).

51. On Bartolomeo's admission to the Accademia, see Leatrice Mendelsohn, "The Panciatichi *Holy Family*," in Falciani and Natali, *Bronzino*, 172; Aloia, *I Panciatichi degli Uffizi*, 12; and for an account of praise for Bartolomeo, see Passerini, *Genealogia e storia della famiglia Panciatichi*, 69, who recorded that Anton Francesco Doni dedicated his lectures on Dante to Bartolomeo (published in Florence, in 1547); Bartolommeo Sermartelli acknowledged Bartolomeo in his *Vita Nuova* of Dante (1576); Pietro Angeli da Barga wrote poetic praise of Bartolomeo, preserved in a manuscript in the Magliabechiana (Classe VII, Cod. 243, Carte 57); and Baccio Baldini dedicated his *Dell'essenza del Fato e della forza sua sopra le cose del mondo* (1578) to Bartolomeo.

52. On Marguérite d'Angouême, Queen of Navarre, see Jonathan Reid, *The King's Sister: Queen of Dissent Marguérite of Navarre (1492–1549) and her Evangelical Network*, 2 vols. (Leiden: Brill, 2009), 7, says of Marguérite's religious pursuits, "… she absorbed many influences and brought them into an arrangement all her own, which defies categorization but not exposition." Lucien Fébvre, *Amour sacré, amour profane: Autour del' Heptameron* (Paris: Gallimard, 1994), 194, characterizes Marguerite as "A Catholic Marguérite, an evangelical Marguérite, a Protestant Marguérite, a Lutheran Marguérite; a Calvinist Marguérite … Marguérite lived the religion of Marguérite, a religion that she made herself, for herself, little by little, with unceasing changes, transformations, retouches, and adaptations that

modified the form of her ideas ... while keeping them in permanent accord with her own profound nature." Among the intellectuals who were either befriended by Marguerite or became part of her court were Erasmus, François Rabelais (1494–1553), Clément Marot (1496–1544), Claude de Bectoz (d. 1547), Pierre de Ronsard (1524–85), John Calvin (1509–64), and Jacques Lefèvre d' Étaples (1455–1536). Caponetto, *La riforma protestante nell'Italia del Cinquecento*, 354–56, discussed Bartolomeo's involvement with French reform movements.

53. Piovan, "Gli studi padovani di Bartolomeo Panciatichi," 122.

54. Falciani, in Falciani and Natali, *Bronzino*, 153.

55. Falciani, in Falciani and Natali, *Bronzino*, 153.

56. Émile Picot, *Les Français Italianisants au XVe Siècle* (Paris: Honoré Champion, 1906), 134–35.

57. Falciani, in Falciani and Natali, *Bronzino*, 154.

58. Massimo Firpo, *Gli affreschi di Pontormo a San Lorenzo* (Turin: Einaudi Editore, 1997), 170–207, discussed the atmosphere at the *Accademia* and gives additional bibliography. For a sense of the larger context, see *Il Rinascimento italiano di Fronte alla Riforma: Letteratura e Arte/Sixteenth-Century Italian Art and Literature and the Reformation*, eds. Chrysa Damianaki, Paolo Procaccioli, and Angelo Romano (Rome: Vecchiarelli Editore, 2005); and the review by Elisabeth G. Gleason, in *Renaissance Quarterly* 59, no. 4 (Winter 2006), 1186–88.

59. Benedetto Varchi, *Orazione funerale, fatta già, et recitata nell'Accademia Fiorentine ... sopra la morte dell'Illustrissima, et Ecc. Signora Madonna maria Salviata de' Medici, Madre dell' Ecc. et Illu. Signor Duca de Firenze, con un Sermone fatto alla Croce, et recitato il Venerdì santo nella compagnia di S. Domenico, l'anno 1549* (Florence: Lorenzo Torrentino, 1549); A.L. De Gaetano, "G.B. Gelli and the Questione della lingua," *Italica* 44, no. 3 (1967), 263–81; idem, *Giambattista Gelli and the Florentine Academy: The Rebellion Against Latin* (Florence: Olschki, 1976); M. Sherber, "The Accademia Fiorentina and the Question of the Language: The Politics of Theory in Ducal Florence," *Renaissance Quarterly* 56 (2003), 26–55; Barzman, *The Florentine Academy and the Early Modern State*.

60. Massimo Firpo, "Bronzino and the Medici," in Falciani and Natali, *Bronzino*, 97.

61. Litta, loc. cit., "Panciatichi."

62. Litta, loc. cit., "Panciatichi," loc. cit.; Passerini, *Genealogia e storia della famiglia Panciatichi*, 70–72, described how Bartolomeo was taken captive and forced, on 4 February 1552, to abjure his heresy in a procession around the Duomo, wearing a black and yellow *bavaglio* and carrying a torch in his hand, with which he was forced to burn his heretical books. Passerini stated that Cosimo's intervention had saved Bartolomeo. He

added the information that Lucrezia had been forced to recant in a procession from where she had been jailed to the Church of San Simone. However, Bertoli, "Luterani e anabattisti processati a Firenze nel 1552," demonstrated that Passerini's information was not accurate, as there is no record of Lucrezia's arrest or forced recantation at San Simone and Bartolomeo was not required to wear the black and yellow costume.

63. On Manelfi's confession, see Carlo Ginzburg, ed., *I costituti di don Pieitro Manelfi* (De Kalb: Northern Illinois University Press; Chicago: Newberry Library, 1970). The events of Bartolomeo's arrest and process were summarized by Bertoli, "Luterani e anabattisti processati a Firenze nel 1552," 59–122. The inquisitorial process against Bartolomeo, and others accused at the same time, was recorded by Bernardo Milanesi, ducal Secretary to Cosimo I, on 28 March 1552. A letter from Pope Julius III, dated 24 December 1551, confirmed Alessandro Strozzi as the commissary in charge of conducting the hearing against those accused of Lutheran heresy by the Anabaptist Pietro Manelfi, this charge having been made on 17 October 1551. Manelfi, who was a priest born in Senigallia, confessed his heresy to the Dominican Inquisitor Leandro Alberti, who was stationed in Bologna at the time. The Dominican Inquisitor Girolamo Muzzarelli was in charge of the Florentine investigation. By 26 December, Duke Cosimo, who was in Pisa, agreed to the papal order to arrest the accused. On 5 January 1552, about forty Florentine citizens were paraded through the streets, as was reported by Cardinal Gyens to Charles V. Bartolomeo was arrested on 6 December 1551 and, as recorded in the *Cronica* attributed to Orazio da Sangallo, was accused of a "specie di santità" engaging in "interpretare le sante scritture." Bartolomeo was imprisoned along with thirty-five men, fifteen of whom were imprisoned in the *Stinche* until 4 February 1552. On 6 February, twenty-two of the thirty-five arrested were declared heretics, and sixteen of them were made to march through the streets of Florence wearing yellow *bavagli* with crosses stamped on them, and six were obliged to march without the *bavagli*, but all carried lit torches. The accused, who were repenting, were stopped in front of the Duomo, where they were blessed, and then they were marched to the Baptistery, where their heretical books were burned. Those who were not wearing the *bavagli* were allowed to go free after paying 10 scudi; the others were again imprisoned, some for up to ten years. Bartolomeo was among those who were released.

64. Bertoli, "Luterani e anabattisti processati a Firenze nel 1552," 59–122.

65. Bertoli, "Luterani e anabattisti processati a Firenze nel 1552," 80: "L'identità delle tre donne che furono benedette in san Simone una settimana dopo la dà il Memoriale; esse sono monna Antonia moglie di Fan-

cesco (del Gabelliere, monna Giovanna moglie di ser Lorenzo Niccolucci e monna Lisabetta moglie di ser Bartolomeo Ducci." Lucrezia Panciatichi is not mentioned in the documents studied by Bertoli; therefore, it is not recorded that she was arrested nor can it be assumed.

66. Bertoli, "Luterani e anabattisti processati a Firenze nel 1552," 69. In Manelfi's accusatory document, there is mention of a "Bartolomeo e sua moglie," but this Bartolomeo is not Bartolomeo Panciatichi, because he and his wife are identified as citizens of Monte Vettolini. This Bartolomeo, "Ser Bartolomeo Notaro, was the son of ser Sebastiano Ducci di Monte Vettolini colla moglie" was accused of being an Anabaptist. This Bartolomeo was further imprisoned until Duke Cosimo obtained his release; see Bertoli, "Luterani e anabattisti processati a Firenze nel 1552," 69, "il notaio Bartolomeo e la moglie."

67. Firpo, *Gli affreschi di Pontormo a San Lorenzo*, 360, note 22.

68. Nieto, *Juan de Valdés*, 5–7, gives the list of works by Valdés: a *Diálogo de la doctrina christiana*, 14 January 1529, published in Alcalá de Henares, while he was a student at the University; a *Diálogo de la lengua*, c. 1535, written in Naples; the *Alfabeto Cristiano*, written in Naples during Lent of 1536, in Spanish, with the Italian version published in Venice in 1545; a *Comentario a los Salmos*, written in Naples c. 1537; a *Comentario sobre la epístola del Apostol San Pablo a los Romanos* and a *Comentario sobre la I epístola del Apostol San Pablo a los Corintios* written in Naples c. 1538–39; *Le cento e dieci divine considerazione* (the original is lost, with the first copy published in 1550); and *El Evangelio de San Mateo declarado por Juan de Valdés*, written c. 1539.

69. De Gaetano, *Giambattista Gelli and the Florentine Academy*; Jacopo Rilli, *Notizie Letterarie, Ed Istoriche Intorno Agli Uomini Illustri Dell'Accademia Fiorentina* (Ann Arbor: University of Michigan Press, 2009).

70. Emily Michelson, *The Pulpit and the Press in Reformation Italy* (Cambridge, MA: Harvard University Press, 2013); Elizabeth L. Eisenstein, *The Printing Press as an Agent of Change*, 2 vols. (Cambridge: Cambridge University Press, 1980); and Mark Edwards, *Printing, Propaganda, and Martin Luther* (Augsburg: Augsburg Fortress Publishers, 2004).

71. Bertoli, "Luterani e anabattisti processati a Firenze nel 1552," 66.

72. Christopher F. Black, *The Italian Inquisition* (New Haven, CT: Yale University Press, 2010); Francisco Bethencourt and Jean Birrell, eds., *The Inquisition: A Global History 1478–1834* (Cambridge: Cambridge University Press, 2009); Jane K. Wichersham, *Rituals of Persecution: The Roman Inquisition and the Prosecution of Philo-Protestants in Sixteenth-Century Italy* (Toronto: University of Toronto Press, 2012); J.T. Betts, *A Glance at the Italian Inquisition: A Sketch of Pietro Carnesecchi* (London: Ulan Press, 2012); John Dillemberger, *Images and Relics: Theological Perceptions and Visual Images in Sixteenth Century Europe* (Oxford: Oxford University Press, 1999).

73. Bertoli, "Luterani e anabattisti processati a Firenze nel 1552," 66.

74. Bertoli, "Luterani e anabattisti processati a Firenze nel 1552," loc. cit.

75. Passerini, *Genealogia e storia della famiglia Panciatichi*, 68–72; and Aloia, *I Panciatichi degli Uffizi*, 24. Carlo Falciani, "Bronzino e i Panciatichi," in Falciani and Natali, *Bronzino*, 153–55, describes Bartolomeo's career.

76. Antonio Natali, "Percorso iniziale d'Agnolo Bronzino: Firenze e poi Pesaro," in Falciani and Natali, *Bronzino*, 37–55.

77. Craig Hugh Smyth, *Bronzino as Draughtsman; an Introduction* (Locust Valley, NY: J.J. Augustin, 1971), 2–3; and Brock (2002), who summarizes the earlier literature on the chronology of the Panciatichi paintings.

78. Angelo Maria Monaco, in Falciani and Natali, *Bronzino*, 258, for a synopsis of the portrait's historiography.

79. Cropper, in Falciani and Natali, *Bronzino*, 250.

80. Simone Giordani, in Falciani and Natali, *Bronzino*, 58.

81. Martina de Petris, in Falciani and Natali, *Bronzino*, 74.

82. Cécile Beuzelin, in Falciani and Natali, *Bronzino*, 82.

83. Bridget Heal, *The Cult of the Virgin Mary in Early Modern Germany: Protestant and Catholic Piety, 1500–1648* (Cambridge: Cambridge University Press, 2007), 1–63, for a discussion of Luther's position on the Virgin Mary and his suppression of her cult and the cult of the saints.

84. Falciani, in Falciani and Natali, *Bronzino*, 166.

85. Falciani, in Falciani and Natali, *Bronzino*, 168.

86. Cropper, in Falciani and Natali, *Bronzino*, 250.

87. Janet Cox-Rearick, "St. Sebastian," in Falciani and Natali, *Bronzino*, 296.

88. Carlo Falciani, "Crucified Christ," in Falciani and Natali, *Bronzino, Christ*, 170–71.

89. On the categorization of beards, see Allan Peterkin: *One Thousand Beards. A Cultural History of Facial Hair* (Vancouver: Arsenal Pulp Press, 2001); Helen Bunkin and Randall Williams, *Beards, Beards, Beards* (Pasadena, CA: Green Street Press, 2000); Reginald Reynolds, *Beards: Their Social Standing, Religious Involvements, Decorative Possibilities, and Value in Offence and Defence Through the Ages* (Garden City, NY: Doubleday, 1949).

90. Roberta Orsi Landini, *Moda a Firenze 1540–1580: Cosimo I de' Medici's Style* (Florence: Mauro Paglia Editore, 2011), 49–50.

91. Orsi Landini, *Moda a Firenze 1540–1580*, 152–54.

92. Falciani, in Falciani and Natali, *Bronzino*, 154.

93. For the dating of Lucrezia's dress and hair, see Orsi Landini and Niccoli (2005), 30.

94. Falciani, in Falciani and Natali, *Bronzino*, 166–67, for a description of the underpainting of Lucrezia's portrait in relation to Bartolomeo's.

95. Passerini, *Genealogia e storia della famiglia Panciatichi*, Tavola IV.

96. Cropper, in Falciani and Natali, *Bronzino*, 250.

97. Caponetto (1997), 356, and Massimo Firpo, "Il Bronzino e I Medici," 91–99, in Falciani and Natali, *Bronzino*, who state (96): "Lo stesso ausero crocifisso dipinto per Bartolomeo Panciatichi, processato dall'Inquisizione nel 1551–52 sembra esprimere una spiritualità tutta incentrata sul Beneficio di Christo e sull' esclusivo valore salvifico." Firpo does not take into consideration that the commission of the *Crucified Christ* predates the publication of the *Beneficio*, in 1543. He also decontextualizes the painting by not taking into consideration the long tradition of *Crucifixions of Christ* that included Donatello's and Brunelleschi's in Sta. Croce and Sta. Maria Novella and which begins in medieval representations of the Crucifixion. The Crucifix as a salvific image is not a Protestant invention, as the significance of the image of the Crucifixion as an icon of salvation was part of Catholic visual culture since the Holy Roman Empire began. The same mistake is made by Carlo Falciani, op. cit., "Il Bronzino e I Panciatichi," 153–65, 156, in writing about the Panciatichi *Christ*, when he asserts that the *Beneficio* provides an interpretive vehicle for the Panciatichi works, along with the *Alfabeto Cristiano*, which was written by Juan de Valdés. Indeed the *Alfabeto Cristiano* was composed earlier than Bronzino's works, in 1536, but it was not available for public distribution until it was published in Venice in 1545—see Nieto, *Juan de Valdés*, 5–7. Possibly a manuscript might have circulated in the Neapolitan inner circle of Valdés and could have made its way to Florence before its publication, but Falciani does not put forth proof that this happened. As Lucrezia's costume and hairstyle and her late 1544/45 pregnancy rule out a date later than c. 1541–42 for her portrait, neither the *Beneficio* nor the *Alfabeto Cristiano* can be used as an interpretive filter for the Panciatichi paintings. Elizabeth Cropper, in Falciani and Natali, *Bronzino*, "Per una lettura dei ritratti Panciatichi del Bronzino," 245–55, 254, suggests an alternative, and more applicable, context for Bartolomeo's heterodoxy, i.e., French reformist ideas circulating at the court of Marguerite d'Angoulême, something that Litta had already noted in his biography of Bartolomeo.

98. See Falciani, in Falciani and Natali, *Bronzino*, on 156.

99. See note 68 above for a list of the works by Valdés.

100. On the *Beneficio*, see Benedetto da Mantova, *Il Beneficio di Cristo con le Versioni del Secolo XVI, Documenti e Testimonianze*, ed., Salvator Caponetto (DeKalb: Northern Illinois University Press, 1972); and John Martin, *Venice's Hidden Enemies: Italian Heretics in a Renaissance City* (Baltimore, MD: Johns Hopkins University Press, 2003), 84, note 3, where there is extensive bibliography on the *Beneficio*.

101. See Benedetto di Mantova (1972), 501.

102. Caponeto/Mantova (1972), 473.

103. Salvatore Caponetto, "Benedetto da Mantova," *Dizionario Biografico degli Italiani*, vol.8 (1966), quotes Carnesecchi, who during his Inquisitorial interrogation on 31 August 1566, stated: "Il primo autore di questo libro fu un Monaco nero chiamato don B. da Mantova il quale disse averlo composto mentre stette nel monastero della sua religione in Sicilia presso Monte Etna; il qual don B., essendo amico di messer Marcantonio Flaminio, li comunicò il detto libro pregandolo che lo volesse pulire e illustrare sul suo bello stile acciò fusse tanto più leggibile e dilettevole ..." See also Alessandro Pastore, "Marcantonio Flaminio," in *Dizionario Biografico Italiano*, vol. 48 (Rome: Treccani, 1997).

104. For discussions of influence on the Spirituali on members of the *Accademia*, see Abigail Brundin and Matthew Treherne, eds., *Forms of Faith in Sixteenth-Century Italy* (Aldershot: Ashgate, 1988); Paolo Simoncelli, *Evangelismo Italiano del Cinquecento* (Rome: Istituto storico italiano per letà moderna e contemporanea, 1979).

105. Gigliola Fragnito, "Un pratese alla corte di Cosimo I," *Archivio Storico Pratese* 62 (1986), 31–83, 41.

106. Gigliola Fragnito, "The Central and Peripheral Organization of Censorship," in Gigliola Fragnito, ed., and Adrian Belton, trans., *Church, Censorship and Culture in Early Modern Italy* (Cambridge: Cambridge University Press, 2001), 13–49, 16.

107. Caponetto/Mantova (1972), 501.

108. Anne Overell, *Italian Reform and English Reformations, c. 1535–1585* (Aldershot: Ashgate, 2013), gives a thorough and succinct summary of the *Beneficio*'s content and context.

109. Dermot Fenlon, *Heresy and Obedience in Tridentine Italy: Cardinal Pole and the Counter Reformation* (Cambridge: Cambridge University Press, 2008).

110. Fragnito, "The Central and Peripheral Organization of Censorship," 30.

111. On Erasmus, see Reinhard Paul Becker, *German Humanism and Reformation: Erasmus, Luther, Müntzner, and Others* (London: Continuum, 1982); Desiderius Erasmus, *The Essential Erasmus* (New York: Plume, 1964); and Sylvia Fitzpatrick, *Erasmus and the Process of Human Perfection: The Philosophy of Christ* (London: Stauros, 2012).

112. Andrew Pettegree, *The Reformation World* (London: Routledge, 2001), 289–90. The *Beneficio* was banned in Venice in 1549 and burned publicly in Naples.

113. Thomas à Kempis, *The Imitation of Christ* (New York: Simon and Brown, 2013); and Girolamo Savonarola, *The Triumph of the Cross* (Hong Kong: Forgotten Books, 2012).

114. St. Ignatius Loyola, *The Spiritual Exercises of Saint Ignatius* (Cicero, NY: Image, 1964); St. John of the Cross, *The Collected Works of St. John of the Cross* (Washington, DC: ICS Publications, 1991); St. Teresa of Avila, *Collected Works*, 2 vols. (Washington, DC: ICS Publications, 1980).

115. Edoardo Barbieri, "Tradition and Change in the Spiritual Literature of the Cinquecento," in Gigliola Fragnito, ed., and Adrian Belton, trans., *Church, Censorship and Culture in Early Modern Italy* (Cambridge: Cambridge University Press, 2001), 111–33.

116. Barbieri, "Tradition and Change," 119.

117. Barbieri, "Tradition and Change," 121.

118. Barbieri, "Tradition and Change," 123.

119. Barbieri, "Tradition and Change," 123–24.

120. Barbieri, "Tradition and Change," 125–26.

121. Roman Missal, "The Canon of the Mass," 206–11.

122. Dermot Fenlon, *Heresy and Obedience in Tridentine Italy: Cardinal Pole and the Counter Reformation* (Cambridge: Cambridge University Press, 2009).

123. See note 69 above for bibliography on the dissemination of Luther's writings and those of other reformists in Italy.

124. Elizabeth Cropper, "Per una lettura dei ritratti Panciatichi del Bronzino," in Falciani and Natali, *Bronzino*, 245–55, 254, suggests an alternative, and more applicable, context for Bartolomeo's heterodoxy, as being based on French reformist ideas circulating at the court of Marguerite d'Angoulême, something that Litta had already noted in his biography of Bartolomeo.

125. In Falciani and Natali, *Bronzino*, these authors treat Lucrezia as an echo of Bartolomeo and ignore evidence of Catholic devotional adherence that is emphasized in her portrait, discussed in this chapter. See Carlo Falciani, "Il Bronzino e I Panciatichi," 153–65, who identifies Lucrezia as a Lutheran on the basis of the necklace she wears on which are inscribed the words "Amour Dure Sans Fin," 156. These words were linked by Elizabeth Cropper ("Per una lettura dei ritratti fiorentini del Bronzino," 245–55) to translations of Psalms made by Jacques Lefèvre d'Étaples and Clément Marot in which she sought to find these words. However, neither translation renders the Psalms Cropper cites with words that include the motto "Amour Dure Sans Fin," and the concept of everlasting love expressed in the Psalms is as appropriate for Catholics as for Protestants. It was the Catholic Church which originally linked the Psalms to God's everlasting love for humanity when they were incorporated into the Roman liturgy. There is nothing specifically Lutheran about the Psalms or about the concept expressed in the necklace, which could just as easily apply in a Catholic context—more applicable to Lucrezia, given that she holds a Book of Hours written in accordance with the use of Rome, not Luther.

126. See The Catholic Encyclopedia, "Lauds," for a discussion of this service, which especially emphasizes praise or *Laudes*—and which evokes the Alleluia recited during the Mass in praise of God.

127. Marina Warner, *Alone of all Her Sex* (Victoria, CA: Vintage Books, 1983).

128. Heal, *The Cult of the Virgin Mary*, 3–63, discusses the respective positions of Catholic and reformers towards the Virgin Mary, clarifying that while the Virgin was honored by the reformers, the Catholic cult of the Virgin was erased, as was the cult of the saints, because the reformers, starting with Luther, believed that emphasis on the Virgin and the saints as intercessors took away emphasis from Christ as the Savior. Thus, while Luther retained liturgical acknowledgment of the Virgin, he did away with exclusive devotion to the Virgin other than to laud her as an exemplar of faith, patience, and virtue, deserving of salvation. See also Anja Ghiselli, "The Virgin Mary," in *Engaging Luther*, ed. Vainio, 173–85.

129. Cropper, in Falciani and Natali, *Bronzino*, 249–51.

130. On Veronica's Veil, see Ewa Kuryluk, *Veronica and Her Cloth: History, Symbolism and Structure of a True Image* (London: Blackwell, 1991).

131. Aloia, *I Panciatichi degli Uffizi*, 23–24.

132. For Grafton's identification, see Elizabeth Pilliod, "Regarding the Hebrew in Bronzino's Holy Family for Bartolomeo Panciatichi," *Artibus et Historiae* 61, no. 31 (2010), 148–58, 157, note 21, who gave her analysis of the Hebrew letters in the accompanying article, touching on similar issues presented here regarding Hebrew letters and the significance of the use of Isaiah, although with some differences.

133. In February/March 2013, I consulted Rabbi Zachary Silver and Deborah Huacuja for their opinions on the Hebrew letters. Both concurred as is presented here in the text on the spelling and significance of the name Isaiah. Rabbi Silver cited the Brown-Driver-Briggs Hebrew and English Lexicon as an authoritative source for translations and transliterations, and it was he who provided the translation of Isaiah, the context for the relation the Tetragrammaton to Isaiah's name, and the observation about the flipped letters in Isaiah being an allusion to the spelling of Jesus in Hebrew.

134. On the Aramei, see Paolo Simoncelli, *La Lingua di Adamo: Guillaume Postel, tra accademici e fuorosciti fiorentini* (Florence: Olschki, 1934), and Pilliod, "Regarding the Hebrew in Bronzino's Holy Family for Bartolomeo Panciatichi," 148–58.

135. Aloia, *I Panciatichi degli Uffizi*, 21–25, discusses the Panciatichi tombs in Santa Maria Novella and in Santa Maria Maggiore.

136. Costamagna and Falciani (2010), 48–49, contextualize the Christ within Savonarolan influence and link it to Fra Bartolomeo's *Christ* and

the *Crucifix* of Baccio da Montelupo, Benedetto da Maianao, and Giuliano da Sangallo, as well as the Brunelleschi and Donatello *Christs* and think it influenced Allori's *Crucifixion* in the Cenacolo di Foligno. Falciani, in Falciani and Natali, *Bronzino*, links it to Donatello's *Crucifix* in Bosco ai Frati and to the *Crucifix* drawing by Michelangelo for Vittoria Colonna and links the architecture of the niche to *il Cronaca*.

137. For the Allori Christ, see F. Saracino, "Alessandro Allori 'arameo,'" *Mitteilungen des Kunsthistorschen Institutes in Florenz* 48 (2003), 371, and in Falciani and Natali, *Bronzino*, 169 and 330.

138. Roman Missal, "Corpus Christi," 256–59; "Canon of the Mass," 206–11; "Inventione Sanctae Crucis," 329–31; "In Exaltatione Crucis," 380–81.

139. On the Church's position on Transubstantiation, see Reverend H.J. Schroeder, trans., *The Canons and Decrees of the Council of Trent* (Charlotte, NC: Tan Books, 1911, 72–75.

140. Roman Missal, "Canon of the Mass," 206–09.

141. Roman Missal, "Corpus Christi," 256–59. The Feast of Corpus Christi was instituted by Pope Urban IV in 1264 with the bull "Transiturus de hoc mundo." The Feast confirmed Transubstantiation.

142. The *Processionale* for Santa Maria Novella is in the collection of Rare Printed Books, British Library, London.

143. Roman Missal, "Corpus Christi," 256–59.

144. For the hymn, see David Hiley, *Western Plainchant: A Handbook* (Oxford: Oxford University Press, 1993), Section II.22, pp.172–95; and Roman Missal, 256–58.

145. Roman Missal, 258–59.

146. Roman Missal, "Inventione Sanctae Crucis," 329–30, and "In Exaltatione Sancte Crucis," 380–81.

147. Jan Eillem Drijvers, *Helena Augusta: The Mother of Constantine the Great and the Legend of Her Finding of the True Cross* (Leiden: Brill Academic Publishers, 2004).

148. Roman Missal, 380–82.

149. Falciani, in Falciani and Natali, *Bronzino*, 153–65; Cropper, in Falciani and Natali, *Bronzino*, 248–51; and Aloia, *I Panciatichi degli Uffizi*, 34–36. Cropper's analysis of Lucrezia's portrait emphasized that the words visible at the top of the right-hand page—"Viderunt eam"—were derived from the Song of Songs (6:9), and she also discussed the hymn "O Gloriosa Domina," the opening words of which can also be read. Additionally, Cropper identified the word "Pulchra"—legible next to the thumb of Lucrezia's right hand—as a reference to the Virgin and Lucrezia. The text of Lucrezia's Hours was similarly discussed by Carlo Falciani, who pointed out that the "Gloria Patri" can also be read right after the text

of the Psalm. Falciani also identified the source of "Pulchra" as Song of Songs 6:4 and gave Song of Songs 6:9 for the source of "Viderunt Eam." Falciani also provided the full text of Psalm 150, the pertinent lines of the Song of Songs, and the text of "O Gloriosa Domina," pointing out that Lucrezia's hand is posed to rest in a way that indicates emphasis on the words of these texts.

150. Aloia, *I Panciatichi degli Uffizi*, 34–36; and Falciani and Natali, *Bronzino*, 168.

151. See Roger S. Wieck, *Painted Prayer: The Medieval Book of Hours in Medieval and Renaissance Art* (New York: Braziller, 1999); and idem, *Time Sanctified: The Book of Hours in Medieval Art and Life* (New York City: Braziller, 2001), for an overview of the history of the Book of Hours and their content and determinations of usage and localization.

152. On the cult of the Virgin in the Church, see Luigi Gambero, *Mary and the Fathers of the Church: The Blessed Virgin Mary in Patristic Thought* (New York: Ignatius Press, 1999); Hilda Graf, *Mary: A History of Doctrine and Devotion* (Notre Dame, IN: Ave Maria Press, 2009); Jaroslav Pelikan, *Mary Through the Centuries: Her Place in the History of Culture* (New Haven, CT: Yale University Press, 1998); and Luigi Gambero, *Mary in the Middle Ages: The Blessed Virgin Mary in the Thought of Medieval Latin Theologians* (New York: Ignatius Press, 2005).

153. Benedict XVI, *Mary: The Church at the Source* (New York: Ignatius Press, 2005).

154. Cropper, in Falciani and Natali, *Bronzino*, 253–54.

155. Silvia Malaguzzi, "Un amore senza fine," *Arte e Dossier* 17, no. 180 (Luglio–Agosto, 2002), 33–37.

156. Cropper, in Falciani and Natali, *Bronzino*, 250.

157. Wieck (2001), Introduction, discusses the history of the Book of Hours and its development from the Breviary.

158. Wieck (1999) illustrates the traditional representations of women with Books of Hours, praying in ecclesiastical interiors, to which Lucrezia's portrait belongs.

159. Wieck (2001) discusses the prayers and other content of Books of Hours.

160. Ordinary Time or the *Quattuor Temporum* is the time in between the major preparation and observance of Advent and Christmas and Lent and Resurrection Sunday that follows Pentecost and ends with the preparation for Advent. On the history of the Catholic liturgy, see Marcel Metzger, *History of the Liturgy: The Major Stages* (Collegeville, MN: Liturgical Press, 1991); Keith F. Pecklers, S.J., *Liturgy: The Illustrated History* (Mahwah, NJ: Paulist Press, 2012); and Joseph A. Jungmann S.J., *The Mass of the Roman Rite: Its Origin and Development* (Grand Rapids, MI: Christian Classics, 2012).

161. Psalm 150: "Laudate Dominum in sanctis ejus; laudate eum in firmamento virtutis ejus. Laudate eum in virtutibus ejus; laudate eum secundum multitudinem magnitudinis ejus. Laudate eum in sono tubae; laudate eum in psalterio et cithara. Laudate eum in tympano et choro; laudate eum in chordis et organo. Laudate eum in cymbalis benesonantibus; laudate eum in cymbalis jubilationis. Omnis spiritus laudet Dominum! Alleluja."

162. Falciani, in Falciani and Natali, *Bronzino*, 169, noted this text, as did Aloia, *I Panciatichi degli Uffizi*, 7.

163. Falciani, in Falciani and Natali, *Bronzino*, 168; and Aloia, *I Panciatichi degli Uffizi*, 7.

164. "*O Gloriosa domina/excelsa super sidera, /qui te creavit provide,/ lactas sacrato ubere./Quod Eva tristis abstulit,/ tu reddis almo germine;/ intrent ut astra flebiles,/ Caeli fenestra facta es./ Tu regis alti ianua/ et porta lucis fulgida;/ vitam datam per Virginem,/ gentes redemptae, plaudite./ Patri sit Paraclito/ tuoque Nato gloria,/ qui veste te mirabili/circumdederunt gratiae. Amen.*"

165. Richard A. Norris, Jr., *The Song of Songs: Interpreted by Early Christian and Medieval Commentators* (London: Wm. B. Eerdmans Publishing Co., 2003); Ann W. Astell, *The Song of Songs in the Middle Ages* (Ithaca, NY: Cornell University Press, 1995); Saint Bernard of Clairvaux, *On the Song of Songs I* (Spencer, MA: Cistercians Publications, 2005); Origen, *The Song of Songs, Commentary and Homilies*, ed. R.P. Lawson (Mahwah, NJ: Paulist Press, 1957).

166. *The Catholic Encyclopedia*, "Liturgical Colors."

167. On the use of red for the Pentecost and the feasts of the Cross, see *The Catholic Encyclopedia*, "Liturgical Colors."

168. See Carolyn Valone, "The Pentecost: Image and Experience in Late Sixteenth-Century Rome," *Sixteenth Century Studies Journal* 24, no. 4 (Winter 1993), 801 ff.

169. See Roman Missal, "Corpus Christi," 256–59, for the place of *Corpus Christi* in the Roman calendar in relation to Pentecost.

170. *The Catholic Encyclopedia*, "Pentecost," describes the lighting of the Paschal candle lit on Holy Saturday during the celebration of Pentecost.

171. Roman Missal, "Pentecost," 249–52.

172. For red as the symbolic color of Charity, see Richard Stemp, *The Secret Language of the Renaissance: Decoding the Hidden Symbolism of Italian Art* (London: Duncan Barid, 2006), 44; and *The Catholic Encyclopedia*, "Faith, Hope and Charity," traditionally identified as Roman martyrs, who represent the three virtues of the Church. In this context, Charity is the spirit of good works, which are necessary for salvation. See *The Catholic Encyclopedia*, "Liturgical Colors," under "Symbolism": "...red is the language of fire and blood, which indicates burning charity and the martyr's generous sacrifice."

173. See Valone (1993) for illustrations of the Pentecost.

174. Roman Missal, 239–40: "Wisdom I: Spiritus domini replevit orbem terrarium alleluia. et hoc quo continent Omnia scientiam habet vocis. alleluia. alleluia. alleluia."

175. Acts 2:1–11 is read on "Pentecost," Roman Missal, 238.

176. On the Panciatichi's veneration for the Feast of the Assumption of the Virgin, see Aloia, *I Panciatichi degli Uffizi*, 38–39.

177. On Eleonora's Hours, see Watson, "Book of Hours," 2:851–57; and idem, "Manual of Dynastic History or Devotional Aid?" 179–95.

178. The signature is on the flyleaf of the Hours of Eleonora de Toledo and on the Prayer Book in Spanish, where the dates are also found for each manuscript, both dated to 1541 (1540, Florentine style).

179. The Hours of Alessandro de Medici and Margaret of Austira are in Rome, in the collection of the Biblioteca Corsiniana, MS Cod. 55.K.16. A limited number facsimile edition of the "Hours of Alessandro de' Medici and Margaret of Austria" was published by the Treccani Institute, in 2012, limited to 750 copies.

180. Myra Orth, *French Renaissance Manuscripts: The Sixteenth Century* (Turnhout: Brepols, 2013); eadem, "A French Illuminated Treaty of 1527," *The Burlington Magazine* 122, no. 923 (Feb. 1980), 125–26, 129; eadem, "Marguerite de Navarre's Illuminated Protestant Catechism and Confession," *The Sixteenth Century Journal* 24, no. 2 (Summer 1993), 383–427; and eadem, "Francis Du Moulin and the Journal of Louise of Savoy," *The Sixteenth Century Journal* 13, no. 1 (Spring 1982), 55–66.

181. On Tory, see Bernard Auguste, *Geoffroy Tory, Peintre et Graveur* (Premier Imprimeur Royal) (Paris: Nabu Press, 2010).

182. Leatrice Mendelsoh, in Falciani and Natali, *Bronzino*, 172 and 300.

183. Firpo, 91–99; Falciani, 153–65, and Elizabeth Pilliod, 248–51, all in Falciani and Natali, *Bronzino*.

184. Graham Smith, "Bronzino's Holy Family in Vienna: A Note on the Identity of Its Patron," *Source: Notes in the History of Art* 2, no. 1 (1982), 21–25.

185. Bart Eherman and Zlatko Plese, *The Apocryphal Gospels: Texts and Translations* (Oxford: University Press, 2011); and *The Catholic Encyclopedia*, "Apocrypha."

186. Roman Missal, 341–43.

187. Roman Missal, 342.

188. Roman Missal, 343: "Tua domine muneribus altaria cumulamus: illius nativitatem honore debito celebrantes. qui salvatorem mundi et cecinit affuturum. et adesse monstravit dominum nostrum iesum christum filium tuum. Qui tecum."

189. Roman Missal, 343: "Sumat ecclesia tua deus beati iohannis baptiste generatio letititam: per quem suae regenerationis cognovit auctorem dominum nostrum iesum christum filium tuum."

190. Cropper, in Falciani and Natali, *Bronzino*, 252.

191. Elena Aloia expressed this opinion during a conversation we had in Perugia on 11 June 2013.

192. Aloia, *I Panciatichi degli Uffizi*, 21–25.

193. Aloia, *I Panciatichi degli Uffizi*, 92–93, identified the buildings in the Uffizi *Holy Family* as Volterra and the ones in the Vienna *Holy Family* as the Villa Corsini in Mezzomonte.

194. On Luther's dogma on transubstantiation, see Jari Jolkkonen, "Eucharist," in Vainio, *Engaging Luther*, 108–37, who explains how William Dilthey, Friedrich Schliermacher, and Adolf von Harnack propagated the concept that Luther did not retain transubstantiation. For Luther's position, see Robert C. Croken, S.J., *Luther's First Front: The Eucharist as Sacrifice* (Ottawa: University of Ottawa Press, 1990); M. Brecht, *Martin Luther: Shaping and Defining the Reformation 1521–1532*, trans. J.L. Schaaf (Minneapolis, MN: Fortress Press, 1990), 293–334; Dennis Ngien, *The Suffering of God According to Martin Luher's "Theologia Crucis"* (Berne: Lang, 1995); and idem, "Chalcedonian Christology and Beyond: Luther's Understanding of the Communicatio Idomatum," *Heythrop Journal* 45 (2004), 54–68: "Luther retained the traditional interpretation, that the properties of Christ's two natures are communicated to the concretum of his person. But he went beyond it, affirming a real communication between the two natures. The logic of his usage of this doctrine enabled Luther to move beyond the Chalcedonian understanding of Christology and also set him apart from the Reformed tradition." See G. Macy, *The Theologies of the Eucharist in the Early Scholastic Period* (Oxford: Clarendon Press, 1984), 27–31.

195. Anne D'Evroye-Stiltz (2011), 14.

196. Jolkkonen, "Eucharist," 108–37, 109.

197. Jolkkonen, "Eucharist," 109.

198. Jolkkonen, "Eucharist," 109.

199. Jolkkonen, "Eucharist," 108. Luther was definite in his belief and in his difference with the Church, as he stated in the Sixth Proposition (Seventh in the 1551 version of The Large Catechism) that Christ was indeed present in the host at the moment of reception, but not before or after.

200. On the Council of Trent's ruling on the Eucharist and Transubstantiation, see David Pietrusza, ed., *Sursum Corda: Documents and Readings on the Traditional Latin Mass From the Council of Trent to Benedict XVI's Motu Proprio* (Seattle, WA: Createspace, 2008), 5–59, and especially 39–44 for the teaching on Transubstantiation.

201. For information on the various positions that Protestants had on the Virgin, the saints, and relics, see Carol Piper Heming, *Protestants and the Cult of the Saints in German Speaking Europe, 1517–1531* (Kirksville, MO: Truman State University Press, 2003).

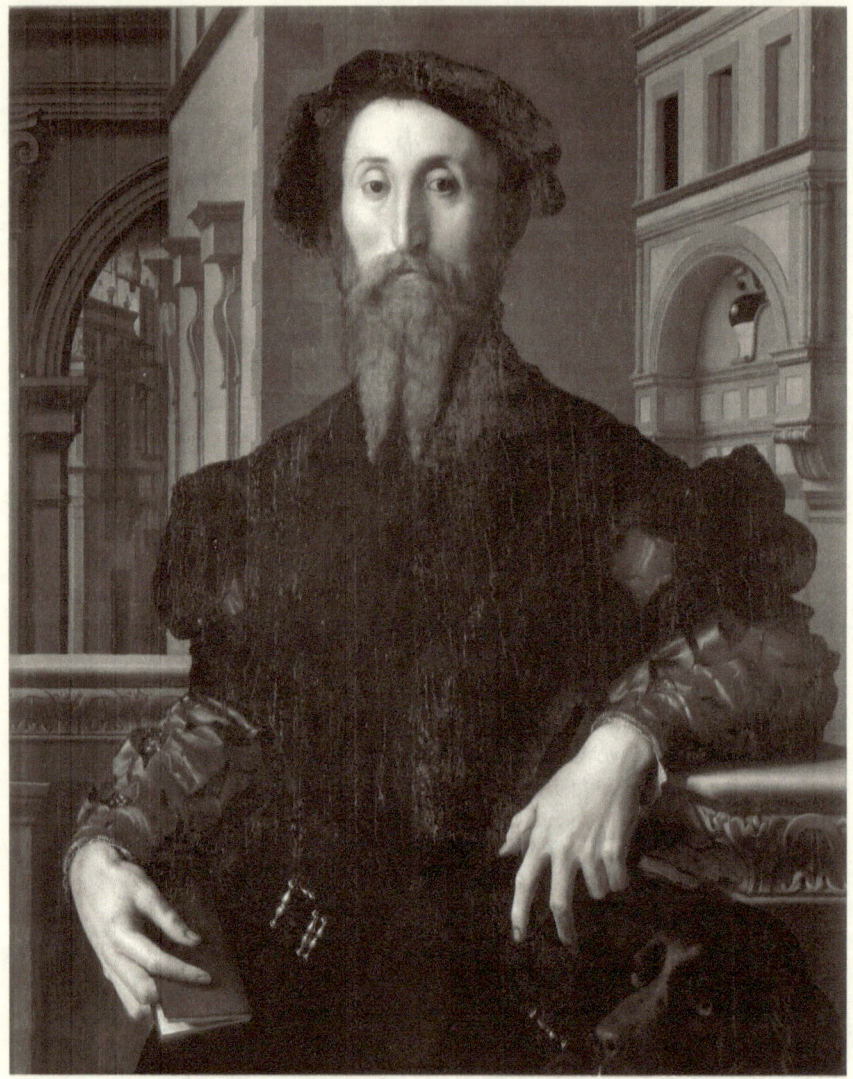

Fig. 1. Agnolo Bronzino, *Portrait of Bartolomeo Panciatichi*, 1540–42. Galleria degli Uffizi, Florence. Photo credit: Scala/Art Resource, NY.

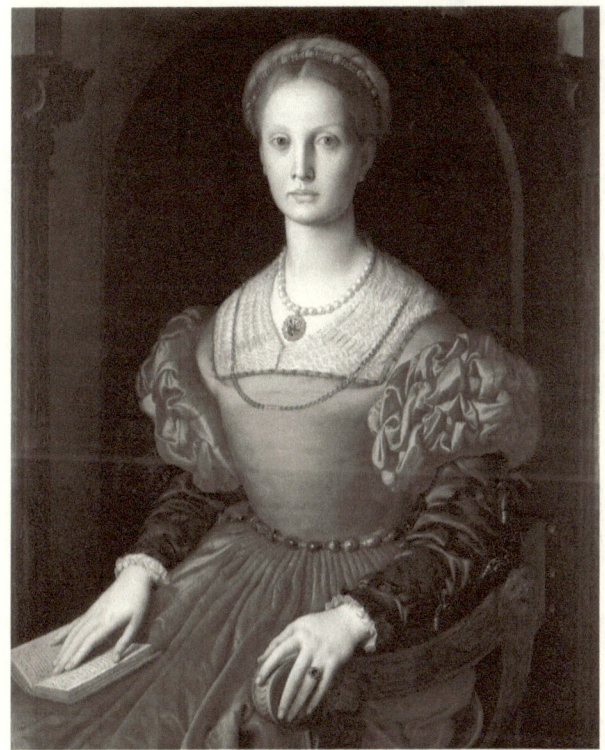

Fig. 2. Agnolo Bronzino, *Portrait of Lucrezia Panciatichi*, 1540–42. Galleria degli Uffizi, Florence. Photo credit: Scala/Ministero per i Beni e le Attività culturali/Art Resource, NY.

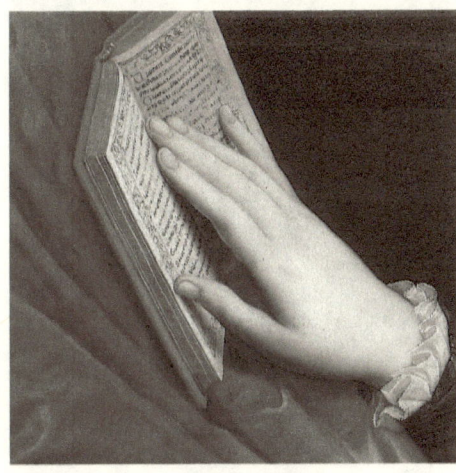

Fig. 3. Agnolo Bronzino, *Portrait of Lucrezia Panciatichi* (det.), 1540–42. Galleria degli Uffizi, Florence. Photo credit: Scala/Ministero per i Beni e le Attività culturali/Art Resource, NY.

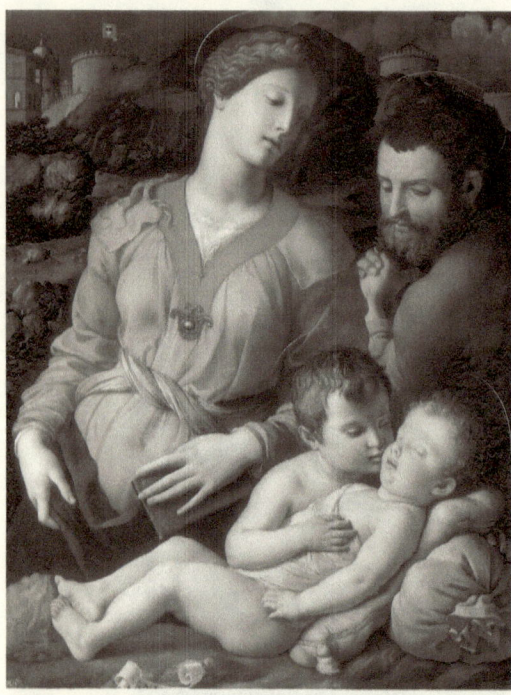

Fig. 4. Agnolo Bronzino, *Panciatichi Holy Family*, 1540. Galleria degli Uffizi, Florence, Italy. Photo credit: Alinari/Art Resource, NY.

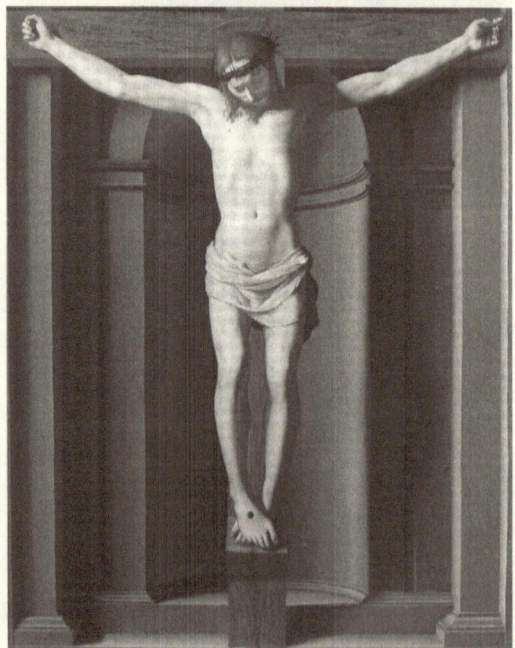

Fig. 5. Agnolo Bronzino, *Crucified Christ*, 1538–40. Musée des Beaux-Arts, Nice, France. Photo credit: Musée des Beaux-Arts, Nice, France.

Fig. 6. Agnolo
Bronzino, *The Madonna
and Child with Saint John
the Baptist and Elizabeth*
(or *Saint Anne*) (*Madonna
Hertford*), 1540–50.
National Gallery,
London, Great Britain.
Photo credit: National
Gallery London/Art
Resource, NY.

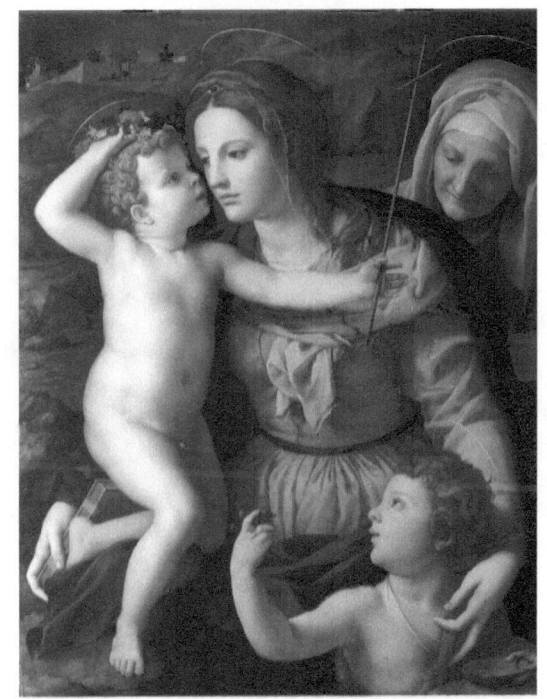

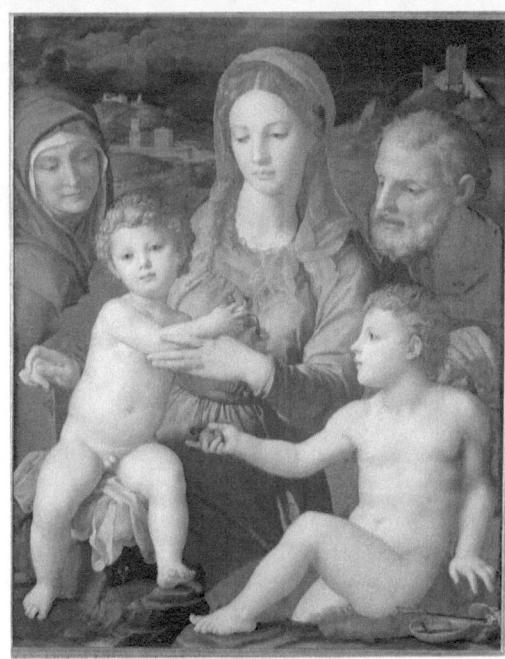

Fig. 7. Agnolo Bronzino,
*Holy Family with Saint Anne
and Young John the Baptist*,
1550s. Kunsthistorisches
Museum, Vienna, Austria.
Photo credit: Erich Less-
ing/Art Resource, NY.

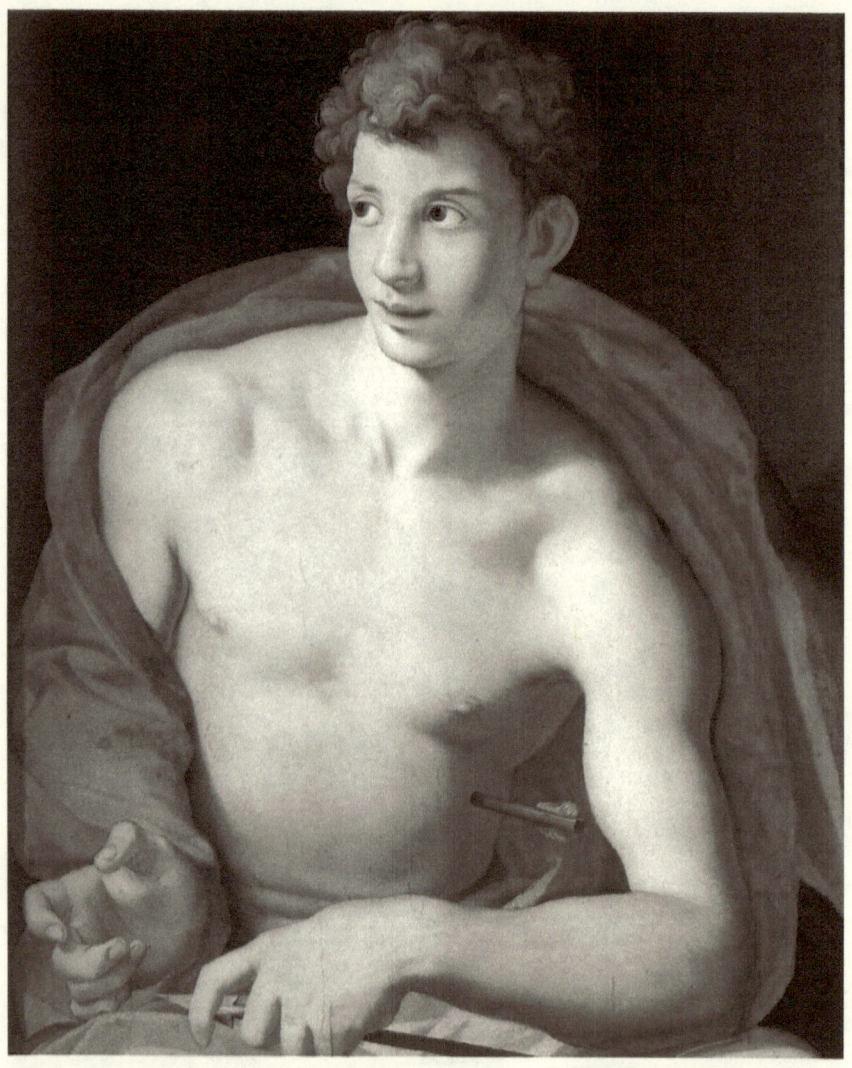

Fig. 8. Agnolo Bronzino, *Saint Sebastian*, c. 1533. Museo Thyssen Bornemisza, Madrid, Inv. 64 (1985.2). Photo credit: Museo Thyssen Bornemisza, Madrid, Scala/Art Resource, NY.

Culture, Faith, and Love:
Bartolomeo Panciatichi

Elena Aloia

For Bartolomeo Panciatichi, Bronzino painted two large pictures of Our Lady with other figures, wonderfully beautiful, and carried out with infinite care, and, besides these, portraits of him and his wife, so natural that they really seem to live, lacking nothing but breath. For the same man he painted a picture of Christ Crucified, which is executed with so much study and pains that it is clearly evident that he copied it from a real dead body fixed on a cross, such is the supreme excellence and perfection of every part.[1]

Giorgio Vasari devotes only one paragraph of the *Vita* to the memory of the intense relationship that united the painter to Bartolomeo Panciatichi, one of his most important private commissioners, a distinguished man of letters, and Florentine merchant of the first half of the sixteenth century. Bronzino completed five paintings for Panciatichi, three of which are now displayed in the Uffizi: Bartolomeo's and Lucrezia's portraits, and a *Holy Family* (Figs. 1–3).

The solemn composure and elegance of the portraits reveal the image of a strong man, confident of the trust that the Medici family had placed in him, and experienced from his life outside of Italy. Beside his portrait hangs the representation of a virtuous lady, Lucrezia Pucci, intelligently involved in daily offices and proudly aware of her role as wife.

Bartolomeo Panciatichi was born on 21 June 1507 in Lyons from an adulterous[2] relationship. Luigi Passerini, the main biographer of his family, states that he was legitimated on 29 March 1531[3] by Alessandro Campeggi Count Palatine. When he was baptized, he was named Giovanni, but his parents preferred the paternal name of Bartolomeo. His birth in France was due to his father's owner-ship of a large trading company: his father, Bartolomeo of Fran-cesco of Piero Panciatichi, had been born on 1 February 1468 in the San Giovanni[4] district but directed a commercial business[5] in Lyons that made him a very rich merchant. As his biographer acknowl-edges, however, he remained very active in Florence and became prior of the city in 1515, the same year the Medicean Pope Leone X made his entry.

Leo X granted Panciatichi the Elder the honor of being Count Palatine, "with the privilege of adding one of the Medicean balls between the two letters L.X. to the coat of arms of his house."[6] Louis XII, King of France, gave him some lands to rule in Lombardy, per-haps to reward him for a loan of money (this might confirm the prosperity of the family business in France) and also took Bartolo-meo the Younger to court as page[7]—an experience that significantly impacted his future role as ambassador.

Vasari tells that Bartolomeo Panciatichi the Elder had the paint-er Andrea Feltrini[8] decorate the facade of the family palace in the Agli Square in Florence. When Vasari wrote Bronzino's *vita*, this property had already passed to Ruberto de' Ricci. As a matter of fact, the catalog concerning the Panciatichi[9] in the *Gargano Index* confirms that Bartolomeo's house in the Agli Square was sold by the Officials and Deputies of the Supreme Magistrate to Federigo di Roberto Ricci in 1557. Luigi Passerini, the historian of the Pan-ciatichi family, reports that the painter of the external decorations of the house in the Agli Square was Morto da Feltre,[10] but a second reading of the life of the artist reveals that the actual painter was Andrea Feltrini. Their biographies appear in the same chapter, with Feltrini's immediately following the life story of the master from Feltre, whence I presume the mistake of Passerini is derived.

The palace in the Agli Square was probably part of the works of restoration carried out between 1885 and 1895, when Florence was the capital of Italy. Many old buildings were demolished to give space to new edifices and better respond to the prestige that the city had acquired, its changing social conditions, and above all its new economic demands. The layout of the streets around the Church of Santa Maria Maggiore was partly twisted, and the house of the Panciatichi is no longer identifiable today. Fortunately, carto-graphic documents reveal the old road network layout of the area and the location of the buildings and prove the truthfulness of the sources that disclose the information. In the map *Il centro di Firenze (Mercato Vecchio) nel 1427 Studio di Guido Carocci R° Ispettore degli scavi e dei monumenti*, visible in the room of the inventories of the Archivio di Stato of Florence, the streets and the buildings are de-tailed with the names of the corresponding owners. It is possible to notice the house of the Panciatichi on the corner between the Agli Square and the *Chiasso dei Buoi* and opposite the Palace of Gabriello and Giovanni of Master Bartolomeo Panciatichi.

To conclude his biography, Bartolomeo the Elder, father of the Bartolomeo portrayed by Bronzino, died in Lyons in 1533, and his son had to succeed him in the economic interests of the family's company. Bartolomeo the Younger completed his studies both at Padova University, between 1528 and 1531, and in Lyons, where he developed an interest in the ideas of renewal of the Church coming from Germany and Switzerland. He also had a direct knowledge of Jaques Le Fevre d' Etaples' and Guillaume Briconnet's movement for spiritual renewal.

In France, Bartolomeo devoted himself to his studies and took little interest in running the family business, which he delegated to some relatives. He translated the religious works by Pietro Are-tino, *L'umanità di Cristo* (*Christ's Humanity*) and *La Passione di Cristo* (*Christ's Passion*) into English. In 1528[11] or 1531,[12] he married Lucre-zia of Gismondo Pucci. The couple lived beyond the Alps, possibly until about 1538, and then went back to Florence.

Bartolomeo was a merchant but favored literary studies; in particular, he applied himself to Latin poetry, and on 20 January 1541, he was received by the *Accademia degli Umidi*, which soon was renamed the *Accademia Fiorentina*. In 1542, Bartolomeo appears as member of the renewed institution. In this milieu, he became ac-quainted with Bronzino, who joined the *Accademia* on 25 March 1541, but the two had already met at Cosimo's Court, perhaps at the time of the duke's wedding with Eleonora of Toledo[13] that was celebrated in 1539, a year after Bartolomeo presumably returned to Italy.

In 1545, Bartolomeo succeeded Benedetto Varchi as a Consul in the *Accademia*. His consulate was memorable both for the reforms to the statutes and for "the importance of the academic lectures."[14] Bartolomeo received important political tasks from Cosimo I, who invited him to France in 1547[15] or in 1549[16] and appointed him his Ambassador at the French Court. Cosimo had confidence in Bartolomeo's knowledge of the language and the nation, and he appointed him in order to re-establish the diplomatic relationships between Florence and France which had deteriorated because of an offense against Giovanni Battista Ricasoli, the duke's ambassador.

In his *vita* of Bronzino, Vasari writes about a painting sent to the King of France, Francis I, "in which there was a naked Venus with Cupid." In that gift, critics recognize the work known as *Allegory of Love*, now in the London National Gallery and dated to the first half of the fifth decade of the Cinquecento. Alessandro Cecchi[17] suggests that the painting was commissioned by Bartolomeo Panciatichi rather than the duke and believes it is the result of a "scholarly invention" of the same man of letters. Antonio Paolucci[18] reiterates the same assumption. Presumably, however, the painting was taken to the king directly by Bartolomeo in his capacity of ambassador at the French Court, probably by 31 March 1547, the day on which the sovereign died at Rambouillett. It might be argued, then, that Bartolomeo's diplomatic journey took place in the first months of 1547, or that he frequently traveled beyond the Alps to take care of Cosimo I's and his own business.

His frequent visits to France allowed Bartolomeo to keep abreast of the novelties of Church Reform, and take possession of Reformist books, including Calvin's text. As a man of letters and a scholar, he deepened his knowledge of such theories and brought them over to Florence by disseminating them among the cultural elite of the city. Thus, he ran up against the Inquisition, was taken to trial, and condemned along with his wife Lucrezia. Afterward, he no longer dealt with religious matters and actively devoted himself to his literary studies. The incident of the Inquisition, however, did not deprive Bartolomeo of the favor of Cosimo I, who nominated him Senator in 1567 and later sent him to Pisa in 1568 and to Pistoia in 1578 as an official Commissioner. According to Massimo Firpo, he died in Pistoia[19] on 23 October 1582.[20]

Passerini's family tree shows that Bartolomeo had four children with Lucrezia. Carlo, the most long-lived, was born on 17 August 1545 and died on 29 February 1620. He had a descendant born on 12 July 1577 whom he called Bartolomeo and who died before 1651. In Carlo's house, Raffaello Borghini had the opportunity to see the portraits of his parents, Bartolomeo and Lucrezia, painted by Bronzino.[21]

On 1 November 1540, to follow the example but also contrast the *Accademia degli Infiammati* of Padova, the *Accademia degli Umidi* was founded in Florence; it gathered in Giacomo Mazzuoli's house thanks to the initiative of Anton Francesco Grazzini called "il Lasca." The institution consisted of artisans and petit bourgeois, but mostly merchants who wanted to cultivate and promote the Tuscan language, read and talk about Dante and Petrarca, and devote themselves to the composition of sonnets.

On 25 March 1541, the *Accademia* became public in accordance with the wishes of Cosimo I and changed its name to *Accademia Fiorentina*. The objects of this change were many and not purely cultural: gathering together the men of culture who were at the duke's service; strengthening the Tuscan identity through language and literature; and consolidating the "culture" of the Medici and creating the myth of Duke Cosimo. Eventually, the *Accademia Fiorentina* became the center of the official literary production, approved and promoted by the dukedom. Cosimo accepted the request of support made by the *Umidi* but failed to keep the spontaneity of the original literary coterie by turning it into an organ of the absolute regime he was creating, for which he needed good bureaucrats and learned men faithful to him. The entrance into the Accademia of Cosimo Bartoli and Pierfrancesco Giambullari, intellectuals who were close to the duke and also welcome to the *Umidi*, facilitated the change by modifying rapidly as well as drastically the cooperation, as wished by Cosimo I.

A strategic consequence of the renewal of the *Accademia* was the entrance of many men close to the government—such as Bartolomeo Panciatichi, who had already become a member on 20 January 1541 prompted by personal interests. Panciatichi immediately worked on the new statutes, which were approved on the following 11 February and which, among other things, established that some public lectures were to be taken in Santa Maria Novella. Within the *Accademia*, Panciatichi held important offices and was Consul on 23 August 1545. According to the Decree of 23 February 1542 by Cosimo I, this role entitled him of the office of Rector of the Studies, which was considered equivalent to the office of a public magistrate and allowed him to supervise the literary diffusion. The importance of the offices held by Bartolomeo in the *Accademia Fiorentina* symbolizes the reliance the duke placed on him and confirms once again that he was an important instrument of Cosimo's policy. Later on, in the first semester of 1547, he became Counselor of the Accademia together with Cristofano Rinieri.

Soon after entering the *Accademia Fiorentina*, on 27 August 1541, Bartolomeo held a lesson on the three songs by Bembo and on the second canto of Dante's *Paradise*, and in the following month, again on Dante and the phases of the moon. The choice and the quality of these lectures probably contributed to the great success that Bartolomeo Panciatichi had in his function as Consul.[22]

Bronzino entered the *Accademia* on 11 February 1541; he was one of the forty-two new members added that year, the largest adhesion ever in the history of the institution. Bronzino was a member for six years; during this time he was particularly inspired and had a prolific pictorial production.[23] In particular, he painted the portraits of some members of the *Accademia*, such as those of Luca Martini, Ugolino Martelli, and Bartolomeo Panciatichi with his wife Lucrezia Pucci. The meeting between Bartolomeo Panciatichi and Bronzino was probably facilitated by their common friend Benedetto Varchi, a great admirer of the painter whose letter on the primacy of painting is preserved. The meeting between Bronzino and Bartolomeo Panciatichi also led Bronzino to negotiate on behalf of Panciatichi for the acquisition of a *Madonna* by Pontormo, sold by a dealer, as Vasari narrates in the *vita* of Pontormo.[24]

In 1549, with the death of Paul III, the danger that Florence would experience the influence of the Farnese faded away as Julius III Del Monte, the new pope, was supported by the Medici family. As a result, Cosimo had to change his attitude towards those who were anticlerical or had approached Protestantism. In the times of hostility with the Farneses, Protestants were not a cause of trouble, but the new need for the dukedom to get near the pontificate again made it necessary to guide all those who had supported the heresy towards the most rigorous Catholicism. In this action, however, Cosimo I was careful to protect his favorites, whose guilt would have damaged the dukedom of Tuscany.

In 1550, after Lorenzo Davidico made known his name to the Roman Inquisition, Bartolomeo was called to face the tribunal. Cosimo I wrote to his Ambassador in Rome in his defense and ensured the pope of the Catholic faith of all the Florentines.[25] On 17 October 1551, the religious Pietro Manelfi, who was a Catholic but later became Lutheran and eventually Anabaptist, went to Bologna and then to Rome in front of the Inquisition. In his abjuration to the reformist doctrines, he denounced all the other Protestants he had known directly or indirectly: Bartolomeo Panciatichi was among them. Indeed, the *Accademia Fiorentina* itself, which considered him a distinguished member, was the close and culturally active milieu in which the Protestant novelties proliferated. After that accusation, the Florentine Inquisition imprisoned him, his wife Lucrezia, and other thirty-four other citizens. Trial, tortures, and convictions followed. Cosimo I, however, intervened in favor of Bartolomeo and was able to mitigate the punishment at the price of public abjuration: Bartolomeo "was condemned to go in procession through the city, accompanied by the satellite of the Holy Office, dressed in black with a yellow gag and holding a torch; he also had to make solemn abjuration in the Cathedral of the heterodox doctrines and burn the books considered suspected; and after that, he had to absolve himself from the censures with the usual rites."[26] The rite ended in the Florentine Cathedral on 4 February 1552. Another source,[27] however, tells that the rite of public abjuration and the burning of the Lutheran books that took place soon after the procession occurred on 6 February 1552.

Not all agree in saying that Bartolomeo really participated in this expiatory rite. As a matter of fact, Cosimo I presumably relieved the nobles of his circle[28] of the shameful procession and protected them. Also, those who possessed a high status partially satisfied the Inquisition by sending the people of lower rank to the procession. Moreover, the same source[29] informs that on 6 February 1552, the process against Bartolomeo Panciatichi had not yet finished.

Since 1552, Cosimo urged the court of the Florentine Inquisi-

tion to determine guilt or innocence in order to avoid any preju-
dicial repercussion on the ducal affairs in France. Without other
real proofs, he also hoped the proceeding would come to an end.
The duke reasserted his determination to free Bartolomeo from the
accusations with a letter addressed to the city Inquisition, dated 9
April 1552, in which he explained how the gentleman's good Christianity had in no way damaged the religious institutions. Had he
privately adhered to Lutheranism, he surely had never shown it
in public.[30] Bartolomeo Panciatichi served his sentence in prison,
but he was soon released thanks to the payment of a considerable
sum. The anonymous Jesuit who wrote about the arrests in his diary notes that Bartolomeo Panciatichi was "rich in thirty thousand
scudos" and "paid twenty thousand scudos to get out of prison."[31]
The price of liberty was obviously very high.

Some letters of Bartolomeo Panciatichi sent from France contrast
with the chronicles that reveal the pretense of his arrest, process,
and penitential procession. A letter of 13 December 1551, written
by Pierfrancesco Riccio to the duke, contained a bundle from Bartolomeo; a letter from Bartolomeo to the duke dated 24 December
1551;[32] and letters dated 5 and 18 February 1552 sent to Cosimo in
Pisa.[33] Considering the dates the letters were written, it is possible
to presume that Bartolomeo was arrested and tried in the month
of January 1552 and quickly returned beyond the Alps, or that he
resided in France between December 1551 and February 1552. As a
matter of fact, as Luigi Passerini reports,[34] it seems difficult to believe that Panciatichi took part in the penitential rites, which ended
on 4 February 1552, and was back in France the following day, as
the letters sent to the duke testify.

If we exclude the pecuniary penalty, we can say that Bartolomeo Panciatichi remained almost unspoiled. In fact, on 24 February 1552, twenty days before the penitential procession that supposedly involved him and about four months after the accusation
made by Pietro Manelfi, he became Counselor of the *Accademia*. In a
letter dated 5 April, he complained to the duke about some troubles
with the Inquisition and asked for his protection. Meanwhile, Bartolomeo agreed to lend Cosimo 4000 scudos and remained a good
servant of the duke.[35] Criticized by some of his Florentine subjects,
Cosimo I did his best to save the inquired people that were close to

him, Panciatichi included, in order to close a trial that could have had even more scandalous and detrimental implications for the dukedom as soon as possible.

To reconstruct the figure of Bartolomeo Panciatichi, it was useful to search in the heraldic and genealogical records of the Archivio di Stato of Florence, in particular in the Ceramelli Papiani,[36] a source of about 8000 files concerning the ancient Tuscan families compiled by Enrico Ceramelli Papiani (1896–1976). My work is also based on additional documents kept in the same Archivio di Stato of Florence and in other Florentine archives and libraries. Additional support came from the Raccolta Sebregondi.

The name Panciatichi might have an ancestor from the Patrician Gente Pansia, but the ethnic origin of the family (Latin, Longobard, or Frank) remains unknown. A possible origin of the last name might be related to Pancio di Bellino from Vignole who appeared in 1067; by the beginning of the twelfth century, however, the last name had the form we know. The first document that shows the last name of Panciatichi is a parchment dated 10 April 1208 from the Community of Pistoia,[37] kept in the Archivio di Stato of Florence. Nonetheless, the powerful family asserted itself in Pistoia and its surrounding areas since the second half of the eleventh century. It was one of the "primarie Prosopie" and later became worthy of the title of *Knights of the Golden Spur*;[38] among its members were captains and generals,[39] lords of manors in Tuscany and Lombardy;[40] and the family possessed palaces in Pistoia and Florence and their countryside. In 1352,[41] some members of the family moved to Florence. The branch of Bartolomeo the Elder originated from this branch and was later bestowed the priorate. The documents[42] also report that a Master Bartolomeo "established a branch of his house in Florence" in 1375, obtained his citizenship in 1376, and bought a house in Via Boni in compliance with all the regulations.

The ancient progenitor of the Panciatichi was Pollo, lord of Licciano, from whom descended Infrangilasta, who generated Lanfranco. He differentiated the branch of our interest, which dies in the seventeenth century. It is also reported[43] that the family lived "in a part of an edifice" in the Agli Square, among the people of Santa Maria Maggiore, where it is possible to see their coat of arms.

The documents I examined present a variety of drawings of

the heraldic coat of arms that consists of a blazon cut off into two halves: the upper part is black colored with a red crossed ball, and the lower one is silver. There are, however, some variants. The records contain a list of the places and monuments that represent the coat of arms. It was placed on the family tomb that presented the following inscription: "Filiorum et descendentium Egregii Militis D. Bartolomei de Panciatichi 1430. S. Magistri et Egregii Militis D. Bartolomei Bandini de Panciatichis, conditoris et dotatoris huius capituli 1401." The people buried in the tomb were Giuliano of Piero of Gabriello Panciatichi, Prior in 1483; Pietro of Francesco of Pietro Panciatichi, Prior in 1494 and in 1500; Bartolomeo of Francesco of Piero Panciatichi, and Prior in 1515, belonging to the people of San Giovanni (father of the Bartolomeo portrayed by Bronzino). Unfortunately, it was not possible for me to identify this tomb and the gravestone mentioned by the sources of the Archivio. In addition to looking in the church of Santa Maria Novella, I looked in the *Chiostro Verde* (Green Cloister) and in the *Chiostro dei Morti* (Cloister of the Dead), both of which hold numerous graves, mainly from the nineteenth century. There are a few gravestones from the previous period, some of them next to the entrance of the *Cappellone degli Spagnoli*, others visible in the first cloister but dedicated to single people and not to families. The passage that leads to the *Chiostro dei Morti* has numerous stony coats of arms, many of which are unrecognizable or in very bad condition. Other gravestones are now kept in storage at the museum which comprises the cloisters, but it is impossible to inspect them, since they are piled up and have not been catalogued. Should they be rearranged, it would be worth continuing the research. It cannot be excluded that the gravestone of the Panciatichi family in Santa Maria Novella was destroyed. Since almost all of the gravestones in the cloisters date back to the nineteenth century, it is possible to presume that the oldest graves were demolished to create space for new ones and that the remains were moved to the ossuary under the *Cappellone degli Spagnoli*. Luigi Passerini's words support the assumption of the loss of the gravestone. According to him, in fact, the marble of the tombstone of Giovanni Panciatichi, in the cloister of the same church with the title of "regalis eques," had been "destroyed many centuries before" (Fig. 4).[44] Moreover, one of the manuscripts[45] of the Repertorio Gargani under the name of Panciatichi notes that "the Arch of the Panciatichi in the internal cemetery" (perhaps the *Chiostro dei Morti*) is listed among "the lost tombs of the cemeteries of the church of Santa Maria Novella." Passerini probably drew on this source in his book published in 1858; if that is the case, though, he omitted the detail of the sepulchral Arch. It is a significant element which suggests the family had a tomb of undeniable value, and it would be important to discover its craftsman.

The coat of arms also appears in the church of Santa Maria Maggiore, where the family lived.[46] I was able to verify that the coat of arms is still noticeable on the unfinished facade of the church (Fig. 5), and the chapel of the family is the first on the right aisle. The coat of arms of the gravestone is reproduced on the two sides of the altar and on the high top of the pointed arch toward the nave; this arch was made of serena stone or sandstone and appears damaged. In front of the chapel is the gravestone with the coat of arms of the Panciatichi set in the center and surrounded by elegant vegetable patterns in black. Along the perimeter of the stone a Gothic inscription appears; it is particularly damaged on the side toward the high altar, but I decoded the following words: "S' Filio e desciendenzium Egregii Militis Dm Bartolomei de Panciatichis q anc capellam fecit fieri e dotavit e Giovanes eius filius fecit och sepulcrum ano dom M CCCC XXX[47] anime reqescant i pace." Thanks to the precious text by Luigi Passerini,[48] I identified "Giovanes" with Giovanni Panciatichi, who lived in Buda as treasurer of the king. In the Hungarian city he had a business house described as the richest in Buda and among the most respected in Europe. He went back to Florence in old age and in 1430 prepared a tomb in Santa Maria Maggiore for himself and his descendants, where he was buried on 7 October 1442.

This man was the great-great-grandfather of Bartolomeo and lived from 1355 to 1442. Giovanni was the son of Bartolomeo,[49] man at arms at the service of Florence and usurer, who died in 1402 and was buried in the above mentioned church at the foot of the altar that he himself had ordered be erected and where, according to Passerini, 28 years after the father's death, the son prepared the family tomb. The altar was dedicated to Saint Mary Magdalene. Giovanni begot Piero, who later fathered Francesco, our Bartolomeo's grandfather. Undoubtedly, then, the tomb built in this church belongs to the branch of the family from which Bartolomeo descended. By comparing the inscription in Santa Maria Maggiore with the one reported in the Ceramelli Papiani archive about an unidentified tomb in Santa Maria Novella, it is possible to notice an important detail: the first part of the two texts coincides, both giving the date 1430. But it is strange to believe that the same person, Giovanni, prepared two tombs in two different churches; I wonder if the archival source merged the details of two different Panciatichi tombs together. While the circumstances in Santa Maria Maggiore are certain and easily provable, it is not simple to unfold the details of the tomb in Santa Maria Novella.

The coat of arms of the Panciatichi was put in different Tuscan towns such as Volterra, Barberino del Mugello, Scarperia, and others where members of the family held public offices of podesta or captain. The stony inscription on the main facade of the Palace of Justice of Pistoia is worthy of note. It states: "Bartolomeus Panciatichi, patricius et senator Flor.nus, commissarius generali an 1578"; and it confirms the office held by the Bartolomeo portrayed by Bronzino four years before he died.

The Ceramelli Papiani documents report the genealogy of the Panciatichi family on the male line and prove that "Bartholomeo" Panciatichi was born on 21 June 1507, was son of Bartolomeo of Francesco, of the people of San Giovanni (Fig. 6). He was prior of the dominion of Florence in 1515. The same source shows Carlo Panciatichi as the son of Bartolomeo of Bartolomeo, born on 17 August 1545.

Carlo of Bartolomeo was sentenced to death in absentia in 1556 for killing one of his servants, but Cosimo I granted him a pardon in 1567 when Carlo agreed to marry Eleonora degli Albizzi, Cosimo I's lover, who was later taken by an incestuous passion for her son Don Giovanni dei Medici. Carlo had his wife locked in the Monastery of Saint Onofrio in Foligno.[50]

It is also reported that Carlo had two male children, Bartolomeo (of Carlo of Bartolomeo), born on 12 July 1577 (the document is mistaken: the date reported is 1477, while the chronological sequence goes from 1545 to 1647), and Cosimo (of Carlo of Bartolomeo), whose day of birth is missing.

Two Florentine Senators belonged to the Panciatichi family (from 1567 to 1680). The first was Bartolomeo the Young. The family had Knights of Malta and Knights of Saint Stephen. The Repertorio Gargani in the Biblioteca Nazionale Centrale of Florence was also very useful to discover the past of the old Florentine families.

By consulting the cards of the volume relative to the Panciatichi family, I found information, with place and dates, about the burial of Bartolomeo and Lucrezia Panciatichi, one of their daughters, and a grandchild.[51] The original source is the Necrology of the Grascia, kept in the Archivio di Stato of Florence. The register is divided by first names, then by year and month. Each volume includes a defined period. Additionally, the date of the burial, not the date of death, is reported. It inform us that on January 1571: "mª Lucrezia donna di Bartolomeo Panciatichi sep in Sª mª mag. Re 26,"[52] so we know that the lady was buried in the tomb prepared by Giovanni Panciatichi in the fifteenth century on the day that followed her death on 25 January, according to what Passerini[53] affirms.

As for the husband, he is registered on the month of October 1582 as follows: "m. Bart.º di bart.º Panciatichi sep.º in sª mra magg. 23";[54] the date of 23 October coincides with the one reported by Passerini,[55] so Bartolomeo was almost certainly buried on the same day of his death, in contrast to what Firpo asserts.[56] On 28 March 1572, Bartolomeo of Carlo Panciatichi, the grandchild of Bartolomeo and Lucrezia, died at the age of one, and he, too, was buried in Santa Maria Maggiore. It is evident that the familiar branch of Bartolomeo Panciatichi chose the tomb built in that church a century before, and it is also possible to suppose that they preserved the chapel of the same name. As a matter of fact, the home of Bartolomeo and Lucrezia was only a few meters from the Christian church, so they certainly attended to it. The Repertorio Gargani also reports the burial of a "fratella" of Carlo Panciatichi in Santa Maria Maggiore[57] on 8 April 1590, but it was not possible to find it in the Necrology of the Grascia, as the first name is not known. In any event, it should be one of Bartolomeo and Lucrezia's daughters, probably Maria, given the fact that Passerini reports neither the date of birth nor that of death but writes that Margherita died in October 1599.[58]

In 1584, Raffaello Borghini synthetically resumed Vasari's words in the dialogue entitled *Il Riposo* by adding that the two *Our*

Lady and two spouses portraits were located in the home of their son Carlo.[59]

In the portrait, Bartolomeo is half-length, standing and facing front; his horsy face[60] with its fine nose is thin, angular, and seems to be framed by the thick, long, and forked reddish beard and a moustache. The look is calm and steady. The painting is traditionally dated to 1540–41, when Bartolomeo was thirty-four, but he actually looks older. The work was probably performed during the peaceful period that preceded the trial of the married couple, that is to say between 1538, when they settled in Florence after their sojourn in France, and 1550, when Lorenzo Davidico informed the Inquisition about Bartolomeo. By hazarding a postponement that contrasts with the dates largely accepted by the critics, and by supposing that they were painted toward the end of the 1540s, we can better justify the age that Bartolomeo shows, especially if we consider that he was forty in 1547. Furthermore, we can read the two portraits as a manifesto or declaration of intents of Bartolomeo's fine intellect and can assume that the portrayal of his wife holding a Book of Hours and her concentration in prayer were made to confirm the couple's adherence to Catholicism, or better, to the Roman Church and dispel suspicions of Protestant leanings (which a few years later will bring them in front of the Inquisition), especially in consideration of the alarm raised by the decrees of January 1547 against the supremacy of the Holy Writ and the justification by faith issued at the end of the first phase of the Council of Trent.[61]

As for the older age that Bartolomeo shows in the portrait, if dated 1545 or later, Cropper[62] believes it is an imitation of Christ to match that of Lucrezia, which, according to the scholar, presents symbols of the reformed doctrines. Bartolomeo wears a black suit with red openwork sleeves and a soft black headdress. In his tapering and skinny hands he holds gloves on the left and a book on the right. As in other gentlemen's portraits, a black dog appears beside him. It has a nice, shiny, and well-kept coat that reflects the light and a sweet calm look turned to the observer.

The figure is placed in a rigorous and realistic architectural scene. It is propped against the balustrade of dressed stone, and in the background appears a palace that is a two-part structure: on the right side, under a big grey stone arch, the coat of arms of the Panciatichi depicted. A door or a sort of monumental arch and other buildings are discernible. Luisa Becherucci notices how the architectural background behind the figure "presents the crystalline precision of Giuliano da Sangallo."[63] Maurizia Tazartes observes the "strictly Florentine architectural setting" of the background.[64]

Brock[65] detects the manneristical form of the background and describes it as a sort of assembly penetrated with what he calls "une allure éminemment florentine,"[66] that is to say a manner, a flavor, or a look that is really Florentine. According to Brock, Bronzino borrows from the real and coeval architectures of Michelangelo. In the portrait of Bartolomeo, the French critic has recognized a resemblance between the foreshortened view of the windows of the facade to the left of the man and those inside the reading room of the Libreria Laurenziana; we can all agree with this suggestion.

I believe Bronzino worked very accurately and did not neglect any detail of his paintings, least of all the backgrounds. Unfortunately, I was unable to find the real sight or the architectural backgrounds that inspired the painter of Bartolomeo's portrait. The picture probably represents the Florentine home of the Panciatichi, but it is now impossible to verify such a conjecture, as Bartolomeo's home was probably destroyed, as previously stated,[67] and the area in which the family lived has changed drastically. It seems to me, however, that the blind arch on the right side of the picture speaks a bit of Quattrocento style. In fact, it seems to have similarities with certain architectural elements used by Filippo Brunelleschi and Leon Battista Alberti, but this might depend on the typical Florentine buildings of the background. I also partially agree with Brock, but I think it is reductive to think of Bronzino as an imitator of the manner of Michelangelo.

The biographical information about Lucrezia is very limited. We are unfamiliar with her date of birth, but we know that she married Bartolomeo Panciatichi in 1528 or, according to others, in 1534[68] and was younger than her husband. She lived in France with Bartolomeo, shared his interest for the Protestant doctrines, and brought some reformed books, such as the text by Calvin, *Christianae religionis institutiones*, to her homeland, which did not save her from the same destiny that awaited her husband. In 1551, she was imprisoned in the jail of Stinche and was tried by the Tribunal of the Inquisition. On 14 February 1552, she abjured in the church of San Simone. She died on 25 January 1572.

Lucrezia is portrayed full bust, in a three-quarter view, sitting on a Dante chair with her left arm posed on the armrest in "a composed, noble and harmonious posture appropriate to the serene eurhythmy and the balance of the volumes."[69] The wooden chair is decorated with two big carved masks that symbolize vices but help to give more prominence to Lucrezia's virtues. Maurice Brock[70] sees an animal in the monstrous face under Lucrezia's hand and a satyr in the other one. I personally find monstrous anthropomorphous figures in both of them. In the background, Lucrezia's figure is framed by a dark niche that clearly hints at the domestic realm,[71] where the woman was the "tutelary deity" and pursued the virtues of bride and mother.

With her right hand she keeps the Book of Hours of the Virgin open in her hand, and it is possible to read some excerpts. In order to read the words, however, it is necessary to get very near the painting and lower the head on the left. Her look seems melancholic, although it is not easy to understand the reason for her sadness. She wears a scarlet red satin gamurra vest with low and large gathered shoulder straps and wide violet sleeves decorated with horizontal ribbons ending in a bow; the rectangular neckline is covered with light pleated fabric embroidered in gold. Carlo Falciani[72] reads Lucrezia's dress in the light of Juan de Valdes' texts *Alfabeto Cristiano* and *Beneficio di Cristo*, which theorize how the dress of true Christians must reflect the likeness of the crucified Lord; thus the red color reproduces the blood of Christ. Lucrezia wears jewels proper to a woman of her rank. She shows a pearl necklace with a pendant medallion in gold and stones. According to Silvia Malaguzzi,[73] women of high birth wore pearls in the sixteenth century as symbol of nobility, whereas the diamonds of the pendant stand for strength, courage, and firmness. Finally, the central ruby symbolizes charity and generosity, all virtues that well suited a lady like Lucrezia.

On her long and outer gold necklace with bars, the French words "amour dure sans fin" are engraved. It was probably a gift given by her husband on their engagement or wedding day. The motto in the French language resembles Bartolomeo's connection with the land beyond the Alps. Silvia Malaguzzi points out the meaning of the necklace as a jewel: it signifies the sentimental bond between husband and wife but also shows the beauty and ornamental value of their union. Thus, it could be a marital gift. Elizabeth Cropper,[74] however, reads the chain worn by Lucrezia in the light of Lefevre d'Etaple's translation of the Bible into French: in their modern translation, the versets of the Psalms 136 (135) end with the sentence "car son amour n'a pas de fin" and refer to divine love. Cropper also clarifies how the eternal power of love, in the Christian sense, was at the center of the Florentine Evangelism.

Lucrezia's blond hair is gathered up into a crown and decorated with a garland in damascened gold. The dress is tightened at the waist by a belt of hard stones and gold. The annular finger of the left hand wears a gold ring with stone, symbol of their marriage. Again, Silvia Malaguzzi points out that Lucrezia's jewels should be valued as documents because they underline the rank and qualities of the lady and her husband. They are few and sober jewels but of great elegance and style, and they quite probably belonged to the noblewoman.[75] It would also seem unusual for an artist like Bronzino to leave the choice of such important details to his imagination.

The painter executes a very polished and patinated pictorial surface, with metal tinges that, particularly in the scarlet satin, reproduce the person of Lucrezia as formal, cold, beautiful, and chaste: the ideal gentlewoman of the Renaissance. Under Lucrezia's left cheek, in a section that should all have been in the shadow, Bronzino paints a thin blade of light whose origin might only be the reflection of the pearl necklace. The effect is the closing of the perfect oval of the face and the creation of a harmonious series of geometric references with the other curved lines painted between the head and the bust of the lady.[76]

Particularly interesting is the booklet of prayers that Lucrezia keeps on her lap. The pages are decorated with frames illuminated with monochromatic vegetable patterns. In the external high corners, we see two little female figures with long dresses and hoop headdresses; the one on the right is a bit wider. Since it is a religious book, we might think of two saints, but the characteristics that could identify them are missing.

The booklet is richly bound, and the thickness of the pages is golden. Some scholars[77] believe that it is a hymn to the Virgin, while others[78] notice the presence of a Psalm on the left side. By reading the words partially worn and unrecognizable, and partly covered by Lucrezia's hand, I initially discerned Psalm 150 on the left page, very short and therefore suitable for such little space, and also characterized by the imperative "Laudate" at the beginning of each paragraph, with the exception of the last one. The structure of the text is easily recognizable even without being able to read all the words. I will quote hereby the whole Psalm; the legible letters or words will be written in bold: "**Laudate Dominum in Sanctis** eius/ laudate eum in firmamento virtutis eius./**Laudate** eum in virtutibus eius/laudate eum secundum multitudinem magnitudinis eius/laudate eum in sono tubae./Laudate eum in psalterio et cithara./Laudate eum in tympano et choro./Laudate eum in chordis et organo/ Laudate eum in cymbalis benesonantibus,/Laudate eum in cymbalis iubilationis;/omnis spiritus laudet Dominum."

In the painting, the Psalm is transcribed in ten lines, whereas it consists of eleven lines in both Latin and Italian. Possibly, the last line, which only has four words in Latin, was written after the second to last line, or perhaps the painter omitted it for lack of space. The hypothesis that it is Psalm 148 cannot be completely excluded, as Caponetto writes. In fact, the content and the structure of this second Psalm also could be found in the words painted by Bronzino. In this case, though, only the first part of the Solomon prayer was transcribed. In my opinion, the decay of the pictorial film in that particular point does not allow us to give a definite answer about the source of the text. It must be noticed, however, that the meaning of both Psalms is the same. It is a praise to God.

The *Gloria* is readable after the Psalm. I will also quote this prayer by highlightening the parts that are visible: "Gloria Patri et Filio et Spiritui Sancto,/Sicut erat in principio,/et nunc et semper/ et in secula seculorum." Underneath, the following antiphon appears: "Pulcra es et decora" from the *Song of Songs*. What follows is not easy to read also for the overlapping of Lucrezia's fingers on the text.

The right page is less ruined and easier to read; here is the antiphon taken from the sixth chapter of the *Song of Songs*; verset 9 is quoted in full in the painting: "Viderunt Eam filiae Sion et/beatissimam praedicaverunt et re-/ginae laudaverunt eam. Deo gr(atias)."[79] Then the hymn to Mary: "O Gloriosa d(omin)a[80] eccelsa super si-/ dera Qui te creavit provide lactas/sacrato ubere. Quod eva tristis/ abstulit tu reddis almo germine"; below the beginning of the third stanza with "Tu regis."

The two pages of the text painted by Bronzino outline the structure of a complete prayer with the Psalm, the Gloria, the antiphon, and the hymn. This hymn is important in order to put these prayers together in the Little Office of the Virgin, to whom the words of the passage of the *Song of Songs* also refer. The most important Marian feasts have an old origin: 1 January has been devoted to Holy Mary since the eighth century; 2 July has been the Visitation since 1389; the Assumption has been celebrated on 15 August since the eighth century, while the Orthodox Church has celebrated the Dormitio Virginis on this day since the sixth century; and 8 September has been Mary's birthday since the sixth century. It is not easy, however, to know the importance that was given to each of these religious celebrations in the course of the centuries. In fact, the days of the year dedicated to the Virgin tend to be the same since the origins of Christianity, but the dedication of the feast has sometimes changed, as in the case of 8 December that became the day of the Immaculate Conception only in 1854, when the dogma was proclaimed; but the same day had been dedicated to the Conception of Mary since 1440.

As to the booklet that the woman keeps on her lap, the text is for the recitation of the Liturgy of the Hours, a form of prayer that dates back to the origins of Christianity. Derived from similar Jewish traditions, it was already practiced in the second–third centuries by the first communities and originally centered on the morning praises and the Vespers; it was then modified and adapted up until the Second Vatican Council. From its origins until the fourth–sixth centuries, it was a prayer for the clergy and secularists, recited in the cathedral and presided over by the bishop; in the sixth century, it was embraced and enriched by the Benedictines; and in the Middle Ages it was collectively recited in church with the use of the books of Psalms located in the choir and the readers. Around the thirteenth century, this practice lost its importance as a communal rite and became an individual act, privately practiced by the religious with the breviary (a book containing the abbreviations necessary to the recital of the Liturgy of the Hours). The Council of Trent, in fact, ratified the use of the breviary and made recital of the Liturgy mandatory for the clergy, but in the form of a private devotional practice. By becoming a prerogative of the consecrated people, the community became excluded from this prayer simply because it was no longer performed in church with the guidance of the priest. Only after the Second Vatican Council was the Liturgy of the Hours recommended to laymen as a form of individual prayer to be practiced at home, and thus began the simplification of its structure and the spreading of the texts.

Lucrezia's open book, the fact that the text is readable, and the precise and identifiable prayers quoted on the pages cannot be unintended. Although it seems odd that a laywoman had a Book of Hours, there are numerous examples of these types of books owned by nobles and sovereigns, such as the Book of Hours of the Medici kept in the Libreria Laurenziana[81] and dating back to the fifteenth century, probably one of the five "Booklets of Women's Sermons" documented in 1492, after Lorenzo the Magnificent's death. The fact that they were identified as female objects tells us that Lucrezia Panciatichi also could have possessed one. Certainly, the lady's devotion to the Virgin is exposed in the painting, but in my opinion, by considering the accuracy of the transcribed prayers, the intention might rather have been to point out a precise day of the year or, even better, a precise feast. In fact, the hymn "O Gloriosa Domina" is recited exclusively on the occasions of Mary's celebration, and this is still true in our time, although the Liturgy of the Hours has been modified several times over the years. By using the expedient of Lucrezia's book of daily prayers, it is possible to assume that the Panciatichi wanted to highlight a very precise day: a Marian Feast.

In his history of the Panciatichi family, Passerini writes about Sigerio, son of Bellasta, and reports that in 1204, for the good of his own soul and parents' souls, he donated some "rents and surfaces" to the parsonage of San Zeno on condition that the canonicals prepared luminaries on the evening before the Assumption. This donation also exempted him from paying the tithes.[82] This event certainly dates back three centuries before Bartolomeo and Lucrezia's time, but I wonder if the Panciatichi family had a special devotion to our Lady of the Assumption, celebrated on 15 August. If this is the case, the sequence of prayers painted by Bronzino on Lucrezia's booklet might be a reminder to that specific day.

It is important to keep in mind that Florence was particularly devoted to Mary. The city, in fact, was consecrated to Christ King and Mary Queen on 9 February 1527 with a public act of the Signoria. But I believe an important date to consider for our analysis is 25 March, the Annunciation. This feast was felt to such an extent that it decreed the beginning of the civil year, and the year was calculated "ab Incarnatione." This practice remained an irremissible tradition until 1750, even if the Gregorian Calendar had fixed the beginning of the year to 1 January. The celebrations had a religious, civil, and spring importance, and Florence gathered around the church of the Santissima Annunziata, one of the most important churches of the city, where an image of the Announced Virgin by an unknown Tuscan painter of the fourteenth century is kept. The church still receives the devotion of the Florentines at present. Probably the hymn "O Gloriosa Domina" was adopted in the Little Office of the Virgin also on 25 March, one of the Marian feasts, and it might be the date that the prayers contained in Lucrezia's booklet are meant to indicate.

Vasari notes that Bronzino painted Bartolomeo's and his wife's portraits as well as two large pictures of *Our Lady* with other figures for the Panciatichi.[83] The *Holy Family* by Bronzino, kept in the Uffizi, is undoubtedly one of the two mentioned by the author of the *Lives*, because a red flag with the coat of arms of the Panciatichi flies high on the left, on one of the bastions of the fortress in the background: a clear reference to the commissioning. Raffaello Borghini[84] confirms the presence of the portraits of the Panciatichi and the *Holy Family* in the home of Carlo, the couple's son.

Mary, Joseph, and Jesus are accompanied by Saint John the Baptist, perhaps in memory of the real Christian name of the commissioner, Giovanni, later called Bartolomeo in honor of his father. We might also think of a homage to the patron of the city of Florence, where the Panciatichi then resided as permanent citizens.

Mary is portrayed half figure, with her bust and head lightly inclined toward the children and gently leaning on the left arm. She wears an old pink-colored dress with a simple belt of indigo fabric tied to the waist and a blue mantle on her lap. A golden brooch with a dark and precious stone set in the middle is pinned on the neckline of the classic dress. The gold and curly hair is gathered behind her nape. The left hand of the Virgin lays on a closed book, symbolizing the Marian quality of "Sedes sapientiae." Saint Joseph is depicted as a rather young man, especially if compared to the man of advanced years who appears in traditional iconography. His bust is seen in a profile view, while the head is turned three-quarters towards the children. His hands are crossed in front of the chest, and he seems to sit in meditation rather than in prayer. He wears a simple purple tunic. Joseph is traditionally placed in the background of sacred paintings, but in Bronzino's work he seems to receive more prominence. Indeed, his young age and pose contribute to represent Joseph as father and husband, protective toward his family and intimate with his wife. Mary and Joseph truly offer themselves as parents by guarding and meditating over their little child.

Jesus is represented as a one- or two-year-old child. He is sleeping on a precious light blue cushion in golden finishes, but a travelling bag is well visible underneath. This element, together with the age of Jesus, make critics think that Bronzino represented one of the stops where the Holy Family rested during their journey back from Egypt. Moreover, according to an apocryphal tradition, Mary, Joseph, and Jesus visited their cousin Elizabeth, mother of Saint John, during this journey home. This could be an additional motivation for the presence of the little precursor in the picture.

The unusual pose of the baby Jesus reveals signs and symbols of the Passion and the Death of the Savior. In fact, the Child is represented as in the descent from the cross; his closed eyes anticipate his death, even if here he is only asleep; his white vest reminds of the Shroud; his little right foot is placed on top of the left one, as it will be on the cross; and his feet are also located against a stone, which seems to symbolize Mount Calvary. On this stone Bronzino left his signature in capital letters: "BRONZO–FIORETI." Next to the child's little legs, a curled cartouche presents the text "GNUS" from the sentence "Ecce Agnus Dei" pronounced by the Baptist when he recognized Jesus as the Savior.

The Cabinet of Drawings and Prints of the Uffizi houses the charcoal drawing number 6639 that was a preparatory study of the baby Jesus of the *Holy Panciatichi Family*. The drawing was initially considered a work by Pontormo, until Frederick Mortimer Clapp compared it to Bronzino's painting in 1914.[85]

The little Saint John the Baptist, who appears slightly older than his cousin, curiously looks at Jesus sleeping and puts an arm on his chest in a protective gesture. His face comes near the child as if he is about to kiss him. In his attitude, the little saint seems to foretell Jesus' destiny. The sanctity of the four figures is represented through very thin and fine haloes: they are golden circles that are hardly noticeable and do not overwhelm the characters.

The scene takes place at the foot of a hill, and a town fortified by walls and bastions stands on its top. On the left, some towering buildings are noticeable inside the walls. A circular-planned, sacred building with a dome stands out for its richness, possibly a baptistery or a church, in a perfect Cinquecento style, decorated with circles, volutes, semicolumns, blind arches, and lanterns. Further back, a palace is depicted, and beyond its roof another dome rises.

Outside the walls, a three-storey house is depicted, sober and elegant, with a covered loggia that looks toward the town on the top floor. It is decorated with string, course and round windows on the second floor, and architraves on the third floor. Overall, the style of these buildings perfectly simulates a contemporary Tuscan town.

The Staatliche Graphische Sammlung of Munich preserves the pen and ink drawing number 2249 that seems to be one of the first sketches of the *Holy Family*. It was initially attributed to the Michelangelo school but was ascribed to Bronzino by Hanns Schulze in 1911.[86] The background of the *Holy Family* kept in the Uffizi is so precise and detailed that it seems a punctual continuation of an existing landscape. As Natali suggested, I focused my research on the particular perspective vision of the steep rocky ascent and on the walls on its top. There is a significant resemblance to the view that Volterra offers by following the road from the sea into the hinterland, with some obvious differences between the pictorial view and the real one. Moreover, the walls and bastions around the hill have analogies with the Medicean fortress built on the highest point of Volterra and structured in two bodies: the Duke of Athens wanted the oldest one, while the Magnificent demanded the most recent one after 1472. The cylindrical shape of the towers and their base, the regularity, and the gravity of the massive structure are not dissimilar to the elements painted by Bronzino. Even if the artist drew the walls with merlons, whereas the fortress in Volterra has brackets, the scenic effect is very similar. For its remarkable dimension, the structure painted by Bronzino is also similar to the Medicean one. It already presented the current characteristics when the artist painted the *Holy Family*, but is visible by coming from San Gimignano, and the massive presence can be perceived from its high position. Bronzino was probably inspired by Volterra in the representation of his background. Certainly, the Panciatichi had ties with this town; in fact, in 1256 Inghiramo "had the office of podesta in Volterra";[87] Piero was podesta of the town in 1332;[88] another Piero had the same office in 1416;[89] and finally there was also a Bandino, named Giovanni,[90] who had the authority in Volterra in 1395, according to the civic sources, but, as Passerini notices, Bandino was still too young at that time. Carlo Falciani[91] also provides a very interesting reading of the background of the painting by assuming that the rock is the symbol of God in accordance with a Psalm of David.

I believe it is more problematic to identify the circular building with the dome that towers behind the house and the walls. It does not have any elements in common with the baptistery of Volterra, and it does not seem to resemble any particular Florentine or Tuscan monument. It actually presents some elements in affinity with some other well-known domes: the vaulting ribs of the dome calotte and the oculus windows in the tambour of Santa Maria del Fiore, the fairly large windows in the drum similar to those of the Medicean chapels, and the blind arches comparable to the ones in the baptistery of San Giovanni in Florence, even if Bronzino located them at the same height of the tambour with a central window. In all probability, the painter began working on the elements he knew, but also left space to his mind's eye by realizing an imaginary building and elaborating, for instance, the beautiful curls located on the second floor of the temple that alternate with the oculi. Overall, the building completely appears as a sixteenth-century structure, even if it is hard to connect it to specific monuments. Bronzino might have adopted the similar technique employed for the background of the portrait of Bartolomeo Panciatichi, by painting a real landscape that evokes real places but without selecting any precise place and by following his own inspirational creativity.

Vasari mentions that Bronzino realized "two large pictures of Our Lady with other figures"[92] for Bartolomeo Panciatichi. Critics have always recognized one of the two works in the *Holy Family* kept in the Uffizi that undoubtedly can be connected to the Florentine lineage for the coat of arms hoisted on the bastion of the fortress in the background. The second painting has not yet been identified with certainty. The hypothesis so far developed takes into consideration two *Madonne* from the Bronzino-catalogue.

The first is the *Madonna and Child with Saints*, also known as the *Madonna Hertford* (Fig. 7) for it origin and now the collection of the National Gallery of London—a painting in oil on wood, 102 x 81 centimeters. Mary appears in the center of the scene, and her face is shown in a three-quarters view; her right arm holds the Child while the left one surrounds Saint John the Baptist. She wears a red dress tightened with a thin belt at the waist, and a light blue mantle is draped over her shoulders and chest. From the shoulders down to the legs falls a blue mantle where Jesus places his little feet. A thin and transparent veil covers her head where a little golden diadem is depicted. The Virgin appears not as a noblewoman, but rather, as a woman of the lower class or a country-woman. The clothes are not sophisticated or precious, and she only wears a simple jewel; in her right hand she holds a closed book.

The Child seems to be about three years of age and stands naked beside his Mother. With his left arm, extended in front of her chest, he raises a thin cross, while with his right hand he removes a small garland of flowers[93] from his head in a gesture of humbleness that confirms his "becoming a man" on the cross until his death. His features are delicate and soft, and his attitude is confidential and intimate towards the Mother: the two faces almost touch, indeed, and Jesus seems to be contemplating a kiss on her cheek.

Saint John the Baptist is portrayed in profile, half bust, in the lower part of the scene. With his right hand he offers some wild strawberries[94] to the Child, and with the left one he carries a small bowl with water, symbol of the baptism he will administer to Jesus.

He wears a camel-skin cloak and a narrow blue piece across his chest. Behind the Virgin the figure of Saint Elizabeth is represented, mother of Saint John the Baptist and Mary's cousin. The elderly female saint wears a wide loose white veil on her head and looks down tenderly as an attentive observer.

A fine golden halo, similar to that of the *Panciatichi Holy Family*, surrounds the heads of the four sacred figures. The characters are placed in a rocky scenery painted with dark tones of brown and grey against which the gleam of the group stands out and shines. As in the *Panciatichi Holy Family*, there is no vegetation. On the high left corner, the painting presents light surrounding walls with a crenellated door, and stonework structures on both of its sides, probably benches: on the left side, in fact, two human figures appear to be seated. Beyond the wall, on the right, a white house is visible, whereas the building on the left, further away, is more difficult to interpret: it might be a circular building, a bastion,[95] or a chapel. Some tree-tops emerge. Overall, the buildings recall a country estate or a small village. Even though the work has been repainted, the artist's signature appear in the low left corner on the rock, where it is possible to read "B.ONZO FL . . ETINO,"[96] which clearly stands for Bronzino Fiorentino. The painting is dated between 1541 and 1543, more or less contemporary to the two portraits and the *Panciatichi Holy Family*.

In their efforts to identify the second *Madonna* commissioned by Bartolomeo Panciatichi, some scholars turned their attention to the London painting, by noticing affinity of style with the picture of the Uffizi. Claude Phillips[97] wrote an article on this painting shortly after Sir Faudell-Phillips had acquired it from a sale at Christie's. He noticed similarities between the right hand of the Virgin and the same right hand of Mary in the *Panciatichi Holy Family*, and between the two heads of Saint John the Baptist. Moreover, the figures that the British historian calls "subsidiary," San Joseph in the *Panciatichi Holy Family* and Saint Elizabeth in the one of London, are "introduced" in the same manner, by occupying the same location in the composition and presenting a resemblance in their poses and in the inclination of their looks. As a matter of fact, they both have the same function in the economy of the pictures and balance the scenes.

Arthur McComb[98] believed this was the other *Madonna* commissioned by the Panciatichi family. Both Luisa Becherucci,[99] less so, and Andrea Emiliani[100] carry forward McComb's hypothesis. Maurice Brock[101] denies a superimposition among the characters and notices how they each have a clear and understandable role in the scene. Only Jesus is a dynamic figure: both his legs, lightly bent in an attempt to keep his balance, and his arms indicate a sense of movement. The scholar, however, defines his "dancing pose" as excessively artificial. The scene does not generate a dramatic tone, even though the gestures of the Child prophesy his death. Finally, Brock suggests that by offering fruit and baptismal water, the figure of Saint John the Baptist acts as an intermediary between the sacred characters and the profane world and encourages the viewer to an attitude toward giving similar to the one experienced during the offertory at the Mass.

According to Charles McCorquodale, the *Madonna Hertford* is qualitatively inferior to the *Panciatichi Holy Family*, and therefore, cannot be identified with the second painting of *Our Lady* recorded by Vasari. McCorquodale draws on Michael Levey's idea according to which the iconography of the painting in London represents the exact opposite of the painting in the Uffizi. The strawberries that Saint John the Baptist keeps in his hands are a symbol of justice or prosperity for his own life or that of Jesus, while the Child's gesture of removing the garland of flowers that signifies innocence or serenity and his grasp of the cross with his left hand indicate the acceptance of his destiny. The characters' pose in the *Madonna Hertford* appears more artificial, as they lack naturalness and softness of lines and contribute little to the harmony of the composition.

Scholars[102] have also been fascinated by the *Holy Family with Saint Elizabeth and Saint John the Baptist* in the Kunsthistorisches Museum in Vienna (Fig. 8). The painting dimensions are slightly bigger than the *Panciatichi Holy Family*, measuring 124,5 x 99,5 centimeters. It is signed by Bronzino and has been dated between 1545[103] and 1550.[104] When compared to the other two *Holy Families*, this work introduces an additional figure: five characters, in fact, are represented.

The Virgin is represented in the center, wearing a dark pink dress tightened at the waist with a fabric belt. Underneath the dress, the neckline and the sleeves reveal a light vest. On her shoulders a light blue mantle is draped; her head is covered with a thin transparent veil tied softly over the shoulders. The Virgin's head seems to echo the ancient classical models: her face is an almost perfect oval with a marble-like pallor; her features are precise and steady, very regular, without lacking traits of grace and gentleness. Also, the rendition of her hair seems to be modeled after the classics: her fawn-colored wavy hair is neatly arranged with a fine circlet, and a lock of hair falls about her right shoulder. Mary shows thin tapering hands, a distinctive characteristic that distinguishes all the women depicted by Bronzino; on the left wrist of the Virgin is hanging a small pendant; the left hand is posed on a preciously bound book, another recurrent feature of Bronzino's art.

Behind Mary's shoulders, two figures are represented. On the left appears Saint Joseph, very similar, in my opinion, to the one depicted in the *Holy Family* in the Uffizi. He seems exactly the same person but more advanced in age; his beard and hair, in fact, are slightly grey, and his face shows some wrinkles, but I believe he has the same aquiline nose profile, and the pose appears less complex because it is frontal. The other female figure is located on the opposite side; she has been alternatively recognized as Saint Anne[105] or Saint Elizabeth.[106] The woman is no longer young, and her face has lost its freshness, but she still reveals a certain beauty and elegance under the white veil and the violet-brown mantle that wraps her head completely.

In the foreground of the painting, Jesus sits on a rocky mass, which functions as a balustrade, or almost a windowsill that frames the representation, as happens in the picture commissioned by the Panciatichi. The Child is naked and sits on a white cloth, perhaps his garment. The little body with its round shapes and delicate complexion seems to be three or four years of age. The Mother holds him with her arm while he gives her a bright-colored bird, probably a goldfinch. Jesus' look appears careful and aware. His head is framed with curly and golden hair.

Saint John the Baptist, the fifth figure of the painting, is depicted in the right inferior corner of the painting. He lies on an animal skin, surrounded by the bowl with baptismal water and the cross wrapped in the ribbon that announces the Advent of the Lamb of

God, both elements that specifically characterize the Precursor. He, too, is naked, and turns his profile toward his cousin, while giving him an apple with the right hand, and he points his finger toward the sex of the Child to show the complete and true nature of the Savior. The gaze of all four characters converges on Jesus, who looks straight at the viewer of the painting.

Behind the figures stretches a green landscape: on the right, a fortified boundary wall arises; on the left, between the two female heads, a villa located on a tableland, with tower and merlons, is depicted. Further back, on top of a hill, other buildings with a tower are represented.

The sky is leaden, overcast with clouds foreboding, perhaps, the events that will take place on the Golgotha. The Louvre museum in Paris keeps a *Holy Family*, analogous to this one in Vienna, which is considered a replica. According to Emiliani,[107] however, this French picture is the prototype, whereas the Austrian one is a copy to be dated back to the beginning of the decoration of the chapel of Eleonora of Toledo, around 1542.

McCorquodale[108] indicates that the *Holy Family* in Vienna, together with the painting on the same subjects kept in the Louvre and the *Deposition* in Besançon, display Bronzino's inconsistent approach toward images of religious themes, which culminates in the *Resurrezione di Cristo* (*Resurrection of Christ*) and in the *Discesa di Cristo al Limbo* (*Descent of Christ to the Limbo*). As in the reproduction of the *Deposition* in Besançon, also in the replica of the *Holy Family* in the Louvre, Bronzino makes changes by creating a more sober atmosphere. The shadow dominates the whole painting, while in the first version, the light impressively dominates the scene: pessimism takes the place of optimism.

In the attempt to discover the second of *Our Lady* painted by Bronzino for Bartolomeo Panciatichi, McCorquodale examines the faces of the Virgin in the three paintings now kept at the Louvre, in Portland, and in Moscow. The face of the Virgin of the *Holy Family* at the Louvre possesses a delicacy very close to that of the *Madonna* of Moscow and Portland. The three faces share features that characterize the female figures of the late Bronzino. The face of the *Madonna* in Vienna has an affinity with the one of the *Holy Family* in the Uffizi in its style, and by considering only this one element, it seems more plausible to identify the painting from Vienna with the second of *Our Lady* for the Panciatichi, not the one from London.

By the late 1550s, Bronzino developed a more naturalistic approach in the religious paintings of the *Holy Family with Infant Saint John the Baptist* (Madonna Stroganoff) in the Pushkin State Museum of Fine Arts in Moscow (Fig. 9) and the *Madonna and Child with Infant Saint John the Baptist* in the Portland Art Museum in Oregon. Though they are still permeated with Manneristic elements, the children, in particular in the Moscow painting, acquire a fascinating spontaneity, and the depiction of the Madonna in both paintings is undoubtedly less rigid than the one in Vienna. The second painting of *Our Lady*, commissioned to Bronzino by the Panciatichi, still remains an unresolved question, but I would personally opt for the *Holy Family* of Vienna, which offers a more studied composition: the artist's care and attention to details used to depict characters (as well as the classic references) emerge, and a stronger elegance and refinement characterize their faces. The painting also offers many symbolic and allusive elements that surely would have been understood and appreciated by a literary man like Bartolomeo. Finally, I believe, this painting presents more affinities to the *Holy Family* of the Uffizi, equally studied, accurate, and sophisticated enough to satisfy the commissioner's expectations. With regard to the second version of the same *Holy Family with Saint Elizabeth and Saint John the Baptist* at the Louvre, I presume it is a replica of the one in Vienna: the use of the tones appears visually lighter in the latter; the representation of the children's faces seems less accurate and expressive; and Mary's face looks more unnatural and less sober.

Maurizia Tazartes thought the recognition of the villa in the background of the painting could have potentially revealed the identity of the client who commissioned the work.[109] It would be then possible to clarify whether or not the painting was the second *Our Lady* specially made for the Panciatichi. Seeing that the villa of the work appears as a punctual reproduction of something already existing, I personally examined the properties of Bartolomeo Panciatichi by consulting the Grand Ducal Tithes[110] kept in the Archivio di Stato of Florence, which registered the estates of the Florentine citizens according to the area in which they lived. In Bartolomeo's case, it was San Giovanni. The first *arroto* analyzed dates back to

1540.[111] A property "located in san piero in gersole with a house for the master and labourer ...," together with other declared possessions, is part of the inheritance that Bartolomeo received from his father. The *arroto* ends by stating the following: "These properties are registered in 1532," and in 1532, Bartolomeo of Francesco, the father, made his last registration before dying in 1533.

The *arroti* of the following years[112] only report the new acquisitions and the possible alienations of Bartolomeo Panciatichi, while the properties already declared are consolidated in conformity with the method of registration of the citizens' properties. Bartolomeo, therefore, remained the owner of the estate mentioned above that already belonged to his father before 1532. A second confirmation is provided by the *arroto* of the son Carlo, written in 1582, the year of his father's death. Among the numerous properties inherited, which include the ones of his mother who died before her husband in 1572, it is possible to find again "a property in san Piero in Gersolè parish of Santa Maria Impruneta ... and a house of the master."[113] In this specific case, it could be useful to assume that the "house of the master" was a villa with lands, houses for laborers, and all the belongings typical of the villa-farms that, around Florence, had the double function of country residence and farm for the nobles or the landlords of the time.[114] The toponym of San Piero in Gersolè, still in use, is the dialectical corruption of the entitlement of the local church of Saint Peter in Jerusalem in the parish of Impruneta, that is to say the area of influence of the parish of Santa Maria in Impruneta.

Despite the large number of luxury residences located among these hills in the southeast of Florence, we might assume that the villa possessed by Bartolomeo Panciatichi is the present Villa Corsini at Mezzomonte, which belonged to the Panciatichi until 1630, when Carlo, Bartolomeo's son, sold it to Prince Giovan Carlo de' Medici, as shown in the Grand Ducal Tithe (**Figs. 10 and 11**).[115] This property was, perhaps, already possessed by the Medicis in the 1630s, if we consider that the family possessed other estates at that time in the same area, as has been clearly documented. As a matter of fact, the *arroto* of Prince Giovan Carlo of 1630 that declares the purchase of the villa from Carlo Panciatichi and provides a detailed description of the real estate uses the toponym "mezzo monte," even if the name referred to a butcher's *bottega* possessed by Bartolomeo. Moreover, the many documents analyzed prove that other farms belonging to Bartolomeo Panciatichi were located in the area of Mezzomonte, which can be located by using the still applicable toponyms such as San Gersolè, Tavarnuzze, and Morgiano. Guido Carocci[116] refers to Villa Corsini as "Mezzo Monte già Morgiano," which confirms the dislocation of the toponym that appears in the registrations of 1540[117] and 1582,[118] respectively completed by Bartolomeo and Carlo Panciatichi and where Morgiano is mentioned with San Gersolè or shortly after. It can be assumed, then, that Bartolomeo's and his father's properties were located on these hills in the southeast of Florence among Impruneta, San Piero in Gersolè, la Capannuccia, and Tavarnuzze. San Lorenzo a Collina is also mentioned, but it was not possible to identify it. The villa at "Mezzo Monte" had to be at the center of their land properties and was part of the large estate of the Panciatichi family. By consulting the *arroti*, it can also be deduced that this property continuously belonged to Bartolomeo and expanded with the years. The sum of 30,000 scudos mentioned by the anonymous Jesuit[119] with reference to the trial by the Inquisition probably referred to the monetary liquidity of the gentleman and not the whole estate.

The present aspect of the villa is the result of a variety of modifications made in the course of time, even by Bartolomeo Panciatichi himself. Built as a fortified farm, perhaps around the year 1000, it initially belonged to the Buondelmonti family. Only parts of the southern walls with merlons date back to that period. The first luxury residence dates back to the fourteenth century, and the small tower, still visible today, is perhaps a trace of it. Lorenzo the Magnificent owned the place as well, but only for two years. I believe there are similarities between the villa that is known today as Villa Corsini and the one represented by Bronzino in the background of the *Holy Family* kept in Vienna: it is located on a tableland known as Villa Mezzomonte, has a small tower, and the section on the right presents those fourteenth-century merlons that are no longer visible on Villa Corsini at present but were described in the *arroto* of Prince Giovan Carlo in 1630.[120] Even the garden which surrounds the building shares some affinities: the painting only depicts a green strip, but this element also suggests the wide dimensions of the real garden documented in the *arroto* of Prince Giovan Carlo: it "is 240 long and 20 wide attached to the mentioned palace."[121] Finally, the boundary walls that appear on the right background of the *Holy Family* in Vienna resemble the Florence walls near the gate of San Niccolò that guides right along the hills where Mezzomonte rises. Should further research clarify whether the Panciatichi already possessed the villa in the fourteenth century, it would be possible to validate the idea that the *Holy Family* kept in Vienna is the second *Our Lady* painted by Bronzino for the Panciatichi family, on the basis of evident resemblances between the villa painted by Bronzino and the one of Mezzomonte, dated back to about 1545, based on the style considerations. If the villa was already in possession of the father, we might assume that Bartolomeo had a particular affection for this place, so much so as to want it represented in the picture commissioned to Bronzino. Also, since the villa was located at the center of the land estates of the Panciatichi, its representation in the background of the painting of the *Holy Family* becomes particularly symbolic.

We must also remember the interesting topics by Graham Smith[122] if we want to consider this painting to be the second *Holy Family* commissioned by Bartolomeo. The critic interprets the shadow projected by the cross of Saint John the Baptist as a possible coat of arms of the Panciatichi. In this work, the shield would therefore appear in a cryptic form and be recognizable only by few, whereas in Bartolomeo's portrait and in the *Holy Family* of the Uffizi, it is small but easily legible.

The reasons behind Bartolomeo Panciatichi's desire to commission two paintings with the same subject of the *Holy Family* to Bronzino is still open. Even if we acknowledge that the painting in Vienna is the second of *Our Lady*, clear differences still emerge between the work at the Uffizi, dated 1538–40, and the one in Vienna, 1545–50. Beyond devotional or collecting reasons, we could imagine the desire to display the pictures in different places of the Florentine house or in different residences that belonged to the family, perhaps just in the villa at Mezzomonte where the *Holy Family* of the Kunsthistorisches Museum could have been admired; or, maybe, the most recent with the villa in the background was exhibited in Panciatichi's house, while the other was displayed in the chapel of the family in Santa Maria Maggiore.

These few notes can only partially satisfy the questions and the interest aroused by the complex figure of Bartolomeo Panciatichi, a man who fully lived his time, a humanist with an open mind full of curiosity. Bronzino painted with his brush what a writer would have evoked in a biography.

NOTES

1. Giorgio Vasari, *Le vite de' più eccellenti pittori scultori e architettori nelle redazioni del 1550 e del 1568*, eds. Rosanna Bettarini and Paola Barocchi, 6 vols. (Florence: Sansoni, 1966–87) [hereafter Bettarini-Barocchi], 6:232.

2. See Luigi Passerini, *Genealogia e storia della famiglia Panciatichi* (Florence: M. Cellini and C. alla Galileiana, 1858), 68.

3. Passerini, *Genealogia e storia della famiglia Panciatichi*, 68.

4. Archivio di Stato di Firenze [hereafter ASF], Raccolta Sebregondi, piece number 4000.

5. Passerini, *Genealogia e storia della famiglia Panciatichi*, 66.

6. Passerini, *Genealogia e storia della famiglia Panciatichi*, 66.

7. Passerini states that Bartolomeo "was keeping his son among the pages of the French King"; Passerini, *Genealogia e storia della famiglia Panciatichi*, 66.

8. He was born in Florence in 1477 and was called Andrea del Fornaio and Andrea di Cosimo because he was a pupil of Cosimo Rosselli, as well as being a pupil of Morto da Feltre. See Bettarini-Barocchi, 4:523.

9. Biblioteca Nazionale Centrale di Firenze, Repertorio Gargani, piece n° 1469, "Panciatichi." Repertorio Gargani, sheet 230, refers to the *Miscellanea Fiorentina d'Erudizione*, year I, n. 4, April 1886. Hereafter BNCF.

10. Passerini, *Genealogia e storia della famiglia Panciatichi*, 67.

11. Passerini, *Genealogia e storia della famiglia Panciatichi*, genealogical tree, Table IV.

12. Maurice Brock, *Bronzino* (Paris: Éditions du Regard, 2002), 72; and Alessandro Cecchi, *Agnolo Bronzino* (Florence: Antella, 1996), 46.

13. Eleonora di Toledo entered Florence on 29 June 1539; she left Naples on 11 June and went ashore in Livorno on 22 June; the nuptial ceremony was celebrated in San Lorenzo, even if the marriage had been signed by proxy on 29 March of the same year. The celebration lasted many days, the city was decorated for the festivity, as well as the spouses' palace in Via Larga where many artists, Bronzino among them, painted stories of illustrious Greek, Roman and Medicean characters.

14. Passerini, *Genealogia e storia della famiglia Panciatichi*, 69.

15. Salvatore Caponetto, *La riforma protestante nell'Italia del Cinquecento* (Turin: Claudiana, 1997), 355, refers to two journeys, in 1539 and in 1547.

16. See Massimo Firpo, *Gli affreschi di Pontormo a San Lorenzo. Eresia, politica e cultura nella Firenze di Cosimo I* (Turin: Giulio Einaudi Editore, 1997), 359.

17. See Cecchi, *Il Bronzino*, 46–47.

18. See Antonio Paolucci, *Bronzino* (Florence: Giunti, 2002), 40.

19. See Firpo, *Gli affreschi*, 7, 370, n. 253.

20. The date is confirmed by the burial documentation in the *Necrologio della Grascia*, ASF, Office then *Magistrato della Grascia, Necrologio della Grascia*, piece 192, bobbin 8.

21. See Raffaello Borghini, *Il Riposo*, vol. 3, book IV (1584; Milan: Società Tipografica de'Classici Italiani, 1807), p. 98.

22. See Cecchi, *Gli affreschi*, 22, with note.

23. For this argument, see Cecchi, *Gli affreschi*, 17–28.

24. See Bettarini-Barocchi, 5:319.

25. See Firpo, *Gli affreschi*, 359–60 and previous bibliography.

26. Passerini, *Genealogia e storia della famiglia Panciatichi*, 71.

27. This information is reported in Firpo, *Gli affreschi*, 368, and is derived from Bernardino Bonsignori's *Memorie*, 101 and 102.

28. Firpo, *Gli affreschi*, 368–69.

29. See Firpo, *Gli affreschi*, 369, and previous bibliography.

30. For all the missives, see Firpo, *Gli affreschi*, 370–71.

31. See Firpo, *Gli affreschi*, 359.

32. For both letters, see Firpo, *Gli affreschi*, 358 and n. 217.

33. For both letters of the month of February, see Firpo, *Gli affreschi*, 369 and n. 251.

34. Passerini, *Genealogia e storia della famiglia Panciatichi*, 71.

35. See Firpo, *Gli affreschi*, 370 and n. 253.

36. ASF, Carte Ceramelli Papiani, piece n° 3570.

37. Passerini, *Genealogia e storia della famiglia Panciatichi*, 5.

38. In 1329, Ridolfo Panciatichi was armed Knights of the Golden Spur together with his sons and his brother with an official decree of the City Hall of Florence "for the contribution and dedication of Pistoia to the Florentines," and in 1352 he was granted Florentine citizenship.

39. The Panciatichi obtained public offices also in Perugia.

40. Passerini reports that the King of France, Louis XII, granted some lands in Lombardy to Bartolomeo the Young's father. See Passerini, *Genealogia e storia della famiglia Panciatichi*, 68.

41. See note 11.

42. ASF, Carte Ceramelli Papiani, piece n° 3570.

43. ASF, Carte Ceramelli Papiani, piece n° 3570 and Bettarini-Barocchi, 4:523.

44. Passerini, *Genealogia e storia della famiglia Panciatichi*, 156.

45. BNCF, Class 25, cod. 401, Magliabechiano, 262.

46. "In the outside facade towards midday *the marble coat of arms of the Panciatichi is visible, exactly in the location where inside their chapel is placed. And this coat of arm is still detectable in those antique and magnificent buildings near the church and make a corner to go into the Agli Square*"; ASF, Archivio Ceramelli Papiani, piece n° 3570.

47. Two letters of difficult interpretation are available, especially in relation to the previous date to which they are connected.

48. Passerini, *Genealogia e storia della famiglia Panciatichi*, 77.

49. Passerini, *Genealogia e storia della famiglia Panciatichi*, 62.

50. See Passerini, *Genealogia e storia della famiglia Panciatichi*, 74.

51. BNCF, Repertorio Gargani, vol. 1469, "Panciatichi," sheet n° 101, 102, 110, 136.

52. ASF, Office then *Magistrato della Grascia, Necrologio della Grascia*, piece 192, bobbin 8.

53. Passerini, *Genealogia e storia della famiglia Panciatichi*, Table IV.

54. ASF, Office then *Magistrato della Grascia, Necrologio della Grascia*, piece 192, bobbin 8.

55. Passerini, *Genealogia e storia della famiglia Panciatichi*, 72.

56. See Firpo, *Gli affreschi*, 359–60

57. BNCF, Repertorio Gargani, vol. 1469, "Panciatichi," sheet n° 136.

58. See Passerini, *Genealogia e storia della famiglia Panciatichi*, Table IV.

59. Borghini, *Il Riposo*, 98.

60. See Renato Barilli, *Maniera moderna e manierismo* (Milan: Feltrinelli Editore, 2004), 92.

61. By suggesting a different reason, that is, the election as Consul of the Accademia in 1545, McCorquodale presumes a postponement of the work; Charles McCorquodale, *Bronzino* (London: Chaucer Press, 2005), 60.

62. See Elizabeth Cropper, *Bronzino. Pittore e poeta alla corte dei Medici*. Catalog of the exhibition (Florence: Mandragora, 2010), 252.

63. See Luisa Becherucci, *Manieristi toscani* (Bergamo: Istituto Italiano di Arti Grafiche, 1944). The brief introduction to the text does not have page numbers; the quotation is from the third page.

64. See Maurizia Tazartes, *Bronzino* (Geneva and Milan: Skira-Rizzoli, 2003), 114.

65. See Brock, *Bronzino*, 119–20.

66. See Brock, *Bronzino*, 122.

67. See n. 8 above.

68. See Tazartes, *Bronzino*, 114.

69. See Mario Tinti, "Agnolo Bronzino pittore 'platonico'," in *Dedalo*, I (Milan and Rome: Bestetti e Tumminelli, 1920–21), 1-14.

70. See Brock, *Bronzino*, 72.

71. See Silvia Malaguzzi, *Un amore senza fine*, in *Arte e Dossier* 17, no. 180 (Florence: Giunti, July/August 2002), 33–37, and 36.

72. Carlo Falciani, *Bronzino. Pittore e poeta alla corte dei Medici*. Catalog of the exhibition (Florence: Mandragora, 2010), 168.

73. Malaguzzi, *Un amore senza fine*, 36.

74. Cropper, *Bronzino*, 250–55.

75. See Malaguzzi, *Un amore senza fine*, 33–37.

76. See Brock, *Bronzino*, 74.

77. See Brock, *Bronzino*, 72.

78. Caponetto, *La Riforma*, 356. In my opinion, the critic indicates an incorrect psalm: he refers to Psalm 149 but reports the incipit of 148.

79. Word abbreviated as "gr" in addition to an appropriate font irreproducible with the screenwriting software.

80. Word abbreviated as "dna" with a dash above the "n" letter.

81. See Biblioteca Medicea Laurenziana, MS Ashburnham Code 1874.

82. Passerini, *Genealogia e storia della famiglia Panciatichi*, 21.

83. Bettarini-Barocchi, 6:232.

84. Borghini, *Il Riposo*, 98.

85. See Frederick Mortimer Clapp, *Les dessins de Pontormo: catalogue raisonné précédé d'une étude critique* (Paris: Universitè de Paris, 1914), 49n3, and 199.

86. See Hanns Schulze, *Die Werke Angelo Bronzinos* (Strassburg: Heitz, 1911), XIII.

87. Passerini, *Genealogia e storia della famiglia Panciatichi*, 28.

88. Passerini, *Genealogia e storia della famiglia Panciatichi*, 40. Piero also became podesta in Perugia in 1360.

89. Passerini, *Genealogia e storia della famiglia Panciatichi*, 87.

90. Passerini, *Genealogia e storia della famiglia Panciatichi*, 167.

91. Falciani, *Bronzino*, 158.

92. Bettarini-Barocchi, 6:232.

93. See Brock, *Bronzino*, 254.

94. See Claude Phillips, "An Unknown Bronzino," *The Burlington Magazine* 26 (1914–15), 3.

95. See Tazartes, *Bronzino*, 118.

96. Phillips, "An Unknown Bronzino," 4.

97. Phillips, "An Unknown Bronzino," 3–4.

98. See Arthur K. McComb, "Agnolo Bronzino: His Life and Works," *The Art Bulletin* 11, no. 298 (1928–29), 43.

99. Becherucci, *Manieristi*, 45.

100. See Andrea Emiliani, *Il Bronzino* (Busto Arsizio: Bramante Editrice, 1960), Table 64.

101. See Brock, *Bronzino*, 254.

102. Fritz Goldschmidt, *Pontormo, Rosso und Bronzino* (Diss., University of Leipzig, 1911), 55, theorized that this painting was the second of *Our Lady* depicted by Bronzino for the Panciatichi.

103. McCorquodale, *Bronzino*, 138.

104. See Edi Baccheschi, ed., *L'Opera completa del Bronzino* (Milan: Rizzoli, 1973), 99.

105. Baccheschi, *L'Opera completa del Bronzino*, 99.

106. See Tazartes, *Bronzino*, 148.

107. Emiliani, *Il Bronzino*, Table 29.

108. McCorquodale, *Bronzino*, 135. The critic also identifies the palace in the background of the *Madonna* in Vienna with the Medicean villa of Cafaggiolo, but I disagree with his opinion.

109. See Tazartes, *Bronzino*, 148.

110. I owe the consultation of the Gran Ducal Tithes to the reading of *Il giardino di Villa Corsini a Mezzomonte: Descrizione dello stato di fatto e proposta di restauro conservativo*. The text quotes the following *Arroti*: 2997, 3020, 3024, 3119, 3234 that I later examined.

111. ASF, Gran Ducal Tithe, piece 2997, *Arroto* number 47, 103.

[112]. I examined the *Arroti* for the year 1551, piece 3020, *Arroto* number 26, 51 and piece 3032, Arroto number 487, 293.

113. ASF, Gran Ducal Tithe, piece 3119, *Arroto* number 354, 60.

114. Noblemen's villas often derived from medieval fortified farms.

115. ASF, Gran Ducal Tithe, piece 3234, *Arroto* number 163, 393.

116. See Guido Carocci, *I dintorni di Firenze* (Florence: Galletti & Cocci, 1906–07), 256.

117. ASF, Gran Ducal Tithe, piece 2997.

118. ASF, Gran Ducal Tithe, piece 3119.

119. See n. 14 above.

120. ASF, Gran Ducal Tithe, piece 3234, *Arroto* number 163, 393.

121. Ibid.

122. See Graham Smith, "Bronzino's Holy Family in Vienna: A Note on the Identity of Its Patron," *Source: Notes in the History of Art* 2, no. 1 (Fall 1982), 21–25.

Fig. 1. Agnolo Bronzino, *Portrait of Bartolomeo Panciatichi*, 1540–42. Galleria degli Uffizi, Florence. Photo credit: Scala/Art Resource, NY.

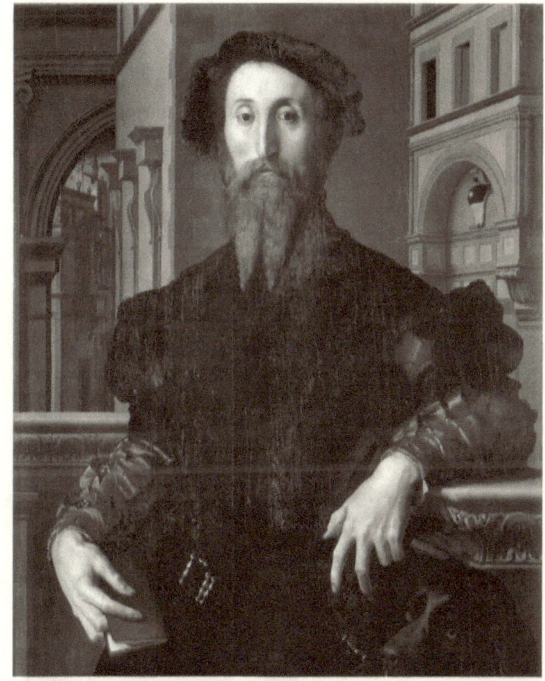

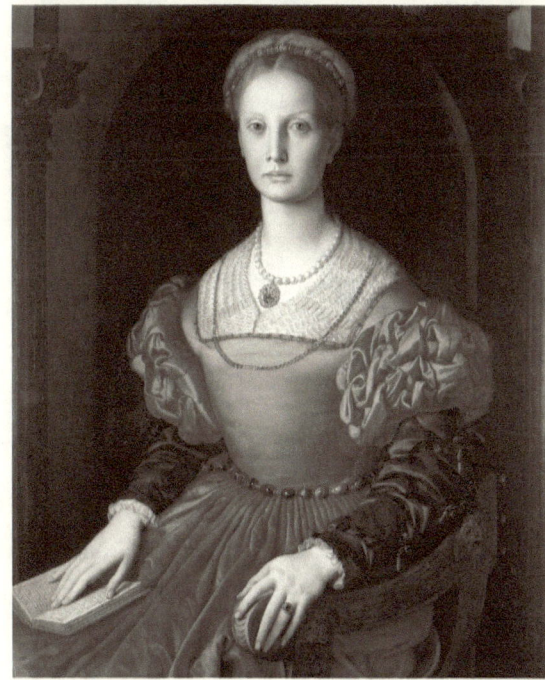

Fig. 2. Agnolo Bronzino, *Portrait of Lucrezia Panciatichi*, 1540–42. Galleria degli Uffizi, Florence. Photo credit: Scala/Ministero per i Beni e le Attività culturali/Art Resource, NY.

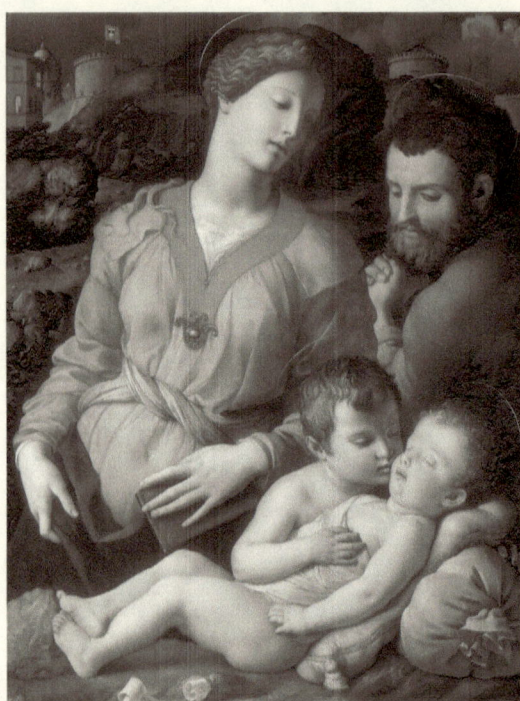

Fig. 3. Agnolo Bronzino, *Panciatichi Holy Family*, 1540–42. Galleria degli Uffizi, Florence, Italy. Photo credit: Alinari/Art Resource, NY.

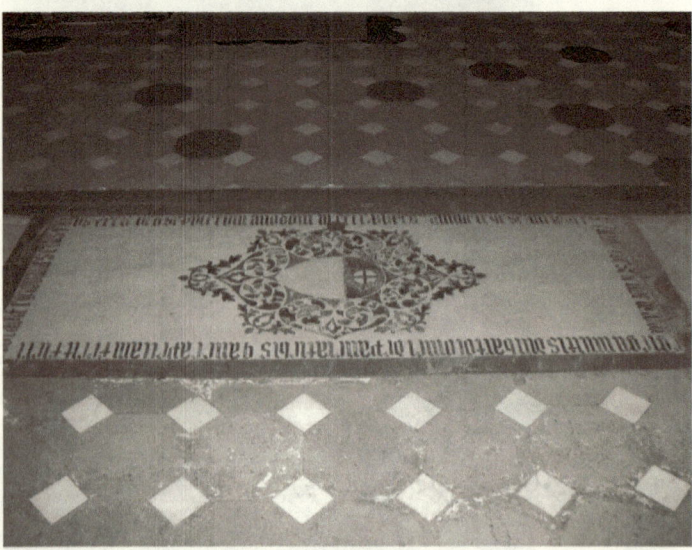

Fig. 4. Panciatichi Family Gravestone, 1430. Church of Santa Maggiore, Florence, Italy. Photo credit: author.

Fig. 5. Panciatichi Family
Coat of Arms (n.d.).
Church of Santa Maria
Maggiore, Florence, Italy.
Photo credit: author.

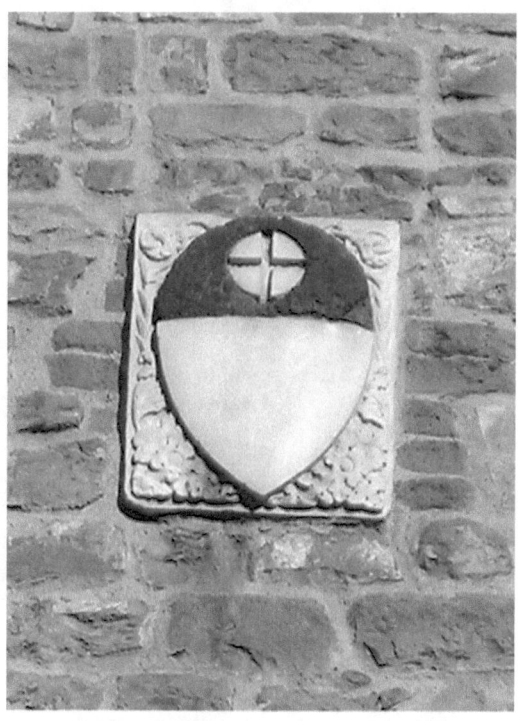

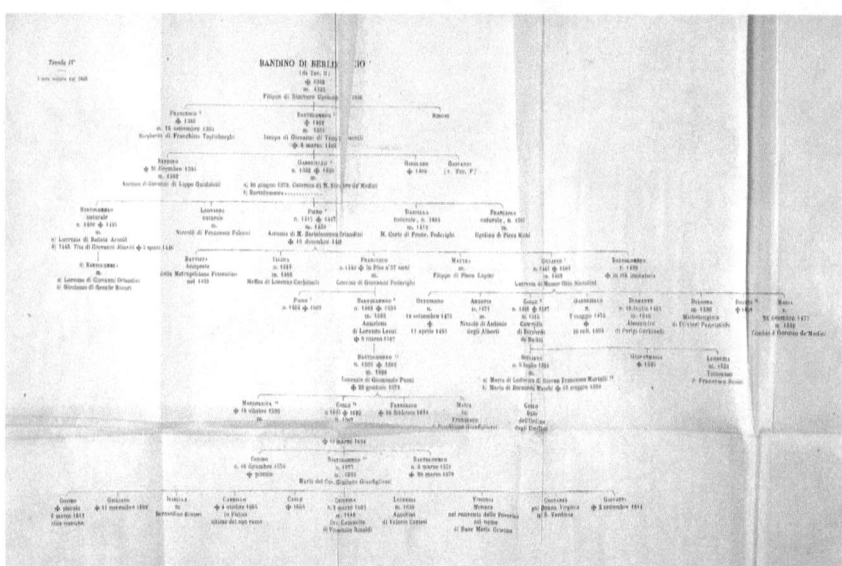

Fig. 6. Ceramelli Papiani's Genealogy of the Panciatichi Family (Table IV).
Photo credit: author.

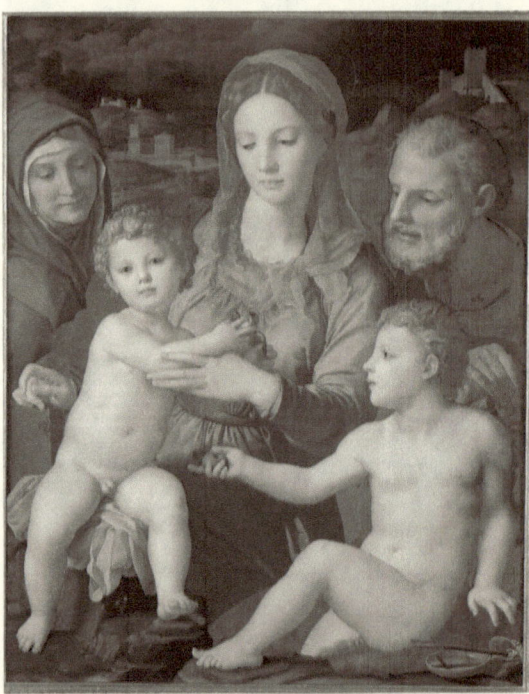

Fig. 7. Agnolo Bronzino, *The Madonna and Child with Saint John the Baptist and Elizabeth* (or *Saint Anne*) (*Madonna Hertford*), 1540–550. National Gallery, London, Great Britain. Photo credit: National Gallery London/Art Resource, NY.

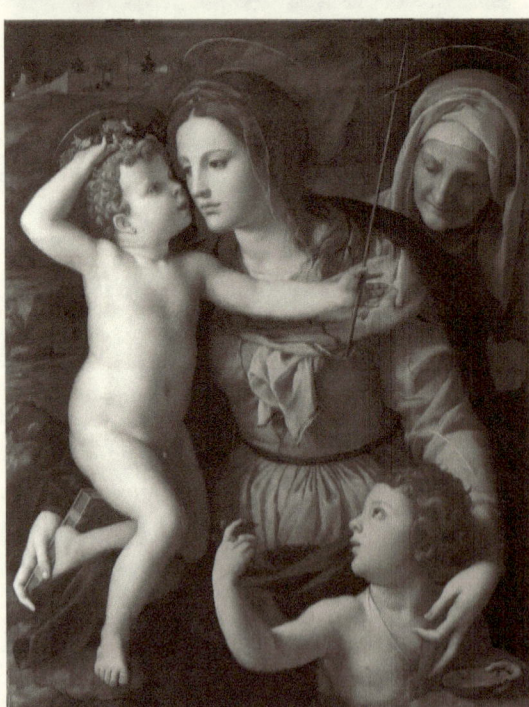

Fig. 8. Agnolo Bronzino, *Holy Family with Saint Anne and Young John the Baptist*, 1550s. Kunsthistorisches Museum, Vienna, Austria. Photo credit: Erich Lessing/Art Resource, NY.

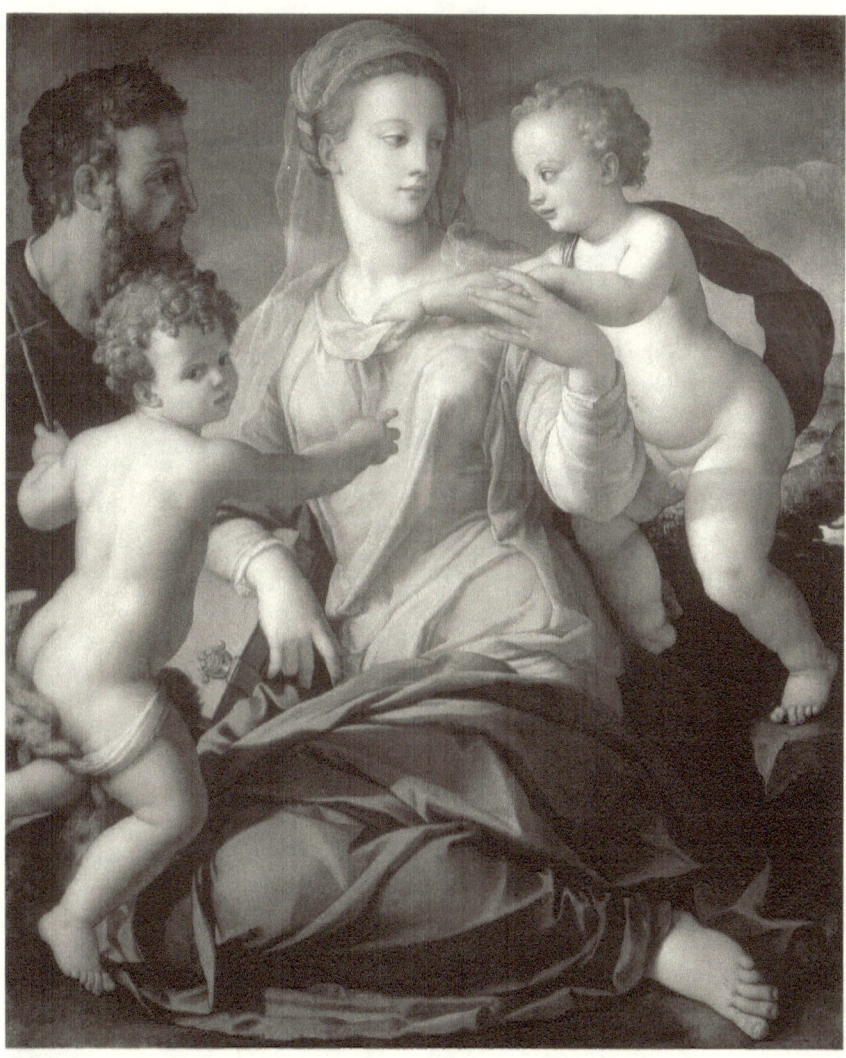

Fig. 9. Agnolo Bronzino, *Holy Family* (Stroganoff), 1540. Puskin Museum of Fine Arts, Moscow, Russia. Photo credit: Scala/Art Resource, NY.

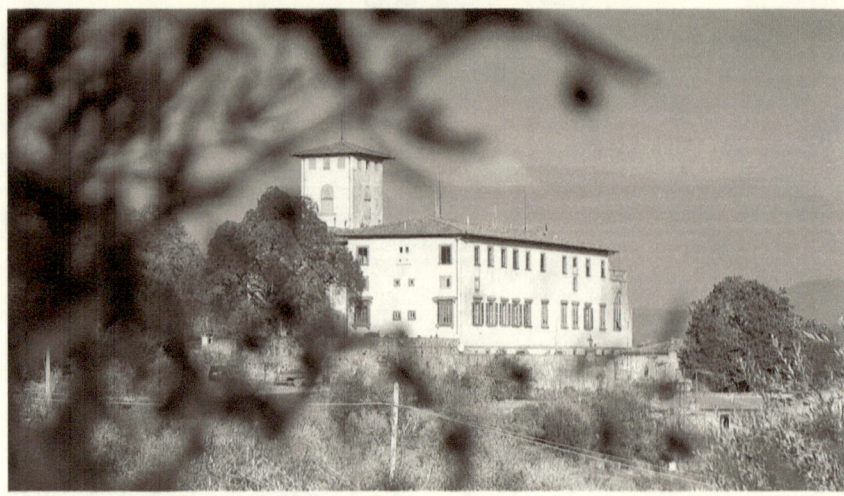

Fig. 10. Villa Corsini, Mezzamonte, Florence. Photo credit: Corsini Family.

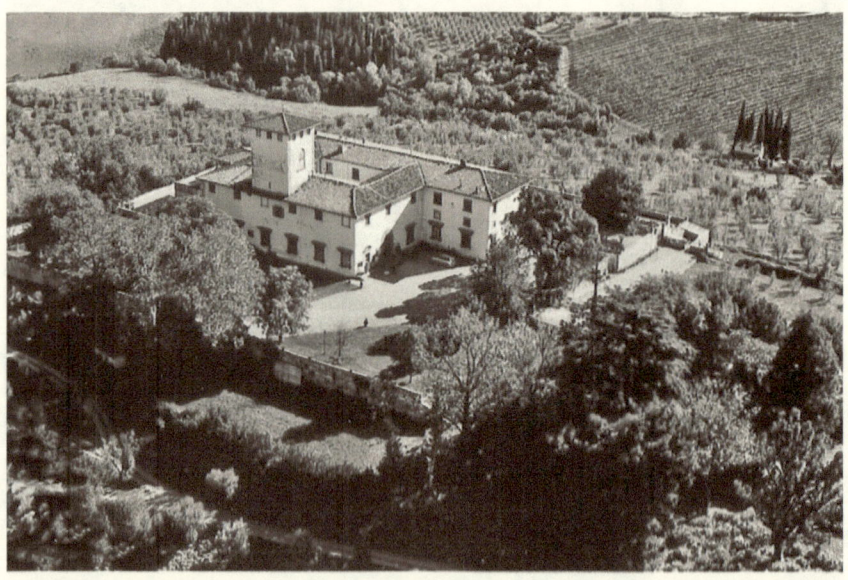

Fig. 11. Villa Corsini, Mezzamonte, Florence, aerial photo. Photo credit: Corsini Family.

"A Room With Many Views": Eleonora de Toledo's Chapel by Agnolo Bronzino in The Palazzo Vecchio

Lynette M.F. Bosch

The Chapel of Eleonora de Toledo, located within Florence's Palazzo Vecchio, is an outstanding sixteenth-century decorative ensemble executed by Agnolo Bronzino for Duke Cosimo I de' Medici and his Spanish wife, Eleonora de Toledo (Figs. 1–6).[1] From 1541 to 1543, Bronzino frescoed the walls with scenes depicting key events from the life of Moses. On the chapel's ceiling, Bronzino frescoed images of Saints Francis, John the Evangelist, and Jerome along with the Archangel Michael. The ceiling's center was originally decorated with the Medici/Toledo arms (quartered), and in the interstices between the panels with the saints there are garlands of fruits, flowers, and *putti*. There were two versions of the chapel's altarpiece, each with a central *Pietà*. (Fig. 1) The first altarpiece was completed in 1545–46 and was composed of a *Pietà* with lateral panels depicting *Saint John the Baptist* and *Cosmas*. The second altarpiece consisted of a copy of the first *Pietà*, installed in 1553, and lateral panels of *The Annunciation*. In addition to the altarpiece, the altar wall was decorated with frescoes of *The Erythraean Sybil* and *King David*. In the capitals of the chapel's fictive corner columns, there appear the virtues of Fortitude, Justice, Prudence, and Temperance. The progress of Bronzino's work on the chapel is chronicled by primary sources, payment documents, and inscriptions found in the chapel's doorway.

The construction and decoration of Eleonora's chapel coincided with the events that led to the Council of Trent (1545–63) and with the challenges faced by the Church represented by reformist movements outside and within its ranks.[2] The chapel is documented to have been an actual liturgical space, not simply a room for Eleonora's private prayer. It is argued here that the room's liturgical function is reflected in its core program, which is based on the Lenten readings of the Roman liturgy as it was celebrated before the Council of Trent.

That Masses were celebrated in Eleonora's chapel, even before the decorations were fully complete, is documented by a *guardaroba* inventory of April 1544, which records a bequest of liturgical objects from Maria Salviati (d. 29 December 1543) to Eleonora. The bequest included a silver cross and two candlesticks given to Andrea, the chaplain, to store and use in the chapel.[3] Throughout its history, the chapel continued to receive other liturgical embellishments in the form of statues, altar cloths, chalices, and patens, leaving no doubt about its liturgical function.[4] However, the chapel lacked a sacristy in which to store these objects, and, as Janet Cox-Rearick suggested, they likely were stored in the *Cappella de Priori's* sacristy, where the service books used to celebrate Masses would also most likely have been kept.[5]

How frequently Masses were celebrated in Eleonora's chapel is not documented, but Eleonora had a reputation, among close observers, of being constantly at prayer in scrupulous daily, devotional observance.[6] While a specific Missal used in the chapel has not been identified, Eleonora's Book of Hours (Victoria and Albert Museum—MSL/1953/1792) follows the prayers to the Virgin in accordance with Roman forms, and her Prayer Book (private collection), written in Spanish, contains a prayer written by Pope Leo X, indicating its content also conforms to Rome use.[7] Missals used in Florence would also have conformed to the usage of Rome, making the chapel a *locus* of orthodox, Roman ritual practice on the eve of the Counter-Reformation. Yet, even at the Catholic courts of Europe, reformist ideas existed, and it was the task of Catholic rulers to know when confessional debates needed to be suppressed for the safety of the court and their personal and political interests.[8]

EARLY SIXTEENTH-CENTURY FLORENTINE INTELLECTUAL AND SPIRITUAL DEVELOPMENTS

In Florence, the religious and intellectual climate of the early sixteenth century was a heterogeneous mixture of traditional religion and continuing humanistic inquiry, combined with the aftermath

of the Neoplatonic interest in comparative religious and philosophical systems.[9] The new confessional issues also played an important
role in the intellectual climate generated by the *Accademia Fiorentina*,
formerly the *Accademia degli Umidi*, renamed and reorganized on 11
February 1541.[10] As a court painter and a member of the *Accademia*,
Bronzino was at least an observer of, if not a leading participant in
these debates and a creator of the visual culture that accompanied
them.[11] With the award of the chapel's commission, Bronzino was
given the task of rendering the most significant religious statement
made by Cosimo and Eleonora within the precincts of the palace.
In so doing, Bronzino communicated with Pierfrancesco Riccio, the
ducal *majordomo*, and with Cosimo and Eleonora.[12] Thus, Bronzino's decorations in the chapel were directed by three individuals
fully aware that the statement made in Eleonora's chapel would be
scrutinized by visitors from the Imperial, papal, and other European courts. This expected scrutiny meant that the chapel's religious
statement needed to protect the best interests of the Medici court,
and the most certain way to ensure this was with a core program
that conformed to the Church's orthodox dogma and liturgy.

Geographically and politically, Florence was close to Rome and
dependent for support on the Holy Roman Emperor, Charles V,
who was pledged to defend the Roman Church, which legitimized
his title.[13] Retaining the support of the emperor was especially important for Cosimo, who had a strained relationship with Pope
Paul III (reigned 1534–49), so much so that, by 1545, the pope was
having Cosimo investigated for heresy. Nothing came of this politically motivated attempt on the part of the pope to make Cosimo
bow to him, and the Inquisition never proceeded with its investigation after Pope Paul III died.[14] Hence, neither Cosimo nor Eleonora
could afford to be charged with either apostasy or Nicodemism.
Yet, the Medici court temporarily accepted the intellectual diversity
represented by certain members of the *Accademia*, such as Bartolomeo Panciatichi and Pietro Carnesecchi, whose interests in reformist ideas was known.[15] However, in the 1550s, Cosimo's initial leniency to confessional debate ended, and the Inquisition arrested
and tried Panciatichi and Carnesecchi, later executing Carnesecchi
and releasing Panciatichi. Cosimo's repression of heterodoxy and
heresy, after 1549, was not a sudden change of policy, as even dur-

ing his conflicts with the Farnese pope, Cosimo had worked assiduously to develop influence at the Vatican and at other religious institutions in Florence and in his territories.[16] Cosimo's Vatican policy was documented by Gregory William Murry in his study of Cosimo's employment of contemporary concepts of sacral monarchy to advance his image and power in Florence and beyond.[17]

Knowing that he would outlast the Farnese pope, Cosimo prepared a more favorable Vatican climate for Florence by ingratiating himself with individual cardinals and prelates in what Murry identified as a deliberate formation of a network of influence at the Roman Curia. This policy worked well for Cosimo after the election of Julius III (reigned 1550–55), with whom Cosimo was on good terms. However, as Murry noted, by 1544, Cosimo was already ordering processions in Florence, intended to stop the spread of Lutheranism, as he actively pursued heretics.[18] Hence, even as Cosimo allowed the *Accademia*'s members to engage in diverse intellectual and spiritual inquiry in the 1540s, he was establishing a state policy of hewing to Roman orthodoxy. By 1550, Cosimo's improved relations with the papacy, under Julius III, were accompanied by his ceding religious control to the Roman Inquisition, and the arrests of accused heretics, including Bartolomeo Panciatichi, Pietro Carnesecchi, and other prominent Florentines, followed.[19] Even as the program for Eleonora's chapel was being planned, in 1540–41, Cosimo understood that long-term stability for Florence meant that the Medici court would be a court that would remain in the service to the Holy Roman Emperor and the Roman Church and that the chapel's program needed to reflect current and future compliance with Roman orthodoxy.

RECENT INTERPRETIVE STRATEGIES FOR ELEONORA'S CHAPEL

This point requires emphasis in view of recent interpretations of the chapel's program by Carlo Falciani and Massimo Firpo, who have suggested an intentionally heterodox, even heretical, meaning for Eleonora's chapel.[20] Firpo identified a treatise by Juan de Valdés, a lay spiritual writer and courtier to Don Pedro de Toledo, who resided in Naples from 1530 until his death in 1540, as a source for the chapel's program. The treatise forwarded by Firpo, the *Qual maniera si devrebbe tenere a informare insino dalla fanciullezza e figliuoli de' chris-*

tiani delle cose della religione, was published in 1545 (four years after the chapel was planned and painted). This text is a catechism for young people, which Firpo identified as being foundational for the Medici court's spirituality and for the chapel's program.

To Firpo, "... valdesianismo ...divenne una sorta di ideologia ufficiosa della corte ducale...echi valdesiani furono gli scritti di numerosi membri dell'Accademia Fiorentina ..." As proof of Cosimo's adherence to Valdesianism, Firpo cited a sermon given by Benedetto Varchi, at San Lorenzo on 20 March 1548, which was declared to be "Lutheran," by a "diarista fiorentino."[21] Yet, at most, Varchi's sermon (and other instances of confessional debate and reformist influence in Florence) represents Cosimo's tolerance of such inquiry, until Paul III's death in 1549. After the pope's death, Cosimo allowed the Inquisition into Florence; and even before Paul III's death, by 1544, Cosimo had engaged in persecution of the unorthodox, even as he expanded his sphere of influence in Rome, as was noted above.

With hindsight, it seems clear that, until the death of Paul III, Cosimo allowed confessional debates as a way of resisting Paul III, and perhaps for other political reasons. Yet, even before and especially after the pope's death, Cosimo's tolerance had limits. Perhaps Cosimo wanted Florentine intellectuals to occupy themselves with critiquing the Church instead of him. Thus, his tolerance of spiritual diversity may also have been a policy of political expediency instead of agreement with heterodoxy. Varchi's spirituality, or that of other members of the *Accademia*, is neither proof nor evidence that the Medici court or Cosimo and Eleonora had an ex-officio policy of heterodoxy officially expressed in Eleonora's chapel.

Similarly inclined to see the Florentine court as a hotbed of Valdesianism and the chapel as a locus of Nicodemism, Carlo Falciani identified, as the source for the chapel's program, the Valdesian *Beneficio di Cristo*, written by Benedetto di Mantova and edited by Marcantonio Flaminio and others. The *Beneficio* belongs to the group of treatises linked to the type of eclectic and personalized spirituality promoted by Valdés.[22] The *Beneficio* was published in Venice in 1543, afterwards becoming one of the most widely read spiritual treatises in Europe. Before its publication, the *Beneficio* circulated in manuscript form, in a limited manner.[23] Firpo and Falciani emphasized Pierfrancesco Riccio's ownership of a manuscript copy of the *Beneficio*, now in the Biblioteca Riccardiana, implicitly assuming that Cosimo's majordomo owned the manuscript before the chapel's program was determined and that Riccio was able to form the chapel's program as an example of Valdesian spirituality.

However, the content of Riccio's manuscript does not support these suppositions, as Salvatore Caponetto and Gigliola Fragnito have pointed out, because on the manuscript's flyleaf, Riccio identifies himself as being the Provost of Prato's Church of Santo Stefano, a title he did not have until 1550.[24] This inscription implies that Riccio acquired the manuscript after 1550, long after the chapel was completed. Caponetto also pointed out that Riccio's *Beneficio* is very close to the edition published in 1543, which suggests a late date for the manuscript. Furthermore, the manuscript also contains Cardinal Gasparo Contarini's contribution to the Conference at Regensburg, dated 25 May 1541, which means that Riccio's manuscript postdates the planning of the chapel in 1540–41. Thus, Riccio's *Beneficio* could not have been used to design the chapel's program because it had not been written before 1540, when the chapel's core program was being planned. Printed copies would not have been available until after 1543, these also being too late to have served as the source for the chapel's program.

Likely understanding that there were chronological problems for proposing the *Beneficio* as the chapel's source, Falciani found his proof that the chapel's program is Valdesian in a comparison between Christ and the sun made in Juan de Valdés' *Cento e dieci divine Considerazioni* (Basel, 1550), which was published five years after the chapel's program was developed.[25] Falciani argues that the light in Eleonora's chapel is Valdesian and that it is a special light inspired by this text, which was written towards the end of his life and read to his Neapolitan friends. Thus, the chapel's Heavenly light conforms to orthodox adherence to traditional symbolic forms.

The use of Heavenly light in the chapel to denote the blessing of Christ to the world has a clear and obvious Florentine precedent in the *Sol Iustitiae* found in Cosimo's *Sala dell'Udienza*. In the *Sala dell'Udienza*, the room most significant for Cosimo's self-presentation as a ruler, the IHS monogram of Christ was inscribed inside the disk of the sun, and the location of this *Sol Iustitiae* aligns it with Cosimo's virtue as a Heaven-sent ruler. In the Medicean context of the palace, the light in Eleonora's chapel referenced the Sun of Christ in the *Sala dell'Udienza*, not the Valdesian text, itself formulated on the basis of the Church's traditional use of this *figura*. Thus, even in a Valdesian context, the use of this conceptual motif returns attention to orthodox, traditional practices. In an Italian and Florentine context, the *Sol Iustitiae* of the *Sala dell'Udienza* found a parallel in the employment by St. Bernardino, when he preached carrying a tablet inscribed with the IHS monograph in the center of a glowing sun.[26] The *Sala dell'Udienza* was the room in which Cosimo held audience, as the ruler of Florence blessed by Christ, in a configuration of sacral monarchy that was prevalent in the symbolic systems of Catholic European courts. In the chapel, the Divine light showering blessings on the Medici court is not a covert statement of Nicodemist Valdesianism but an overt example of an artistic statement used to denote Cosimo's sacral monarchy, a topos studied by Murry. As Murry discussed, Cosimo was a ruler who adhered to an orthodox religious position in order to strengthen his power as the head of a European, Catholic court, dependent on the Holy Roman Emperor.[27] Thus, the light in Eleonora's chapel was indeed linked to Christ but also to Florentine and Italian precedent linked to allegiance to the Roman Church.

Similarly ignoring ties to orthodox Catholicism found in the imagery of the chapel's *Pietà*, Falciani identified as Valdesian the inclusion of the chalice and veil found in both versions of Bronzino's *Pietà*, citing a sentence in the *Beneficio di Cristo* which refers to *"velature"* in connection with the Last Supper.[28] The veil in the chapel's *Pietà* is the corporal used during the Mass, as discussed by Janet Cox-Rearick.[29] The corporal is the humeral altar cloth on which the priest rests the Host and the chalice during the Eucharistic part of the Canon of the Mass. As such, the corporal in Bronzino's painting is an allusion to the Mass and to the Eucharistic dogma of Transubstantiation, the focus of the Mass. In the chapel's context, the *Pietà's velature* are part of Catholic tradition, and spectators seeing Bronzino's painting would have immediately identified the "veils" in the painting with the celebration of the liturgy of the Church and not with a phrase in the *Beneficio*.

Additional links between the Church and Bronzino's depiction of the corporal were noted by Antonio Natali, who pointed out that Bronzino's second *Pietà* bears the imprint of Christ's face, thereby evoking Veronica's Veil. Veronica's Veil is one of the Church's most venerable relics, believed to have been in Rome since the Middle Ages.[30] Thus, Bronzino's image directly and contextually linked Florence to Rome, while evoking the Church's ritual practices and its icons, such as the Veronica's Veil. In arguing for a Valdesian interpretation for Eleonora's chapel, Firpo and Falciani neglected to consider the Catholic content and context of the heterodox Valdesian texts, and as a result they overlooked the orthodox content and context of the core program of Eleonora's chapel.

Firpo and Falciani's Valdesian arguments have been offset by Cox-Rearick and Natali's consideration of the central role played in the chapel by the Easter liturgy and the evidently orthodox Eucharistic imagery of the altar wall, which emphasizes the Church's dogma of Transubstantiation.[31] Natali's assertions about the chapel's traditional presentation of Paschal and Eucharistic themes amplified Cox-Rearick's foundational work, in which she already identified the importance of the Easter liturgy for the chapel's Eucharistic themes.[32] Thus, the recent vogue for interpreting Eleonora's chapel as being Valdesian should be tempered by a recognition of the predominantly orthodox content that defines the chapel's orthodox, core program.

There is, however, evidence that the liturgical sources for the chapel's frescoes and paintings were composite. As Robert Gaston noted, the chapel's images also conform to the Spanish Mozarabic Rite's liturgy, wherein the Lenten liturgy contains readings from Exodus that correspond to the chapel's Mosaic scenes.[33] In the sixteenth century, the Mozarabic Rite's liturgy was celebrated mainly in the Mozarabic Chapel in the Cathedral of Toledo. Yet, this Rite's liturgy was also considered orthodox by the Roman Church, which accepted it as different but dogmatically correct. In Eleonora's chapel, the employment of imagery from the Mozarabic liturgy intentionally resonated with the city of Toledo, Eleonora's ancestral seat, and with her Spanish identity.

Towards A New Understanding of Eleonora's Chapel

To a degree, this essay expands Cox-Rearick's and Natali's assertions that the chapel should be interpreted in accordance with the Roman liturgy and orthodox dogma. Additionally, it presents a detailed consideration of the correspondences that emerge when the chapel's frescoes and paintings are juxtaposed with the Lenten Roman and Mozarabic liturgies.[34] My focus is not narrowly on the Easter Liturgy, from Holy Thursday to Resurrection Sunday, as discussed by Cox-Rearick and Natali, but rather on the whole Lenten liturgy and its reverberations throughout the liturgical year. This approach also achieves a more comprehensive understanding of how the chapel's images resonated with the Roman liturgy as a whole, which emphasizes the sources for the Church's Eucharistic dogma and ritual. Any number of texts can be brought to an interpretation of a work of art. However, in the case of Eleonora's chapel, the only texts that can be securely ascertained to have been directly brought into relation with the chapel's frescoes are the texts of the liturgy. In correspondence to the chapel's function as a liturgical space where Masses were celebrated, it would be the liturgy of the Church that provided the primary interpretive filter for the frescoes. Any other texts (and interpretations) can only be secondary to the primary meaning for the frescoes, as derived from the Church's liturgical texts. Given the primacy of the liturgy, additional interpretations of the meaning or meanings of Bronzino's frescoes have to consider the intentionality and resonance—for the patrons—of the significance of the liturgy's texts for the chapel's program.

Building again on the work of Cox-Rearick, a more focused interpretation of the dynastic aspects of the chapel is given here. This aspect of this study expands on Cox-Rearick's suggestion that the birth of Francesco, Cosimo's first-born son and heir, was an important element in the chapel's program.[35] However, Francesco's birth was even more specifically important for developing the chapel's program than has been noted in the literature on this topic. It is argued here that the catalyst for the full development of the chapel's program was Francesco's Lenten birth, as he was born on 25 March 1541, on the Feast of the Annunciation, which is part of the Lenten observances of feasts. Thus, the chapel's program, which is focused on Lent, resonates with the significance of the birth of the Medici heir. In 1541, Easter fell on April 17, and Francesco's birth occurred slightly more than a month earlier, during the forty days of Lenten preparation.[36] The timing of the child's birth would have been anticipated, once the pregnancy was established, and the program could have been determined in 1540. When Francesco was born on the first day of the Florentine year, the program could have been finalized to include references to the child's dynastic importance.

Another contentious issue in the literature on the chapel is that of the respective patronage roles of Cosimo and Eleonora. This controversy is the result of a debate that ensued in the aftermath of the publication of Cox-Rearick's book, as Bruce Edelstein, Elizabeth Pilliod, and Robert Gaston have debated Cox-Rearick's assertion that Cosimo was the chapel's dominant patron.[37] Despite attempts to claim Eleonora as the chapel's dominant patron, in all of the decorative stages of the chapel's history, analysis of the primary sources and documents leaves no doubt that Cosimo was the chapel's initial patron, who later ceded control of the room to Eleonora. The sources and documents discussed below make the chapel's patronage succession clear, although, even in the early stages, Cosimo consulted Eleonora. Hence, the chapel is a product of coordinated and successive patronage by the ducal couple, where first one then the other was in control of the room's decorations, which they coordinated together from its inception.

Finally, a comprehensive analysis of Eleonora's Spanish lineage is presented here, which demonstrates her close kinship to Emperor Charles V, who was a distant cousin of Eleonora's. This familial tie, or *emparentado*, brought the Medici into a family relationship with Europe's most powerful Catholic ruler. In considering the program of Eleonora's chapel, it is important to understand her identity, as a Catholic, and her heritage and lineage, as the descendant of families that had a venerable history of supporting the Church. Thus, for Eleonora, for whom Catholic orthodoxy was a marker of her identity as a Spanish aristocrat and a kinswoman to the Holy Roman Emperor, only an orthodox Catholic program for her chapel could have been acceptable.

ELEONORA'S ANCESTRY

Eleonora (Leonor/a) de Toledo was a prize bride for Cosimo de' Medici, as she was the daughter of Don Pedro Álvarez de Toledo y Zuñíga (1484–1553), Viceroy of Naples (1532–52), and María Osorio Pimentel, the second Marquesa de Villafranca del Bierzo (1498–1539).[38] In 1539, when Eleonora married Cosimo de' Medici, she was in her late teens. Likely born in her father's family home at Alba de Tómes, near Salamanca, Eleonora was raised in Spain and then at the Neapolitan court, to which she was brought in 1534, two years after Don Pedro became its Viceroy.[39]

Born in Spain and living at the Spanish Neapolitan court, Eleonora did not learn Italian until her engagement to Cosimo, and, although she learned to write and speak Italian, she always preferred Spanish and the company of Spaniards.[40] Because the Neapolitan court was closely linked to the emperor's court, Eleonora was raised in an aristocratic atmosphere of luxury superior to that of the Florentine court.[41] Charles V's approval of Eleonora's marriage to Cosimo meant that he understood that Cosimo's fealty was important, and to secure it he allowed him to marry into one of Spain's most illustrious families and one to which he was closely related. Cosimo demonstrated appropriate gratitude in the complex wedding *apparato* that celebrated his marriage to Eleonora (1539) and his special connection, through her, to the emperor.[42]

Eleonora and the emperor shared royal ancestors. They were third cousins, as they were both descended from Alfonso XI de Castilla (1311–50)—she from the wrong side of the royal blanket. While the emperor was the product of official lines of descent, Eleonora's side was descended from Don Fadríque Alfonso, Maestro de la Orden de Santiago and first Conde de Haro (1335–58), the illegitimate son of Alfonso XI and Leonor de Guzmán (1310–51), the great-great-granddaughter of King Alfonso IX de Castilla and León.[43] Charles V was also descended from Alfonso IX, this descent providing another family tie between the Medici and the emperor. Thus, the Trastámara ancestors shared by Eleonora and Charles V, were founded by a woman named Leonor—a resonance and an ancestral history that would have been clear to the Spaniards at the Florentine court and to the emperor as well. As a result of this history, Eleonora's children were fourth cousins to the emperor, and the Medici carried illustrious blood in their veins henceforth.

Eleonora's direct line of descent from kings began with Alfonso XI and Leonora de Guzmán, who was the great-granddaughter of Alfonso IX, King of Castile and León. Attached to Eleonora's name is a history of succession that is intertwined with that of the family of Charles V and the history of Spain that Eleonora brought to Florence. This history and its significance for the Medici is briefly outlined below. Their son Fadrique Alfonso married Juana de Mendoza, and their son, Fadrique Enriquez de Mendoza, married Mariana Fernández de Córdoba y Ayála y Toledo. Fadrique and Mariana's son García Álvarez de Toledo y Carrillo married María Enríquez de Quiñones y Cossines, and García and María's son Fadrique Álvarez de Toledo married Isabel de Zúñiga, and they in turn begat Don Pedro Álvarez de Toledo, who married María Ossorio de Pimentel, these being Eleonora's parents.

The liaison between Alfonso XI and Leonor de Guzmán produced ten children, something that augured well for Eleonora's fecundity. The Guzmáns, although Catholic, were reputedly of Jewish blood, as Francisco Layna Serrano stated in his history of the Mendoza, although he did not provide documentation for this assertion.[44] If Layna Serrano's statement is accurate, this Jewish ancestry would have made the Mosaic scenes in Eleonora's chapel especially resonant for her.

King Alfonso so loved Leonor de Guzmán that he left Queen María de Portugal to live with Leonor in Seville, where Leonor was allowed to be present during governmental discussions.[45] Despite Leonor's privileged position and birth, she met an untimely end: soon after Alfonso's death in 1350, Pedro de Castilla and María de Portugal had Leonor imprisoned and later executed. Nonetheless, Eleonora's name was associated with a very unusual and accomplished woman who played a role in governing Castile. When Cosimo left Eleonora in charge of the government of Florence, as his Consort, there was family resonance for her stewardship, in the example provided by Eleonora's ancestress. However, although Eleonora performed competently during Cosimo's absences in 1541 and 1543, assisted by the ducal secretaries, it should be noted that court records document that she was not comfortable either being without Cosimo's presence or ruling in his absence.[46] Thus, Eleonora was not as comfortable with playing a prominent role at court as the original Leonor had been. Nonetheless, Eleonora's ancestry had destined her for the role of occasional regent, and she performed it well, with assistance from the capable court secretaries.[47]

Eleonora's direct line of descent continued with Leonor and Alfonso XI's son, Don Fadríque Alfonso, Maestre de la Ordén de Santiago y Señor de Haro (1334–58). Don Fadríque Alfonso's son, Don Alfonso Enríquez, Primer Admiral de Castilla and Duque de Medína de Ríoseco (1354–1429), married Juana de Mendoza (1360–1431), the daughter of Pedro González de Mendoza (1340–85) and Aldónza de Ayála (c. 1354–1451). Juana de Mendoza became the great-grandmother of King Fernando de Aragón, as her granddaughter, Juana Enríquez (1425–68) was his mother. Eleonora's Mendoza ancestors became supporters of the Castilian monarchs through these marriages, which connected them to the Trastámaras; hence, they aligned themselves with Henry II, the first Trastámara King of Castile (1333/34–79), after Henry defeated Pedro de Castilla (1313–57) at the Battle of Montiel (1369).

When Fernando de Aragón married Isabel de Castilla (1469), of the house of Trastámara, two lines of descent connected to Eleonora came together in the grandparents of Emperor Charles V, lines of ancestry that passed to Cosimo and Eleonora's children. Spanish courtiers visiting Florence, as well as the Mendoza at the Florentine court, familiar with the Mendoza's reputation for fecundity would have been able to place Eleonora within this familial and cultural history, as the descendant of royal houses and a member of this prolific family. Hence, Eleonora de Toledo's acclaimed fecundity was a trope that had a basis in the reputation possessed by her Mendoza ancestors of being remarkably fecund, as a result of their large and surviving families.

Juana de Mendoza's father, Don Pedro González de Mendoza, Senor de Híta y Buitrago, was another noble ancestor of Eleonora's, who linked her family to the powerful Mendoza supporters of the monarchs of Castile.[48] Eleonora's direct ancestral line continued with Don Fadríque Enríquez de Mendoza (1390–1473), who was the son of Don Alfonso and Juana de Mendoza. Don Fadrique was also the second Admiral de Castilla, Conde de Melgar y Rueda and Segundo Duque de Medína del Ríoseco, Maestro de la Orden de Santiago, Señor de Castroverde y Torrelogatón. He married Mariana Fernández de Córdoba y Ayála y Toledo (1394–1431), and it was their daughter, Juana Enríquez (1425–68), who became the mother of Fernando de Aragón—the offspring of her marriage to King Juan II, de Aragón (1398–1479), Charles V's grandfather.

Eleonora's next set of ancestors were descended from Don Fadríque and Mariana's daughter, Maria Enríquez de Quiñones y Cossínes, who married García Álvarez de Toledo y Carrillo, first duke of Alba de Tórmes (1451–1504). García Álvarez de Tórmes' father, Hernándo Álvarez de Toledo, Primer Conde de Alba de Tormes, was a supporter of King Enrique IV, another member of the Trastámara family. Hernando Álvarez's marriage to Mencía de Carrillo, Señora de Bercimuelle, introduced another aristocratic line into Eleonora's ancestry, one to which the famous Archbishop of Toledo, Alfonso Carrillo (1410–82), belonged.[49]

In the war of the Castilian Succession (1475–79), Hernando Álvarez fought on the side of Queen Isabel de Castilla against the claims to the Crown of Castilla being made by Juana, "La Beltráneja" (1460–1530), the daughter of the wife of King Enrique IV de Castilla (1425–74), Juana de Portugal (1439–35).[50] As Enrique IV was known to be impotent—at best—Juana "La Beltráneja" was thought to be the child of Juana de Portugal and Beltrán de La Cueva, one of Enrique's courtiers. In 1476, at the Battle of Toro, Isabel won over Juana "La Beltráneja's" army with the assistance of the Mendoza family, especially that of Cardinal Pedro González de Mendoza (1428–95), Archbishop of Toledo from 1482.[51]

At the Battle of Toro, Eleonora de Toledo's ancestor Hernándo Álvarez de Toledo supported Isabel so thoroughly that the de Toledo family became part of the group of families who were especially favored by Isabel and Fernando. In 1527, Charles V declared these families, identified by historian Helen Nader as the Nájera families (those closest to the Crown for faithful service since the Middle Ages), to be *Famílias Primadas de España*—foremost among them were Eleonora's Mendoza ancestors.[52] To be counted among the *Famílias Primadas* meant that Eleonora and her children belonged to some of the highest ranking families of European aristocrats, linked to the emperor by ties of blood, religious affiliation, and politics. Thus, Eleonora was multiply related to Charles V. This is a heritage that was noted in the chapel's program, in the quartered Toledo/Medici arms that were placed at the center of the chapel's ceiling.

Closer to Eleonora's birth were her next set of ancestors, Fadríque Álvarez de Toledo, Segundo Duque de Alba (1460–1531), whose wife was Isabél de Zúñiga, Condesa de Sevilla (1470–1520). Fadrique was the son of García Álvarez de Toledo and María Enríquez, the sister of Juana Enríquez (mother of Fernando de Aragón). Fadríque and Isabél were the parents of Eleonora's father, Don Pedro Álvarez de Toledo y Zúñiga (1484–1553). Don Pedro married María Osorio de Pimentél, Marquesa de Villafranca del Bierzo (1497/99–1530), whose mother was Juana Osorio de Pimentél, Segunda Marquesa de Villafranca del Bierzo (1470–91). Juana Osorio died when María Ossorio was a child, thus María Ossorio was raised at the court of Isabél de Castilla, as was discussed by Robert Gaston.[53]

Eleonora de Toledo, Cosimo's ducal consort, was descended from the kings of Spain, from the fecund Mendoza, and from the reputedly *converso* Guzmáns — altogether an illustrious and prominently Catholic ancestry, rich with iconographic material for the programs that would be devised at the Medici court to extol the advantages she brought to Florence. Charles V, knowing Eleonora's family history, approved this marriage for Cosimo, understanding that it would tie their families together and make Cosimo a very close ally. A fortunate name, resonant with love and rule and fecundity, also gave Eleonora (Leonor) de Toledo the same name as that of Charles V's sister, Leonor (1498–1558), who married Manuel I of Portugal and then Francis I of France. With his marriage to Eleonora, Cosimo acquired family ties to the French court as well as to the Spanish court, compounded for him by Maria de Medici's marriage to Henry II, son of Francis I.[54]

It is not then surprising that subsequent marriages of the ducal offspring to aristocratic and royal houses were made easily, as, through Eleonora, they too were of high aristocratic and royal blood. In marrying Eleonora, Cosimo inextricably linked himself to a Catholic history that encompassed the dominant Catholic powers of European religious politics — the Holy Roman Emperor and the King of France. Additionally, he had married a woman whose own adherence to orthodox Catholicism was made manifest in her documented observance of daily devotions and in her patronage of the Jesuits she brought to Florence, starting in 1546. It is, therefore, doubtful that the descendant of such Catholic, Spanish royalty and aristocracy would worship in a chapel that was not in keeping with the dogma and ritual of the Church.

Eleonora, The Jesuits and Florentine Orthodoxy

Eleonora's support of the Jesuits was a strong statement of her allegiance to Rome and its orthodox traditions, as the Jesuits were the order that most faithfully served the pope.[56] The first Jesuit to arrive in Florence was Juan de Polanco, who arrived in 1546. In 1547, Diego Laínez replaced Polanco. Elpidio Ugoletti replaced Laínez in 1551. The Jesuits in Florence served as Eleonora's confessors and as her children's spiritual tutors. The lack of Jesuit censure of the chapel is additional evidence that its program was orthodox. After the first arrival of the Jesuits, Eleonora was instrumental in persuading Cosimo to allow the Jesuits to establish a school in Florence, something that Cosimo was reluctant to do, as he was suspicious of Jesuit connections to the Savonarolan *piagnoni*, who were still in Florence. Cosimo allowed the Jesuits to organize a school only after the Jesuits had distanced themselves from the problematic Dominicans.

In supporting the Jesuits, Eleonora was not just providing her family with spiritual instruction; she was also enacting the good works necessary for salvation advised by the Roman Church. Both Eleonora and Cosimo regularly donated money to Roman Catholic churches and charities, in keeping with the Roman prescription of good works as being a necessary part of the process of salvation.[57] Good works on the part of the ducal couple and their Roman devotional practices matched Cosimo's consistent policy of developing influence at the papal court assisted by Eleonora's kinsman, Cardinal Juán Álvarez de Toledo (1488–1557).[58] Thus, Cosimo's Vatican politics, family ties, and good works presented a comprehensive allegiance to Rome.

As Eleonora's chapel arguably provided a statement of fealty to the Roman Church, it supported Cosimo's agenda of increasing his control among members of the high Roman clergy. In her devotional space, Eleonora immersed herself in the liturgical season in which her son had been born. Surrounded by scenes of Moses and of the virtuous Israelites, who adhered to the orthodox path along which Moses led them, Eleonora worshipped in a Florence guarded by Cosimo, who performed the leadership role exemplified by Moses, depicted on the walls of her chapel. Moses was the leader known for his unwavering adherence to the path of orthodoxy, and the choice of Moses in the chapel, figuratively corresponding to Cosimo as the Duke of Florence, was an intentional statement that Cosimo would uphold orthodoxy, as had his alter ego.

As the descendant of families so intrinsically linked to the Roman Church that their support of the Church was part of their lineage and their personal identities, Eleonora's understanding of her chapel's program, based on the Lenten readings of the Church, encompassed a historical as well as devotional awareness of its significance. In her chapel and in Florence, Cosimo was the exemplary leader and Eleonora the virtuous ducal consort who had fulfilled her destiny, bringing honor, wealth, and offspring to the Medici duke.[59] Eleonora's consistent affiliation to the Roman Church was evident in her choice of a Book of Hours and a Prayer Book written in accordance with the usage of Rome.

THE ROMAN LITURGY AND ELEONORA'S BOOK OF HOURS AND PRAYER BOOK

In their discussions of Eleonora's chapel, both Cox-Rearick and Gaston briefly mentioned the existence of Eleonora's Book of Hours, now in the Victoria and Albert Museum (MSL/1953/1792).[60] This manuscript was comprehensively published and interpreted by Rowan Watson, who brought attention to a matching Prayer Book, in Spanish (private collection).[61] Both manuscripts are dated to February 1540 (Florentine style 1541), which indicates that the devotional books were completed about six weeks before Francesco's birth and two years after Eleonora and Cosimo's marriage.

Neither the miniatures nor the *marginalia* of Eleonora's Hours or Prayer Book were the work of a major artist, but the selection of the artists was significant, because the workshop to which they belonged had already produced at least one Medici manuscript. In determining authorship for the illustrations, Watson concurred with an earlier attribution of the larger miniatures to Michele Tosini or his circle, suggesting that the *marginalia* was the work of Boccardino Giovane.[62] Boccardino Giovane and his father, Boccardino

Vecchio, were the illuminators of the Book of Hours made for Alessandro de' Medici and his Spanish bride, Margaret of Austria, the illegitimate daughter of Charles V. This Hours is now in Rome in the collection of the Biblioteca Corsiniana (MS Cod. 55.K.16).[63]

The commission of Eleonora's Hours from the workshop that produced the Hours for Alessandro de' Medici and Margaret of Austria could be understood as a matter of expediency, as the workshop was familiar with Medici insignia and able to provide devotional manuscripts in accordance with the use of Rome. It could indicate that Cosimo played a patronage role in the commission of Eleonora's Hours and that he made a selection in keeping with traditions binding the Medici and Florence to the emperor and Rome. For Cosimo, who inherited the title of duke from Alessandro, continuity was important, as was placing emphasis on his relationship to Charles V, who officially mourned Alessandro's death, with great pomp.[65] Thus, selecting the Boccardino workshop to produce a Rome Use Book of Hours and a corresponding Prayer Book indicates a political decision that emphasized interaction between the Roman Church, the Medici, and the Imperial court, and these were *topoi* that also governed the programmatic choices made in Eleonora's chapel.

In Eleonora's Hours, style had meaning, and that meaning was linked to Eleonora's position as a member of international, European, Catholic aristocracy. While the style of the miniatures conforms to a late Quattrocento Florentine style, similar to that of Ghirlandaio or even very early Raphael, the borders are in the Ghent-Bruges style popular in the Netherlands and Spain during the early sixteenth century. The Ghent-Bruges style also emerged in Toledan manuscripts made from the end of the fifteenth century to the middle of the sixteenth, and the employment of this style in Eleonora's Hours alluded to her family's source city.[63] The political implications of a style associated with Spain and the Netherlands would have been clear to those who understood the connections between the Medici and the Imperial court. Linked to Rome, through the devotional content of the Hours and the Prayer Book, Eleonora's devotional books indicate that her prayers conformed to orthodox practice.[64]

Coordinated Patronage in Eleonora's Chapel

The primary function of Eleonora's chapel was to provide her with a space for the private celebration of the Mass and for personal prayer. Yet, the room was part of a larger renovation project that was controlled by Cosimo, as he shaped his family home to reflect his role as Florence's hereditary ruler. Developing the chapel's program required cooperation between Cosimo and Eleonora, and between the ducal couple and Bronzino, all three working with a program adviser. Such an adviser needed to be familiar with the history, emblems, and iconographic devises of the Medici and the liturgy of the Roman and Mozarabic Rite. Among the court's scholars, Pierfrancesco Riccio, an ordained priest, would have possessed the theological and liturgical knowledge required by the chapel's program. As Cosimo's childhood tutor and the palace's *majordomo*, Riccio also had the requisite secular knowledge of Medici history and emblems necessary for providing the political and dynastic aspects of the chapel's program.[66]

In *The Crossing of the Red Sea*, Cox-Rearick identified a portrait of Riccio in the face of the priest, Eleazar, depicted standing next to Moses.[67] The face and long, black beard of the fresco's priest matches Riccio's appearance, as recorded in the contemporary portraits to which Cox-Rearick compared Eleazar's features. Riccio's priesthood and his relationship to Cosimo is a correlate to Eleazar's position as high priest to Moses. Yet, Cox-Rearick rejected the possibility that Riccio was the program's iconographer in favor of Giambattista Gelli, whom she considered to be a better humanistic scholar than Riccio. However, the combination of religious, secular, and Medicean knowledge required for the chapel's program makes Riccio a stronger candidate than Gelli for having been the program adviser, as does his hands-on approach to administration. In his study of Riccio's interaction with Cosimo's court artists, Alessandro Cecchi pointed out that Riccio's control of the administration of the palace's repurposing was extensive and suggested that it was Riccio who devised and administratively coordinated the palace's programs.[68] The inclusion of his portrait in the chapel argues for his having played an important role in its development. Here, it is assumed that Riccio was the adviser for the chapel's program.

Riccio's intimate knowledge of the Lenten liturgy would have enabled him to select passages with possibilities for the multiple religious, political, and dynastic meanings the program required. The incorporation of the Mozarabic Rite into the program also argues for a priestly ability to work within different liturgical traditions and to understand the connections and parallels that the different orthodox liturgies of the Church shared. In the scenes selected for the chapel, from Exodus, Deuteronomy, and Numbers, the Eucharistic significance of the chapel's central *Pietà* was emphasized in a visual representation of the Old and New Covenants, the fulfillment of which is Christ. Included in the program are dynastic references to the Medici and to Eleonora's fecundity, as has been noted in the chapel's literature, incorporated in the numerous women with children depicted in the room's frescoes.[69] The necessary allusions to the histories and goals of the Medici court would have been easily devised by Riccio, who knew the family's history and would have been familiar with the 1539 wedding decorations in which these themes were first formulated in reference to Eleonora, whose role was defined by the need for an heir and by expectations of exemplary virtue and piety.[70]

Despite the flattering portrayal of Eleonora's virtues and accomplishments found in court visual and literary panegyrics, it is unlikely that she was allowed to unilaterally determine her chapel's program or to work independently with Riccio to develop it. In 1541, Eleonora was still too new to the Florentine court to be completely entrusted with controlling the religious and political statement required for her chapel. Thus, it is suggested here that Cosimo and Riccio, in consultation with Eleonora and Bronzino, devised the chapel's core program, and the sources and documents recording the chapel's progress indicate that this was the process whereby the chapel was decorated, as is discussed below.

Yet, as the sources and documents record, once the initial program was set, Cosimo's interest in the room faded, and Eleonora took control of her chapel, as Cox-Rearick noted.[71] By September 1549, Eleonora had the room's only set of keys, as is documented by a letter from Riccio, asking for the keys, sent from Florence to Poggio a Caiano, where the ducal couple was staying. Riccio's letter, which was published by Cox-Rearick, reported water damage in the *scrittoio*, and he requested Eleonora's keys so that he could check on the chapel to see if damage had occurred there (it had not). It is clear from the available data that Eleonora's chapel was a project undertaken by the ducal couple at the beginning of their marriage and continued by Eleonora as she matured and became a more independent patron. Throughout the changes that are part of the room's history, three programmatic elements remained consistent in the ducal agenda: religion, politics, and dynastic ambition. These linked concerns were evident in the first letter written by Cosimo to Don Pedro soon after he and Eleonora moved into the palace that became their home.

Sources, Documents, History, and Identity in Eleonora's Chapel

The ducal family moved from the old Medici Palace, on the Via Cavour (Via Larga) to their new home on the Piazza della Signoria on 14 May 1540, when Maria, their first child, born on 3 April 1540, was an infant.[72] Afterwards, Cosimo wrote to Don Pedro de Toledo that "The Duchess is vigorous and in good spirits, and today, in the name of Our Lord, she and I took possession of the great palace, where there are regal rooms. May it please our divine Lord for it to turn out well, with good health and increase for us and our offspring ..."[73] Eleonora's regal rooms (*stanze regali*) were on the second floor of the family's new home.[74] They were connected to Cosimo's rooms, on the first floor, by a staircase. Her apartment was constructed under the supervision of Giovanni Battista del Tasso, with the chapel being located on the east side of the *Camera Verde*—the most private area of the *"stanze regali."*[75] The chapel that Tasso constructed for Eleonora is a small room—approximately 14' x 14'—and would not have taken more than a couple of months to construct.[76]

Soon after the move, Eleonora became pregnant with Francesco and the hopes for increased offspring were fulfilled the following Lent, when Francesco was born—on 25 March, the Feast of the Annunciation to the Virgin.[77] The renewal promised by the Feast of the Annunciation, which marked Christ's Incarnation and the beginning of the Florentine New Year, indicated that Francesco's birth was an auspicious Florentine event, and as such, the child's birth was referenced in the chapel's decorations.[78] The ducal heir

was born in the former Palazzo della Signoria or Palazzo dei Priori, which in becoming the ducal residence transformed into a sign
of the new Florentine order of government formed by a dynastic
and religious destiny that would become Francesco's inheritance.[79]
Within six months of Francesco's birth, Bronzino began to work on
the chapel's decorations.[80] Thus, the initiation of the chapel's decorations and Eleonora's fulfillment of her role as *genitrix* were tem-
porally proximate.

As is recorded in the inscriptions scratched into the frame of the
chapel's door, Bronzino had begun work on the frescoes before 6
September 1541, having already finished the ceiling by that date.[81]
Using the door's inscriptions, the *giornate* for the walls, and the surviving documents, Cox-Rearick developed a comprehensive chronology for the chapel's frescoes.[82] The chronological parameters
suggested by Cox-Rearick were: the chapel's ceiling took forty-sev-
en days and was finished by 6 September 1541, when work began
on *The Crossing of the Red Sea* (Fig. 3) on the south wall (completed 30
March 1542), which took sixty days to finish; next came *The Brazen
Serpent* (Fig. 4) on the west wall (begun 5 June 1542) and finished
in forty-six days; followed by *Moses Striking the Rock and the Gathering of Manna* (Fig. 5), on the north wall, which took fifty-five days;
with, perhaps, *The Erythraean Sibyl* and *King David* (Fig. 1) begun
after June 1542, when *Moses Striking the Rock* was completed; and, at
some point, there were painted the Virtues found in the spandrels:
Prudence, Justice, Temperance, and *Fortitude*.[83] However, Cox-Rearick
did not assume that Bronzino worked non-stop; hence, her chronology allows for some deviation from the dates stated in the inscriptions. Documents supporting the general dates for Bronzino's
work recorded by the inscriptions and proposed by Cox-Rearick
have survived, and they record that Cosimo made payments to
Bronzino beginning on 26 May 1543 until 7 July 1543.[84]

The chapel's chronology corresponds to Francesco's Lenten
birth, predictable because the pregnancy began in July 1540. This
pregnancy would have enabled the development of a projected
general Lenten program that could include the specific reference to
the birth of an heir, if the child was male. After Francesco's birth on
25 March, and before the walls were begun on 6 September, there
was ample time to develop additional programmatic details that

would directly reference the new heir. This aspect of the program was discussed by Cox-Rearick, who focused attention on the presence of the ceiling's Saint Francis and on other dynastic references in the chapel's program.[85] If the general plan for the chapel's decorations and program began with Eleonora's pregnancy in July 1540 and was finalized after Francesco's birth on 25 March 1541, there was close to a year for developing the chapel's general and then its more specific program, which emphasized Francesco's significance.

Had the child been a girl, the Lenten program would still have fulfilled the devotional function of the room as well as its religious politics, as such a program would have identified the Medici court as supporters of the Roman liturgy and its dogmatic foundation. References to a male heir would have been omitted from such a program, but its overarching message of orthodox religious allegiance would have been desired and appropriate nonetheless. The ducal couple was, however, fortunate in Francesco's birth, which enabled the chapel's program to encompass religious, political, and dynastic elements. The chapel's program thus became multi-valent, and, as Vasari described, Cosimo and Eleonora each took part in making the decisions about the chapel's permanent and changing decorative parts.

Vasari's *Vite* and Eleonora's Chapel

In the 1550 edition of his *Vite*, Vasari included an account of Bronzino's work in his biography of Raffaellino del Garbo, where he described the commission of Eleonora's chapel as follows: "... ne fanno fede alcuni ritratti et opera di sua mano appresso lo illustríssimo et eccellentissimo signor Duca Cosimo nella guardaroba, e per la illustríssima signora duchessa la cappella lavorata in fresco ..."[86] For those who seek to identify Eleonora as the chapel's sole patron, this account could seem to be conclusive evidence for Eleonora's patronage.[87] However, Vasari's 1568 *Vite* tells a different story.

In the 1568 *Vite*, Vasari gave Bronzino his own *Vita*, and he began his discussion of the chapel's decorations by associating Bronzino's work in the chapel with his designs for the 1539 wedding decorations when he wrote: "E nelle nozze ... fece [Bronzino] ... le migliori pitture ché fussero fate in quell' apparato. Lá dove il duca, conosciuta la virtú di quest'uomo, gli fece metter mano a fare

nel suo ducale palazzo una cappella non molto grande per la detta
signora duchessa." As noted above, the chapel measures approximately 14 sq. ft. and is a small room.[88] In this description, Vasari
stated that it was Cosimo who ordered Bronzino "gli fece metter
mano a fare nel suo ducal palazzo una cappella ... per la detta signora duchessa," thus clarifiying, in 1568, the syntax and meaning
of his earlier statement—"per la illustríssima signora duchessa"—
by giving explicit patronage credit to Cosimo, who had the chapel
painted "per" Eleonora.[89] Unless Vasari deliberately lied in the second edition, the 1568 account provides a straightforward record of
events: Cosimo hired Bronzino to paint the chapel for Eleonora's
possession as her personal devotional space.

But, as time passed, the chapel's patronage changed, and Vasari
proceeded, in 1568, to describe Eleonora becoming more active in
her control of the chapel, after he credits Cosimo with initiating the
commission. Specifically, he noted that she made changes to the
altar wall:

> Nella tavola di questa cappella, fatta a olio, che fu posta so-
> pra l'altare, era Cristo deposto di croce in grembo alla ma-
> dre; ma ne fu levata dal duca Cosimo per mandarla, come
> cosa raríssima, a donare a Granvela, maggiore uomo che
> già fusse appresso Carlo V imperatore. In luogo della qual
> tavola ne ha fatto una simile il medesimo, e postála sopra
> l'altare in mezzo a due quadri non manco belli che la tavola;
> dentro i quali sono l'Angelo Gabriello e la Vergine da lui
> annunziata. Ma in cambio di questi, quando ne fu levata
> la prima tavola, erano un San Giovanni Batista ed un San
> Cosimo, che furono messi in guardaroba quando la signora
> duchessa, mutato pensiero, fece fare questi altri due.[90]

Thus, Vasari records that the first *Pietà* (1545) was given—by
Cosimo—to Nicolas Perrenot de Granvelle, the Keeper of the Seals
for Charles V.[91] The second *Pietà* was placed on the altar wall in
1553, as is recorded in surviving documents and published by Cox-
Rearick; as Vasari described, it was placed there between the new
lateral panels of *The Annunciation* which Eleonora commissioned.[92]

Vasari does not tell us what, if anything, took the place of the first *Pietà* between 1545 and 1553. But he was explicit in stating that the second *Pietà* was placed between the panels of *The Annunciation*, which are surely those still in place.[93] This seems a very precise statement recording the contemporary manufacture of the second *Pietà* and *The Annunciation*. Vasari also noted that the panels featuring "San Giovanni Batista ed un San Cosimo" were then placed in the "guardaroba" after they were removed from the chapel, and they were indeed inventoried there in 1553.[94] Unless it is accepted that the second *Pietà* stood alone on the altar wall for the rest of Eleonora's life, it would seem that Vasari correctly described the order of replacement and the chronology of this change.

In the 1568 edition of the *Vite*, Vasari recorded, in a detailed straightforward manner, a changing situation of alternating patronage decisions. The first set of lateral panels featured St. John the Baptist, patron saint of Giovanni delle Bande Nere, Cosimo's father, and Cosmas, Cosimo's patron. These panels were more meaningful to Cosimo than to Eleonora, and they were decidedly masculine in subject. In the second set of panels, Eleonora exchanged the male saints for the more feminine subject of *The Annunciation*, which explicitly celebrated her son's birth on 25 March, the event that secured her increasing power at court. Commissioning *The Annunciation* was in keeping with Eleonora's special veneration for the Virgin, expressed in her Book of Hours, in a special Mass of the Virgin illustrated with a full-page miniature of the Annunciation, the second Annunciation in the Hours.[95] This special veneration preceded Francesco's birth but became charged with new meaning after he was born. Thus, the chapel's Annunciation reflects Eleonora's special devotion to the Virgin Mary and to the Catholic cult of the Virgin, as well as to the Lenten Feast, which commemorates Christ's Incarnation.

SALVIATI'S LAMENTATION AND THE SECOND PIETÀ

Although Vasari does not tell us what replaced the first *Pietà* during the eight years that separate the first from the second *Pietà*, it is unlikely that the center of the altar wall was left empty for so long. Cox-Rearick suggested that a tapestry of *The Lamentation* (Fig. 6), now in the Uffizi, designed by Francesco Salviati and woven by Nicholas Karcher, filled the gap left by the removal of the first *Pietà*.[96] Karcher was the Flemish weaver brought to Florence by Cosimo to oversee his newly founded enterprise intended to make Florence a center of tapestry manufacturing. Support for Cox-Rearick's suggestion that the Salviati *Lamentation* replaced the first *Pietà* is found in a letter, from Sforza Almeni to Riccio, dated 8 April 1550, which records that Eleonora ordered a copy of it to be made to be sent to Spain as a gift, and it states that the tapestry is in the "oratorio," which is how the chapel was also identified (it was also called a *cappella*).[97] As Cox-Rearick discussed, the Salviati/Karcher tapestry was delivered on 31 July 1546, a year after the first *Pietà* was removed, and as it is the same size as that work, its placement on the altar wall did not require additional changes for it to be placed between the panels of *Sts. John the Baptist and Cosmas*. The replacement of the first *Pietà* by a tapestry that was the first product of Cosimo's tapestry works suggests that the decision to have a tapestry occupy the center of the altar wall developed from Cosimo's desire to show off this new Florentine product in the chapel. In 1553, when the second *Pietà* was installed in the chapel, the tapestry was put away in the *guardaroba* and identified as a "panno d'altare."[98] This nomenclature makes the room's liturgical function specific, and the timing of the tapestry's being sent into storage argues that it was on the altar wall until the second *Pietà* replaced it.

The design of the Salviati *Lamentation*'s border is notably similar to that found in the *marginalia* of the Hours of Eleonora, as both are decorated with similarly disposed arrangements of Medici heraldic devices and both include the combined Medici/Toledo arms. Among emblems shared by the tapestry and the Hours are: Cosimo's Capricorn *impresa*, on the lower right (which he shared with Charles V and the Emperor Augustus), and the interlaced Medici *diamante*, in the middle on the left.[99] As the manuscripts were completed in 1541 and the tapestry was delivered five years later, it is clear that the tapestry's border was designed to match Eleonora's Hours. After using the Hours in the chapel for five years, it is likely that it was Eleonora who wanted the tapestry's border to match those in her Hours. If so, this may be the earliest instance of Eleonora's personal patronage expressed in the chapel, although her patronage became evident in a tapestry that was the product of Cosimo's founding of Florentine tapestry manufacturing. As such, this indicates coordinated patronage on the part of the ducal couple, as they continued to share decisions about the chapel.

The Chapel's Annunciation: Patronage and Liturgy

By 1553, Eleonora was not the inexperienced young bride who was consulted by her husband as he made decisions about her chapel. Instead, she was fully the Duchess Eleonora in charge of her chapel and free to express her preferences, which she did, as Vasari chronicled, by exchanging the Medicean/male subjects of the first panels for the more feminine *Annunciation*, which directly referenced 25 March, the birthday of Francesco and the day on which she secured her place at court. In 1553, when the second *Pietà* was installed in the chapel, Eleonora had been married to Cosimo for fourteen years and had borne several sons and daughters.[100] She had also developed working relationships with Florentine artists, such as Bronzino, Cellini, and Bandinelli and had made the real estate purchase of the Pitti Palace (1549).[101] Working with financial advisers, she had increased her wealth, which she used to furnish and renovate the Medici homes and to purchase clothing, jewelry, and textiles, all of which she used to enhance her family's status and social position.[102]

If Vasari accurately recorded the placement of the *Annunciation* on the altar wall at the same time as that of the second Pietà, in 1553, it would be a commission reflective of Eleonora's new status in Florence. However, dating *The Annunciation* presents problems, because there are a series of documents in the Medici *guardaroba* that seem to conflict with Vasari's assertion that *The Annunciation* was placed at the same time as the second *Pietà*.

The documents in question were published by Cox-Rearick, and they record that in 1563–64, there were additional purchases of wood for a *tavola* for the chapel, followed by payments for making and gilding frames for *The Annunciation*.[103] These documents can be construed as a progression—-from purchase for wood, completion of painting, followed by frames—that would date *The Annunciation* to 1564, two years after Eleonora's death, the date suggested by Cox-Rearick for the panels.[104] There is also a letter dated 15 April 1564 from Bronzino to Cosimo, thanking the duke for continuing to pay his stipend, which Cox-Rearick linked to *The Annunciation*, although the letter does not mention the work.[105] Yet, Vasari clearly states that *The Annunciation* was put in place, with the second *Pietà*, which was delivered in 1553, thus the documents seem to contradict Vasari.

However, Carolyn Smyth suggested that this chronological conundrum could be resolved if the documents recording a purchase of wood respond to the desire for new frames for *The Annunciation*.[106] Smyth proposed that when *The Annunciation* was placed alongside the second *Pietà*, in 1553, it was put in the old frames made for the first set of lateral panels, as the four panels are the same size. Thus, she interpreted the later documents as being payments for new frames for the work, thereby resolving the existing conundrum—if her suggestion is accepted as accurately reflective of the situation. Whether the panels were placed in the chapel in 1553 or 1564, their meaning in the chapel's program and context remains the same—they record Eleonora's veneration for the Annunciation, the birth of Francesco on that Feast, and a feminization of the room that was an expression of her patronage.

After Eleonora's death, Cosimo again took charge of the room. In 1564, *The Annunciation* was fitted for new frames, as the chapel was being readied for Joanna of Austria's occupancy of the room, prior to her marriage to Francesco on 18 December 1565.[107] As additional preparation for this event, Bronzino finished cleaning the room on 17 February 1565, six months before the wedding. In the early 1580s, it was Bianca Cappello who used the room, after her marriage to Francesco, announced on 10 June 1579.[108] At that time, the last stages of the room's decoration were enacted.

Bianca Cappello's tenancy coincided with structural changes, made in the early 1580s, which included a door being cut into the east wall and the blocking of the window that had been there when Tasso finished the room for Eleonora.[109] To cover the plaster over the closed-up window, there was commissioned, possibly from Alessandro Allori, *The Angels with Chalice, Host and Globe* and perhaps the replacement of the ceiling's Medici/Toledo arms with *The Trinity*. Neither the *Angels* nor *The Trinity* have anything to do with the chapel's original program. They reflect a later, post-Counter Reformation, religious climate, and they should be discounted in interpretations that seek to elucidate the programmatic intentions of Cosimo and Eleonora, coordinated with the chapel's function.

However the issue of the 1560s documents and Vasari's information about *The Annunciation* is interpreted in developing a chronology for the chapel's decorations, the subject of the Annunciation, represented twice in Eleonora's Hours and in the lateral panels of her chapel's altarpiece, can be linked to the Roman liturgical significance of this Marian feast, an expression of the Church's cult of the Virgin. Thus, the chapel's *Annunciation* reinforces the Roman aspects of Eleonora's devotional practices, confirmed by the Rome Use of her Hours and the prayer, written by Pope Leo X, found in her Prayer Book.[110] Additionally, the chapel's *Pietà* indicates Lent as the liturgical season most applicable to the chapel's devotional program, and the panels of the *Annunciation* emphasize this season and its special devotional and dynastic significance for Eleonora.

Lent and The Annunciation

The direct celebration of the Annunciation to the Virgin emerges in the Roman Lenten liturgy on 25 March in the Communion reading, which is Isaiah 7:14: "Behold a Virgin shall conceive, bring forth a Son, and His Name shall be called Emmanuel."[111] On the Feast of the Annunciation, the liturgy of that day emphasizes the connections between the Annunciation, the Incarnation, and salvation through the Resurrection, linking these to Eucharistic Transubstantiation.[112] The special Mass to the Virgin found in Eleonora's Hours (fols. 92v–112) expands on the significance of Christ's birth, with the words of John 1 (fol. 92v): "In the beginning was the word ..." and ends with the passage:

> ... Out of his full store we have all received grace upon grace; for while the Law was given through Moses, grace and truth came through Jesus Christ. No one has ever seen God; but God's only Son, he who is nearest to the Father's heart he has made him known.

John's text for the special Mass appears by the page featuring the Annunciation, and the text's content would have brought attention simultaneously to the Mosaic scenes on the walls and to the second set of lateral panels, every time this Mass was celebrated in the chapel or its text was read as part of Eleonora's devotions. Given Eleonora's special devotion to the Virgin and to the Annunciation, twice depicted in her Hours, Francesco's birth must have seemed a miraculous confirmation of Eleonora's faith in the Virgin Mary. With the Lenten celebration of the Feast of the Annunciation, which includes Isaiah's prophecy, attention would again be drawn to the altarpiece and to Eleonora's veneration of the Feast and to her dynastic triumph. When the child was born male, the celebratory program was set, and it had a personal as well as a religious meaning for the ducal couple. Thus, the role played by Lent in the chapel's program can be directly seen as being connected to Francesco's birth, which was predictable as being destined to occur during Lent.

THE CHAPEL AND THE LENTEN LITURGY OF THE ROMAN RITE

Eleonora's chapel, as Cox-Rearick pointed out, is not unique in employing the Lenten liturgy for its essential program.[113] In her study, Cox-Rearick noted that the closest precedent for Eleonora's chapel is the Sistine Chapel, thereby linking Eleonora's chapel to the most important Roman chapel. The similarity of the program, most evident in the frescoes featuring Moses, would have provided an immediate and clear connection between Florence and Rome that would have been perceived by visitors to Eleonora's chapel.[114] The Sistine Chapel's program, as Carol Lewine has discussed, is based on the Lenten liturgy, and the connections between Lent's readings and the images in the Sistine Chapel would have been clear to Renaissance visitors to the room. Visitors at the Florentine court familiar with the Lenten readings and with the Sistine Chapel's program would have immediately understood the program of Eleonora's chapel and its connections to Lent and to the Roman chapel of the popes. [115]

Lent significantly consolidates the Church's teachings on the Eucharist, Transubstantiation, Baptism, Penance, and healing through Salvation. These themes are part of the core program of Eleonora's chapel, and they are given visual form in the selection of scenes and saints found in the chapel's paintings and frescoes, which together express the core beliefs of the Roman Church. Lent, in the Catholic Church, began and still begins with the *Tempus Septuagesimae*, on the sixth Sunday after the Feast of the Epiphany (January 6). [116] In Lent, *Septuagesima* Sunday is followed by *Sexagesimae*

Sunday and *Quinquagesimae* Sunday, followed by Ash Wednesday. After Ash Wednesday, each daily Mass is a Stational Mass, commemorating a specific Roman church and continuing until the first Sunday after Easter.[117] The official Lenten Sundays are: *Dominica Prima in Quadragesima, Dominica Secunda in Quadragesima, Dominica Tertia in Quadragesima, Dominica Quarta in Quadragesima*, Passion Sunday (*Tempus Passionis*), Palm Sunday, and Easter Sunday, following by the Octave of Easter, which ends Lent. The most important days of Lent which are not Sundays are Ash Wednesday, the Ember Days, Holy Thursday, Good Friday, and Holy Saturday, the day on which the catechumens were baptized in the early Church.

The Lenten liturgy emphasizes sacrifice, penance, and salvation, as well as the preparation for Baptism, along with healing and exorcisms of demons from the catechumens, with the greatest emphasis reserved for the Church's teaching on the Eucharist and Transubstantiation. Lent includes passages from Exodus, Deuteronomy, Leviticus, and Numbers, which recount the story of the life of Moses. From the perspective of the Roman Church, these passages prefigure the future events of the life of Christ. As Lent progressed, different parts of Eleonora's chapel were activated by the resonance between the words of the Lenten liturgy and the chapel's paintings and frescoes.

On a more personal level, for Cosimo and Eleonora, the Lenten liturgy incorporated references to the Bridegroom and Bride of the Song of Songs, which enabled suitable allusions to the ducal couple's wedding. Because the Lenten liturgy includes the promises God made to the Israelites about the increase of their descendants who would be "as numerous as the stars in the sky," even the chapel's depiction of numerous women and plentiful children corresponds with Lent's themes and readings. For the recently married Cosimo and Eleonora, who were blessed with the birth of Francesco on the Feast of the Annunciation, these Lenten themes provided a perfect vehicle through which to transmit their political and dynastic good fortune, along with their fealty to the Roman Church and the emperor, who supported the Church.

The Lenten liturgy also emphasized unity for all within the Church, including Jews and Gentiles. Hence, on the chapel's altar wall, the images of the Erythraean Sybil and King David are important for the core program.[118] Angelic themes recur in Lent, as angels assist with casting out demons to enable the souls of the catechumens to achieve the innocence of children, a theme exemplified by the prominent placement of the Archangel Michael, on the ceiling directly above the *Pietà*. Michael is a key image that resonates with the chapel's core program, because he is the Archangel who assists in salvation during the Last Judgment. Lenten associations linked to Baptism and healing exist for Saints John the Baptist and Cosmas. Lent also includes eschatological references represented by *The Brazen Serpent*, an event directly referenced in Lenten readings, such as John 3:13–16 and 1 Corinthians 10:9–11, both being readings that evoke the events recorded in Numbers 21:9, which recounts the incident of the Brazen Serpent.

Numbers 21:9 is read in the Spanish Mozarabic Rite's liturgy of the Feast of the Exaltation of the Cross, a feast thematically linked to Lent.[119] Thus, *The Brazen Serpent* provided a link between Eleonora's national liturgy and that of Rome, as the Roman Church accepted the Mozarabic liturgy as orthodox. As Natali discussed, in his study of the chapel, Lenten eschatological associations, identifiable in *The Brazen Serpent*, also exist for the ceiling's saints: St. John the Evangelist is the author of Revelation; St. Jerome had a special devotion for the events of the Last Judgment; and St. Francis had connections to the Crucifixion, indicated by his Stigmatization.[120] Hence, *The Brazen Serpent* functioned as an ideological and programmatic hinge for the chapel's program, enabling multiple connections to be made, which responded to the room's religious politics. But it is the representations of the events from Exodus and the prominent presence of Moses, in conjunction with the *Pietà*, which explicitly indicate the chapel's Lenten program.

Moses and the Liturgy of the Roman Rite

Moses is introduced into the Lenten liturgy on *Septuagesima* Sunday, with the first *Oratio* of 1 Corinthians 10:1–4:

> You should understand, my brothers, that our ancestors were all under the pillar of cloud, and all of them passed through the Red Sea; and so they all received baptism into the fellowship of Moses in cloud and sea. They all ate the

same supernatural food, and all drank the same supernatural drink; I mean, they all drank from the supernatural rock that accompanied their travels—and that rock was Christ.[121]

The three Mosaic events described in 1 Corinthians 10:1–4 are depicted in Eleonora's chapel and were charged with special meaning at the beginning of Lent: *The Crossing of the Red Sea*, *The Gathering of Manna*, and *Moses Striking Water From The Rock*.

Mosaic passages recur on *Feria IV Quatuor Temporum in Quadragesima*, in the first *Lectio*, when Exodus 24:12–18 was read as the post-Communion *Oratio*, a passage that recounts how God called Moses to the top of the mountain and gave him "the law and the commandments." This reading presented Moses as the guardian of religious orthodoxy, a task in which Joshua assists.[122] The same theme is continued with Deuteronomy 26:15–22, the first *Lectio* read on *Sabbato Quatuor Temporum in Quadragesima*, which promises the reward of "milk and honey" for faithful service.[123] The application of these passages to Cosimo in the service of the Roman Church and the emperor is clear. Expansive territories are part of the reward for fealty to orthodoxy, as is expressed in the second *Lectio* of the same day in Deuteronomy 11:22–25: "... the Lord will drive out all these nations before you and you shall occupy the territory of nations greater and more powerful than you."[124] For the ducal couple, this territorial expansion alluded to their desire to expand into Siena and Pisa, something that was their divine right and blessing, as the result of their fealty to the teachings of the Roman Church.[125]

On *Feria III Post Dominican IV in Quadragesima*, the *Lectio* after the *Secreta* was Exodus 32:7–14 recounting the blasphemous worship of the Golden Calf. This event is not represented in the chapel. Instead, the comparable scene of *The Brazen Serpent* depicts a similar message, through contiguous substitution and linked to the Spanish Mozarabic liturgy's Feast of the Exaltation of the Cross—a feast liturgically related to Lent. The end of Exodus 32:7–14 identifies Moses as the intercessor for his people, who dissuades God from punishment, reminding him that he had promised Abraham that his descendants would be "... countless as the stars in the sky ..." and that he would give them, "... all this land, of which I have spoken, ... for ever."[126] This passage expresses Cosimo's role as defender of orthodoxy, protector of the Florentines, and the head of a dynasty that would be as "countless as the stars in the sky." The message of Exodus 32:7–14 is clear and appropriate for the contemporary religious situation of Cosimo's Florence, which needed to control heterodoxy in order to preserve its standing with the Roman Church. This passage also expresses a desire for the unity for which many hoped, until the Council of Trent made reconciliation impossible.[127] For the ducal couple, the closing promise of this reading—of plentiful posterity and boundless territories—would have been another iteration of their dynastic and political ambitions—their reward for maintaining orthodoxy in their territories.

Abundant progeny is a recurring theme in Lent that corresponded to the wedding *apparato*'s praise of Eleonora's fecundity, as was discussed above. This theme recurred in the Epistle for Ash Wednesday, Joel 2:12–19: "… gather together the people, sanctify the Church, assemble the ancients, gather together the little ones and those who suck at the breasts: let the bridegroom go forth from his bed and the bride out of her bride chamber…"[128] The reference to the Bride and Bridegroom in this passage related directly to Cosimo and Eleonora's marriage, and its explicit description of the little ones and the ones who suck at the breast enables a link to Maria and Francesco, as well as to additional children to come to the ducal couple.

The balance between guardianship of orthodoxy and its reward recurred on the *Feria V Post Dominicam III in Quadragesima*, with the first *Lectio*—Exodus 20:12–24, the text of the Ten Commandments.[129] This theme was reinforced on *Feria IV Post Dominicam de Passigne*, with a similar passage—Leviticus 19:1.2 and 11–19.[130] The extension of God's care for those who preserve correct worship was explained on *Feria VI Post Dominicam III in Quadragesima*, with Numbers 20:2–3 and 6:13, the reading that corresponds to *Moses Striking Water from the Rock*.[131] This passage describes how the unruly Israelites, who doubted in God and Moses, were saved by the intercession of Moses, who asked God to provide drink for the thirsty group. The miracle represented by this narrative is linked simultaneously to the Eucharistic wine and to the sacrament of Baptism, water being liquid life in each case, simultaneously material and spiritual.

The counterpart miracle to the water from the rock was the fall of manna, described in the first *Lectio*, that accompanied the blessing of the palms on Palm Sunday—*In Benedictione Palmarum*, Exodus 15:27 and 16:7.[132] Thus, Bronzino's *Fall of Manna* and *Moses Striking Water from the Rock* were twice referenced in the Lenten liturgy, first by 1 Corinthians 10:1–4 and again on Feria IV after the third Sunday of Lent and on Palm Sunday. The Eucharistic significance of these Mosaic miracles is clear and discussed by Cox-Rearick and Natali. The emphasis on the Eucharist—"the supernatural food"— emphasizes the Roman Church's teaching on Transubstantiation and is an explicit statement of ducal adherence to this dogma.[133]

In *Feria Sexta in Parasceve*, Exodus 12:1–11 was the first *Lectio*, which recounts the institution of Passover, by Moses and Aaron, an event that prefigures the institution of the Eucharist.[134] The reading describing the subsequent destruction of the Egyptians after the crossing of the Red Sea was recited on Holy Saturday, when the fourth *Lectio* read was Exodus 24:24 and 25:1. In this passage, God asks Moses to "Stretch out your hand over the sea, and let the water flow back over the Egyptians ..." This act of Moses caused the Egyptians to be "... swept out to sea ..." and "... not one man was left alive ..." while the Israelites, who had passed over, "... saw the Egyptians lying dead on the sea-shore" ... and then "... Moses and the Israelites sang this song to the Lord."[135] This passage is illustrated on the left side of Bronzino's fresco, and its Eucharistic significance is emphasized by its placement alongside the altar wall, as was discussed by Cox-Rearick and Natali.[136]

The scene on the right side of the Red Sea fresco was identified by Cox-Rearick as *The Investiture of Moses*.[137] Here, this scene is identified as *The Last Teaching of Moses*, because it is this event which corresponds to the readings of the Lenten liturgy, and the chapel's Mosaic scenes closely follow this liturgy. This event corresponds to Deuteronomy 31:22–30, the reading for the eleventh *Lectio* of Holy Saturday. [138] In this narrative, God informed Joshua that he was the leader destined to bring the Israelites to the promised land, as a prelude to instructing Moses to write down the correct form of the teaching, after which Moses was to give his last oral transmission of God's instructions to the Israelites. This last teaching, as God instructed Moses, was given to the assembled Israelites, especially to the elders of the tribes and to the officers of the Israelite army.

The passage emphasizes adherence to orthodoxy but also teaching, stewardship, and continuity—themes that accord with the role that Cosimo assumed as Duke of Florence and, later, Siena and Pisa—which he would pass on to Francesco. Thus, Cox-Rearick's idea that this scene represented the investiture of Joshua and signified a passing on to Francesco's of Cosimo's rule was correct, but the scene itself corresponds not to actual investiture but to the Lenten liturgical passage of the last teaching of Moses. During this teaching, Joshua is instructed to continue leading as Moses had on the path of orthodoxy.

In her interpretation of this scene as *The Investiture of Joshua*, Cox-Rearick identified, as Joshua, the idealized, semi-nude youth who looks at Moses while resting his right hand on a rock, as he gestures out of the fresco with his right. But this beautiful young boy is a generic Israelite who responds to the words of Moses much as a similar idealized youth does in Signorelli's *Last Teaching of Moses*, in the Sistine Chapel. In Signorelli rendition of this scene, the idealized youth is located in the same compositional place, to the spectator's left, as is Bronzino's idealized youth, serving a parallel function. In Bronzino's rendition, the young Israelite reacts to the teaching of Moses, as he points towards the chapel's *Pietà* and to Christ, the rock of salvation of the Lenten Gospel, visible in the *Pietà* and indicated by the rock on which the youth rests his hand.[139]

In Bronzino's rendition of the group surrounding the speaking Moses, he included the "elders" and the "officers" mentioned in Deuteronomy, represented by the standing man with the long, black beard and the kneeling man who wears clothing evocative of armor, as well as by the group of older, bearded men visible behind Moses. A semi-nude youth, in the lower right of the group, reclines against a sword, emphasizing the idea of "officers" and their weapons. Standing, kneeling, sitting, and reclining around Moses are the generations of Israelites—"as plentiful as the stars in the sky"—who will occupy the territories promised to them by God. Among the assembled, the best candidate for Joshua, the next leader described in the Lenten text from Deuteronomy, is the mature, kneeling man, evocatively dressed as a soldier. His dress, age, and beard are indicative of Joshua's role as an adult general of the army that protected the Israelites. In Bronzino's fresco, he kneels before

Moses, looking up at him with great attention and aligned with the rod that will be passed on to him, as soon as Moses concludes his last teaching, followed by his death.

Standing next to Moses is a man with a long, black beard, whose hand gestures intertwine with those of Moses and whose hand almost touches the rod Moses holds in his right hand. This is the high priest Eleazar, Aaron's son, who is the counterpoint to Aaron, as Eleazar's behavior was always exemplary and orthodox whereas Aaron occasionally fell from the path of orthodoxy, as recounted in the incident of the worship of the Golden Calf. In *The Crossing of the Red Sea*, Moses sits and Eleazar stands, both placed in front of the kneeling man in a manner that indicates that they acknowledge him as the passage's "... son of Nun ..." to whom God said, "Be strong, be resolute; for you shall bring the Israelites into the land which I swore to give them, and I will be with you." Joshua gave faithful service to Moses and was an indefatigable warrior who demonstrated his leadership ability and his adherence to the orthodox teaching in repeated instances. Thus, this scene incorporates the three major leaders of the Israelites at the time of the last teaching and death of Moses—Moses, Eleazar, and Joshua—three leaders who never wavered from the path of orthodoxy.

The recurrence of Moses in the liturgy of the Roman Rite extends beyond Lent into the post-Lenten liturgy, and on the Saturday after Pentecost, the first *Prophetia* was Leviticus 23:9–11, 15–17, 20, 21.[140] In this passage, Moses is given instructions about the Sabbath and the offerings he should prepare to celebrate it. The third *Prophetia*, on the same day, was Deuteronomy 26:1–3, 7–11.[141] This passage reminded the Egyptians how they were saved from Egypt "with a strong hand and outstretched arm," similar to how Bronzino depicted Moses in the Red Sea fresco, and brought into the land "flowing with milk and honey." The fourth *Prophetia* on the same day was Leviticus 26:3–12, which promises the Israelites a life of ease in the promised land.[142] The last time that Moses recurs in the liturgy, before the Lenten liturgy recycles, is on the fourth Saturday of the *Temporum Septembris*, when Leviticus 23:27–32 is read as the first *Prophetia*[143] and Leviticus 23:39–43 is read as the second *Prophetia*.[144] The first passage describes additional details about how the Sabbath is to be observed. The second passage describes how the

Israelites are to pass on the prescribed commemorations to their descendants. While the liturgy used for the chapel's themes was the Roman liturgy, the scene of *The Brazen Serpent* directed attention to the Spanish Mozarabic liturgy, thereby emphasizing Eleonora's national origin.

The Chapel and the Mozarabic Liturgy

The remaining Mosaic scene, *The Brazen Serpent*, illustrates Numbers 21:4–11:

> But on the way they grew impatient and spoke against God and Moses. "Why have you brought us up from Egypt," they said, "to die in the desert where there is neither food nor water? We are heartily sick of this miserable fare." Then the Lord sent poisonous snakes among the people, and they bit the Israelites so that many of them died. The people came to Moses and said, "We sinned when we spoke against the Lord and you. Plead with the Lord to rid us of the snakes." Moses therefore pleaded with the Lord for the people; and the Lord told Moses to make a serpent of bronze and erect it as a standard, so that anyone who had been bitten could look at it and recover. So Moses made a bronze serpent and erected it as a standard, so that when a snake had bitten a man, he could look at the bronze serpent and recover.[145]

This text is read on the Feast of the Exaltation of the Cross (September 4), in the Mozarabic liturgy, and, in Eleonora's chapel, *The Brazen Serpent*'s resonance with the Spanish Mozarabic liturgy emphasizes Eleonora's national origin. This visual affirmation of the two liturgies associated with Rome and Toledo reflects the Italian and Spanish heritage of the ducal family, as an evocation of the dual lineages of Francesco, the heir to these traditions of orthodoxy, which he will, in turn, uphold.

The Spanish Mozarabic liturgy was the rite that Spanish Catholics celebrated during the years of Islamic rule, when they were cut off from direct contact with Rome.[146] Its forms were different enough from those of the Roman Rite that it was examined for orthodoxy soon after the initial stages of the Reconquista restored

Toledo to Catholic control, in 1095.[147] The papal examination of the Mozarabic Rite concluded that the Rite was orthodox and had remained uncorrupted despite its isolation from Rome. The Mozarabic Rite continued to be celebrated in Spain, but it was limited to the six Mozarabic parishes of Toledo.[148] In the late fifteenth century, the dwindling numbers of Mozarabic Catholics meant that the Rite was in danger of disappearing. To preserve it, Cardinal Francisco Jiménes de Cisneros ordered the publication of the Mozarabic Missal, in 1500, and he instituted the celebration of this liturgy in perpetuity in a special chapel in the Cathedral of Toledo, where it continues to be celebrated.[149] The Toledan associations for this liturgy indicated Eleonora's family's city of origin and Spain's fidelity to Rome through centuries of Islamic occupation. In Florence, it was perhaps Don Pedro, Eleonora's father, who was visiting as the chapel was being decorated, who provided information about the Mozarabic liturgy.[150] However, Eleonora should not be overlooked as a contributor to the decision to use this liturgy for *The Brazen Serpent*.

The texts that directly reference *The Brazen Serpent*, John 3:13–16 and 1 Corinthians 10:9–11, are found in different parts of the liturgies of the Mozarabic and the Roman Rite, these associations forming a network of textual links connected to this image. John 3 recurs in the Roman Rite's liturgical readings for *Dominica II Post Pentecosten*, where it is read as the Epistle reading.[151] Also in the Roman Rite, the liturgy of *Dominica IX Post Pentecosten* includes 1 Corinthians 10 as the Epistle reading on that day.[152] John 3 is read in the Roman Rite as the Gospel reading for the Feast of the *Inventione Sanctae Crucis*, celebrated on 5 May.[153] In the Mozarabic Rite, John 3 is read on Palm Sunday.[155] Thus the connections between Moses, Lent, and the events of Lent that lead to the institution of the Eucharist, the Crucifixion, and the Resurrection are evoked throughout the liturgical year in connected sequences of related readings.

As with the Roman Rite, the Mozarabic Rite included Mosaic passages in the Lenten liturgy as follows: on the first Sunday in *Quadragesima*;[155] on the fourth Sunday in *Quadragesimae*;[156] on Feria IV in *Hebdomada Maiore*;[157] on Feria V in *Cena Domini*;[158] on the *Vigilia Paschalis*, in the Oratio *post benedictionem lucernae ante altare*; on Holy Saturday, which was also the day of Baptism in the Mozarabic Rite;[159] and on Feria IV of the Octave of Easter.[160] In the post-

Easter liturgy, the Mozarabic liturgy included passages from Revelation.[161] Mosaic passages were also read on: VI Dominico;[162] VII Dominico in the *Oratione post Gloriam*;[163] VIII Dominico, after the Gloria;[164] IX Dominico, after the Gloria;[165] X Dominico;[166] XI Dominico;[167] XII Dominico;[168] and XX Dominico.[170] The texts of Exodus, Numbers, Deuteronomy, and Leviticus were read in the Mozarabic Rite as they were in the Roman. For Spanish visitors to Eleonora's chapel, who were familiar with the Mozarabic Rite, Bronzino's frescoes would have functioned equally well for evoking the Mozarabic Lenten liturgy's readings for *The Crossing of the Red Sea* and the *Last Teaching of Moses*, *The Gathering of Manna* and the *Water from the Rock*, as well as for *The Brazen Serpent*. Thus, the Mosaic scenes in Eleonora's chapel flexibly accommodated the two Rites, both orthodox, applicable to the bicultural identities of the ducal couple.

The interaction between the Roman and Mozarabic liturgies celebrated respectively in Florence and Toledo can be construed as a statement of the Medici court's hybridity. The frescoes narrating the story of Exodus, were the first works Bronzino painted in the chapel, and their references to the Florentine and Spanish identities of Cosimo and Eleonora can be understood as a statement of dual heritage of Francesco, whose role as the next Florentine duke was specifically indicated by the depiction of St. Francis, the child's patron saint, on the ceiling. The scenes representing the events of the life of Moses and their significance for the Church were followed by Bronzino's delivery of the chapel's first altarpiece in the form of the first version of the *Pietà*, in 1545, subsequently given by Cosimo to Nicholas Perrenot de Granvelle, and the accompanying lateral panels of *St. John the Baptist and Cosmas*. Whereas the scenes depicting the story of Moses blended the Roman and Mozarabic liturgies, the altar wall adhered to the liturgy of Rome. Thus, when the first version of the *Pietà* was given to Granvelle to be placed in his chapel, the orthodox religious connotations were suitable for a gift that carried diplomatic and religious significance. As examples of patronage, the first and second altarpieces for the chapel indicate how Cosimo and Eleonora negotiated the room's patronage and their interaction with each other and with their artists, as well as their consideration of works of art as objects that were useful in building networks of political influence in a context of orthodox, religious observance.

The Chapel's Altar Wall: The First Pietà

In the 1568 *Vite*, Vasari recorded that it was Cosimo who decided to give the first *Pietà* to Nicholas Perrenot de Granvelle, upon its completion in 1545.[170] Among the documents Cox-Rearick published, tracing the progress of the inception of the *Pietà* eventually given to Granvelle, is a letter, dated 10 November 1542, from Cosimo to Bandinelli.[171] The letter informs Bandinelli that Cosimo had consulted Eleonora and that the duchess was pleased with Bandinelli's design for the *Pietà* but that the commission is being given to Bronzino, who is to paint it following Bandinelli's composition. On 12 August, Pagni writes to Riccio, informing him that the *Pietà* is in the chapel, but the painting was scarcely a month in the chapel when it was packed up to be sent to Besançon.[172]

The letters recording the process whereby Cosimo gave the first *Pietà* to Granvelle do not mention Eleonora, and it was Cosimo who made all of the arrangements. These letters were exchanged between Cosimo, his secretary Lorenzo Pagni, Riccio, and Don Francisco de Toledo, Count of Oropesa, one of Eleonora's kinsmen, who was in Brussels with Charles V.[173] The letters begin on 12–13 August 1545 and continue until 19 September, and it is assumed that the *Pietà* arrived in Besançon soon after the last letter.

Prior to the painting's departure from Florence, Cosimo, who was still in charge of the chapel's decorative decisions, ordered Bronzino to prepare to make a second version of the painting by recording its composition in a drawing. In a letter that Bronzino sent to Riccio on 22 August 1545, Bronzino wrote that the duke instructed him to reproduce the first version as closely as possible.[174] Bronzino explained that the duke had told him to make a drawing of the *Pietà* and that he did not want the artist to make any changes or to try to make the painting more beautiful than the original. Clearly, Cosimo wished to return to Eleonora a *Pietà* as beautiful as the first, which he had removed from her chapel.

It is clear that in the early stages of the chapel's history, it is Cosimo who is the dominant patron, although Eleonora's participation in making decisions is noted. The documents and Vasari establish that, from the beginning of the process of decorating the chapel and through 1545–46, it was Cosimo who was in charge of making most of the decisions about its decoration. However, in the eight years that passed between the removal of the first *Pietà*, in 1545, and its replacement, in 1553, Eleonora became more dominant; Vasari tells us that it was she who commissioned the second set of lateral panels of *The Annunciation*.[175] Yet, prior to Eleonora's control of the room, Cosimo's influence is evident in three other works—the lateral panels of *Saints John the Baptist and Cosmas* and, perhaps, in the selection of the temporary replacement of the first *Pietà* in the interim between its removal and replacement with the second *Pietà*.

THE LENTEN LITURGY AND THE CHAPEL'S ALTAR WALL

The Pietà

Bronzino's *Pietà*, discussed by Cox-Rearick and Natali as a Lenten liturgical image, is a compositionally and thematically complex work.[176] In both versions of the subject, Bronzino's assembly of participants in the event incorporates: the Virgin holding Christ in her lap, as John and Mary Magdalene hold his torso and feet; a group of four women, with a fifth woman placed in the painting's center, who leans over to look down at Christ two angels holding a chalice and a veil; three men, one of whom is Nicodemus (holding the jar of spices), while the other is Joseph of Arimathea (holding the nails of the Crucifixion) and a third, who represents the *Nicodemi*—the helpers of Nicodemus. Bronzino's first version is lighter in color and in tone, whereas the second version is darker in tonality and has a somber air that emphasizes the sorrow of the subject of the Lamentation.

The extended group of participants assembled by Bronzino presents not a symbolic assembly of personages but is a gathering of those named in the Gospels as being engaged in preparing the body of Christ for burial during the sequence of events that includes the Virgin's understanding that the human body of Christ is dead. The other participants in the scene stand by waiting for the Virgin to relinquish Christ's body to their care, while John supports his torso, as the Magdalene gestures while holding his feet in her hand. Bronzino signed the painting on the rock that is identified in the Lenten liturgy as the Rock that *is* Christ, and in so doing, he identified himself with the chapel's program and with one of the more important Eucharistic texts of Lent, which underscores the Roman dogma of Transubstantiation.[177]

The group of men and women gathered around Christ were identified by Cox-Rearick, who pointed out that on the left, the man with the spice jar is Nicodemus, and the man holding the nails is Joseph of Arimathea.[178] Cox-Rearick identified the woman who leans solicitously over the Virgin as Mary Cleophas but did not specifically identify the other women, except to say that they included the other Maries, who attended the Virgin.[179] This woman, who may be either Mary Cleophas or Mary Salome, was identified by Richelson as a portrait of Eleonora.[180] While the woman's face has a generic resemblance to Eleonora, and her costume indicates high rank and a style of elegance associated with Eleonora, she does not look enough like Eleonora to be considered a portrait of the duchess. Yet, the woman's distinction nonetheless alludes to Eleonora, who would have looked at her as a mirror echo of herself, spiritually participating in the scene. The question to be asked about her identity is—who did Bronzino think she was in the context of the Lenten Gospels?

The group of participants depicted in the *Pietà* are identified in the Eastern Orthodox Church as The Myrrhbearers, being: Mary Magdalene, Mary Salome (sister of the Virgin and mother of James and John, the sons of Zebedee, Christ's cousins), Mary of Bethany (sister of Lazarus), Martha of Bethany (sister of Lazarus), Mary Cleophas (wife of Cleophas), Joanna (wife of Chuza, the steward of Herod Antipas), Susanna, Joseph of Arimathea, and Nicodemus, as well as additional *Nicodemi* who assist Nicodemus and Joseph of Arimathea with the body of Christ.[181] Bronzino's *Pieta* features seven of the possible nine Myhrrbearers, who can be identified by name, and one generic *Nicodemi*.

The men are easily identified by their attributes, but the group of women presents more of a dilemma because the Gospels do not specifically and clearly differentiate them. The woman who leans over the Virgin and Christ, identified by Cox-Rearick as Mary Cleophas (Clopas), is mentioned by specific name only in John 19:25.[182] The Gospels of Matthew and Mark supplement the names of the women, adding to the list the mother of the sons of Zebedee, who were John and James, who may be the Salome, mentioned in Mark: 16:1. However, the syntax of the text of the Gospels is such that it is impossible to say precisely which women were present at each instance. John 19:25 lists the Virgin and the Virgin's sister and Mary the wife of Clopas, standing by the Cross, in such a way that the text can be interpreted to be recounting the presence of either three women (the Virgin, the Virgin's sister, and Mary Cleophas) or two women (The Virgin and her sister, who is Mary Cleophas). Of the women mentioned in the Gospels, the two most important were Mary Cleophas and Salome, who came to the tomb with Mary Magdalene in Mark: 16:1 and who may also be the mother of the sons of Zebedee, James, and Joses.

Among the group depicted by Bronzino, two of the women are dressed in a style that distinguishes them from the other women. The woman who leans towards Christ is the one who is most elaborately dressed, and the one directly to her left is also distinguished with a more aristocratic costume. Since the two most prominent women listed in the Gospels are Mary Cleophas and Mary Salome, it seems that Bronzino distinguished two of the women, in keeping with the Gospels' descriptions of events. For Bronzino, who would have been looking for a participant to whom Eleonora could be linked spiritually, the Virgin's sister would be the woman who would best serve a symbolic Eleonora, among those who "followed" Christ and "ministered" to him.

We cannot know whether Bronzino considered Mary Cleophas to be the Virgin's sister, but we can be certain that Eleonora's *alter ego* would have required such status, echoing the hierarchy of the Florentine court, wherein Eleonora would have been surrounded by her women in descending order of status, much as the *Pietà*'s women reflect in their dress their varying social positions. As such, the gathering in the *Pietà* echoes the Florentine Court, where Eleonora would have had primacy, as the other women of the court, of varying standing, would have surrounded her in her daily activities. Within the context of the Gospels, the women in Bronzino's *Pietà* reflect an unspecified combination of Mary Cleophas, Mary Salome, and the "many" women mentioned by Mark 15:40–41 who followed Christ and ministered to Him, among whom the Eastern Church speculatively includes Mary and Martha of Bethany, Joanna, and Susanna, wife of Chuza.[183]

The Christ of the *Pietà* was referenced by the Lenten readings of Holy Thursday, the day of the *Cena Domini* on Feria V and the day that marks the Institution of the Eucharist, in the first *Lectio*, 1 Corinthians 11:20–32:

> [Christ] … took bread and giving thanks broke, and said, "Take and eat. This is my body which shall be given up for you; do this in remembrance of Me" … "This cup is the new Covenant in My Blood: do this … in remembrance of Me." (184)

On Holy Thursday, these words explicitly express the Church's teaching that the Eucharist is the Body and Blood of Christ, which the faithful "eat" after its miraculous Transubstantiation.

In 1 Corinthians 11:20–32, Paul admonished the Corinthians for having deviated from orthodoxy in the celebration of the Eucharist, as he states explicitly that the Eucharist is the body and blood of Christ and reminds them of Christ's words: "'This is my body, which is for you' … In the same way, he took the cup after supper, and said: 'This cup is the new covenant sealed by my blood' …" This passage includes a very explicit condemnation of those who do not believe in Transubstantiation, lest they be "… condemned with the rest of the world." Within the context of early sixteenth-century religious controversies, the words of Paul would have resonated — if the Church's teachings are not accepted, damnation follows — and these words would have functioned as a warning from the ducal couple that they expected their court to heed the words of Paul and retain their fealty to the Church.

The Eucharist and Moses were explicitly connected in the Lenten liturgy by the post-Communion versicles recited on Good Friday, which emphasize Moses as the leader of the Israelites and the guardian of orthodoxy.[185] These versicles, which were Eucharistic in context, would have returned attention to each of the chapel's walls as follows: "Ego eduxis te de Aegypto demerso Pharaone in mari rubro …" brings the Crossing of the Red Sea back into focus; "Ego ante te aparvi mare …" repeats the attention to the *Red Sea* fresco; "Ego te potavi aqua salutis da petra …" brings attention to the scene of the *Water from the Rock*; and "Ego te pani manna per desertum ..." brings the attention to the *Gathering of Manna*. Thus, the post-Communion versicles connect the *Pietà* to Transubstantiation in the Eucharist and the chapel's Mosaic frescoes to the Eucharistic meaning of the miracles Moses performed, while emphasizing the adherence to orthodoxy which is the holy task of faithful leaders.

In effect, the Good Friday versicles encapsulate all of the themes found on the three walls visible to the participants standing, kneeling, or sitting in Eleonora's chapels, who, hearing these words, would have seen their illustration on the walls of the chapel. These themes were reiterated on Holy Saturday, when the story of Moses is repeatedly referenced throughout the readings of the day, with special attention given to the Crossing of the Red Sea.[186] Direct attention to the Eucharistic significance of the *Pietà* and the body of Christ recurred on Passion Sunday (the Sunday before Palm Sunday) with the Communion reading 1 Corinthians 11:24–25: "This is My Body which shall be given up for you: this is the cup of the new covenant in My Blood; says the Lord."[187] With these passages and on different days of Lent, the chapel's *Pietà* and its Mosaic scenes were united in the Lenten liturgy.

King David and the Erythraean Sybil

On the altar wall, the figures of King David and the Erythraean Sibyl hold scrolls that link them to Lent. King David holds a scroll with the words "Foderunt Manus Meas Et Pedes/Meos Dinumeraverunt Omnia/Ossa Mea—David" (They have pierced my hands and my feet; they have numbered all my bones—David).[188] These are the words of Psalm 21, which bring attention to Passion Week, the culmination of Lent. The Erythraean Sybil's scroll has the words "Morte Morietur Trib[u]s Diebus/somno subscepto et T[u]nc Ab/Inferis Regressus Ad Lucem Veniet [Primus]—Erithrea" (And return from the lower world and come again to the light—Erythraean), a quote from the Oracula Sibyllina.[189] The Sibyl's text directly evokes the Resurrection and Easter Sunday.

The placement of David and the Sibyl forms a triangle with the body of Christ in the *Pietà* that joins Jews, Pagans (Gentiles), and Christians in a visual parallel to the desire for unity that is expressed in the Lenten liturgy. David is directly evoked in the liturgical readings for Palm Sunday, in the opening Antiphon, which was Matthew 21:9: "Hosanna to the Son of David! Blessed is He who comes in the name of the Lord. O King of Israel. Hosanna in the highest."[191] This reference to King David would have resonated with the manner in which David looks down at the body of Christ, as one King of Israel recognizes and acknowledges another.

As the Sibyl, who represents the Gentiles, mirrors David's posture and gaze, she too recognizes Christ as the King of Israel. In so designing the altar wall, Bronzino responded to the program's core message and refined it by enabling his compositional structure to encompass the hope for unification that is part of Lent's themes. In the early sixteenth century, when the idea that unification among the disputing Christians under the aegis of the Roman Church could still happen, even at the Council of Trent, the altar wall of Eleonora's chapel graphically expressed this hope. And David's Florentine tradition as one of the symbols of the city and of the Medici would have emphasized the leadership role and the tradition of governmental and religious stewardship of the Medici in Florence, as Cox-Rearick pointed out in her discussion of this figure.[191]

Sts. John the Baptist and Cosmas: Florence and the Medici

The chapel's original altar wall featured the *Pietà* placed between two lateral panels in which Saints John the Baptist and Cosmas were represented. The visual effect of this ensemble would have emphasized masculinity on this wall and in the chapel, as the two male saints of the wings would have emphasized the Christ, John the Evangelist, and the other men included in the *Pietà*'s composition. Saint Cosmas was Cosimo's patron saint; hence, the selection of this saint emphasizes the duke's presence in the chapel. Associations for Cosimo with John the Baptist were explored by Paul Richelson, who discussed how Cosimo employed the image of Florence's patron saint on coins that he ordered to commemorate his victory at Montemurlo.[192] St. John the Baptist also had Medicean significance for Cosimo, as the patron saint of Cosimo's father, Giovanni delle Bande Nere.[193] Hence, it is likely that the selection of the first set of lateral panels also indicates Cosimo's initial patronage control of the room.

When Cox-Rearick discussed the first set of lateral panels, she suggested that the panel featuring John the Baptist, now in the Getty, was intended as a portrait of the famous *condottiere* and that the then-lost *St. Cosmas* was a portrait of Cosimo. However, a recently discovered candidate for the panel of *St. Cosmas* is not a portrait of Cosimo, as Cox-Rearick suggested.[194] Nonetheless, the first set of panels were clearly Medicean in context and dynastic in intention, emphasizing the duke and his father. They were also part of the program of localization and heredity exemplified by the ceiling's saints — pointing to Florence and the Medici, as Francesco's seat of power and family lineage on his father's side. These panels also had Lenten significance.

The Liturgy and Saints John the Baptist and Cosmas

Bronzino's first set of lateral panels for the chapel depicting Sts. John the Baptist and Cosmas were also part of the Lenten program. On the first Sunday of Lent, *Quadragesima* Sunday, the Stational Mass was celebrated at St. John Lateran, which is dedicated to Christ and St. John the Baptist, and on the Thursday of the third week of Lent, the Stational Mass was celebrated at the Church of Saints Cosmas and Damian, on the Via Sacra of the Imperial Forum.[195] Thus, on these days, attention was brought to the Saints on the Altar Walls in connection with the Roman churches of Lent.

John the Baptist is the saint who initiated Baptism, and he symbolized the Baptism of the Catechumens on Holy Saturday, the day in which Christ is in his tomb preparing for the Resurrection. Thus, his presence on the altar wall resonates with one of the major Lenten themes.[196] The Lenten liturgy celebrated Cosmas (and Damian) on Thursday of the third week of Lent with the Prayer "May the blessed solemnity of your saints, Cosmas and Damian, glorify You, O Lord: Whereby you have both given to them everlasting glory, and to us Your aid in Your ineffable providence. Through Our Lord, Amen."[197]

While John the Baptist resonated with Lent's Baptismal theme, Cosmas evoked Lenten themes of healing and salvation, represented by the healing miracles exemplified by the Pool of Bethesda, John 5:1–15, read on Friday of Quadragesima.[198] On the third Thursday of Lent, when the designated Stational Church is Sts. Cosmas and Damian, the Gospel reading was Luke 4:38–44, which recounts the miraculous healing of Simon's mother-in-law, which occurred after Christ laid hands on her; Christ then proceeded to heal and cast out the devils from those who were possessed.[199] The reference to Cosimo found in the depiction of Cosmas linked the Duke Cosimo to the healing miracles of Lent and to the role of Cosmas and Damian as doctors and saints, renowned for their powers of healing.

Represented in the chapel by his patron saint, Cosimo emerges in an evocative reminder of the healing powers of kings, such as St. Louis, who reputedly possessed the ability to heal their subjects, as aspect of sacral monarchy discussed by Murry.[200] In Eleonora's chapel, Cosmas reminds the spectator that the performance of actions that will repair the spiritual and political breaches that could threaten a court is part of the duke's responsibilities. Such a reminder in troubled times was an explicit vow on the part of the ducal couple that Florence would be kept safe in a time of confessional strife. The promise of stability and continuity in troubled times was also the organizing thematic principle for the chapel's ceiling, which brought together references to the birth of Francesco, to the Heavenly plan that fated the Medici to rule Florence, and to the place of the Medici court in Europe's dynastic and religious politics.

The Modello for the Chapel's Ceiling: Identity and Hybridity

The original plan for the ceiling of Eleonora's chapel is preserved in a *modello* for the central part of the ceiling (excluding the fictive columns and spandrels), which is in the Louvre. The ceiling's *modello* was first published by Hermann Voss in 1920 and was later discussed by Craig Hugh Smyth.[201] This *modello* represents the ceiling's design, including the central Medici/Toledo arms, the festoons of flowers and fruit with *putti*, and the four saints—Saints Francis, John the Evangelist, and Jerome, and the Archangel Michael.[202]

Bruce Edelstein recently dated the ceiling's *modello* prior to Francesco's birth and mistakenly stated that the *modello* was "first published" by John Shearman.[203] In his analysis of the drawing, Edelstein argued for an original design intention to place St. Jerome above the altar wall; St. Michael above *The Brazen Serpent*; St. John the Evangelist over *The Crossing of the Red Sea*; and St. Francis above the wall with *The Gathering of Manna*. Edelstein's proposal argued that before Francesco was born the child's name was undetermined, and that Bronzino placed St. John above the scene Cox-Rearick identified as *The Investiture of Joshua* and interpreted as symbolic of Francesco's future title because Giovanni was a Medici name that might have been considered, whereas Francesco was not. Edelstein argued that this initial plan was changed after Francesco was born and Giovanni was not the name selected: Bronzino therefore "rotated" the drawing to place St. Francis in his current location, indicating Francesco's future as Duke of Florence. However, contextual data found in the *modello* indicates that Bronzino always planned to place St. Michael above the altar wall and that the drawing was not "rotated," because Eleonora vowed to name the child Francesco, if male, almost as soon as she realized she was pregnant.

Francesco's name was selected when Eleonora was scarcely a month into the pregnancy, during a pilgrimage that she made to the Franciscan shrine at La Verna.[204] La Verna is the place where St. Francis received his stigmata, and when Eleonora reached La Verna, she swore to name the child Francesco, if a boy. At the point when Eleonora made the vow, the child's name was set, and any plans for the chapel's decorations would have begun with the knowledge that a male child's name would be Francesco. The *modello* for the ceiling was planned and executed once the child's name was selected, in conjunction with the placement of the wall frescoes — for which the shape of the room established the decorative schema. *The Crossing of the Red Sea* could only have been placed on the south wall, as it required an undisrupted wall space, whereas the *Moses Striking the Rock* and the *Gathering of Manna* could be accommodated on the north wall, suitably split into two parts by its central window. Employment of the *modello* awaited only the confirmation of the birth of a male child, which was received on 25 March. Additional data found in the content of Bronzino's *modello* indicates that it was not developed until after the birth of Francesco.

The ceiling's *modello* is a preliminary design for the vault and records the original appearance of the Medici/Toledo *stemma*, still visible through the obscuring *Trinity*, as described by Cox-Rearick: "... to the left, the (red) Medici *palle* and, to the right, the (blue and silver) squares of the Toledo arms; above is Cosimo's ducal coronet embraced by the imperial eagle of Charles V."[205] The arms in the drawing are quartered, which is indicative of heredity, as opposed to marriage, which is represented by an impaled shield (split in half by the two sets of arms).[206] The quartered arms, surmounted by the ducal coronet, indicate that the ceiling's shield was designed to reflect the fact that the ducal couple had an heir. Thus, the quartered arms in the *modello* provide additional support that the drawing was designed after Francesco was born and the location of Francis above the *Crossing of the Red Sea*, with the Archangel Michael above the altar, was part of the original design.

Additional evidence for dating the *modello* after Francesco's birth is found in another drawing, where Bronzino also studied the *stemma*.[207] This drawing, now in the Uffizi, is a small black-chalk drawing on which Bronzino sketched the double-headed eagle of Charles V, Cosimo's protector, Eleonora's kinsman, and Francesco's godfather. This sketch is found on the verso of a life-study for the figure of the Archangel Michael. The final version of the quartered *stemma*, surmounted with the ducal coronet and enfolded by the Imperial eagle, could only have been designed after Francesco was born and perhaps even after the emperor had agreed to be the child's godfather. As the chapel is only about 14 sq. ft. in size, the five months between Francesco's birth on 25 March and the beginning of the wall frescoes on 6 September gave ample time for Bronzino to design and execute the ceiling's content, after Tasso completed the room's construction and in the aftermath of the child's birth.

An outstanding element of the chapel's ceiling design, already incorporated into the *modello*'s composition, is the light that streams into the chapel from the Heavenly space above the *stemma*, which was identified by Falciani as being Valdesian.[208] Cox-Rearick interpreted this light as Divine and orthodox approval, which transformed the vault into an apotheosis of the ducal couple's marriage.[209] The light acknowledged by the ceiling's saints, who are transfixed and transformed by its Heavenly nature, changes the central *stemma* into a symbol of God's approval of the ducal family and the role they play on earth.

This *topos* of Medici apotheosis was later more ostentatiously employed in Vasari's *Apotheosis of Cosimo* (1565), on the ceiling of the *Salone de' Cinquecento*, as was discussed by Murry.[210] The pictorial rendition of Medici apotheosis, studied by Murry, found in Bronzino and Vasari's work had a literary correlate in the panegyrics of courtiers such as the priest-scholar Giovanni Fabrini di Figline, Antonio Brucioli, the canon Matteo Saminiati, Bernardo Segni, and Prete Francesco Da Trivigi. Thus, the Heavenly light that streams from above the ceiling's *stemma* emphasizes the transformation of the Medici into sacred personages, as was noted by Cox-Rearick and Murry. The use of this light in the chapel's ceiling was thus deliberately linked to contemporary ideas about sacred monarchy and the Church's traditional manner of indicating the presence of God through metaphors of light and illumination.

Because the saints, who look at the light of Heaven, are linked to the Medici/Toledo *stemma* through their gazes and gestures, their interaction with the Heavenly zone of the *stemma* links the earthly sphere to Heaven. As such, the saints function as indexical indicators of connection between the Medici and God, as they bring attention to the lineage and territories that Francesco would inherit from his Florentine and Toledan parents. These earthly territories are blessed by God, whose light shines down on the Medici arms and on the symbolic program that extols the birth of a child so blessed by God that he was born on the Feast of the Annunciation, the day on which Christ was conceived. As the ceiling's saints gaze, kneel, and gesture in recognition of Divine presence and favor, the continuity of the Medici dynasty is ensured as God's will on earth. As such statements could not be formulated unless the child was born, this internal evidence dates the *modello* after Francesco's birth.

The ceiling's saints—John the Evangelist, Jerome, Francis, and the Archangel Michael—are saints with multiple roles in the history of the Church. Each saint has cult centers in multiple places, where special devotions in their honor are enacted; thus, they are international saints. Cox-Rearick characterized Saints John, Jerome, and Francis as either "Florentine" or "Medici" saints, with John the Evangelist and Francis being "Medici" as well as "Florentine."[211] She considered Saints John and Francis because they are, respectively, the patron saints of Giovanni di Bicci de' Medici (founder of the family) and of Francesco. Cox-Rearick also characterized St. Jerome as the saint favored by Florentine Humanists, and she linked the Archangel Michael's presence to the Mosaic frescoes because he was the Archangel who led the Exodus.

In ascertaining the reasons for the selection of these specific saints in the ceiling's design, Cox-Rearick pointed out that these saints occur on two terracotta altarpieces at La Verna.[212] One of these altarpieces was designed by Andrea della Robbia, is in the Chapel of the Stigmata at La Verna, and includes Saints Francis, John, and Jerome. The other altarpiece is by Giovanni della Robbia and is found in the Chapel of the Pietà. This altarpiece features Saints Francis, Jerome, John, and the Archangel Michael. Eleonora saw these altarpieces, in August of 1540, when she went—already pregnant with Francesco—on her pilgrimage to the place where St. Francis received the stigmata, in order to perform her vow to name the child Francesco if she was blessed with an heir.[213] The inclusion in the ceiling of the La Verna saints also argues for dating the *modello* after the birth of Francesco, as his birth was proof that God had answered Eleonora's prayer.

That Eleonora went to a Franciscan shrine to make her vow was in keeping with the special devotion she and Cosimo had for St. Francis, indicative of the widespread devotion Francis received in Italy and Spain. As Cox-Rearick noted, their devotion to the Saint manifested in their support of Franciscan churches,[214] and Gigliola Fragninto pointed out that Cosimo's confessor was a Franciscan named Raffaele Sannini da Firenze.[215] Had Eleonora's pregnancy not yielded an heir, it is doubtful that St. Francis would have been represented on the ceiling, as his appearance would have symbolized an act of Divine disfavor and a failed petition. Nor could Eleonora, once she made the vow, have considered naming the child anything other than Francis when the prayer was granted, as this would have represented breaking her vow, and such action would have been an invitation to Divine punishment.

Francesco was not a traditional Medici name, nor were Eleonora's immediate male relatives named Francisco, but the name recurred among members of the Álvarez de Toledo and among the Mendoza family, one of the highest-ranking Spanish families, from which Eleonora was also descended.[216] A close relative to Eleonora, with the name Francisco, in diplomatic proximity to the ducal couple, was Francisco de Toledo, Count of Oropesa (1515–84), who was a close attaché of Charles V and with whom Cosimo corresponded to make arrangements when he sent Bronzino's first *Pietà* for the chapel to Nicolas Perrenot de Granvelle as a gift.[217] Among the Mendoza at the Florentine court was Don Francisco Mendoza de Burgos, Cosimo's governor and captain general of Siena after the death of Pedro di Toledo in 1553.[218] As one of the copies of Bronzino's *Pietà* for Eleonora's chapel went to the Iglesia de Castrogeríz, near Burgos, it is likely that it was either commissioned by or given to Don Francisco Mendoza de Burgos—as a sign of connection to the Florentine court.[219] Thus, the selection of Francesco as a name was suitable for political as well as religious reasons, as the Mendoza were powerful allies and were *emparentado* with Eleonora through ties of blood kinship and marriage.

The selection of the chapel's saints, with their Spanish and Florentine family associations for the ducal couple, represents the hybridity of the Florentine court, which blended Italian and Spanish culture in devotional, dynastic, and political contexts.[220] As such, the ceiling's saints are multivalent and should be considered both from Cosimo's Florentine/Medici perspective and from a Spanish perspective corresponding to Eleonora. Therefore, the ceiling's saints exist in the hyphen between the diverse cultural/ethnic/national identities of the ducal family, and they are also indicative of Franciscan religious affiliations on the part of Cosimo and Eleonora.

Bruce Edelstein and Robert Gaston, who have examined the ceiling's saints from an ethnic perspective, have suggested Spanish associations for the ceiling's saints. Edelstein pointed out St. Jerome's Spanish associations and the development of the Jeronimite Order in Spain and "in Toledo, the ancestral home of Eleonora's family."[221] Gaston's "Spanish" interpretation of the chapel's ceiling focused on Spanish and Italian devotional treatises, which included discussion of the ceiling's saints.[222] In his Eleonoran interpretation for the chapel, Gaston attempted to counter Cox-Rearick's interpretation, which placed Cosimo as the chapel's patron.[223] Gaston argued that the chapel's program was assembled from a variety of texts and diverse objects in which the ceiling's saints were included, such as Isabel de Castilla's last testament; the decorative imagery of San Juán de los Reyes in Toledo; tapestries, manuscripts, and paintings also commissioned by and for Isabel de Castilla; and a treatise entitled *The Impregnable Castle* by Fray Gonzálo de Arredondo y Alvarado (where Don Pedro de Toledo and Charles V participate in a dialogue that features references to the Archangel Michael and

John the Evangelist).[224]

In addition to interpretations that privilege Spain, Italy, or Florence as the *locus* for the inclusion of these specific saints in the ceiling, a Roman interpretation linked to the Catholic Church is also possible. Natali provided such an interpretation, from a perspective based on the traditional beliefs of the Church.[225] His Roman interpretation pointed out the role played by John the Evangelist in the Lenten liturgy, where he is the author of one of the more important Gospel narratives of the Passion. Natali also discussed the Evangelist's authorship of Revelation, which he linked to the chapel's program and described as being eschatological.[226] Additionally, he suggested that John the Evangelist was included because he is the author of one of the Passion Gospels, as well as Revelation, and he linked the other saints to the writings of John, providing an interpretation based on the texts of the Church. John is also the Evangelist who most focuses on the theology of the Eucharist, when he describes the events of the Last Supper, and it is his ideological presentation of the conceptual importance of the Eucharist that the Church used to develop its Eucharistic dogma.[227] The connection between Lent, The Last Supper, and the Eucharistic doctrine of Transubstantiation pronounced by the Church are thus linked in Eleonora's chapel.

THE CHAPEL AND THE EUCHARIST

The Eucharist and the Last Supper are joined, in the Church's dogma, to the celebration of Passover and to the Covenant between the Israelites and God manifested in their salvation from Egypt and their Exodus.[228] The Covenant between God and the Israelites was offered in two species—blood and flesh—and in the New Covenant of Christ, the substances are matched by Christ's Body and Blood. The Exodus narrative specifically describes how after the sacrifice that marked the Covenant was completed, the blood of the sacrificial lamb was placed in vessels. In the chapel, Bronzino depicted a set of vessels located in the foreground of the *Crossing of the Red Sea* (itself a *figura* of the Passover). These vessels are placed next to the figure of the idealized youth, whose left hand stretches out over them, drawing attention to their sacrificial role. In front of the youth, Moses sits with his left arm raised and his hand and finger pointing out of the fresco towards the chapel's altar wall. The youth, whose hand is stretched over the vessels, looks at Moses in a reactive manner, as Moses raises his arm, pointing in the direction of the chapel's *Pietà*. In the context of the chapel, the pointing gesture of Moses draws the spectator's attention to the body of Christ, visible above the chapel's altar table. The visual and gestural interaction so devised is a graphic explication of the Eucharistic context of the chapel's *Pietà*, as Moses and the youth explicitly draw attention to the old and the new Covenants, sealed with blood and flesh.

For the Church, the important texts that emphasize the two Covenants are Luke 22:20 ("This cup that is poured out for you is the new covenant in my blood"); Mark 14:24 ("This is the blood of my covenant, which is poured out for many"); and Exodus 24 ("Moses took half of the blood and put it in basins, and half of the blood he dashed against the altar"). The blood used by Moses was taken from the lamb that was sacrificed as the flesh of the sacrifice.[229] As the Lenten readings featuring Moses were read, the chapel's Mosaic frescoes graphically recalled the Old Covenant made by the Israelites with the Lord. This realization would have brought attention to the youth who gestures towards the vessels or basins, as Moses stretches his arm and hand towards the altar wall—with the altar referenced in Exodus 24. Whenever Masses were held in the chapel, the words linking Christ's sacrifice to the Eucharist and to the New Covenant fulfilled in the Church brought attention to the Eucharistic *Pietà*, in which Christ's body was placed next to the depicted chalice and the actual chalice used to celebrate the Mass in the chapel. These liturgical objects would have drawn attention to the ceiling's John the Evangelist and to the Eucharistic message of his Gospel.[230]

THE CEILING SAINTS

The chapel's ceiling and its interaction with the wall frescoes was complex and multivalent. Thus, depending on who looked up at the ceiling, different meanings came into play, including a Roman meaning in keeping with the Church's doctrines. When Eleonora looked up at the ceiling with the Spanish eyes of an Álvarez de Toledo, she saw the saints of her family's city. St. Francis, founder of the Franciscan order, would have reminded her of Toledo's monastery of San Juán de Los Reyes—a Franciscan monastery, paid for by Isabél de Castilla and Fernando de Aragón, the grandparents of Charles V, Francesco's godfather and Eleonora's kinsman. The double-eagle *impresa* originated with Isabel de Castilla and recurs throughout the decorative program of San Juán de los Reyes enfolding the arms of the Reyes Católicos. In Eleonora's chapel, the double-headed eagle surrounding the Medici/Toledo arms was also reminiscent of the protection Charles V offered the child, as his godfather, and of the allegiance and *emparentado* between the Florentine and Imperial families.

St. John the Evangelist was equally important for the Medici, as he was the patron saint of their founder, Giovanni di Bicci. For the Trastámaras, the family name of the house of Castilla, to which Charles V and Eleonora traced their ancestry, John the Evangelist was the saint to whom San Juán de Los Reyes was dedicated and for whom their families had special veneration. Thus, the heraldic devices of the chapel and of San Juán de Toledo evoked *emparentado* of blood and religious observance and served as a reminder of Francesco's Spanish and Medici family heritage. As such, the double-headed eagle of St. John was significant in a Spanish/Toledan and in a Florentine/Medicean context, with the eagle becoming a trope of hyphenated identities for Francesco, who was Spanish and Florentine. Similarly evocative of dual identities are St. Jerome and the Archangel Michael, who were important in both Toledo and in Florence.

In different ways, the ceiling's saints are place saints for Florence, Spain, and Toledo, as they localize the origin of Francesco's paternal and maternal ancestry in Toledo and Florence. Their place in the Church's history also aligns them with the Lenten readings and with the chapel's core program, which emphasized the foundation of the Eucharist, the fulfillment of the New Covenant with the Crucifixion, and the promise of eternal salvation of the blessed—in this case, that of the Medici/de Toledo family.

When Cosimo looked up at the ceiling with a Florentine and Medicean point of view, John the Evangelist and Francis would have reminded him of the founder of the Medici family, Giovanni di Bicci, and of his son and heir. Thus, for Cosimo, the ceiling's saints represented his family's origin and its dynastic future. St.

Jerome, as Cox-Rearick pointed out, is a Florentine, Humanist, scholar-saint; thus, he would have localized Francesco's family to its ancestral city, while exemplifying Medicean traditions of piety and scholarship.[231] When the ducal couple looked up at the ceiling together, the ceiling's saints could have reminded them of the altarpieces at La Verna and could have focused their attention on the blessing they received from Heaven of a healthy son and heir, who enabled their dynastic ambitions to be fulfilled.

In the hyphenated cultural space of the Florentine court, the chapel's ceiling delineated Francesco's dual identities and the status of his *emparentado* with the emperor, whose protective eagle encircled the ceiling's quartered *stemma* representative of his ancestors. The devotional postures of the assembled saints who gaze up at the light of God, illuminating Francesco's heritage, emphasize the message of sacral monarchy that Murry described as a prevalent *topos* at the Florentine Court, applied here to the heir. They also represent the ducal couple's adherence to the Roman Church, a fealty indicated by Cosimo's consistent assembly of support and influence at the papal court and by the patronage favors he received from the emperor.[232]

Similar multiple Toledan/Hispanic and Florentine meanings to those evident in the *stemma* exist for the pomegranates so evident in the ceiling's fruit and flower friezes. Identified with fertility and the Resurrection, by Cox-Rearick, the pomegranates would have had a different meaning for Eleonora.[233] Within a Spanish referential system, Eleonora would have seen the pomegranates as *granadas*, symbolic of the conquest of Granada in 1492 by Isabel de Castilla and Fernando de Aragón, which was quickly followed by the expulsion of Spain's Jewish and Islamic populations on 2 August 1492.[234] The goal of the expulsion was the establishment of a nation united by a Roman Catholic identity equated with "purity" of blood. Once Granada was conquered, the Catholic kings, Isabel and Fernando, placed the pomegranate on their joint shield as a symbol of the unification of Spain. Cosimo and other Florentines or Italians seeing the chapel's pomegranates would have identified them as symbols of fertility and the Resurrection. Eleonora and Spanish visitors would have associated them with the conquest of Granada and with the arms of the Catholic kings, the expulsion of Spain's

Jewish and Islamic populations, and with Charles V, who also bore the pomegranate on his shield. They would also have understood them as symbols of Roman orthodoxy because Granada was a victory for the Catholic Church.

In Eleonora's chapel, the ceiling's heraldry is one prominent key to unlocking the religious and political meaning of the chapel's core program, focused on Francesco's birth during Lent and the attendant dynastic and political programmatic messages found in the readings of this liturgical season. As such, it is interesting to note, given the chapel's scenes from the life of Moses, that the origins of heraldry are identified with Moses, as described in Numbers 1: 2, 18, 52: "And the children of Israel shall pitch their tents, every man by his own camp, and *every man by his own standard*, throughout their hosts," and Numbers 2:2: *"Every man of the children of Israel shall pitch by his own standard, with the ensign of their father's house,"* as well as Numbers 2:34: "And the children of Israel did according to all that the Lord commanded to Moses: *so they pitched by their standards, and so they set forward, every one after their families, according to the house of their fathers."* Thus, heraldry and Moses come together in the chapel's Lenten program, which features scenes from Exodus, Numbers, Leviticus, and Deuteronomy, all Mosaic texts read during Lent—the liturgical season centrally indicated on the altar wall by the chapel's *Pietà*.[235]

Lent, and the Chapel's Ceiling

In keeping with the chapel's core Lenten program, the ceiling's saints also have connections to the Lenten liturgy. As Cox-Rearick and Natali respectively noted, the Archangel Michael is the angel who leads the Israelites out of Egypt, and he is the guardian of souls, as well as the angel of the Judgment.[236] In the chapel, Michael appears in the pose of the Judgment. Although Gaston suggested that Bronzino used a book cover illustration for the pose of Michael, it was actually studied from life, as is clear from a preparatory drawing, now in the Louvre.[237] Michael's placement above John the Baptist emphasizes the Church's tradition of performing Baptism for the catechumens during Lent, in order to ensure their salvation at the Last Judgment.[238] In their process towards salvation through Baptism, the catechumens were guarded and guided by

angels, of which Michael is representative. During Lent, the catechumens were exorcised of demons as part of their preparation to
receive Baptism, and Michael's role as the protector from demons is
emphasized in the chapel's image of the Archangel.

On the chapel's ceiling, Bronzino represented Michael in the act
of vanquishing a demon, and in the first Oratio of Ash Wednesday,
Michael is invoked as an aid to fighting sin.[239] Michael, with John
the Baptist and Cosmas, represented the conquest of evil and the
bestowal of healing through the commission of Original Sin that
Baptism brought. To establish all of these connections, Michael had
to have been planned to appear above the altar wall as soon as the
Lenten program was composed. This coordinated symbolic and
liturgical arrangement also argues against Edelstein's suggestion
that the ceiling *modello* was rotated, as the pertinent connections for
Michael could only be made by placing the Archangel above John
the Baptist.

Michael's depiction, above the altar, as an angel who fights demons resonates with several Lenten readings. On the first Sunday
of Lent, the text for the Gradual is Psalm 90:11–12: "To His angels
God has given command about you, that they guard you in all your
ways. Upon their hands they shall bear you up, lest you dash your
foot against a stone."[240] This reading is followed on the same day
by the Gospel of Matthew 4:1–11, which recounts the Temptation
of Christ, the narration of which closes with the words "Begone
Satan, for it is written, 'The Lord your God shall you worship and
Him only shall you serve.' Then the Devil left Him; and behold, the
angels came and ministered to Him."[241] An additional text that addresses the casting out of devils is the Gospel of Mathew 15:21–28,
which is read on the Thursday of the first week of Lent, in which
Christ casts out the Devil, this being the same text that identifies
Christ as a son of David; thus Michael and David are related to each
other.[242]

Michael's placement above the altar encapsulates all the Lenten
themes: Baptism, salvation, and healing through Christ, but also
the theme of Judgment for which he serves as the chief angel, who
separates the saved from the damned. Natali's study of the chapel
discussed Michael's participation in the events of the Last Judgment in relation to *The Brazen Serpent*, itself a prefiguration for

Christ's Crucifixion and of the Last Judgment.[243] By placing Michael directly across from *The Brazen Serpent*, the program aligned the Archangel with his role as defender of souls and minister of punishment. On Monday of the First Week in Lent, the Gospel text was Matthew 25:31—" When the Son of Man shall come in His glory, and all the holy angels with him, then shall he sit upon the throne of glory"—which reminds the participants of the second coming of Christ and the day of Judgment. The reading of this passage would have drawn attention to the ceiling's Michael and to John the Evangelist, the author of Revelation.[244]

At the Last Judgment, those who fell away from the orthodox path of righteousness dictated by the Church would be damned. To those at the Florentine court who were experimenting with heterodoxy, a clearer message of warning could not have been given. As visitors entered and left the chapel, they would have seen the pairing of the representations of *St. Michael* and *The Brazen Serpent* intended to remind them of the outcome of the final Judgment. With *St. Cosmas* there as Cosimo's alter ego, the watchful eye of the duke was summoned on the altar wall as an additional warning to those who strayed too far into spiritual experimentation. Yet, forgiveness is always available for those who strayed, and the combination of the Archangel's presence with the healing Saint Cosmas alongside John the Baptist indicated the possibility for salvation through renewal. The implicit message of the necessity to adhere to orthodoxy found in the chapel ceiling's juxtaposition of Michael, John the Evangelist, John the Baptist, The Brazen Serpent, and St. Cosmas/Duke Cosimo would have been clear to those attending Mass in the chapel.

Similar associations exist for Jerome, the saint whose order provided the confessors of choice for Spanish aristocrats and who was a penitent saint linked to the Apocalypse, as Natali indicated.[246] As such, Jerome is aligned on the chapel's axis with Michael as he gazes towards *The Brazen Serpent* and its eschatological prefiguration. As a saint associated with sin, penitence, the texts of the Church, and the Last Judgment, Jerome joins the chapel's Lenten themes into his personal devotional concerns.[246] In Bronzino's rendition, Jerome kneels in a penitential pose, looking at the light of God that illuminates the chapel. His gaze echoes the advice given to the Israelites, who were instructed to look beyond the Brazen Serpent to their salvation; and, indeed, Jerome's pose and gaze make him a participant in the events of *The Brazen Serpent*, described in Numbers 21:8–9:

> The Lord said to Moses," make a snake and put it up on a pole; anyone who is bitten can look at it and live." So Moses made a bronze snake and put it up on a pole. Then when anyone was bitten by a snake and looked at the bronze snake, they lived.

Jerome was the scholar saint who expurgated the Vulgate of error, and he represents the Church's orthodox dogmatic and textual traditions. His presence in the chapel, as a participant in the events of *The Brazen Serpent* and aligned with Michael's association with the Last Judgment, is a strong statement about the necessity of orthodoxy for salvation, in a context that is unequivocally Catholic.

Francis, the place saint indicative of Francesco's birth and of Eleonora's vow at La Verna, is also associated with the penitential themes of Lent and with Christ's Crucifixion during this liturgical season. His *stigmata*, the sign of the Cross manifested on his body, connects him to the altar wall, which he faces. In Bronzino's *modello*, Francis faced *The Brazen Serpent*, but in execution he was turned around. Had Francis faced *The Brazen Serpent*, his position would have resonated with certain unorthodox associations of Francis as the *alter christus*, as opposed to the orthodox consideration of Francis as a *typus christus*.[247] At a time when complying with orthodoxy was important for the religious politics of the Medici court, turning Francis around was part of ensuring that the chapel's program could not be misinterpreted as deviating from orthodoxy.

In turning Francis around, Bronzino also changed the compositional structure of this section to match that of Saints John the Evangelist and Jerome, whose attributes (eagle and lion) are on the left of the scene. By moving Francis to face the altar, Brother Leo appears on the left, with his size reduced in relation to that of Francis in a manner that mimics the proportion and arrangement of the compositional structure of John the Evangelist and Jerome. Thus, turning Francis towards the altar avoided unorthodox interpretations for his inclusion and rendered his section of the ceiling more harmonious with the rest of the ceiling's compositional structure.

The chapel's Lenten program, which established the Medici court as a bulwark of Rome, extended to the ceiling and encompassed Francesco's significance as the heir and future of the Medici dynasty and its religious politics. In effect, the chapel's message indicated that Francesco would also become a leader—a Joshua—who would uphold the traditions of orthodoxy, similar to those Moses passed to the Israelites and which Cosimo supported and Eleonora embodied. For the Medici and for Spanish aristocrats, for whom the association with Roman Catholicism was embedded in their identity, the meaning of Eleonora's chapel would have represented the Medici court—as defenders of the Church. This message was in accord with the mandate inherited by Charles V from his grandparents—*Los Reyes Católicos*. Through the family ties that existed between the Medici and the Royal houses of Spain, the Imperial mandate became a Medici mandate that was upheld by Cosimo and Francesco, who remained loyal to Rome before, during, and after the Council of Trent.

Heraldry and Identity In the *Crossing of the Red Sea* Fresco

When Cox-Rearick analyzed the pictorial content of the chapel's *Crossing of the Red Sea*, she interpreted heraldic aspects of the fresco's content—namely, a flag and a shield in the section with the defeated Egyptians—as indicating connections between the fresco and current Florentine and European events. Specifically, Cox-Rearick identified a red flag with a single crescent that appears on the fresco's upper right as representing the Strozzi arms (which are three silver crescents on a red band against a yellow background).[248] With this identification, Cox-Rearick suggested that the flag could be linked to the defeat of Filippo Strozzi, Cosimo's main opponent at Montemurlo.[249] Likely, the battle alludes to Cosimo's victory at Montemurlo. However, the heraldic incongruence of the depicted crescents and the Strozzi shield argues against a specific reference to Filippo Strozzi, whose suicide could not have been a memory Cosimo wished to permanently recall in Eleonora's chapel. Suicide was considered a sin that damned the suicide to Hell, so a permanent reminder that Cosimo had been responsible for Strozzi's suicide could not have been a desired part of the chapel's program.

To the right of the red flag with the single crescent there is a light-colored shield floating on the water, decorated with a single, upturned crescent and two stars on a band. Cox-Rearick identified this shield as linked to the flag of the Islamic Ottoman Empire, which she characterized as having a "crescent and two stars" found on "the Turkish flag."[250] Cox-Rearick also noted, based on information given to her by Edward Mader, that the armor worn by the Egyptians in *The Crossing of the Red Sea* conforms to that worn by Turkish soldiers in the sixteenth century.[251] Based on these elements, Cox-Rearick deduced that the *Red Sea* fresco contained allusions to recent European-Christian/Ottoman-Islamic conflicts, in which the Ottomans had been defeated.[252] However, the red flag in the fresco conforms more to the Ottoman flag than to the Strozzi arms, and it is likely that the flag, the shield, and the battle against the Egyptians are generalized references to the Ottomans. Although Cox-Rearick did not convincingly establish her analysis of the flag as indicating Filippo Strozzi, she did identify that *The Crossing of the Red Sea* recalls Cosimo's victory at Montemurlo and the Roman triumph over Ottoman incursions in Italy. Prior to Cox-Rearick's analysis of the *Red Sea*, Richelson had drawn attention to its significance, and after Cox-Rearick, Gason expanded on its meaning contextualized within the European/Ottoman conflicts.[252]

In a Spanish context, the defeat of the Ottomans, to which the *Red Sea* fresco alludes, would have had special resonance, as on 2 August 1492, Spain expelled its Jewish and Islamic populations.[254] The expulsion of Spain's Jewish and Islamic populations by Emperor Charles V's grandparents—Isabel and Fernando—was enacted in order to achieve religious purity and Catholic orthodoxy in a united Spain—the first European nation. Thus, the *Red Sea* fresco had topical references for Eleonora, whose family history was intertwined with the expulsion of Spain's Muslim population. It also had significance in the context of the confessional debates of the early 1540s.

In Exodus, the Egyptians were destroyed because they did not follow the orthodox teaching given to Moses and recorded in Exodus, Numbers, Deuteronomy, and Leviticus, from which passages are read during Lent as confirmation of the correct dogma of the Roman Church, which is the manifestation of the New Covenant

with God that replaced the Old Covenant of Moses and the Israelites. Given the contemporary religious debates of the 1540s, the *Red
Sea* fresco can also be understood as referring to the destruction
of European heretics and the salvation of the Roman Church—the
keeper of the orthodox tradition descended from Moses. Thus, the
Red Sea fresco's heraldic content can also be interpreted as containing allusions to contemporary military and confessional issues,
while metaphorically visualizing the Roman Church's hope that
their opponents would be swept out to sea, as the Egyptians had
been in Exodus. In Eleonora's chapel, it is very clear on which side
the Medici stood, as they remained standing on the shore, aligned
with Moses and with the Roman Church.

For Spanish Jews or for families which, reputedly, had once
been Jewish—such as that of Leonor de Guzmán, Eleonora's ancestress—the subject of the *Red Sea* fresco would have been a poignant
reminder of the Spanish Exodus forced upon the rejected populations. Jewish Spaniards would have had even more complicated
and complex reactions to the scene, as it would have reminded
them simultaneously of the triumph of the Israelites and of their
recent loss of a country they had called home. This emotional territory belonged to one Jewish woman close to Eleonora—Benvenida
Abravanel—who belonged to the family that had been the financial
advisers to the kings of Spain and who, in exile, advised Eleonora's
father and Eleonora.[255]

Cox-Rearick's publication of an early characterization of Eleonora's interaction with Benvenida makes the relationship clear:

> Siendo allí [in Naples] Visrey Don Pedro de Toledo, se cre-
> ase debaxo de la disciplina de la Señora Benvenida y en su
> casa, y después que casó con el Seieníssimo gran duque Cos-
> mo de Medices ... siempre en sus cosas se le valía de la
> Señora Benvenida que havitava en Ferrara, a quién llamava
> madre, como a tal la tratava, y venerava.[256]

The passage states that Don Pedro appointed Benvenida as Eleonora's substitute mother and that Eleonora called her "madre"
and venerating her as such. This passage also describes how Eleonora turned to Benvenida for advice and saw her frequently, as

Benvenida lived in Ferrara, after Italy's Jews were expelled from Naples.

In her consideration of Eleonora's perspective on the frescoes, Cox-Rearick linked Eleonora's relationship with Benvenida to the Mosaic scenes, considering that these scenes had special meaning for Eleonora because of her relationship with Benvenida. Cox-Rearick also published a document that records a visit to Eleonora by a "Jewish woman" with whom she discussed many aspects of religion in a beautiful manner.[257] It is very likely that this woman was Benvenida Abravanel, with whom Eleonora remained in contact. For someone of reputed Jewish blood, who maintained close relations with a Jewish family, the meaning of the chapel's Mosaic scenes would have been personally and emotionally significant reminders of such connections.

The levels of intertwined identities and loyalties that defined Eleonora may have been brought together in the *Red Sea* fresco in the symbolic figure of an aristocratic, very pregnant woman, dressed in red, green, gold, and white, who stands behind Moses as he gives his last teaching. Cox-Rearick identified this figure as "intended to allude to Eleonora herself" and "not ... an actual portrait likeness of the duchess ..."[258] In identifying the woman as an allusion to Eleonora's fecundity, Cox-Rearick pointed out that her placement beneath the depiction of St. Francis allows an association to be made between the woman and Francesco's birth and that she is an allusion to Eleonora's successful fecundity, which produced the Medici heir.

The association with fecundity and Eleonora encapsulated in this figure would have been even more meaningful to a Spaniard familiar with the heraldic colors of the Mendoza family and with Eleonora's familial connection to the Mendoza. The Mendoza colors were green, red, gold, and white—the colors of the woman's costume.[259] The Mendoza were prolific, and dressing Eleonora in their colors was a visual pun that referenced her lineage and the expectations for her as the *genitrix* of a new Medici dynasty. To Eleonora, familiar with the Mendoza history and colors, the pregnant woman would have been a constant reminder of her role and her triumph, and the colors of the woman's costume indicate that Eleonora was consulted to determine this very specific and unusual color combination, which would not have been well known in Florence at the time of the composition of the *Red Sea* fresco. To visiting Spaniards, who would have been familiar with the Mendoza colors and would have understood the reference being made in the colors of the pregnant woman's costume, this detail would have been a subtly humorous reminder of Eleonora's family alliances, as well as of the continuous manifestation of the famed Mendoza fecundity. In effect, the Mendoza were comparably as numerous as the Israelites, whose descendants were numbered by the stars in the sky.

To the Mendozas at the Florentine court, the figure of the pregnant woman dressed in the colors of their family would have been a reminder of their kinship with the ducal family. Thus, when Don Diego Francisco Mendoza (the likely patron for the Castrojeriz *Pietà* that is a copy of the chapel's *Pietà* and Charles V's ambassador to Florence) and Don Diego Hurtado de Mendoza (later, the Viceroy of Mexico), likely visitors to the chapel, would have seen this figure, they understood its implications of *emparentado* for the ducal family to the Nájera group and to them.[260] The inclusion of these topical references indicates Eleonora's participation in the design of the fresco, as such a trope required very specialized knowledge about Spanish families and their history, and only Don Pedro and Eleonora would have possessed such knowledge. Hence, this detail could be another indication of Eleonora's participation in shaping the chapel's content to emphasize her descent from the *Famílias Primadas* of Spain.

Gaston's consideration of the chapel sought to establish familial connections for Eleonora found in the *Red Sea* fresco by arguing that the kneeling man in the fresco's right foreground was intended as a portrait of Don Pedro de Toledo, Eleonora's father.[261] This identification is rejected here for several reasons. Scrutiny of the kneeling man's face reveals that, although he is emphasized, he is not particularized enough to be a portrait. Furthermore, the clear parallels made in the chapel between Moses and Cosimo also argue against Gaston's identification, because court protocol would never have had Don Pedro kneeling before Cosimo (or his *alter ego*), as Don Pedro's rank as Viceroy was superior to Cosimo's as duke. Such a representation would have represented a violation of hieratic protocol and would have been personally insulting to Don Pedro, as would have been a portrait in which his face was obscured.

Thus, Gaston's suggestion does not accord with courtly protocols. Joshua was a general in the army Moses assembled to protect the Israelites. Hence, the semi-military clothing worn by the kneeling figure indicates his rank as a soldier, in keeping with Joshua's role. In the chapel's symbolic system, Moses/Cosimo was matched by Joshua/Francesco, who was a baby at the time of the painting of the fresco. Perhaps this figure's face is obscured because the features of the adult Francesco were not yet manifest. Yet, his future role is clear, as he is Florence's next duke and the heir to the title, territories, stewardship, and guardianship of orthodoxy passed on to him by Cosimo, with the blessing of God, as Moses had done for Joshua.

As was discussed above, the kneeling man is correctly placed as the successor to Moses and identifiable as the next leader who will be responsible for observing the orthodox teachings that Moses passes to his followers. Appropriately, Joshua kneels at the feet of Moses in proximity to the baton of rule that will pass to him once Moses has died after delivering his last teaching. Standing next to Moses is Eleazar, the priest of unquestioned orthodoxy, who will assist Joshua in bringing the Israelites to the Promised Land. As Cox-Rearick indicated, Eleazar is a portrait of Riccio as Eleazar, and, as such, the use of Riccio's features for the face of Eleazar carries specific meaning that would seem to indicate that Riccio, like Eleazar, is being represented in the chapel as a priest of impeccably orthodox standing.

Riccio, Orthodoxy, and Heterodoxy

In his discussion of Eleonora's chapel, Falciani pointed to the inclusion of Riccio's portrait in the chapel's *Crossing of the Red Sea* as confirmation that the chapel's program is intentionally Valdesian.[262] Falciani considered Riccio to have been a follower of Juan de Valdés and that Cosimo and Eleonora desired a Valdesian program for the chapel. Falciani's assertion was based on Riccio's ownership of a manuscript copy of the *Beneficio* and because he knew individuals who exhibited an interest in reforming the Church and/or in the intellectual and spiritual aspects of confessional controversies. Falciani, therefore, assumed that Riccio's friendship indicated Cosimo and Eleonora's spiritual allegiance.[263]

Yet, Gigliola Fragnito's study of Riccio's life and of his ecclesiastical and courtly career provides counter evidence for the wholesale recent assignment of Riccio to the ranks of the heterodox, and she specifically cautions against the "recente" tendency to assign Riccio "posizione religiose sospette."[264] Fragnito's study traced the traditional education—religious, literary, and artistic—which Riccio gave Cosimo, after September 1527, when Maria Salviati engaged him as Cosimo's tutor. In 1532, Riccio accompanied Cosimo to Bologna, where Riccio ensured that Cosimo made a good impression on Emperor Charles V and Pope Clement VII. After Cosimo's confirmation as duke, Riccio, with Maria Salviati, assisted Cosimo in his careful domestic and international political agenda designed to secure the Medici court's safety in the changing political and religious climate. Riccio's role as *majordomo* was made official on 1 March 1545, although he had been fulfilling that role for some years, managing much of the daily affairs of the court and overseeing the decoration of the palace. At a time when it was crucial to secure the ongoing support of Charles V, it is unlikely that Riccio, with Cosimo's approval, would have devised a heretical program for Eleonora's chapel.

In March 1548, Riccio fell ill and almost died. When Riccio recovered, he continued his management of the court until 1553, when he fell ill again and was forced to retire from court service. Upon his retirement, Riccio drew income from a series of Church appointments, including the chaplaincy of St. Catherine; the canonicate of San Lorenzo and Santa Maria del Fiore, Santo Stefano di Campi, San Leonardo di Cerreto Guidi, San Giovanni di Petroio, San Romolo di Firenze, Ss. Jacopo e Cristofano a Cornazzaro, San Martino a Montughi; and the prefecture of Santo Stefano di Prato. On 6 November, 1561, Riccio was awarded the title of Apostolic Protonotary by Pope Pius IV, this being one of the highest titles that can be awarded by the college of prelates of the Roman Curia and a title that that would not have been awarded to someone whose religious loyalties were suspect. In effect, the receipt of these benefices and the title of *Protonotario Apostolico* indicate that Riccio passed the test of orthodoxy several times, as he advanced in his ecclesiastical career, while serving the Medici court. The data thus argue against the proposition that Riccio and the ducal couple were Valdesian sympathizers, much less avowed Valdesians.

Although Fragnito asserted the orthodoxy of Cosimo and Riccio's religious politics, she did identify that intellectual and spiritual diversity had political value for Cosimo. In the varied interests exhibited by the intellectual pursuits of the *Accademia's* members, which included interest in Egyptian, Hebrew, and contemporary evangelical culture, Fragnito identified a plan on Cosimo's part to deliberately taunt Paul III.[265] Fragnito noted that once Julius III became pope, Cosimo aligned his religious politics with those of the Church by allowing the Inquisition to control Florentine spirituality. Fragnito also pointed out that the identification of Riccio with heterodoxy, as a result of his ownership of a copy of the *Beneficio*, is not sufficient to demonstrate that Riccio subscribed to unorthodox beliefs or practices, as clerics owned a wide range of books so that they could study and prepare to defend the Church.

The premise that anyone who owned a copy of the *Beneficio* was a Valdesian is comparable to assuming that anyone owning a copy of the *Communist Manifesto* is a Communist and that anyone who has leftist friends is a fellow traveler. Ownership of controversial texts by ecclesiastics is not a situation of fixed meaning, as sixteenth-century clergy were expected to read the available confessional literature in order to debate it. Riccio may indeed have been sympathetic to ideas of reform, as were many within the Church, but caution should be used in attaching too much meaning to the ownership of controversial books. Reformists were also orthodox Catholics, as a desire for reform did not render individuals automatically Protestant.

Before the Diet of Ratisbon (February 1541), clerics and intellectuals interested in religious issues read treatises arguing all of the points of debate, and even after the Diet, these collections increased, as clerics kept up with what was being published about confessional controversies. After the failure of the Diet to bring about a reunification of the Church, books that forwarded positions counter to the Church's orthodoxy became increasingly problematic but were still owned, read, passed around, and discussed. [266] Specifically, Fragnito cautioned against using the *Beneficio* as proof that Riccio created unorthodox programs at the Medici court, such as Pontormo's frescoes at San Lorenzo. As Fragnito pointed out, while Riccio may have had a wide range of intellectual interests and diverse input into the creation and enactment of programs, only Cosimo would have controlled the decision about the nature of the program. The creation of heterodox programs would have been against Cosimo's careful and traditional politics and personal religious practices; therefore, it is unlikely that Riccio would have been allowed (had he even wished to) create problematic programs at the court.

Following Fragnito's study of Riccio, Alessandro Cecchi presented his findings on Riccio's role as *majordomo* in charge of overseeing the decoration of the palace.[267] Cecchi suggested that Riccio's portrait in the *Crossing of the Red Sea* was an allusion to his role as an administrator and adviser for the decorative programs in the palace. Ignoring Cox-Rearick's identification of the priest as Eleazar, Cecchi noted that Moses had two high priests—Aaron and Eleazar—and that Riccio could have been one or the other in the fresco. The conundrum created by Cecchi's statement is easily resolved in favor of Cox-Rearick's identification of the "priest" as Eleazar, through a comparison of the relative ages of the depictions of Moses and his priest. Aaron and Moses were contemporaries, and Eleazar belonged to the next generation, as he was Aaron's son, clothed by Moses in the garments of his father after Aaron was buried on Mount Hor. Eleazar, in contrast, was the priest of consummate orthodoxy, who received his teaching from Moses when Moses passed on to him the teachings he had received from the Lord. In the *Crossing of the Red Sea*, the priest next to Moses is Eleazar, so identified by his relative youth in comparison with Moses' clearly advanced years, indicated by his white hair and seated posture. Thus, in the *Red Sea* fresco, Riccio is portrayed as Eleazar, the priest of unquestioned adherence to orthodoxy, as an indication that the chapel's program was intentionally orthodox.

Falciani, in identifying Riccio's portrait in the chapel as confirmation of heterodoxy bordering on heresy, did not sufficiently take into consideration that Riccio was represented as Eleazar, nor did he consider the history and characterization of Eleazar as a signifier of Riccio's characterization.[268] Had Riccio been portrayed as Aaron, Falciani's assertion that Riccio's portrait indicated a heterodox program could have held, but it must be set aside because Riccio was depicted as Eleazar.

Riccio's depiction as Eleazar, the priest of impeccable orthodoxy, accords with the interpretive approach employed in this chapter, which analyzes the chapel's decorative program from the perspective of the Roman and Mozarabic liturgy. This approach was based on the primary function of the chapel as a liturgical space, in which Roman Catholic Masses were celebrated and in which Eleonora de Toledo prayed from devotional books written in accordance with the use of Rome. The liturgical approach employed here is grounded in the sixteenth-century liturgies of Rome and Toledo, and it follows the methodological approach exemplified in Carol Lewine's study of the Sistine Chapel.

As a means of understanding and decoding religious works of art in liturgical spaces, the application of the method employed in this chapter extends beyond the chapel and can be used for any number of works commissioned for churches and chapels. The constancy and consistency of the liturgy and the Church's dogma meant that patrons, such as Cosimo and Eleonora, could employ artists to illustrate programs based on the Church's liturgy, which could be easily apprised by spectators familiar with the readings of the liturgical year. In Catholic countries, such messages were easily deciphered by the elite familiar with the content of the services, which they regularly attended to mark the holy days of the Church. The employment of a liturgical approach to the chapel has revealed a cohesive core program based on the Lenten liturgy of the Church that also accommodated ancillary themes, such as territorial and political ambition, dynastic succession, and religious politics.

The decorative program of Eleonora's chapel reflects coordinated patronage on the part of Cosimo and Eleonora in a room designated for her use. As part of her apartment in the palace, the chapel was key for Eleonora, who preferred the company of the select few who composed her personal court, shunned socializing with Italians in preference of Spaniards, and chose to worship privately in her chapel instead of publicly in the city's churches. Because the chapel's core and extended programs address the larger and more communal concerns of religious identity, dynastic union, and political hierarchies, the individual at the center of the room became submerged in these representative agendas. The Duchess Eleonora is the person who occupies the chapel, but she emerges in it transformed into a sign or symbol of the role her birth and marriage destined her to play in the international sixteenth-century politics. Thus, the concluding section of this chapter seeks to balance the depersonalization of Eleonora that was the inevitable outcome of the political nature of her chapel by outlining a path to a reconsideration of the personal Eleonora.

CONCLUSION: PROBLEMATIZING THE TRIUMPHALIST ELEONORA AS PATRON

In Florence, Eleonora began her patronage career by initially coordinating the decoration of her private chapel with her husband, his court advisers, and with Bronzino, the artist selected by Cosimo because his work on the wedding *apparato* had pleased him, as Vasari noted. By 1549, Eleonora had the chapel's keys, and by 1553 she had control of the chapel's imagery and was working independently with Bronzino. It is clear from the sources and documents that Eleonora learned quickly, and, as she matured in her role as duchess, she fashioned a material culture of dress and interior design for her family, court, and palaces that emphasized the cross-cultural and international nature of the Florentine state.[269] It was her increasing wealth, the result of her investments, and her growing power at court, the result of the birth of her numerous children, that gave Eleonora the status and confidence that made her an indefatigable coordinator of her court's image.

As a demanding and discerning patron of costume, jewelry, furnishings, textiles, paintings, and tapestries, Eleonora demonstrated, in the later 1540s and 1550s, a shrewd and pragmatic manipulation of objects and comestible gifts that enabled her to aggrandize her family and her social position among European aristocrats. As Eleonora increasingly manifested her control of the Florentine court's image, the purchase of the Pitti Palace (1549) provided her with another theater in which she could express her personal taste, characterized by an eclectic blend of international style.[270] Eleonora's personal style fused elements of dress and decor from Spain, Italy, France, England, and Germany into an internationally oriented visual presentation expressed through costume, jewelry, and furnishings (which included paintings). Thus, every aspect of the material culture which surrounded Eleonora consistently projected a message (public and private) of cosmopolitan sophistication, almost as though she were saying "because I'm here, this is a court of international culture."

Future study of Eleonora's patronage of visual and material culture should be contextualized within current studies being conducted by Evelyn Welch and Michele O' Malley, focused on the purchase of commodities and their display.[271] Such studies, which explore the employment of material culture as a measure of wealth in order to signify rank and power through image making, enable the consideration of how such activities communicated religious and political positions, as well as social standing and lineage. Eleonora knowingly and expertly engaged in such statements as she grew more confident, wealthier, more aware of her role at the Florentine court and more ambitious for her children's future marriages and connections.

As she employed her money to enhance her family, Eleonora purchased, displayed, and gave away jewels, furnishings, tapestries, textiles, works of art, and other gifts that indicated wealth, with gifts of comestibles indicating ownership of agricultural territories.[272] Gifts of charitable endowments and contributions to churches and other religious organizations were also expressions of Eleonora's patronage and her religious views—and in giving gifts to religious institutions and charity to individuals, Eleonora asserted the Roman Church's beliefs that good works were salvific. Hence, Eleonora's patronage was also an indicator of the orthodox ducal position in the religious controversies of the sixteenth century.[273]

Eleonora was introduced to artistic patronage at the Florentine court with Bronzino's decoration of her chapel and Bandinelli's participation in the design of the chapel's altarpiece, and her patronage of artists with whom she felt comfortable continued. The portraits of the ducal family, which were commissioned from Bronzino by Cosimo and Eleonora, whether they remained in Florence or were sent away as gifts, actualized the presence of the Medici in Florence and in far away courts.[274] There can be little question that Eleonora appreciated the beauty and quality of execution of Bronzino's portraits, but did she select Bronzino because of the nature of his stylistic statement and its intellectual implications or because the quality of his craftsmanship enabled him to represent her family's costumes and jewels to best effect? This is an important question that should be answered by anyone considering a patronage study of the Florentine duchess, because the direct and pragmatic style of her patronage is much more evident in her high expenditures on clothing, jewelry, and furnishings than it is in her purchase of works of art. Thus, her commissions from Bronzino should, perhaps, be contextualized more within the purchasing patterns of Eleonora than within the intellectualized world of artistic theory and intellectual history that is given to Bronzino by modern scholarship, from perspectives other than those found in Eleonora's pragmatic agendas.

Bruce Edelstein recently attempted to document that Eleonora assessed Bronzino's work from a connoisseurship perspective and that she played a dominant role in the majority of the commissions of Bronzino's portraits. [275] However, the manner whereby the portraits were commissioned parallels that of the cooperative nature of the chapel's commission, where at different times either member of the ducal couple took the lead in overseeing the content and destination of portraits. For a portrait of the duchess and Francesco, which had already been ordered by Cosimo, Eleonora, expectedly, took charge of deciding the clothing to be depicted and the manner in which this clothing presented her son.[276] In other instances, it was Cosimo who ordered portraits from Bronzino, as Vasari noted in Bronzino's *Vita*.

In another instance, discussed by Alessandro Cecchi, a copy of a portrait of Giovanni was ordered from Luigi Corto (a Flemish painter working in Florence), and it was Eleonora who was anxious to see the finished portrait, which pleased upon arrival.[277] Vasari records that Bronzino completed the famous Uffizi portrait of Eleonora and Giovanni to Eleonora's satisfaction—"siccome piacque a lei"—but this casual remark can mean simply that she liked the portrait or that she was satisfied with the portrayal of their clothing and jewels, as opposed to its being a connoisseurship position.[278]

Edelstein also noted another instance of coordinated ducal patronage, when Vasari meets with the ducal couple to discuss his planned program for Eleonora's *stanze*. Vasari recounted, in a letter to Vincenzo Borghini dated 21 November 1561, that he had met with Cosimo and Eleonora and had spent half as much time with

Cosimo as he had with Eleonora.[279] Six months later, Vasari told Borghini that "If I have succeeded in satisfying the duchess it will be no small thing."[280] Edelstein's discussion of Vasari's statements implied that he considered Eleonora to be the dominant patron for Vasari's work and that her questions originated from a context of sophisticated consumption of artistic theory and intellectual production.

Yet, perhaps Vasari spent two hours with Eleonora and one with Cosimo because Cosimo either grasped Vasari's concepts faster and/or he needed to be moving on to more important things. Perhaps Eleonora needed more explanations to grasp Vasari's plan; or, she had more time and interest because they were discussing her rooms and she did not have pressing state business to attend to. Although there is little question that Eleonora was a demanding patron, it is important, when considering her patronage, to carefully distinguish the nature of her demands in order to assess her style and type of patronage. There is a difference between the demanding personality of a difficult person and a demanding patron of art who is working from the perspective of a connoisseur determined to develop a collection of art of outstanding artistic merit based on knowledge of artistic theory and the history of art.

If Eleonora's patronage is studied for its intentionality, it become clear that her patronage interests were predominantly and pragmatically preoccupied with the material use of the objects she purchased as elements of display and image-making, not as conveyors of artistic or literary culture. Recent study of Eleonora's costumes conducted by Roberta Orsi Landini and Bruna Niccoli have established that Eleonora spent much more money on clothing, furnishings, textiles, and jewelry than she did on paintings or statues.[281] This accords with Benevenuto Cellini's assessment of her patronage, which was focused on personal décor and objects that increased her status or her devotional practices.[282] Even the purchase of the Pitti was not an architectural commission; it was a real estate acquisition intended to accommodate her growing family. Gaetano Pieraccini, in his assessment of Eleonora's patronage interests, noted, as did Cellini, that her taste for things ran to those which could be used for personal embellishment.[283]

Eleonora's demanding patronage was an extension of her exacting and difficult personality, recorded by the court secretaries Ugolino Grifoni and Leonardo Pagni, who noted that the duchess was prone to hysteria when she was crossed. This behavior is documented by Pieraccini, who published extracts from letters which record that, when Cosimo was away in 1541 and 1543 Eleonora would cry, scream, tear at her face, and pull her hair in fits of childish, histrionic behavior, in protest at being left behind. These displays left the courtiers nonplussed.[284] Eleonora would also refuse to eat or sleep until Cosimo returned. As part of this discussion, Pieraccini noted that Eleonora's handwriting was nearly illegible, even to Cosimo, and that during her regencies of Florence, she paid little attention to ruling, did not sign a single document in 1541, and could only be persuaded to attend to state business when she was not entertaining herself. It is difficult to think that someone who spoke Italian with difficulty and wrote badly could have fully participated in Florentine intellectual culture. Countering Pieraccini's assertion would require documented proof that Eleonora actively spent time reading and discussing literature and treatises with a peer group of intellectuals, as opposed to being pressed into service for show, as she sometimes was made to do. Balancing Eleonora's less ideal qualities were the manners of a consummate courtier, and ducal secretaries do record that Eleonora could be gracious and that she was the perfect partner to Cosimo.[285]

Eleonora's demanding personality and her concern with status and personal appearance focused her attention on a show of courtly wealth through material display. Her interest in manipulating dress and jewelry to create effective and elaborate pageants and other special occasions resulted in her extensive and ingenious commissions of clothing and jewelry, intended to make the Medici court appear resplendently sophisticated. There is not, however, enough evidence to support a characterization of Eleonora as a connoisseur comparable to Isabella d'Este. Nor can it be established that Eleonora regarded paintings and sculpture or architecture as being significantly different from the artistic designs she commissioned for her clothing and jewelry. Instead, it seems that Eleonora appreciated luxury goods, including works of art, which could be used to advance her personal agendas and her family's position through display and gifts made to influential individuals. If money spent is a judgment of interest, then Eleonora was much more interested in clothing, jewelry, textiles, embroideries, and furnishings than she was in art.[286] In her commissions for works of art, Eleonora's patronage focused on religious or meritorious subjects and portraits, all subjects that were useful in furthering a straightforward representation of herself as the model woman, wife, and mother who brought abundance to the Medici court.

Orsi Landini and Niccoli's study also describes how Eleonora's apartments became workrooms for the creation of the style and costumes of the family and the court.[287] Eleonora oversaw the weaving of the cloth used to make her family's clothing, and she worked closely with tailors and embroiderers and jewelers, who provided her with the furnishings and clothing she commissioned. These craftsmen were steady visitors at the court and had access to her apartments, access which may well have been denied to Florentines of higher class, as while Eleonora did commission works from artists such as Bronzino, Bandinelli, Vasari, and Cellini, the volume of her commissions were not given to the artists of the world of fine arts. Instead, Eleonora's passion for developing and purchasing unusual textiles, inventive costumes, original jewels, and for styling the court's image meant that she lived in the world of designers and craftspeople. It is intriguing to consider that the woman who snubbed Italian aristocrats worked so well with the Italian working classes and that she was able to develop such successful collaborative relations with them that crossed the boundaries of the accepted class lines. As a study in class behavior and in crossing social boundaries, a consideration of this aspect of Eleonora's life could be a study with larger application in the consideration of social and class interaction in early modern Europe.

The image that develops of Eleonora's apartment, based on the results of Orsi Landini and Niccoli's study, is one of constant activity, noise, bustle, and movement, all focused on manufacturing the style of the court that Elenora designed with the help of a variety of manufacturing experts. She may not have been an Isabella d'Este or an Isabel de Castilla, but Eleonora was a brilliant coordinator of image making and self-fashioning and an innovative designer of fashion in personal adornment and domestic furnishings. She was ahead of her time in understanding the connection between status,

presentation, design, and the messages inscribed in the manipulation of material culture. That she exercised her talent in a domestic
sphere is very much the product of Eleonora's acceptance of her
role as a sixteenth-century aristocratic woman and it was through
her adherence and expansion of this role that she became remarkable.

In fulfilling all of the expectation for her role, Eleonora acquired
power, and she used it to help her family—as any wife and mother
would do. As an unfortunate comparison of a woman of similar
rank but bad fortune, one can think of Jeanne d'Evreux, whose
failure to produce an heir meant that she was never able to gain
a position comparable to Eleonora's. In a feminist study of Jeanne
d'Evreux's Book of Hours, Madeline Caviness demonstrated how
an aristocratic woman of Jeanne's rank was constrained and tutored
in the expected performance of her assigned role as the bearer of
children and the manager of her husband's reputation.[288] Eleonora
was similarly tutored, with the difference being that she succeeded
where Jeanne d'Evreux failed. One cannot help but wonder what
would have happened to Eleonora if she had not produced an aver-
age of one child a year for as long as she could or an heir who survived. That she did produce an heir and multiple spares meant that
she was free to pursue her interests in accordance with her abilities
and talents, which were focused on making money and spending it
to enhance her family's social position at home and abroad.

Because Eleonora's chapel has drawn attention from a feminist
perspective, it is important to conclude by addressing the implications the chapel has for study from this perspective. The point
of feminist studies, especially of feminist Renaissance studies, is to
elucidate the circumstances of women's lives and how they negotiated power in a patriarchal society. Such studies fail if they seek to
make pseudo-men of women or if their goal is to construct a triumphalist narrative akin to that constructed for a history that is focused on the great accomplishments of great men. Finding heroines
may be part of feminist studies, and such studies do bring to prominence and attention remarkable women who otherwise would have
continued to be overlooked. But, it is not possible to remove wom-
en from their time or their place or their social conditioning or circumstances. Nor should the record of history be distorted to enable

a politically correct reading of evidence in an attempt to create a narrative that may not be the complete or accurate story. If it is the purpose of feminist studies to clarify the circumstances of women's lives, then their lives need to be clarified in the context in which they were lived, taking into consideration all the evidence that exists about women's lives, activities, character, and personality.

Eleonora was a woman who was remarkably adept at situating herself as a woman of consequence within the world into which she was born, but she did not do it by competing with Cosimo or by imitating male patronage or behavior in an attempt to compete on male terms. Instead, she made herself notable by deliberately embodying the virtues that a male-dominated society favored for women: fecundity, courtly manners, high birth, money, and domestic display. Her fits of hysteria were also displays of power, as they paralyzed the court, but they were essentially feminine. By not overtly participating in occupations that did not overly interest her, she was able to concentrate on those aspects of court life that suited her talents. By emphasizing her female role, as the duchess consort to Cosimo, Duke of Florence and Siena, Eleonora enhanced her family's prestige and gathered all the praise that was duly accorded to a woman who fulfilled all of the expectations of her role. Eleonora succeeded because she enacted the traditional feminine role expected of her and because she understood precisely how to manipulate that role into her personal sphere of power, using her lapses into states of hysteria and the capricious temperament of a woman who enjoyed undue privilege to control her surroundings. Whether this behavior was deliberate staging or a sign of mental imbalance, the outcome was an increase of her power.[289]

Orsi Landini and Niccoli framed their study of Eleonora's costumes as a study of history and legend in which they juxtaposed two different stories about Eleonora's life, using data and the romantic legend created about her by earlier literature. In so doing, they avoided the pitfalls of romanticizing Eleonora, as they brought together diverse sources and documents to present their findings about her social world. A study sensitive to Eleonora's character and the events of her life could trace how Leonor de Toledo, the young girl, who arrived at Livorno for her wedding, transformed into Eleonora da Toledo, Duchess of Florence and Pisa, taking into account all of the available data.

The studies of Eleonora's patronage and her role as ducal consort by Cox-Rearick, Edelstein, Gáldy, Smyth, and Gaston have relied on revisionist history for their idealized Eleonora; crafted in a triumphalist mode, they thus omit her less than sterling personality traits. The newer, feminist revisionism has suppressed the less ideal aspects of Eleonora's behavior and has rendered an incomplete picture of her, even as it has sought to force Eleonora into a mode imitative of and defined by the social roles of men. A new consideration of Eleonora must take into consideration all of the available evidence that could clarify her life in a more balanced and less idealizing but no less noteworthy manner. Otherwise, the lines blur between modern, critical writers of history and the sixteenth-century panegyrists, who were paid to praise Eleonora to the skies no matter what—and who were so successful that today's triumphalist Eleonora is based on their *facture* of Eleonora the paragon of virtue, omitting evidence, found in primary sources, that Eleonora had a dark side.

As the link between Florence and Spain, Eleonora performed a key role in cementing relations between Cosimo and Charles V. At a time of tension in European religious politics, Eleonora's orthodox Catholicism, along with her economic and courtly activities, played an important role in safeguarding Florence. This adherence to the faith of her childhood and to the marker of her Spanish identity was the foundation on which her chapel's program was built, and the statement made in the chapel was part of Cosimo's religious politics. Eleonora's contribution to Florentine politics and religious and social life was important, yet it is a contribution that should be studied by contextualizing Eleonora's capabilities alongside her imperfections.

As the *genetrix* of aristocrats, Eleonora was successful beyond the expectations expressed at her wedding in leaving her imprint on the royal houses of Europe. Her descendants have kept her heritage alive, long past the time when the Medici dynasty she founded with Cosimo came to an end. Today, her legacy continues through her granddaughter, Maria de' Medici, Francesco's daughter, who married Henri IV of France. One of Maria de' Medici's descendants was Diana Spenser, Princess of Wales, and her son, William, Duke of Cambridge, is a direct descendant of Eleonora de Toledo. History records that Eleonora was so successful in producing a dynasty that, even today, as Prince William waits to ascend the British throne, the family she founded continues to produce monarchs.[290]

NOTES

I thank Liana De Girolami Cheney for providing me with the opportunity for presenting this essay in honor of Craig Hugh Smyth. I am indebted to my husband, Charles Burroughs, for his thoughtful discussions, throughout the process of this project. I thank Gregory Clark for his help with issues related to the content and use of devotional books. For assistance with the Eleonora Hours, I thank Rowan Watson. I also thank Paul Barolsky, Dorothy Limouze, and Larry Silver for their support and encouragement of the project and for their comments about the manuscript during preparation. I thank Cristiano Giometti for assistance in locating hard-to-find sources. A series of publication support grants from SUNY at Geneseo provided funding towards this project, including a Small Senate Grant and a Research Grant from the Geneseo Foundation. Finally, I thank Janet Cox-Rearick, whose pioneering work on the Eleonora Chapel will continue to stand as the touchstone and benchmark study for Bronzino's Chapel for Eleonora de Toledo, for the personal and professional support she gave me during three and one-half decades of friendship.

1. The more pertinent publication on the chapel are: Janet Cox-Rearick, "Les Dessins de Bronzino pour la Chapelle d' Eleonora au Palazzo Vecchio," *Revue de l'Art* 14 (1971), 7–22; eadem, "Bronzino's *Young Woman with Her Little Boy*," *Studies in the History of Art* 12 (1982), 67–79; eadem, "Bronzino's Crossing of the Red Sea and Moses Appointing Joshua: Prolegomena to the Chapel of Eleonora di Toledo," *The Art Bulletin* 69 (1987), 45–67; eadem, "From Bandinelli to Bronzino," *The Burlington Magazine* 129 (1987), 155–62; eadem, *Bronzino's Chapel of Eleonora in the Palazzo Vecchio* (Berkeley: University of California Press, 1993); Bruce Edelstein, *The Early Patronage of Eleonora di Toledo: The Camera Verde and its Dependencies in the Palazzo Vecchio* (Ph.D. diss., Harvard University, 1995); Maurice Brock, *Bronzino* (Paris: Flammarion, 2002); Andrea Gáldy, "Tuscan Concerns and Spanish Heritage in the Decoration of Duchess Eleonora's Apartment in the Palazzo Vecchio," *Renaissance Studies* 20, no. 3 (June 2006), 293–319; Carmen C. Bambach et al., *New York, Metropolitan Museum of Art, The Drawings of Bronzino* (New York: The Metropolitan Museum of Art/New Haven, CT, and London: Yale University Press, 2010) [henceforth Bambach, *The Drawings of Bronzino*], 118–49 and 196–97; and Carlo Falciani and Antonio Natali, eds., *Bronzino, Artist and Poet at the Court of the Medici*

(Florence: Mandragora, 2010) [henceforth Falciani and Natali, *Bronzino*].

2. On the Council, see John W. O' Malley, *Trent: What Happened at the Council* (Cambridge, MA: Belknap Press, 2012); and John A. McHugh and Charles J. Callan, *The Catechism of the Council of Trent* (Charlotte, NC: Tan Books, 1982).

3. Cox-Rearick, *Bronzino's Chapel of Eleonora*, 72.

4. Cox-Rearick, *Bronzino's Chapel of Eleonora*, 81, notes that the new furnishings included a new altar frontal, six silver statues of the Apostles, and a *pax* (1550) and vestments for the chaplain (1553). The purchase of new vestments coincided with the installation of the second *Pietà*.

5. Cox-Rearick, *Bronzino's Chapel of Eleonora*, 81.

6. For Eleonora's attendance at daily Mass, see Cox-Rearick, *Bronzino's Chapel of Eleonora*, 45. See ibid. for a letter from Ugolino Griffoni, one of the court secretaries to Riccio, dated 1541, reporting that while the duke was away, Eleonora spent her time attending to business and entertaining women who came to visit and in prayer—so much so that Griffoni thought that he was locked up in a monastery. Cosimo attended Mass in the Cappella de Priori or at the Duomo or SS Annunizata, depending on his desires. For Cosimo's traditional piety and his adherence to the Church, see Henk Th. Van Veen, *Cosimo I de' Medici and His Self-Representation in Florentine Art and Culture* (Cambridge: Cambridge University Press, 2006), 185; and Gregory William Murry, *The Making of a God: Culture, Religion, and Sacral Monarchy in Duke Cosimo de' Medici's Florence* (Ph.D. diss., The Pennsylvania State University, 2009; Ann Arbor, MI: ProQuest, UMI Dissertation Publishing, 2012), for a study of how Cosimo presented himself as a monarch appointed by God to rule. Van Veen's study also addresses Cosimo's employment of self-apotheosis to style his self-fashioning as a ruler. See also Gregory William Murry, *Monarchy and Sacral Politics in Duke Cosimo de' Medici's Florence* (Camridge, MA: Harvard University Press, 2014), for additional consideration of Cosimo de' Medici's engagement with employing apotheosis as an iconographic theme.

7. For a description of these manuscripts, see Rowan Watson, "Manual of Dynastic History or Devotional Aid? Eleanor of Toledo's Book of Hours," in *Excavating the Medieval Image: Manuscripts, Artists, Audiences: Essays in Honor of Sandra Hindman*, eds. David S. Areford and Nina A. Rowe (Aldershot: Ashgate, 2004), 179–95; idem, "Book of Hours (The Eleanor of Toledo Hours), Use of Rome, in Latin," in *Western Illuminated Manuscripts*, 2 vols. (London: V & A Publishing, 2011), 2:851–57. See also Cox-Rearick, *Bronzino's Chapel of Eleonora*, 37, 39, 277; and Robert W. Gaston, "Eleonora di Toledo's Chapel: Lineage, Salvation and the War Against the Turks," in *The Cultural World of Eleonora di Toledo: Duchess of Florence and Siena*, ed. Konrad Eisenbichler (Aldershot: Ashgate, 2004), 167. Gaston noted that

in the *guardaroba*'s inventory, there is listed "... an Hours of the Virgin, in Spanish, in accordance with Rome use, made in León, in 1531; a Psalter, in Spanish, which included other devotional prayers; an Hours of Jesus Christ, in Spanish [likely an Hours of the Cross]; a Spanish *Devocionario*; a manuscript, in Spanish, with a special Prayer to Christ and the Virgin; and a Gospel of John, translated into Tuscan, dedicated to Eleonora." For a general discussion of the contents of Books of Hours and the significance of usage, see Roger Wieck, *Painted Prayers: The Book of Hours in Medieval and Renaissance Art* (New York: George Braziller, 1999).

8. For a very brief summary of confessional debates, see Steven Ozment, *The Age of Reform, 1250–1550: An Intellectual and Religious History of Late Medieval and Reformation Europe* (New Haven, CT: Yale University Press, 1981); and Hans J. Hillerbrand, *The Protestant Reformation* (New York City: Harper Perennial, 2009).

9. On the intellectual climate of the Florence and the Accademia, see Detlef Heikamp, "Rapporti fra accademici ed artisti nella Firenze del '500," *Il Vasari*, 1 (1957), 139–63; Armand L. De Gaetano, *Giambattista Gelli and the Florentine Academy: The Rebellion Against Latin* (Florence: Olschki, 1976); S.J. Batomsky, "Noah, Italy, and the Sea-Peoples: The Problem," *The Jewish Quarterly Review*, n.s. 67 (1977), 146–53; Cesare Vasoli, "Considerazione sull'Accademia Fiorentina," *Revue des etudes italiennes* 25 (1979), 41–72; G. Cipriani, *Il mito etrusco nel rinascimento fiorentino* (Florence: Olschki, 1980); Alessandro Cecchi, "Il Bronzino, Benedetto Varchi e l'Accademia Fiorentina: ritratti di poeti, letterati e personaggi illustri della corte medicea," *Antichità Viva* 30 (1991), 17–28; and M. Sherberg, "The Accademia Fiorentina and the Question of Language: The Politics of Theory in Ducal Florence," *Renaissance Quarterly* 56 (2003), 26–55.

10. On the *Accademia*'s history, see Iacopo Rilli, *Notizie letterarie ed istoriche intorno agli uomini illustri dell'Accademia Fiorentina* (Florence: Piero Matini, 1700); and Salvino Salvini, *Fasti Consolari dell'Accademia Fiorentine* (Florence: Tartini, 1717). For a modern summary of the *Accademia*'s history, see Karen-edis Barzman, *The Florentine Academy and the Early Modern State: The Discipline of Disegno* (Cambridge: Cambridge University Press, 2000).

11. Bronzino became a member of the Accademia on 11 February 1541; see Leatrice Mendelsohn's entry on the Panciatichi Holy Family in Falciani and Natali, *Bronzino*.

12. For a discussion of Riccio and the religious climate at the court, see Gigliola Fragnito, "Un Pratese alla corte di Cosimo I, *Archivio Storico Pratese* 62 (1986), 31–83, especially 41–44; Firpo, "Il Bronzino e I Medici," in Natali and Falciani, *Bronzino: Pittore e poeta alla corte dei Medici* (Florence: Mandragora, 2010), 91–99; and Alessandro Cecchi, "Il Maggiordomo Du-

cale Pierfrancesco Riccio E Gli Artisti Della Corte Medicea," *Mitteilungen des Kunsthistorischen Institutes in Florenz* 42, no. 1 (1998), 115–43.

13. For a discussion of the religious politics of Charles V, see John H. Elliott, *Imperial Spain: 1469–1716* (New York: Penguin Books, 2002); James Reston, Jr., *Defenders of the Faith: Charles V, Suleyman the Magnificent and the Battle for Europe* (New York: Penguin Press, 2009); Harald Kleinschmidt, *Charles V: The World Emperor* (Gloucestershire: The History Press, 2004); and Wim Blockmans, *Emperor Charles V: 1500–1558* (New York: Bloomsbury USA, 2001).

14. Cosimo's troubled relations with Paul III were discussed by Fragnito, "Un Pratese alla corte di Cosimo I"; Van Veen, *Cosimo I de' Medici and His Self-Representation*; and Murry, *Making of a God*.

15. For Panciatichi and Carnesecchi's Inquisitorial process, see Carlo Ginzburg, *I Costituti di Don Pietro Manelfi* (DeKalb: Northern Illinois University Press, 1970); and John T. Betts, *A Glance at the Italian Inquisition: A Sketch of Pietro Carnesecchi: His Trial Before the Court of the Papal Inquisition and His Martyrdom In 1566* (Whitefish, MT: Kessinger Publishing, 2010); and Lynette M.F. Bosch's chapter on the Panciatichi in this book.

16. On Cosimo's interaction with religious institutions, see Konrad Eisenbichler, ed., *The Cultural Politics of Duke Cosimo I De' Medici* (Aldershot: Ashgate, 2001); Van Veen, *Cosimo I de' Medici and His Self-Representation*; and Murry, *Making of a God*.

17. Murry, *Making of a God*, 190–215, discussed how carefully Cosimo cultivated supporters and patrons in the Roman Curia during his entire time as duke, as well as his close relations with Cardinal Juan Álvarez de Toledo (1488–1557), the son of Fadríque Álavarez de Toledo and Isabél de Zuñíga, who was closely related to Eleonora. Cosimo also worked with Medici relations in the Church, such as Onofrio Bartolini Medici, Bishop of Pisa, and Bernardo Antonio Medici, Bishop of Forlí, Francesco Minerbetti Medici, Bishop of Arezzo, and Guido Sforza Riario, Bishop of Lucca, his half uncle, and also others similarly related.

18. Murry, *Making of a God*, 202–04, noted that in 1544, Cosimo was ordering processions in the city for peace and the conversion of Lutherans, and in 1549, he wanted to burn the heretic Francesco Puccerrelli. In the early 1550s, Cosimo gave full support to Inquisitorial inquests, and in 1552, forty Florentines were arrested, including Bartolomeo Panciatichi. Later, Cosimo turned Carnesecchi over to the Inquisition. These actions are not those of a sympathetic Nicodemist; they are the acts of a ruler enacting a policy of abiding by Rome.

19. Murry, *Making of a God*, 183–214, discussed Cosimo's alignment with Roman religious politics.

20. Massimo Firpo, "Bronzino and the Medici," 91–99, in Falciani and

Natali, *Bronzino*, especially 96–97, links Cosimo, Bronzino, and Pontormo, as well as the majority of the members of the *Accademia*, to the religious thought of Juan de Valdés. Carlo Falciani, *"Della pittura sacra, ma anche di "fianchi, stomachi, ecc.,"* in Falciani and Natali, *Bronzino*, 277–95, makes a similar argument. The benchmark study on Valdés remains Jose C. Nieto, *Juan de Valdes and the Origins of the Spanish and Italian Reformation* (Geneva: Droz, 1970).

21. Firpo, "Bronzino and the Medici," 97, where Firpo also interprets Pontormo's San Lorenzo frescoes as being Valdesian.

22. Falciani in Falciani and Natali, *Bronzino*, 279–80.

23. For the *Beneficio*'s early circulation, see C. Ginzburg and A. Prosperi, "Le due redazioni del Beneficio di Cristo," in *Eresia e riforma nell' Italia del Cinquecento, Biblioteca del Corpus Reformatorum Italicorum, Miscellanea I*, ed. Albano Biondi et al. (Chicago, IL: The Newberry Library, 1974), 135–205. For a discussion of the *Beneficio* and its hybrid spirituality, as well as pertinent bibliography, see Anne Overell, *Italian Reform and the English Reformations, c. 1535–c. 1585* (Aldershot: Ashgate, 2008).

24. Fragnito, "Un Pratese alla corte di Cosimo I," 49–50, discusses Riccio's ownership of the *Beneficio* and its significance. For an analysis of the content and date of Riccio's manuscript of the Beneficio, see Benedetto da Mantova, *Il Beneficio di Cristo*, ed. Salvatore Caponetto (DeKalb: Northern Illinois University Press, 1972), 499–504. Riccio's manuscript is in Florence, at the Biblioteca Riccardiana, Cod. 1785, and it contains the text of Cardinal Gaspare Contarini's contribution to the meeting at Regensburg, dated 25 May 1541. Caponetto noted that the text of the manuscript is very close to the printed version of 1543, printed in Venice, which makes the manuscript late. Additionally, on folio 1r there is written, "Petri Francisci Riccij praepositi Pratensis mancipium Cosimi Medicis Florentiae et Senarum totiusque fere Thusciae regni Ducis optimi principis," which indicates that Riccio likely owned the manuscript after 1550, when he was Provost at Prato.

25. Falciani, *op. cit.* in Falciani and Natali, *Bronzino*, 279–80.

26. On San Bernardino, see Franco Mormando, *The Preacher's Demons: Bernardino of Siena and the Social Underworld of Early Renaissance Italy* (Chicago, IL: University of Chicago Press, 1999).

27. Van Veen, *Cosimo I de' Medici and His Self-Representation*, 27–29; and Murry, *Making of a God*, 22–67.

28. Falciani, *op cit.* in Falciani and Natali, *Bronzino*, 280, quotes from the *Beneficio*, "a fideli distribuito nell'ultima cena sotto il velame del santissimo sacramento; il quale fu da Cristo instituito, perché clebrassimo la memoria della morte sua, e con questo sacramento visibile rendessimo le nostre afflite conscienze sicure della nostra reconciliazione con Dio."

The "velame" referenced in the *Beneficio* correspond to the altar cloths employed during the Catholic Mass, during the Canon of the Mass, when the Last Supper is commemorated. There is nothing specifically Valdesian or Lutheran or Protestant about the statement found in the *Beneficio*, which is indicative of the Catholic influence that coexists in the text with more heterodox ideas. For a discussion of the diverse sources of the text, see Overell, *Italian Reform and the English Reformations*, 32–33.

29. On the use of corporals, see "Corporal," The Catholic Encyclopedia, which describes the corporal as "A square, white, linen cloth ... on which the Sacred Host and chalice are placed during the celebration of the Mass." See also Cox-Rearick, *Bronzino's Chapel of Eleonora*, 382, note 15, for a discussion of the representation of humeral veils on other Florentine paintings; and Natali, in Falciani and Natali, *Bronzino*, 102, who linked the corporal in the *Pietà* to the image of the face of Christ or to Veronica's Veil.

30. On Veronica's Veil, see Ewa Kuryluk, *Veronica and Her Cloth: History, Symbolism and Structure of a True Image* (London: Blackwell Publishers, 1991).

31. Antonio Natali, "I duchi e l'eucarestia: La cappella d'Eleonora di Toledo," in Falciani and Natali, *Bronzino*, 101–11; and Cox-Rearick, *Bronzino's Chapel of Eleonora*, 191–94.

32. Cox-Rearick, *Bronzino's Chapel of Eleonora*, 388, note 9.

33. See Gaston, "Eleonora di Toledo's Chapel," 157–80, for a discussion of the correspondences between the chapel's frescoes and the Spanish Mozarabic Rite. For a discussion of the history and significance of the Mozarabic Rite, see Lynette M.F. Bosch, *Art, Liturgy and Legend in Renaissance Toledo* (University Park: Pennsylvania State University Press, 2000), 55–64.

34. The Roman Renaissance liturgy, while corresponding to the twentieth-century liturgy in many ways, differed significantly, as can be seen by comparing the Renaissance and twentieth-century rites, respectively, in the *Missale Romanun Mediolani*, 1474, ed. Robert Lippe, LL.D, vol. 1, Text (London: Henry Bradshaw Society, 1899); and the Rev. Hugo H. Hoever, ed., *St. Joseph Daily Missal*, (New York: Catholic Book Publishing Co, 1959). For the Mozarabic Rite, see *Missale Hispano-Mozarabicum*, Conferencia Episcopal Espanola (Toledo: Arzobispado de Toledo, 1991)—each henceforth cited as "Roman Missal" and "Mozarabic Missal."

35. For Francesco and the chapel, see Cox-Rearick, *Bronzino's Chapel of Eleonora*, 33, 314, 318–19, 325. Cox-Rearick identified references to Francesco: in the ceiling's St. Francis; in the scene she identified as *The Investiture of Joshua* and interpreted as a reference to Francesco's future role as Duke of Florence; and in a wingless *putto*, among the ceiling's angels—"a mortal child." On Francesco and Cosimo, see B. Baldini, *Vita di Cosimo de' Medici Primo Gran Duca di Toscana* (Florence, 1578); G.B. Cini, *Vita del*

Serenissimo Signor Cosimo de' Medici Primo Gran Duca di Toscana (Florence, 1611); A. Mannucci, *Vita di Cosimo de' Medici primo Granduca di Toscana* (Bologna, 1586); G. Spini, *Cosimo I de' Medici: Lettere* (Florence, 1843–44); C. Booth, *Cosimo I, Duke of Florence* (Cambridge: Cambridge University Press, 1921); L.A. Ferrai, *Cosimo de' Medici Duca di Firenze* (Bologna, 1882); and R. Galluzzi, *Istoria del Granducato di Toscana sotto il governo della casa Medici*, 2 vols. (Florence, 1781).

36. For the dates of Easter, see Sir Nicholas Harris, *The Chronology of History* (London: Longham, Rees, Orme, Brown, Green & Longman and John Taylor, 1833), 64. Lent always encompasses the Feast of the Annunciation.

37. For other interpretations of the chapel and its patronage, see Bruce Edelstein, Review of *Bronzino's Chapel of Eleonora in the Palazzo Vecchio*, *The Art Bulletin* 76, no. 1 (March 1994), 171–75; Yael Even, "Bronzino's Chapel of Eleonora in the Palazzo Vecchio by Janet Cox-Rearick," *The Sixteenth Century Journal* 25, no. 4 (Winter 1994), 957–58; Bruce Edelstein, *The Early Patronage of Eleonora di Toledo: The Camera Verde and its Dependencies in the Palazzo Vecchio* (Ph.D. diss.: Harvard University, 1995); Elizabeth Pilliod, Review of "Bronzino's Chapel of Eleonora in the Palazzo Vecchio by Janet Cox-Rearick," *The Burlington Magazine* 138, no. 1118 (May 1996), 333–35; Carolyn Smyth, "An Instance of Feminine Patronage," in *Women and Art in Early Modern Europe: Patrons, Collectors, and Connoisseurs*, ed. Cynthia Lawrence (University Park: Pennsylvania State University Press, 1997); Bruce Edelstein, "L'usco di una porta e sei apostoli in cerca d'autore: Ipotesi su due committenze al Tribolo per la Cappella di Eleonora," in *Niccolo detto il Tribolo: Tra arte, archiettura e paesaggio*, eds. Elisabetta Pieri and Luigi Zangheri, *Quaderni di ricerche storiche Poggio a Caiano* 7. Proceedings of a meeting held in Poggio a Caiano, November 10–11, 2000, on the occasion of the 500th anniversary of the birth of *Il Tribolo* (Poggio a Caiano: Banca d'Italia, 2001), 37–50; Bruce Edelstein, "Nobildonne napoletane e committenza: Eleonora d'Aragona ed Eleonora di Toledo a confronto," *Quaderni Storici* 104 (2000), 295–329; idem, "Bronzino in the Service of Eleonora di Toledo and Cosimo I de' Medici: Conjugal Patronage and the Painter-Courier," in *Beyond Isabella: Secular Women Patrons of Art in Renaissance Italy*, ed. Sheryl E. Reiss and David G. Wilkins, Sixteenth Century Essays and Studies 54 (Kirksville, MO: Truman State University Press, 2001), 225–61; idem, "Bronzino's Frankfurt *Modello* for the Vault Decoration in the Chapel of Eleonora," in *Coming About: A Festschrift for John Shearman*, eds. Lars R. Jones and Louisa C. Matthew (Cambridge, MA: Harvard University Art Museums, 2001), 157–63; Maurice Brock, *Bronzino* (Paris: Flammarion, 2002), 181–211; Gaston, "Eleonora di Toledo's Chapel," 157–80; Antonio Natali, "The Dukes and the Eucharist: The Chapel of Eleonora da Toledo,"

in Falciani and Natali, *Bronzino*, 101–11; and Bambach, *The Drawings of Bronzino*, 118–49. Cox-Rearick defended her position in Janet Cox-Rearick, "A Question of Patronage," *The Art Bulletin* 78, no. 3 (September 1996), 572–74, and "Concerning Bronzino's Chapel of Eleonora in the Palazzo Vecchio," *The Sixteenth Century Journal* 26, no. 3 (Autumn 1995), 665–66.

38. Eleonora's name was originally Leonor, the Spanish version of the name. On the use of Leonor, see Cox-Rearick, *Bronzino's Chapel of Eleonora*, 26, where Eleonora signs "Donna Leonor de T.o" when writing to Cosimo soon after their engagement, hence recording her own name's preferred form. In the Prayer Book commissioned for Eleonora soon after her arrival in Florence, her name is written as either "Leonor" or "Leonora"; see Watson, "Manual of Dynastic History or Devotional Aid?" 180–82. For details about Eleonora's life, see Konrad Eisenbichler, "Introduction," in Eisenbichler, *The Cultural World of Eleonora di Toledo*, 2, note 1, where he gives Eleonora's age at the time of her marriage as seventeen. The standard biography of Eleonora is Anna Baia, *Leonora di Toledo, Duchessa di Firenze e Siena* (Todi: Z. Foglietti, 1907), which is available at the Kunsthistorisches Institutes, in Florence.

39. See Eisenbichler, *The Cultural World of Eleonora di Toledo*, 2 for the date of Eleonora's arrival in Naples.

40. Eisenbichler, *The Cultural World of Eleonora di Toledo*, 4.

41. On Naples and its culture, see Jennifer D. Selwin, *A Paradise Inhabited by Devils: The Jesuits' Civilizing Mission in Early Modern Naples* (Rome: Jesuit Historical Institute, 2004); Jordan Lancaster, *In the Shadow of Vesuvius* (London: Tauris Parke Paperbacks, 2009); Benedetto Croce, *History of the Kingdom of Naples* (Chicago, IL: University of Chicago Press, 1972); and William S. Maltby, *The Reign of Charles V* (London: Palgrave Macmillan, 2004).

42. Eisenbichler, *The Cultural World of Eleonora di Toledo*, 2–4. On Eleonora's wedding decorations, see Cox-Rearick, *Bronzino's Chapel of Eleonora*, 27 and 29–30; and Bruce Edelstein, "La fecundissima Signora Duchessa: The Courtly Persona of Eleonora di Toledo and the Iconography of Abundance," 71–97, both in Eisenbichler, *The Cultural World of Eleonora di Toledo*.

43. The biographical and lineage information provided in this section was taken from the *Diccionario de Historia Eclesiástica de España*, eds. Quintín Aldea Vaquero, Tomás Marín Martínez, and José Vives, Instituto Enrique Flórez, 4 vols. (Madrid: Consejo Superior de Investigaciones Científicas, 1972–75); Eloy Benito Ruano, *Los Infantes de Aragón* (Madrid: Escuela de Estudios Medievales, 1952); Luis Suárez Fernández, *Los Trastámaras de Castilla y Aragón en el Siglo XV* (Madrid: Espasa-Calpe, 1982); Angus MacKay, *Society, Economy, and Religion in Late Medieval Castile* (Lon-

don: Variorum Reprints, 1987); José Manuel Nieto Soria, *Fundamentos ide-ológicos del poder real in Castilla (Siglos XIII–XVI)* (Madrid: Departamento de Historia Medieval, 1988); Julio Valdeón Baruque, *Enrique II de Castilla: La Guerra civil y la consolidación del regimen, 1366–1371* (Valladolid: Universidad de Valladolid, 1966); Helen Nader, *The Mendoza Family in the Spanish Renaissance, 1350–1550* (New Brunswick, NJ: Rutgers University Press, 1979); and Francisco Layna Serrano, *Historia de Guadalajara y sus Mendozas en los Siglos XV y XVI* (Madrid: Aldus, 1942). Baia, *Leonor de Toledo*, 11, noted that Jacopo Riguccio Galluzzi, the historian of the *Granducato di Toscana*, had stated (*Istoria del Granducato di Toscana sotto il Governo della Casa Medici*, 5 vols. (Florence: Pier Gaetano Cambiagi, 1801), 1:43) that Eleonora was descended from the kings of Castile.

44. Layna Serrano, *Historia de Guadalajara y sus Mendozas*, 67–69, traces the line from the Mendoza to Eleonora and mentions the Jewish ancestry of the Guzmáns. On issues of ancestry, see Linda Martz, "*Converso* Families in Fifteenth and Sixteenth Century Toledo: The Significance of Lineage," *Sefarad*, 48 (1988), 118–19; Antonio Domínguez Ortíz, *Los judeoconversos en España y America* (Madrid: ISTMO, 1971); and Henry Kamen, *A Society of Conflict* (New York and London: Longmans, 2005), 38–44.

45. On Alfonso and Leonor, see Juán Victorio, *Alfonso XI, el Justiciero* (Madrid: Ediciones Nowtilus, 2009) and on his diplomatic relations and judicial actions, see Francisco de Moxó y de Montoliu, *Estudios sobre las relaciones entre Aragón y Castilla (ss. XIII–XV)* (Madrid: Institución Fernando el Católico, 1997).

46. Cox-Rearick, *Bronzino's Chapel of Eleonora*, 34–35, discussed Eleonora's role as regent ducal consort on two occasions when Cosimo left her in charge of Florence. The first time was in August/September 1541, when Cosimo went to Genoa to meet with Charles V; Cox-Rearick, *Bronzino's Chapel of Eleonora*, 355, note 44. Lorenzo Pagni reported to the duke that Eleonora ecstatically received a letter from the duke and that she was attending to business (ASF, MDP 353, fols. 259r–260r—letter from Lorenzo Pagni in Florence to Ugolino Grifoni in Genoa, 26 August 1541). On 28 August, Pagni wrote to Cosimo on Eleonora's behalf, conveying her distress that the duke could not read her handwriting (note 12— Gaetano Pieraccini, *La stirpe de' Medici di Cafaggiolo. Saggio di ricerche sulla trasmissione ereditaria dei caratteri biologici*, 3 vols. (Florence: Nardini, 1924–25), 2:62–63, on Eleonora's handwriting, which was indecipherable). In May 1543, Cosimo went to Genoa, to negotiate with Charles V for control of the fortresses of Florence and Livorno. Eleonora accompanied him as far as Pietrasanta and then went to Poggio a Caiano, where she was lonely and feeling threatened and stated in a letter, "Mi doggo della mia fortuna, poi che mi veggo in pericolo di restare senza voi in una città nemica del

nome Spag.lo et di questo modo di reggimento, e non so in che modo in sì strano accidente potrò mantenere me, et I fig. li in stato" (I lament my lot: I see myself in danger staying here without you in a hostile city, with a Spanish name and under the present government; I don't see how I'll be able to maintain myself and the children here in such a strange situation.), Cox-Rearick, *Bronzino's Chapel of Eleonora*, 355, note 48 (BNF, MS Magl. VIII.80, I, fol. 203v—the letter is annotated "Della Duchessa Leonora al Duca Cosimo ammalato," and it states "Queste Parole furno causa, che li Spag.li già levati dal Duca furno rimessi nelle fortezze." Cox-Rearick thought this incorrect, but possibly, some soldiers did remain until Cosimo's return to quiet Eleonora's worries. In a letter dated 2 September 1543, Eleonora tells Cosimo, "If your Excellency could make out better the way I write, I might write many other things that I have to tell you—but since they might be spread around, I'd better be discreet and tell them to you in person rather than put them on paper in a hand other than mine. Duchess Eleonora") (ASF, MDP 354, fol. 18). None of this correspondence indicates that Eleonora was comfortable taking a dominant role in Florence's administration, although, surrounded by helpful secretaries, she acquitted herself well enough the first time that Cosimo left her in charge one more time. Pieraccini, *La stirpe de' Medici di Cafaggiolo*, 2:55–62, discusses letters exchanged between Grifoni and Riccio, where Grifoni states that, in Cosimo's absence, Eleonora "piange, grida et si straccia i cappelli cosa pazza a vederla"—in a letter dated 8 May 1943. The secretaries also report that Eleonora refused to eat when Cosimo left her and that she did not sleep but would rally when she heard from him. Pagni, another of the ducal secretaries, wrote to Riccio informing him that it was difficult to get Eleonora to stop gambling and pay attention to business—in a letter dated 13 June 1543. On 26 October 1543, Pagni writes Riccio that the duchess pays little attention to business.

47. Cox-Rearick, *Bronzino's Chapel of Eleonora*, 26–53, describes the partnership between Cosimo and Eleonora during their marriage.

48. On Pedro González de Mendoza, Señor de Hita y Buitrago, see Jaime de Salazar y Acha, *La casa del Rey de Castilla y León en la Edad Media* (Madrid: Centro de Estudios Políticos y Constitucionales, 2000); and Ana Belén Sánchez Prieto, *La Casa de Mendoza* (Madrid: Palafox Y Pezuela, 2001). This Pedro González was a poet, an army general; and the *Mayordomo Mayor* of King Juan II of Castilla (1405–54). During his life, he was almost as powerful as the king, and his daughter Juana linked the Mendoza's to the Crown with her marriage to Don Alfonso. Don Alfonso and Juana's first offspring of twelve were a set of triplets.

49. Bosch, *Art, Liturgy and Legend*, 72–79.

50. On Juana de Castilla "La Beltraneja," see Tarsicio de Azcona, *Juana de Castilla, mal llamada la Beltraneja* (Madrid: La Esfera de los Libroa, 2007).

51. Bosch, *Art, Liturgy and Legend*, 106–14.

52. On the families who composed the Nájera group, see Nader, *The Mendoza Family*, 128–49.

53. See Gaston, "Eleonora di Toledo's Chapel," 159, on Maria Osorio being raised at the court of Isabél de Castilla.

54. Cosimo had diplomatic relations with the French Court in 1544–47 as a result of this connection, when he sent ambassadors and gifts to the French Court; see Janet Cox-Rearick, *The Collection of Francis I: Royal Treasures* (New York: Abrams, 1995), 226–28.

55. Cox-Rearick, *Bronzino's Chapel of Eleonora*, 45–46, and Franceschini, in Eisenbichler, *The Cultural World of Eleonora di Toledo*, 182, 185–92, describe how Eleonora's intercession was necessary for the foundation of a Jesuit school in Florence. The first Jesuit at the Medici court was Juan de Polanco (1516–77), sent by Ignatius Loyola in 1546. He was replaced by Diego Laínez, in June 1547, followed by Elpidio Ugoletti in 1551.

56. Franceschini, in Eisenbichler, *The Cultural World of Eleonora di Toledo*, 187–89. It was not until 1551 that Cosimo agreed to fund a Jesuit school in Florence after the Jesuits had realized that they needed to distance themselves from the *piagnoni*. Baia, *Leonor de Toledo*, 54–56, discussed how it was Eleonora who accepted the Jesuits into Florence in 1551, after Cosimo turned down Cardinal Capri's offer of two Jesuit priests in 1546. The arrival of Jacopo Lainez, as Eleonora's confessor, was arranged by her uncle, Cardinal Giovanni Álvarez de Toledo, with dispensation from Pope Julius III.

57. Cosimo and Eleonora's support of Florentine institutions is discussed in their biographies by Richard Fremantle, *God and Money: Florence and the Medici in the Renaissance* (Florence: Olschki, 1992); see also Baia, *Leonora di Toledo*, 36, who notes that Eleonora had prayers said for Cosimo, while he was in Genoa (August 1541), by the nuns at the monastery of S. Pietro in Pistoia, and Cosimo himself was moved, as Eleonora wrote to the abbess of the convent, to whom she gave 50 scudi for the needs of the nuns and the poor (letter dated 27 August 1541). Baia also noted (61) that there were records of extensive donations from Eleonora to convents, schools, and the poor, all recorded in the *Libri Maestri*, C.D., which would seem to attest to a steady stream of good works in keeping with Catholic practice.

58. Murry, *Making of a God*, 190–215, discussed how carefully Cosimo cultivated supporters and patrons in the Roman Curia during his entire time as duke and his close relations with Cardinal Juan Álvarez de Toledo (1488–1557), the son of Fadríque Álvarez de Toledo and Isabél de Zuñíga who was closely related to Eleonora. Cosimo also worked with Medici relations in the Church, such as Onofrio Bartolini Medici, Bishop of Pisa, and Bernardo Antonio Medici, Bishop of Forlí, Francesco Miner-

betti Medici, Bishop of Arezzzo, and Guido Sforza Riario, Bishop of Lucca, his half uncle, as well as others similarly related.

59. Eleonora's role as the *genitrix* of a new Medici dynasty was expounded in the 1539 wedding *apparato*; see Cox-Rearick, *Bronzino's Chapel of Eleonora*, 27 and 29–30; and Edelstein, "La fecundissima Signora Duchessa," 71–97.

60. See Cox-Rearick, *Bronzino's Chapel of Eleonora*, 37, 39, 277; and Gaston, "Eleonora di Toledo's Chapel," 167.

61. Watson, "Manual of Dynastic History or Devotional Aid?" 179–95, and Watson, "Book of Hours," 2:851–57 described the Hours and analyzed its text and illumination and gave information about the Prayer Book, summarized here. Both manuscripts are signed by the scribe "Aloysius." Both books have similar sixteenth-century Spanish bindings and are the same size (130 x 85 mm.), and the style of their script and the marginalia found in both books indicates that they were intended to be a matching pair. In Madrid, the Hours was reviewed by one of the Inquisitors—"El Doctor Heredia"—who pronounced the Hours to be correct and orthodox in content on 22 September 1576. The same can be assumed for the Prayer Book; otherwise it would have been destroyed. The Hours contains: the Hours of the Virgin from Matins to Vespers; a special Mass for the Virgin; The Seven Penitential Psalms; the Hours of the Cross; and prayers for leaving home safely, a prayer to a guardian angel; the prayer *Deus qui contritorum non despicis gemitum*; and from the St. Bernard's Psalter *O bone iesu. Illumina oculos meos*, with verses from *O Adonai, O Messias, O Rex Fili David, O Eloy, O Emanuel, O Christi*—and concludes with the Pater Noster. The Prayer Book's content, as described by Watson, refers to Eleonora as "Leonora" or "Leonor" and contains a prayer given to Pope Leo, which begins with the words "Señor Dios todo poderoso ... concede a mi Leonor tu sierva remission de todos mis pecados" (All powerful God, grant to Leonor, your servant, remission of all of my sins). The miniatures found illustrating the text are: *The Annunciation* for Matins (fols. 2v–3r); *The Nativity* for Prime (fols. 41v–42r); *The Annunciation to the Shepherds* for Tierce (fols. 48v–49r); *The Adoration of the Magi* for Sext (fols. 55v–56); *The Presentation at the Temple* for None (fols. 62v–63r); *The Flight into Egypt* for Vespers (fols. 69v–70r); another *Annunciation* for the Mass of the Virgin (fols. 92v–93r); *King David* for the Penitential Psalms (fols. 98v–99r); and *The Crucifixion* for the Hours of the Cross (fols. 125–126v).

62. Watson, "Manual of Dynastic History or Devotional Aid?" 183.

63. A limited number facsimile edition of the "Hours of Alessandro de' Medici and Margaret of Austria" was published by the Treccani Institute in 2012, limited to 750 copies.

64. The Ghent Bruges style of marginalia was used in the Misal Rico

de Cisneros. See Anna Muntada, *Torrellas, Misal rico de Cisneros* (Toledo: Real Fundación de Toledo, 1992); Jesús Domínguez Bordona, *Ars Hispaniae: Miniatura, Grabado, Encuadernación* (Madrid: Editorial Plus Ultra, 1962); Jesús Domínguez Bordona, *El arte de la miniature española* (Madrid: Plutarco, 1932); and José Janini and Ramón Gonzálvez, *Catálogo de los Manuscritos Litúrgicos de la Catedral de Toledo* (Toledo: Diputación Provincial, 1977).

65. For biographical information on Riccio, see Paolo Simoncelli, "Jacopo da Pontormo e Pierfrancesco Riccio: Due Appunti," *Critica Storica* 17 (1980), 331–41.

66. Fragnito, "Un Pratese alla corte di Cosimo I," provides a thorough chronology with archival citations and previous bibliography that traces Riccio's life and career in the Church and at court.

67. Cox-Rearick, *Bronzino's Chapel of Eleonora*, 321–26.

68. Cecchi, *Mitteilungen des Kunsthistorischen*, 115.

69. On Eleonora's fecundity and the part that praise of her as *genitrix* played in Medicean program, see Cox-Rearick, *Bronzino's Chapel of Eleonora*, 22–53.

70. Eleonora's role as ducal consort was extensively discussed by Cox-Rearick, *Bronzino's Chapel of Eleonora*, 80–84. See also Edelstein, "Bronzino in the Service of Eleonora di Toledo and Cosimo I de' Medici," 225–61. In Eisenbichler, *The Cultural World of Eleonora di Toledo*, see: Gabrielle Langdon, "A 'Laura' For Cosimo: Bronzino's Eleonora di Toledo and her Son Giovanni," 40–70; Ilaria Hoppe, "A Duchess' Place at Court: The Quartiere di Eleonora in the Palazzo della Signoria in Florence," 98–118; Paola Tinagli, "Eleonora and her 'Famous Sisters.' The Tradition of 'Illustrious Women' in Paintings for the Domestic Interior," 119–35; and Pamela J. Benson, "Eleonora di Toledo Among the Famous Women: Iconographic Innovation after the Conquest of Siena," 136–56. See also Andrea M. Gáldy, "Tuscan Concerns and Spanish Heritage in the Decoration of Duchess Eleonora's Apartment in the Palazzo Vecchio," in *Renaissance Studies* 20, no. 3 (2006), 293–319; Valentina Zucchi, "The Medici Guardaroba in the Florentine Ducal Residences, c. 1550–1565," in *Collecting and the Princely Apartment*, eds. Andrea M. Gáldy, Susan Bracken, and Adriana Turpin (Newcastle Upon Tyne: Cambridge Scholars Publishing, 2011), 1–23; Andrea M. Gáldy and Robert G. La France, "Golden Chambers for Eleonora of Toledo: Duchess and Collector in Palazzo Vecchio," in *Women Patrons and Collectors*, eds. Susan Bracken, Andrea M. Gáldy, and Adriana Turpin (Newcastle Upon Tyne: Cambridge Scholars Publishing, 2012), 1–34; and Valentina Zucchi, "The Medici Guardaroba in the Florentine Ducal Residences, c. 1550–1565," in Gáldy, Bracken, and Turpin, *Collecting and the Princely Apartment*, 1–23.

71. Cox-Rearick, *Bronzino's Chapel of Eleonora*, 225–26.

72. Cox-Rearick, *Bronzino's Chapel of Eleonora*, 54.

73. Cox-Rearick, *Bronzino's Chapel of Eleonora*, 54–55.

74. For descriptions of Eleonora's *stanze*, see Cox-Rearick, *Bronzino's Chapel of Eleonora*, 80–84; Hoppe, "A Duchess' Place at Court," 71–97; Tinagli, "Eleonora and her 'Famous Sisters," 119–55; Galdy, "Tuscan Concerns and Spanish Heritage," 293–319; and Gáldy and La France, "Golden Chambers for Eleonora of Toledo," 1–34.

75. On Tasso's work, see Cox-Rearick, *Bronzino's Chapel of Eleonora*, 9, 10, 56–57, 115, 252–53, 321.

76. Cox-Rearick, *Bronzino's Chapel of Eleonora*, 13.

77. Cox-Rearick, *Bronzino's Chapel of Eleonora*, 33, 54.

78. For Francesco and the chapel, see Cox-Rearick, *Bronzino's Chapel of Eleonora*, 33, 314, 318–19, 325.

79. For the history of the Palazzo Veccio before it became the home of Cosimo and Eleonora, see Nicolai Rubinstein, *The Palazzo Vecchio, 1298–1532: Government, Architecture and Imagery in the Civic Palace of the Florentine Republic* (New York: Oxford University Press, 1995); and Alessandro Cecchi, Antonio Paolucci; and Raffaello Bencini, *Le stanze del Principe in Palazzo Vecchio* (Florence: Lettere, 1991).

80. Cox-Rearick, *Bronzino's Chapel of Eleonora*, 59–66.

81. These inscriptions were first described by Andrea Emiliani and were fully published by Cox-Rearick, *Bronzino's Chapel of Eleonora*, 60–62, who provided a translation: "On Tuesday 6 September (1541) the story of the pharaoh was begun; on 30 March 1542 the story of the pharaoh was completed. On Monday 5 June 154(2) the story of the serpent was begun. On the 15th … the story of the water was completed."

82. See Cox-Rearick, *Bronzino's Chapel of Eleonora*, 67–68, for information on the *giornate*.

83. For Cox-Rearick's chronology for the frescoes, see Cox-Rearick, *Bronzino's Chapel of Eleonora*, 60–66.

84. Cox-Rearick, *Bronzino's Chapel of Eleonora*, 328–34, reproduces the payments made to Bronzino for the frescoes and the first altarpiece.

85. Cox-Rearick, *Bronzino's Chapel of Eleonora*, 33, 314, 318–19, 325.

86. See Cox-Rearick, *Bronzino's Chapel of Eleonora*, 70–71, for a discussion of Vasari's descriptions of the chapel.

87. Giorgio Vasari, *Le vite de' più eccellenti architetti, pittori, et scultori italiani, da Cimabue insino a' tempi nostril nell'edizione per I tipi di Lorenzo Torrentino Firenze, 1550*, eds. L. Bellosi and A. Rossi (Turin: Einaudi, 1986), 592–93.

88. See Cox-Rearick, *Bronzino's Chapel of Eleonora*, 13, for the chapel's size and location. The chapel is on the second floor, to the left of the *Camera Verde* and the *Studiolo*, which are to left of the larger *stanze*, such as the *Sala delle Sabine*.

89. Vasari's assignment of initial patronage for the chapel to Cosimo in the 1568 *Vite* is clear. Yet, Carmen Bambach, in Bambach, *The Drawings of Bronzino*, 118–19, ignored Vasari's statements in the 1568 *Vite* and the documentary evidence Cox-Rearick published to support Cosimo's initial dominant patronage of the chapel and stated: "That Eleonora di Toledo was the patron of the Chapel decorations, rather than her husband, Cosimo ..." In making her assertion that Eleonora was the chapel's patron, Bambach cited Edelstein as the authority on the chapel's patronage, and only the 1550 Torrentino edition, even though the 1568 edition is explicit in identifying Cosimo as the initial patron. For a modified position by Edelstein, on Cosimo and Eleonora's patronage, see Edelstein, in Reiss and Wilkins, *Beyond Isabella*, 226–61.

90. Giorgio Vasari, *Le Opere di Giorgio Vasari*, ed. Gaetano Milanesi, 8 vols. (Florence: Sansoni, 1906; repr. Florence: Sansoni, 1973), 7:597 [hereafter Vasari-Milanesi].

91. For a detailed description of the documents connected with this gift, see Cox-Rearick, *Bronzino's Chapel of Eleonora*, 74–92.

92. Cox-Rearick, *Bronzino's Chapel of Eleonora*, 185–88 and 342–43, Documents 22–26. See also Smyth, *Women and Art in Early Modern Europe*, 80–81, for a discussion of the documents about *The Annunciation*'s frame.

93. Vasari-Milanesi, 7:597: "In luogo della qual tavola (the first *Pietà*), ne ha fatto una simile il medesimo, e postala sopra l'altare in mezzo a due quadri non manco belli che la tavola; dentro I quali sono l'Angelo Gabriello e la Vergine da lui annunziata." Support for Vasari's statement is found in the inventory dated 27 October 1553, which records that the Salviati *Lamentation* and the panels of *Sts John the Baptist and Cosmas* were stored in the *guardaroba*—see Cox-Rearick, *Bronzino's Chapel of Eleonora*, 341, Document 20, for this document.

94. Cox-Rearick, *Bronzino's Chapel of Eleonora*, 341, Document 20, ASF, *Guardaroba Medicea* 28, dated 27 October to 7 November 1553, records on fol. 30r: "[nella prima stanza della guardaroba secreta...3 November 1553] Uno San Cosimo pitto in sul legname, di mano del Bronzino. Uno San Giovan Batista pitto in sul legname, di mano del Bronzino." These panels were again mentioned as being in the *guardaroba* on 1 July 1560, fol. 59r: "Dua quadri compagni, dentrovi in uno Sto Cosimo et nel'altrao S.to Giovanbatista, di man del Bronzino, sanza ornamento." For this document, see Cox-Rearick, *Bronzino's Chapel of Eleonora*, 342, Document 21. The panels were later moved, and on 19 June 1574, they hung, "Nella stanza Prima principale della Guardaroba dove è la Mostra, per quale si passa alla stanza dell'horologio. Adì 19 Giugno 1574...Ritratti dua, di S.to Giovanni et S.to Cosimo aovati"; see Cox-Rearick, *Bronzino's Chapel of Eleonora*, 344, Document 27.

95. Watson, "Book of Hours," 2:851–57, noted the special Mass with the second *Annunciation* on fols. 92v–93r.

96. Cox-Rearick, *Bronzino's Chapel of Eleonora*, 82.

97. Cox-Rearick, *Bronzino's Chapel of Eleonora*, 82, drew attention to a letter from Sforza Almeni to Riccio, dated 8 April 1550, which recorded that Eleonora wished to have Bronzino instructed to make a copy of the Salviati tapestry "che stave quella del suo oratorio" to be sent to Spain, presumably as a gift. It would appear that Eleonora was following Cosimo's lead in giving away the first *Pietà* but keeping the original for herself and sending the copy. See also Cox-Rearick, *Bronzino's Chapel of Eleonora*, 3, 57, 90, 254, 274 for additional discussion of Salviati's work.

98. Cox-Rearick, *Bronzino's Chapel of Eleonora*, 341, Document 20, ASF, Guardaroba Medicea 28, fol. 37r. Also see Cox-Rearick, *Bronzino's Chapel of Eleonora*, 341 (Document 20, ASF, Guardaroba Medicea 28, fols. 30r and 37r) who records that *Sts. John the Baptist and Cosmas*, along with a *panno d'altare* made by Nicholas Karcher (the Salviati *Lamentation*) were in the *guardaroba* on 7 November 1553, coinciding with the installation of the second *Pietà*. On 1 July 1560, the same three items were inventoried in the *guardaroba*; see CR, 342 (Document 21, ASF, Guardaroba Medicea 45, fols. 28r and 59r). By 19 June 1574, the two panels were hanging "Nella stanza Prima principale della Guardaroba"; CR, 344 (Document 27, ASF, Guardaroba Medicea 87, fol. 68v).

99. On Medici *imprese*, see Paul William Richelson, *Studies in the Personal Imagery of Cosimo I de' Medici, Duke of Florence* (New York: Garland Dissertation Publishing, 1978), 25–27; and Janet Cox-Rearick, *Dynasty and Destiny in Medici Art: Pontormo, Leo X, and the Two Cosimos* (Princeton, NJ: Princeton University Press, 1984), 185, 257, 265, 270–82. Watson's survey of the *imprese* in the Hours is as follows: on fols. 2v–3r — the Medici/Toledo arms supported — on the Medici side — by snakes with red objects (they are Medici *palle*) in their mouths and on the Toledo side — red and white flags; Capricorn astrological emblem (used by Emperor Augustus and Charles V and used at the wedding); fols. 26v–27r — three interlaced diamond rings, the *broncone fiorito*, roses, swan walking on grass (Averardo de' Medici (1360–1429)), two doves on a gold branch (arms of Cosimo il Vecchio upon his return from exile); fols. 41v–42r — Capricorn, Mercury, and Caduceus (Vasari — motif from the wedding with an image of Cosimo being made duke and the arms of Alessandro Vitelli, Charles V's commander in Florence), Pegasus (also from wedding, associated with the downfall of three cardinals who had tried to raise troops to help Cosimo's enemies and with Jacopo de' Medici (1497–1555), Marquess of Marignano and general of Charles V; fols. 48v–49r — imperial emblem twin pillars and scroll *Plus Ultra*, flanked by the imperial double-headed eagle beneath

a crown both emblems of Charles V; fols. 55v–56r—anchors crossed in saltire, with a scroll inscribed *Duabus* (Duke Cosimo indicating he and Charles were tight); fols. 62v–63v—Medici yoke with a scroll *Semper* (Cosimo il Vecchio, on return from exile 1434); Cardinal Giovanni de' Medici also used the device after the Spanish drove him from Rome to Florence in 1512 (yoke was used by Isabel and Fernando) (*semper* was used with the *diamanti* of Piero and the *diamanti* with feathers of Piero di Cosimo. Other items in the *marginalia* are cameos, antique figures, reminiscent of the Medici collections of coins, gems and cameos, classical deities (Athena, Hera, Aphrodite), personifications of Italy, and Apollo flaying Marsyas; fols. 55v–56r—Hercules strangling snakes and Hercules awakened by Mercury. The program of the Hours is clear—orthodox piety (signified by the celebration of the Roman liturgy) is combined with Medici family history with parallels drawn between Cosimo and Charles V, with whom he is *emparentado* through Eleonora.

100. Cox-Rearick, *Bronzino's Chapel of Eleonora*, 24–25, provides a genealogical chart of the ducal children who survived childhood and adolescence: Lucrezia (1545–61), Isabella (1542–76), Maria (1540–57), Pietro (1554–64), Garzia (1547–62), Giovanni (1543–62), Ferdinando I (1549–1609), and Francesco (1541–87).

101. Eleonora's patronage of artists other than Bronzino was discussed by Cox-Rearick, *Bronzino's Chapel of Eleonora*, 9, 10, 56–57, 115, 252–53, 321. Cox-Rearick, *Bronzino's Chapel of Eleonora*, 2–12, identifies Pontormo, Salviati, Bandinelli, Tribolo, Vasari, and Bachiacca among the artists who worked for Eleonora.

102. On Eleonora's finances, see Bruce Edelstein, "Nobildonne napoletane e committenza: Eleonora d'Aragona ed Eleonora di Toledo a confronto," *Quaderni Storici* 104 (2000), 295–329.

103. Cox-Rearick, *Bronzino's Chapel of Eleonora*, 343, Document 25, ASF, Fabbriche Medicee 10, fol. 66v and Document 26, ASF, Fabbriche Medicee 10, fol. 73.

104. Cox-Rearick, *Bronzino's Chapel of Eleonora*, 185–88, dated *The Annunciation* to the early 1560s, based on documents that record new frames for the panels, 343, Documents 25 and 26; Smyth, *Women and Art in Early Modern Europe*, 86–87, dates *The Annunciation* to 1553 in accordance with Vasari's statement and considers that the documents paying for wood indicate that *The Annunciation* received a new frame at that time, not that it was painted then; Natali, *Bronzino*, 110, dates them to the early 1560s, in agreement with Cox-Rearick, as does Bambach, *The Drawings of Bronzino*, 196–97, without reference to either Vasari's text or Smyth's discussion.

105. Cox-Rearick, *Bronzino's Chapel of Eleonora*, 342, Document 24, New York, Pierpont Morgan Library 1346–47: "... ringrazio vostra infinita

coretesia, e larghissima liberaliata, dell'havermi fatto pagare li danari di quell salario…" Later, Bronzino expressed a desire to continue working for the duke, and on 17 February 1565, Cosimo pays Bronzino for "… per spese fatte el Bronzino pittore nel rassettare La cappella che è nella Camera Verde, in diverse spese come in detta poliza …" (Document 27, ASF, Fabbriche Medicee 10, fol. 91r). The document does not specifically refer to individual works.

106. Smyth, *Women and Art in Early Modern Europe*, 86–87.

107. Cox-Rearick, *Bronzino's Chapel of Eleonora*, 344, Document 27, ASF, Fabbriche Medicee 10, fol. 91r.

108. *Feste nelle nozze del serenissimo don Francesco Medici grand duca di Toscana; et della serenissima sua consorte la signora Bianca Cappello*, author Raffaello Gualterotti, Accursio Baldi, and Sebastiano Marsili (Charleston, SC: Nabu Press, 2011). The marriage was announced on 10 June 1579, and Bianca Cappello was crowned Grand Duchess of Tuscany on 12 June. She and Francesco seem to have died from malarial fever in October 1587 at Poggio a Caiano.

109. Cox-Rearick, *Bronzino's Chapel of Eleonora*, 225–26.

110. Watson, "Manual of Dynastic History or Devotional Aid?" 179–95, 182.

111. "Roman Missal," 325.

112. "Roman Missal," 324–25.

113. Cox-Rearick, *Bronzino's Chapel of Eleonora*, 214–18, discussed the chapel of Bastie d'Urfé by Sicolante da Sermoneta and the paintings by Battista Franco, Niccolò del Abrigia, and Domenico Beccafumi in the Pisa Duomo.

114. Cox-Rearick, *Bronzino's Chapel of Eleonora*, 219–20, discussed similarities between the Sistine Chapel and Eleonora's Chapel.

115. Carol Lewine, *The Sistine Chapel Walls and the Roman Liturgy* (University Park: Pennsylvania State University Press, 1993).

116. Lewine, *The Sistine Chapel Walls*, 1–19.

117. Celebration of the daily Stational Masses of Lent begin on Ash Wednesday and continue to the last day of the Fifth Week of Lent. In the early Church, the Lenten Masses were literally celebrated at each of these churches. In later times, the Stational Churches have become commemorative. For a list of the Stational Churches which correspond to each daily Mass, see *Saint Joseph Daily Missal*, ed. Rev. Hugo H. Hoever (New York: Catholic Book Publishing Co., 1960), 123–400.

118. For a description of the hope for unification of the peoples of the world expressed during Lent, see Lynette M.F. Bosch. "Genesis, Holy Saturday, and the Sistine Ceiling," *The Sixteenth Century Journal* 30, no. 3 (Autumn 1999), 643–52.

119. Mozarabic Missal, 475

120. Natali, *Bronzino*, 105–08.

121. Roman Missal, 41.

122. Roman Missal, 61: "The Lord said to Moses, 'Come up to me on the mountain, stay here and let me give you the tablets of stone, the law and the commandment, which I have written down that you may teach them.' Moses arose with Joshua his assistant and went up the mountain of God; he said to the elders, 'Wait for us here until we come back to you. You have Aaron and Hur; if anyone has a dispute, let him go to them.' So Moses went up the mountain and a cloud covered the mountain or six days; on the seventh day he called to Moses out of the cloud. The Glory of the Lord spoke to the Israelites like a devouring fire on the mountain top. Moses entered the cloud and went up the mountain; there he stayed forty days and forty nights."

123. Roman Missal, 67: "Look down from heaving, thy holy dwelling-place, and bless thy people Israel and the ground which thou hast given to us as thou didst swear to our forefathers, a land flowing with milk and honey. This day the Lord your God commands you to keep these statutes and laws: be careful to observe them with all your heart and soul. You have recognized the Lord this day as your God; you are to conform to his ways, to keep his statutes, his commandments, and his laws, and to obey him. The Lord has recognized you this day as his special possession, as he promised you, and to keep his commandments; he will raise you high above all the nations which he has made, to bring him praise and fame and glory, and to be a people holy to the Lord your God, according to his promise."

124. Roman Missal, 67: "If you diligently keep all these commandments that I now charge you to observe, by loving the Lord your God, by conforming to his ways and by holding fast to him, the Lord will drive out all these nations before you and you shall occupy the territory of nations greater and more powerful than you. Every place where you set the soles of your feet shall be yours. Your borders shall run from the wilderness to the Lebanon and from the River, the river Euphrates, to the western sea. No man will be able to withstand you; the Lord your God will put the fear and dread of you upon the whole land on which you set foot, as he promised you."

125. For considerations of Cosimo's territorial ambitions and accomplishments, see Richard Fremantle, *God and Money: Florence and the Medici in the Renaissance including Cosimo I de' Medici's Uffizi Collection* (Florence: Olschki, 1997); Eisenbichler, *The Cultural Politics of Duke Cosimo I De' Medici*; Baccio Baldini, *Vita Di Cosimo I de' Medici* (Whitefish, MT: Kessinger Publishing, LLC, 2009); Henk Th. Van Veen, *Cosimo I de' Medici and His*

Self-Representation in Florentine Art and Culture (Cambridge: Cambridge University Press, 2006); Michele Lupo Gentile, *Studi Sulla Storiografia Fiorentina alla Corte Di Cosimo I de'Medici* (Cambridge: Ulan Press, 2011).

126. Roman Missal, 103: "But the Lord said to Moses, 'Go down at once, for your people, the people you brought up from Egypt, have done a disgraceful thing; so quickly have they turned aside from the way I commanded them. They have made themselves an image of a bull-calf, they have prostrated themselves before it, sacrificed to it and said, "These are your gods, O Israel, that brought you up from Egypt"' so the Lord said to Moses, 'I have considered this people, and I see that they are a stubborn people. Now, let me alone to vent my anger upon them, so that I may put an end to them and make a great nations spring from you.' But Moses set himself to placate the Lord his God: 'O Lord,' he said, 'why shouldst thou vent thy anger upon thy hand? Why let the Egyptians say, "So he meant evil when he took them out, to kill them in the mountains and wipe them off the face of the earth."' But Moses asked, 'Turn from thy anger, and think better of the evil thou dost intend against thy people. Remember Abraham, Isaac and Israel, thy servants, to whom thou didst swear by thy own self.' And God said to Moses, 'I will make your posterity countless as the stars in the sky, and all this land, of which I have spoken, I will give to them, and they shall poses it for ever.' It is written that So the Lord relented, and spared his people the evil with which he had threatened them."

127. On the continuing hope for unification among Protestants and Catholics, which continued even after the Council of Trent met, see Dermot Fenlon, *Heresy and Obedience in Tridentine Italy: Cardinal Pole and the Counter Reformation* (Cambridge: Cambridge University Press, 2008). On the Council, see John W. O' Malley, *Trent: What Happened at the Council* (Cambridge, MA: Belknap Press/Harvard University Press, 2013); Hubert Jedin, *A History of the Council of Trent Volume I: The Struggle for the Council* (New York: American Council of Learned Societies Press, 2008); and idem, *A History of the Council of Trent: Volume II: The First Sessions at Trent, 1545–1547* (New York: American Council of Learned Societies Press, ACLS, 2008).

128. "Roman Missal," 78.

129. "Roman Missal," 90.

130. "Roman Missal," 120–21.

131. "Roman Missal," 93–94: "There was no water for the community; so they gathered against Moses and Aaron. The people disputed with Moses and said, 'if only we had perished when our brothers perished in the presence of the Lord! Why have you brought the assembly of the Lord into this wilderness for us and our beasts to die here? Why did you fetch us up from Egypt to bring us to this vile place, where nothing will grow, neither

corn, nor figs, vines nor pomegranates? There is not even any water to drink.' Moses and Aaron came forward in front of the assembly to the entrance of the Tent of the Presence. There they fell prostrate, and the glory of the Lord appeared to them. The Lord spoke to Moses and said, 'Take a staff, and then with Aaron your brother assemble all the community, and, in front of them all, speak to the rock and it will yield its water. Thus you will produce water for the community out of the rock, for them and their beasts to drink.' Moses left the presence of the Lord with the staff, as he had commanded him. Then he and Aaron gathered the assembly together in front of the rock, and he said to them, 'Listen to me, you rebels. Must we get water out of this rock for you?' Moses raised his hand and struck the rock twice with his staff. Water gushed out in abundance and they all drank, men and beasts. But the Lord said to Moses and Aaron, 'You did not trust me so far as to uphold my holiness in the sight of the Israelites; therefore you shall not lead this assembly into the land which I promised to give them.' Such were the waters of Meribah, where the people disputed with the Lord and through which his holiness was upheld."

132. "Roman Missal," 128–29: "They came to Elim, where there were twelve springs and seventy palm trees, and there they encamped beside the water. The whole community of Israelites set out from Elim, and came into the wilderness of Sin, which lies between Elim and Sinai. This was on the fifteenth day of the second month after they had left Egypt. The Israelites complained to Moses and Aaron in the wilderness and said, 'If only we had died at the Lord's hand in Egypt, where we sat round the fleshpots and had plenty of bread to eat! But you have brought us out into this wilderness to let this whole assembly starve to death.' The Lord said to Moses, 'I will rain down bread from heaven for you. Each day the people shall go out and gather a day's supply, so that I can put them to the test and see whether they will follow my instructions or not. But on the sixth day, when they prepare what they bring in, it shall be twice as much as they have gathered on other days.' Moses and Aaron then said to all the Israelites, 'In the evening you will know that it was the Lord who brought you out of Egypt, and in the morning you will the glory of the Lord' …"

133. For the Church's teachings on Transubstantiation, see David Pietrusza, ed., *Sursum Corda: Documents and Readings on the Traditional Latin Mass from the Council of Trent to Benedict XVI's Motu Propio* (Seattle, WA: Createspace, 2008), 7–8. The Church's teachings on Transubstantiation were expressed at Trent but had been formulated during the early councils from Nicea to Constantinople III. Succinctly expressed at Trent, the doctrine was stated as follows: "And because that Christ, our Redeemer, declared that which He offered under the species of bread to be truly His own Body, therefore has it ever been a firm belief in the Church of God,

and this holy Synod doth now declare it anew, that, by the consecration of the bread and of the wine, a conversion is made of the whole substance of the bread into the substance of the Body of Christ our Lord, and of the whole substance of the wine into the substance of His Blood; which conversion is, by the holy Catholic Church, suitably and properly called Transubstantiation."

134. "Roman Missal," 162–63: "The Lord said to Moses and Aaron in Egypt: 'This month is for you the first of months; you shall make it the first month of the year. Speak to the whole community of Israel and say to them: On the tenth day of this month let each man take a lamb or a kid for his family, one for each household, but if a household is too small for one lamb or one kid, then the man and his nearest neighbor may take one between them. They shall share the cost, taking into account both the number of persons and the amount each of them eats. Your lamb or kid must be without blemish, a yearling male. You may take equally a sheep or a goat. You must have it in safe keeping until the fourteenth day of this month, and then all the assembled community of Israel shall slaughter the victim between dusk and dark. They must take some of the blood and smear it on two doorposts and on the lintel of every house in which they eat the lamb. On that night they shall eat the flesh roast on the fire; they shall eat it with unleavened cakes and bitter herbs. You are not to eat any of it raw or even boiled in water, but roasted, head, shins and entrails. You shall not leave any of it until morning; if anything is left over until morning, it must be destroyed by fire.'"

135. "Roman Missal," 182–83: "In the morning watch the Lord looked down on the Egyptian army through the pillar of fire and cloud, and he threw them into a panic. He clogged their chariot wheels and made them lumber along heavily, so that the Egyptians said, 'It is the Lord fighting for Israel against Egypt; let us flee.' Then the lord said to Moses, 'Stretch out your hand over the sea, and let the water flow back over the Egyptians, their chariots and their cavalry.' So Moses stretched out his hand over the sea, and at daybreak the water returned to its accustomed place; but the Egyptians were in flight as it advanced, and the Lord swept them out into the sea. The water flowed back and covered all Pharaoh's army, the chariots and the cavalry, which had pressed the pursuit into the sea. Not one man was left alive. Meanwhile the Israelites had passed along the dry ground through the sea, with the water making a wall for them to right and to left. That day the Lord saved Israel from the power of Egypt, and the Israelites saw the Egyptians lying dead on the sea-shore. When Israel saw the great power which the Lord had put forth against Egypt, all the people feared the Lord, and they put their faith in him and in Moses his servant. Then Moses and the Israelites sand this song to the Lord ..."

136. Cox-Rearick, *Bronzino's Chapel of Eleonora*, 213–33; and Natali, *Bronzino*, 101–03.

137. Cox-Rearick, *Bronzino's Chapel of Eleonora*, 234–36.

138. "Roman Missal," 186–87—Deuteronomy 31:22–30: "That day Moses wrote down this rule of life and taught it to the Israelites. The Lord gave Joshua a son of Nun his commission in these words: 'Be strong, be resolute; for you shall bring the Israelites into the land which I swore to give them, and I will be with you.' When Moses had finished writing down these laws in a book, from beginning to end, he gave this command to the Levites, who carried the Ark of the Covenant of the Lord: 'Take this book of the law and put it beside the Ark of the Covenant of the Lord your God to be a witness against you. For I know how defiant and stubborn you are; even during my lifetime you have defied the Lord; how much more, then, will you do so when I am dead? Assemble all the elders of your tribes and your officers; I will say all these things in their hearing and will summon heaven and earth to witness against them. For I know that after my death you will take to degrading practices and turn aside from the way which I told you to follow, and in days to come disaster will come upon you, because you are doing what is wrong in the eyes of the Lord and so provoking him to anger.'"

139. Janet Cox-Rearick, "From Bandinelli to Bronzino: The Geneseis of the Lamentation from the Chapel of Eleonora di Toledo," *Mitteilungen des Kunsthistorischen Institutes in Florenz* (1989), 37–84, here 40, notes that Bronzino signed his name on the Besançon *Pietà*, on the rock by the Magdalen's hand, OPERA/DEL BRONZINO/FIORENTINO.

140. "Roman Missal," 249–50: "The Lord spoke to Moses and said, 'Speak to the Israelites in these words: When you enter the land which I give you, and you reap its harvest, you shall bring the first sheaf of your harvest to the priest. He shall present the sheaf a special gift before the Lord on the day after the Sabbath, so as to gain acceptance for yourselves … From the day after the Sabbath, the day on which you bring your sheaf as a special gift, you shall count seven full weeks. The day after the seventh sabbath will make fifty days, and then you shall present to the Lord a grain-offering from the new crop. You shall bring from your homes two loaves as a special gift; they shall contain two tenths of an ephah of flour and shall be baked with leaven … You shall also prepare one he-goat for a sin-offering and two yearling sheep for a shared-offering, and the priest shall present them in addition to the bread of the firstfruits as a special gift before the Lord. They shall be a holy-gift to the Lord for the Priest. On that same day you shall proclaim a sacred assembly for yourselves; you shall not do your daily work. This is a rule binding on your descendants for all time wherever you live.'"

141. "Roman Missal," 250: "When you come into the land which the Lord your God is giving you to occupy as your patrimony and settle in it, you shall take the first-fruits of all the produce of the soil, which you gather in from the land which the Lord your God is giving you, and put them in a basket. Then you shall go to the place which the Lord your God will choose as a dwelling for his Name and come to the priest, whoever he shall be in those days ... Then we cried to the Lord the God of our fathers for help, and he listened to us and saw our humiliation, our hardship and distress; and so the Lord brought us out of Egypt with a strong hand and outstretched arm, with terrifying deeds, and with signs and portents. He brought us to this place and gave us this land, a land flowing with milk and honey. And now I have brought the first fruits of the soil which thou, O Lord, hast given me. You shall then set the basket before the Lord your God and bow down in worship before him."

142. "Roman Missal," 251: "If you conform to my statutes, if you observe my commandments and carry them out, I will give you rain at the proper time; the land shall yield its produce and the trees of the countryside their fruit. Threshing shall last till vintage and vintage till sowing; you shall eat your fill and live secure in your land. I will give peace in the land, and you shall lie down to sleep with no one to terrify you. I will rid your land of dangerous beasts and it shall not be ravaged by war. You shall put your enemies to flight and they shall fall in battle before you. Five of you shall pursue a hundred and a hundred of you ten thousand; so shall your enemies fall in battle before you. I will look upon you with favour, I will make you fruitful and increase your numbers: I will give my covenant with you its full effect. Your old harvest shall last you in sore until you have to clear out the old to make room for the new. I will establish my Tabernacle among you and will not spurn you."

143. "Roman Missal," 286: "The Lord spoke to Moses and said: Further, the tenth day of this seventh month is the Day of Atonement. There shall be a sacred assembly; you shall mortify yourselves and present a food offering to the Lord. On that same day you shall do no work because it is a day of expiation, to make expiation for you before the Lord your God. Therefore every person who does not mortify himself on that day shall be cut off from his father's kin. I will extirpate any person who does any work on that day. You shall do no work; it is a rule binding on your descendants for all time wherever you life. It is for you a Sabbath of sacred rest, and you shall mortify yourselves. From the evening of the ninth day to the following evening you shall keep your Sabbath-rest."

144. "Roman Missal," 286: "Further, form the fifteenth day of the seventh month, when the harvest has been gathered, you shall keep the Lord's pilgrim-feast for seven days. The first day is a sacred rest and so

is the eighth day. On the first day you shall take the fruit of citrus-trees, palm fronds, and leafy branches, and willows from the riverside, and you shall rejoice before the Lord your God for seven days. You shall keep this as a pilgrim feast in the Lord's honor for seven days every year. It is a rule binding for all time on your descendants; in the seventh month you shall hold this pilgrim feast. You shall live in arbors for seven days, all who are native Israelites, so that your descendants may be reminded how I made the Israelites live in arbors when I brought them out of Egypt. I am the Lord your God."

Mosaic passages also occur in other passages of the Roman liturgy, inter-liturgical connections also exist in the chapel's texts and images, and the scenes of *The Gathering of Manna, Moses Striking Water from the Rock, The Crossing of the Red Sea*, and *Baptism* exist in the Roman liturgy of Advent, as recorded in the "Roman Missal." The connections existing between Christ and salvation and the damnation of unbelievers, like the Egyptians (made explicit in the fresco of the *Crossing of the Red Sea*), were also made during Advent. The first Lesson of Advent's Saturday Mass was Isaiah 19, wherein Isaiah prophesies the coming of the Messiah with the words: "In those days, they shall cry to the Lord because of the oppressor and He shall send them a Savior and a defender to deliver them. And the Lord shall be known by Egypt … And the Lord shall strike Egypt … and the Lord Our God shall heal them" — a reading that evokes the Crucifixion and the Brazen Serpent. The second Lesson is Isaiah 35:1–7: "… for waters are broken out in the desert, and streams in the wilderness. And that which was dry land shall become a pool, and the thirsty land springs out of water …" — a reading that evokes baptism and Moses Striking Water from the Rock. The same text from Isaiah is also read on the fourth Sunday of Advent at the Introit, which was Isaiah 45:8: "Drop down dew, you heavens from above, and let the clouds rain the just: Let the earth be opened and bud forth a Savior" — thus is the theme of salvation that is crucial for Lent and Easter introduced at the beginning of the liturgical season focused on the birth of Christ. On the same Sunday, the Gospel reading is Luke 3:1–6, which tells the story of John the Baptist baptizing the catechumens, a reading that resonates with the Lenten theme of Baptism. Hence, the images on the walls of Eleonora's chapels, while focused on Lent, would also have been activated by readings throughout the liturgical year that reference Lent's events and texts.

145. "Mozarabic Missal," 475, Feast of the *Exaltatio Crucis*.

146. On the Mozarabic liturgy, see Don Ramón Gonzálvez Ruíz, "The Persistence of the Mozarabic Liturgy in Toledo after A.D. 1080, Santiago, Saint-Denis and Saint Peter," in *The Reception of the Roman Liturgy in León-Castile in 1080*, ed. Bernard F. Reilly (New York: Fordham University

Press, 1985), 157–85; idem, "*Una Empresa del Cardenal Cisneros: la Reforma de la Liturgia Hispano-Mozárabe*," *XX Siglos* 15, no. 53 (2004), 49–61; and Bosch, *Art, Liturgy and Legend*, 55–64.

147. Bosch, *Art, Liturgy and Legend*, 57–62.

148. Bosch, *Art, Liturgy and Legend*, 60–61; Don Ramón Gonzálvez Ruíz, "*Elipando de Toledo: La crisis de la comunidad Mozárabe*" in *Ars Longa, Vita Brevis: Homenaje al Doctor Rafael Sancho de San Román* (Toledo: Real Academia de Bellas Artes y Ciencias Históricas de Toledo, 2006), 287–326.

149. Bosch, *Art, Liturgy and Legend*, 62–63; Don Ramón Gonzálvez Ruíz, "*El Cabildo de la Capilla Mozárabe*," *La Catedral Primada de Toledo: Dieciocho siglos de Historia* (Burgos: Catedral de Burgos, 2010), 112–19.

150. Gaston, "Eleonora di Toledo's Chapel," 173, notes that Don Pedro visited Florence in September 1541, the same month when the Red Sea fresco was being worked on.

151. "Roman Missal," 257.

152. "Roman Missal," 264.

153. "Roman Missal," 330.

154. "Mozarabic Missal," 308.

155. "Mozarabic Missal," 176–77, *I Dominico Quadregesimae* (Deut. 7:13; Exod. 12:16; Lev. 26).

156. "Mozarabic Missal," 323; Deut. 9:15–18 and 16:1–2, 4b.

157. "Mozarabic Missal," 325, *Feria IV in hebdomada maiore* (Exod. 24:86; 35:1; 4:10; 20:19–20).

158. "Mozarabic Missal," 331–32, *Feria V in Cena Domini* (Exod. 24:4–5; 19:9–11; 14:19).

159. "Mozarabic Missal," 375, *Vigilia Paschalis* (Holy Saturday), after the blessing of the lights.

160. "Mozarabic Missal," 438, *Feria IV Paschae* (Exod. 12:14; 14:13–14).

161. "Mozarabic Missal," 445, 474, 482, 497, 498, 511 for passages from Revelation.

162. "Mozarabic Missal," 597, *VI Dominico Paschae* (Exod. 24:4–4; 17–12; 34:2–5; 8:10).

163. "Mozarabic Missal," 605 *VII Dominico Pascae*.

164. "Mozarabic Missal," 612, *VIII Dominico*.

165. "Mozarabic Missal," 620, *IX Dominico*.

166. "Mozarabic Missal," 625, *X Dominico Paschae* (Exod. 31:1–2; 24:4; 25:9; 40:24–25).

167. "Mozarabic Missal," 630, *XI Dominico Paschae* (Exod. 31:1–2; Num. 18:8; Exod. 35:30–32; Num. 18:8–9).

168. "Mozarabic Missal," 635, *XII Dominico Paschae* (Exod. 40:24–25; 32).

169. "Mozarabic Missal," 715, *XX Dominico*.

170. Cox-Rearick, *Bronzino's Chapel of Eleonora*, 75, identified Nicolas Perrenot de Granvelle as the Keeper of the Seals for Charles V, who had helped Cosimo when he asked Charles V to return the fortresses of Florence and Livorno in 1543. Granvelle had also assisted Cosimo in securing the Order of the Golden Fleece, which he received from Charles V in 1545.

171. See Cox-Rearick, "From Bandinelli to Bronzino: The Genesis of the 'Lamentation' for the Chapel of Eleonora di Toledo," 38, for a response from Agnolo Marzi, the duke's secretary to Bandinelli, dated 9 November 1542, that the duke has been given the *modello* for the chapel's altarpiece. On 10 November, Cosimo wrote to Bandinelli informing him that Eleonora approved the design but that Bronzino would be painting the altarpiece based on Bandinelli's design.

172. Cox-Rearick, *Bronzino's Chapel of Eleonora*, 74–81, discusses the correspondence that traces the gift, especially 74–76, for the payment document that records that the *Pietà* received a frame in July 1545, establishing its completion date.

173. Cox-Rearick, *Bronzino's Chapel of Eleonora*, identifies Don Francesco di Toledo or Francisco de Toledo as Eleonora's brother. He was actually a cousin removed, although descended from King Alfonso IX of Leon, as was Eleonora.

174. See Cox-Rearick, *Bronzino's Chapel of Eleonora*, 79–80, for this letter.

175. See Cox-Rearick, *Bronzino's Chapel of Eleonora*, 84–86 and 184–86, for information on the installation of the second *Pietà*.

176. Cox-Rearick, *Bronzino's Chapel of Eleonora*, 191–212; and Natali, *Bronzino*, 101–02.

177. On Eucharistic dogma, see Edward Schillebeeckx, *The Eucharist* (London: Burns & Oates, 2005); Reverend James T. O'Connor, *The Hidden Manna: A Theology of the Eucharist* (San Francisco: Ignatius Press, 2005).

178. For identification of the participants in the *Pietà*, see Cox-Rearick, "From Bandeinelli to Bronzino," 37–84; and Cox-Rearick, *Bronzino's Chapel of Eleonora*, 191–212.

179. Cox-Rearick, *Bronzino's Chapel of Eleonora*, 264–65, identified the woman who leans over the body of Christ as Mary Cleophas. There is a preparatory drawing for this figure, now in the Uffizi, that was linked to the painting by Cox-Rearick and which she identified as a sketch of Eleonora, recently described by Bambach, *The Drawings of Bronzino*, 142–44. The drawing is in the Gabinetto Disegni e Stampe degli Uffizi, Florence (10894F), "Black chalk on off-white paper (now faded beige), glued onto a secondary paper support." The face of the young woman in the Uffizi drawing resembles that of the model for a fragment of a cartoon for *Moses Striking Water from the Rock*, now in the Louvre, for the face of a young

Israelite. It could be that Bronzino used the same model for both faces, although in the *Pietà*, she was intended to evoke the duchess. On this drawing, see Bambach, *The Drawings of Bronzino*, 138–41, Musée du Louvre, Département des Arts Graphiques, Paris (17), "Charcoal and black chalk (with stumping), highlighted with white chalk, on off-white paper, silhouetted and glued onto secondary paper support; some outlines stylus-incised, and traces of framing outlines in brown ink by a later hand."

180. Richelson, *Studies in the Personal Imagery of Cosimo I de' Medici*, 110.

181. In the Eastern Orthodox and the Greek Catholic Churches, the Second Sunday after Easter is the day dedicated to commemorating "The Myrrhbearers," those who assisted in the Crucifixion, Deposition, Burial, and Resurrection of Christ, and the readings are from Mark 16:9–20, Acts 6:1–7, and Mark 15:43–16:8. On the traditions for the Myrrhbearers, see Richard Bauckham, *Jesus and the Eyewitnesses* (Grand Rapids, MI: Eerdmans Publishing Company, 2006); B. Gerhardsson, "Mark and the Female Witnesses," in H. Behrens, D. Loding, and M.T. Roth, eds., *Dumu-E2-Dub-Ba-A, A.W. Sjöberg FS; Occasional Papers of the Samuel Noah Kramer Fund 11* (Philadelphia, PA: The University Museum, 1989), 219–20, 222–23; S. Byrskog, *Story as History—History as Story Wissenschaftliche Untersuchungen zum Neuen Testament Jerusalem Talmud 123* (Tübingen: Mohr, 2000; repr. Leiden: Brill, 2002), 75–78; and C.H. Dodd, *The Interpretation of the Fourth Gospel* (Cambridge: Cambridge University Press, 1953).

182. In the Gospels, Mary Cleophas is identified as the Mother of the sons of Zebedee, who are James and John. John 19:25 lists the women: "Now there stood by the cross of Jesus, His mother and His mother's sister, Mary the wife of Clopas and Mary Magdalene." In Matthew 28:1, the women are identified as: "Now after the Sabbath, as the first day of the week began to dawn, Mary Magdalene and other Mary came to see the tomb." In Mark 16:1, he stated: Now when the Sabbath was past, Mary Magdalene, Mary the mother of James, and Salome bought spices, that they might come and anoint Him." Another version of the list is found in Mark 27:55–56: "And many women were there beholding afar off, which followed Jesus from Galilee, ministering unto him: Among which was Mary Magdalene, and Mary the mother of James and Joses, and the mother of Zebedees children." In Mark 15:40–41, the list is: "There were also women looking on afar off: among whom was Mary Magdalene, and Mary the mother James the less and of Joses, and Salome. Who also, when he was in Galilee, followed him, and ministered unto him; and many other women which came up with him unto Jerusalem." In Matthew 27:61, there is another version: "And there was Mary Magdalene, and the other Mary, sitting over against the sepulcher." Some assistance with the identification of the women is found in Matthew 4:21, the account of the calling of James

and John, the sons of Zebedee: "And going on from thence, he saw other two brethren, James the son of Zebedee, and John his brother, in a ship with Zebedee their father, mending their nets; and he called them." In Luke 24:13–27, Cleopas appears as one of the two who travelled with Jesus to Emmaus: "Then the one whose name was Cleopas answered and said to Him, 'Are you the only stranger in Jerusalem, and have you not known the things happened there in these days?'"

183. Mark 15:40–41: "There were also women looking on afar off: among whom was Mary Magdalene, and Mary the mother James the less and of Joses, and Salome. Who also, when he was in Galilee, followed him, and ministered unto him; and many other women which came up with him unto Jerusalem." I thank Charles Burroughs for the observation that the women in the *Pietà* reflect the hierarchy of court life.

184. "Roman Missal," 156.

185. "Roman Missal," 171–73.

186. "Roman Missal," 173–97.

187. "Roman Missal," 116.

188. Cox-Rearick, *Bronzino's Chapel of Eleonora*, 190, 194, 271.

189. Cox-Rearick, *Bronzino's Chapel of Eleonora*, 191, 271, 381, note 4.

190. "Roman Missal," 128.

191, Cox-Rearick, *Bronzino's Chapel of Eleonora*, 271.

192. Richelson, *Studies in the Personal Imagery of Cosimo I de' Medici*, 108–09, described coins minted by Cosimo that identified him with John the Baptist, patron saint of Florence. See also Cox-Rearick, *Bronzino's Chapel of Eleonora*, 269, for John the Baptist's significance in a Florentine context.

193. Cox-Rearick, *Bronzino's Chapel of Eleonora*, 266–67.

194. The panel of *St. Cosmas* is in a private collection and was described by Philippe de Costamagna, *"St. Cosmas,"* in Falciani and Natali, *Bronzino*, 122.

195. "Roman Missal," 55 (St. John Lateran) and 91 (Cosmas and Damian).

196. Lewine, *The Sistine Chapel Walls*, 22.

197. "Roman Missal," 92, "Magnificat te domine sanctorum tuorum cosme et damiani beata solemnitas: qua et ilis gloriam sempiternam et opem nobis inefabili providential contulisti. Amen."

198. "Roman Missal," 55.

199. "Roman Missal," 92, Luke 4:38–44: "At that time, Jesus rose from the synagogue and entered Simon's house. Now Simon's mother-in-law was suffering from a great ever, and they besought Him for her. And standing over her He rebuked the fever, and it left her; an she rose at once and began to wait on them. Now when the sun was setting, all who had

persons sick with various diseases brought them to Him. And He laid his hands upon each of them and cured them. And devils also came froth from many, crying out and saying, 'you are the Son of God ...'"

200. Murry, *Making of a God*, 9–21. The relationship between Heavenly divinity and the Medici had been noted by Cox-Rearick, *Bronzino's Chapel of Eleonora*, 280, for the chapel's ceiling design.

201. See Hermann Voss, *Die Malerei de Spåtrenaissance in Rom und Florenz*, 2 vols. (Berlin: G. Grote, 1920), 1:217, note 2: Frankfurt, Stådelsches Kunstinstitut (4344). For a description, see Bambach, *The Drawings of Bronzino*, 118, "... pen and brown ink, brush and brown wash, highlighted with white gouache, over black chalk, and stylus-ruling, on gray-glue prepared paper, framing outlines in pen and dark brown ink, silhouetted and glued onto secondary support."

202. For a recent discussion of the *modello*, see Bambach, *The Drawings of Bronzino*, 118–21.

203. For Bruce Edelstein's argument, see "Observations on the Genesis & Function of Bronzino's Frankfurt *Modello* for the Vault Decoration in the Chapel of Eleonora," in *Coming About ... A Festschrift for John Shearman* (Cambridge, MA: Harvard University Art Museums, 2001), 157–63, especially 157. Edelstein argued that St. Michael represents The Last Judgment and should have been above the entrance wall, "the traditional site for such images." As proof for this tradition, Edelstein cites only Giotto's Arena Chapel as an example of Last Judgments being placed on entrance walls, among the "myriad" that he claims exist (162, n. 10). Bambach, *The Drawings of Bronzino*, 120 concurred with Edelstein but did not add to his one example. Given that Last Judgment altarpieces were placed on altars facing the spectator—(Rogier Van der Weyden, Beaune *Last Judgment*), on the entrance doors of Gothic Cathedrals (Chartres, Royal Portal; Puerta de Gloria, Santiago de Compostela; Notre Dame; Paris, St. Lazare, Autun), and on altar apses and walls (in the old Cathedral of Salamanca and in St. Thomas Beckett Church, Salisbury, and by Michelangelo, Sistine Chapel). It would seem that Last Judgment scenes are more often placed to be seen as audiences enter than as they leave.

Bambach, in *The Drawings of Bronzino*, 120, did correct Edelstein's error of crediting Shearman with the drawing's initial publication. Bambach also suggested that Bronzino designed the *modello* before the chapel's construction was finished "from memory" and that the difference between the design of the *modello* and the finished product is the result of architectural changes that ensued. The *modello* focuses on the ceiling's central section and curves at the edges to allow for the illusionistic pillars that belong to the design of the upper part of the walls, which suggests that the chapel was completed before Bronzino finished the design of the *modello*.

204. On the selection of Francesco's name, see Cox-Rearick, *Bronzino's Chapel of Eleonora*, 66–67, who quotes Scipione Ammirato, *Istorie fiorentine con l'aggiunte di Scipione ammirato il Giovane*, 11 vols. (Florence: Ranalli, 1846–49), 6:262, 40.

205. Cox-Rearick, *Bronzino's Chapel of Eleonora*, 276. Baia, *Leonor de Toledo*, 20, noted that when Cosimo and Eleonora arrived at the Medici Palace on the via Larga, as a newly married couple, there was above the door a shield with the combined arms of the Medici/Toledo, surmounted by the Imperial eagle, arms that were evoked in the depiction of arms in her Book of Hours, et al. These arms were not quartered, as they represented the marriage.

206. For heraldic terms and usage, see Stephen Friar, *A Dictionary of Heraldry* (New York: Harmony Books, 1987); and Thomas Woodcock and John Martin Robinson, *The Oxford Guide to Heraldry* (New York: Oxford University Press, 1988).

207. For the smaller drawing, see Cox-Rearick, *Bronzino's Chapel of Eleonora*, 277, Fig. 171, Paris, Louvre (6346v). The drawing is in black chalk on the verso of the life-drawing for St. Michael, Département des Arts Graphiques, Musée du Louvre, Paris (6356); see Bambach, *The Drawings of Bronzino*, 122–25: "… black chalk on off-white paper colored with blue-gray wash, framing outlines in pen and black-brown ink, verso: black chalk on off-white paper (unprepared)." Gaston, "Eleonora di Toledo's Chapel," 162–63, suggested that the style of the painted St. Michael, which Cox-Rearick described as reflective of an "emblematic, decorative flatness," was dictated to Bronzino by Eleonora, based on a woodcut frontispiece of Françesc Eiximénis' treatise *De natura angelica* (1392), published in Burgos (1516), although Gaston could not demonstrate that this edition was known at the Florentine court. Gaston revived Cox-Rearick's observation that St. Michael was the Archangel who led the Israelites across the Red Sea — Cox-Rearick, *Bronzino's Chapel of Eleonora*, 241.

208. Falciani, in Falciani and Natali, *Bronzino*, 277–95.

209. Cox-Rearick, *Bronzino's Chapel of Eleonora*, 280–81: "The radiance emanating from the central Medici-Toledo *stemma* that bathes all the figures, garlands, and fruits in the heavenly zone of the chapel reads as both a supernatural light illuminating the ecstatic saints and a blatant assertion of Medicean dominance, as if from Heaven itself, that transforms the vault into an apotheosis of the Medici-Toledo marriage." See also Cox-Rearick, *Bronzino's Chapel of Eleonora*, 404, note 79, where she cites B.B. Davanzati, "Orazione in morte del Granduca Cosimo I recitata nell'Accademia degli Alterati," in *Operette del Signor Bernardo Davanzati Bostichi tratte dall'edizione di Padova di Giuseppe Cosimo* (Livorno, 1779), I, 162: "La famiglia de' Medici è … come stele folgorante nel Cielo"; and B. Baldini, *Vita di Cosimo*

de' Medici Primo Gran Duca di Toscana (Florence: 1578), 16, where Cosimo as duke is described as, "una nova luce la quale apprisca et risplenda nel mezzo di molti oscuri et soliti."

210. Murry, *Making of a God*, 22–32.

211. Cox-Rearick, *Bronzino's Chapel of Eleonora*, 239–40, summarized previous ideas about the saints and put forward her own arguments for their assembly, based on Florentine and Medici traditions.

212. Cox-Rearick, *Bronzino's Chapel of Eleonora*, 243–46.

213. Cox-Rearick, *Bronzino's Chapel of Eleonora*, 318–19.

214. Cox-Rearick, *Bronzino's Chapel of Eleonora*, 413, note 77; and Gaston, "Eleonora di Toledo's Chapel," passim.

215. Fragnito, "Un Pratese alla corte di Cosimo I," 47.

216. Members of the Mendoza family named Francisco included: Cardinal Francisco Mendoza de Bobadilla (1508–66); Francisco Fernández de Córdoba y Mendoza, Bishop of Jaén and Counselor to Charles V (died 1536); Francisco de Mendoza y Pacheco (died 1543); Don Francisco de Mendoza y Vargas "El Indio" (1523–63) and Francisco Sarmiento de Mendoza (1525–95). For details on their lives, see *Diccionario de Historia Eclesiástica de España*, ed. Quintín Aldea Vaquero, Tomás Marín Martínez, and José Vives, Instituto Enrique Flórez, 4 volumes, organized alphabetically (Madrid: Consejo Superior de Investigaciones Científicas, 1972–75).

217. On the Count of Oropesa, see Arthur Franklin Zimmerman, *Francisco de Toledo: Fifth Viceroy of Peru 1566–1881* (London: The Caxton Printers, Ltd., 1938). Cox-Rearick, *Bronzino's Chapel of Eleonora*, 75, misidentifies Don Francisco de Toledo, Count of Oropesa, as a brother of Eleonora, but none of Eleonora's brothers were named Francisco.

218. See Cox-Rearick, *Bronzino's Chapel of Eleonora*, 85, for the Mendozas at court. Although the Mendoza with whom the Florentine dukes had closest relations, Don Diego Hurtado Diaz de Mendoza, who was Charles V's ambassador to Florence, was not named Francisco, he too would have recognized the name as one that recurred in his family.

219. Cox-Rearick, *Bronzino's Chapel of Eleonora*, 85.

220. Later, the complex cultural identities of the Florentine court would be expressed through the material culture of fashion and style, in the costumes, jewelry, and furnishings that Eleonora commissioned for herself, her family, and court. Eleonora's manipulation of Spanish, Italian, and German style was discussed by Roberta Orsi Landini and Bruna Niccoli, *Moda a Firenze 1540–1580: Lo stile di Eleonora di Toledo e la sua influenza* (Florence: Edizioni Polistampa Pagliai, 2005). For a discussion of the bicultural identity of the court, see Robert G. La France, "Bronzino and His Friends: The Medici-Toledo Tapestries," in Andrea Gáldy, *Agnolo Bronzino: Medici Court Artist in Context* (Newcastle upon Tyne: Cambridge Scholars Pub-

lishing, 2013), 67–80. On the tapestries by Bronzino, see also Lynette M.F. Bosch, "Bronzino's *Primavera* and the *Vindication of Innocence*," *Mitteilungen des Kunsthistorischen Institutes in Florenz* (June 1983), 74–82.

221. Edelstein, Review of *Bronzino's Chapel of Eleonora in the Palazzo Vecchio*, 173; and Edelstein, "Nobildonne napoletane e committenza," 295–329, 313, n. 29.

222. Gaston, "Eleonora di Toledo's Chapel," 157–80.

223. Cox-Rearick, *Bronzino's Chapel of Eleonora*, 321, stated that Eleonora was reminded of her role as the mother of the Medici dynasty "each time she attended Mass in her chapel."

224. Gaston, "Eleonora di Toledo's Chapel," 162–63, discussed these connections but did not follow them through to a comprehensive program for the ceiling indicative of Toledo.

225. Natali, *Bronzino*, 101–11.

226. Natali, *Bronzino*, 104.

227. For a succinct discussion of the Church's position on the Eucharist, see Johannes H. Emminghaus, *The Eucharist: Essence, Form, Celebration* (Collegeville, MN: The Liturgical Press, 1997).

228. Emminghaus, *The Eucharist*, 5–11.

229. Emminghaus, *The Eucharist*, 5–6.

230. See Emminghaus, *The Eucharist*, 11–20, for a discussion of the relationship between the Eucharist and Passover and the new and old covenants they represent.

231. Cox-Rearick, *Bronzino's Chapel of Eleonora*, 265–71.

232. Murry, *Making of a God*, 177–96, discussed Cosimo's adherence to the Church, despite his disagreements with Paul III, which included pro-Roman campaigns to flush out heretics in Florence, beginning in 1544. Murry's discussion asserts that Cosimo's fealty to Charles V guaranteed his fidelity to the pope and the teachings of Rome—a position in keeping with Cosimo's conservative nature. Murry's work is in contrast with more recent attempts to interpret. 233. Cox-Rearick, *Bronzino's Chapel of Eleonora*, 276–77.

234. On the reign of Isabél and Fernanco and their policies, see Peggy K. Liss, *Isabél, the Queen* (New York and Oxford: Oxford University Press, 1992); and Nancy Rubin, *Isabella of Castile: The First Renaissance Queen* (New York: St. Martin's Press, 1992). On the Conquest of Granada, see David Coleman, *Creating Christian Granada: Society and Religious Culture in an Old-World Frontier City* (Ithaca, NY: Cornell University Press, 2003); and Henry Edward Watts, *The Christian Recovery of Spain, being the story of Spain from the Moorish conquest to the Fall of Granada (711–1492)* (Cambridge: Ulan Press, 2011).

235. A.C. Fox Davies, *The Art of Heraldry* (London and Edinburgh: T.C.

& E.C. Jack, 1904), Chapter 1, "The Origins of Armory," 3, quoting Sloane Evans, *Grammar of Heraldry,* ix: "The Antiquity of standards and symbols may be proved by reference to the Holy Writ."

236. Cox-Rearick, *Bronzino's Chapel of Eleonora,* 241.

237. Lewine, *Bronzino's Chapel of Eleonora,* 89.

238. Lewine, *Bronzino's Chapel of Eleonora.*

239. "Roman Missal," 47: "Omnipotens sempiterne deus parce metuentibus propitiare supplicantibus et mittere digneris sanctum angelum tuum de celis qui benedicat et sanctificet hos cineres: ut sint remedium salubre omnibus nomen sanctum tuum humiliter implorantibus ... pro redemption peccatorum suorum ..." Healing and exorcism are also linked and invoked by: the fourth *Oratio* of Ash Wednesday: "Almighty and Everlasting God, You granted Your healing pardon upon the Ninivites ..." ("Roman Missal," 47); on the Saturday after Ash Wednesday, in the Gospel text of Mark 6:47–56, which recounts the healing that Christ performed at Genesareth ("Roman Missal," 55); and on the third Sunday of Lent, the casting out of devils is again mentioned in the Gospel text of Luke 12:14–28 ("Roman Missal," 85).

240. "Roman Missal," 56.

241. "Roman Missal," 56–57.

242. "Roman Missal," 64.

243. Natali, *Bronzino,* 102.

244. "Roman Missal," 58.

245. On St. Jerome in the chapel, see Natali, *Bronzino,* 109–10; Edelstein, Review of *Bronzino's Chapel of Eleonora in the Palazzo Vecchio,* 173; and Gaston, "Eleonora di Toledo's Chapel," 157, 161, 162.

246. On St. Jerome, see Stefan Rebenich, *Jerome* (London: Routledge, 2002); J.N.D. Kelly, *Jerome: His Life, Writings, and Controversies* (London: Hendrickson Publishers, 1998); and Raymond E. Brown, S.S. Joseph A. Fitzmyer, and Roland E. Murphy, *New Jerome Biblical Commentary* (Upper Saddle River, NJ: Pearson, 1999).

247. On the problematically heretical beliefs of the Franciscan Joachimites, see Marjorie Reeves, *Joachim of Fiore and the Prophetic Future* (London: Sutton Publishing, 1999); George H. Tavard, *The Contemplative Church: Joachim and his Adversaries* (Milwaukee, WI: Marquette University Press, 2005); and Delno C. West, *Joachim of Fiore: A Study in Spiritual Perception and History* (Bloomington: Indiana University Press, 1983).

248. Cox-Rearick, *Bronzino's Chapel of Eleonora,* 305–07, identified the Strozzi arms on the flag with the single crescent. However, the Strozzi arms are three crescents on a band.

249. Cox-Rearick, *Bronzino's Chapel of Eleonora,* 305, cites Venetian use of this theme to indicate military victory. See also Gaston, "Eleonora di

Toledo's Chapel," 164 and 168, for a discussion of the use of the rout of the Egyptians as a trope indicative of the contemporary defeat of Islam.

250. Cox-Rearick, *Bronzino's Chapel of Eleonora*, 305.

251. Cox-Rearick, *Bronzino's Chapel of Eleonora*, 411, note 47. The armor worn by the soldiers in the Red Sea fresco is generically exotic, and more study of its details would need to be done to determine if they are specifically based on the armor worn by the soldiers of the Ottoman Empire.

252. On the European/Ottoman conflicts, see Daniel Goffman, *The Ottoman Empire and Early Modern Europe* (Cambridge: Cambridge University Press, 2002); Donald Quataert, *The Ottoman Empire, 1700–1922* (Cambridge: Cambridge University Press, 2005); and Christine Isom-Verhaaren, "Allies with the Infidel: The Ottoman and French Alliance in the Sixteenth Century," *The American Historical Review* 117, no. 5 (2012), 1543–44.

253. See Richelson, *Studies in the Personal Imagery of Cosimo I de' Medici*, 127, on Red Sea and Montemurlo; Cox-Rearick, *Bronzino's Chapel of Eleonora*, 302–06; and Gaston, "Eleonora di Toledo's Chapel," 166, 168.

254. On the Expulsion of Spain's Jewish and Moslem Populations, see Jane S. Gerber, *Jews of Spain: A History of the Sephardic Experience* (New York: Free Press, 1994); Matthew Carr, *Blood and Faith: The Purging of Muslim Spain* (New York: New Press, 2009); and Lauro Martines, *Furies: War in Europe, 1450–1700* (London: Bloomsbury Press, 2013). For the situation prior to the expulsion, see María Rosa Menocal, *The Ornament of the World: How Muslims, Jews and Christians Created a Culture of Tolerance in Medieval Spain* (New York: Back Bay Books, 2003).

255. Cox-Rearick, *Bronzino's Chapel of Eleonora*, 321 and 414, notes 1 and 2, cites A. Balletti, *Gli Ebrei e gli Estensi* (Modena: Soc. Tip Modenense, 1913), 65–66; C. Roth, *The History of the Jews in Italy* (Philadelphia, PA: Jewish Publication Society of America, 1946), 215; U. Cassuto, *Gli Ebrei a Firenze nel rinascimento* (Florence: Galletti e Cocci, 1918), 89, and quoted by Cassuto from Aboab, *Nomologia* (Venice, 1629), 304, the text that describes Eleonora's close relationship with Benvenida. See also Edelstein, "Nobildonne napoletane e committenza," 299, who points out that Benvenida was married to Don Pedro's treasurer, Don Samuele Abravanel, and that in 1541, the Abravanels were expelled from Naples and went to Ferrara. The Abravanels handled finances for Cosimo and Eleonora, and in 1553, Cosimo exempted the Abravanels from the usury laws, which allowed them to lend money in Florence without penalty. Don Jacob Abravanel, Benvenida's son, in 1562 lived in the neighborhood of Santa Croce, and he was Cosimo and Eleonora's chief banker in Ferrara. See also Benzion Nethnyahu, *Don Isaac Abravanel: Statesman and Philosopher* (Ithaca, NY: Cornell University Press, 1998).

256. Cox-Rearick, *Bronzino's Chapel of Eleonora*, 414–15, note 2.

257. Cox-Rearick, *Bronzino's Chapel of Eleonora*, 45, 356, note 67—ASF, MDP 353, f. 324 (letter of 29 August 1541).

258. Cox-Rearick, *Bronzino's Chapel of Eleonora*, 317–19.

259. See Bosch, *Art, Liturgy and Legend*, Plates I, II, and V, for the red, green, gold, and white Mendoza arms.

260. Cox-Rearick, *Bronzino's Chapel of Eleonora*, 85, 366, note 44, cites information from Col. D. Gutierrez, *Historia genealógica de la casa de Mendoza* (Cuenca: Instituto Jerónimo Zurita, 1946), 498 (Don Diego Hurtado) and 484 (Don Francisco).

261. Gaston, "Eleonora di Toledo's Chapel," 170 and 172, identifies the kneeling man's outfit as a *sayo*, a Spanish garment, and links it to one identified in the inventory of Don Pedro's belongings made at his death, which included a pair of leather boots and helmets. Gaston, 173, identified the helmet worn by the kneeling man as Spanish. However, while soft leather boots, *sayos*, and helmets were standard wear for Spanish military men and were not specific or particular to Don Pedro. Bronzino's approximation of a *sayo* in this fresco may be an acknowledgment of Eleonora's Hispanic identity, inherited by Francesco, and a way of indicating that the Israelites were foreign and exotic, just as he indicated that the Egyptians were foreign and exotic by giving them eclectic armor. However, the *sayo* or *saio* was such a ubiquitous garment among men's fashion that its employment does not by itself mean that the kneeling man can only be Don Pedro or even that it has strictly militaristic connotation. For the *sayo* as a garment of popular wear in Italy's material culture, see Roberta Orsi Landini, *Moda A Firenze 1540–1580Z: Cosimo de' Medici's Style* (Florence: Maruo Pagliai, 2011), 41–42.

262. Firpo, "Bronzino and the Medici," 91–99, in Falciani and Natali, *Bronzino*; and Falciani, in Falciani and Natali, *Bronzino*, 277–95.

263. Falciani, in Falciani and Natali, *Bronzino*, 280: "Nell'affresco col Passaggio del Mar Rosso, il volto di Pier Francesco Riccio, documentato possessore di una copia del Beneficio, è forse testimonianza di una possibile chiave di lettura eterodossa dell'intero ciclo."

264. Fragnito, "Un Pratese alla corte di Cosimo I," 41–42.

265. Fragnito, "Un Pratese alla corte di Cosimo I," 48–51.

266. Fragnito, "Un Pratese alla corte di Cosimo I," 50–53.

267. Cecchi, *Mitteilungen des Kunsthistorischen*, 115.

268. Falciani, in Falciani and Natali, *Bronzino*, 279–80.

269. Orsi Landini and Niccoli, *Moda a Firenze 1540–1580 (Eleonora di Toledo)*, and Landini, *Moda a Firenze 1540–1580 (Cosimo I)*, are the best sources for information about Eleonora's formation as a stylist of the Medici court.

270. See F. Morandini, *Mostra documentaria e iconorafica di Palazzo Pitti e Giardino de Boboli* (Florence, Archivio di Stato, 1960), p. 13, Document 11 records the transference of the court, in 1550.

271. Evelyn S. Welch, *Shopping in the Renaissance: Consumer Cultures in Italy, 1400–1600* (Cambridge: Cambridge University Press, 2009); Michele O'Malley and Evelyn Welch, *The Material Renaissance* (Manchester: Manchester University Press, 2010); and Rembrandt Duits, *Gold Brocade and Renaissance Painting* (London: Pindar Press, 2008).

272. For a discussion of Eleonora's activities in the area of finances and gifts, see Edelstein, *The Early Patronage of Eleonora di Toledo*; Edelstein, "L'usco di una porta e sei apostoli in cerca d'autore," 37–50; Edelstein, "La fecundissima Signora Duchessa," 71–97; and especially Edelstein, "Nobildonne napoletane e committenza," 295–329. Baia, *Leonor de Toledo*, 63, recorded how indefatigable Eleonora was when it came to acquiring land, possessions, and money, animals, grain, and wine—some of which she sent to Spain as gifts—and that she used the money to buy clothing and to fund her gambling. The records Baia consulted were in the ASF Mediceo, Registro Strozziano della II Serie.

273. An example of which is the gift she made to the Prioress of S. Pietro in Pistoia on 27 August 1543, cited by Cox-Rearick from Cantini, 1805, 516. See also Franceschini, in Eisenbichler, *The Cultural World of Eleonora di Toledo*, 185–92, for a discussion of Eleonora's patronage of the Jesuits.

274. For a discussion of the portraits, see Brock, *Bronzino*, 60–181.

275. Edelstein, "L'usco di una porta e sei apostoli in cerca d'autore," 225–31, attempted to present Eleonora as an independent patron of Bronzino, focusing on a few portraits, in which Eleonora became involved in their commissions, such as two portraits of Don Giovanni, the famous Uffizi portrait of Eleonora and Giovanni, a portrait of Eleonora and Francesco, and a portrait of Garzia. Edelstein, 228, also discussed a portrait of Don Giovanni ordered by Eleonora to be sent to the pope, for which she wanted Cosimo to send Bronzino to her to execute—a document that indicates that it was Cosimo who had control of Bronzino's schedule. When the documents are analyzed, it appears that the ducal couple coordinated commissions, as Edelstein admitted, 228: "It is clear, however, that Eleonora took an active interest in such projects, which may be more accurately understood as products of both the duke's and the duchess's patronage."

276. Eleonora's interest in a double portrait of herself and Francesco, which had been commissioned by Cosimo to be given to Antoine Perrenot, Bishop of Arras, was focused on making sure that his clothing reflected his more grown-up position at court. See Edelstein, "L'usco di una porta e sei apostoli in cerca d'autore," 226–27. Yet, Eleonora did commission some works of art independently, as Cox-Rearick, *Bronzino's Chapel of Eleonora*, 82, noted in her publication of a letter from Sforza Almeni to Riccio, documenting Eleonora's ordering Bronzino to copy the Salviati *Lamentation* in her chapel so that a copy could be sent to Spain.

277. Some of the documents Edelstein discussed had been published and studied by Fragnito, "Un Pratese alla corte di Cosimo I," 31–83, and Cecchi, *Mitteilungen des Kunsthistorischen*, 115–43, with conclusions somewhat different from those Edelstein reached. Most notably, Fragnito and Cecchi identified the unknown Flemish painter from whom a copy of a portrait of Don Giovanni was commissioned as the painter Luigi Corto. They cited a letter from Lorenzo Pagni to Pierfrancesco Riccio, dated 16 March 1547: "Il ritratto del S.or Don Giovanni non è se non piacciuto a S. Ecc.a, per quello che mi disse quando lo scoperse, che ero presente" (The portrait of Don Giovanni was nothing if not pleasing to His Excellency, according to what he told me when he discovered it, in my presence) as the source for this information. This statement indicates approval for the portrait, not disapproval. Edelstein wished to interpret the Italian phrase as disapproval on Eleonora's part so that he could demonstrate her demanding patronage. Even though Edelstein, "L'usco di una porta e sei apostoli in cerca d'autore," 259, note 69, admitted that he mistakenly translated the double negatives, which cancel each other out, he did not alter his text to reflect an accurate reading of this phrase. Edelstein identified the "S. Ecc.a" in the document as indicating Eleonora, but Pieraccini, *La Stirpe de' Medici a Caffagiuolo*, 2:116, interpreted the document's form of address as indicating Cosimo. Hence, the letter may record Cosimo's pleasure, although Eleonora may have been equally pleased. A closer reading of the actual document is needed to establish whether it is recording Cosimo or Eleonora's pleasure.

278. Vasari-Milanesi, 7:597–98: "Il signor duca, veduta in queste ed alter opera l'eccellenza di questo pittore, e particolarmente che era suo proprio ritrarre dal natural quanto con più diligenzia si può imaginare, fece ritrarre sè, che allora era giovane, armato tuto d'arme bianche e con una mano sopra l'elmo: in un altro quadro la signora duchessa sua consorte; ed in un altro quadro il signor don Francesco loro figliuolo e prencipe di Fiorenza. E non andò molto che ritrasse, sì come piacque a lei, un'altra volta la detta signora Duchessa, in vario modo dal primo, col signor don Giovanni suo figliuolo appresso."

279. Edelstein, "L'usco di una porta e sei apostoli in cerca d'autore," 234, discussed Vasari's description to Vincenzo Borghini of his meetings with Cosimo and Eleonora, on 21 November 1561, at which he discussed his plans for his frescoes for her rooms; he states that he spent one hour explaining his work to Cosimo and two hours explaining it to Eleonora.

280. Edelstein, "L'usco di una porta e sei apostoli in cerca d'autore," 234, for the letter, dated 9 May 1562.

281. For a context for Eleonora's clothing and on Renaissance clothing, see Carole Collier Frick, *Dressing Renaissance Florence: Families, For-*

tunes and Fine Clothing (Baltimore, MD: Johns Hopkins University Press, 2005); Ann Rosalind Jones, *Renaissance Clothing and the Materials of Memory* (Cambridge: Cambridge University Press, 2001); Ann Rosalind Jones and Margaret F. Rosenthal, *The Clothing of the Renaissance World: Europe–Asia–Africa–The Americas* (Oxford: Oxford University Press, 2012); Janet Cox-Rearick, *Splendor of the Renaissance: Princely Attire in Italy: Reconstructions of Historic Costumes* (New York: Art Gallery of The Graduate Center, CUNY, 2004); and Orsi Landini, *Moda a Firenze 1540–1580 (Cosimo I)*. Baia, *Leonor de Toledo*, 66–68, recorded how in the ASF Mediceo, Registro Strozziano della II Serie, there is a record of the extensive collection of luxury jewelry and objects of personal adornment Eleonra owned.

282. Benvenuto Cellini, *The Autobiography of Benevenuto Cellini*, eds. Charles Hope and Alessandro Nova (New York: St. Martin's Press, 1983), 152–207. Baia, *Leonor de Toledo*, 52–60, discussed how in documents she had read, she found Eleonora to be capricious, lacking in justice, manipulative, and meddlesome in people's affairs, to the discomfort of others. Baia recounts how Eleonora persecuted a young woman, Lucrezia Bertolini, who was in the convent of San Giovannino and from which Eleonora ordered her out, to live with a relative, Alessandra Bertolini. Eleonora informed the girl, who did not want to leave the convent, that if she disobeyed her, she would call the bargello and remove her by force and would then ruin the convent. The abbess had to write to Cosimo to intercede for the poor girl. The girl herself wrote Cosimo, begging him to let her stay in the convent. The outcome of the situation is unknown, but it makes Eleonora look to be as malicious of character as Benvenuto Cellini opined that she was in his autobiography. Yet, as Baia noted, 63, when it came to certain political matters, Eleonora was very active in managing relations for Cosimo and different special interest groups and was very astute when advising him.

283. Pieraccini, *La stirpe de' Medici di Cafaggiolo*, 2:64, reproduced documentation for a conversation between Eleonora and Jacopo Cappoini, who was about to leave for Egypt, in which Eleonora tells him that if he finds "qualcosa bella et rara da quelle parti 'Egitto per donne, non manchi mandarla.'" Baia, *Leonor de Toledo*, 78, asserted that Eleonora was interested in the reform of the University of Siena and in poetry and that she regularly attended the meetings of the *Accademia degli Elevati* (founded 1547); also that Benedetto Varchi translated Seneca at her request and that, soon after the marriage, Cosimo ordered a "commedia" that the duchess wanted. Baia also noted (80) that in 1545, Pietro Aretineo sent Eleonora a verse chapter of his work, which implies that her interest in poetry was known.

284. Pieraccini, *La stirpe de' Medici di Cafaggiolo*, 2:55–64.

285. Cox-Rearick *Mitteilungen des Kunsthistorischen*, 26–33, published correspondence written by the court secretaries praising Eleonora's performance at the wedding.

286. See Orsi Landini and Niccoli, *Moda a Firenze 1540–1580 (Eleonora di Toledo)*, Appendices, for inventories of Eleonora's clothing and a discussion of costs for clothing, textiles, and jewelry for herself, her family, and the court.

287. See Orsi Landini and Niccoli, *Moda a Firenze 1540–1580 (Eleonora di Toledo)*, 171–95, for information on the process of making the items of clothing and furnishing that Eleonora commissioned and for information about the tailors, weavers, and embroiderers she regularly employed.

288. Madeline H. Caviness, "Patron or Matron? A Capetian Bride and a Vade Mecum for Her Marriage Bed," *Speculum* 68, no. 2 (April 1993), 333–62.

289. For a summary of the praise bestowed on Eleonora at her funeral, see Cox-Rearick, *Bronzino's Chapel of Eleonora*, 50–53; and Janet Cox-Rearick, "La Ill.ma Sig.ra Duchessa felice memoria: The Posthumous Eleonora di Toledo," in Eisenbichler, *The Cultural World of Eleonora di Toledo*, 225–47.

290. Prince William, Duke of Cambridge is descended from Marie de' Medici, daughter of Francesco de' Medici and granddaughter of Eleonora, through his mother, Diana, Princess of Wales, who is a descendant of the Dukes of Grafton and Richmond (on different sides of her family tree), who were the illegitimate sons of Charles II, the son of Charles I and Queen Henrietta Maria, the great-granddaughter of Eleonora.

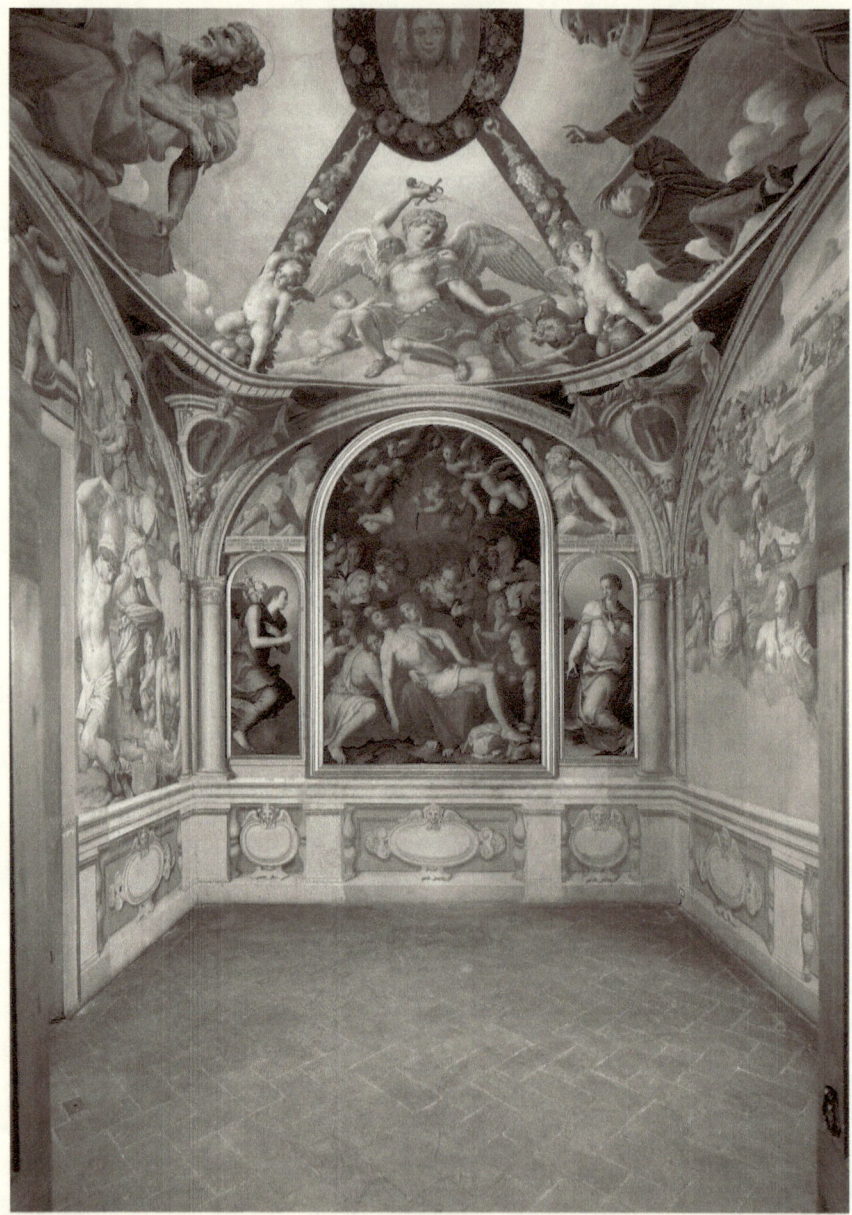

Fig. 1. Agnolo Bronzino, The Chapel of Eleonora de Toledo, Interior view, 1541–46. Palazzo Vecchio, Florence. Photo credit: Scala/Art Resource, NY.

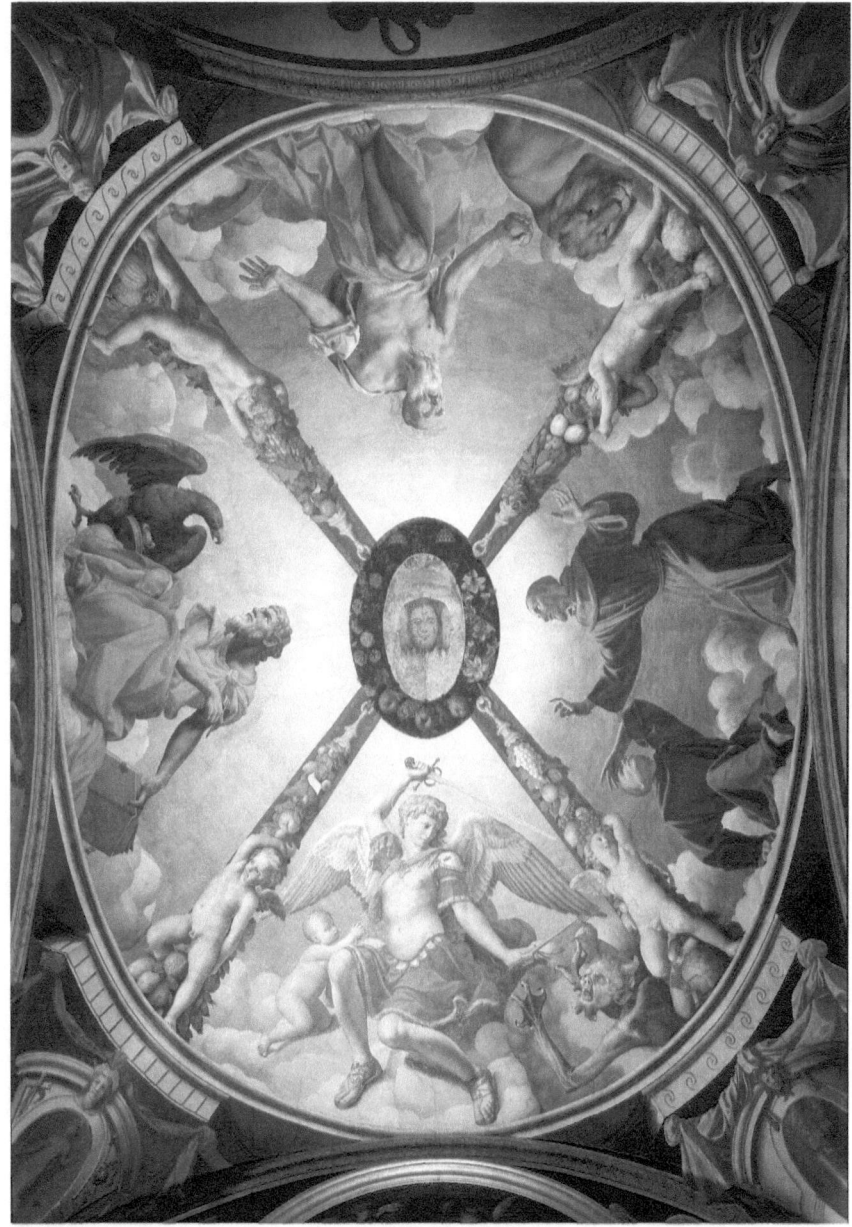

Fig. 2. Agnolo Bronzino, *Vault of the Chapel of Eleonora de Toledo*, 1541. Chapel of Eleonora de Toledo, Palazzo Vecchio, Florence. Photo credit: Scala/Art Resource, NY.

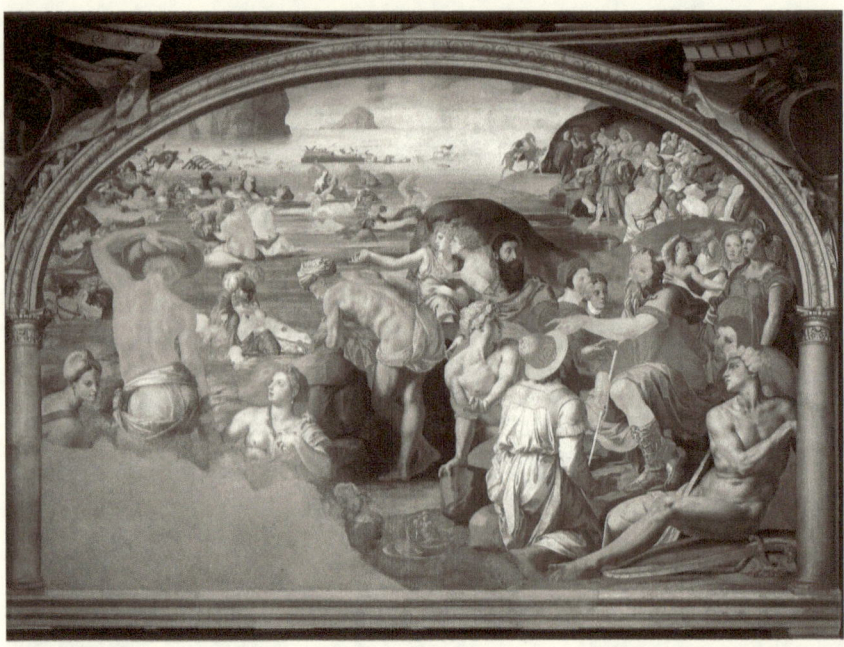

Fig. 3. Agnolo Bronzino, *Crossing of the Red Sea*, 1541–42. Chapel of Eleonora de Toledo, Palazzo Vecchio, Florence. Photo credit: Scala/Art Resource, NY.

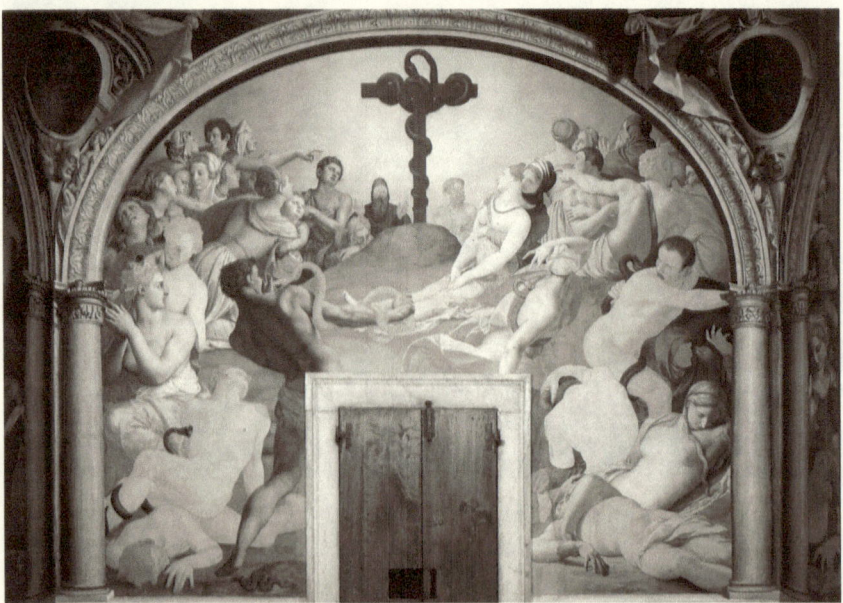

Fig. 4. Agnolo Bronzino, *The Miracle of the Brazen Serpent*, 1542. Chapel of Eleonora de Toledo, Palazzo Vecchio, Florence. Photo credit: Scala/Art Resource, NY.

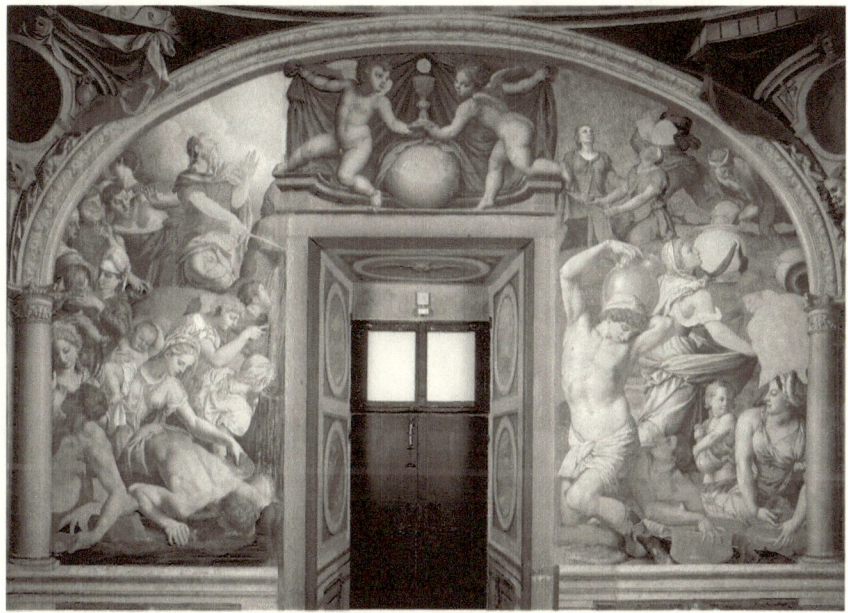

Fig. 5. Agnolo Bronzino, *Moses Striking the Rock and the Gathering of the Manna*, 1542–43. Chapel of Eleonora de Toledo, Palazzo Vecchio, Florence. Photo credit: Scala/Art Resource, NY.

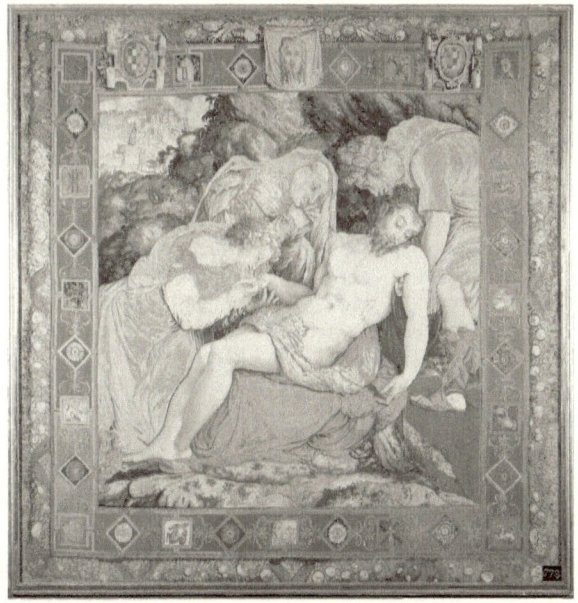

Fig. 6. Francesco Salviati, *The Lamentation*, 1546, tapestry. Galleria degli Uffizi, Florence. Photo credit: Scala/Art Resource, NY.

A Color Inventory of Selected Paintings by Agnolo Bronzino From 1540 to 1546: The Panciatichi Paintings and the Chapel of Eleonora de Toledo

Thomas MacPherson

As a contemporary egg tempera painter with an interest in the historic pigments used by artists in the sixteenth century, I have been interested in Bronzino's colors since 2009, when I began studying them while on a research trip. During the summer of 2009, I began to inventory Bronzino's colors, focusing on the portraits of Bartolomeo and Lucrezia Panciatichi and the Uffizi *Holy Family*. I also studied the frescoes and altarpiece of the Chapel of Eleonora de Toledo in the Palazzo Vecchio. For the Panciatichi paintings, I took detailed color notes on site, but not for the frescoes in the chapel or for the Vienna *Holy Family* or the Nice *Crucifixion*, which are also surveyed here. For these works, I used the reproductions in the recent Bronzino exhibition, held in the Strozzi Palace in 2010. In this article, I will limit my study to those works generally accepted as belonging to Bronzino's mid-career paintings, completed between 1540 to 1546. I will begin this inventory with the Eleonora Chapel, after which I will inventory the Panciatichi paintings. The goal of my study is to provide a list of colors that Bronzino used in his work during this stage of his development, in order to provide information that can be used in a variety of ways by art historians interested in Bronzino's use of color and changing patterns of color selection.

My inventory of pigments is a speculative venture based on years of using the same historic pigments in my own work. While the name of some of these pigments may have changed since the days of Bronzino, I am confident that I am accurate in most instances. I am not a restorer, so my analysis and conclusions are based on several sources: viewing the original art, locating slides from the

Web Gallery of Art, relying on my experiences of using and mixing paints as a painter, and from the web site of the art supply company, Natural Pigments, where I purchase the historic dry pigments that I use to make the paints for my egg tempera paintings. This company has a web site, www.NaturalPigments.com, and it is an invaluable resource on historical and technical information about each pigment, as well as for articles on technique about fresco and egg tempera painting. My primary goal for this project is to start a resource that includes the names of pigments used in the sixteenth century so that researchers can have a common ground for what to call colors. In the future, the list can be reviewed, expanded, and revised as needed, as more pigments are accurately identified. It is by no means an authoritative list, just a starting point for discussion.

From an artistic point of view, the undertaking of this project has altered my own way of seeing and using colors. I am now using color combinations in my own work that either never occurred to me or ones that I rejected as being too "mundane" when compared to many of the brilliant, modern pigments used in contemporary painting today. I have come to appreciate the subtlety and brilliance of these ancient pigments as I studied closely the synthesis of color harmonies and technique in the hands of a master like Bronzino.

INVENTORY OF COLORS

The Chapel of Eleonora de Toledo 1541–46. Palazzo Vecchio, Florence (Fig. 1).
Vault of the Chapel of Eleonora de Toledo, 1541. Fresco, Palazzo Vecchio, Florence (Fig. 2).

Lapis Lazuli—Sky (medium to light values), garments of St. Michael (deep, rich color).
Italian yellow earth + *Red Sartorius earth* + *Verona green earth*—Face, shoulders, and arms of devil.
Ercolano red + *lead white*—Pale red brown behind devil and on his arms and torso.
Lead white + *lamp black (Gray)*—Clouds, wings on St. Michael, and beards of St. Jerome and St. John the Evangelist. I think Bronzino used lamp black. It is a color that can be

warm or cool and is known for its intensity and blue-black properties, especially when mixed with lead white.

Lead-tin yellow—Glow around center trinity.

Dragon's blood (Sangue di drago)—Various red brown tints and shades are found on the garments of Saints Jerome, Michael, and John the Evangelist; tip of horn on devil; sash on St. Michael.

Cold (violet) Hematite + Dragon's blood—Dark violet brown garment behind St. Michael.

Burnt umber + lead white + lamp black—Eagle, St. Francis and Brother Leo, ends of wings of St. Michael, and Bible of St. John.

Red Sartorius earth + Verona green earth—Angel hiding behind St. Michael in shadow.

Italian yellow earth + Red Sartorius earth + lead white—Basic yellowish skin tone of St. Michael's torso.

Dragon's blood + Verona green earth—Red tones and warm shadows on St. Michael's torso, red tones on the devil's arms and back.

Lamp Black—Dark tones on devil and saints.

Pale yellow ochre + white—Light tones on St. Michael's hair, belt, sandals; trim on garments; and sword hand.

Raw sienna—Deep golden tones of hair, gold belt, trim on garments, and sandals on St. Michael.

Italian yellow earth + Red Sartorius earth + lapis lazuli + lead white—Basic skin tones of other saints, gray skin tones (more lapis in color).

Goethite—Medium, dull yellow parts of lion,

Cold hematite—Deeper brown violet parts of the lion.

The Crossing of the Red Sea, 1541–42. Fresco (right hand wall). Chapel of Eleonora de Toledo, Palazzo Vecchio, Florence (Fig. 3).

Lapis lazuli (intense blue to various light variations)—Moses' boots and cloak, hood on the figure with a dark beard behind Moses, headdress on the figure to the right of him, various figures on the shore in the background, and some headdresses of figures in the sea.

Nicossia green earth—Pale bluish green sections of rocks in foreground, cloak of the figure in front of Moses, and water and rock in foreground.

Verdigris—Deeper blue-green on the garment of the figure sitting behind the dark rock, green shore near rock, and hill on the end of the shore.

Verdigris + Italian yellow earth—Warm parts of the grass behind Moses' head.

Lead white + lamp black (gray)—Cloak of figure in foreground, silver jug in foreground, headdress of figure leaning on rock, various figures and horses in water, and the distant landscape.

Burnt Umber (pure burnt umber and burnt umber + lamp black)—Dark rock in middle ground.

Ercolano Red (a rich, historic red oxide)—Garment on figure extending his hand located in the left foreground, headdress and figure on the shore in the background.

Vermillion—Glazed on top of fresco with tempera on hat and loincloth of standing male figure on left.

Dragon's blood—Deep red headdress and garment of figure next to Moses, deep shades on the dress of woman behind Moses, interspersed throughout the crowd on the shore, and flag in the sea.

Dragon's blood + white—I think this is the pinkish color found in Moses' garment and light parts of the dress of the blond woman behind the black rock motioning to the sea.

Raw sienna + dragon's blood—Darker earth color on Moses' shirt and the headdress of the main figure in the left foreground, and light areas on the dress of the woman behind Moses.

Raw sienna—Deep earth yellow on the hat of the main figure kneeling in the right foreground, the front of Moses, the vessel in the foreground, and rich blond hair.

Pale yellow ochre—Light color on the hat of the kneeling figure in front of Moses, the light blond hair, light areas of vessel with figure in the foreground, and garment on leg on figure in the extreme lower right corner.

Dragon's blood + Verona green earth—Warm skin tones on the main figure in the left foreground, all other warm skin tones.

Italian yellow earth + Sartorius red earth + Lapis lazuli + lead white—Neutral skin tones.

Cold hematite—When painted over a light warm ground, the color tends to be a warm reddish purple. The color can be found in the light and deep reddish purple brown areas of the sea.

Cold hematite +lead white—When mixed with white, it produces excellent purple grays and purple lakes because of its purple bias. This mixed color can be found in the purple gray cloak of the man with dark beard next to Moses, Moses' garment, and the clothes of various figures through out the fresco.

Moses Striking the Rock and the Gathering of the Manna, 1542–43. Fresco (left hand wall). Chapel of Eleonora de Toledo, Palazzo Vecchio, Florence (Fig. 4).
Moses Striking the Rock

Raw sienna + dragon's blood—Lighter parts, Moses' cloak, the man's cloak to his left.

Dragon's blood—Deeper red areas of Moses' cloak, cloak of the semi-nude female figure next to him, and the darker red shadowed area on the cloak of blond mother holding her baby and dipping her bowl into the spring.

Pale yellow ochre—Lightest parts, of all of the blond hair and Moses' "horns," and the heaven at the top of the fresco.

Dragon's blood + lead white—Pink areas of Moses' robe and the pink highlight areas found on the headdress of the woman with her back to viewer.

Lapis lazuli—Shadow areas of the woman's (with her back to the viewer) cloak and the headdress and dress of the woman giving her baby a drink.

Lead-tin yellow + lead white—Light yellow found in the cloak of the woman turned toward the spring and highlight area of the cloak of blond mother figure holding her baby.

Lamp black + lead white (gray)—Clouds, rocks, spring, and shadows in the white clothing.

Lead white + lamp black + lapis lazuli (blue-gray)—This appears have some lapis lazuli added to the gray mixture. This color can be found in the some clothing, rocks, the spring, and the clouds.

Verdigris—Deep blue-green sleeves worn by the woman giving her baby a drink, the man drinking directly from the spring, and shawl of the blond woman holding a baby dipping a bowl in the spring.

Verdigris + Italian yellow earth—Grassy area in the middle of fresco.

Carmine lake—Deep red skin tones on the crying baby, all other warm skin tones.

Yellow Italian earth + Sartorius red earth + Verona green earth + vermillion + white—Warm skin tones on face of the crying baby, all other warm skin tones. The vermillion was possibly glazed over onto the fresco with egg tempera.

Yellow Italian earth + Sartorius red earth + lapis lazuli—Neutral or gray skin tones.

Italian yellow earth + Red Sartorius earth + lead white—Basic yellow skin color on the figures.

Italian yellow earth—Light parts of brown hair.

Burnt umber—Dark areas of brown hair.

Cold hematite—Water.

Lamp black—Deepest dark areas throughout fresco.

Moses Striking the Rock and the Gathering of the Manna, 1542–43. Fresco (left hand wall). Chapel of Eleonora de Toledo, Palazzo Vecchio, Florence (Fig. 4).

Gathering of the Manna

Lead tin yellow + lead white—Headdress and loincloth of dominant figure in left foreground.

Lapis lazuli—Shadows on dominant figure with loincloth, shadows on cloak of young child to the right.

Cold hematite—Warm reddish purple on the cloak of the figure at the very top walking away, and inside of vessel on side at extreme right.

Cold hematite + lead white—Light areas of both the shirt of the retreating figure and vessel lying on its side.

Yellow Italian earth + Sartorius red earth + lapis lazuli + lead white—Neutral skin tones.

Yellow Italian earth + Sartorius red earth + Verona green earth + vermillion + white—All other warm (red) skin tones.

Carmine lake—Deeper red areas of skin, I think were glazed with tempera.

Pale yellow ochre—Lightest areas in the dress of the woman in the middle of the fresco, the same woman's hair.

Yellow ochre + cold hematite—Middle and dark tones of same dress.

Dragon's blood—Cloak of man crouching in upper right corner, part of his hat, and piece of fabric below young child.

Yellow ochre + dragon's blood + lead white—Hat and object the crouching man is holding.

Lead white + lamp black + Lapis lazuli—Blue-gray of the sky, hat of man to the right middle of the composition.

Lead white + lamp black—Cloak of female figure in the center, headdress of female figure in lower right corner.

Lead white + lamp black + cold hematite—Clothing of woman in lower right corner.

Ercolano red + lead white—Vessel main figure is holding.

Raw sienna—Containers at the bottom of the fresco, trim on boots of main figure.

Deep verdigris—Boots of the main figure, vessel at the top of the page, and dark areas of figure in green, looking up at sky.

Green earth + verdigris—Clothing of figure at the top, looking toward heaven, various colors mixed with yellow earth on the ground.

The Miracle of the Brazen Serpent, 1542. Fresco (wall at entrance). Chapel of Eleonora de Toledo, Palazzo Vecchio, Florence (Fig. 5).

Lapis lazuli—Cloak of the distressed male figure looking to heaven on left, headdress and robe of figure just above distressed figure, robe of man to left of cross, and strap of man pointing to cross.

Lapis lazuli + lead white—Sky, shadows in the dress of the supported woman in the center, headdress of two women in the background to the right, and the drapery of the reclining woman in the lower right corner.

Ercolano red + Dragon's blood—Loincloth of man in left foreground cut off by door and woman's headdress in lower left corner.

Ercolano red + lead white—Pale orange cloak on the woman at the extreme right.

Vermillion—Applied to medium and darker areas of the pale orange cloak.

Light lead-tin yellow—Cloaks of the women in the lower left corner, the one holding her child and leaning toward the brazen serpent, drapery on reclining male figure in foreground and the figure fleeing in the foreground in the right corner of the door.

Nicosia green earth—The green shadows in figure in left corner, the woman with baby leaning toward the cross.

Verdigris + red Sartorius earth—Center mound, hat of man next to cross and hooded figure on the right.

Verdigris + Italian yellow earth—Warm parts of ground.

Red Sartorius earth—Red areas of cross and serpent.

Red Sartorius earth + lamp black—Dark areas on cross and dark serpents.

Dragon's blood + lead white—Cloak of man in background by cross.

Pale yellow ochre—Light areas of blond hair.

Raw sienna—Deeper areas of cloak of person fleeing, bust of sitting woman in the middle that has been bitten by a snake, and the all of the blond hair.

Yellow Italian earth + Sartorius red earth + lapis lazuli + lead white—The gray, white, pale yellow and brown skin tones.

Verona green earth—Face on distressed figure looking up on the left of the fresco.

Yellow Italian earth + Sartorius red earth + Verona green earth + vermillion + lead white—Nude figures fleeing on the right and standing by the cross and other warm (reddish) skin tones.

Burnt umber + lamp black—Dark hair.

Yellow Italian earth + Sartorius red earth + lamp black—Male figure in foreground to the left of the door being attacked by a snake.

Cold hematite + lead white—Robe of man by right column in shadow.

Portrait of Bartolomeo Panciatichi c. 1540. Oil on panel, 104 x 85 cm. Galleria degli Uffizi, Florence (Fig. 6).

Lamp black with glazes of burnt umber and lapis lazuli—Hat and coat, dog, third window in upper left, and robe on legs (the darkest).

Raw sienna with glazes of Ercolano red and burnt umber—Beard, eyes of dog, and edge of pages of book.

Carmine (scarlet) lake—Medium red areas of sleeves.

Carmine lake + lead white—Lightest areas of sleeves.

Madder (alizarin) lake—Deep red areas of sleeve.

Azurite blue—Patch sky in the distance.

Italian yellow earth + lead white—Building below blue patch.

Lead white + Italian yellow earth + Ercolano red + lapis lazuli—Pale skin color. I think that Bronzino used lapis to neutralize the skin color in Bartolomeo rather than an earth color.

Italian yellow earth + red Sartorius earth + lapis lazuli—Shadow on face and hands.

Carmine lake—Reddish glazes on cheeks and side of face.

Lapis lazuli—Glazing on face to create dark shadows.

Lead white + lamp black + Italian yellow earth—Warm gray in building facades.

Blue-gray glazes—On the warm gray facade to create the sense of depth and on yellow building below sky.

Ercolano red—Very delicate glazes on yellow building.

Lead white + lamp black + lapis lazuli—Blue-gray on trim of buildings and arm of chair.

Italian yellow earth—Glazes on window in upper right.

Burnt umber—Glazes of window in the middle on upper right.

Yellow ochre—First window in the upper left.
Red Sartorius earth—Second window in upper left.

Portrait of Lucrezia Panciatichi c. 1541. Oil on panel, 102 x 85. Galleria degli Uffizi, Florence (Fig. 7).

Lead white + Italian yellow earth + red Sartorius earth + lapis lazuli—Very pale skin on face, neck, and hands.

Carmine lake—Glaze on book cover, cheeks, lips, side of face and fingers.

Italian yellow earth + red Sartorius earth + lapis lazuli—Shadow on face and hands.

Lapis lazuli—Glazing on face to create dark shadows.

Yellow ochre + with glazes of raw sienna + Ercolano red + burnt umber—Hair.

Deep lapis lazuli—Eyes, brooch, and ring.

Madder (crimson) lake—Center of brooch and middle to deep shadows of the dress.

Lead white + dragon's blood + burnt umber—Delicate to light colors and glazes on pearls, top of dress, and ruffles.

Burnt umber—Glazing in deep shadows of dress and ruffles and side of arm of chair.

Lamp black—Glazing in the darkest furrows of dress, darkest shadows in hair, and in the darkest areas around Lucrezia.

Azurite—Glazed on top of black background on columns.

Lead white glazed with raw umber—Lace part on top of dress, pearls.

Burnt umber with lead white swirls—Wooden beaded belt.

Burnt umber—Glazing on column on the right side of painting.

Deep burnt umber + lamp black—Sleeves.

Cold hematite + lead white—On violet highlights on brown sleeve.

Raw sienna—Carved part of chair arm, gold on necklace and ring.

The Madonna and Child with St. Elizabeth and the Infant St. John the Baptist c. 1545–46. Oil on panel, 124 x 99 cm. Kunsthistorisches Museum, Vienna (Fig. 8).

Lead white + Italian yellow earth + red Sartorius earth + lapis lazuli—Very pale skin on face, neck, and hands.

Italian yellow earth + red Sartorius earth + lapis lazuli— Shadow on face and hands of figures.

Carmine lake—Reddish glazes on cheeks and side of head.

Lapis lazuli—Glazing on the skin of the faces and bodies to create subtle and dark neutral shadows. Vibrant areas on Madonna's cloak, Joseph's robe, prayer book, sky in upper left hand corner, and bird in the Christ child's hand.

Pale yellow ochre—Under painting and lightest parts of blond hair, cushion under St. John, crucifix, wings of bird, and fruit.

Raw sienna with glazes of Ercolano red + burnt umber + lamp black—Blond hair, cushion under St. John, and book edge.

Lead white + dragon's blood + burnt umber—Light and middle areas of the Madonna's robe and veil.

Burnt umber + dragon's blood + lamp black—Deeper tones in lower half of robe.

Dragon's blood—Glazed areas on the sleeve and over darker tones on the lower torso and hips.

Madder lake—Glazed over darker tones on the lower torso and hips.

Raw sienna—Glazes on fruit, crucifix, and wings of bird.

Vermillion—Glazing on fruit, glow on the under side of sleeve on left arm.

Cold hematite—Shirt of St. Elizabeth.

Cold hematite + lead white—Violet-gray parts of St. Elizabeth's blouse.

Verdigris—Hills in landscape in the background.

Italian yellow earth + verdigris—Yellow green areas in landscape in the background.

Lead white + lamp black—Cowl of St. Elizabeth, garment under Christ, building in background, veil on Madonna, gray beard and hair of St. Joseph, the Madonna's shawl, and other drapery.

Cold hematite + burnt umber + lamp black—Cloak around St. Joseph, building in the right background, and pillow under St. John the Baptist.

Ercolano red—Glazes on tower and wall in the top right corner of background, roof and stairs of buildings on the left, and cloak of Joseph and comb (barrette).

Lead white + lamp black + glazes of verdigris—Clouds in sky. Various amounts of lead white and lamp black are used as an under painting to create the middle and deep tones then glazed.

Cold hematite glazes—Applied to the darkest clouds in the top right that interacts with the verdigris and deepens the clouds into an ominous deep color.

Verona green earth + lead white + lamp black—Rocks in foreground, leaves of fruit.

The Madonna and Child with the Infant St. John the Baptist c. 1540–42 (*Panciatichi Holy Family*). Tempera on panel, 117 x 93 cm. Galleria degli Uffizi, Florence (Fig. 9).

Vermillion + lead white—Various tints on cloak.

Lapis lazuli—Sash on Madonna, jewel on clasp and pillow.

Lead white + Italian yellow earth + Ercolano red + lapis lazuli—Very pale skin on face, neck, and hands.

Italian yellow earth + Ercolano red + lapis lazuli—Shadow on face and hands of figures.

Carmine lake—Reddish glazes in middle tones on face color.

Lapis lazuli—Glazing on face to create dark shadows.

Vermillion—Intense application on parts of cloak of the Madonna and flag in the distance.

Raw sienna with glazes of Ercolano red + burnt umber + lamp black—Edge of pages of book, blond hair and beard of St. Joseph.

Raw sienna—Brooch.

Burnt umber + lamp black — Dark hair.

Deep lapis lazuli — Bottom garment on the Madonna. Possibly indigo and black were added to lapis to deepen it.

Cold hematite — Shirt of St. Joseph, rocks in distance.

Cold hematite + lead white — Violet-gray parts of St. Joseph's cloak.

Lead white + burnt umber — Sack under pillow, parts of rock in left front corner, and rocks in the background.

Ercolano red — Glazed in foreground, the rocks and the buildings in the far distance.

Lamp black — Darkest parts of picture.

Lead white + lamp black — Gray clouds, parts of buildings.

Verdigris — Glazes on clouds.

Hematite — Delicate glazes on clouds.

Italian yellow earth + Ercolano red + verdigris — Book cover.

The Crucified Christ c. 1540. Oil on panel, 145 x 115 cm. Musée des Beaux-Arts, Nice, France (Fig. 10).

Lead white + Italian yellow earth + red Sartorius earth + lapis lazuli — Very pale skin on body.

Italian yellow earth + red Sartorius earth + lapis lazuli — Shadow on body.

Carmine lake — Reddish glazes in middle tones on flesh.

Lamp black + lead white (gray) — Various grays for the background of niches and columns.

Lamp black — Darkest areas at the very top and deepest shadows in background.

Lapis lazuli — Glazes on body to create dark shadows, niches and columns in background.

Lead white + lamp black — Blue-gray in background.

Tyrian purple — Delicate glazes and dark, rich areas in loincloth and hair in the vicinity of the thorns. A color similar to magenta or red-violet sometimes confused with madder lake (crimson). Pliny the Elder thought it looked like the color of "freshly coagulated blood."[1]

Madder lake — The color of the blood oozing from the nail holes in the feet.

Yellow ochre—Highlights in hair and cross.
Raw sienna—Medium tones in cross, hair, and beard.
Ercolano red—Probably glazed onto cross.
Burnt umber—Darker shadows in cross, hair, and beard.

The Crucified Christ, 1540, is an unusual painting in terms of the color palette Bronzino used when it is compared to the frescoes in the Eleonora Chapel and the other oil paintings produced around the same time. *The Crucified Christ* has some of the same color mixtures Bronzino used in the works inventoried above, but Bronzino also added unusual colors for this painting. His use of these unexpected colors yielded a painting that is unique for his *oeuvre*. One major difference is the use of the color Tyrian purple and his almost exclusive use of blue-gray in the architecture in the background. In Bronzino's works, this is the only instance I can find where he used Tyrian purple. Thus, the employment of this color raises questions: Did this color have a special symbolic connotation? Did Tyrian purple represent blood or the idea of the transubstantiation? Or did he try experimenting with Tyrian purple and the cool blue-gray background in this painting but did not like the effect so did not return to it in later works? Perhaps, the use of Tyrian purple in this painting was the result of a very special request from the patrons? Or, does this difference in color indicate that *The Crucified Christ* is not by Bronzino?

The other paintings by Bronzino that I studied and that can be assigned to his early years are similar and were painted with comparable colors and color combinations. In these, Bronzino relied on a customary and preferred palette. Yet, *The Crucified Christ* diverges from the expected for its supposed chronological place in Bronzino's work. *The Crucified Christ* seems to be either a very special commission with specific requests or an experiment on Bronzino's part that failed pictorially; hence, he never again utilized these colors. More likely, this was an artistic experiment that he considered to have not accomplished the effect he sought, because even if the color scheme had been a special order, had it worked, he would have repeated it. Thus, the evidence argues for considering the uniqueness of *The Crucified Christ* as an experiment that Bronzino did not repeat.

NOTE

1. J.N. Liles, *The Art and Craft of Natural Dyeing: Traditional Recipes for Modern Use.* (Knoxville: University of Tennessee Press, 2006), 156.

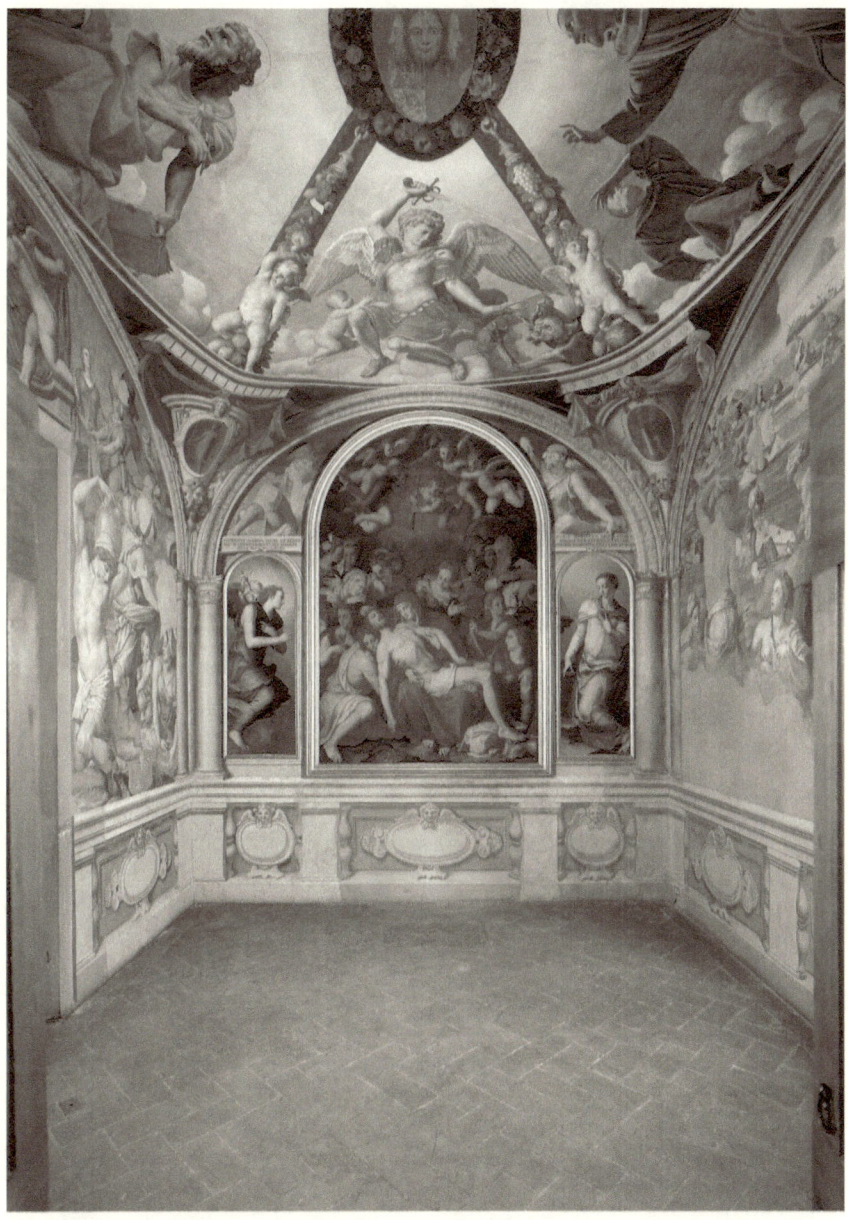

Fig. 1. Agnolo Bronzino, The Chapel of Eleonora de Toledo, Interior view, 1541–46. Palazzo Vecchio, Florence. Photo credit: Scala/Art Resource, NY.

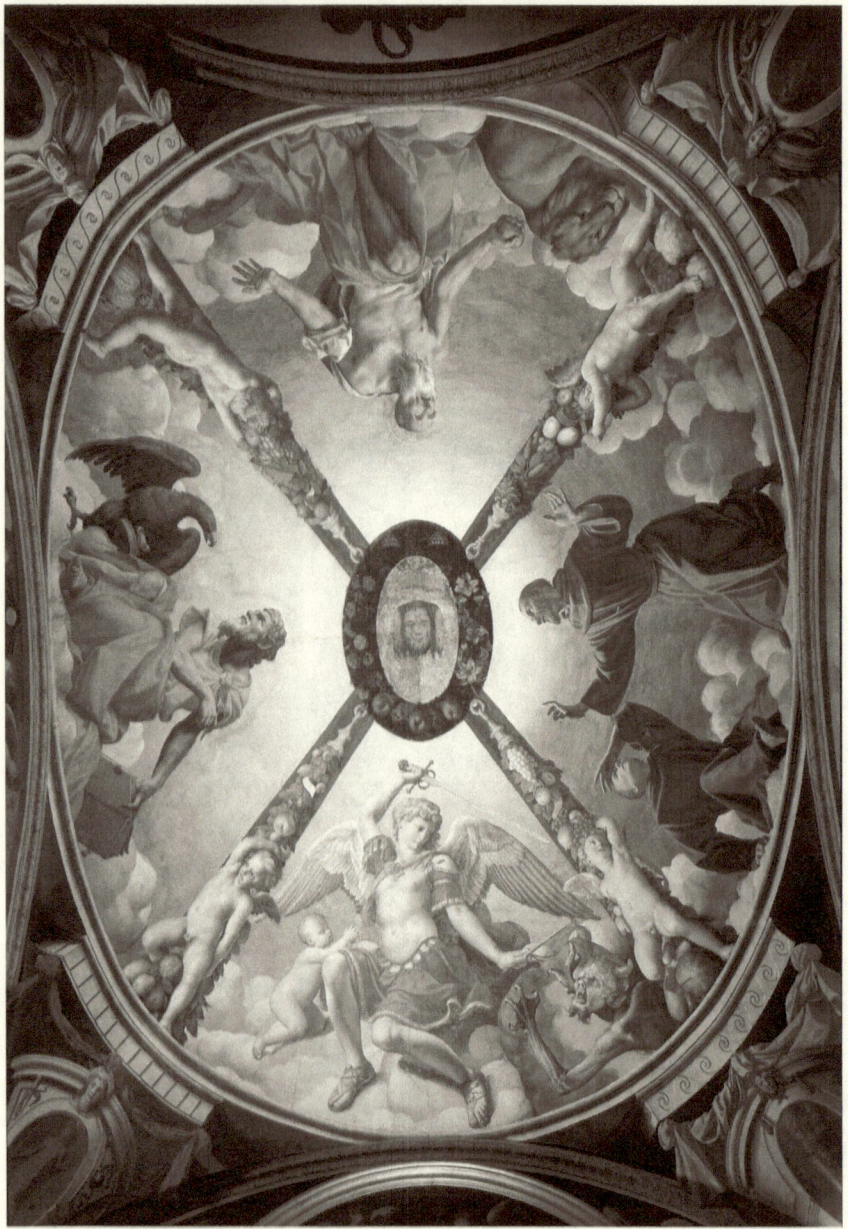

Fig. 2. Agnolo Bronzino, *Vault of the Chapel of Eleonora de Toledo*, 1541. Chapel of Eleonora de Toledo, Palazzo Vecchio, Florence. Photo credit: Scala/Art Resource, NY.

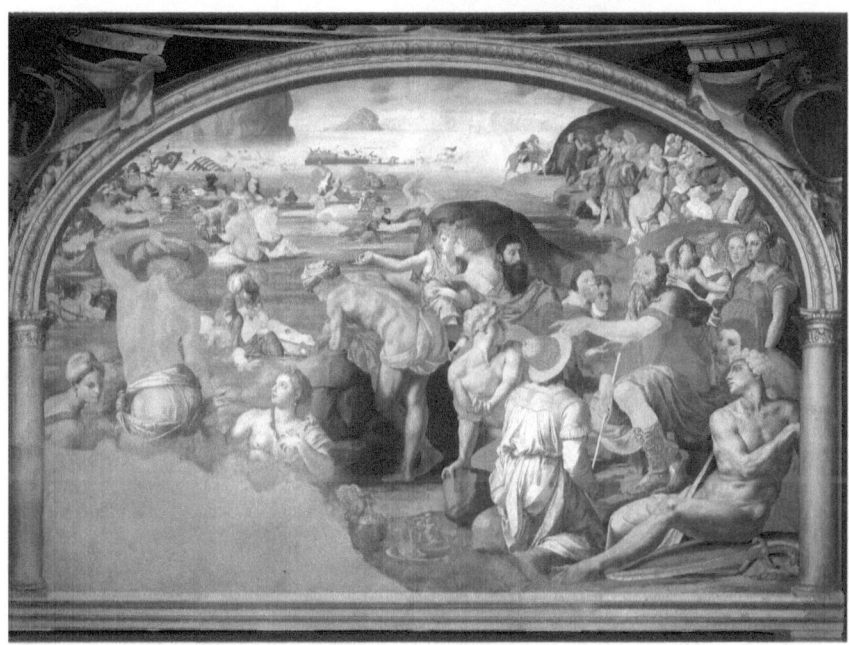

Fig. 3. Agnolo Bronzino, *Crossing of the Red Sea*, 1541–42. Chapel of Eleonora de Toledo, Palazzo Vecchio, Florence. Photo credit: Scala/Art Resource, NY.

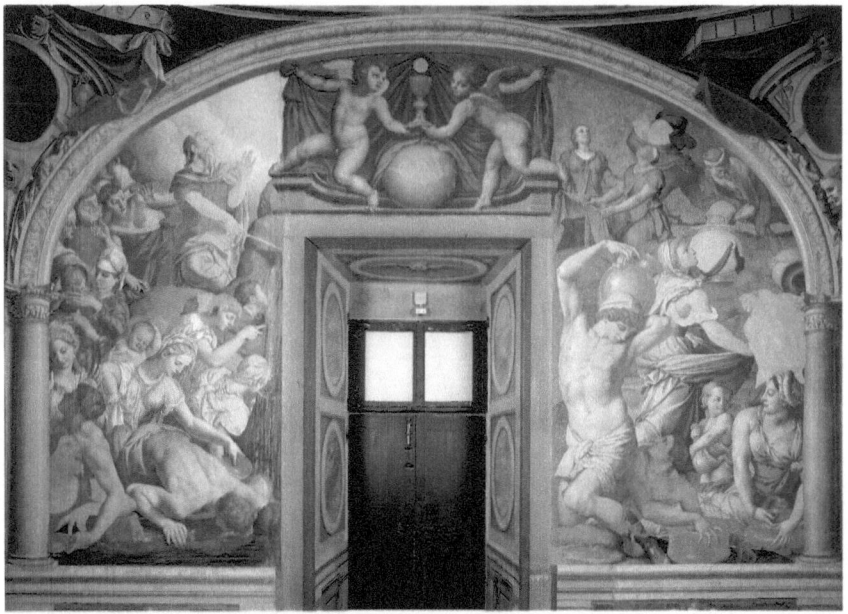

Fig. 4. Agnolo Bronzino, *Moses Striking the Rock and the Gathering of the Manna,* 1542–43. Chapel of Eleonora de Toledo, Palazzo Vecchio, Florence. Photo credit: Scala/Art Resource, NY.

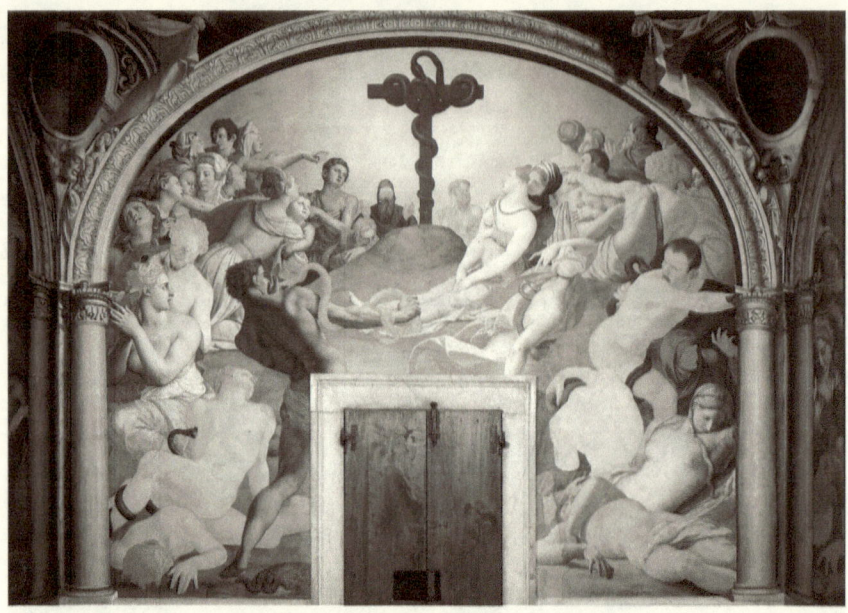

Fig. 5. Agnolo Bronzino, *The Miracle of the Brazen Serpent*, 1542. Chapel of Eleonora de Toledo, Palazzo Vecchio, Florence. Photo credit: Scala/Art Resource, NY.

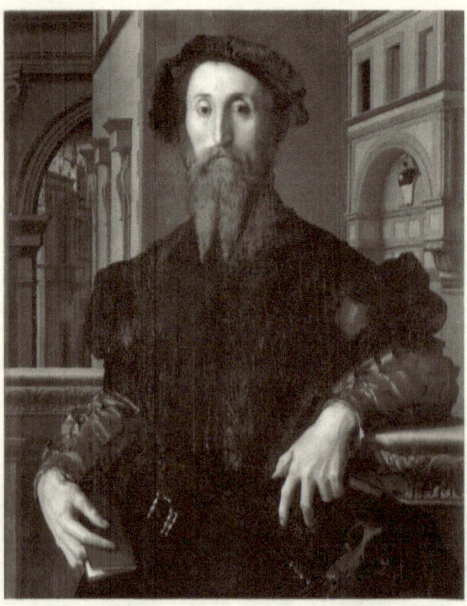

Fig. 6. Agnolo Bronzino, *Portrait of Bartolomeo Panciatichi*, 1540–42. Galleria degli Uffizi, Florence. Photo credit: Scala/ Art Resource, NY.

Fig. 7. Agnolo
Bronzino, *Portrait of
Lucrezia Panciatichi*,
1540–42. Galleria degli
Uffizi, Florence. Photo
credit: Scala/Ministero
per i Beni e le Attività
culturali/Art Resource,
NY.

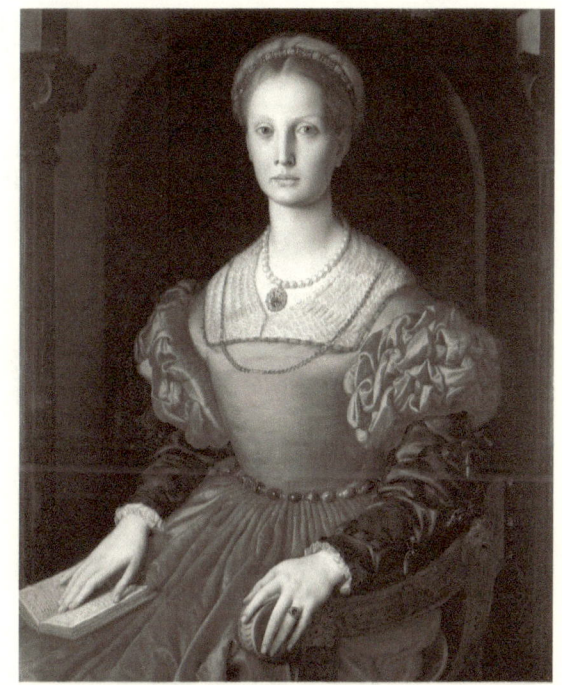

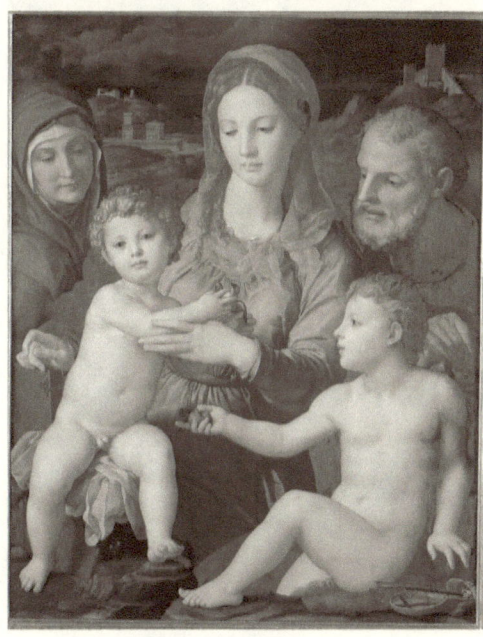

Fig. 8. Agnolo Bronzino, *Holy
Family with Saint Anne and
Young John the Baptist*, 1550s.
Kunsthistorisches Museum,
Vienna, Austria. Photo credit:
Erich Lessing/Art Resource,
NY.

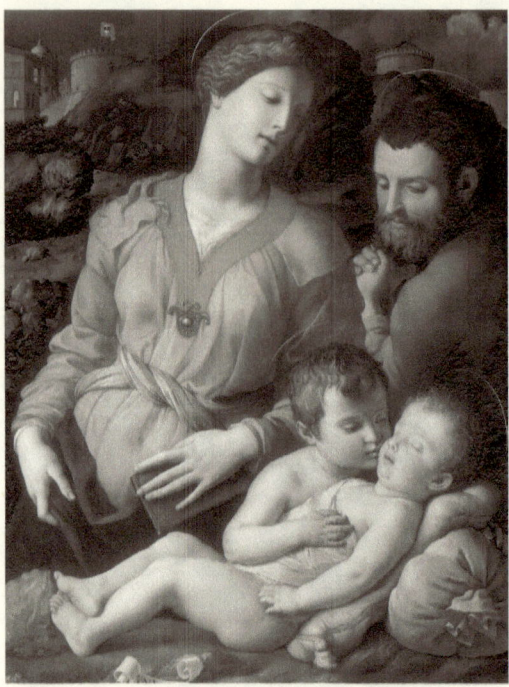

Fig. 9. Agnolo Bronzino, *Panciatichi Holy Family*, 1540–42. Galleria degli Uffizi, Florence. Photo credit: Alinari/Art Resource, NY.

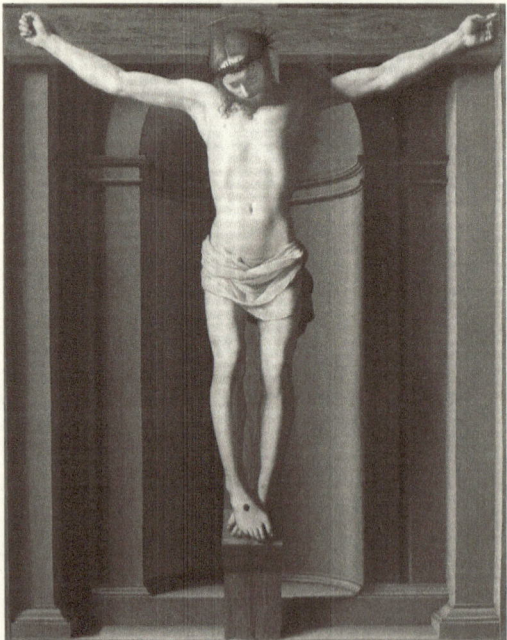

Fig. 10. Agnolo Bronzino, *Crucified Christ*, 1538–40. Musée des Beaux-Arts, Nice, France. Photo credit: Musée des Beaux-Arts, Nice, France.

"The Bystander" in the Chapel of Eleonora: A Lucretian Image in Bronzino's Work

Massimiliano Rossi

Many times we ask ourselves about the focus of the *Zuschauer*, leaning on a rocky riverbank, who, thoughtful yet relaxed, observes Pharaoh's troops drowning within the now calm Red Sea. To demonstrate an idiosyncratic topic full of reversibility, Carlo Falciani has included this character among those who appear both in Bronzino's painting and in his poetry, particularly in Capitolo (Chapter) III of *Il piato*. There, the protagonist, climbing the giant Arcigrandone's foot, which is an allegory of "che cosa è il mondo e ciò che gl'uomin fanno" (what is the world and what do men do in it),[1] pauses to watch "un fetido piano,/qual è presso a Viterbo o a Fucecchio" (a stinky plain,/similar to the land around Viterbo or Fucecchio), in which "chi ci s'imbratta par che goda e schiva/per se d'uscirne o che ne '1 tragga altrui" (he who smears himself appears to enjoy or avoid/one might leave or draw others).[2] Consequently,

> Quel viaggiatore che osserva da un costone roccioso la palude (…) ci sembrerà quasi una descrizione dell'uomo che, come distaccato dal soggetto della storia, nell'affresco (…) si affaccia a guardare chi è stato travolto dalle acque scure e limacciose del mare: alcuni di quegli uomini non si disperano per la fine prossima, ma continuano a mordersi e lottare fra di loro senza ragione.[3]

> (That traveler from a rocky coast observes the marsh … it appears almost like the description of a man depicted as a distant subject in the fresco painting … The figure that gazes outwardly is noticing those who have been crushed

by the dark and muddy waters of the sea and those who do not seem to despair about the fatal outcome and continue fighting and hitting each other without a purpose.)

If in the frescoes located in the Chapel of Eleonora de Toledo, painted from 1541 to 1545, "The Bystander" appears for the first time to represent himself as a protagonist, in *Il piato* (but the dates of the composition of Bronzino's "humble" poetry have yet to be determined),[4] its privileged placing, visual focus, and fitting element of the scene that approaches the *Crossing of the Red Sea* (Fig. 1), as well as his posture and expression in contrast to the spectacle of death, forces us to rethink his role and significance in light of his successive and more dynamic appearance.[5] There is, in fact, a substantial change in the type of observation in *Il piato* by the itinerant condition of the *agens* and of his guide: "Cosi n'andava e 'ntanto io vidi pieno/il brutto limo di genti, ch'in quello/erano immerse, chi più e chi meno" (As I was going I fully saw/the ugly silt of people, that were immersed in it, some more and some less).[6] He will be permitted to stop only briefly to contemplate and meditate—but always from a lofty position—following the model of Dante's stops intended for the vision of infernal torments through immersion, complicated by bursts of flame or by rituals of violence: brawls between devils and swindlers around Malebolge's lake of boiling pitch or Cocito's frozen horror, whose atrocious retaliation among the Damned perhaps could also have been inspired the desperate battle among the horsemen who are drowning.[7]

Il piato, as it is known from the title and then later on in the vision of numerous scenes of brawls and human disputes, reproduces in the form of a dream-vision the gigantic cosmic battle among the elements to which the chapter is dedicated praising *Sdegno* (Disdain):

Entra lo sdegno in tutte le create
cose, intendendo giù sotto la luna,
e per lui sono corrotte e generate.
Se non fusse egli, ogni cosa tutt'una
sarebbe stata in poche settimane,
né ci sarebbe varietà nessuna.
Stan gl'elementi come gatta e cane

verso l'un l'altro; l'acqua ha a sdegno il fuoco,
l'aria la terra e son nimiche e strane.[8]

(Disdain is in all the creation
of course under the Moon,
and it is generated and ruined by him.
Weren't it, everything whole
would have been in few weeks,
and no variety would exist.
Elements are each other like cat and dog
Water disdains Fire,
Air Earth and both of them
are adverse and extraneous.)

However, just because *Il tutt'una* becomes the object of different praise,[9] the hybrid demonstration of every aspect of reality preached in Bernesque poetry (and even in the impartial and therefore incomplete answer to Varchi's investigation),[10] it seems inherent in the charter itself of "Terra over Natura" (Earth that is Nature) as a primordial and intrinsic *concordia discors*. This radical pyrrhonism, which explicitly characterizes such a production and which Bronzino ties in this way to the well-known skeptical professions of Anton Francesco Doni, a contemporary in the 1540s,[11] comes to the same reductionism, to that "materiaccia, ch'è tra pelle e pelle" (horrible matter between skin and skin), extracted from the doubly praised mosquitoes.[12] At the same time, since "questo corpaccio che mondo e chiamato/pel suo disordinar sempre si trova/in qualche parte corrotto e malato" (this ugly body that we call world/for its intrinsic chaos/is always somehow corrupted and ill), it becomes necessary to "un composito, un conserto/o per dir meglio una triaca vera" (a compound, an amalgam,/or better stated a real theriac), and "quivi si vede quanto giova e vale/la mescolanza d'infinite cose/che metton dentro [the apothecaries] in questa lor cotale" (here you see how beneficial and valuable is/the mixture of countless things/that [apothecaries] combine in their medicines).[13] If, therefore, every futile object, degrading place, or negative condition paradoxically overturns into its positive condition, expanding into cosmic proportions and becoming a perfect specularity, then a bond takes place between the universe and the individual's nature and activities, including the creation of art;[14] it is not surprising that such breathtaking dynamics may influence poetical production. Thanks to the reconstruction of Giuliano Tanturli, it is now established that the final sequence of files that makes up Bronzino's first book of poetry[15] may have been intended to redesign an interrupted cycle "in vita" (in life) and "in morte" (in death)—not by chance does the "canzone alla morte" (song of death) *A che dolersi ogn'or, misera e cieca* (*Why pine daily, miserable and blind [Life]*) transform itself in the earnest praise of one for whom "'n cambio ogni contrario apporta" (instead every opposite attracts).[16] Elsewhere Bronzino reveals explicit strategies—macro-textual and even more radical, as in:

> Raviggiolo (A type of fresh cheese)
> Io che cantai già le cipolle e vanto
> diedi al pennello e lodai la galea
> duo volte, ch'una non mi parve tanto,
> (…)
> e 'l me' ch'io seppi celebrai l'umane
> bellezze di colei ch'in gioia e 'n duolo
> mi tenne un tempo e non se ne rimane;
> or (…)
> (…) per mio spasso ho voglia
> di ragionar del cacio raviggiuolo.[17]
> (I, who have already sung onions and celebrated
> the brush and praised galley twice,
> while once wasn't enough,
> (…)
> and, at my best, the human
> beauty of the woman which made me
> enjoy and cry and she doesn't give up yet;
> now (…)
> (…), for my fun, want to speak
> about cheese raviggiuolo)

Facing the misleading dawn of a dual and contrasting perspective in Bronzino's paintings, e.g., the bifocality in *Portrait of Bartolomeo Panciatichi*;[18] the front and back of the portrait of *Nano Morgante*;[19]

the nocturnal and diurnal *Panciatichi Holy Family*,[20] immediately negated by the obsessive and unrelenting reversibility, the space that is ultimately revealed to Man's self-consciousness takes shape in stoically narrow terms, characterized by a "vitetta quieta" (quiet life), by appearing "dappoco" (negligible), by "esser chiaro" (by being clear), and, above all, by "starsi" (existing/being)—to which Bronzino even dedicates three sequential *capitoli* (chapters) praising a chosen condition and still accessible to all, because it is bestowed by the "gran madre" (Great Mother):[21]

> Starsi (Existing or Being)
> Non già ch'al pigro, al vile o al nighittoso
> voglia accostarmi o diventare amico,
> anzi guardargli ognor torto e ritroso,
> che questo starsi, ch'io vi lodo e dico
> e vi ridico, non vuol perdigiorni
> sgratiati o goffi o di cervel mendico.
> (...)
> E poi che la natura ce lo presta,
> chi non s'e n'è avveduto se n'avvegga
> e faccia conto aver avuto festa.[22]
> (Don't think that I want to be close or to become friend
> of those who are vile or lazy, on the contrary
> I want to remain far from them as an enemy,
> as this "staying," which I intend and praise
> once more, doesn't desire idler, rough, or stupid men.
> (...)
> And as Nature offers us it,
> who is still unaware of this, wakes up
> and think he gained a lot.)

It is therefore, in my opinion, it is the archetypal Lucretian metaphor that opens the second book of *De rerum natura*—"Suave, mari magno turbantibus aequora ventis,/e terra magnum alterius spectare laborem"[23]—which inspired the insertion of "The Bystander" at the center of the fresco in the Chapel of Eleonora. Bronzino, without minimally altering the "letter" of the biblical text depicted, or its typologically Eucharistic worthiness,[24] has taken the opportunity to offer a further meaning, exploiting the analogy between the shipwreck and the drowning, perfectly comprehensible or peacefully avoidable depending on skills and, above all, not in any way conflicting with the encomiastic declension—so many times underlined—of the *Stories of Moses*.[25] This is the same operational modality brought into evidence in his late altarpiece for Santa Croce in *Christ's Descent into Limbo* (1552), in which, nonetheless, the multiplication of characters—some of which are detectable in *Il piato*—forces the artist to a noticeable complication of the compositional scheme linked to such iconography.[26] It therefore will be worthwhile to approach the entire Lucretian sequence of "naufragio con spettatore" (drowning with the viewer) and the image located in his fifth book of the cosmos as a living organism which cyclically regenerates itself, in order to rethink the reception of both in the existential key peculiar to Bronzino:

> Suave, mari magno turbantibus aequora ventis,
> e terra magnum alterius spectare laborem;
> non quia vexari quemquamst iucunda voluptas,
> sed quibus ipse malis careas quia cernere suave est.
> Suave etiam belli certamina magna tueri
> per campos instructa tua sine parte pericli.
> *Sed nil dulcius est, bene quam munita tenere*
> *edita doctrina sapientum templa serena,*
> *despicere unde queas alios passimque videre*
> *errare atque viam palantis quaerere vitae,*
> certare ingenio, contendere nobilitate,
> noctes atque dies niti praestante labore
> ad summas emergere opes rerumque potiri.[27]

> ('Tis sweet, when, down the mighty main, the winds
> Roll up its waste of waters, from the land
> To watch another's labouring anguish far,
> Not that we joyously delight that man
> Should thus be smitten, but because 'tis sweet
> To mark what evils we ourselves be spared;
> 'Tis sweet, again, to view the mighty strife
> Of armies embattled yonder o'er the plains,

Ourselves no sharers in the peril; but naught
There is more goodly than to hold the high
Serene plateaus, well fortressed by the wise,
Whence thou may'st look below on other men
And see them ev'rywhere wand'ring, all dispersed
In their lone seeking for the road of life;
Rivals in genius, or emulous in rank,
Pressing through days and nights with hugest toil
For summits of power and mastery of the world.)

....

Principio quoniam terrai corpus et umor
aurarumque leves animae calidique vapores,
e quibus haec rerum consistere summa videtur,
omnia nativo ac mortali corpore constant,
debet eodem omnis mundi natura putari.
Quippe etenim quorum partis et membra videmus
corpore nativo ac mortalibus esse figuris,
haec eadem ferme mortalia cernimus esse
et nativa simul. Quapropter maxima mundi
cum videam membra ac partis consumpta regigni,
scire licet caeli quoque item terraeque fuisse
principiale aliquod tempus clademque futuram.[28]

(And first,
Since body of earth and water, air's light breath,
And fiery exhalations (of which four
This sum of things is seen to be compact)
So all have birth and perishable frame,
Thus the whole nature of the world itself
Must be conceived as perishable too.
For, verily, those things of which we see
The parts and members to have birth in time
And perishable shapes, those same we mark
To be invariably born in time
And born to die.)

Figurative confirmation, certainly not unique to Florence after
the great fortune of Lucretius in the Soderinian age,[29] of an exten-

sive albeit disguised presence is evidenced in this case, and that
might have been filtered down to Bronzino through Varchi's lyrics
and treatises.[30] "The Bystander," from the safety of the riverbank
overlooking the Red Sea, seems to be musing within himself rather
than watching the massacre of the Egyptians—which should cause
a fugitive Jew to rejoice, "non quia vexari quemquamst iucunda
voluptas,/sed quibus ipse malis careas quia cernere suave est" (not
because any man's troubles are a delectable joy, but because to perceive what ills you are free from yourself is pleasant).[31]

In the copperplate engraving of the *Crossing of the Red Sea*
(Fig. 2), in which Hieronymus Cock infers the "secure" attitude of
"The Bystander" in obvious counterpart, could have suggested the
moral allegory in the patristic tradition in the four hexameters below:

Tutus agit vir iustus iter, vel per mare magnum,
ecce Dei famulis scissim, freta rubra dehiscunt,
quum peccatores rabidos, eadem freta mergunt,
obruitur Pharao, patuit via libera Mosi.[32]

(The wise man proceeds on a safe road or on the sea,
the red waves open for the servants of God,
while the same waves overwhelm the evil and furious men,
this is ruin for the Pharaoh but the way is free for Moses.)

At the end of the century, in specular harmony, even Antonio
Possevino, in *De rerum natura*, could appreciate a similar lesson,
the only acceptable one: "E contrario non negaverim perlegi posse
in Lucretio quae de morte contemnenda, de amore fugiendo, de
coercendis cupidatibus, de sedandis animorum motibus, de mentis
tranquillitate comparanda ... ac plerisque eiusmodi rebus dispu-
tat" (On the contrary, I am allowed to affirm that in Lucretius it is
possible to read what he maintains about the disdain of the death,
love, and desire, about the way to deal with the passions of the soul
and the quiet of the mind ... and much more).[33]

Immediately visible, yet simultaneously unrecognizable, the
image of "The Bystander" in the chapel of Eleonora de Toledo has
had the same fate as the text from which it was taken, but with a
far more lasting obfuscation. Similar to "The Figure in the Carpet"

and "The Purloined Letter," the image of "The Bystander" coaxes Bronzino's exegetes to a global reconsideration of his pictorial and poetic work; and these analyses, we believe, are still at the beginning of its due rediscovery.

NOTES

1. See Franca Petrucci Nardelli, ed., *Agnolo Bronzino, Rime in burla* (Rome: Istituto della Enciclopedia Italiana, 1988), Chapter 3, v. 48, p. 233.

2. Petrucci Nardelli, *Rime in burla*, Chapter 3, vv. 84, 95–96, p. 234–35.

3. See Carlo Falciani and Antonio Natali, eds., *Bronzino: Artist and Poet at the Court of the Medici* (Florence: Mandragora, 2010), 288–89.

4. *Il piato* is dated between 1552 and 1555, on the grounds that the initial verses corroborated. See Petrucci Nardelli, *Rime in burla*, 426; and Deborah Parker, *Bronzino: Renaissance Painter as Poet* (Cambridge: Cambridge University Press, 2000), 133–34. An allusive dedication to Vincenzio Borghini, nominated by Cosimo I de' Medici as Director of the Hospital of the Innocents in 1552, remains to be demonstrated.

5. Martin Hirschboeck, *Florentinische Palastkapellen unter den ersten Medici-Herzögen (1537–1609): Verborgene Orte frommer Selbstdarstellung und konfessioneller Identität (I Mandorli Bd. 12)* (Berlin and Munich: Deutscher Kunstverlag, 2011), 62–63, who, however, remains in the framework of the political-encomiastic meaning of the frescoes (see below, n. 25, for a different conclusion).

6. See Petrucci Nardelli, *Rime in burla*, Chapter 3, vv. 100–03, p. 235.

7. Respectively: "Pur a la pegola era la mia 'ntesa,/per veder de la bolgia ogne contegno/e de la gente ch'entro v'era incesa" (Ever upon the pitch was my intent,/To see the whole condition of that Bolgia,/And of the people who therein were burned), *Inferno*, XXII, vv. 16–18; "Perch'io mi volsi, e vidimi davante/e sotto i piedi un lago che per gelo/avea di vetro e no d'acqua sembiante" (Whereat I turned me round, and saw before me/ And underfoot a lake, that from the frost/The semblance had of glass, and not of water), *Inferno*, XXXII, vv. 22–24; see Anna Maria Chiavacci Leonardi, ed., *Dante Alighieri, Commedia-Inferno* (Milan: Mondadori, 1991), respectively, 658 and 949–50). At the end of *Il piato* (Petrucci Nardelli, *Rime in burla*, Chapter 8, vv. 130–47, p. 268), the "pegola" is recalled in the "lago" formed by the gastric juices of Arcigrandone, into which, this time, the protagonist also ends up falling, together with "tanta gente" (crowds).

8. See Petrucci Nardelli, *Rime in burla*, Lo sdegno, 356.

9. See Petrucci Nardelli, *Rime in burla*, Lo sdegno, 344–50.

10. Carlo Falciani, "Il Bronzino e i Panciatichi," in Carlo Falciani and Antonio Natali, eds., *Bronzino: Pittore e poeta alla corte dei Medici*, Exh. Flo-

rence, Palazzo Strozzi, 24 September 2010–23 January 2011 (Florence: Mandragora, 2010), 153–65, in particular 281, asks himself, rather, "se la sua scelta di non finire la lettera non sia da intendere come un espediente retorico per sottolineare, in modo polemico, la negazione da parte dell'Accademia [*scil.* Fiorentina, da cui era stato espulso proprio nel'47] del suo status di letterato" (whether his choice to leave the letter unfinished may be interpreted as a rhetorical device to polemically underline the Accademia's refusal [the Florentine Accademia, which expelled him precisely in 1547] to recognize him as a man of letters).

11. Paolo Procaccioli, "Cinquecento capriccioso e irregolare. Dei lettori di Luciano e di Erasmo; di Aretino e Doni; di altri peregrini ingegni," in Paolo Procaccioli and Angelo Romano, eds., *Cinquecento capriccioso e irregolare. Eresie letterarie nell'Italia del classicismo* (Manziana (Rome): Vecchiarelli, 1999), 27–28; Massimiliano Rossi, "Artisti e discorsi sull'arte nei *Marmi*," in Giovanna Rizzarelli, ed., *I* Marmi *di Anton Francesco Doni: la storia, i generi e le arti*, Mangiar libri e inghiottir scritture (Florence: Olschki, 2012), 181–87; and Francesco Paolo Campione, *La regola del Capriccio: Alle origini di una idea estetica* (Palermo: Centro Internazionale di Studi di Estetica, 2011), 67–83.

12. Petrucci Nardelli, *Rime in burla, A Messer Benedetto Varchi in lode delle zanzare*, v. 83, p. 48; and Petrucci Nardelli, *Rime in burla, Esortazione del Bronzino pittore alle zanzare*, 55–63.

13. Petrucci Nardelli, *Rime in burla, In lode della galea*, Chapter 2, vv. 31–33, 49–51, p. 79.

14. Rossi, "Artisti e discorsi sull'arte nei *Marmi*," 177–93.

15. Agnolo Bronzino, *Delle Rime (…) libro Primo*, MS Biblioteca Nazionale Centrale di Firenze, II.IX.10, cc. 113v–116r, in particular vv. 101–05; Giuliano Tanturli, "Formazione d'un codice e d'un canzoniere: Delle Rime del Bronzino pittore libro primo," *Studi di filologia italiana* 62 (2004), 195–224.

16. Also, in this case, the observance of the Petrarchan form, which entrusted the overcoming of amorous errors to the sonnets of spiritual theme, welcomes, if need be, a non-Christian dynamic of cyclicity.

17. Petrucci Nardelli, *Rime in burla, Il Raviggiuolo*, vv. 1–15, p. 135.

18. Two perspectives are presented in the background of Bartolomeo's portrait, where the triumphal arch with a pilaster of mixed arrangement on the one hand allows allows a glimpse of a fifth façade, which one could say is still of the fifteenth century; on the other hand, it literally collides in mid-archivolt with a modern wall, punctuated by the profiling of three windows, in which the memory of the Classical order is deconstructed into fragments of corbels and blocks jutting out of the lintels. See Rossi, "Artisti e discorsi sull'arte nei *Marmi*," 311–29. See also Natali and Falciani, *Il Bronzino e i Panciatichi*," 153–65, on Bronzino's commissions for the

Panciatichi family.

19. See S. Endler, Bronzino Entry card IV.7, in Natali and Falciani, *Bronzino: Pittore e poeta alla corte dei Medici*, 214–17.

20. See E. Pilliod, respectively, Bronzino Entry card VI.3 (Vienna, Kunsthistorisches Museum), and Bronzino Entry card VI.4 (Paris, Louvre), in Natali and Falciani, *Bronzino: Pittore e poeta alla corte dei Medici*, 300–03; not to mention the shifting from the monumental measurements of the Guadagni altarpiece in the Santissima Annunziata to the quasi-miniature dimensions of the secular *Allegoria* in the Uffizi, painted on tin, in which the compositional scheme used is almost identical (see L. Morini, Bronzino Entry card VI.6, in Natali and Falciani, *Bronzino: Pittore e poeta alla corte dei Medici*, 306–07; and A. Geremicca, Bronzino Entry card II.18, in Natali and Falciani, *Bronzino: Pittore e poeta alla corte dei Medici*, 148–49.

21. Petrucci Nardelli, *Rime in burla, Del Bisogno*, Chapter 1, v. 97, p. 283.

22. Petrucci Nardelli, *Rime in burla, Dello Starsi*, Chapter 3, vv. 160–65; 172–74, pp. 377–78.

23. See Lucrezio, *De rerum natura*, ed. A. Schiesaro (Turin: Einaudi, 2003), Chapter II, vv. 1–2, p. 64.

24. See Antonio Natali, "I duchi e l'eucarestia. La cappella d'Eleonora di Toledo," in Natali and Falciani, *Bronzino. Pittore e poeta alla corte dei Medici*, 101–13; and Hirschboeck, *Florentinische Palastkapellen*, 51–56.

25. See Janet Cox-Rearick, "Bronzino's 'Crossing of the Red Sea and Moses Appointing Joshua': Prolegomena to the Chapel of Eleonora di Toledo," *The Art Bulletin* 69 (1987), 45–67; Janet Cox-Rearick, *Bronzino's Chapel of Eleonora in the Palazzo Vecchio* (Berkeley: University of California Press, 1993), 250–51; Maurice Brock, *Bronzino* (Paris: Flammarion, 2002), 183–211; and Hirschboeck, *Florentinische Palastkapellen*, 56–64, who notes how the identification between Cosimo and Moses is anything but peaceful.

26. See Carlo Falciani, "*Della pittura sacra, ma anche di 'fianchi, stomachi, ec.',*" in Falciani and Natali, *Pittore e poeta alla corte dei Medici*, 285–97; and L. Morini, Bronzino Entry card VI.5, in Natali and Falciani, *Bronzino. Pittore e poeta alla corte dei Medici*, 304–05.

27. See Lucrezio, *De rerum natura*, Chapter II, vv. 1–13, p. 64, trans. by William Ellery Leonard, *On The Nature of Things*; see <http://classics.mit.edu/Carus/nature_things.2.ii.html>.

28. See Lucrezio, *De rerum natura*, Chapter V, vv. 235–46, p. 269, trans. by William Ellery Leonard, *On The Nature of Things*; see <http://classics.mit.edu/Carus/nature_things.5.v.html>.

29. See especially Benedetta Matucci, "'Ornamentation symbolique': una rilettura del cenotafio Soderini di Benedetto da Rovezzano," *Artista. Critica dell'arte in Toscana* (2007), 74–109, who sees in the decoration of the

cenotaph of Soderini di Benedetto by Rovezzano, in the Carmelite church, "il simbolo di una vita perenne, soggetta ad una lenta e continua trasmutazione e in accordo, direi, con la concezione lucreziana sul sottile passaggio fra disgregazione e rinascita" (the symbol of an eternal life, subject to a slow and continuous transformation and according, I say, to what Lucretius conceives about the subtle passage between disintegration and rebirth) (84).

30. See Valentina Prosperi, *Di soavi licor gli orli del vaso: La fortuna di Lucrezio dall'Umanesimo alla Controriforma* (Turin: Aragno Editore, 2004), 141–42 and 170–73. As for his fate in the fifteenth century, see Stephen Greenblatt, *The Swerve: How the World Became Modern* (New York: Norton, 2011), passim.

31. See Lucrezio, *De rerum natura*, Chapter II, v. 550, p. 92. See also Hans Blumenberg, *Schiffbruch mit Zuschauer. Paradigma einer Daseinsmetaphe* (1979; Frankfurt am Main: Suhrkamp Verlag, 1997), 33: "Der Zuschauer genießt nicht die Erhabenheit der Gegenstände, die ihm seine Theorie erschießt (…). Der Kosmos ist nicht mehr die Ordnung, deren Anschauung den Betrachter mit Eudämonie erfüllt. Er ist allenfalls ein Rest der Zusicherung, daß er solchen festen Grund überhaupt gibt, an den das feindliche Element nicht heranreicht" (The Bystander doesn't enjoy the sublimity of the Whole. The Cosmos is no longer the Order, the contemplation of which filled him with the harmony of the soul, on the contrary it is what remains of the guarantee that the adverse elements don't get to such a solid ground).

32. Keep in mind Michelangelo's precursors in the Sistine Chapel; personifications of the stops of the Chosen People in the desert, which, because of a figurative link, become a narrative *plaque tournante* against the subordinate stories of Moses and Christ, allegorical in relation to the above celestial creation, to which every human being should aspire, once he has left the "Egypt" of this world (as Creighton Gilbert, *Michelangelo: On and Off the Sistine Ceiling. Selected Essays* (New York: Braziller, 1994), 115–49, has demonstrated). Bronzino's engraving is reproduced also in Hirschboeck, *Florentinische Palastkapellen*, 63, who dates it in the 1550s, while Cox-Rearick, "Bronzino's 'Crossing of the Red Sea,'" dates it c. 1550.

33. See Antonio Possevino, *Tractatio de Poësi et Pictura ethnica, humana et fabulosa collata cum vera, honesta et sacra* (Lugduni: Apud Ioannem Pillehotte, 1595); and see *De Lucretio Caro*, Caput XIV, 148–51, cited in Prosperi, *Di soavi licor gli orli del vaso*, 104.

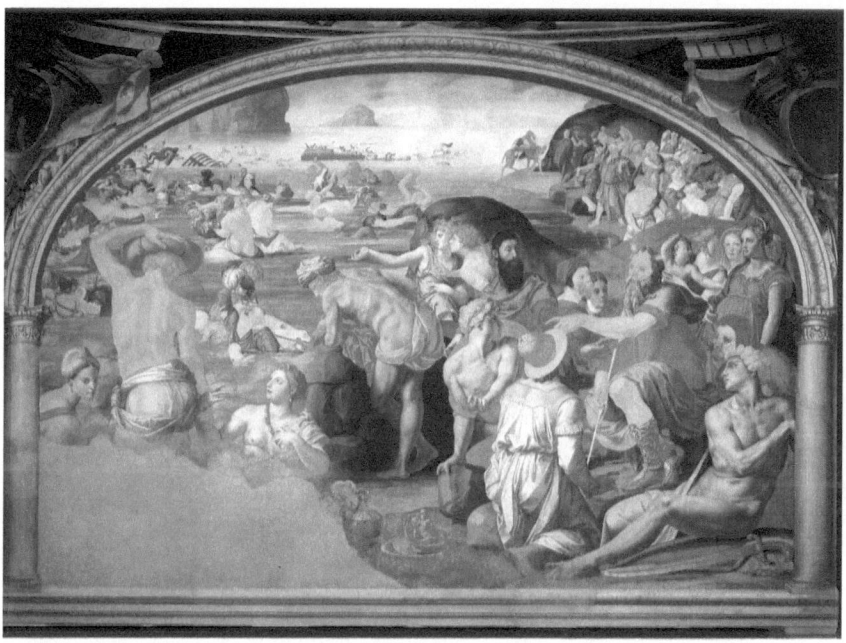

Fig. 1. Agnolo Bronzino, *Crossing of the Red Sea*, 1541–42. Chapel of Eleonora de Toledo, Palazzo Vecchio, Florence, Italy. Photo credit: Scala/ Art Resources, NY.

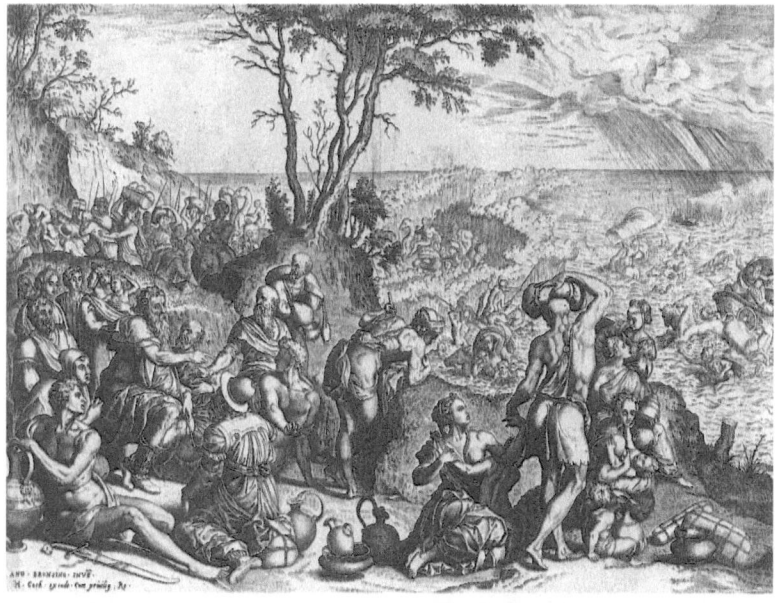

Fig. 2. Hieronymus Cock, engraving after Bronzino, *Crossing the Red Sea*, 1550. Gabinetto Disegni e Stampe degli Uffizi, Florence. Photo credit: Gabinetto Disegni e Stampe degli Uffizi, Florence.

PART THREE

SECULAR PAINTINGS, PORTAITS, AND ALLEGORIES

Bronzino's Art of Emblazoning:
The Young Man with a Book,
Lucrezia Panciatichi,
Saint Bartholomew, and *Laura Battiferri*

Michael J. Giordano

The word *blazon* was originally a heraldic term used in the fifteenth and early sixteenth centuries to designate the description and interpretation of coats of arms. Technically speaking, it referred not to the shield itself (*écu*) but to the analysis of such components as tinctures, areas, partitions, ordinaries and subordinaries, cadence marks, and charges.[1] During the sixteenth century, the word also meant the art of isolating, partitioning, or putting into relief a component of an organic series for close observation and display. The myriad objects emblazoned ran the gamut from colors, flowers, and wines to animals, furniture, and the virtues. Also, emblazoning cut across national lines and could serve many purposes in such fields as literature, descriptive anatomy, the fine arts, emblematics, pedagogy, cartography, satire, or public performance. Thanks to such studies as Alison Saunders' *Sixteenth Century Blason Poétique* and Jonathan Sawday's *The Body Emblazoned*, we know a great deal more about what is termed the "anatomical blazon."[2] This is a vivid verbal description of a part of the human body, generally of a woman, written as a love poem in which a poet-lover addresses the body component with praise or blame.

Francesco Petrarca may be considered one of the main sources of this genre, as in the *Rime sparse*, where he emblazoned Laura's head, face, eyebrows, eyes and tears.[3] In *canzone* 199, Petrarch's persona cannot but shower praise on his beloved's fingers and nails, which resemble five oriental pearls and ivory roses but which, like her white gloves, cruelly hold his heart in captivity: "et sol ne le mie piaghe acerbi et crudi" (v. 6).[4] Petrarch's fifteenth- and sixteenth-century imitators continued in this vein by using repetitive apostrophe to address and praise the beautiful body part. For instance, Giusto de Conti wrote a work titled *La bella mano*, where in a sonnet to his beloved he uses the vocative to laud the woman's exquisite white hand ("O Bella, e Bianca Mano, o Man soave" v.1) and to avow that she holds the power of life and death over him: "Et da voi attenda vita, e da voi morte" (v. 11).[5] Similarly, Angelo Poliziano opens a poem invoking his beloved's eyes ("Occhi leggiadri, grazioso sguardo") and repeats the apostrophe twice to re-enact the *innamoramento* and the effects of those "occhi" that enflame, ensnare, and put him at their mercy: "Sperar debbo mercè di tanti guai."[6] In the *Opera nova amorosa*, Nocturno Napolitano addresses praise to the woman's golden hair whose threads are the captivating chains of love: "O chiome relucente piu che lo avaro/di che mi fece amor al collo un laccio."[7] One of the most popular and notorious sixteenth-century Petrarchans was Olimpo de Sassoferrato, who distinguished himself in composing erotic, anatomical love poetry honoring a number of ladies. Two of these works bear titles that tell us much about the literary forms and sensuality of his poetics, namely, *Capitolo del bianco petto de madonna Pegasea* and the *Capitolo delle poppe tette de pegasea*.[8]

The influence that Italy exerted on France in the sixteenth century in many aspects of exchange cannot be exaggerated, and this is indicated by Francis I's invitation to Leonardo da Vinci to take up residence there and provide an inspiring presence to enhance its prestige and spark artistic initiatives. According to Vasari, Cosimo I commissioned a *Venus and Cupid* painted by Bronzino as a diplomatic gift to Francis.[9] One of the main French figures to initiate the Italian manner in literature and create a poetic bridge between the two countries was Clément Marot. In fact, our general knowledge of the anatomical blazon is enhanced by following the poetic development of this genius and his relations with Italy. Marot single-handedly created the circumstances and the model poem that launched the genre in France and ignited its popularity.[10] In 1535, having sought exile in Ferrara from religious persecution and stimulated by the type of poetry written by the Italian neo-petrarchans, he composed a poem titled "On the Beautiful Breast" ("Du Beau tétin") and sent it to France to challenge other writers to emulate him. His knowledge of court politics and his dramatization of his

own poetic creativity resulted in a successful harvest of blazons—
on the woman's hair, heart, thigh, hand, eye, mind, mouth, tear-
drop, and ear.[11] Under Alfonso and Ercole of the House of Esté,
Ferrara became a spiritual haven for Protestants and Jews as well as
a center for cultural and scientific exchange. Marot knew Renée de
France, Duchess of Ferrara, wife of Ercole II d'Esté and a strong advocate of Protestantism and evangelism who no doubt welcomed
his presence at court. While there, Marot provided the impetus for
a *concours des blasons* consisting of the poems sent to Ferrara by the
French *blasonneurs* who took up his challenge. According to Marot's account, Renée de France who was the central French figure at
the court judged the poems and awarded the poetic laurel to Maurice Scève's *Blason du sourcil* featuring a highly Platonized praise of
the eyebrow.[12]

The anatomical blazons quickly became very popular, and this
is indicated by the publication of six editions in France from 1536
to 1554. Each was illustrated with pictures of the body part head-
ing the love poem, and the best of these editions was produced by
Charles Langelier in Paris (1543) titled *Blasons anatomiques du corps
femenin* [*sic*].

In looking back at both Italian and French anatomical poems,
we see that they could display great variance in tone and vision
ranging from the obscene to the highly spiritual. In either the Italian
or the French poems, it would not be rare that the most lubricious
verses could veer off into far-flung, witty conceits, or as the French
call them, *pointes*. While it is true that Italy's innovations were para-
mount in the eyes of the French and a vital source of literary models and inspiration, it is nevertheless true that France developed
its blazons in the context of its native traditions. In any case, the
artistic and literary ties between Italy and France in relation to the
anatomical poems collectively help us understand Bronzino.

It is interesting and useful to transfer the concept of the literary,
anatomical blazon to the art of emblazoning in Agnolo Bronzino's
portraits. The title of Deborah Parker's book, *Bronzino: Renaissance
Painter As Poet*, as well as her enlightening argument demonstrate
that "similar modes of signification underlie Bronzino's work in
both mediums."[13] In my estimate, Bronzino, while he does not
use the adjective "anatomical," was himself writing blazons in his

burlesque *capitoli*, and it would be a fruitful enterprise to look for signs of this style in his painting. Emblazoning is most apparent in his *Rime in burla*, where the isolation and facetious encomium of a single object not literally a part of the human body is eventually revealed to be a sexually charged anatomical feature. This is the case in "Del pennello," where a paintbrush is described in such a way was to imply a penis and in "Loda della galea," where references to receptacles and enclosed spaces such as "albergo," "sentina," and "stanza" are actually allusions to the anus and the vagina.[14] It is important to point out that these words are not merely facetious double entendres but the core matrices of descriptive, erotic allegories. For instance, "Del pennello" does not merely mention a paintbrush but devotes some eighteen verses (ll. 13–30) to describing how men and women receive pleasure from what the "paintbrush" creates. The brush is said to be "born from the hair of a bristle or tail," which can draw people "on the bed or in tiring positions, standing, or seated" and create perspectives "from behind, from in front, diagonally, [and] foreshortened."[15] In this description of the pleasures brought by the paintbrush, the switch from literal to figurative is precisely the opposite of what the *blasonneurs* do, since they explicitly mention the body part such as the face, the eyes, the teeth, or the genitals. But both they and Bronzino end up by doing the same thing, namely, composing a sustained, verbal depiction of a body part often in conceits with or without sexual intent.

Bronzino's lyric poems do not give the impression of isolating, compartmentalizing, and eroticizing parts of the body with the same degree of emphasis as Sassoferrato, nor do they engage in the accumulation of obscene puns cascading in fetishistic symbols of sexual acts found in the burlesque *capitoli*. Rather, Bronzino's lyrics are serious in tone and subject matter (friendship, mourning, love, art, and poetry) and imitate the sweet, elegiac voice of Petrarch in ways that tend to integrate the physical and spiritual. Synecdoche veers towards the whole, and fracturing metonymies are rare. But it is also true that the collection of Bronzino's lyrics edited by Domenico Moreni[16] show a repetitive use of *mano, man,* and synonyms of these words that are uttered not only by Bronzino but also by his interlocuters. This is particularly true of the exchange of sonnets commenting on his portrait of Laura Battiferri. Benedetto Varchi begins a poem with "La vostra man, chiaro *Bronzino*" (M, p. 2, v. 1) to praise his beloved friend for immortalizing the outer beauty of Laura in painting and the inner virtue in poetry. Of Bronzino's portrait, Lasca says that he must be an Angel, since no divine thing can be portrayed by a mortal hand ("da mortal mano," M, p. 3, v. 4). In his *reposta*, Bronzino humbly replies that merit for the work is not his but, rather, should be accorded to the "alto favor" (v. 1) guiding his hand and mind ("e la mano, et la mente," M, p. 3, v. 10). Varchi returns in another sonnet on behalf of himself and his colleagues to offer Bronzino the gift of a rod girt with gold. But he adds that Bronzino has no need to be grateful since by his learned hand ("tua dotta mano," M, p. 4, v. 9) he has painted a work beyond all praise. Finally, Spini, more prone to give counsel than to panegyrize, urges Bronzino to forego portraying Laura by his "dotta man" (M, p. 12, v. 5), that is, by painting, since that would only imitate the frailty of outward beauty. Rather, he should depict her inner beauty with "pure, sweet eternal notes" ("Con le tue pure dolce eterne note," M, p. 12, v. 13), that is, by poetry.

There are other lyrics that do not directly bear on the Battiferri portrait but that also refer to the hand. In the poems that Bronzino devotes to works of art, he lauds only one figure, and that is Michelangelo. Bronzino moves beyond reverence to adoration of this paragon whose painting, sculpture, and architecture make him a "God on Earth" ("Terrestre Dio," M, p. 26, v. 7) to whom he consecrates his hand and intellect ("la mano, e l'intelleto," M, v. 8). In another poem, Bronzino as in a vision sees Michelangelo as championing heaven over darkness "with his strong hand" ("con forte/ Mano," M, p. 26, vv. 1–2), and he is raised to transport by his "lofty mind" and "hand, happy above all others" ("o mente altra, ed o mano/Sovr'ogni altra felice," vv. 9–10). Bronzino confers every conceivable power on this terrestrial god, associating his praises with symbols of the hand. It is of no small significance that the master image of the Renaissance is Michelangelo's Sistine Chapel scene of God the Creator extending his index finger to touch that of humanity.

It is valid to approach Bronzino's painting from the angle of anatomical emblazoning, considering his creation of one of the most body-conscious works of art ever invented, the London *Alle-*

gory of Venus and Cupid (1544–45) (Fig. 1).[17] Like the highlighting of beautiful body parts depicted in the Italian and French anatomical blazons, this painting throws into eye-catching relief the scene of nude Cupid, buttocks prominently extended, fondling the porcelain breasts of nude Venus, fingering her left nipple forever frozen in the bliss of a lustful kiss. Flanking the central scene are other allegorical figures without complete (human) bodies and showing only specific anatomical parts. On the right, we see the bald head of an old man stretching out his right arm (Time?), an apparently floating head of a young girl with a grotesque body proffering a honeycomb (Duplicity?), and two realistic masks placed at Venus' left foot of disembodied faces that at first glance seem like two severed but living heads. On the top left of the painting, there is the left profile of a head with eyeless sockets, and just below it, one finds the top right head and chest of a man in agony tearing out his hair (Folly?, Jealousy?, symbol of syphilis?). Maurice Brock, commenting on this painting, says, "The minutiae of the details and painstaking facture exert an attraction that, like sexual desire, incites one to approach the object as closely as possible."[18] These details of body parts, as Robert W. Gaston has shown, have crucial intertexts in vernacular Italian works, such as Sassoferrato's *Gloria d'amore*, and it is essential to remember the reciprocal influences between literature and painting in approaching the subject of anatomical emblazoning.[19]

The London *Venus and Cupid* and the *Rime in burla* are but the most conspicuous examples of a central technique in Bronzino's paintings that in more formal, decorous, and dignified ways emblazon a body part with or without erotic allure. I will examine four of them in chronological order from this perspective, the first being the diverging left eye of the courtier and the mascarons flanking him in *The Young Man with a Book* of the 1530s, at the Metropolitan Museum of Art in New York (Fig. 2). Then I will move to the puffed-out shoulder sleeves in the *Portrait of Lucrezia Panciatichi* of 1540–42, at the Galleria degli Uffizi in Florence (Fig. 3). My third example will be the flayed foot of the *St. Bartholomew* fragment in the pala for the *Altar of the Graces* (1554–56) in Pisa Cathedral but conserved in Rome at the Accademia di San Luca (Fig. 4). Finally, I will study the aquiline nose of *Laura Battiferri* (1558), whose portrait is found in the Palazzo Vecchio (Fig. 5).

I will consider emblazoning the painterly act of drawing attention to, putting into relief, or making stand out a particular component that is treated as semi-autonomous part, a partial whole, or a
highly worked element of an organic series that is made prominent
to the viewer's eyes. In this respect, there are two broad functions of
the emblazoned component. First, the artist uses either anatomical
or costume emblazoning to create a microcosmic condensation of
mutually supporting or antagonistic ideas. Second, Bronzino emblazons to provide an artistic matrix that reveals the poetic principles permeating the painting as a whole. By focusing on emblazoning, we may have a better idea of how Bronzino treated Vasari's
aesthetic recommendation to create "invenzione copiosa di tutte le
cose" ("abundant invention continued in the smallest things").[20]

The portrait of *The Young Man*, likely done in the 1530s, is frequently cited as a depiction of many of the traits of the ideal courtier
described by Baldassare Castiglione in *Il Cortigiano* (1528). It is one
of at least three paintings by Bronzino where the subject's left eye
stands out as drifting towards the viewer's right. One will see a
similar, pronounced divergence of the left eye in *The Portrait of
Bartolomeo Panciatichi* of 1540–42, at the Galleria degli Uffizi in Florence (Fig. 6), and *Portrait of Young Man with a Hat with a Feather* of
1550–55, at the Nelson Gallery in Kansas City (Fig. 7). From a medical perspective, this deviation of the eye is symptomatic of exotropia—a type of strabismus in which both eyes cannot turn to the
same point at the same time.[21] However, without contradicting the
clinical diagnosis, it may be more useful to consider the left eye as a
technique of emblazoning, which creates two contrary viewpoints
of the young man. It is characteristic of Bronzino's emblazoning
that other features of a portrait evoke a dissonance similar to the
emblazoned part and create a poetic painting of tense illusions. In
the *Young Man*, the main discrepancy concerns the opposition of
two psychological states. While the right eye looks defiantly at the
viewer in a state of condescending *hauteur*, the left eye appears to
be straining in apprehensive surveillance of the door behind him
and to the side. Doubling these contrasting attitudes are plays of
light and dark where the left side of his face is half covered with a
shadow but the right side is bathed in brightness.

These color contrasts of light and dark on the young man's face that redound to the difference in eye focus invite us to consider the subtly communicated political tensions. He is dressed in the Spanish style of a black doublet associated with the shadows of the left side of his face, but his right hand that receives the same light illuminating the right side of his face is likely holding a copy of Petrarch's poems. How could a Florentine miss the political connotations of the portrait that would suggest an intersection of dissonances between Spain and Italy, Charles V and Cosimo I, the Duchy and republic?[22]

If we observe the young man's left forearm jutting outward with left hand on the hip, we again see a double sign. Certainly there is a gesture of imperturbability mixed with defiance. However, this may also been viewed as a defensive precaution in which the assertive thrust of the left arm and elbow painted over the door frame would keep an intruder at bay. Shall we not say that Bronzino imparts a kind of taut exotropia to the viewer, since we must see two opposing emotional states at the same time from different angles? Only a quarter of the door is visible as it turns diagonally beyond the picture frame, carrying whatever threatens the young man into an unseen and menacing mystery. The play between the eyes and architecture is also instructive. The young man's right side gaze is forthright and straightforward and his chest boastful, but this part of his body parallels a diagonal wall which itself turns into a right-angle projection that encloses him from the rear. Similarly, on either side of the young man puffed up with pride is a table and armrest that appear to crowd him at the flanks, giving a pressing sensation. Thus, the gaze of the young man is direct and defiant in spite of the overall mood of the painting that is oblique, confining, and encroaching. Maurice Brock has seen in this painting an allegory of virtue overcoming vice that is depicted in an ascending movement beginning from the mascarons flanking the courtier to his idealized and perfectly poised face.[23] However, I would rather view the painting as a simultaneous contrariety of self-possession and self-skepticism.

There are two mascarons flanking the young man at belt level: one at the viewer's left of a crumpled human head with a dour squinting face; and another at the right, which is a hybrid head mixing dog and lion with an oversized ear. These two figures, by virtue of their grotesque prominence, are among the most conspicuously emblazoned elements of the painting.[24] The comic effect of these mascarons is to deflate the young man's self-possession and to pin-prick the balloon of pride. Like the self-skeptical attitude of the courtier, they undermine his mien of *odi profanum vulgus*. But they also take the viewer into a zone of even more uncertainty by contributing to the effects of illusion where one meaning is superposed over another and contrary one. This point requires clarification. Though the table and armchair rest convey encroachment relative to the man, the comic faces open up the psychological "space" of humor, which lightens the mood, diverts attention from enclosure, or temporarily dispels the feeling of confinement. There is also a grotesque figure obscurely adumbrated in the man's doublet, and while it is in the same metaphorical line of comic conceits as the furniture mascarons, it cannot be part of the real world of fashionable doublets and is obviously the external intervention of the artist interposing his own ludic, impish outlook. Bronzino's witty joke is like a narrator's comic aside commenting on his/her own narrative. It also has some similarity with the literary technique of authors or narrators departing from recounting the main story events to speak directly to the reader. Frequently, this breaking of the aesthetic distance is used to allow narrators to give their own views on characters or self-reflexively muse on their own poetics.[25] To a certain extent, Bronzino's play with the figure in the doublet makes a knowing gesture to his culture's elite that thrived on unexpected and ingenious intellectual play. This meta-comment adds another level of signification to the two internal but opposing moods of arrogance and skepticism and creates a third perspective, namely, that of the comic associated with semi-autonomous objects of elusiveness bordering on mirage. The mascarons mime this by their complex, kaleidoscopic effects now showing one thing, now another, not only in respect to figure (the dog-lion head topped by a painter's cap)[26] but also in regard to media. As Brock observes, the deformed human head to the viewer's left combines wood or perhaps stone with fabric, and "it emerges from what looks like a piece of cloth tied behind the scroll to the right."[27] In a similar way, the table-top appears overly extended, implying it is made of some fabric rather than of wood.

In the relationship between the grotesques and the man's right hand fingers, there is an analogous sensation in the viewer of seeing an object, watching it dissolve, and finally refocusing on a reconfiguration. At first sight they have all the beauty of elegant, elongated features typical of mannerism,[28] but at the same time, the pointed index finger and little finger with their tactile nails reconfigure the finger group to suggest a hand of talons. (Can we see both views of the fingers, the sleek and grotesque, at the same time or only successively?[29]) Also, the fingers' spatial grouping of three components—index and small fingers at the top separated from the two middle fingers pressed together to form one unit, and the separated little finger—conjure up a trident. Benedetto Varchi authored a treatise titled *Della Generazione del corpo humano et de' mostri* (1547) in which he defined *mostro* as "tutte quelle cose, le quali avvengono fuori dell'ordine consueto, & usitato corso della Natura in qualunche modo."[30] Amid numerous definitions of *mostro*, he gave one meaning as physical deformity and another as display of rare accomplishment. Putting Bembo, Michelangelo, Petrarch, and Cosimo I in the second category, he also placed Bronzino in the same rank for having done a "splendid representation" ("fu ritratto egregiamente") of the surgical separation of Siamese twins.[31] How does this point bear on the *Young Man*? It would seem that his left hand fingers show *mostro* in both senses, namely, irregularity in shape and length but also the striking singularity of slender grace rarely achieved. We see both nearly at the same time. By contrast, the index finger of the right hand is extended into the pages of a momentarily closed book to keep place and this symbolizes the "learned hand" or what Varchi (as we have already seen) called the "dotta mano."[32] Bronzino himself uses "dotta man" (M, v. 7, p. 42) in a sonnet dedicated to Cellini for his exceptional ability to make Perseus reborn in glory "more alive than ever" ("Più che mai vivo," v. 9). Thus, *The Young Man*'s right hand suggests superiority of knowledge, talent, and skill and is thereby associated with his confident if not imperious right eye.

In the *Young Man*, there is a dialogue of pictorial components exchanging surprises and incompatibilities which in their reversals are the more formal but less shocking version of the discontinuities and disruptions of Bronzino's burlesque *capitoli*. Juxtaposed to the grotesque head supporting the table, there is a scroll carved in a graceful S-form whose symmetry, elegance, and homogeneity contrast sharply with the bizarre, hybrid strangeness of the mascarons. Though the scroll surely bears these characteristics, the careful viewer of Bronzino's art may justifiably anticipate that objects, concepts, and sensations will keep morphing and that the components will vie for attention with the whole. Deborah Parker shows that in Bronzino's *capitolo* titled "Lo sdegno," the author culminates his burlesque on disdain with "a raucous tribute to the letter S."[33] Bronzino facetiously praises the powers of the letter "S" and shows that by adding the letter "S" to certain words, he can make them figuratively speaking produce an erection. This satirical effect is evident in such terms as "sforarsi," "spenzolarsi," and "smorza."[34] Returning to *Young Man* portrait, we see that there is a decorative scroll supporting the table top taking the shape of the letter "S" and placed right above the youth's codpiece.[35] Read in conjunction with the *capitolo*, the letter "S" of the scroll has now become the signifier of comic deflation. However, the burlesque connotations of the "S" go beyond the parody of virility, for they reflexively comment on the scroll's own aesthetics (grace, homogeneity, symmetry, balance, elegance), which, of course, redound to the courtier's physical bearing and attitudinal posture. One must marvel at the many and complex levels of meaning that Bronzino is able to coordinate and condense and that in spite of their tensions remain as formally rigorous as a well-crafted poem.

The anatomical emblazoning of the *Young Man*'s drifting left eye commences a deeply ambivalent story where in a feat of *sprezzatura* the subject not only maintains but projects a prepossessing posture while subjected to subtle, pervasive tensions that threaten to undermine his superiority and smug composure.

Appointed by Cosimo I as an official court painter, Bronzino did portraits of important officials in the service of the Florentine duchy. One is of Bartolomeo Panciatichi, consul of the Florentine Academy and ambassador to the Court of France under Francis I. Bronzino also did a portrait of Lucrezia Panciatichi, Bartolomeo's wife, capturing in flickering crimson and purple lights his admiration of her devout nature, virtuous character, and ideal beauty. Among the countless riches of this portrait is the complicated working of Lucrezia's left, puffed-up shoulder sleeve. It is one of at least three portraits having similar sleeves, the other two being *Bia de' Medici* (1542, Galleria degli Uffizi) called the "infantile version of Lucrezia,"[36] and the *Lady in a Red Dress with a Little Boy* of 1540 at the National Gallery of Art in Washington DC (Fig. 8). As Lucrezia's left shoulder sleeve vies for our attention, we see numerous satin folds arching and interpenetrating with the complexity of an ever-bourgeoning rose. But for what purpose? In the enamel plaques of Lucrezia's gold chain, she offers the onlooker not only her moral device but also her symbol of infinity. That is the French motto "Amour dure Sans Fin."

I take the woman's sleeve as the poetic matrix of infinity that is everywhere present in the portrait. The contemporary French philosopher Gilles Deleuze points out in his book *The Fold* that the types of folds in Mannerist and baroque costume suggest an inexhaustible puzzle that can never be fully unfolded.[37] In Lucrezia's portrait, the onlooker's response can partake of Lucrezia's limitless love by deciphering the beautiful morphology of her shoulder folds. The painting encourages us to capture the pattern of various fold forms just long enough before they morph into transformations, nodal points, multiplicities, and vanishing points. Curiously, one fold takes the shape of a diagonal "S" with loops coiling inward in concentric circles at opposite ends similar to the "S"- shaped support of the table in the *Young Man* portrait. Others are like bracelets looping around a cylinder, some of them clamp into one another like interlocking brackets, and a few rise up like crying or yawning mouths. An enfolded eye descends into a tearful nose, others bulge upwards to reflect the light and then retreat into the depths of mysterious involutions. Even as Bronzino offers a somber, hagiographic portrait of Lucrezia, he cannot avoid adumbrating two mascarons hiding in the complex folds of both shoulder sleeves. One in the inner left bottom of the left shoulder shows an elongated, narrow nose, left eye, and grotesque smile. Another mascaron molded into the right shoulder sleeve looks out from the side with a smile at the nothingness of the neutral brown background. The concentration imposed on the viewer by the complexity of the folds is complemented by Lucrezia's posture of meditation, her eyes fixed outward towards the onlooker in an impassive mask of dignity, but inwardly enjoying introspective harmony while holding a Book of Hours posed on her gown.

Lucrezia's shoulder folds communicate two types of infinity that Bronzino drew into this portrait. The first is the infinity of unlimited development and constant change, or, to put in mathematical terms, the infinity of calculus. This is opposed to the second type of infinity seen in the Panciatichi's pearl necklace, gilded hair band, and cylindrical neck that is the completed perfection of the circle. We can term this the infinity of geometry. Out of this contrast, one can see the fundamental Pythagorean distinction, echoed in Plato's *Timaeas*, between bounded and unbounded, limited and unlimited, or, in Greek, *peras* and *apeiron*.[38] For an understanding of unlimited development, we can revert to three Renaissance models derived respectively from metaphysics, alchemy, and anatomy. The first is Nicholas of Cusa's concept of the individual as a microcosm having a *complicatio* or enfolding of virtual powers out of which the individual performs acts of *explicatio*, namely, the unfoldings of human knowledge and creativity.[39] The second model stems from Paracelsus and is suggested by Lucrezia's involuted folds, which appear to be an arsenal of heterogeneous forms and movements. This is alchemical concept of *prima materia* that contains the primitive agglomerations and elements from which humanity, assisting the worker Archei, transmutes into quintessences or gold.[40] A third model of Lucrezia's many-folded left sleeve is suggested by a woodcut in Andreas Vesalius' *De Fabrica* and by his shorter and beautifully illustrated *Epitome*.[41] In its wrinkles, fissures, convolutions, and labyrinthine curvatures, the agglomeration of folds resembles a human brain.[42]

Lucrezia's shoulder folds show that in Bronzino's painting, emblazoning a detail is an invitation to the viewer to explore multiple microcosms and thereby activate their ongoing dialogue of reconfigurations that have an infinite quality reminiscent of contemporary metaphysical and alchemical concepts.

The third work I wish to examine is the figure of Saint Bartholomew flayed alive, which, because it emblazons so many anatomical structures, is highly relevant to our subject. It is a high point of *disegno* and *colore*. The Saint Bartholomew fragment was originally intended as part of the Pala of the Altar of Graces in Pisa

Cathedral, and it is one figure of a seven-part group consisting of Christ bearing the Cross, Saint Andrew, Saint John the Evangelist, Saint Michael the Archangel, Saint Peter Martyr, and Saint Stephen. Unfortunately, the pala was irreparably damaged only decades after its installation, and it is now conserved in fragments at the Accademia di San Luca in Rome.[43]

In his *Art and Anatomy: Images from a Scientific Revolution*, Domenico Laurenza points out that the sixteenth century was the "century of anatomy,"[44] and his focus is to trace the relations between artists and anatomists. The first phase is dominated by printers such as the brothers De Gregori, who conceived of the idea of collecting illustrated medieval medical manuscripts and in 1491 published the very first of this kind under the title *Fasciculus medicinae*.[45] In a second phase, the artist-anatomist came to the fore by creating independent images such as those of Leonardo da Vinci, who emphasized the scientific method of meticulous observation, and of Michelangelo, who was "more strictly artistic anthropocentric" and "studied anatomy exclusively as a function of his art."[46] Both did dissections, and their works were scrutinized by Raphael, who, according to Vasari, "devoted himself to studying the nude and to comparing the muscles of anatomical subjects of flayed human bodies with those of the living."[47] Andreas Vesalius' *De humani corporis fabrica*, published in 1543 as was his *Epitome*, is considered the first modern descriptive anatomy, and while emphasizing the scientific viewpoint, he also produced an aesthetic masterpiece of anatomical illustration.[48] In a third stage, the scientific objective predominates, as exemplified by Charles Estienne's *De dissectione partium corporis humani* (Paris, 1545), which improved on Vesalius by carving minute strokes into woodblocks that offered better representation of muscle volume and texture.[49] As the scientific gaze became more pronounced, illustrated works on anatomy began to stress the observation of single organs in great, perhaps overwhelming, detail, but this method could incur criticism such as that of Vasari, who thought that Battista Franco "wasted his time beyond all reason over the minutiae of muscles ... while paying no attention to other fields of art."[50]

Where do we place Bronzino's *Saint Bartholomew* in the context of these three phases of anatomical art and illustration? On the one hand, there is a decidedly scientific dimension to his work, and Laurenza cites Vasari's estimate that it "has the appearance of a true anatomical subject and of a man flayed in reality, so natural it is and imitated with such diligence from an anatomical subject."[51] Bronzino emblazoned the saint's left foot and ankle, minutely detailing the *tendon achillis*, the *superior peroneal retinaculum*, the *peroneus tertius*, and the *extensor hallucis longus*, and the silver color of the tendons is an accurate scientific representation. In this regard, it should be pointed out that observation of live, exposed, human tendons will, in fact, show a silvery white glow as painted by Bronzino.[52] On the other hand, there is a great deal of art in the service of scientific anatomy, but this quality can be best shown by studying the fragment as a whole from the perspective of the *paragone*. Quite simply, the question may be asked how many perspectives of the human body can a single painting, drawing, or sculpture produce? For example, Laurenza cites Cellini's opinion that sculpture was seven times superior to painting since the latter could only represent one point of view while the former eight. But Leonardo, as Laurenza points out, developed a drawing method of the eight-pointed star, each point able to represent a point of view, and Rubens drew the left arm from six points of view from a three dimensional *écorché* model.[53]

It can be seen that Bronzino utilized two strategies to multiply perspective, keeping in mind that we are speaking of single painting of a single subject, the saint's body as a whole. This would be different from making more than one drawing with each giving a different perspective of the same object or body part. One of Bronzino's methods is based on the use of curvature of exterior anatomy to increase angles and viewpoints difficult to display, but the principal method is to enhance the third dimension by moving from surface to deeper components.

The first technique I have mentioned stresses variations in angles and positions which, for the most part, are based on exterior anatomy or, to use a metaphor, topography. Examining the painting from top to bottom, we see that it takes a well-defined serpentine shape. Our eyes move from the saint's head and then left to his raised arm, which, since it is extended, turns right to the thorax and continues to the stomach and hip. From the hip, we follow the left thigh in a leftward line diagonally, which then turns right at the knee. This serpentine form is the basic design that allows Bronzino to multiply perspective. The open right hand showing the palm contrasts with the back of the left hand. Also, we are given two views of the right forearm, the outermost and the lateral areas. In addition, Bronzino offers us a more or less flat view of the full chest and abdomen, but, thanks to a curvature, he also shows a lateral area of the left hip or, in other words, the ribcage left side angle. Standing back and looking at the painting, we can see that Bronzino gives relief to the admirable symmetry of the body, for he clearly outlines three aspects of the torso: the horizontal pectoral arc, the ribs right below, and the more elliptical circle enclosing the abdominal muscles. The white figure on Bartholomew's shoulder and chest that looks like a running stick-man gives color and line to enhance and brighten the symmetry. Just above this figure, forming a "V" in the neck, there are two bulging muscles, the sternocleid mastoideus structures, which descend into the middle of the horizontal clavicle. From precisely the middle of the clavicle, there descends a vertical white line, the sternum, which bisects the pectoral muscles. Finally, let us note that just as Leonardo was interested in how movement affected anatomy,[54] so does Bronzino emphasize what happens to body parts when they are bent. This is evident in the tightening of skin at the right elbow and the left knee, which also reveals a bony prominence on its lateral surface.

Aside from exterior anatomy, the more pervasive anatomical aspect of the Saint Bartholomew pala is the play between surface and depth which gives more of a three-dimensional view. This is particularly relevant to the treatment of skin and other surfaces. Let us examine this by moving from the most interior parts of the saint's body to the most external ones. According to Laurenza, Michelangelo emphasized "external anatomy,"[55] meaning the outer surface of the body. However, Bronzino gives his audience variations in anatomical depth. As a result of dissection, we see the innermost, subcutaneous parts of the left foot and ankle, especially the tendons. At a level just above this, Bronzino takes us to the surface of the left arm muscles whose anatomical characteristics are their braiding and involutions. The flaying of the chest allows Bronzino to show the inner rib cage appearing through the surface of chest muscles. One can appreciate that the glistening, smoother surfaces of the reddish brown muscle surfaces act like an X-Ray of the chest bones, which are so highly articulated that we can count them. If we look at the flayed ankle extending to the middle of the foot, there is a movement of depth going from exterior to interior, first with the peeled away outer skin, then the tendons, and finally to structures just below. Bartholomew's raised right hand, flayed up to the fingers, brings us to the border of inner and outer layers, precisely marking that transition with a horizontal white cut below the outer, overlapping skin. Finally, the painter has the viewer look upward to see the healthy, smooth flesh of a young face brightened by the contrast with his black hair, eyebrows, and beard, which are components outermost to the skin. In fact, the saint's face is illuminated by mystical transport. The meticulously folded skin on the floor, repulsive as it is, takes us to the border of nature and art, for, on the nature side, the precision of its folds is like the high degree of articulation of the ribs and, on the artistic side, its overlapping folds are of a similar color and morphology as the drapery thrown over Bartholomew's right shoulder and left thigh. According to Brock, Bronzino imitates Pontormo's view that the body is composed of an outer, "physical envelope," and this can be seen in the figures of the Capponi Chapel pala.[56] However, unlike his predecessor who made the reader guess whether one sees clothing or skin, Bronzino disambiguates the metaphor by throwing drapery of a slightly different color over the saint's body which takes the form of a loosely fitting, convex curve whose verticality contrasts with horizontal bend of the right rib section. Saint Bartholomew appears in Michelangelo's *Last Judgment* with a grotesque bag of floppy, flayed skin sagging down from his left hand. In the center of this doughy, limp envelope not yet carrion is the anamorphosis of Micheangleo's distorted, tortured face, neither alive nor dead and set within a drooping socket of stretched out flesh. Here we see even more the stark contrast with Bronzino's different objective of combining the science of anatomy with the anatomy of martyrdom.[57]

But the anatomist is predominantly an artist offering other messages that galvanize the various bodily topographies to produce discrete but related philosophical, aesthetic, religious, and theological statements that move vertically but by compartments, reliefs, and color contrasts. The viewer's eyes move up an ascending order of ontological perfection that begins in the dissected ankle and foot with scientific knowledge and pedagogical mastery. Then moving upward, we see the aesthetic beauty and nobility of the human body sublime, and even its grace, in spite of being precariously posed between resting on the right knee and two left toes and rising to the pull of rapture. But biological science is also the bearer of a religious allegory of knowledge, since in the *Golden Legend* Jacobus de Voragine tells us through an onomastic study of the name "Bartholomew" that the saint is "a son of God, who lifts up the minds of the doctors so that they may pour down the waters of their teaching."[58] Then there is the theological dimension superposed over these staccato-like levels worked through the paradox that the skin, here luminous in the chest, is the veil of the transfigured body. This is the doctrine of the flesh turned sacred, indicated by the saint's effulgent face which operates through the mystery of Christ's incarnation, transfiguration, and resurrection. Understood this way, all negative values are reversed into positive transvaluations.[59]

Bronzino has painted an anatomy of emotions into the pala that, in spite of some very abrupt changes in feeling, sensation, and affect bordering on dissociation, maintain a progressive direction. First, one experiences repulsion in the dissected foot and flayed skin folded on the floor. But revulsion changes into admiration of the body sublime that reminiscent of Leonardo's heroic, male model of the nude.[60] If Bartholomew is not Hercules, he has similar heroic qualities symbolized by his beard, broad shoulders, and muscles, thereby connoting force, strength, and courage, though it must be stated that here such human powers are also impelled by the irresistibility of divine grace. This brings us to the culminating emotions, which are also expressed through paradox. From the viewpoint of aesthetics, the miracle of martyrdom is transferred to the reader as a marvel of a psychological split. Saint Bartholomew is gripped by transport, and this ecstasy appears to disconnect him from the torture of cuts and slashes. Though in viewing the pala the onlooker may feel excruciating pain, Saint Bartholomew himself is oblivious to his flaying and is transported by the rapture of already glimpsed salvation and beatitude. The body of the saint has a certain hardness typical of Bronzino's portraits that reminds one of sculpture, and if that is the case, the blade of agony is sublimated through the artist's chisel.[61]

When we turn to the *Portrait of Laura Battiferri*, we find a case in which the emblazoned body part in spite of its symbolism of nobility and artistic achievement is a condensation of unresolved tensions ranging from admiration to angry frustration. Battiferri was born in Urbino but married to the Florentine sculptor-architect Bartolommeo Ammannati.[62] An accomplished poetess who sought guidance and inspiration from Benedetto Varchi and his circle of literati, she published a collection of lyrics in 1560 titled *Il primo libro dell'opere toscane*, followed by a free translation into Tuscan of seven Penetential Psalms (*I sette salmi penitenzali di David con alcuni sonetti spirituali*," 1564).[63] Bronzino was in love with the pious and chaste Battiferri and painted her portrait in highly dignified profile which emphasized her accomplishments by depicting her holding or displaying a book of poems. Laura responded in a sonnet which, by commenting on her image, gave a voice to her painted countenance.[64] These were sentiments of profound gratitude, thanking Bronzino for his bond of friendship by comparing herself to the stem of a growing laurel cultivated by his literary counsel: "Com'io, la tua mercé, di doppio vanto/Cingo il mio basso oscuro umile stelo" (M, vv. 12–13, p. 6).

As one can see from Laura's prominent aquiline nose, Bronzino intended to praise Battiferri's poetic talent by comparing her to the author of the *Divine Comedy*. Since Boccaccio's *Life of Dante*, artists from Giotto to Raphael had created a virtual iconographic topos of Dante's profile.[65] Bronzino thoroughly assimilated to Laura other characteristic traits of Dante, such as the hooked nose, sloping forehead, pinched cheeks, fleshly lips, and jutting chin. Thus, it is not Beatrice, Dante's spiritual guide, to whom Laura is directly compared but, rather, the very author of Tuscany's greatest work. Thanks to the research of Parker, Plazzotta, Kirkham, and Brock,[66] we have highly instructive and intricate analyses of epistolary interchanges between Bronzino and Battiferri that offer informative insights into their views on the *ut pictura poesis* debate. Suffice it point out that in a sonnet addressed to Laura, Bronzino elevates Battiferri to a higher place in the pantheon than Laura and Beatrice and makes her the equal of Petrarch and Dante. In fact, the Battiferri portrait is consistent with such adulation, since Laura is shown holding a book of Petrarch's poems opened to sonnets 64 and 240.[67] In the second of these sonnets, Laura's index and middle finger appear to point to Petrarch's words "dal dritto mio sentier" (v. 4), thereby echoing Dante's famous opening of the *Divine Comedy*. Bronzino even brings Laura into association with Boccaccio as one of the paragons of writing in the Toscan vernacular. In a drawing of Dante now in Munich sketched by Bronzino's for lunettes he painted for Bartolomeo Bettini's palace, we see depictions of Dante, Petrarch, and Boccaccio respectively, where Dante's profile closely resembles that of Laura's portrait.[68] However, there is another side to the Battiferri portrait.

As an emblematic picture is glossed by an accompanying poem, so do a chain of poems contextualize Bronzino's angry frustration towards his painted subject. A sonnet written by Bronzino himself, which ostensibly refers to Battiferri, describes her as "within, all iron, and without, all ice—with tardy hand and all fire spent."[69] No doubt "fero" is a pun on her name. Other poems directly or indirectly refer to Laura as distant, remote, and aloof, for she has a hard heart of iron ("fero, e duro cor"), and is cold and hard ("geluta, e dura"), with a disdainful appearance ("disdegnosa vista").[70] It is no small irony that these adjectives are typically used to describe Bronzino's own portrait style and the chilly fashion in which he depicts his subjects such as *Lucrezia Panciatichi*. Bronzino's poems give credence to the suspicion that the Petrarchan sonnets that he cites in the Battiferri portrait are not merely conventional sentiments but personal feelings. In Petrarch's sonnet 64 on the verso, the lover complains of the beloved's disdain, anger, and flight from his attentions and implies that if he could he would tear his laurel from his heart. In sonnet 240 on the recto, the speaker confesses that reason cannot restrain his passions and imagines Laura saying, "What else can this man do? My face consumes him. Why is he so desirous and why am I so beautiful" (vv. 12–14).[71]

Seen from the angle of Bronzino's pangs of thwarted passion, Battiferri's aquiline nose not only symbolizes her assimilation to Dante but also serves as the painterly matrix for the artist's cutting, piercing, slashing, hatcheting, and ripping that are connoted in other features of the portrait. The incisiveness and flatness of the profiled face resemble those decoupages in anatomy books like Vesalius' *Epitome*, in which students were instructed to cut out an illustrated organ around its borders and glue it on the right place of a nude manikin.[72] The long, open fingers pointing to Petrarch's verses are also scissors prepared to cut up the pages, pages that can just as easily cut Laura's fingers. Because her veil is so gauzy, thin, and diaphanous, it too makes for easy clipping and puncturing. Laura's high forehead that shows intelligence and dignity is made prominent because her hair is very tightly and severely pulled back, and her chignon bonnet, like her jutting chain and thinly cut eyebrow, appears to be sharply pointed. Battiferri's long, column-like neck that would solicit admiration from Fierenzuola and Parmigianino provides a good beheading target for the hatchet face. The fact that Bronzino paints her in stark and distant profile cuts her off from emotional connection with the viewer. Why is the low-cut ruché collar fitted so tightly around her neck, and is the button or pin that fastens it also piercing Laura's trachea? Her unusually wide shoulders emphasize the cut ridges in her partlet, and her wine-colored puffed sleeves are slashed. There is a suggestion of blood in that wine color, which also appears in the redness of Laura's lips. The white, transparent muslin guimpe, which seems to be detachable, cuts a razor thin boundary across the chest and over the shoulder because of its sharp color contrast with the much darker tones of Laura's dress. Bronzino's transcription of Petrarch's sonnets is hand-written and therefore made personal. But all verse is etymologically and visibly a furrow, fissure, or groove cutting across the page, and a page resembles skin.[73]

Bronzino's Battiferri portrait is as conflicted about his subject as his love poems, a fact that gives us yet another reason to read his paintings and literary work side by side as translations of one another.

In conclusion, it is useful to evaluate the effects of emblazoning in Bronzino by reference to Claude Lévi-Strauss' definition of a myth. In *Anthropologie structurale*, Lévi-Strauss states that the function of a myth is to express or explain a contradiction by bringing to the fore the abstract relations of values in tension with one another.[74] Following this idea, one can find in Bronzino's logic of the blazon at least this—that instead of seeking to perfect the whole, he preferred semi-autonomous or partial wholes that vie with the illusion of overall unity. But to what end? In his burlesque poem "Dell'Esser Chiaro,"[75] Bronzino engages in a fundamental meditation on the problems of truth and deception, of whether we can distinguish reality from a dream, and if it is possible to overcome ambiguity, irresolution, and perpetual suspension. Can one make progress in differentiating the *di dentro* from *di fuori*? In his portraits, it is tempting to see in the ever-morphing partial wholes not only an expression of vigilance against illusion by the use of illusion but also an instrument of knowledge, frequently ludic, seeking protection from a too-easy commitment to belief. It is on the bodies of his painted figures that Bronzino challenges his viewers to make similar discriminations amid the complexities of ever-transforming configurations and perpetually transposable, semi-autonomous parts. In *The Young Man with a Book*, this translates as the challenge to grasp a mitosis of double visions, and, as such, this portrait may serve as the meta-communicational statement of Bronzino's poetics of skepticism. In *Lucrezia Panciatichi*'s complicated shoulder folds, we find the more positive side of illusion used as an exploration of the limitless powers of human creativity involuted in a sometimes comic interpenetration of morphing rose petals. In the *Saint Bartholomew* pala, the compartmentalization of emblazoned body parts creates a corresponding succession of abrupt emotional shifts in viewers that keep them edgy and unsure about precisely what they are encountering. It first draws attention to itself by repulsion in displaying peeled back skin but then becomes a scientific anatomy lesson offering a bracing vivisection of human tendons then, in a wonder of metamorphosis, is psychologically turned inside out as it loops from what should be excruciating martyrdom to detached transport. And what a paragon of human nobility is Bronzino's *Laura Battiferri*, which is everywhere admiration and everywhere anger and frustration.

NOTES

1. On the armorial blazon, see Michel Pastoureau, *Traité de l'héraldique* (Paris: Picard, 1993).

2. Jonathan Sawday, *The Body Emblazoned: Dissection and the Human Body in Renaissance Culture* (London and New York: Routledge, 1995), 191–212. See also Alison Saunders, *The Sixteenth-Century Blason Poétique* (Berne: Peter Lang, 1981), 9–51.

3. *Petrarch's Lyric Poems: The Rime Sparse and Other Lyrics*, trans. and ed. Robert M. Durling (Cambridge, MA: Harvard University Press, 1976). See *canzone* 157, 302. On Petrarch's division of Laura into individual anatomical features compared to objects such as precious metals, see Leonard Forster, *The Icy Fire: Five Studies in European Petrarchism* (Cambridge: Cambridge University Press, 1969), 8–10.

4. *Petrarch's Lyric poems, op. cit.*, 344.

5. Giusto de Conti, *La bella mano di Giusto de' Conti romano senator e una raccolta delle rime antiche di diversi Toscani* (Florence: J. Guiducci e Santi Franchi, 1715; and Verona: Giannalberto Tumermani, 1732), 14.

6. Angelo Poliziano, *Poesie italiane di messer Angelo Poliziano* (Milan: G. Silvestri, 1825), 124.

7. Nocturno Napolitano, *Opera nova amorosa de Nocturno Napolitano* (Milan: Jo. Jacobo et fratelli da Legnano, 1518). MIIr.

8. Olympo de Sassoferrato, *Parthenia. Pegasea. Olimpia. Nova Phenice. Gloria d'Amore. Linguaccio. Aurora. Ardela* (Venice, 1538–1539). For these two works, see *Pegasea*, B5r–B5v.

9. Giorgio Vasari, *Le opera di Giorgio Vasari*, ed. Gaetano Milanesi, 8 vols. (Florence: Sansoni, 1906), 7:598–99. Maurice Brock clarifies Vasari's account of a *Venus and Cupid* sent to Francis I: "The reasonable conclusion is that the painting was commissioned probably by the duke himself, for purposes of diplomatic largesse and that Bronzino painted it somewhat expeditiously sometime in 1544–45"; see Brock, *Bronzino*, trans. David Poole Radzinowicz and Christine Schultz-Touge (Paris: Flammarion, 2002), 218.

10. Saunders, *The Sixteenth-Century Blason Poétique*, 88–112. See also Verdun-Louis Saulnier, *Maurice Scève*, 2 vols. (Paris: Klincksieck, 1948), 1:72–87.

11. See the poem "A ceulx qui, après l'Epigramme du beau Tetin, en feirent d'aultres," in *Marot: Œuvres completès*, ed. François Rigolot, 2 vols. (Paris: G.F. Flammarion, 2009), 1:418–21.

12. Ibid.

13. Deborah Parker, *Bronzino: Renaissance Painter as Poet* (Cambridge: Cambridge University Press, 2000), 12.

14. "Del pennello," in *Agnolo Bronzino: Rime in burla*, ed. Franca Petrucci Nardelli, intro. Claudio Mutini (Rome: Instituto della Enciclopedia Italiana, 1988), 23–26, vv.13–30. For the sexual meanings of "albergo," "sentina," and "stanza" in "In lode della galea" (Petrucci Nardelli, 64–77), as well as their English translations, see Parker, *Bronzino*, 30.

15. Translation taken from Parker, *Bronzino: Renaissance Painter as Poet*, 25.

16. See *Sonetti di Angiolo Allori detto il Bronzino ed alter rime inediti* ed. Domenico Moreni (Florence: Magheri, 1823). Henceforth, all references to this edition are indicated by M plus the page number and lines.

17. On the relationship between literature and the London *Venus and Cupid*, see Robert Gaston, "Love's Sweet Poison: A New Reading of Bronzino's London *Allegory*," *I Tatti Studies* 4 (1991), 247–88. On Bronzino's anatomical drawings, see *The Drawings of Bronzino*, Exhibition Catalogue, The Metropolitan Museum of Art in collaboration with the Gabinetto e Stampo degli Uffizi and the Polo Museale Fiortino, Florence, ed. Carmen C. Bambach et al. Information on the *Venus and Cupid* is found on 3, 7, 29, 89, 116, 152, 254. *On Jealousy*, 39, 146–47. See also Lynette M.F. Bosch, "Bronzino's London Allegory: Love versus Time," *Source: Notes in the History of Art* 9, no. 2 (Winter 1990), 30–35.

18. Brock, *Bronzino*, 218.

19. Gaston, "Love's Sweet Poison," 281. See also Elizabeth Cropper on Bronzino's determined integration of the Tuscan vernacular into his overall poetics; she emphasizes its importance over the canons of antiquity and straightforward naturalism given impetus by Bembo: "Bronzino's interest in the formation of a canon of vernacular literature, and in the relationship between painting and poetry was not confined, however, to the representation of Tuscan poets or their themes. He also embarked on a search for a visual style that would enable him to signify the Florentine character of his work and that of his subjects." See Andrew Morrough, Fiorella Gioffredi Superbi, et al., eds., "Prolegomena to a New Interpretation of Bronzino's Florentine Portraits," in *Renaissance Studies in Honor of Craig Hugh Smyth* 2 vols. (Florence: Giunti Barbère, 1985), 2:150.

20. Gaetano Milanesi, ed., *Le Opera di Giorgio Vasari*, 4:9.

21. Brock, *Bronzino*, 144. Other studies I have consulted are: Arthur McComb, *Agnolo Bronzino: His Life and Works* (Cambridge, MA: Harvard University Press, 1928); Craig Hugh Smyth, *Bronzino Studies* (Ph.D. diss., Princeton University, 1955); Craig Hugh Smyth, *Bronzino as Draughtsman: An Introduction* (Locust Valley, NY: J.J. Augustin, 1971); Charles McCorquodale, *Bronzino* (New York: Harper and Row, 1981); Leatrice Mendelsohn, *Paragoni: Benedetto Varchi's "Due Lezzioni" and Cinquecento Art Theory* (Ann Arbor, MI: UMI Research Press, 1982); Janet Cox-Rearick, *Dynasty and Destiny in Medici Art: Pontormo, Leo X, and the Two Cosimos* (Princeton, NJ: Princeton University Press, 1984); Marcia B. Hall, *Color and Meaning: Practice and Theory in Renaissance Painting* (Cambridge: Cambridge University Press, 1992); Craig Hugh Smyth, *Mannerism and Maniera*, intro. Elizabeth Cropper (Vienna: IRSA, 1992); Janet Cox-Rearick, *Bronzino's Chapel of El-*

eonora in the Palazzo Vecchio (Berkeley: The University of California Press, 1993); Alessandro Cecchi, *Agnolo Bronzino* (Florence: SCALA, 1996); Liana De Girolami Cheney, ed. *Readings in Italian Mannerism*, foreword by Craig Hugh Smyth (New York: Peter Lang, 1997); Elizabeth Cropper, *Pontormo: Portrait of a Halberdier* (Los Angeles, CA: Getty Museum, 1997); Jodi Cranston, *The Poetics of Portraiture in the Italian Renaissance* (Cambridge: Cambridge University Press, 2000); and Elizabeth Pilliod, *Pontormo, Bronzino, Allori* (New Haven, CT: Yale University Press, 2001).

22. In my estimate, Cosimo I succeeded preeminently in consolidating powers that would keep Charles at a distance and create a resurgence of Florentine pride and power that would expand into a Tuscan territorial state. Not only his autocratic rule and military build-up, but also his investment in cultural propaganda through literature and the arts enabled him to balance the precarious tensions tugging outwards and inwards. It was no small part of Cosimo's amalgamation of cultural power to take over the *Accademia degli Umidi* and give it official footing as the new *Accademia Fiorentina* in 1541. These points are symbolically written all over the *Young Man* portrait and its background. In spite of Cosimo's political successes, we cannot take his dominance for granted, since control over the innumerable, pressing demands of the duchy required constant vigilance—like the wary left eye of the young man, his body turning to see someone or some event that has surprised him, and the extension of his left arm and elbow outward and painted in front of the closed door. The status of Florence as a duchy ultimately under Charles V's control but creating its own identity as a semi-autonomous political entity is not unlike the partial whole of the anatomical blazon. On the political background of Cosimo's Florence, see J.R. Hale, *Florence and the Medici: The Pattern of Control* (Plymouth: Thames and Hudson, 1977), 109–43; 146.

23. Brock, *Bronzino*, 135.

24. On these mascarons, see Paul Barolsky, *Infinite Jest: Wit and Humor in Italian Renaissance Art* (Columbia: University of Missouri Press, 1990), 141.

25. See the beginning of Chapter 9 of Charlotte Brontë's *Jane Eyre*, especially the first line that reads: "A new chapter in a novel is something like a new scene in a play ...," ed. Stevie Davies (London: Penguin, 2006), 11.

26. I am indebted to Liana De Girolami Cheney for pointing out to me in conversation that this is a painter's cap.

27. Brock, *Bronzino*, 132.

28. Pierre Barucco, *Le maniérisme italien* (Paris: Presses Universitaires de France, 1981), 91, in the section titled *"La morphologie maniériste,"* 90–98.

29. This may be a play on figure and ground (bi-stability), which is

a distinction made by Gestalt psychology. In Edgar Rubin's famous example called "Rubin's Vase," one is confronted with ambiguity. There appears to be a white vase against a black background, but if one reverses figure and ground, what was background is now two faces looking at one another. Only one of these two views can be maintained at a given moment. If I think of Mannerist style as the ground, my original impression of seeing fingers as talons changes to an appreciation of their graceful elongation. See "Gestalt Theory," *Encyclopedia of Philosophy*. 4 vols., ed. Paul Edwards (New York: Macmillian, 1967), vol. 3, 319. It is not surprising that artists would describe the art of painting as requiring the distinct but coordinated operation of the hand, eyes, and mind. For example, Vasari, in his Preface to *Le Vite*, writes: "Design means the imitation of the most beautiful parts of nature, and this requires that the hand and mind of the artist be capable of reproducing them exactly upon the flat surface of the picture or relief" (Liana De Girolami Cheney, *Giorgio Vasari's Prefaces: Art & Theory* (New York: Peter Lang, 2012), xxix; 188 for the Italian). But Bronzino appears to carry over this sense of the separateness among the artist's faculties to the physical description of the object painted. He does this with emphasis. For, in the *Young Man*, the different gazes of each of his two eyes and the double appearance of the right hand as elegantly long but talon-like bespeak a painterly accent on either the separateness of the objects (eyes) or the double nature of the hand. And as I have noted, the *Young Man* is of two minds.

30. *La prima parte delle Lezzioni di M. Benedetto Varchi, nella quale si tratta della Natura, Della Generazione del corpo humano e de' mostri: lette da lui publicamente nella Accademia Fiorentina* (Florence: Giunti, 1560), 98v. This is largely a reprint of the 1547 edition.

31. See Gaston, "Love's Sweet Poison," 267. Varchi's text reads as follows: "Quanti sono in questa luogo, che si ricordano d'hauer veduto quel Mostro che nacque dalla porta al Prato, circa dodici anni sono, il quale fu ritratto egregiamente dallo eccellentissimo Bronzino, il quale cra cosi fatto" (104v).

32. *Sonnetti*, ed. Moreni, 44. In the first tercet of his sonnet, Varchi says: "Grato non giá, ch'aver tua dotta mano/Spresso con arte tal tanto lavoro/Et di qual anche pregio opra maggiore" (vv. 9–11).

33. Parker, *Bronzino: Renaissance Painter as Poet*, 165.

34. Parker, *Bronzino: Renaissance Painter as Poet*, 167.

35. On codpieces in Bronzino's paintings, see Konrad Eisenbichler, "Bronzino's *Portrait of Guidobaldo II della Rovere*," in *Desire and Discipline: Sexuality in the Premodern West*, eds. Jacqueline Murray and Konrad Eisenbichler (Toronto: University of Toronto Press, 1966), 21–33.

36. Gabrielle Langdon, *Medici Women: Portraits of Power, Love, and Be-*

trayal from the Court of Duke Cosimo I (Toronto: University of Toronto Press, 2006), 100.

37. Gilles Deleuze, *The Fold: Leibniz and the Baroque*, trans. Tom Conley (Minneapolis: The University of Minnesota Press, 1993), 121.

38. *The Pythagorean Sourcebook and Library*, comp. and trans. Kenneth Sylvan Guthrie, ed. and intro. David Fideler (Grand Rapids, MI: Phanes Press, 1988), 22–24.

39. Clyde Lee Miller, *Reading Cusanus: Metaphor and Dialectic in a Conjectural Universe* (Washington, DC: Catholic University of America Press, 2003), 36.

40. "God created all things, something from nothing. This something is a seed; the seed contains the end of its predestination and office. And ... there is nothing that is created in its final form, but *Vulcan* must complete it ... all things are created as *prime matter* and after that the *Vulcan* follows and turns them into *ultimate matter* through the art of alchemy." Paracelsus' words are translated by Walter Pagel in "The Prime Matter of Paracelsus," *Ambix: The Journal of the Society for the Study of Alchemy and Early Chemistry* 9, no. 3 (1961), 118.

41. See John B. de C.M. Saunders and Charles D. O'Malley, *The Illustrations from the Works of Andreas Vesalius of Brussels: Annotations and Translations* (New York: Dover, 1950), 188. See also *De humani corporis fabrica* (Basel: Johannes Oporinus, 1555). The first edition was published in 1543.

42. Bronzino uses the phrase "un gran cervello" in "Del Pennello" "Nè bisogna a impararla un gran cervello,/Perche se un non è grosso qual bue/ Gli ha chi gl'insegna, purche voglia avello."

43. From a historical perspective and in comparison with Bronzino's pala, it is useful to mention two related references. The first is an article by Sara Kay titled "Original Skin: Flaying, Reading, and Thinking in the Legend of Saint Bartholomew and Other Works" (*Journal of Medieval and Early Modern Studies* 36, no. 1 (Winter 2006), 35–74). The author analyzes a medieval miniature painting by Jean de Vignay of Bartholomew's flaying which also has anatomical realism as its subject. Less detailed than Bronzino's work, the miniature shows the saint lying on a trestle table where two torturers slit open his lower right leg just before peeling back the skin. Kay also explores the very interesting aesthetic question of how changes and depredations in the material substance of the manuscript over time enrich and give added meaning to the miniature (47–52). Does this not suggest that a similar experiment can be conducted on the pala by comparing its damaged state with the saint's flaying? Also, one will also want to compare Bronzino's painting with a contemporary sculpture of Marco d'Agrate's 1562 statue of Saint Bartholomew — slashed, cut, and deeply furrowed but standing unperturbed outdoors in the Milan Duomo.

44. Domenico Laurenza, *Art and Anatomy: Images from a Scientific Revolution* (New York: Metropolitan Museum of Art, 2012), 5. This informative essay should be read in conjunction with Laurenza's related studies such as *De figura umana: Fisiognomica, anatomia e arte in Leonardo* (Florence: Olschki, 2001).

45. Laurenza, *Art and Anatomy*, 20.

46. Laurenza, *Art and Anatomy*, 13.

47. Laurenza, *Art and Anatomy*, 17.

48. In the preface to the *De Fabrica*, Vesalius upbraids his medical contemporaries for too bookish an approach to teaching anatomy, and he points out to them that by leaving dissection to barbers and surgeons, they have lost first-hand knowledge of the human body. He emphasizes that the physician no longer used his own hands in dissection but dictated instructions to butchers "out of a manual alone matters he has never subjected to dissection by hand." See Daniel Garrison and Malcolm Hast, *On the Fabric of the Human Body: An Annotated Translation of the 1543 and 1555 Editions of Andreas Vesalius' De Humani Corporis Fabrica*, historical introduction by Vivian Nutton. An on-line work in progress accessible at <http://vesalius.northwestern.edu>. My quotation is from Vesalius' Preface, 3r. As if to underscore the importance of the hand but primarily to emphasize Vesalius' own authority, the frontispiece shows a picture of him highly confident and self-assured, highlighting his hands which hold forward for display the dissected arm of a standing cadaver. See Garrison and Hast, *On the Fabric of the Human Body*.

49. Laurenza, *Art and Anatomy*, 20; 23. This is hardly a one-sided affair, and one improvement in Estienne's *De Dissectione*, however significant, does not surpass Vesalius overall. As Laurenza states, "The success of Vesalius' work was due above all to the extraordinary orchestration of images in his treatise" (22).

50. Laurenza, *Art and Anatomy*, 30. Laurenza points out "a tradition of anatomical study practiced in the studio of Pontormo (1494–1557), which included Bronzino (1503–72), Alessandro Allori (1535–1607), and [Ludovico] Cigoli, each the pupil of his predecessor and each the author of dissections carried out in the Florentine milieu of San Lorenzo" (34).

51. Quoted from Laurenza, *Art and Anatomy*, 36. Bronzino and his fellow Florentines had ample opportunity to educate themselves on and contribute to anatomical investigation through the official auspices of the *Accadema del Disegno*, founded in 1563, which provided facilities for dissection during winter months. See Laurenzo (2012), 33; 36.

52. I offer my gratitude to Dr. George Rudden, M.D., for assistance in identifying the anatomical components of the pala.

53. Laurenza, *Art and Anatomy*, 42–43.

54. Laurenza, *Art and Anatomy*, 13.

55. Laurenza, *Art and Anatomy*, 13.

56. Brock, *Bronzino*, 303.

57. Brock makes the observation that Bronzino's Saint Bartholomew takes basically the same pose as Michelangelo's in the bent legs, folded right arm, and the turned head (Brock, *Bronzino*, 303).

58. Jacobus de Voragine, *The Golden Legend*, 2 vols. (Princeton, NJ: Princeton University Press, 1993), 2:109.

59. On the useful concept of transvaluation, see James J. Liska, *The Semiotic of Myth: A Critical Study of the Symbol* (Bloomington: Indiana University Press, 1989), 14–15.

60. Laurenza, *Art and Anatomy*, 10.

61. On the relationship of sculpture to the *paragone* in the context of Bronzino, one will profit from Janet Cox-Rearick's observations in *Bronzino's Chapel*, 112–18.

62. See Carol Plazzotta, "Bronzino's Laura," *The Burlington Magazine* 140 (April 1998), 252.

63. *Il primo libro delle 'opere toscane*, ed. Enrico Maria Guidi (Urbino: Accademia Raffaello, 2000); *I sette salmi*, ed. Enrico Maria Guidi (Urbino: Accademia Raffaello, 2005).

64. The first line of the sonnet is "Così nel volto rilucente, e vago," *Sonnetti*, ed. Moreni, 6.

65. Richard Thayer Holbrook, *Portraits of Dante: From Giotto to Raffael* (London: Philip Lee Warner, 1911).

66. See Parker, *Bronzino: Renaissance Painter as Poet*, 16, 17, 96–103, Plazzotta, "Bronzino's Laura," 251–63; and Brock, *Bronzino*, 93–101. See also Victoria Kirkham, "Laura Battiferri degli Ammannati's 'First Book' of Poetry: A Renaissance Holograph Comes out of Hiding," *Rinascimento* 36 (1996), 351–91; and Victoria Kirkham, "Dante's Phantom, Petrarch's Specter: Bronzino's Portrait of Poet Laura Battiferra," in *Visibile parlare: Dante and the Art of the Italian Renaissance*, special issue of. *Lectura Dantis*, ed. Deborah Parker, 22–23 (1998), 63–139. Also, Kirkham is the editor and translator of *Laura Battiferra and her Literary Circle: An Anthology* (Chicago, IL: University of Chicago Press, 2006). For an anthology on the ways in which Bronzino makes Battiferri resemble Dante, see Luciano Bellosi, "Il ritratto fiorentino del Cinquecento," in *Firenze e la Toscana dei Medici nell'Europa del Cinquecento: Il Primato del disegno* (Florence: Centro di edizioni, 1980), 45.

67. Brock, *Bronzino*, 96.

68. Brock, *Bronzino*, 100.

69. "Tutta dentro di ferro e furor di ghiaccio," *Sonnetti*, ed. Moreni, 121. Graham Smith observes that the *Battiferri* is unique in Bronzino's works,

since it depicts her in profile, and that Bronzino shows a Laura who is reserved in contrast to the more coy figure in Andrea Del Sarto's *Portrait of a Young Woman with a Volume of Petrarch*. See *Source* 15 (1996), 30–32. Parker points out that the words *dentro* and *fuori* are also found in burlesque and sexual lexicons: "expressions in burlesque poetry indicating interiority or exteriority generally refer to one's proximity to the genitals" (*Bronzino: Renaissance Painter as Poet*, 30). She refers us to Jean Toscan, *Le carnival du langage. Le lexique érotique des poètes de l'équivoque de Burchiello a Marino (XVe–XVIe siècles)* 4 vols. (Lille: Reproduction des thèses, Université de Lille, 1981), 1:435.

70. *Sonnetti*, ed. Moreni, 11, v. 5, 104, v. 2, v. 8.

71. "Che po questi altro? Il mio volt oil consuma./Et perché igordo, et io perché si bella?" (vv. 13–14). *Petrarch's Lyric Poems*, 403.

72. See *The Epitome of Andreas Vesalius*, trans. L.R. Lind, with anatomical notes by C.W. Asling and a foreword by Logan Clendening (New York: Macmillan, 1949). Also, Andreus Vesalius, *Von des menschen cörpers Anatomey* (Basel, 1543), 12. See also Michael Giordano, "The *Blason anatomique* and Related Fields: Emblematics, Nominalism, Mannerism, and Descriptive Anatomy as Illustrated by Maurice Scève's *Blason de la gorge*," in David Graham, ed., *An Interregnum of the Sign: The Emblematic Age in France: Essays in Honor of Daniel S. Russell* (Glasgow: University of Glasgow, 2001), 121–48.

73. Kay, *op. cit.*

74. Claude Lévi-Strauss, *Anthropologie structurale* (Paris: Plon, 1958), 236.

75. Petrucci Nardelli, *Rime in burla*, 379–89.

Fig. 1. Agnolo Bronzino, *Allegory of Venus and Cupid* (*Allegory of Love*), 1544–45. National Gallery, London, Great Britain. Photo credit: National Gallery, London/Art Resource, NY.

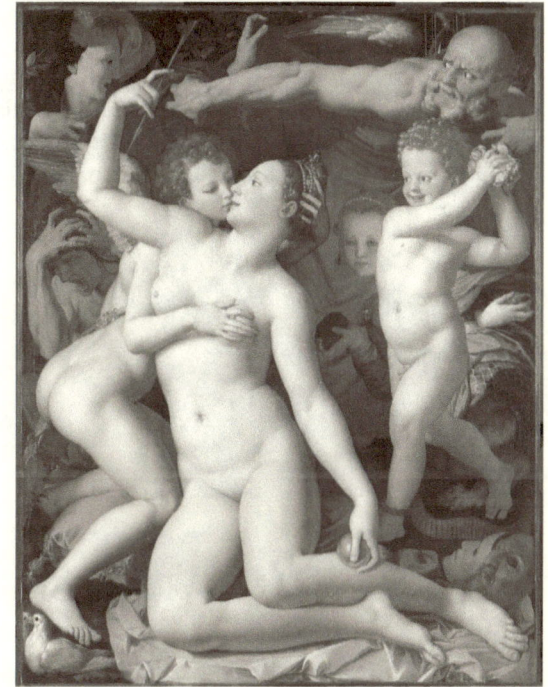

Fig. 2. Agnolo Bronzino, *The Young Man with a Book*, 1530s. Metropolitan Museum of Art, New York. Photo credit: The Metropolitan Museum of Art, NY/Art Resource, NY.

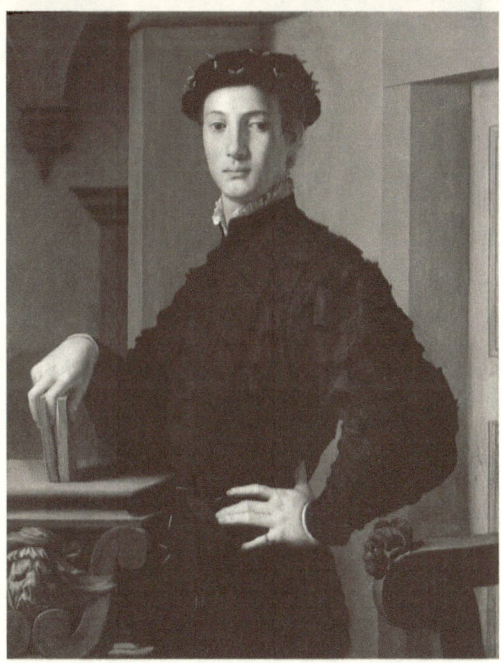

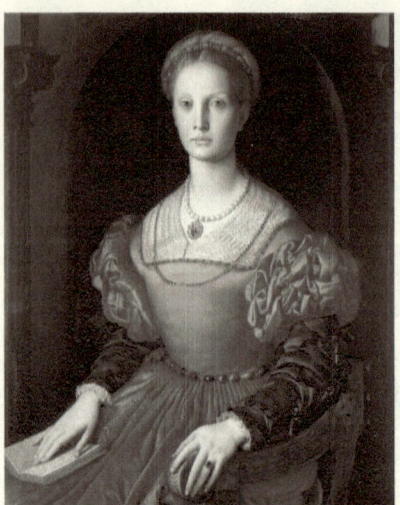

Fig. 3. Agnolo Bronzino, *Portrait of Lucrezia Panciatichi*, 1540–42. Galleria degli Uffizi, Florence. Photo credit: Scala/Ministero per i Beni e le Attività culturali/Art Resource, NY.

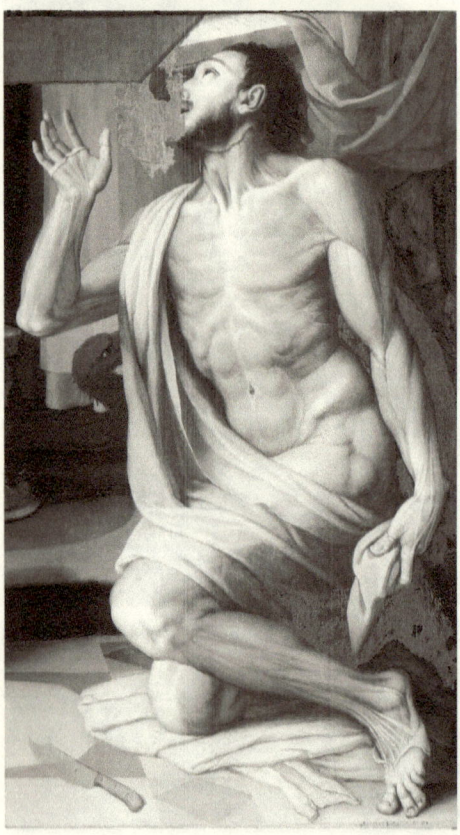

Fig. 4. Agnolo Bronzino, *Saint Bartholomew* (det.), Altar of the Graces, 1554–56. Cathedral of Pisa (now in the Accademia di San Luca, Rome). Photo credit: Scala/ Art Resource, NY.

Fig. 5. Agnolo Bron-
zino, *Laura Battiferri*,
1558. Penelope Room
(Loeser Collection),
Palazzo Vecchio, Flor-
ence. Photo credit:
Scala/Art Resource,
NY.

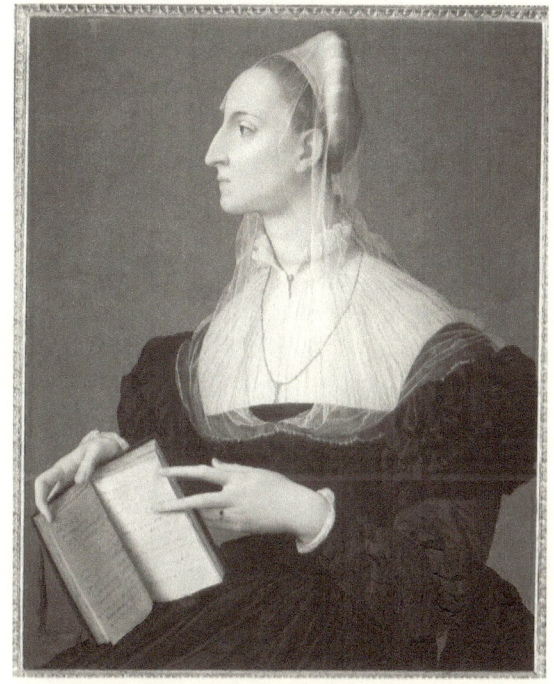

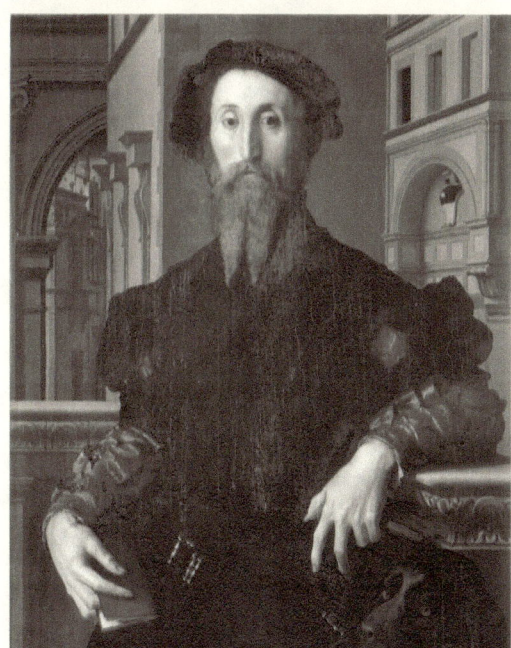

Fig. 6. Agnolo Bronzino,
*Portrait of Bartolomeo
Panciatichi*, 1540–42.
Galleria degli Uffizi,
Florence. Photo credit:
Scala/Art Resource, NY.

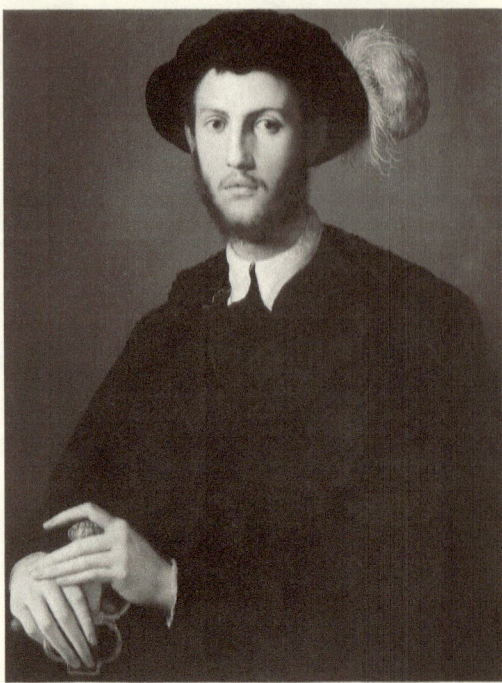

Fig. 7. Agnolo Bronzino, *Portrait of Young Man in a Hat with a Feather*, 1550–55. Nelson Gallery, Kansas City, Kansas. Photo credit: Nelson Gallery, Kansas City, Kansas.

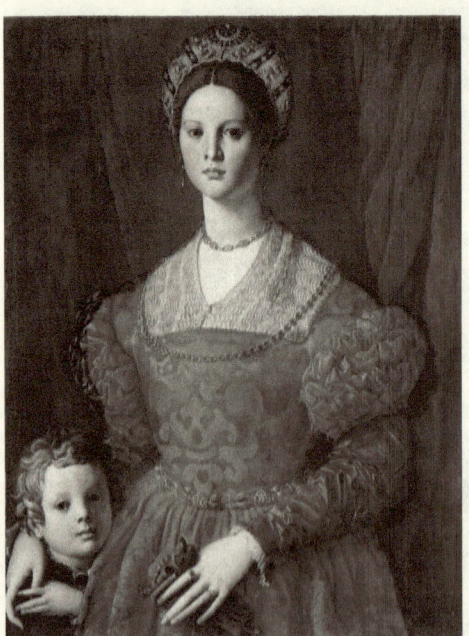

Fig. 8. Agnolo Bronzino, *Lady in a Red Dress with a Little Boy*, 1540. National Gallery of Art, Washington, DC. Photo credit: Album/Art Resource, NY.

Decoding Bronzino's *Portrait of Eleonora di Toledo* (c. 1539): An Iconography of Jewels and Dress

Donna A. Bilak

The Národní Galerie in Prague holds an oil-on-panel portrait by Agnolo Bronzino of Eleonora di Toledo (1522–62), which was created c. 1539 (Fig. 1).[1] Eleonora was the Spanish consort of Cosimo I de' Medici (1519–74), who, on 30 September 1537, at the age of seventeen, was made Duke of Florence by the Holy Roman Emperor Charles V. Over the course of his thirty-seven years in power, Cosimo revitalized Florentine culture, emerging as a renowned patron of artists and intellectuals. He reopened the University of Pisa and, among other cultural initiatives, sponsored the *Accademia Fiorentina* and the *Accademia del Disegno*. Cosimo's achievements earned him his elevation in 1569 to Grand Duke of Tuscany by Pope Pius V at imperial behest, the designation under which he ruled until his death in 1574.

Bronzino's portrait of Eleonora was painted around the time of her marriage to Cosimo in 1539. It is a bust length depiction of the duchess wearing a red-colored dress that is embellished with an embroidered gold border, whose interlacing pattern frames her bodice and shoulders and runs along the length of her sleeves. Eleonora gazes out at the viewer from against a deep *azzurro* blue background made from ground lapis lazuli, her seemingly impassive face and pale marble-like skin a hallmark of Bronzino's style of portraiture. The panel dimensions are 23¼ x 18⅛ inches, or 59 x 46 cm, portraying Eleonora on a life-sized scale, and thus evoking a powerful sense of the duchess's physical presence. We do not know, however, who commissioned it, or where it was originally displayed, or whether it comprised one half of a pendant in which a portrait of Cosimo would have completed a matched pair of pictures.[2] We only know that Eleonora's jewelry and dress in this painting relates to her 1539 wedding to Cosimo and that at some point this portrait became a Hapsburg possession and had made its way into the ducal collection at Konopiště Castle (about 30 miles south-east of Prague) until 1939.[3] A muted reminder of its journey through time and ownership is found at the bottom edge of the portrait where a painted inscription of the number 26, most likely an old inventory number, is faintly visible just below Eleonora's fingers.[4]

This portrait of Eleonora is known to scholarship on the basis of her dress, for it corresponds with the one she is described as wearing in contemporary accounts of her *entrata*, her formal entry, into Florence on 29 June 1539 en route to the wedding festivities at the Palazzo Medici. Yet, despite its significance as a Medici state portrait marking Eleonora's new role as Cosimo's consort, the 1539 painting by Bronzino is eclipsed by his double portrait of the duchess and her second son Giovanni from circa 1545, which is part of the permanent collection at the Galleria degli Uffizi in Florence.[5] Painted about five years into her marriage, here Eleonora wears a sumptuous dress that features a striking pattern of large gold brocade pomegranates boldly accentuated by a framework of interlacing black velvet arabesque scrolls applied to a white satin ground, while her young son (a future cardinal) is resplendent in a dark velvet doublet under which the gold embroidered collar and cuffs of his white shirt, the *camicia*, is visible at his neck and wrists. Eleonora's dress in the 1545 state portrait harnesses sartorial splendor to proclaim the family's dynastic ascendancy within European court culture through the depiction and placement of the pomegranate motif upon the duchess's body. As a focal point upon Eleonora's bodice, this design effectively "emblazoned" her with a traditional symbol of fertility, an association established by virtue of the prodigious quantity of seeds that this fruit contains.[6] Indeed, this symbolic display of the pomegranate dominates Eleonora's upper body, and its central placement upon her bodice assumes heightened significance, for it approximates the area of her womb. Moreover, while parts of an overall pomegranate pattern are visible in the rest of her dress, there is, notably, only one other fully rendered pomegranate in this portrait. This second pomegranate is depicted at a slight angle upon Eleonora's lap. It is located directly below the one that adorns her bodice; however, it is subtly different in design and slightly smaller in size. Bronzino draws the viewer's attention to this second pomegranate by framing its sides with Eleonora's left hand as well as with Giovanni's left hand, which is placed upon his mother's skirt. Symbol and gesture thus work in tandem to signify that, with the birth of her second son, Eleonora's fertility has guaranteed Medici rule into the next generation.[7]

Analysis of Eleonora's grand attire in the 1545 double portrait has ensured its iconic status in art history studies. Comparatively, scholarly opinion contends that the 1539 portrait "is not Bronzino's most splendidly depicted of Eleonora's dresses."[8] Be that as it may, iconographic interpretation of the 1539 portrait reveals the duchess's dress and jewelry to be embedded with auspicious marital symbols; intriguingly, it also contains a discreetly rendered love token worked into the composition. This study, therefore, explores Bronzino's 1539 portrait of Eleonora as a specific visual encapsulation of the decorative program and entertainments that comprised the ducal couple's wedding festivities of 29 June 1539, which were structured around the explicit promotion of a tripartite message of fecundity, security, and continuity, the dynastic promises advanced by the new *principato*. As such, the creation of the 1539 portrait of Eleonora constitutes an important visual document commemorating the series of ceremonial events that marked the nuptial proceedings, establishing this painting as a significant work amongst Bronzino's canon of Medici ducal portraits. Notably, it is also one of Bronzino's first commissions as court painter to Cosimo, a position he held throughout most of the duke's reign.[9] In executing this portrait, Bronzino was vested with the responsibility of introducing the duchess through her painted likeness into the European court system in which Cosimo intended to participate, wherein the circulation of paintings functioned as an important conduit of information and as mode of communicating propaganda among the elite milieu of sixteenth-century European aristocracy. In her capacity as a patroness of state portraits, over the course of her marriage, Eleonora commissioned Bronzino to execute paintings of herself and her children (such as the 1545 Uffizi double portrait) that were intended as diplomatic gifts.[10] Thus, Eleonora demonstrated that, as the ducal consort, she was well attuned to the importance of dress and jewelry as a fundamental vehicle of Medici political representation and the family's declaration of status amongst their European peers.

From a historical standpoint, Bronzino's 1539 portrait of Eleonora contextualizes both the uncertainties and aspirations that characterized the start of Cosimo's rule as Duke of Florence. Eleonora was the second daughter of Signor Don Pedro Alvárez de Toledo, Hapsburg viceroy of Naples and trusted lieutenant of Charles V, and her marriage to Cosimo joined the Neapolitan house of Alvárez to that of the Medici in Florence. Cosimo needed this prestigious connection and its attendant imperial backing to consolidate his own power base, for his rule began in an unstable and volatile political environment, the aggregate of decades of war, invasion, and rival claims to power. Cosimo's political debut occurred on 9 January 1537, when he was unexpectedly elected by the *ottimati*, the civic aristocracy, as "first citizen" of Florence in the wake of Duke Alessandro de' Medici's assassination, which had occurred three days earlier. The Senate had decided to advance Cosimo's candidacy because of his lineage: as the son of Giovanni dalle Bande Nere and Maria Salviati, Cosimo could trace his family tree back to Giovanni di Bicci, founder of the Medici line, from both sides. Even more appealingly, Cosimo was perceived as an untried youth, which powerbrokers thought to use to their advantage. Cosimo, however, had different plans. He swiftly and effectively sidelined the Florentine oligarchs who had mistakenly viewed him as a pliable youth they could control. He also sufficiently impressed the emperor with his decisive action in affirming his rulership in both the Florentine political arena and with the battle at Montemurlo, where the rival Strozzi family and their supporters were defeated, to be granted the ducal title nine months later.[11] Thereafter, Cosimo essentially wanted to "obtain Charles V's favor while simultaneously attempting to eliminate the emperor's presence in Florence."[12] Basically, he wished to rule his duchy without imperial interference, yet he recognized imperial approbation as vitally important to maintaining and extending his power.

From the outset of his investiture as duke, Cosimo and his supporters implemented a carefully crafted program promoting themes of Medici rejuvenation and dynastic continuity designed to uphold his claim to rule through commissioned artworks.[13] Cosimo's personal device, the *broncone* (the laurel branch traditionally associated with the Medici family), aptly encapsulated this propagandistic strategy. The 1559 treatise *Dialogo dell'imprese militari et amorose*, by the Florentine humanist and prelate Paolo Giovio, describes Cosimo's device as a new green shoot of laurel sprouting out from a severed stump, symbolizing the continuity of the Medici dynasty after the murder of his predecessor and cousin, Alessandro.[14] Medici supporters heralded Cosimo's marriage to Eleonora as an assurance of renewal, certainty that a thriving new branch was growing on the Medici laurel. Indeed, the successful promotion of this campaign relied on the fertility of Cosimo's bride, through whom a Medici dynasty would be established. Therefore, Eleonora held a pivotal role as the vessel through which legitimate Medici heirs would issue, ensuring the family's continued rule into future generations—so went the rhetoric.

Even as the union between Cosimo and Eleonora was a strategic alliance, by all accounts it was also an early modern love story, an unusual circumstance in the pre-modern marriage contract.[15] The Florentine ambassador at the Spanish court, Giovanni Bandini, was Cosimo's advisor in the matter of seeking a suitable bride, for the match had to reflect Cosimo's imperial loyalty as well as his political and cultural aspirations in his duchy.[16] Cosimo's first choice was Margaret of Austria, Alessandro de' Medici's widow and the emperor's natural daughter, but his hopes for this match ended in 1538 when Charles V decided that she was to marry the grandson of Pope Paul III, Ottaviano Farnese. The emperor's viceroy, Don Pedro de Toledo, however, had two marriageable daughters, Isabella and Eleonora. Cosimo had seen Eleonora, the younger and prettier of the two sisters, when he accompanied his cousin Alessandro on a visit to Naples in 1535, and while Bandini secured Don Pedro's approval for Cosimo to marry Isabella, the young duke insisted on a union with Eleonora. "No sooner was the agreement reached than Eleonora and Cosimo began to correspond and she, for one, visibly showed her pleasure at the match and her growing love for the groom."[17] At a time when marriages were used as a political tool to gain titles, territory, and power, contemporary observers noted the ducal couple's loving union with wonder.

Cosimo and Eleonora's marriage unfolded in stages over the course of several months in accordance with Florentine marriage custom, which was characterized by its secular nature.[18] Once the match had been proposed, dowry negotiations were undertaken, followed by the promise before witnesses. In this case, once Cosimo's representatives reached an agreement with Don Pedro for Eleonora, a proxy wedding was held in Naples on 29 March, which was contractually sealed by the presentation of the gift of a diamond ring to Eleonora by Iacopo de' Medici and Luigi Ridolfi on Cosimo's behalf. Thereafter, Eleonora's ceremonial public transfer from her family home in Naples to her new home in Tuscany transpired when she arrived in Livorno on 25 June with a fleet of seven galleys (she was accompanied by her brother Garcia as well as her retinue of Spanish nobles and their servants), whereupon she was greeted by Onofrio Bartolini de' Medici, the archbishop of Pisa. Later that day, Cosimo met her with an entourage of Florentine nobles. On 29 June, they journeyed from the Medici villa at Poggio a Caiano to Florence for the wedding festivities. Eleonora's formal entry into the city and public procession, the *ductio*, on this day was a critical part of the traditional wedding ceremony, in which the groom led his bride through the streets under the eyes of all the community to his house. Indeed, the *ductio* was a vitally important public event and a crucial point within the wedding procedure, for it constituted the moment of display when the public saw the bride, who "sartorially embodied the honor of the entire social transaction."[19] For this occasion, Eleonora is recorded as having worn a crimson satin dress with gold embroidery that had been chosen by Cosimo, as was his right as the groom. The ensuing wedding festivities completed the cycle of Cosimo and Eleonora's nuptial ceremonies, which culminated in the production of a theatrical entertainment created for the marriage as well as a banquet held at the Palazzo Medici.

Let us now undertake a close examination of Bronzino's 1539 portrait of Eleonora di Toledo, for its details and composition are key to unlocking its relationship with the ducal wedding and to illuminating the aims of the new *principato* that this union was to bring about. From this perspective, Eleonora's dress and jewelry come together as a masterpiece of statecraft. The duchess is depicted in the fashionable *moda alla spagnola*, as it was known to Cinquecento contemporaries, which dominated Italian fashion for both men and women at the time. The crowning of Charles V in 1530 had fueled its taste in Italy, and Eleonora's dress and adornment embodies the Spanish style in every respect. Her cap-like head covering, the *cuffia* (called *cofia* in Spanish) is designed as a braided gold net decorated with pearls. The duchess's hairstyle features a center part from which extends a row of narrow rolled braids that edge the top of her brow, and her hair is swept back over her pierced ears, which are adorned with large drop-pearl earrings suspended from gold hoops. The neckline of Eleonora's dress is squared in shape, although there is a slight upward curve to its line, a characteristic of the *moda alla spagnola*. Eleonora's bodice and sleeves feature a wide embroidered gold border, whose raised design creates an embossed effect upon the fabric. A fashionable form of embellishment, such embroidery typically used gold thread, either drawn or spun or *de orilla*.[20]

Bronzino has subtly angled Eleonora's body to her right, affecting a position that shows off her left sleeve. The *spagnolesco* dress sleeves ("sleeves in the Spanish style") are attached to the shoulders by ribbons tied into double-looped bows.[21] The sleeves themselves are puffed and slashed, decorated with aglets designed as pearl pins interspersed with gold balls of matching size. This type of jewelry was a functional and ubiquitous fashion accessory for both men and women throughout Europe.[22] Typically pinned, sewn, or tied with ribbon in clusters to the clothing (usually upon the sleeves, but they were also popular as hat ornaments), aglets were decorative, small-sized perforated metal receptacles designed as two fitted halves, which contained tiny scented balls that perfumed the immediate air around the wearer. Aglets were commonly filled with pieces of ambergris or other such pungent materials as gum amalgam scented with musk, and the gold balls that were placed in between the pearls that comprised Eleonora's aglets would have held such aromatic substances.[23] The duchess's décolletage is covered up by a lattice-like partlet (*gorguera* in Spanish).[24] It is made of a heavy netting of blue silk cord and raised loops of gold thread (a type of stitch called *punto real* in Spanish) set atop a fine, sheer, net-like foundation.[25] Eleonora's partlet is also studded with pearls at the interstices, thus matching her *cuffia*, and it features a modest V-shaped opening at the front that has an upturned collar at her neck. Just below the collar, near the base of Eleonora's throat, a light blue-colored cord is threaded into the edges of the partlet. It features a double knot that is placed in the middle of her neck, tied in such a manner that it creates a single loop, leaving the two ends of the cord to dangle from below the knot. The edge of Eleonora's chemise is just visible over the top of her bodice, and it is finished with a delicate embroidered band (called a *cabezón* in Spanish), whose pattern is also seen on the edge of the cuff that encircles her right wrist. This effectively draws attention to the duchess's right hand, which is placed upon her midriff, showcasing the large table-cut diamond ring that adorns her forefinger and the intaglio onyx ring upon her fifth finger.[26]

Symmetry of form distinguishes this portrait of Eleonora, and Bronzino's sense of balance and proportion in rendering the duchess's dress and figure is representative of established tenets of Cinquecento beauty. These were codified in the 1552 publication of Agnolo Firenzuola's *Dialogo delle bellezze donne*, which considered and evaluated the female body according to discrete parts that possessed particular characteristics. This idealized concept of outer beauty signaled inner virtue, embodied as the attributes *leggiadria*, *grazia*, *vaghezza* (elegance, grace, charm). These qualities were enhanced, and proclaimed, by fashionable attire. Eleonora exemplifies this Cinquecento feminine ideal. Her inner virtue is made manifest by her beautiful outer appearance, befitting of a woman of her noble rank as the daughter of a Spanish aristocrat and the consort of the Duke of Florence. In accordance with this cultural construct of beauty, the duchess's jewelry calls attention to her various body parts, enhancing their fine features. Notice that the bejeweled partlet coordinates with the *cuffia*, effectively creating a golden aureole about the duchess's head and shoulders and casting a radiant glow about her face. Observe the way in which the pearl-and-gold aglets decorate the sleeves, and thus adorn her arms. Look how the drop-pearl earrings accentuate Eleonora's dainty ears and graceful neck, delicately filling in this space. And see how the eye is drawn to Eleonora's shapely hand, whose elegant fingers are decorated by rings. Their prominent display is highlighted by Bronzino's careful positioning of the duchess's fingers. Her bejeweled index and fifth fingers are slightly separated from the others, and her thumb has been tucked behind her palm to better foreground the two rings.

Indeed, these two rings form a point of convergence within the painting as the very manifestation of Eleonora and Cosimo's conjugal union. In this, each ring represents a discrete embodiment of particular elements from the wedding process. The diamond ring on Eleonora's index finger marks her as a Medici consort because of this gemstone's direct association with the *impresa* used by Medici family members since the mid-Quattrocento.[27] Moreover, it is likely the same one that Eleonora received from Cosimo's representatives at the 29 March proxy ceremony in Naples. In this context, this piece of jewelry was not only an appropriate Medici gift but also constituted a legal document of this event, as the wedding procedure required such a token as witness to the contract between Cosimo, as the groom, and Eleonora's father, Don Pedro. Its presence in this portrait makes a pointed proclamation of Medici dynastic continuity, which dictated the thematic scope of the wedding festivities four months later: the diamond's unsurpassable durability paired with the Medici motto, *semper*, formulates a fitting symbol of Eternity.[28]

The intaglio ring depicted on Eleonora's fifth finger survives, and it is on display at the Museo degli Argenti in Florence.[29] The term "intaglio" refers to a type of carved gemstone that features a flat surface into which the design is engraved. An intaglio is generally created for use as a seal, in which case the design is carved in reverse, thereby rendering an embossed impression when pressed into a malleable substance, like wax.[30] Eleonora's intaglio is carved from banded onyx, a variety of agate comprised of alternating layers of white and black that occur as straight, parallel bands within the stone. The intaglio's white-and-black aesthetic was achieved by slicing the hardstone along its horizontal axis so as to feature a white surface in which the incised design appears in black (i.e., the next layer beneath the white stratum). Eleonora's intaglio is oval-shaped and bezel-set (a type of setting referring to the rim of metal that surrounds the stone and is pushed over the stone's edges to hold it in place). The ring's shank (the term for the metal hoop that encircles the finger) shows traces of colored enamel.

Eleonora's intaglio is set in gold. While its setting is contemporary, the stone is Roman, its iconography dating to the Augustan period.[31] The engraved design on this intaglio is symmetrically arranged, depicting two cornucopiae that flank a circular-shaped altar surmounted by a bird (possibly the raven, which was sacred to Apollo), below which two conjoined hands fill the space in the stone's lower register.[32] These classical symbols articulate propitious marital augurs. The cornucopia is a signifier for abundance and fertility through its association with the horns of Amalthea, the goat which nursed the infant Jupiter in Crete. The cornucopiae featured in Eleonora's intaglio are distinguished by an ear of corn that juts out the top of each horn, another symbol of plenty, and the opening of each horn is further embellished with what may be a pair of poppies. A sphere-shaped element dots the lowermost point of both horns, possibly put forth by contemporaries as an allusion to the *palle* from the Medici *stemma*.[33] Conjoined hands have been a traditional symbol of matrimony since antiquity, its typology expressed in a variety of media during the Renaissance. Lorenzo Lotto's 1523 double portrait of Messer Marsilio and his wife Faustina (Museo Nacional del Prado, Madrid) provides a representative depiction of conjugal concord and fidelity. It features the couple clasping their left hands together while the husband holds a ring between his right thumb and forefinger, their union encapsulated in its display. Cupid flutters above the couple, his arms stretched wide and his hands placed by either side of them, framing them in his embrace. The material representation of conjugal fidelity is also embodied in the ring type known as the fede ring, which bears the device known as the *dextrarum iunctio*, the clasped hands, understood as a symbol of faith since antiquity. The fede ring is characterized by the way in which the clasped hands join the shank into a single, unbroken circle; typically, the clasped hands in the fede ring are molded into the shank, rather than being executed as a design engraved in the metal. Fede rings were in vogue throughout Europe from about the twelfth to the eighteenth centuries, and they were used for betrothal or given as token of affection.[34] Such rings could also be decorated with gemstones, and often featured amatory inscriptions engraved on the inside of the shank.

The decoration on the exterior of a ring's shank is an important

site of information. On this point, the design of the shank on Eleonora's ring provides valuable insight into its meaning and function as a civic symbol, for its shoulders are designed as fleur-de-
lis that appear on either side of the intaglio, joining the band to
the bezel. Could this decorative element be a reference to the *giglio
rosso*, the red Florentine lily? Compelling material evidence argues
in favor of this interpretation. Designed as the stylized three-leaved
lily, the fleur-de-lis, or Florentine lily, appears on the city's coat
of arms; it decorates the Palazzo Vecchio and the Santa Maria del
Fiore, important Florentine administrative and ecclesiastical centers; and, moreover, its image was disseminated throughout the
wider world, as it was stamped on the obverse of the *florin*, the gold
coin issued from Florence. From this standpoint, the two fleur-de-
lis terminals in the duchess's intaglio ring constitute an appropriate
design element that proclaim Eleonora as a Florentine through her
marriage to Cosimo. Symbolically, then, this ring represented Florence as a civic entity that surrounded the duchess in her new role
as Cosimo's consort.

We can surmise that the diamond ring depicted in Eleonora's
portrait relates to the one she received from Cosimo's representatives in Naples in March 1539. We do not know, however, where
the intaglio ring came from, or who presented it to her. Nonetheless, the engraved symbols in this intaglio ring, together with the
design of the shank, reflect the allegorical program of the June wedding festivities, hence its inclusion in this portrait. The significance
of both rings in representing these aspects of Eleonora's union with
Cosimo deepen, owing to their placement on the duchess's right
hand. This is the oath-giving hand, and, as such, it is the hand that
signifies fidelity.[35]

The full account of Cosimo and Eleonora's June wedding was
assembled by the Florentine court humanist Pierfrancesco Giambullari and presented as a detailed letter to Giovanni Bandini, Cosimo's ambassador to Charles V. This was published shortly after the
event in August 1539 as the *Apparato et feste nelle nozze del Illustrissimo Signor Duca di Firenze, et della Duchessa sua consorte, con le sue
Stanze, Madriali, Comedia, et Intermedii, in quelle recitati.*[36] In all likeli-
hood, Giambullari was charged either by Cosimo or a Medici advisor to document the wedding festivities, because such publications

were not yet *de rigeur* (they would, however, become extremely fashionable by the late sixteenth and seventeenth centuries).[37] But it is noteworthy that Giambullari addressed this work to Bandini, indicating Cosimo's desire to have the details of his wedding known to the emperor.

Giambullari's text recreates the experiences, sights, and sounds that characterized the wedding festivities as they came to pass on 29 June 1539. According to his account, Cosimo and Eleonora set out that morning from the Medici villa at Poggio a Caiano for the Palazzo Medici in Florence, where the festivities were to take place. Their splendid horseback procession was attended by trumpeting heralds and a military escort, as well as the Florentine elite resplendent in their finest attire and arranged in pairs on their horses, their liveried servants following on foot. Upon reaching the outer limits of Florence, they separated just before the city gate, the Porta al Prato, for Cosimo went ahead to the palace in order to formally welcome his bride into his home in accordance with Florentine marital custom. Left with a select company of thirty-six nobles in peacock-blue and crimson livery (the Toledan and Medicean colors), Eleonora, dressed in "crimson satin, richly embroidered all over with beaten gold" was greeted with a resounding artillery salute at the Prato Gate.[38] At this point, Giambullari tells us that Eleonora encountered a great, ornately decorated entryway designed as an Arch of Triumph. This edifice was constructed as an elaborate, tiered Doric composition that consisted of a base of pilasters, an architrave, a frieze, and a cornice. It was created by a team of artists specifically to mark Eleonora's formal entry into Florence as Cosimo's bride, and, as an ephemeral construction, it was made from painted wood, plaster, papier-mâché, and canvas; the entire edifice was dismantled after the festivities. The many artists who participated in its fabrication are immortalized in Vasari's *Vite* of Il Tribolo, and of Bastiano San Gallo.

Giambullari gives an exacting account of the Arch's complex iconographic program. Essentially, its narrative scheme used classical allegory and "Dantesque allusions" to convey the message that a renewed Medici line "would be assured by the children Eleonora would bear," and it also underscored the political importance of Cosimo and Eleonora's families and their connections to the Holy

Roman Empire.[39] Next, Giambullari recounts Eleonora's procession through this majestic monument, teeming with allegorical imagery and classical inscriptions. He draws especial focus to the "stories" that decorated its frontispiece, highlighting this all-important element of the Arch for the reader: "We shall describe these in detail, beginning with that part which was first visible to a person arriving."[40] Thus we learn that the frontispiece is dominated by a large, centrally placed female figure representing Fecundity, who is flanked by two other female figures representing Security (on the right) and Eternity (to the left). Security holds a small branch in her hand that signifies Cosimo's personal device, the *broncone*, while Eternity tramples Time under her feet, depicted as a hairy old man who holds the sun and moon.[41] Giambullari goes on to detail the subsidiary components of the Arch's narrative scheme, but it is significant that Fecundity holds center stage, because the *pubblico bene*, the public welfare of Florence, was dependent on the fecundity of Eleonora.[42] Her future sons and daughters would secure Florence's place in Europe's political arena via marriage or Church careers.

Just past Eleonora's Arch of Triumph, Giambullari relates, are boxed areas positioned on both sides of the processional aisle for the musicians and singers:[43]

> who, at the arrival of Her Excellency, sang as a motet these words, which could be read in carved antique letters in the main frieze of the arch ... INGREDERE INGREDERE FOELICISS. AUSPICIIS URBEM TUAM HELIONORA AC OPTIMAE PROLIS FOECUNDA ITA DOMI SIMILEM PATRI FORIS AVO SOBOLEM PRODUCAS UT MEDICEO NOMINI EIUSQUE DEVOTISS. CIVIBUS SECURITATEM PRAESTES AETERNAM.
>
> ("Enter, enter your city, Eleonora, under the guidance of these most auspicious signs. And, fruitful in excellent offspring, may you produce descendants similar in quality to your father and forebears abroad, so that you may guarantee eternal security for the Medici name and its most devoted citizenry.")

The elaborate allegorical schema that marked Eleonora's entry into Florence through the Arch of Triumph was thus animated by musicians, actors, and dancers. Collectively, the artists and entertainers involved in the festivities of 29 June created a multimedia event that transformed the city of Florence into an *all'antica* vision. Eleonora's Arch of Triumph entwined ancient and contemporary history into a living picture orchestrated to express the hopes and aims of the new *principato* to its citizens.

Giambullari's text revolves around the Medici message of renewal and dynastic continuity, which was conveyed visually by the three figures of Fecundity, Security, and Eternity in the Arch of Triumph and aurally reinforced by the musicians who performed nearby. Significantly, Giambullari's emphasis on the sights and sounds that imbued the Arch with meaning points to a deeper dimension and inherent function of its symbolic program. The key lies with the words "most auspicious signs" (*felicissimis auspiciis*), which were both inscribed in the artwork that surrounded Eleonora inside the Arch and also sung to her as she processed in state through this monumental apparatus. In keeping with the contemporary understanding of how the human anatomy worked, these "most auspicious signs"—Fecundity, Security, Eternity—were being impressed, literally, upon the mind and body of the young bride. How? Early modern society understood the five senses as being conduits of external substances into the body through sight, smell, sound, taste, and touch.[44] These sensations were held to interact with the human mind, organs, and spirit in ways that were either beneficial or harmful to the individual's state of health. These medical ideas were rooted in Galenic and Hippocratic authority and exerted deep influence upon pre-modern cultural constructs of what promoted good health and caused bad health. Renaissance Florentine society operated within this framework of heightened awareness about the impact that environment and experience exerted upon an individual's state of well-being through sensory perception. This idea is especially evident in the kinds of talismans and rituals that Florentine women utilized during pregnancy in seeking to avoid the "visual contagion" afforded by seeing horrific images, as well as in the desire of the newly wedded bride to "visually imprint" herself with positive images by contemplating the beauty of naked men and women depicted inside of *cassone* lids, with the intent of conceiving a beautiful child.[45]

From such perspectives, it is therefore of utmost significance that the first thing Eleonora *sees* upon reaching Florence is the Arch of Triumph, radiating with symbols of fertility and everlasting peace that the new Medici rule promised to bring through this marriage. And the first thing that Eleonora *hears* upon entering into the city is the motet whose lyrics overlaid the very words inscribed upon the Arch. Both the triumphal entryway and its musical accompaniment were expressly designed for Eleonora's personal experience as she crossed the threshold of the Prato Gate into her new city, an action laden with meaning as she literally stepped into her new political role as a Medici consort. Thus, Eleonora commenced her new relationship with Florence and its citizens as the ducal wife in the place where her husband was the ruler. With her entry into the city through the Arch of Triumph, the city itself was party to this celebration, and the people whom Giambullari described as cramming the streets of Eleonora's processional route amplified the Arch's message with their shouted wishes for the bride's fertility on this joyous occasion.[46]

Just as Giambullari described the allegorized program of Medici dynastic ambition in his letter to Bandini, so too did Bronzino articulate this message in paint. His portrait of Eleonora is the material representation of the symbols about fertility and continuity that characterized the duchess's entry into Florence, made manifest in the two rings placed upon her right hand. Bronzino elegantly guides our eye to these rings by means of an implied vertical line that runs down the central axis of the painting, using the duchess's body and dress in its establishment. Thus, the line begins at the top of the portrait with the center part in Eleonora's hair, and it travels down the tapered edges of her partlet, which, arrow-like, point directly to the gold-embroidered border that runs horizontally along the top of her bodice. The embroidered segment that this line pinpoints is formed as a pair of entwined, back-to-back "C"s, for "Cosimo." A closer look at the embroidered border reveals that it delineates a repeating pattern of the monogram:

CMƆ

The centrally placed letter "M" is flanked on either side by the letter "C" to represent Cosimo de' Medici's initials, creating a motif that is duplicated across the duchess's bodice, shoulders, and sleeves like an intricate chain of golden links. An extant table-cut diamond intaglio engraved with Cosimo's initials provides a concrete example of his official monogram, and it is part of the permanent collection at the Museo degli Argenti.[47] This engraved gemstone features the uppercase letter "M" upon which is superimposed a reverse-carved uppercase "C," and the monogram is surmounted by the Grand Ducal crown. In the examples presented pictorially by the embroidery upon Eleonora's dress and in Cosimo's extant diamond intaglio, the "M" is the focal element of the initial's design, proclaiming the family name.

Bronzino's subtle line thus crosses through the pair of entwined "C"s located at the center of the embroidered border and terminates at the two vertically stacked rings upon the duchess's fingers at the bottom of the painting. From a compositional standpoint, Eleonora's dress, appropriately, forms a backdrop for her two finger rings, and the embroidered gold monogram of her husband's name becomes their frame. But Bronzino's implicit vertical pathway also passes through another symbol: the knotted blue cord at Eleonora's throat. In emblematic terms, this is a love knot, representing the joining of two souls (embodied by the two dangling ends) bound together as one (the double knot) through marriage, a popular concept that was expressed in contemporary lyric poetry. This distinctive knot is ubiquitous in Renaissance images of Cupid, as it ties together the ribbon that fastens his quiver to his body, which is full of the arrows he uses to pierce human hearts. Once again, Lorenzo Lotto provides us with contemporary insight into Renaissance marital symbolism through his painting *Venus and Cupid*, which was most likely executed to commemorate a Venetian wedding from the 1520s and that is in the collection of Metropolitan Museum of Art. Cupid's quiver is tied to his torso with a green ribbon, whereby the knot is prominently displayed at his right shoulder, the dexter side signifying the position of honor and fidelity. Cupid's right side is lent even greater significance in this painting, for he holds his tiny penis between his right-hand thumb and forefinger as he playfully urinates upon Venus in a symbolic gesture of fertility. Cupid's love knot is also featured in Lotto's double portrait of Messer Marsilio and his wife, in which the god of love is depicted as hovering behind the couple, his quiver just visible behind him, this time tied to his chest with a yellow ribbon. Here, the love knot is positioned below Cupid's smiling face, and it is in alignment with the ring held in M. Marsilio's right hand; its two dangling ends point to the right and left, that is, to the husband and wife, respectively. Consequently, the location of the love knot within a painting holds specific implications for the sitter(s) depicted therein. In Bronzino's portrait of Eleonora, the duchess's love knot is delicately rendered at her throat, directly below her lips. In this way, Eleonora eloquently voices her love for Cosimo in the painting.

Bronzino's 1539 portrait of Eleonora di Toledo can thus be read according to the information that is embedded along the central axis of the painting. In descending order, we encounter the love knot, the entwined "C"s, the diamond ring, and the intaglio ring. Collectively, these elements evoke the celebration of the ducal marriage with its promise of good government, and Eleonora's own expression of love for her husband, Cosimo, captured by Bronzino's brush.

NOTES

1. Bronzino's painting of Eleonora di Toledo (c. 1539) is part of the permanent collection in Prague at the Národní Galerie (NG), inventory no. O 11971. I wish to thank Liana De Girolami Cheney for the opportunity to present my research about Eleonora di Toledo's jewelry in this portrait at the 2005 Renaissance Society of America meeting in Cambridge, UK ("Emblematic Jewellery in Bronzino's Portrait of Eleonora di Toledo") as well as at the 2008 RSA Chicago meeting ("Visual Narration in Bronzino's Portraiture"). I am indebted to Thomas V. Cohen for providing valuable critique on this study in earlier stages.

2. For a useful discussion about Bronzino's 1539 portrait of Eleonora and the issue of possible pendant matches with portraits of Cosimo, see Carl Brandon Strehlke, *Pontormo, Bronzino, and the Medici: The Transformation of the Renaissance Portrait in Florence* (Philadelphia: Philadelphia Museum of Art in assoc. with the Pennsylvania State University Press, 2004), 136.

3. Ibid., 136.

4. Ibid., 136. Strehlke notes that the inscription of the number 26 "is probably an old inventory number, though Janet Cox-Rearick interpreted

it as Eleonora's age, which would date the portrait to 1545"; see p.138, no. 3, for Strehlke's citation of Cox-Rearick's argument in *Bronzino's Chapel of Eleonora in the Palazzo Vecchio* (Berkeley: University of California Press, 1993), 22–23. Maria Sframeli, *I gioielli dei Medici dal vero e in ritratto* (Livorno: Sillabe, 2003), 64, dates the NG portrait of Eleonora to 1543, following the reassignation of her birth date to 1519 as proposed in Cox-Rearick, "Bronzino's *Young Woman with Her Little Boy*," *Studies in the History of Art* 12 (1982), 79, no. 20.

5. For discussion about Eleonora's dress in the c. 1545 double portrait and the political signification of its design and material to Cosimo's cultural program of Medici rejuvenation and dynasty, see Karla Langedijk, *Portraits of the Medici: 15th–18th Centuries*, vol. 1 (Florence: Studio per edizioni Scelte, 1981), 98–99; Gabrielle Langdon, *Medici Women: Portraits of Power, Love and Betrayal from the Court of Duke Cosimo I* (Toronto: University of Toronto Press, 2006), especially Ch. 2, "Declarations of Dynasty: The State Portrait of Eleonora di Toledo," 59–97; and Cox-Rearick, "Power-Dressing at the Courts of Cosimo de' Medici and François I: The 'moda alla spagnola' of Spanish Consorts Eléonore d'Autriche and Eleonora di Toledo," *Artibus et Historiae* 30, no. 60 (2009), 56–57.

6. Cox-Rearick, "Power-Dressing," 56. See Heather L. Sale Holian, "Family Jewels: The Gendered Marking of Medici Women in Court Portraits of the Late Renaissance," *Mediterranean Studies Journal* 17 (2008), 156–58, for discussion about Eleonora and the practice of her political marking as a Medici consort through jewelry.

7. Konrad Eisenbichler, *The Cultural World of Eleanora di Toledo: Duchess of Florence and Siena*, ed. Konrad Eisenbichler (Aldershot: Ashgate, 2004), 4: "In the course of a long and happy marriage, Eleonora and Cosimo had eleven children together: Maria (1540–57), Francesco (1541–87), Isabella (1542–76), Giovanni (1543–62), Lucrezia (1545–61), Pedricco (1546–47), Garzia (1547–62), Antonio (1548), Ferdinando (1549–1609), Anna (1553) and Pietro (1554–1604)." Langedijk, *Portraits of the Medici*, 98, omits Pedricco, Antonio, and Anna. Ladislav Daniel, *The Florentines: Art from the Time of the Medici Grand Dukes* (Prague: Národní Galerie v Praze, 2002), 54, also counts eight children.

8. Strehlke, *Pontormo, Bronzino, and the Medici*, 136.

9. Bruce Edelstein, "Bronzino in the Service of Eleonora di Toledo and Cosimo I de' Medici: Conjugal Patronage and the Painter-Courtier," in *Beyond Isabella: Secular Women Patrons of Art in Renaissance Italy*, eds. Sheryl E. Reiss and David G. Wilkins (Kirksville, MO: Truman State University Press, 2001), 240: "Between 1539 and 1553 Bronzino executed projects alternately for the duke and duchess with almost surprising regularity." Francesca de Luca, "Bronzino in Florentine Dynastic Collections: *diligenza*

and *prestezza*," in *Bronzino: Artist and Poet at the Court of the Medici*, eds. Carlo Falciani and Antonio Natali (Florence: Mandragora, 2010), 341, notes that by the 1560s, Bronzino was no longer on the duke's payroll, although Cosimo "indulged the elderly painter" by having him work on "demanding public projects" during this period.

10. Edelstein, "Bronzino in the Service of Eleonora di Toledo and Cosimo I de' Medici," 225. See de Luca, "Bronzino in Florentine Dynastic Collections," 339, for discussion about Bronzino's portraits of the Medici family as diplomatic gifts.

11. See Eisenbichler "Introduction," in *Cultural Politics of Duke Cosimo I de' Medici*, ed. Konrad Eisenbichler (Aldershot: Ashgate, 2001), xi and xii; and John M. Najemy, *A History of Florence 1200–1575* (Malden: Blackwell, 2006), especially Ch.15, "The Last Republic and the Medici Duchy," 446–85.

12. Elizabeth Pilliod, "Cosimo and the Arts," in *Florence*, ed. Francis Ames-Lewis (Cambridge: Cambridge University Press, 2012), 332.

13. Langdon, *Medici Women*, 59.

14. Paolo Giovio, *Dialogo dell'imprese militari et amorose di monsignor Giovio ... con la tavola* (Lyon, 1559), 52–53.

15. Mary A. Watt, "*Veni, sponsa*: Love and Politics at the Wedding of Eleonora di Toledo," in *The Cultural World of Eleanora di Toledo: Duchess of Florence and Siena*, ed. Konrad Eisenbichler (Aldershot: Ashgate, 2004), 18–20.

16. Ibid., 19.

17. Eisenbichler, "Introduction," *Cultural World of Eleanora*, 4.

18. See Christiane Klapisch-Zuber, Ch.10, "The Griselda Complex: Dowry and Marriage Gifts in the Quattrocento," in *Women, Family, and Ritual in Renaissance Italy*, trans. Lydia Cochrane (Chicago, IL: University of Chicago Press, 1987), 213–46. Carole Collier Frick, Ch.6, "The Making of Wedding Gowns," in *Dressing Renaissance Florence: Families, Fortunes, and Fine Clothing* (Baltimore, MD: Johns Hopkins University Press, 2002), 115–32, provides a succinct synopsis of the Florentine Quattrocento ceremony and stages marriage and its sartorial culture.

19. Collier Frick, *Dressing Renaissance Florence*, 116.

20. Ruth Matilda Anderson, *Hispanic Costume* (New York: Hispanic Society of America, 1979), 205.

21. Collier Frick, *Dressing Renaissance Florence*, 132.

22. Harold Newman, *An Illustrated Dictionary of Jewelry* (London: Thames and Hudson, 1981), 13.

23. For contemporary recipes about how to make or refresh scented balls for aglets, pomanders, and paternosters, see Gioanventura Rosetti, *Notandissimi secreti de l'arte profumatoria: per far ogli, acque, paste, balle, mo-*

scardini, vccelletti, paternostri, e tutta l'arte intiera, come si ricerca, cosi nella cit-tà di Napoli del Reame, come in Roma, e quini in la città di Vinegia nuouamente ristampati (Venice, 1560).

24. Anderson, *Hispanic Costume*, 181.

25. Ibid., 185.

26. The term "table" was used since the fifteenth century to describe the large, flat central facet on the top of the diamond; for detailed discussion about pre-modern table-cut diamonds, see Herbert Tillander, *Diamond Cuts in Historic Jewellery 1381–1910* (London: Art Books International, 1995), 102–21.

27. Francis Ames-Lewis, "Early Medicean Devices," *Journal of the Warburg and Courtauld Institutes* 42 (1979), 126–31.

28. Ibid., 129: "The diamond ring, the device used by all members of the Medici family from the middle of the fifteenth century onwards and evidently not personal to any particular individual, traditionally symbolizes Eternity."

29. Firenze, Palazzo Pitti, Museo degli Argenti, inv. Depositi, 95. See Constanza Contu's catalogue entry in Sframeli, *I gioielli dei Medici*, 67, for a detailed image of Eleonora's intaglio ring, which is described as "calcedonio, oro con tracce di smalto; diam. mm 22." Contu is incorrect in describing the intaglio's circular altar as "un vasetto all'antica." Strehlke (*Pontormo, Bronzino, and the Medici*, 136) and Cox-Rearick ("Power-Dressing," 53) erroneously use the designation cameo to describe Eleonora's ring instead of intaglio.

30. For a detailed discussion about the materiality of seals, sealing practices, and their relationship with identity in pre-modern Europe, see Brigitte Miriam Bedos-Rezak, "In Search of a Semiotic Paradigm: The Matter of Sealing in Medieval Thought and Praxis (1050–1400)," in *Good Impressions: Image and Authority in Medieval Seals*, eds. Noël Adams, John Cherry, and James Robinson (London: British Museum, 2008), 1–8.

31. I am grateful to Michel Cottier (University of Toronto, Department of Classics) for providing valuable assistance in the dating and identification of the iconographic elements of this intaglio.

32. See the commentary in Andrew C. Minor and Bonner Mitchell, where the authors propose that the image of the bird in the stone's upper register is likely the crow, a symbol of weddings since antiquity; *Renaissance Entertainment: Festivities for the Marriage of Cosimo I, Duke of Florence, in 1539. An edition of the music, poetry, comedy, and descriptive account, with commentary by Andrew C. Minor and Bonner Mitchell* (Columbia: University of Missouri Press, 1968), 135.

33. Sframeli, *I gioielli dei Medici*, 67.

34. Newman, *Illustrated Dictionary of Jewelry*, 122. Sframeli, *I gioielli dei*

Medici, 67, provides a sixtenth-century example of an "anello d'oro con mani in fede."

35. The epigram that accompanies the emblem "Concordia" [B4r] in Andreas Alciati's *Emblematum liber* (Augsburg, 1531) elucidates the concept of the right hand as the oath-giving hand: "When Rome was marshalling her generals to fight in civil war and that martial land was being destroyed by her own might, it was the custom for squadrons coming together on the same side to exchange joined right hands as gifts. This is a token of alliance; concord has this for a sign—those whom affection joins the hand joins also." English translation of the Latin epigram from the academic portal "Alciato at Glasgow" http://www.emblems.arts.gla.ac.uk/alciato/emblem.php?id=A31a028.

36. Minor and Mitchell assert that the 1539 celebrations are notable because this is the first wedding festival for which the music has survived, and that Giambullari's description of the *apparato* is "one of the most interesting of the entire century"; see *Renaissance Entertainment*, vii.

37. Ibid., 26. Minor and Mitchell further note that just prior to its publication in August 1539, the music had been printed in Venice on independent initiative, and it was reprinted in 1566 by Giunti, "doubtless as a result of renewed interest in the 1539 celebrations occasioned by those for the marriage of Cosimo's son Francesco [and heir] in 1565," vii–viii.

38. Pierfrancesco Giambullari, *Apparato et feste nelle nozze del Illustrissimo Signor Duca di Firenze, et della Duchessa sua consorte ... in quelle recitati* (Florence, 1539), 6: "... la Signora Duchessa, uestita quel' giorno di rasi chermisi riccamente per tutto ricamati d'Oro battuto...". See Minor and Mitchell for a translation of this episode in *Renaissance Entertainment*, 97–99.

39. Pilliod, "Cosimo and the Arts," 334, discusses the state wedding and the elaborate *entrata*, asserting that such apparatus had become fashionable amongst contemporary European aristocracy.

40. Minor and Mitchell, *Renaissance Entertainment*, 100.

41. Langdon, *Medici Women*, 67, states: "The twig held by *Securità* was the *broncone*, the lopped but sprouting laurel symbolizing Cosimo as the redemptive new Medici branch ...".

42. Edelstein, "Bronzino," 257, no. 48.

43. Minor and Mitchell, *Renaissance Entertainment*, 103. A CD was recorded in Bologna by Tactus in 1989, entitled *Firenze 1539: musiche fatte nelle nozze dello illustrissimo duca di Firenze il signor Cosimo de Medici et [sic] della illustrissima concorte sua Mad. Leonora da Tolleto*, performed by the Centre de musique ancienne di Ginevra [sic], conducted by Gabriel Garrido. The first track is the "Ingredere" composed by Francesco Corteccia (3:05).

44. For examples of scholarship that investigate pre-modern sensory

perceptions in cultural context, see Constance Classen, David Howes, and Anthony Synnott, *Aroma: The Cultural History of Smell* (London and New York: Routledge, 1994); Penelope Gouk, ed., *Musical Healing in Cultural Contexts* (Aldershot: Ashgate, 2000); and Penelope Gouk and Helen Hills, eds., *Representing Emotions: New Connections in the Histories of Art, Music, and Medicine* (Aldershot: Ashgate, 2005).

45. Jacqueline Marie Musacchio, "Imaginative Conceptions in Renaissance Italy," in *Picturing Women in Renaissance and Baroque Italy*, eds. Geraldine A. Johnson and Sara F. Matthews Grieco (Cambridge and New York: Cambridge University Press, 1997), 48–49; and Dale Kent, "Women in Renaissance Florence," in David Alan Brown, et al., *Virtue and Beauty: Leonardo's Ginevra de' Benci and Renaissance Portraits of Women* (Washington, DC: National Gallery of Art; Princeton: Princeton University, 2001), 34–35. For an interesting analysis of medieval concepts of sanctity and spiritual impression through visual association, see Katharine Park, "Impressed Images: Reproducing Wonders," in *Picturing Science, Producing Art*, eds. Caroline A. Jones and Peter Galison (New York: Routledge, 1998), 272–96.

46. Minor and Mitchell, *Renaissance Entertainment*, 121: "… the streets were so full of spectators that there was hardly room to pass."

47. Sframeli, *I gioielli dei Medici*, 64, catalogue entry no. 7, "Diamante intagliato con monogramma di Cosimo de' Medici," Museo degli Argenti, inv. Gemme 1921, no. 1802.

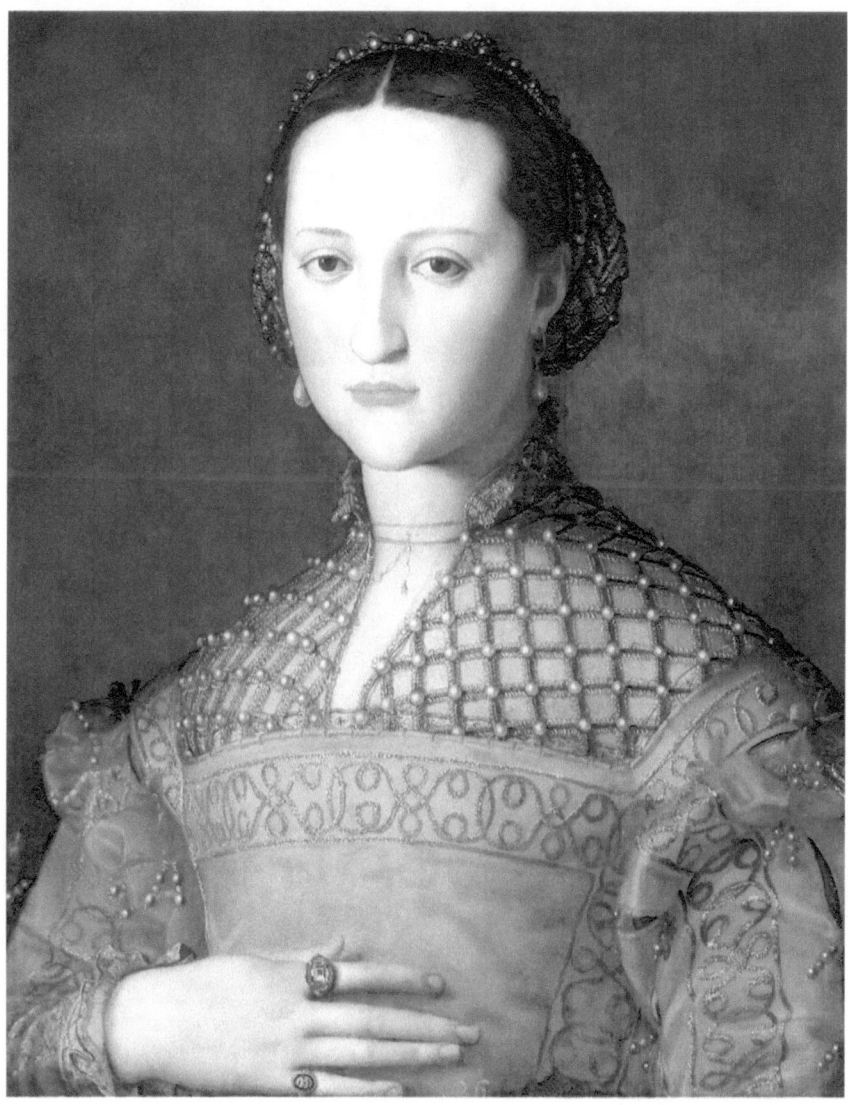

Fig. 1. Agnolo Bronzino, *Eleonora di Toledo*, 1539. Národní Galerie, Prague, Czech Republic. Photo credit: Národní Galerie, Prague, Czech Republic.

The Devil in the Details: Ornament as Emblem and Adage in Two Male Portraits by Bronzino[1]

Leatrice Mendelsohn

... for adages, like jewels, are small things, and sometimes escape your eye as you hunt for them, unless you keep a very sharp lookout. Besides which they do not lie on the surface, but as a rule are buried so that you have to dig them out before you can collect them. (Erasmus, *Adages* (1508) I. iv.25)

The world is still deceived with ornament. In law, what plea so tainted and corrupt but being season'd with a gracious voice, obscures the show of evil? (Shakespeare, *The Merchant of Venice*)

Disguised Details and Eloquent Extremities

The role of pictorial ornament in the creation of a beautiful style as described from antiquity throughout the Renaissance by Marcus Vitruvius Pollio, Leon Battista Alberti, and Giorgio Vasari provides us with a new and valid point of departure for investigating the inventive use of detail in two of Agnolo Bronzino's most studied male portraits: *The Portrait of a Young Man* in New York's Metropolitan Museum (Fig. 1) and *The Portrait of Ugolino Martelli* (Fig. 2) in the Gemäldegalerie, Berlin. Attentive observation of Bronzino's use of detail in his portraits reveals a substratum of ideologies and moral intentions that were not meant to be accessible to viewers outside of a select Florentine circle and that even now continue to confound connoisseurs and scholars. Bronzino's unique approach to portraiture allowed patrons, scholars, poets, friends, and other privileged associates access to hidden areas of meaning beneath the smooth, enamel-like treatment of the painted surface and the impassive expressions of his sitters. The painter was inspired not only by theoretical writing but also by images culled from literary texts and illustrations that circulated in printed matter, frequently of Northern origin, conveying Northern attitudes on art, ethics, and religion. Before identifying these sources and in order to appreciate the ramifications of textual image sources for Italian Renaissance art and its viewers, we must come to terms with the various applications of the word "ornament" in use at that time, especially in the poetry of artists and their literary mentors.

ORNAMENT/ORNAMENTUM

In his three influential treatises *De re aedificatoria, Della pittura,* and *De scultura,* published in the Quattrocento and republished in the Cinquecento for painters, sculptors, and architects, Leon Battista Alberti took special care to acknowledge his Greek and Roman authorities.[2] In *De re aedificatoria,* Alberti made it clear that his Latin model was Vitruvius, but in the same breath he suggested that without the intervention of his own translation and interpretation, "nothing from the ancient treatise worthy of transmitting would have survived."[3] According to the introduction to the 1550 edition of Giorgio Vasari's *Lives of the Painters, Sculptors and Architects,* "the most beautiful style" (*La più bella maniera*) was achieved by "frequently copying the most beautiful things and from those most beautiful hands, heads, bodies, or legs ... to make a figure of as many beauties as possible."[4] The importance played by small body parts in attaining this uniquely "beautiful style" should not be underestimated. In defining that style, Vasari echoed Alberti's statements on the value of the extremities as carriers of grace or *grazia.*[5]

In Alberti's *De scultura,* modules based on *minutia* establish a single measure for a statue. The chosen module number could then be used to determine the proportions of the entire figure.[6] By retaining the model's original proportions, the artist insured the proper relationship of the parts to the whole, regardless of size. Establishing a fixed proportion made possible the replication not only of statues but also figures in all media and in all sizes, from miniscule to colossal.[7] Alberti was unequivocal about the significance of the extremities as transmitters of beauty. He emphasized the fact that even though a human model was often used, measurements taken from ancient sculpture "were more certain to result in a beautiful product."[8] By retaining the model's original proportions, the replica was thought to preserve and transmit the original object's perfect beauty. The words Alberti associated with the production of replicas are not the technical terms we might expect. Instead, they reverberate aesthetically to remind the reader that, in the painter's eye, the smallest parts of the human body were details to be utilized for their inherent grace. Just as inanimate objects when isolated or miniaturized can become "ornamental," hands, heads, and feet seen as objects of perfect proportion, when detached from their original context, may also be viewed as "ornamental." Like a *pars pro toto*, or part taken for the whole, details can function as synecdoches of beauty.[9]

As we might expect, Vasari had a great deal to say about ornament. Like Alberti, Vasari (along with his own correspondents and contributors to the *Vite* [*Lives*]) was equally dependent on Vitruvius for his terminology.[10] In the *Vite*, Vasari compares the new style in painting directly to the *ornamenti* of architecture. It is of some interest that the breakdown of the architectural members of the *New Sacristy* as listed in the proemio to Part III of the *Vite* precisely parallels the parts of the body enumerated in Vasari's definition of *la bella maniera*.[11] Like Alberti, when he applied the ideals of architecture to sculpture and those of sculpture to painting, Vasari openly reveals Vitruvius as his source. By linking architectural theory to sculpture and painting, Vasari transforms what was originally a hierarchy into a tripartite theory of the arts. Gathering the three arts beneath the unifying practice of *disegno*, he establishes a trilogy of siblings under the aegis of father *Disegno* that was codified by Benedetto Varchi in his *Due Lezzioni*, presented in a public lecture and subsequently published shortly before Vasari's first edition appeared in 1550. Varchi too was concerned with ornament, primarily as an aspect of the *paragone*.[12]

At a certain point in *De scultura*, Alberti suddenly shifts away from his text on statues to a discussion of portraiture, repeating his initial statement that "what is true for the sculptor is equally true for the painter and architect."[13] The way in which the term "ornament" was transferred from rhetoric and poetry to sculpture and then reapplied specifically to the portrait genre appears to have been a Northern invention, taken up and adapted by Italian artists. To illustrate this, I have chosen two works by an Italian painter that reflect both Italian and Northern uses of text/image combinations and exemplify a rhetorical use of visual ornamentation. In the sixteenth-century European exchange of portraits (in print and paint) among rulers and the migration of artists from north to south (and vice versa), the portrait became a type of international currency, leaving its imprint across the continent and in England. Bronzino's *Portrait of a Young Man* in the Metropolitan Museum and *The Portrait of Ugolino Martelli* in the Gemäldegalerie have been selected because they illustrate this adaptive dissemination of images from north to south at a specific moment in the history of religious and social change. During the second and third decades of the sixteenth century, contemporary ideological upheavals were reflected in art and spread more rapidly because of the circulation of new ideas through images.

BACKGROUND

After the defeat of the Republic by Imperial forces in 1530, during the interim before the Medici fully regained control of Florence until the closure of the Council of Trent in 1564, world-changing socio-religious and political changes occurred in the known world that left their mark on all levels of society. These events affected art and artists in ways that forced them to reassess their professional self-image. This was especially true in the smaller Italian cities, ripe to be subjugated under the reign of Cosimo de' Medici, the young pre-emptor chosen to replace the unpopular ruler, Duke Alessandro de' Medici, assassinated in 1537.[14] Once secure in his power, Cosimo was determined to create a strong Tuscan empire under the newly restructured, authoritarian Medici rule. The relationship between remaining Florentine artists and *fuorusciti* (political exiles) living in Venice was ongoing, despite decrees prohibiting contacts between citizens of Florence and exiles. Venice, a liaison city aligned geographically with Germany, the Netherlands, and Northern France, inclined toward both its Protestant and Hapsburg neighbors. Venice also alternated between constant conflict and appeasement with papal Rome, where, paradoxically, the emergent Catholic counter-Reformation began to flourish.[15] This access gave exiled Florentines an opportunity to pick and choose their alliances from divergent religious positions and diverse political viewpoints. The new pictorial style that evolved from these external contacts was eventually transmitted and received by artists in northern Italy and Tuscany. There, the new materialism stemming from the secular art market in the North combined with passion imagery flourishing in the Catholic North to transform painting style. This new style was tempered with a degree of conformity sufficient to appease the papal consular rulings coming under consideration at the Council of Trent, filtering down to local Italian prelates.[16] This was a time of apprehension, but with only a faint presentment of the repercussions to follow in the wake of the Inquisition.[17]

In more recent times, art historical writing has designated this style by the term "Mannerism," stemming from *maniera*, the Italian word for style.[18] *Maniera*, the style under consideration here, was to a great extent (greater than is usually acknowledged) determined by the religious controversy in the northern countries that by the 1530s had taken root in Italy.[19] This style was *not* homogeneously created by consensus, nor was it created in one city.[20] At first, it may have been an involuntary reaction to conflicting pressures placed on artists, an attempt to preserve their professional integrity and eventually their independence, but the exigencies of exile soon led to cross-fertilization and a sharing of common traits across borders. Subsequently, the style was disseminated via networks of artists with similar allegiances working for patrons in Florence or *fuorusciti* in exile in Rome, Venice, Parma, and Mantua who were antipathetic towards their local political/religious regimes and equally desirous for the religious reform of the Church of Rome. Nicodemism, reflected in works by Michelangelo and Bandinelli, has been exemplified by Bronzino's *Lamentation* for Eleonora of Toledo, with its subtle references to reform Catholicism.[21] Several factors determined an artist's need for circumspection regarding visually expressed responses to a controversy concerning not only the nature of Christ, but also the very nature and purpose of artistic representation. With respect to Christian worship and its ties to secular politics, the group of artists who later came to be known as *manieristi* reacted to the climate of instability by successfully disguising subversive allusions inserted into their "politically correct" paintings. In portraiture as well as in religious paintings, mid-Cinquecento artists adopted techniques appropriated from late Roman and medieval periods when similar restrictions were imposed on art by the Church acting as Imperial governor.[22] Individualized techniques incorporated by Florentine artists into paintings included the insertion of personalized *bizzarrie* and *fantasie* into non-narrative as well as some religious paintings, such as deliberately ambiguous spatial distortion, pictorial and written allusions to ancient texts, and, occasionally, a darker or harsher palette. The persuasive authority of the Medici pope Clement VII and his ability to impose his personal taste early in the evolution of this new style should, however, be restricted to those artists whose work he commissioned.[23] From 1531 on, after the short-lived resumption of Medici power under Alessandro de' Medici, artists who were sympathetic to Church reform joined covert sects in support of their political and religious ideals; the members soon found it necessary to protect themselves from accusations of disloyalty and, more important, charges of heresy.[24] The escalation of a tense political situation, as Florentines faced the demise of their brief Republic under siege by the army of Charles V, severely affected anti-Medici factions that included artists and literati as well as merchants and nobles. Following the sack of Rome, many artists had already assumed self-imposed exile in Venice, Mantua, Lyon, and other major cities receptive to their cause. There, the *fuorusciti* established cohesive, expatriate Florentine communities.[25]

Those Republican artists who retained Medici ties were few, but Jacopo da Pontormo, who was among those who remained in Florence garnering new commissions, recalled Bronzino from Pesaro, where he was working for the della Rovere duke, to assist him once the Medici regained control. Those who stayed in Florence and continued to serve the new Medici regime, first under Alessandro and later under Cosimo, were constrained to exploit the potency of art as a socio-political force with extreme care for their own safety. Artists saw the need to invent coded images to disguise their opposition to imperialism and their continuing allegiance to the

Republic, all the while dissembling their compliance to the Medici regime and the Medici pope. They witnessed growing support for reform of the mother Church in Rome by foreign diplomats, such as Cardinal Pole and Nicholas Perrenot de Granvelle, first minister to Charles V and religious advisor to Eleonora of Toledo, and by wealthy and powerful exiles and patrons at home and abroad. It was for Granvelle that the *Lamentation* altarpiece by Bronzino was intended.[26] This factor required caution on the part of artists when representing religious themes for reformist patrons.[27] Their advocacy of freedom took visual shape in the form of artistic license (*licenzia*).

LICENZIA

In the *Vite*, as in Vitruvius' treatise on architecture, the word *ornamento* is linked with the word *licenzia*. Originally meaning license or "permission ... requested from the clergy or a person from a higher rank to wear luxuriously beautiful clothes that in their excess were subject to Florentine sumptuary laws or displaying a variety of *bizzarie* or exotic decorations considered extravagantly ornamented," artistic license expanded to representing images of un-natural or immoderate—that is, disproportionate or distorted—beings or objects.[28] Excess, whether applied to clothing ornamented with gold brocade or to jewels, evoked the concept of sin, of *luxuria* or gluttony; speaking behaviorally, "excess" implied sensual licentiousness. This aspect of license was transferred to painting, referencing exaggerated or distorted pictorial effects that were claimed by some clergy to be the *raison d'être* for institutionalizing the "rules of art" drawn up by the Council of Trent during its third and concluding session in 1563.[29]

In the Giunti edition of 1550, Vasari uses the word *licenzia* in a variety of ways. It is clear from his famous passage on Michelangelo, who "broke the rules," that *licenzia* means license to diverge from, or to contest, the "rule." For both Vitruvius and Vasari, the rules or *regole* were first applied to architecture, favoring a strict system of drawing, and then to composition. More particularly, the "rule" was applied to the ordering of the parts and construction of the body. Exaggeration or distortion, even when used to good effect for interpreting or evoking emotion, even in religious images, was strictly forbidden.[30]

Ornament

Not every use of ornament was viewed negatively; ornaments were recommended by Vasari to sustain the interest of the spectator. Like ancient fragments added or attached to statues to restore missing parts, details were meant to be noticed by the viewer, all the while being silently subsumed into the total picture. Bronzino's details can be considered "ornamental" in the way *ornamenta* was defined by Marcus Tullius Cicero and Marcus Fabius Quintillanus (Quintilian) in rhetorical theory and in instructions for ancient stage design. This usage is consistent with Quintilian's application of the word *ornamenta* translated in English as "embellishments" intended to lend a speech "additional brilliance," especially when it refers to "the decorations of the forum or a richly ornamented stage, since they not only adorn but also stand out conspicuously in the midst of other ornaments."[31] Both authors were frequently cited in lectures and poetry delivered in the Florentine Academy in which Bronzino was active in 1541.[32]

Today, detail is most often seen as a technical feature of ornament, a viewpoint perpetuated in the twentieth century by reinforcing an earlier notion that ornament or *parergon* was distinct from the main body of a work of art.[33] This may explain the partial neglect until recently of the subject as a significant element in the history of art despite occasional scholarly attempts to qualify the role of ornament, particularly in reference to architecture. The reverse saying, "more is less," which stems from the modernist "less is more," derives from Immanuel Kant's negative view of ornament that referred back to rhetorical theory. It has, of course, always been possible to use ornament as mere elaboration without imbuing it with additional meanings, but this is not the case in mid-sixteenth-century paintings by Bronzino and his circle.

Detail as Ornament

Using texts, visual metaphors, pictorial jokes, puns, and reversals, Bronzino chose to contrast the outward grace of his figures with their inward intellectual and spiritual unrest. That unrest, I intend to demonstrate, is revealed in the details.[34] In contemporary poetic criticism, the controversy known as the *paragone* argued the superiority of poetry versus painting and sculpture. Bronzino, a disciple of Benedetto Varchi—the linguistic and literary theorist, philosopher-poet, and political chameleon—followed his mentor's approach based on Aristotle's *Rhetorica*, transferring the poetic and rhetorical techniques to painting in order to assert the superiority of the visual. He approached the competition taking on the most difficult task first: making the invisible tangible by rendering man's concealed interiority (*il di dentro*) through external and visibly tangible forms (*il di fuori*).[35] In both Quattrocento and Cinquecento art, inner grace was revealed primarily in the linear patterns of the painting's surface.[36] In his letter answering Varchi's theoretical question, "which of the two arts, painting or sculpture, is the superior," Bronzino, writing in support of sculpture, delegates that same linear surface movement to painting—but as a liability.[37] He begins by presenting the standard arguments in support of sculpture. In this unfinished letter, Bronzino presents the *paragone* from the point of view of the sculptor. He denies the greater *difficoltà* of the sculptor's task caused by the hardness and natural three-dimensionality of the material, insisting that these are merely properties of the sculptor's medium. In denying the raw material as a major factor in the sculptor's claim to superiority, he indirectly reaffirms his support of painting by declaring: "all that belongs to three-dimensional existence does not appertain to art but to nature."[38] Bronzino clearly did not see himself as a decorator of surfaces, as such. Instead, he defined himself as a painter of relief or *rilievo* who created the depth and three-dimensionality of tactile physical matter using contour line to gain a relief effect, and who achieved it with intellect, that is, via *disegno*. Although Bronzino's application of detail may seem entirely unrelated to Quattrocentesque undulating draperies and limbs (for example, in Botticelli) in one respect, Bronzino's portraits are indebted to earlier painted mythological allegories. Both Quattrocento and Cinquecento depend on stylized contour and draw upon ancient sculpture and texts to convey meaning. What differentiates them is their *elocutio*, i.e., their style. In Bronzino's painting, as in ancient drama, techniques directed at the spectator depend on rhetorical texts that engage the use of gesture as ornament. In his *Institutiones Oratoriae* VII and VIII, Quintilian equated *eloquentia* to "style," particularly with respect to its effect on an audience. Everything is geared to its impact on the listener, who is expected, in fact required, to respond in a predetermined manner.[39]

In Bronzino's portraiture, we see line as contour applied to reveal the figure's *grazia*—a grace, however, that, being stilled, neither exudes nor excites emotion. While lacking any extreme activation of the limbs in these portraits, Bronzino nevertheless manages to create tension and a sense of energy through contrast.[40] Perversely, his choice of ornament injects a deviant element in the form of grotesque figures that simultaneously heighten and contest the inner grace of the sitter. Because of their contrasting strangeness, in these two portraits Bronzino's carved details instill a sense of energy (*energia*) that is transmitted to the viewer and through *his* eyes, to the sitter.[41]

Ornament as Metaphor

Bronzino's method of embedding a series of concepts in concrete objects derives from techniques of ancient allegory.[42] The allegorizing of Bronzino's portraiture depends on images that recall and, by being recalled via imitation, transmit written and verbal metaphors.[43] A tradition for this type of portrait was ripe for expansion in the wake of Pontormo's iconic portrait of *Cosimo Il Vecchio Pater Patriae*, painted after the sitter's death (Fig. 3).[44] Although the commission is not documented, it has been dated, with some controversy, to between 1519 and 1520. It is presumed to have been commissioned to commemorate the birth of the "new Cosimo," the Medici hope for a continuation of their line. Vasari was later commissioned to paint two iconic Medici portraits, one of Alessandro de' Medici and one of Lorenzo de' Medici, painted c. 1534.[45] In them, Vasari retained the courtly symbols of identity used by Pontormo in his earlier portrait of *Cosimo Il Vecchio*, since Vasari's portrait of Lorenzo was intended as a pendant. But despite their use of individual emblematic references, owed in part to Paolo Giovio, whose intervention is discussed by Davitt Asmus, in none of these earlier Medici icons did the painters attempt, as Bronzino does, to show more than the outward *persona* of the sitter.[46] In the Renaissance, *persona* signifies an exterior mask that hides the "real" person under a mask or a cover as disguise.[47] Rather than presenting his sitter beneath a mask, Bronzino seeks to grant the viewer visual access to the sitter's "soul" or *anima*, a feat that theoretically was initially assigned to sculpture but not to painting.[48] "Attributes," that is, objects that merely identified saints or rulers, were insufficient to reveal the sitter's true self. In their place, images with direct connections to verbal adages, epigrams, and ancient epitaphs became the indicators of choice. These "details" or "ornaments" are coded devices, based on ancient Greek and Latin texts as well as contemporary authors, which expose the invisible aspects of the persons represented. They are intended to give the viewer insight beyond and beneath the sitter's external *persona*, mask, or title.[49] The use of attributes for saints and ruler portraits was a necessary preliminary stage in the application of symbolic objects as identifiers in paintings; "attributes" preceded the more sophisticated literary messages conveyed by material objects. In literature, ties between image, narrative, and allegory focused more on illustrated narrative, yet introduced a connection with the moral allegories that led to more visually oriented symbols. Medieval dialogues about virtue and vice evolved into illustrated *agons* in narrative form, such as the *Psychomachia* of Prudentius or the allegorical writings of Alain de Lille. These moralizing texts stimulated the creation of allegorical scenarios to activate their personifications that, in turn, resulted in the absorption of moral messages by signified objects acting as empowered attributes inserted into secular as well as religious paintings.

Following Varchi's advice to offer a glimpse into the "interior" of the sitter, Bronzino (following ancient literature) employed substitute carriers of meaning that went beyond mere identification and social classification. As his technique matured, he turned to epigrams and epitaphs, popularized in the books of adages by Desiderius Erasmus published as texts. Only later, when Andrea Alciato illustrated his emblems, were texts that were identified with specific material objects or statues inserted into paintings as ornaments.[50] It was presumed that the sitters and the audience for the portraits were familiar with the text or the allusion alluded to by the objects.

As already noted, in Quintilian's writing on rhetoric, the Greek word φράσιν becomes *elocutio* in Latin and is most often translated into English as "style."[51] In rhetoric, "style" is revealed both in individual words and in sentences, or groups of words. When transposed from rhetorical theory into art theory, an image or a group of images is substituted for words.[52] In the literary-oral presentation as described by Quintilian and Cicero, "word" can be considered equivalent to an ornamental object. When the "word" *qua* ornament is an image, for example in a painting by Bronzino, it can take the form of a carved *mascherone* or a marbleized statue "sculpted in paint" or, as in the *Portrait of Ugolino Martelli*, a hand-inscribed epigraphy on parchment or any other material object that signifies something beyond the pictorial environment. In this way, informed viewers are made aware that they are dealing with a rhetorical "ornament." In a painting, the imaged ornament substitutes for a word or saying or idea and becomes what we might call a "visual metaphor."[53] A definite link exists between Alciato's *Emblemata*, illustrated with figures derived from antique statues or reliefs, and mid-Cinquecento paintings, in which meaning is encapsulated within a "sculpted" object, whether a classically derived statuette or the carved furniture grotesques Bronzino included in these portraits. In attempting to surpass the proportion and grace of surviving masterpieces (as well as of lesser ancient statues and their fragmented parts), artists frequently depended on the broken limbs of antiquities for the body parts of their painted human beings to make whole figures. Like restorers who used the fragments of antique statues to complete the limbs of their figures, they attached visual references to their sitters. In this way, their "painted statues" or inanimate objects could "speak."[54] We know that Alciato and Erasmus corresponded from the time Erasmus was in Venice in 1508 working on the Italian publication of his *Adages* with the publisher Aldus Manutius.[55] What is less commonly known to scholars is that, in 1546, Cosimo de' Medici wrote to his representative in Padua, Francesco di Paolo Vinta, requesting that he continue to "implore" Alciato to join his Studio in Pisa. His persistence did not persuade Alciato, whom Cosimo describes as having been sought after by other universities and patrons in Ferrara and Pavia. In addition, Bartolomeo Panciatichi, a patron of Bronzino's at that time, was mentioned as an intermediary in this attempt to entice Alciato to work for the Medici in Florence.[56] In the third edition of *Adages*, published in Basel in 1515, many of the original sayings from the first edition were included; to these Erasmus added several thousand more and amplified the commentaries of those already published.[57] In the new edition, Erasmus touched on the political and social implications of some of the adages, relating them to the present historical situation.[58] By the mid-Cinquecento, Italian scholars and members of Florentine society were reading many of the works of Erasmus; the *Adages* were of special interest for young students of literature and rhetoric. Since Varchi was in contact with Alciato in Padua, we can assume that his student Martelli, who joined him there, would also have known of the collaboration between Alciato and Erasmus in the creation of the former's *Emblemata*. Martelli would have been cognizant of the appropriate form of an emblem, as well as the fact that, in many instances, an illustrated *Emblema* is a visualization of an adage. When an image is added to a *motto* and augmented with a descriptive saying, it forms a complex (and at times contradictory) tripartite message. An image that recalls a motto and refers to an adage when added to a portrait would most certainly have been understood by the young *letterati* portrayed by Bronzino, especially the poet Ugolino Martelli.

In the 1568 edition of the *Vite*, in the preface on painting, *disegno* is defined as "a concept achieved by the hand." Vasari writes that this concept depends on a Greek proverb in which "a valiant man saw a single lion's claw sculpted in a block (*masso*). From that measure and form, he comprehended intellectually the parts of the whole animal and, beyond it, the entire complex, as if it had been present before.[59] The immediate source of this citation by Vasari is the proverb "on the lion's claw" analyzed by Erasmus and published in Italy by the printer Aldus Manutius.[60] This metaphor for *disegno* is also mentioned by Alberti, so we should expect that it had a wide circulation among artists as well as literati.[61] Not coincidentally, Proverb 138 on Hercules was later published separately with a longer and more personalized explanation (Fig. 4). Thus, the Greek saying would have been accessible *in volgare* at the time Bronzino painted Ugolino, who was, very likely, familiar with the proverb.

In Bronzino's portrait of Ugolino, the foot or paw carved in the table ornament would be understood as a synecdoche for the whole body, just as the lion's claw (*l'ugno del' leone*) in the proverb is a *pars pro toto* referring to *disegno*. The artist's hand, mediating between study and the experience of many years of drawing, became, implicitly, the repository of memory. According to Vasari, the artist is only able to depict the totality of nature by calling upon the memory of this earlier disciplined practice. The concept of *disegno* as envisioned by Vasari, therefore, encodes the concept of remembered experience as a "seed."[62] In the same way, the single talon, the paw or foot, conceived of as the "smallest detail," encodes the full animal or figure in order to convey the meaning of the whole. Linking study and practice to the act of expression, *disegno* may be defined more broadly as the active expression of a concept, a *concetto* or mental plan. Conceived as an activity linking hand to mind, drawing is the means of transmitting the meaning conveyed in the "smallest detail" to the entire painting, in this case, the image of the sitter plus the context in which he is shown. Material ornament, i.e., the details displayed in the portraits, encapsulates information about the sitter's inner as well as outer worlds, first tying him to the physical surroundings, the painting's foreground and background (with messages conveyed by means of a collection of ornaments). Status in Florence, as elsewhere, was conveyed via objects held or pointed out by a gesturing hand, whether embedded in the background or by being included in a sort of scattered still life. Finally, these ornamental objects are given added meaning by their connection to written texts known to the sitter, the recipient of the portrait, and preferred viewers.

It is important for our present subject to insist that even if in a Renaissance painting a detail should appear extrinsic to the uninitiated, the intention was for it to be intrinsic to the art work itself, seen as a totality.[63] In fact, the "eye-catching," immoderate, and often ambiguous nature of ornament is precisely what gave scope to the expression of disparate meanings.

In the fourth decade of the Cinquecento, particularly in Bronzino's works, ornament contributed to a pictorial mood created by intensifying an action or representing an apparent inaction. That is, an action not actually taking place but impending—a movement never realized in the painting but which appears immanent due to the instability of the pose. In this sense, one may speak of a style consciously imbued with potential so as to project multiple meanings into the future. At the very least, there is no attempt to produce a work that has been given a meaning so fixed that the viewer's reaction cannot add or subtract from it. In *Maniera* painting, artifice is accomplished by the artist who energizes unseen powers rather than by an artisan who follows a familiar pattern. The ability to mean without saying—or, to rephrase it, to connect odd images (i.e., *fantasie*) to invisible links or to words with double meanings—contributed to the retrospective denigration of paintings produced in the 1530s and 1540s in this style by Giovanni Andrea Gilio da Fabriano (d. 1584), the counter reformation critic who wrote in the 1560s.[64]

The Early Portraits

Beginning c. 1527 and continuing through the 1540s, Bronzino painted a series of portraits of his contemporaries, friends, and fellow academicians.[65] One or more of this group of portraits has been dated 1527, a time when a group of students fled to the outskirts of Florence, to Bivigliano, to escape the plague.[66] By scholarly consensus, several have been dated after 1532/33, that is, after Bronzino's sojourn in Pesaro, where, assisting in the decoration of the Villa Imperiale of Duke Francesco I della Rovere, he was exposed to the exchange of ideas between Venice and the North in matters of religion as well as the arts.[67] Others of his scholar-patron portraits, particularly those identified and commissioned, have been dated as late as 1547. By then, Bronzino was incorporating portraiture into religious paintings, not as formal patron portraits but by using recognizable individuals in the guise of participants in ritual enactments, somewhat like the sneak appearances of celebrities in modern film-making. That is, the intention was for the illustrious living to become substitutes for righteous immortals; not just to be recognized by the audience but also to be noticed as if they assumed the role of an historical or biblical character.[68]

The portraits of Bronzino's academic friends were intended for a specific group of viewers—the sitters themselves.[69] Friendship was a prime motive for male portraiture, mentioned by Aristotle

(384–322 BCE) and reaffirmed by Alberti.[70] The sitters' shared interests in Greek and Latin literature, as well as political and philosophical principles, formed a sort of young men's "Republic of Letters," as Erasmus called it.[71] Any pictorial allusions, obvious or hidden, would have been made with the approval of the sitters. Details and their meaning were very likely intended to be recognizable and appreciated by the collective group because of their shared beliefs. Based on documents, correspondence, and sonnets exchanged between the students and their teacher/mentor Benedetto Varchi, it would seem that the young scholars were well aware of the precariousness of the Florentine Republic and the impending restoration of Medici rule. They would have been equally up to date on the religious turmoil in the North. Yet, as portrayed, their faces reflect no signs of anxiety or discomfort.

These are friendship portraits in the true sense of the word. In light of their presumed knowledge of one another and their habit of making jokes and puns in coded language, the sitters and their friends would probably have easily recognized any hidden references and examples of wit incorporated into the images.[72]

Portrait of a Young Man[73]

Bronzino's portrait of an unnamed young man, now in New York's Metropolitan Museum, is shown nearly full face, standing in a slightly shifted three-quarter view, a format initiated in the North and employed by Titian for portraits of Charles V of Spain and members of the Mantuan Gonzaga family (Fig. 1). His Florentine precedent is the *Halberdier* painted by Pontormo (Fig. 5), dated earlier than Bronzino's *Young Man*. A significant precedent for the pose of the *Halberdier* may be Donatello's bronze *David* in the Bargello.[74] The inherent Republicanism of the pose has been used to support the identification of the sitter as *Francesco Guardi*, a young soldier, rather than Cosimo I de' Medici, as identified by Janet Cox-Rearick and Costamagna.[75] Cox-Rearick saw the costume, recognizably that of a German-Swiss *Landsknechte*, as an expression of Cosimo de' Medici's youthful flamboyance and preference for military dress recorded in contemporary sources.[76] It is a curiosity of art historical logic that the identities of two different sitters have been supported and rejected on the same basis of the figure's uniform and hat emblem. Regardless of who the living sitter might be impersonating, he wears a garment that, during the Republican period, would identify him as a mercenary soldier fighting for Charles V of Spain, the future Holy Roman Emperor. But if the pose was meant to allude to David, who slew the enemy of his people, can we presume to resolve his identity on the basis of his dress or pose? What then is the relationship between Pontormo's portrait in the J. Paul Getty Museum, Los Angeles, California, and our portrait in the Metropolitan Museum, whose figure was conceived in a pose nearly identical to that of the *Halberdier*? How would the potential identity of Pontormo's sitter and the sculptural antecedents of the *Halberdier* relate to Bronzino's figure dressed in high Spanish fashion? And what of Raphael's lost portrait of Giuliano: was it a model for Bronzino, or was he, like Pontormo, merely representing his sitter in a Herculean pose? The relationship between the master painter and his student demands to be examined in greater depth before arriving at a conclusion. Let us take a more comprehensive look at the painting.

Bronzino situates his *Young Man* between two grotesque furniture ornaments: a table with a carved wooden head stretched into a distorted shape decorates the cornice-like support beneath it; and a second carved head juts out from the curved arm of the wooden chair to his left, suggesting a winged body supporting the sitter. A mid-sixteenth-century table from Lyon, now in the National Gallery of Art in Washington DC, is similarly ornamented, albeit with a carved lion-sphinx, a traditional decorative motif.[77] Bronzino does not appear to be interested in replicating actual furniture designs, and we have no drawings of inventions of his own for decorative designs of household objects such as those we have by Francesco Salviati. Bronzino's grotesque heads, having both classical and Northern antecedents, remain in the realm of *fantasia*, a fantasy, however, that imbued material objects with a sense of magic and power.[78]

A similar, though rarely commented upon, carving is discreetly hidden just above the joined hands of *Giovanni Arnolfini and his Betrothed* in Van Eyck's 1434 portrait of the couple now in the National Gallery in London.[79] A grotesque "verso" of a lion's head faces outward on the arm of a throne-like chair placed on what has been called the "female side" of the room, indicated by the bed. Another scholar has called it "a Master's chair" belonging to the male member of the household. It resembles a throne of Wisdom such as those supporting Roman figures of Wisdom or medieval Madonnas (Fig. 6).[80] A second head looks out from the bedpost, backed by another miniature lion. These carvings recall the protective powers of ancient apotropaic guardians such as Medusa, but with a folkloric, burlesque aspect. In Van Eyck's painting, the small but powerful lion/female heads retain their function as Solomonic ornaments on a throne, sanctifying and protecting the couple.

Still another sort of painting utilized similar bedpost imagery in England. It was titled *Edward VI and the Pope* or *An Allegory of the Reformation under Edward VI* and has been analyzed for its political message by Margaret Aston, *The King's Bedpost: Reformation and Iconography in a Tudor Group Portrait* (Cambridge: Cambridge University Press, 1993). Aston enumerates symbols not unlike Bronzino's carved *mascheron*. In the painting, dated after the portraits under consideration here, Aston points to a bedpost in the form of a grotesque sphinx enacting a demonic role in the complex narrative that has been constructed by the anonymous painter by means of words and symbols. She calls the painting a "text painting—a painting with a message ... Carrying its own message in written captions that are an integral part of the composition."[81] The written slogans, however, had at some later point been erased and were revealed only through X-ray treatment. Painted during the reign of Queen Elizabeth I, the proposed date for this work is c. 1547. The message is both anti-iconoclastic and anti-papal. Henry VIII, apparently on his death bed, is shown sitting up and pointing to his son and heir, Edward VI, a young boy who is enthroned at the center. Edward is depicted crushing Pope Paul III beneath the elevated podium of his kingship. At the same time, the pope is threatening the stability of the throne. At the foot of the bed, a gargoyle-like sphinx with prominent breasts supports the bed with a clawed lion's foot. Below, on a lower level, two monks run from the scene. The painting is a blatant political cartoon, lacking the subtlety of the disguised ornaments of the Italian portraits and closer in type to printed anti-papal and anti-Lutheran propaganda sheets that caricatured their protagonists, transforming them into hybrid monsters. Since the historical figures are clearly labeled, there is nothing hidden for the viewer to discover. At the same time, an open book with the text "The word of the Lord endureth forever" visible to the viewer contributes to the weight suppressing Pope Paul III.

Northern single-sheet prints combined just that kind of detail, adding emotional expressiveness through the artist's manipulation of spatial and figural effects.[82] In early modern Italy, just as in Antiquity, the distortion of figure and space in both secular and religious paintings signifies a deviation from the ideal norm and often, by the use of minor details, implies the presence of a potentially dangerous higher power.[83] One prominent example of this practice in ancient sculpture is found on the armrest of the *River God, Tigris*, one of the monumental reclining male personifications on the Capitoline on which a sphinx-like ornament is carved.[84] Because of the occult status of this statue, the sphinx serves as a hieroglyph alluding to the hidden wisdom possessed by the River God.[85] As it appears on the Arnolfini throne, the lion demon carries an analogous threat to frighten away evil spirits, the invisible powers that menace the sanctity of the sacral space.

Sources for Bronzino's table ornament in the Metropolitan Museum portrait are not easily found in contemporary carved sculpture but are ubiquitous in printed sources that ensured their circulation. The closest resemblance to Bronzino's table carving appears on a two-dimensional engraving belonging to a vocabulary of decorative ornaments specifically intended for painters, that is, in Alciato's *Emblemata*. In the center of the lower border of an emblem in the earliest illustrated edition of Alciato's *Emblemata* we find a similar head functioning as a keystone.[86] Alciato's book was reprinted numerous times after 1531; subsequent illustrated editions reprinted the original border decorations until their surfaces became too worn to reuse, a common parsimonious practice of the period. A probable source for the scroll-like decorative motifs surrounding the head was the thinly carved and curled strap work, part of the ornamental vocabulary of Northern wood carvers.[87] A reflection of the contemporary taste for this type of ornament is seen at Fontainebleau, where decorative framework directly imitates the thin, curled wood carving (Fig. 7).[88] A similar head, somewhat less de-formed, appears (beginning in 1546) in the framing devices of several of the tapestries narrating the story of Joseph, commissioned by Cosimo de' Medici, for which the painters Bronzino and Salviati prepared the central design. In three of the tapestries exhibited in the Florentine Bronzino exhibition (Florence, 2010), another grotesque head also acts as a keystone in the lower portion of the border (Fig. 8).[89] The borders of the Joseph series are attributed to Nicolas Karcher (d. 1562), a Belgian artist and member of the crew of weavers imported by Cosimo to create a Florentine manufactury for tapestry making. Once again a Northern sensibility passed to and fro, to Italy, in this case from Belgium, just as the examples shown above came from the Netherlands, Spain, and France.

It is noteworthy that the decorative sources proposed thus far have all been Northern in origin. We do not know whether Bronzino had a hand in determining the framing borders attributed to Nicolas Karcher. The surrounding garland ornaments include a number of root vegetables such as squash, cauliflower, eggplant, and string beans, along with nude women holding up putti and a ram's head at the mid-point of the upper row. Many of these vegetable names are found in the dictionary of Jean Toscan, where they are defined as code words for body parts or sexual acts.[90] We find many of the same coded words in Bronzino's poetry and capitoli generally dated in the 1550s, which is slightly later than the tapestries.

Bronzino's friend, the architect Bartolomeo Ammannati, who trained in Venice with Jacopo Sansovino, brought back to Florence in 1527 a Venetian ornamental vocabulary that he applied to the Tuscan palaces and villas he designed. Among his motifs were grotesques and fantastic monsters in marble and stone.[91] The newly flourishing print industry, along with a transplanted Belgian weaving industry in Florence, facilitated the rapid exchange of designs between north and south. In prints for Fontainebleau by Domenico del Barbiere, the simulated strap work, a trademark of his creations, derives from antique as well as medieval architectural decoration.[92]

It seems that from the 1530s, ongoing wars between France, Spain, and Germany as well as the dispersal of many Florentines to northern cities hastened rather than impeded the spread of ideas. Bronzino, whom we know was well read and open to influences of this kind, benefited from his connections to his exiled patrons, contact with other *fuorusciti*, and images transmitted via printed matter. More important, perhaps, was the highly inter-European literature exchanged among his young Florentine sitters and their private advocacy of new ideology.

The close relationship between the uses of ornament in architecture and its use in painting brings to mind the famous passage in Book VII of Vitruvius' *De architectura* that proposes a narrative source for the relationship between ornament and political thought. Vitruvius begins his chapter by condemning the decline of wall painting in Rome. He describes how "imitations based upon reality are now disdained by the improper taste of the present."[93] This statement is supported by the related passage that precedes his complaint against stucco decoration in Roman houses. What follows is the litany of monsters and other un-natural forms and distortions of nature that Vitruvius saw replacing "definite representations taken from definite things."[94] Vitruvius condemns the fact that viewers accept these.

> falsehoods ... failing to consider whether any of them can really occur or not ... for pictures cannot be approved which do not resemble reality ... even if they have a fine and craftsman like finish, they are only to receive commendation if they exhibit their proper subject without transgressing the rules of art.

Vasari praised Michelangelo precisely for transgressing the "rules of art," as the one who "broke the chains" of those rules for those who came after him.[95] Vitruvius reaffirmed his condemnation of artistic license for painters by citing the cities of Alabanda and Abdera as examples (as quasi personifications) of foolishness and excess luxury, respectively. In the case of Alabanda, the people were repudiated for their stupidity and inconsistency in placing important statues in inappropriate surroundings—the statues of athletes in the assembly room and those of politicians in the gymnasium. In Abdera, the stage scenery's colors were too bright. Because their civic leaders' reputations were stained, the cities' images as respectable political entities was diminished even after the errors were rectified. A transgression of rules by artists, therefore, reflected on the entire population; a lack of taste and decorum cast a shadow on the political status of their respective cities. The disposition of art works, their perception and decorum observed by its citizens, was critically tied to a city's greatness.[96]

The transfer of the Latin use of the word *licentia* from architecture to painting, as we have seen, is already included in the 1550 edition of Vasari in the third preface, where Michelangelo's freedom to apply license is characterized as a loosening of the rules in his work. That statement acted as the stimulus for opening up new possibilities for painters.[97] Although the practice of artistic license by painters goes back to Roman times, as described by Vitruvius in his well-known lament on the decline of wall painting, it was frequently used in the Middle Ages to describe a sinful Christian, usually female. The codification of the word to characterize a stylistic effect coincides approximately with the period between the 1550 publication of the first edition of the *Vite*, the period during which Vasari conceived his second edition, until its publication in 1568, five years after the release of the edicts of the Council of Trent on art.[98] The word *licenza* as an allusion to sin was strengthened with the Council's decree on images. That depended on the earlier decree of the Second Council of Nicea, held in 787, a reaction against iconoclasm in the Eastern Empire similar to the sixteenth-century reaction to iconoclasm in the northern Catholic countries. The formation of the decree was primarily the work of the French delegate Charles de Guise, who had the backing of the French theological faculty of the University of Paris. This ruling was made a priority, since lascivious images were considered a particular problem in France.[99] The final conciliar decree went further than it had in the eighth century, not only declaring that sacred images were *lecito*, legal and useful for instruction and prayer, but also including limits, stressing that images must be free of all *lascivia*, that is, "sensual appeal." At the issuing of the degree on sacred images 3 December 1563, the religious implication of two significant reformation terms, *licenzia* and *libero arbitrio* (license and free will), not only secured the application of the word *lascivia* to religious images but also subjected all images and their makers to moral scrutiny.[100]

Bronzino's decidedly burlesque carved grotesques appear to

possess powers similar to those of Medusa heads on war shields or family escutcheons attached to the exteriors of domestic palaces—for example, the Medici *palle* placed high on the corner of the Medici Palace or the great Lion escutcheon of the Martelli family, attributed to Donatello, that thrust out from the upper story of the façade in the Palazzo Martelli. Yet, attached to the painted heads is an element of parody as well. More than a mere embellishment or heraldic relic from medieval Florence, Bronzino's *ornamenti*, while less common than hat ornaments, are manifestly more personal; they speak to the unspoken inner life of the sitter. Their meaning, however, does not exclude a satirical and somewhat comedic aspect. The painted carvings in the Bronzino portrait are signs opposing as well as reinforcing other signs in the pictorial field.

The austere, geometric style of the portrait's setting recalls Michelangelo's architectural vocabulary in the New Sacristy, perhaps tempered by the painter's memory of the interior architecture of the Palace of Urbino near Pesaro, designed by Fra Carnevale and the geometer Francesco di Giorgio Martini.[101] Appropriately painted in grisaille, the architecture seems to echo and reify the detachment of the sitter. Resembling fragments of an interior palace courtyard, it provides a tight surface grid against which the eccentric details of the two grotesque furniture carvings stand out more vividly, as if in deliberate opposition. Like the architectural ornaments in the New Sacristy, those in Bronzino's Metropolitan painting literally melt away against the classical severity of the background. In the Medici burial chapel, imaginative details of the princely armor and the ornamented objects connected to it accent the flat surfaces and enliven the detached expressions of the ducal effigies. Rodent-like faces on the armor of the Medici dukes and the frieze of masks limning the entablature of the Sacristy add capricious punctuation marks to the unbroken surface planes of the background.[102] In the portrait's conscious juxtaposition of the beautiful and the ugly, as well as in the demeanor of his model, Bronzino's carved details have earned the title *mascherone*.[103] This is appropriate insofar as they function in a manner similar to the distorted mask placed beneath Michelangelo's figure of *Night*, conceived as a mixture of attribute, emblem, and apotropaic sign (Fig. 9). Beyond this, a licentious or occult aura is projected onto the languorous statue when the distorted mask is contrasted with the beauty of the female nude.[104] Thus, Michelangelo's mask, suggesting the shell of the artist himself, becomes a monster that looks upon the beautiful figure of Night with unseeing eyes. Bronzino's carved demons appear far less frightening and more capricious than Michelangelo's "persona," the sculpted, eyeless mask.

In the portrait of the youth luxuriously dressed in stylish, Spanish black we sense something of the *inganno* permeating the London *Allegory of Love*, c. 1546, the painting that Vasari claims was a gift to Francis I.[105] Instead of conveying a satirical sense of sin such as we see enacted by Venus and Cupid in the guise of illicit love, however, our elegant *Young Man*'s dissimulation is that of assuming the hauteur of a courtier. By pretending an attitude, he presumably follows Baldassare Castiglione's advice to the Courtier to affect a stance of nonchalance, yet he is less than successful in appearing unstudied.[106] The artifice of the pose, including the studied pattern of the left hand on the hip, with fingers spaced apart in a distinctive manner, is neither hidden nor unselfconscious. The sitter embodies the affect of artfulness in assuming a "false front" unrelieved by any casual or relaxed attitude on his part; he is represented as playing a role. The artist, in contrast, displays *sprezzatura* in his ability to depict subtle character distinctions by means of apparently effortless technical skill. It is as if the youth's mask of arrogance and pride is mimicked by the melting grotesque beneath the table top on which our young man rests his book. One finger holds a place in the book, two other fingers keep it upright. Both hands focus our attention on the book as it weighs heavily on the table carving. In exerting visible pressure, the book itself counterbalances the demonic carving that seems to be melting under its weight.

We may not know definitively who our young man is, but we have a clue as to where his interest lies from his immersion in the literature indicated by the hand marking his place in a well-bound yet untitled tome and by his stance.[107] In a sense, he appears to be the converse of Pontormo's *Halberdier* (Fig. 5), in supporting the "word" triumphant over the sword. At this point, the reader may have doubts about the resemblance between this upstanding, *disinvolto* youth and the typology of Hercules. However, the indecisive pose of the Halberdier can be said to resemble a Hercules at the

Crossroads rather than the slayer of the Nemean Lion. Bronzino's self-assured young man would seem to be a Hercules of another color.

The Hercules Factor

In the second century, Herakles-Ogmios was identified with Eloquence.[108] Alciato's Emblem represents this Hercules, and it has been suggested that Alciato got the idea for the emblem from the proverb of Erasmus. The emblem's image shows Hercules' tongue connected by a chain to the ears of the populace, his voice substituting for his weapons, which are ineffectual in the face of his eloquence (Fig. 10).[109] The illustration in the 1531 and subsequent Latin editions of the *Emblemata* have the following motto: "Eloquentia fortitudine praestantior," which in English reads: "Eloquence Surpasses Strength" or, as stated in the *Iliad* of Homer, the open book in the portrait of Ugolino Martelli, eloquence must substitute for (a show of) strength.

Virginia Callahan has demonstrated how, in a variety of published adages on Hercules, Erasmus was referring to his own literary status in Germany.[110] Under a strain while composing the adages and suffering attacks for his religious stance on aspects of Luther's doctrine, Erasmus identified with Hercules, who was compelled to complete twelve difficult labors.[111] Erasmus considered the verbal attacks to be a result of envy (*Invidia*), a sin that was also uppermost in the eyes of Varchi and considered inevitable among his contemporaries, whether academics or theologians. Varchi's preoccupation led to his presenting a lecture on the subject of envy to the Paduan *Accademia degli Infiammati*.[112]

In addition to the emblem on Eloquence, Alciato refers to another Herculean action in the emblem on "Those who venture on what is beyond their powers" (*In eos qui supra vires quicquam audent*; Fig. 4). The image alludes to Hercules' temerity in battling with his enemies, in this case the pygmies. The emblem commentary deals once more with *Elocutio* and its winning battle over strength.

PORTRAIT OF UGOLINO MARTELLI

In this portrait of a young man belonging to an elite Florentine family and Varchi's literary circle, Ugolino Martelli, Bronzino "carved" another ornamental motif into the foreground table. Like the carving on the chair in his *Portrait of a Young Man*, this too should be read as emblematic. Just above the table ornament, Bronzino signed his name by carving "Bronzo—Fiorentino" into the table surface, a signature he would use again in the roughly contemporaneous *Panciatichi Holy Family* commissioned by Bartolomeo Panciatichi.[113]

In using the carved grotesques and a carved signature, the artist emphasizes the material nature of painting as malleable matter that could be shaped or incised like sculpture.[114] Building upon important studies of this painting published by R. Wildmoser, Elizabeth Cropper, and Wolf-Dietrich Lohr,[115] I will focus on S.J. Freedberg's reference to Bronzino's "small truths" that give veracity to the "lie of painting." In this portrait, the nearly illegible detail of a carved fragment partially hidden beneath the lifted veil of the tablecloth is the primary object. After close scrutiny, aided by photographs taken during the portrait's first restoration in Berlin in 1925 (Figs. 11a–g), I find the manner in which the carving was finished in the recent restoration of the painting inconsistent with the original remaining detail, as seen in an X-ray of the underpainting photographed before the portrait's first cleaning (Fig. 12).[116] In the painted relief, before its second, more recent cleaning and conservation in 2004, I distinguished a foot or paw crushing a snake, placed next to what may have been a carved distorted head, partially covered by a piece of cloth.[117] Another scholar has seen an arm reaching out to grasp the horn of an unidentified animal around which a cloth is tied.[118] If the paw was originally a lion's paw, it would relate to the Martelli family *stemma* carved by Donatello, a figure that emits a powerful apotropaic effect when attached to the palace façade.[119]

Before preparing this paper for publication, I reconsidered my earlier response to this carving and sought additional sources. After further study, I came to the conclusion that the design of the table carving resembles a fragment of an antique sarcophagus after one by Lysippos, depicting the *Labors of Hercules*. The sarcophagus, which at one time was in the Medici collection, is now in the Boboli

Gardens in Florence.[120] It remains intact in one example among many others now in Rome (Fig. 13). It seems clear to me that the fragment depicting two of the twelve *Labors of Hercules* now in the Boboli collection would have been recognized by the portrait's select audience, or at least by Bronzino.[121] The citation of an accessible, prized, local antique would certainly have had implications beyond its reference to the sitter. As a condensation of an entire narrative, as well as a statement of a moral virtue, it could be used as an allusion to the laborious and unrewarded work of the young poet and future cleric Martelli. Like the "claw of the Lion," it acts as a synecdoche for the entire sarcophagus, all twelve deeds enacted as a punishment. The fragmentary nature of the sculpture beneath the table, plus the page of hand written Homeric text, informs what one might call a sixteenth-century "philosophy of the fragment."[122] Such chains of associated images were thought to embody occult or divine signification far beyond the apparent meaning that such objects convey in actuality. If the images of a lion's paw, a serpent, or both were depicted in the portrait and were intended as references to a surviving section of a Roman sarcophagus depicting the labors of Hercules, the symbols chosen would be recognized as belonging to an accepted vocabulary of ancient ornamental decoration.

Traces of the signature "Bronzo—fiorentino," carved into the table almost invisibly and placed above the sarcophagus fragment, recall the famous sculptor to whom the Hercules sarcophagus is attributed: Lysippus, a sculptor whom Bronzino sought to emulate in his painting style.[123] The signature, when combined with the text from Homer, relates to a Northern tradition of placing epitaphs on engraved portraits of famous men, both living and deceased.[124] Portraits of Luther and Erasmus made by artists such as Lucas Cranach the Elder (c. 1472–1553) and Albrecht Dürer circulated among friends of Bronzino's sitters. A book, identified by its title plus other painted carvings surrounding the sitter, not coincidentally also appear in Hans Holbein the Younger's *Portrait of Erasmus* of 1523 (Fig. 14). These correspondences seem to reinforce the possibility that Holbein's portrait of Erasmus was in some sense a model for Bronzino's portrait of Martelli. Could it be merely a coincidence that the open page with the text facing the spectator and the carvings (including a Siren, a civic symbol of Nuremberg) are similar in their typology to those in Bronzino's portrait? Possibly the Holbein portrait, painted in England by a northerner, had been circulated as a single-sheet print, as were other images of Erasmus, and in this way found its way into Bronzino's hands.[125]

Like the example of Van Eyck's demonic lion in the Arnolfini portrait, the carvings are signs of the intrusion into everyday life of forces beyond the control of ordinary men. Only the painter, his sitter, and their select circle are meant to be fully aware of the meaning of such hidden allusions. In later works by Bronzino, such messages were directed to an audience that would include the patron (not always identified with the sitter) and his family or coterie as well as the sitter himself. The need for a receptive audience had been stressed by Aristotle in his *Poetica* and *Rhetorica*.[126]Although the Martelli portrait may predate the publication of the *Poetics* by at least a decade, similar writings by Aristotle could be found in manuscript fragments known to be earlier.[127] A second alternative is to give the painting a later date in the 1540s. As Lohr has thoroughly demonstrated, the literary allusions in this painting go beyond contemporary linguistic debates to make a moral point.[128] Scholars, however, continue to disagree on precisely what that point is. We should not forget that linguistic debates at that time had strong political implications.[129] All of the symbolic "figures" used in the painting point to the emblem and the adage that in turn relate to the classical "Triumph of Letters over Arms." Thus, David the poet, author of the Psalms, stands behind Martelli, also the poet. A Martelli family possession, the statue of *David* (as noted above), also refers to the family *stemma* carved by Donatello and showing *Hercules slaying the Nemean Lion*. The portrait refers to both Homer and Virgil, who both wrote of the destruction of an enemy of the state by a citizen acting in the best interest of his fellow citizens. Who was the enemy in c. 1538, and who represented the loyal citizen at the time this was painted? This reference can point to the lost Republican cause to which Martelli was committed or the reform of the Church vs. Rome; I prefer the former, since the reference is to actual war.[130] In a lecture delivered at the Villa I Tatti in the 1980s, Silvana Seidel-Menchi spoke of the "duplice Ercole," an iconographical motif based upon Erasmus' writings on Hercules. She attributed to Luther himself the paternity of a leaf with the image of Luther as

Hercules Germanicus intent on destroying a group of scholastic theologians.[131] This image should be seen in connection with a counter representation of Erasmus as *Hercules Gallicus*, a demi-god capable of winning men's minds with force of his eloquence alone. Alciato's Herculean emblems state that *concetto* textually. As noted above, the *pictura* for "Eloquence, surpassing strength" (Fig. 10) shows an aged Hercules who "chains men's tongues" through the strength of his eloquence. The connection between war and language in the passages by Virgil, which exist in the unopened book held by Ugolino, is further reified by its reference to a Herculean subject. The viewer could more easily make the association between Homer, Hercules, and peaceful reconciliation through speech (i.e., rhetoric or eloquence) as expressed in Alciato's emblem to "Eloquence, surpassing strength." Beneath the illustration, the text reads: "His left hand holds a bow, his right carries a rough club, and the Nemean lion cloaks his naked body."

Is Martelli shown in the likeness of Hercules? The Hercules in the eloquence emblem, "depicted as old and his temples hoary with age ... suggests otherwise" (as quoted under the image). The heroic aspect of Heracles was the prerogative only of rulers. What of Hercules'

> tongue, pierced with light chains, by which he cleaves the ears of men and draws them to him without difficulty? Are the Gauls not saying that with his tongue, not with his might, Alcides excelled in providing nations with laws? Arms yield to the toga, and he who is powerful in speech draws to his wishes even the most resistant hearts.[132]

This triumph of the word over the sword is the message in the table carving; and the "motto" of the portrait, the carving, in its details is the synecdochal message. A hidden narrative, described in a series of visual and written metaphors, is linked to the visible, worded documents; together, metaphors and text transmit the overall meaning to the observant, forewarned, and intellectually astute viewer. One might go so far as to contend that the painting as a whole contains the three parts of an emblem: a motto, the image, and a commentary.

Such literary references, as we have already mentioned, were not accessible to an ordinary Florentine viewer of the painting, only to the chosen audience for whom they were intended. Like Alciato's *Emblemata illustrata*, it was expressly intended for artists. Bronzino's inner circle of fellow artists, as well as academicians, would have immediately grasped any meanings hidden in details. Although it is not possible to explicate each ornamental reference, it is clear that beyond the exterior description of Martelli's role as a young "literary lion" (with references to Hercules), the details tell the story of his inner self. This interiority encoded in external details corresponds to what Varchi termed "il di dentro": that part of the subject which cannot be "seen" in a painting but can easily be "revealed" in poetry.[133] In a possibly intentional reference to the *paragone* between painting and the written word in this portrait, Bronzino makes a claim that the "unseen" locked within the sitter can indeed be made visible in paint (as visible as the word). He does this by replicating in painted words the actual text displayed in an open book that the sitter has been reading; in this case, Homer's *Iliad*. Thus, on a theoretical level, the painting is also a demonstration of the *paragone* between painting and poetry that is, in effect, parallel to the contrast between war and eloquence as Virgil states it in the second unopened and untitled book. Most likely it is the *Aeneid*, containing a passage regarding the word vs. the sword in which the former is victor.[134] All the pictorial details add to Bronzino's secular variation on the traditional Evangelist portrait, e.g., Raphael's *Portrait of Tommaso Inghirami*, to which Martelli's painted image is a successor, combining moral and religious notions of strength as told through a war of words made visible in the open book. Something of a paradox, if you think about it.

The sculpted grotesques and the sarcophagus fragment break the mold of the secular portrait, not only by exposing the *anima* of the sitter but also by alluding to Martelli's political and religious leanings, as well as the painter's legitimate right to poetic license. The head-like masks appear as substitutes for the *chimerae* to which Bronzino refers in his *Capitolo* entitled *le scuse*.[135] The medieval, northern, and pagan origins of these demonic creatures reinforce their function: to make visible those deviations from the norm that identify the sitter politically as well as personally Although *capricci* are said to derive from unseen powers operating in the minds of painter and sitter alike, Bronzino ascribes to the portrait the Horatian dictum *quodlibet* that favored the judicious use of artistic license, rather than the more rigid restrictions imposed by Vitruvius that were echoed in the restrictions on art proposed at the Council of Trent.[136] In defending the artist's right to license, Bronzino expresses not only the acceptance of, but also a preference for, the very excesses condemned by Vitruvius.[137] Although the use of licentious and capricious grotesquerie offered the selective viewer a more profound yet discrete exposure of the sitter's ideology, the message in this painting is an ethical-political one about war and chaos (in the form of demons) versus its antidotes reason and eloquence. This statement takes the form of an open book "speaking" for peace. The aspect of religion does not enter the picture directly, but the moral message of Homer appears as a subtext that, when combined with the allusion to Erasmus, leads us toward the Northern scholar-reformer in the guise of Hercules; a possible paradigm for Ugolino himself.

CONCLUSION

The new *Maniera* style took hold and subsequently migrated north and south because Italian patrons and sitters (often one and the same) and their chosen artists were more closely exposed to Northern art and its burgeoning art market disseminated through prints and trade. At that moment (from the 1530s on), art required discretion and dissimulation to override repression and escape serious repercussion.[138] Under pressure to renounce their claim to artistic license in particular contexts, Italian painters entertained various means of circumventing the restrictions imposed on them. Using art itself, they refashioned style so as to overcome the many imposed obstacles to imaging the imaginary. By appropriating visual cues and adapting literary tropes that veiled their true bias, they continued to elude discovery by their enemies as well as by unsuspecting modern scholars even today. The transmission of "Beauty" remained a principal goal of art throughout this period,[139] yet the newly invented style favored individualism, thus liberating the artist's need, as well as his desire, to adapt to a rapidly changing ideological ambiance. This stance engendered a tendency to enhance the depiction of ugliness as a contrast and contradiction to the primary goal of representing in paint the philosophical ideal of Beauty.

NOTES

1. This paper was initially presented at the annual Renaissance Society of America conference in 2004 in New York City. The session, organized by Dr. Liana De Girolami Cheney, included several other papers in this collection. I owe this publication to the dedication, gentle persistence, and sheer determination of Professor Cheney. I would like to thank her and my colleagues in that session for contributing to this final version. It has not been possible to assimilate, let alone read, all the important scholarship that has appeared in my area of research since this paper was delivered a decade ago. Publications by historian and art historians on Florentine sympathy for Catholic reform ideology and its impact on the art of the period in Tuscany and northern Italy have increased exponentially since then. Revelations of the clandestine adherence of Italian artists and patrons to religious reform—a concept of which I was only subliminally aware during the early stages of my research on Varchi and the *paragoni* in the 1970s was rarely acknowledged and mostly avoided by art historians. That subject has not only been brought out of the closet but is now recognized as a major influence on the art of Cinquecento Florence. I want to thank all the scholars who participated in the clearing of the air, whose scholarship changed the face of mid-Cinquecento studies. Others who have helped in diverse ways are Sharon Oboshi and Marie Tanner, who read a version of the text and made useful suggestions. To Craig H. Smyth I owe my enduring fascination for Bronzino and his cultural ambience, as well as the benefit of his impeccable scholarship, methodology, and discerning eye. Without help in obtaining images of the Berlin portrait of Ugolino Martelli through the intervention of Dr. Eric Schleier and, most recently, Dr. Bernd Lindemann, Director of the Gemäldegalerie, Berlin, I would not have been able to draw the conclusions regarding the portrait presented here. I owe a great debt to Ronny Cohen, who helped with footnotes and bibliography and saw me through to the end of this project. To Richard Brilliant, whose NEH seminar sparked my interest and transformed my perception of portraiture, thank you.

2. I have used the following editions of these books for all citations to follow: Leon Battista Alberti, *On Painting and On Sculpture: The Latin Texts of De pictura and De statua*, ed. Cecil Grayson (London: Phaidon Press Ltd., 1972) [hereafter Alberti, ed. Grayson, *On Painting and On Sculpture*]; *On*

the Art of Building in Ten Books, trans. Joseph Rykwert, N. Leach, and R. Tavernor (Cambridge, MA, and London: MIT Press, 1989) [hereafter *Art of Building*]. In addition, I have consulted the Italian text of *De re aedificatoria* in the 1565 translation by Cosimo Bartoli via a microform in the Frick Research Library, NY.

3. In writing his introduction to the book on ornament, one of his ten books of Architecture, Alberti manages to both compliment Vitruvius's text and stress his own skill in overcoming the difficulties of interpreting the ancient remains. In this way, he distances himself from the written source and asserts his personal competence based instead on familiarity with actual antiquities. In the "Sixth Book of *De re aedificatoria,* On Ornament" (*Art of Building,* 6. I. 154) he writes:

> … so many works of such brilliant writers had been destroyed by the hostility of time and of man, and almost the only sole survivor from this vast shipwreck is Vitruvius, an author of unquestioned experience, though one whose writings have been so corrupted by time that there are many omissions and many shortcoming. What he handed down was in any case not refined, and his speech such that the Latins might think that he wanted to appear a Greek, while the Greeks would think that he babbled Latin. However, his very text is evidence that he wrote neither Latin nor Greek, so that as far as we are concerned he might just as well not have written at all rather than write something that we cannot understand.

On the first illustrated edition of Vitruvius, see Carol Herselle Krinsky, "Cesare Cesariano and the Como Vitruvius edition of 1521" (Unpublished Ph.D. thesis, New York University, 1965).

4. Giorgio Vasari, *Le Vite de'più eccellenti Pittori Scultori e Architettori, scritta da M. Giorgio Vasari, pittore et architetto aretino, con i ritratti loro et con l'aggiunta delle Vite de' vivi & dei morti dallánno 1550, infino al 1567,* ed. Gaetano Milanese, 9 vols. (1878; repr. Florence: Sansoni, 1973) [hereafter cited as *Vite*-Milanese], Proemio to Part III, vol. IV, p. 8. Also in Giorgio Vasari, *Le Vite de'più eccellenti Pittori Scultori e Architettori nelle redazioni del 1550 e 1568,* eds. Rosanna Bettarini and Paola Barocchi (Florence: SPES, 1966–87) [hereafter *Vite*-B-B], Part III, vol. IV, p. 4. See also Leatrice Mendelsohn, "The Sum of the Parts: Recycling Antiquities in the *Maniera* Workshops of Salviati and his Colleagues," *Atti del Convegno: Salviati ou 'La Bella Maniera,'* Academie de France a Rome, American Academy in Rome et l'École Française, 6 March 1998, [special issue of] *Melanges de l'École Française* (2002), 107–148, here 109.

5. On Grazia, see Ulrike Müller-Hofstede, "Grazia," in *Lexikon für Kunstwissenschaft,* ed. Ulrich Pfisterer (Stuttgart: Weimar, 2003), 132–36.

6. Alberti, *Art of Building*, 420, for the translator's commentary on "Beauty and ornament *pulchritudo et ornamentum.*"

7. Alberti, ed. Grayson, *On Painting and On Sculpture, De pictura*, Bk. 2, 75–77:

> ... in assessing the proportions of a living creature we should take one member of it by which the rest are measured. The architect Vitruvius reckons the height of a man in feet. I think it more suitable if the rest of the limbs are related to the size of the head, although I have observed it to be well nigh a common fact in men that the length of the foot is the same as the distance from the chin to the top of the head. Having selected this one member, the rest should be accommodated to it, so that there is no member of the whole body that does not correspond with the others in length and breadth ...

8. Alberti, *On Painting and On Sculpture*, ed. Grayson, *De pictura*, Bk. 2, 76–77 (italics mine).

9. For a Renaissance example of a sculpted limb functioning as a sign of the inner workings of the mind of the subject, see H.W. Janson, "The Right Arm of Michelangelo's *Moses*," in *Festschrift Ulrich Middeldorf*, eds. Antje Kosegarten and Peter Tigler, 2 vols. (Berlin: de Gruyter, 1968), 1:241–47. Janson considers the tangible realization of the unseen in an intangible form that is created by means of the artist's, as he wrote in "The Image Made by Chance in Renaissance Thought," in *De Artibus Opuscula LX: Essays in Honor of Erwin Panofsky* (New York: New York University Press, 1961), 254–55.

10. See "Vasari's Life of Michelangelo," in Giorgio Vasari, *Le Vite de'più eccellenti Pittori Scultori e Architettori, scritta da M. Giorgio Vasari, pittore et architetto aretino, con i ritratti loro et con l'aggiunta delle Vite de' vivi & dei morti dal l' anno 1550, infino al 1567*, originally in 2 vols. (Florence: Giunti, 1568), vol. 6:54 this was downloaded from a copy on the web site of Scuola Normale di Pisa (no longer available on-line) [hereafter *Vite*-Giunti]; and Paola Barocchi, ed., *Giorgio Vasari, La Vita di Michelangelo*, 5 vols. (Milan: Riccardo Ricciardi, 1962), 1:58, commentary on the passage. Here, the New Sacristy's architectural members, viewed as ornaments, are described as parallel equivalents to the tomb effigies in the Medici burial chamber.

11. "Vasari's Life of Michelangelo" in *Vite*-Giunti, 6:54 and Barocchi, *Vita di Michelangelo*, 1:58, with commentary on the passage. The parallels Vasari uses to compare a new style in painting to architecture are not unlike the way Alberti transferred artistic goals from sculpture to painting. The chain begins with Vitruvius and continues through Alberti to Vasari,

linking architecture first to sculpture, then to painting. In sixteenth-century *paragoni* that omit architecture from the hierarchy of the three arts, sculpture takes over the lead, and painting remains secondary. Reasons for this may be due to the dominance of Michelangelo, the freeing of sculpture from the taint of manual labor, the stigma of Plato's diatribe against the deceptive nature of painting, or the permanence and monumentality of sculpture enabling it to sustain the memory of famous men. Not least of these reasons may have been the indestructibility of sculpture in the face of war and the vicissitudes of time (a myth due to the survival of antique sculpture and the loss of its paintings).

12. On Varchi's concept of *ornatus*, see Leatrice Mendelsohn, *Paragoni: Benedetto Varchi and Cinquecento Art Theory* (Ann Arbor, MI: UMI Research Press, 1982), 126–28. Varchi's highest praise for ornament, however, is bestowed on sculpture rather than painting. In his *Lezzione* on the *paragone*, the Roman column of Trajan and Michelangelo's New Sacristy in Florence are judged the highest examples of magnificence and ornament (Mendelsohn, *Paragoni*, 127).

13. Alberti, ed. Grayson, *On Painting and On Sculpture, De scultura*, 133–35.

14. On the period between the fall of the Republic in 1530 and the firm re-establishment of Medici rule under Cosimo, see Paolo Simoncelli, "Republicani fiorentini in esilio nuove testimonianze (1538–41)," in *Renaissance Studies in Honor of Craig Hugh Smyth*, ed. Andrew Morrogh, 2 vols. (Florence: Giunti Barbera, 1985), 1:217–29; and Domenico Zanrè, *Cultural Non-Conformity in Early Modern Florence* (Aldershot and Burlington, VT: Ashgate, 2004), 15–16. See also Giorgio Spini, *Cosimo I e la indipendenza del' principato mediceo* (Florence: Vallechi, 1980), 3–31.

15. See Paolo Simoncelli, "The Turbulent Life of the Florentine Community in Venice," in *Heresy, Culture, and Religion in Early Modern Italy: Contexts and Contestations*, eds. Ronald K. Delph, M.M. Fontaine, and J.J. Martin, *Sixteenth Century Essays & Studies*, 76 (Kirksville, MO: Truman State University Press, 2006), 113–33, including useful bibliography.

16. See Massimo Firpo, "Bronzino and the Medici," in Carlo Falciani and Antonio Natali, eds., *Bronzino: Artist and Poet at the Court of the Medici* (Florence: Mandragora, 2010) [hereafter Falciani and Natali, *Bronzino*], 96–98; and Carlo Falciani, "On religious painting but also on 'sides, stomachs, etc.,'" in ibid., 277 –93, where he refers primarily to the later religious works of the 1550s by Bronzino and other Florentine artists.

17. Duplicity was a skill that courtiers learned to survive at court. The role of duplicity, disguise, and deception in portraiture is discussed in Harry Berger, Jr., *Fictions of the Pose: Rembrandt against the Italian Renaissance* (Stanford, CA: Stanford University Press, 2000), Ch. 3, 95–104, where

he proposes that the posing for one's portrait, especially in the case of ruler portraits, is a performative act and can be transformed or distorted by both sitter and artist. In *The Absence of Grace: Sprezzatura and Suspicion in Two Renaissance Courtesy Books* (Stanford, CA: Stanford University Press, 2000), Berger sets the stage for these attitudes, presenting the reasons and justification for the behavior of the Courtier in contemporary literary manuals of behavior such as Castiglione's Cortegiano and others.

18. According to Sydney J. Freedberg, *Painting in Italy, 1500–1600* (Baltimore, MD: Penguin Books, Pelican History of Art, 1971), 286–95, "High *Maniera*" differs from its earlier form in that it takes the inventions and experiments of the previous generation to another level, "becoming more restrictive and artificial … owing in part to the political and religious context of its time." Freedberg considered the heightened artificiality of style to be a direct response to external social factors, combined with greater acceptance of the influence and appropriation of classical antiquity. In 1970, Freedberg wrote about these causes in the face of a scholarly back-lash against the *zeitgeist* explanation of art history, an attitude that has since mellowed considerably. We will not weigh in on the varying influence of different external factors on the mannerist style of painting cited by Freedberg but, rather, will show how each of his defining factors, the "restrictive and artificial," reveals itself in pictorial details. See also Philip S. Sohm, *Style in the Art Theory of Early Modern Italy* (New York: Cambridge University Press, 2001), 87–97, who devotes a large part of his Vasari chapter to the words *maniera* and "mannerism" and their diverse meanings, often held simultaneously. For Sohm on later critics of mannerist style, see his chapter "Style as Symbolic Form," 22–23, where he states definitively that the name "Mannerism" as a period style was invented only in the seventeenth century. By the end of the sixteenth century the term "Mannerism" had taken on an identity based largely on the negative characteristics emphasized by its critics goes without saying. Here, however, *Maniera* is understood to be the singular style: *la bella maniera*, named by Vasari, a style baptized into existence from 1527 that endured in modified form into the 1560s. In this study, *maniera* is considered a sub-category of the more general style, translatable in English as Mannerism. For a nuanced history of anti-mannerist criticism, see Craig H. Smyth, *Mannerism and Maniera* (Locust Valley, NY: J.J. Augustin, 1963, reissued in *Artibus et Historiae*, IRSA, 1992), 17, where he dates the use of the term *Maniera* to the 1530s, with anticipations of it earlier in Michelangelo (19). The negative connotation of the term "Mannerism," although implied by Lodovico Dolce, was not applied by Florentine artists to their work, nor even by Gregorio Giraldi Gilio, whose later criticisms lay elsewhere, but its negative usage was consistently used by critics in the seventeenth and eigh-

teenth centuries and fully codified by nineteenth-century art historians. In my opinion, although the term *manierismo* eventually acquired a built-in critique, it is not an appropriate noun or adjective to use when discussing the prescient style exemplified by our portraits. That word refers to the style as it evolved decades after its primacy in the 1540s. In the twenty-first century, the English term "Mannerism" has become more neutral; "mannerist" however, is still used occasionally to differentiate "bad" style (excessively stylized) from "good" style (more restrained). In this paper, John Shearman's book *Mannerism* (London: Penguin Books, 1991) has not been pre-eminent because, although he views Mannerism as intrinsically ornamental, my use of the term is actually narrower. I give greater weight to the historical, satirical, and political factors that imbued and defined the use of the word "ornament" with respect to mid-Cinquecento style than to those decorative qualities by which he defined and designated it the "stylish style."

19. In the introduction to *Erasmo in Italia 1520–1580* (Turin: Bollati Boringhieri, 1987), 15ff, Sylvia Seidel Menchi takes issue with previous historical positions taken by scholars that the Italian preference for Erasmus over Luther in the early stages of the Reformation was due to their perception of the former as a moderate and balanced humanist, a critic of society and the Church who did not seek a break between them. According to Seidel Menchi, Erasmus was officially viewed in Italy as a "pestilential heretic, a disseminator of scandal," etc., and was attacked there for his *Enchiridion*. In Ch. 2, 41–72 titled "Erasmo luterano: una costruzione della teologia italiana fra il 1520 e il 1535," Seidel Menchi focuses on the fact that, during that period in Italy, Erasmus was viewed as a Lutheran. In an appendix (68–69), she offers two cases, that of Vergerio and that of Nacchianti, demonstrating the influence of the scholar Erasmus on the Italians. Nevertheless, Seidel Menchi refers to echoes of the Erasmian-Lutheran conflict over Free Will, emphasizing their differences in Italy as early as 1525 in Ferrara. See the appendix to Ch. 3, 95–99, concerning the publication of *De libero arbitrio* in Venice in 1524, copies of which almost entirely disappeared by 1559 after the publication of the index by Pope Paul IV. In 1525, a sort of appendix to the volume published by Fröben came into the hands of the Ferrarese Celio Calcagnini, which, because it was not considered the original volume, did not suffer the same fate as other condemned works of Erasmus (such as the treatise itself, eventually labeled a "Lutheran book"). This is further elaborated by Seidel Menchi in Ch. 4, 100ff, on the doctrine of *Libertà*. It is not clear the extent to which scholars such as Varchi and his students, including Martelli, were aware of the differences between Erasmus and Luther. However, since the works of Erasmus were among those in Varchi's library and well read by his dis-

ciples in Italy, they certainly knew what Erasmus wrote. See also Albano Biondi, "La Giustificazione della Simulazione nel Cinquecento," in idem, *Eresia e Riforma nell'Italia del Cinquecento, Miscellanea I* (DeKalb: Northern Illinois University Press, Chicago, IL: The Newberry Library, and Florence: Sansoni, 1974), 1–68, esp. 7, 9–10, where he distinguishes between simulation and dissimulation.

20. See M. Hall, *Art After Raphael: Painting in Central Italy in the Sixteenth Century* (Cambridge, Edinburgh, and New York: Cambridge University Press: 1999), for another view of the origins of this style.

21. Janet Cox-Rearick, "From Bandinelli to Bronzino: The Genesis of the *Lamentation* for the Chapel of Eleonora di Toledo," *Mitteilungen des Kunsthistorischen Institutes in Florenz* 33 (1989), 37–84; and Massimo Firpo, *Gli Affreschi di Pontormo a San Lorenzo, Eresia, politica e cultura nella Firenze di Cosimo I* (Turin: Einaudi, 1997). For a perspective on *Vittoria Colonna*'s reception to the writings of Juan de Valdés and her connections to Varchi, Vasari, and Michelangelo, see Leatrice Mendelsohn, "Der Florentiner Kreis—Michelangelos Sonett an Vittoria Colonna, Varchis *Lezzione* und Bilder der Reformation" (Catholic reform), in *Vittoria Colonna, Dichterin und Muse Michelangelos*, Exh. Kunsthistorisches Museum, Vienna, 1997, Catalogue, ed. Sylvia Ferino-Pagden (Vienna: Skira, 1997), 265–73. On the influence of reform religious ideas disseminated by the "Spirituali," led by the Venetian Gaspero Contarini until 1542 (convicted of heresy; d. 1542). See also Gigliola Fragnito, "Vittoria Colonna e il dissenso religioso," in *Vittoria Colonna e Michelangelo*, ed. Pina Ragionieri (Florence: Mandragora, 2005), 97–105.

22. The conflation of ruler icons with images of Christ and their potential for a dual reading was one of the means by which the restoration of images was made possible under Constantine. See Jaroslav Pelikan, *Imago Dei: The Byzantine Apologia for Icons*, The A.W. Mellon Lectures in the Fine Arts, 1987, The National Gallery of Art, Washington, DC (Princeton, NJ: Princeton University Press, 1990), 2–3, on the iconoclastic controversies of the eighth and ninth centuries. Citing John of Damascus, "Orations of the Holy Icons," III.19, Pelikan makes clear how the double meaning (Christian and Imperial) of icons is the basis for both Iconoclasm and Iconodulia. At the outset (*Imago Dei*, 7ff., esp. 36–39), he notes the political origins of iconoclasm. The message of this chapter is the essentially political nature of the controversy over images. See also 143–45, on the concept relevant for *la bella maniera*, of the "hidden in the visible"; esp. 145n91, where he quotes William Loerke; and, further, 167–69, on the portrayal of invisible transcendent persons from the Bible based on the fact that "some form must be found in the visible world" to make men aware that these "unportrayable figures" exist. Other discussions in the text regard the oppos-

ing interpretations of both biblical and apostolic statements on the nature of Christ and the "inseparability of the human and divine nature of God," which are transferred to similar dichotomies in visual depictions, by means of both aesthetic and religious veracity (77–83).

23. Kenneth Gowans and Sheryl Reiss, eds., *The Pontificate of Clement VII: History, Politics, Culture* (Aldershot: Ashgate, 2005), contains the following relevant essays: William Wallace, "Clement VII and Michelangelo ...," 189–98; Caroline Elam, "Michelangelo and the Clementine Architectural Style," 199–201, 203–06, 212–18, 220–22; George L. Gorse, "Augustan Mediterranean Iconography and Renaissance Hieroglyphics at the Court of Clement VII: Sebastiano del Piombo's Portrait of Andrea Doria," 318–28 and Appendix I, 329–30; and Alexander Nagle, "Experiments in Art and Reform in Italy in the Early Sixteenth Century," esp. 398–402, where his discussion of free-standing sculpture and its "form as iconography" can be related to Bronzino's inclusion of statue images in his painted portraits. In the context of artistic experiment and reform, the substantial role of sculpture as a metaphorical *figura* as well as a material prototype deserves further investigation.

24. The degree to which members of various academies (in particular the *Umidi* in Florence and the *Infiammati* in Venice) supported anti-Medici factions immediately before and after the demise of the Florentine Republic is difficult to determine or measure, since overt adherence to opposing political or religious institutions could not be openly asserted safely. Even the *Ottimati* members of in the *Academia degli Umidi* were cautious in their expression against the Medici. Having maintained a certain amount of control during the Republic, many were stripped of their possessions and heavily taxed on their return to an oligarchy. The *fuorusciti* in Venice, for example, were divided by class factions; those who were anxious to protect their Florentine property opposed the merchant and labor populace on the question of military opposition.

25. See Simoncelli, "Florentine *Fuorusciti* at the Time of Bindo Altoviti," in *Raphael, Cellini and a Florentine Banker, The Patronage of Bindo Altoviti*, Exhibition Catalog for Boston: Isabella Stuart Gardner Museum of Art, eds. A. Chong, D. Pegazzano, and D. Zikos (Milan: Mondadori Electa, 2003), 285–328.

26. Janet Cox-Rearick, *Bronzino's Chapel of Eleonora in the Palazzo Vecchio* (Berkeley, Los Angeles, and Oxford: University of California Press, 1993), 74–75.

27. For paintings by Pontormo, Bronzino, Vasari, and Michelangelo commissioned by patrons such as Bartolomeo Bettini, Panciatichi, and Bindo Altoviti, see Simoncelli, "Florentine *Fuorusciti*" and eadem, "Republicani fiorentini in esilio nuove testimonianze (1538–1541)," 1:217–29;

Philippe Costamagna, "Portraits of Florentine Exiles," in Exhibition Catalog, *Raphael, Cellini and A Renaissance Banker: The Patronage of Bindo Altoviti*, eds. A. Chong, D. Pegazzano, and D. Zikos (Boston: Isabella Stewart Museum of Art, 2003), 329–22; idem, "De la *fiorentinità* des portraits de Pontormo et de Bronzino," *Paragone* 62 (2005), 50–75; Falciani and Natali, *Bronzino*; and, at a somewhat later moment, the extreme case of Pontormo's frescoes in San Lorenzo for the Medici, as described by Firpo, *Gli Afreschi di Pontormo a San Lorenzo*, 137–39, 408–18.

28. On *bizzarrie*, see Vasari, *Vite*-Giunti, as cited in Barocchi's *Vita di Michelangelo*, 1:10 and *commento*. Speaking of the art of the Quattrocento in comparison with the Cinquecento, Vasari wrote: "Vi mancavano ancora la copia *de'belli abiti, la varietà di tante bizzarie, la vaghezza de'colori* ...," from the *Proemio della terza parte*, *Vita*-Milanese, IV, 8–9 (italics mine). On *bizzarie* and other ornaments as anti-classical and Mannerist, and writing in relation to painting and Bronzino in particular, see Antonio Pinelli, *La bella maniera. Artisti del Cinquecento tra regola e licenza* (Turin: Giulio Einaudi editore, 1993), Section 5, *La grottesca: capriccio, controsenso e improvvisazione*, 131–35.

29. See John W. O'Malley, *Trent, What Happened at the Council* (Cambridge, MA, and London: The Belknap Press of Harvard University Press, 2013), 244, 281.

30. The variety of forms that artistic license might take with regard to the portraits is discussed below. See Vasari, *Vite*-B-B, 6:54, as cited in Barocchi, *Vita di Michelangelo*, 1:58–59:

> Vitruvio e le antichità, per non volere a quello agiugnere. La quale *licenzia* ha dato grande animo, a quelli che ànno veduto il far suo, *di mettersi a imitarlo*, e *nuove fantasie* si sono vedute poi, *alla grottesca più tosto che a ragione o regola, a'loro ornamenti*; onde gli artifici gli hanno infinito e perpetuo obligo, avendo egli rotto i lacci e le catene delle cose *che per via d'una strada comune* eglino di continuo operavano (italics mine).

In a previous article, I suggested that the word *licenza* used in art theory may be related to the contemporaneous debate between Luther and Erasmus concerning the doctrine of Free Will. I plan to elucidate this undeveloped statement in a future publication, since it is too complex to be dealt with here.

31. The '*Institutio Oratoria' of Quintilian*, Latin and English trans. H.E. Butler (Cambridge, London, and New York: W. Heinemann and Harvard University Press, 1922; repr. 1966), vol. VIII, Bk. III, pp. 61–62. Dio Chrysostomo, *Orations*, Eng. trans. Heinemann, 5 vols. (London: Heinemann,

1932–51), vol. 1, *Fifth Oration*. See also Cicero, *De Oratore*, 2 vols., Eng. trans. L.H.G. Greenwood (Cambridge, MA, and London: Heinemann, 1960), Bk. III, Section xxv, pp. 96–97 and Section xxvii, p. 104.

> ... the embellishment (ornamenting) of oratory is achieved in the first place by general style and by a sort of inherent colour and flavour; for that it shall be weighty and pleasing and scholarly and gentlemanly and attractive and polished, and shall possess the requisite amount of feeling and pathos (it) is not a matter of particular divisions of the framework, but these qualities must be visible in the whole of the structure. But further, in order to embellish it with flowers of language and gems of thought, it is not necessary for this ornamentation to be spread evenly over the entire speech but it must be so distributed that there may be brilliant jewels ... (*Inst. Orat.* 96 XXV).

Compare Jacques Derrida, *The Truth in Painting*, trans. Geoff Bennington and I. McLeod (Chicago, IL, and London: University of Chicago Press, 1987), n. 27. It is important, in the context of this paper, not to confuse *ornato/ornatus* with *ornamento/ornamentus*, that is, we must distinguish the word "ornate" from the word "ornament." The characteristics of a room or picture described as being ornate or overly decorated are quite different pictorially from an ornament *per se*, that is, a specific object added to embellish the whole which may or may not be "ornamental," and not necessarily in excess. For additional discussion of *ornato/ornatus* and *ornamento/ornamentus*, see H. Wohl, *The Aesthetics of Italian Renaissance Art: A Reconsideration of Style* (New York and Cambridge: Cambridge University Press, 1999), Ch. 2, *Ornato*, 54–75.

32. In that year, Bartolomeo Panciatichi also became a member of the *Accademia degli Umidi*, prior to its appropriation by Cosimo de' Medici as a state institution under the name *Accademia Fiorentina*. See Carlo Falciani, "Bronzino and the Panciatichi," in Falciani and Natali, *Bronzino*, 153–65, esp. 154; Leatrice Mendelsohn, "Madonna and Child with St. John in the Uffizi," Cat. Entry, in Falciani and Natali, *Bronzino*, 172; and Elena Aloia, "Culture, Faith, and Love: Bartolomeo Panciatichi," and Lynette M.F. Bosch, "Orthodoxy and Heterodoxy in Agnolo Bronzino's Paintings for Bartolomeo and Lucrezia Panciatichi," both in this volume.

33. In his chapter on the *parergon*, Derrida, *Truth in Painting*, 37–82, begins by attacking Kant's *Critique of Judgment* on the existence of a universal value of beauty. As Derrida sees it, Kant's position requires making a sharp distinction (or visual separation) between the "inside and outside" (interior and exterior) of the work "proper." The example he uses is the

separation of the drapery from the body of a nude statue. Reconsidering the notion of "binary opposition," Derrida questions contradictions he finds in Kant's logic and unveils the false assumptions underlying its philosophical structure. He refutes Kant's concept of one intrinsic, reducible quality based on an *a priori* ideal of beauty. Instead, Derrida visualizes an "oppositional limit in the edges of the frame" (i.e., the "frame" acts as a barrier that prevents ornament from escaping its essential role in the enclosed pictorial space). His concept of the *parergon* is emblematic of his method of deconstruction; he reverses the hierarchies within which "signification naturalizes certain discourses."

34. On *Grazia*, see Müller-Hofstede, "Grazia," 132–36.

35. Varchi not only was important in transferring philosophical ideas on love, poetry, and creation to the visual arts but also was instrumental in collating a vocabulary for the new theory of art under construction at that time. In his lectures on the comparison of the arts he set forth the kind of new *regole* necessary for artists. In particular, his transference from Aristotle's *Poetics* and *Nicomachean Ethics* were crucial for defining painting and sculpture. Comparing poetry to painting, to the detriment of poetry, in his *Lezzioni* he wrote: "… i poeti imitano il di dentro principalmente, cioè i corpi e le fattezze di tutti le cose, cose." And "Bene è vero che, come I poeti discrivono ancora *il di fuori*, cosi I pittori mostrano quanto più possono *il di dentro, cioè gli affetti*"; see Paola Barocchi, *Trattati d'Arte dell'Cinquecento, fra manierismo e controriforma*, 3 vols. (Bari: Laterza, 1960–62), 1:55. Elsewhere in his writing, he supported poetry as revealing *il di dentro*, while painting is occupied with externals, that is, *il di fuori*. On *il di fuori* and *il di dentro* in the *Lezzioni*, see Mendelsohn, *Paragoni*, 61–62 and 132–33; regarding his poetic influence, ibid., xvii, 5n18. Umberto Pirotti, in his biography of Varchi, *Benedetto Varchi e la cultura del suo tempo* (Florence: Olschki, 1971), 6n25, writes that he: "… can be credited personally with the infusion of a strong dose of Aristotle into Florence"; and see Paul O. Kristeller, "The Modern System of the Arts," *Journal of the History of Ideas* 12, no. 4 (1951). On Varchi and the new Aristotelian criticism, see Mendelsohn, *Paragoni*, 8–11. Varchi's lecture on the *paragone* took place in 1547; the standard volgare version of *Retorica e Poetica di Aristotele in volgare* by Bernardo Segni (*Aristotle's Rhetoric and Poetics*, trans. and commentary by Bernardo Segni, Florence, 1549) was published in Florence by the *Accademia Fiorentina*, intended for use by its members, the same year as Varchi's *Lezzione sulla maggioranza degli arti* was published. The volgare edition of the Aristotle with Segni's extensive commentary was dedicated to Cosimo I de' Medici, whose interest in the Florentine language was closely connected to the politicized myth of his Etruscan heritage: *L'Ercolano Dialogo Di Benedetto Varchi: Dove Si Ragiona Delle Lingue e in Paticolare Della Toscana E. Fiorentina,*

con la Correzione di Lodovico Castelvetro Girolamo Muzio, note di G. Bottari e G.A. Volpi, eds. rivedata e illustrata da Pietro dal Rio (Florence: L'Agenzia Libraria, 1846); facsimile of original MSS 1 July 1914, repr. n.d. (c. 2012). See also comments on another linguistic *lezzione* by Annalisa Andreoni, "La *Lezzione seconda* sulla grammatica di Benedetto Varchi," *Nuova Rivista di Letturatura Italiana* 6, nos. 1–2 (2003), 137–68.

36. Religious painting in the Quattrocento relied on subject matter as well as line to produce *grazia*, that is, grace in the spiritual sense. However, even comparing earlier religious paintings to Bronzino's expression of *grazia* in his religious paintings, we find little reliance on graceful lines. This is material for another discussion.

37. In his letter on the debate requested by Varchi for publication. See Mendelsohn, *Paragoni*, 143–45 and 150–54, for Bronzino's letter.

38. For elaboration of this idea, see Mendelsohn, *Paragoni*, 152.

39. Through Varchi, Bronzino would have known not only Quintilian's but also Franciscus Robortellus' commentary on "audience," in specifically his volgare translation of Aristotle's *Poetics* 1453a5: "what is, what is probable and verisimilar—all these are known only by reference to the audience and only by consulting the audience do we know whether they have been achieved …"; Francisci Robortelli, *Utinensis in librum Aristotelis de Arte Poetica explicationes* (Basel, 1555), I, 46. Varchi attended Robortellus' lectures in Padua before Segni's volgare publication of the *Poetics* in 1549, which coincided with Vasari's first edition printed in 1550. We owe the rapid dissemination of the *Poetics* in the second half of the Cinquecento to these publications. Aristotle's verbal theatrical directions are transferred by Varchi directly from the *Poetics* to painting theory, an event that also reshaped the characteristics defining portraiture.

40. Selective body parts drawn from well-known statues add to the sitter's male beauty, i.e., his *grazia*. This is heightened by constructing the body with fragments of ancient and contemporary limbs. The hands as well as the torsos are frequently attached in poses that allude to known sculpted or painted portraits of famous rulers whose powers are transferred "by proxy" through these limbs and further reinforced when they interact with significant objects. See Mendelsohn, "The Sum of the Parts," 107–48. In Lucian of Samostrata, "Essays in Portraiture," in *Ikones*, trans. A.M. Harmon, 8 vols. (Cambridge, MA, and London: William Heinemann Ltd., 1919); 4:162, 265, 267, 275, Lucian described his method of taking body parts from famous works of sculpture and adding them together to form a portrait of perfect beauty. In this manner, he created the portrait of the famous courtesan Panthea, meaning "all the goddesses."

41. The rhetorical term *energia* depends on ornamental detail's overtly aggressive, ludicrous, or brutal appearance, on occasion supporting an

emotional expression. At the same time, the effect can be grotesquely co-medic. Consequently they fulfill the role of creating *energia* because they stick in your mind; they are, in fact, memorable. Bronzino's carvings cre-ate ornamental activation generated by their contrast with the stability and seriousness of the remaining context. See Wolf-Dieter Lohr, "... *e nuo-vi Omeri, e Plati* ... Painted Characters in Portraits by Andrea del Sarto and Agnolo Bronzino," in *Poetry on Art: Renaissance to Romanticism*, ed. Thom-as Frangenberg (Donington: Shaun Tyas, 2003), 79n139, where the author justly connects Varchi's expression of Bronzino's *ornato stile* to Quintilian's passages on *evidencia* in his *Institutio Oratoria* (see Lohr's note on 139 for page notations for these passages).

42. The best discussion of the evolution from metaphor to allegory in antiquity is found in Otto J. Brendel, *Prolegomena to the Study of Roman Art*, foreword by Jerome J. Pollitt (New Haven, CT: Yale University Press, 1979), passim.

43. Clues to hidden allegorical meaning were also present in portraits by Rosso Fiorentino, Alessandro Allori, Sebastiano del Piombo, Bacchi-acca, Parmigianino, and Lorenzo Lotto, as well as other contemporaries and followers of Bronzino.

44. Janet Cox-Rearick, *Dynasty and Destiny in Medici Art: Pontormo, Leo X and the Two Cosimos* (Princeton, NJ: Princeton University Press, 1984), 41–59, devotes an entire chapter to this ancestor portrait. She points out that like the family burial chapel in the New Sacristy and its sculptures, commissioned of Michelangelo by Leo X via Cardinal Giulio de' Medici, the portrait of Cosimo shares the themes of "dynastic extinction and re-newal—of Medici glorification and immortality ..." (43). This theme is rep-resented by the laurel bush to which a *fresh new branch* (*broncone*) has been attached, painted on the right-hand side of Cosimo the Elder. According to Cox-Rearick, Pontormo's likeness of Cosimo is based on a medal bearing an effigy of Cicero on which the motto *Pater Patriae Parens* was inscribed. The abbreviated motto *Cosmus Medices P.P.P.* appears here inscribed, writ-ten in antique form on the scroll-like back of the chair in which Cosimo is enthroned. The inscription on the ribbon scroll that wraps around the *broncone* is taken from Virgil's *Aeneid* VI. 143–44: "[Primo] avvulso. No[n] Defic[it] Alter [Aureus]" (As soon as one is torn away another takes its place). See n. 31 above for the related description by Dio Chrysostomo of the transformation of a narrative into a metaphor published in a collec-tion of his lectures. Since the publication of Cox-Rearick's citation of Her-cules' appearance in various prints by Fontainebleau artists (*Dynasty and Destiny*, 41–63), she dates the Michelangelo *Hercules* c. 1519 (here dated 1527), by which time it had already left Florence for Fontainebleau. Like the dating of the *Halberdier*, the pose of the lost Hercules has been debated

by scholars without unanimity or further confirmation of its appearance. Philippe Costamagna, *Pontormo, catalogue raisonné de l'oeuvre peint* (Paris: Gallimard, 1994), 42, 150–52n33, agrees with Cox-Rearick's dating of the Pontormo *Halberdier*. Elizabeth Cropper, in *L'officina della maniera: varietà e fierezza nell'arte fiorentina del Cinquecento fra le due repubbliche (1494–1530)*, eds. Alessandro Cecchi and Antonio Natali (Florence: Giunti, and Venice: Marsilio, 1966), Exhibition Catalog entry, no. 101, 290, disagrees, believing the *Halberdier* to be later and a portrait of a certain Francesco Guardi, whom Vasari mentions as a subject for a portrait Bronzino; see her *Pontormo: Portrait of a Halberdier* (Los Angeles, CA: Getty Museum, 1997). See Leatrice Mendelsohn, "Bronzino in Pesaro and After: The Impact of Raphael and Raphaelism on Bronzino's Florentine Manner," in Henk Van Veen, ed., *The Translation of Raphael's Roman Style*, Conference Proceedings from The Translation of Raphael's Roman Style in Groningen, The Netherlands, November 2002 (Leuven: Peeters, 2007), 102nn111–112, in agreement with Cropper's dating and identification.

On the relationship of portrait medals to painted portraits, and portraits to family lineage, social rank, virtue, and prestige, see the fundamental discussion by Sir John Pope-Hennessy, *The Portrait in the Renaissance*, Bollingen Series 30, Lecture 12, The National Gallery of Art, Washington, DC (Princeton, NJ: Princeton University Press, 1979), 64–73, where he links portrait medals to Northern portraits (89–100) and concludes with comparisons between portraits of Erasmus and Thomas More (1478–1535), both captured in paint and on medals. Recently, Luke Syson and D. Thornton refer to portraits from the Quattrocento in which books or writing materials, written words, fruits, and personal belongings play a major role in defining the function of the portrait with respect to the sitter and his intended audience; see *Objects of Virtue: Art in Renaissance Italy*, Exhibition Catalog, J. Paul Getty Museum (Los Angeles, CA: Getty Publications, 2001), Chapter 1, 12–36, notes 118, 119, and figs. 25, 38. The importance of the value of luxury objects as political gifts and status symbols is discussed throughout, tangentially relevant to our interpretation of *ornamenti* and the more specific use of *ornatus* in the two portraits by Bronzino under discussion.

45. For illustrations of Vasari's portraits, see Laura Corti, *Vasari, catalogo completo* (Florence: Cantini Editore, 1989), 13; and for Lorenzo de' Medici, see Entries 2 and 14 and Entry 3. Both portraits now in the Uffizi: Inv. 1578 and Inv. 1563, respectively. Dated by Corti to 1534 based on the commission requested by Duke Alessandro and communicated by Ottaviano de' Medici, recorded in a letter to Alessandro published by Malcolm Campbell, "Il ritratto del Duca Alessandro de' Medici di Giorgio Vasari: contesto e significato," in *Giorgio Vasari tra decorazione ambientale e storio-*

grafia artistica, ed. G.C. Garfagnini (Florence: Olschki, 1985), 339–61. See Corti, *Vasari catalogo completo*, Entry 1 and 2, 14 and 15 (with illustrations of the two works), and Liana De Girolami Cheney, "Giorgio Vasari's and Niccolò Machiavelli's Medicean Emblems of War and Peace in the Portrait of Duke Alessandro de Medici," in *Artful Armies, Beautiful Battles*, ed. Pia Cuneo (Leiden: Brill, 2001), 107-31.

46. See U. Davitt Asmus, *Corpus Quasi Vas: Beitrag zur Ikonographie der Italienischen Renaissance* (Berlin: Mann, 1977). See also Julian Kliemann, "Il pensiero di Paolo Giovio nelle pitture eseguite sulle sue 'ínvenzione,'" in *Paolo Giovio, Il Rinascimento e la memoria.* Conference Proceedings (Como: Società Storica Comense, 1985), 77–78, 197–23. The relationship of Paolo Giovio's imprese and museum of portraits to the two Bronzino portraits under consideration here deserves more attention, since Giovio appears to be the liaison for Cosimo I, Alciato, and possibly also Erasmus.

47. Portrait covers such as the *Pygmalion* painted by Bronzino were called *Timpani*. For an example of a cover showing the mask as a *persona*, see the *timpano* (outer skin) of a *Portrait of a Lady* attributed to Ghirlandaio, with the inscription *Sua Cuinque Persona*, discussed by Elizabeth Cropper in "Portrait of a Lady (La Monaca)," Entry 39, with related illustration "Portrait Cover with Mask and Grotesques," Entry 36, in *Virtue and Beauty, Leonardo's Ginevra de'Benci and Renaissance Portraits of Women*, Exhibition Catalogue of the National Gallery, London (Princeton, NJ: Princeton University Press, 2001). The Quattrocento portrait of Lucrezia Tornaquinci by Ghirlandaio utilizes an epitaph by Martial that alludes to the inability of a painted portrait to show the beauty of the soul. The painter appears to use personal objects probably belonging to the deceased, such as her jewels and a book that symbolically reflect her inner soul. Covering Pontormo's portrait of Francesco Guardi is a *timpano* by Bronzino of the Pygmalion legend. See Liana De Girolami Cheney and Sonia Michelotti Bonetti, "Bronzino's *Pygmalion and Galatea: l'antica bella maniera*," *Discoveries* 24, no. 1 (2007), 1–5 (posted on 15 September by anydam at <http://www.scrc.us.com/discoveries/bronzinos-pygmalion-and-galatea-1%e2%80%99-antica-bella-maniera/>); and Liana De Girolami Cheney, "Bronzino's *Pygmalion and Galatea*: The Metamorphosis of a Muse," in this volume. For the history and meaning of masks, see Eckhard Leuchner, *Persona, Larva, Maske: Ikonographische Untersuchungen vom 16 bus zum früen 18 Jahrhundert* (Frankfurt-am-Main: Peter Lang, 1997), passim.

48. In Neoplatonic terms, the *anima* of the image exists within the sculptural material (stone, marble, wood, or clay) prior to its transformation from mere matter into an object of art; the "soul" is waiting within to be released by the sculptor through his skill. See Varchi's explication of Michelangelo's sonnet "L'Ottimo Artista ...," "Lezzioni della maggioran-

za delle arti," in Paola Barocchi, *Trattati d'Arte del Cinquecento, fra manierismo e controriforma*, 3 vols. (Bari: Laterza, 1960–62), 1:3–82. For one of many English translations, see Mendelsohn, *Paragoni*, 103–04.

49. See Varchi in Barocchi, *Trattati de'Arte del Cinquecento*, 55. For examples of the origin and use of attributes in antiquity, see Ernst H. Gombrich, "Icones Symbolicae," in idem, *Symbolic Images: Studies in the Art of the Renaissance II*, 2nd ed. (New York: E.P. Dutton, 1978), 132–34.

50. In classical usage, "emblem" has been defined as the "grafting of a cultivated shoot onto a wild one." See Hessel Miedema, "The Term *Emblema* in Alciato," *Journal of the Warburg and Courtauld Institutes* 31 (1966), 234–44, here 239n24. This use of an agricultural metaphor occurs elsewhere in ancient literature, namely, in Dio Chrysostomo, *Orations*, 1:236–47. In "The Libyan Sybil," Dio uses the example to explain the transformation of a fable into a moral message. For Vasari's *Portrait of Cosimo the Elder*, the Medici selected an image of a dying tree to which a young branch has been grafted as the emblem of their renewal and repeated it in images related to the young Cosimo de' Medici, who had just come into power in 1537. In recent lectures delivered at Hunter College (November 2013), Pedro Campa and Peter Daly showed similar revived blossomings of tree stumps in several seventeenth-century ruler emblems. See Kliemann, "Il pensiero di Paolo Giovio," 330ff.

51. Quintilian, *Institutiones Oratoriae*, Bk. VIII, p. 2.ff: "What the Greeks call φράσιν we in Latin call *elocutio* or style."

52.

Well then, the embellishment of oratory is achieved In the first place by general style and by a sort of inherent/Color and flavor; for that it shall be weighty and pleasing And scholarly and gentlemanly and attractive and polished, and/Shall possess the requisite amount of feeling and pathos, is not a Matter of particular divisions of the framework, but these qualities/Must be visible in the whole of the structure. But further, in order to/Embellish it with flowers of language and gems of thought, it is not/Necessary for this ornamentation to be spread evenly over the entire/Speech but it must be so distributed that there may be brilliant jewels. (Quintilian, ibid.)

See Massimiliano Rossi, "Bronzino: Language, Flesh and Painting," in Falciani and Natali, *Bronzino*, 177–93: "… that naturalness and florentinity (so to speak)."

53. Pinelli, *La Bella Maniera*, 130–31, in his rich text, describes the translation of word image to allegory, from Bronzino's poetry to his painting in a different manner and to a somewhat different purpose. Confronting

442   *Agnolo Bronzino: The Muse of Florence*

the paintings of Archimboldo with those of Bronzino, in a turn-around, Pinelli writes: "Più che un raffronto tra i quadri del Bronzino e quelli di Arcimboldi, è istruttivo in proposito un paragone tra le rime bernesche del primo e i capricci in pittura' del secondo." Following this line of thinking, Pinelli cites passages from *La Zucca* of Anton Francesco, which he compares to the word play and *grotesquerie* of *Maniera*. On this subject, see Alessandro Cecchi, "Pratica fiereza e terribilità nelle grottesche di Marco da Faenza in Palazzo Vecchio a Firenze," in *Paragone* (1977), 25n327, on the ornamental *grottesche* of Marco da Faenza in the Palazzo Vecchio, Florence.

54. See Mendelsohn, "The Sum of the Parts," 107–48; and eadem, "Emblemi, Epigrammi e Statue: L'immagine di Eros Nella Pittura Del Cinquecento e La Diffusione Della Cultura Greca Nel Italia Del Nord," in *Storia della lingua e storia dell'arte in Italia: Dissimmetrie e intersezioni*, atti *del 3. Convegno ASLI, Associazione per la storia della lingua italiana, Roma, 30–31 maggio 2002*, eds. Vittorio Casale and Paolo D'Achille (Florence: F. Cesati, 2004), 125–97. Hessel Miedema assumes that Alciato did not concern himself with the illustrations for his published *Emblemata* because these were usually left to the domain of the publisher. The fact that a youthful Alciato had authored and illustrated an inventory of Roman tomb writings or *syllogi* in Lombardy prior to publishing the *Emblemata* would suggest that even if he did not engrave the illustrations himself, the use of famous statues to illustrate and convey moral messages.

55. On contact between Erasmus in Germany and Alciato in Italy, in touch as correspondents, see Silvana Menchi Seidel, *Erasmo in Italia, 1520–1580* (Turin: Bollati Boringhieri, 1987); eadem, "Alcuni Atteggiamenti della cultura Italiana di fronte a Erasmo," in *Eresia e Riforma*; and Virginia W. Callahan, "The Erasmus-Hercules Equation in the Emblems of Alciati," in *The Verbal and the Visual: Essays in Honor of William Sebastian Heckscher*, eds. Karl-Ludwig Selig and Elizabeth Sears (New York: Italica Press, 1990), 41–58 (Kindle edition, location 3345), who writes extensively about the friendship between them and on the special meaning the Hercules adages held for Erasmus. Alciato held a professorship in the faculty of Law at the University of Padua when Martelli joined his mentor Varchi in Padua. At the very least, Martelli would have been familiar with the published *Adages* and the 1531 edition of *Emblemata*.

56. Archivio di Stato di Firenze [hereafter ASF], 7 doc. ID 4160, folio. 277, 1546. Obtained courtesy of The Medici Archive Project online: <http://documents.medici.org/>, accessed 7/28/2010. The competition among the cities and between Cosimo, Ercole II d'Este Duke of Ferrara, and Emperor Charles V Habsburg reflects similar political machinations at the time.

57. See *The Adages of Erasmus*, ed. William W. Barker (London, Buffalo, and Toronto: University of Toronto Press, 2001), xvii ff. See also Aloia,

"Culture, Faith, and Love," and Bosch, "Orthodoxy and Heterodoxy," both in this volume.

58. Barker, *Selected Adages*, Editor's Introduction, ix ff.

59. In his proemio to the section on painting *Della Pittura*, Vasari includes this passage that he clearly has lifted from Alberti; see n. 61 below:

> Perchè il *disegno*, padre delle tre arti nostre, Architettura, Scultura e Pittura, procedono dall' intelletto, cava di molte cose un giudizio universale; simile a una forma ovvero idea di tutte le cose della natura, la quale è singolarissima nelle sue misure … E perchè da questa congnizione nasce un certo concetto e giudizio, che si forma nella mente quella tal cosa che poi espressa con le mani si chiama *disegno* … non sia che una apparente espressione e dichiarazione del concetto che si ha nell'animo, è di quello che altri si è nella mente immaginato e fabbricato nell' idea.
>
> E da questo, per avventura, naque il proverbio dei Greci *Dall'Ugna un leone*; quando quel valente uomo, vedendo scolpito in un masso l'ugna sola d'un leone, comprese con l'intelletto da quella misura e forma le parti di tutto l'animale, e dopo il tutto insieme, come se l'avesse avuto presente e dinanzi agli occhi.

Vasari says it is *disegno* that enables this act, with the help of cognition and discourse. He goes on to elaborate on the meaning of *disegno*. He makes it clear that it is not only a mental process that enables the artist to conceive an entire figure from a detail but also that it depends on *le mani*, his hands, the practiced hand of the artist; Vasari-Milanese, vol. 1, Capitolo 1, pp. 168–69.

60. Erasmus, *Adages* (Venice: Manutius, 1508).

61. Leon Battista Alberti, *Opere Volgari*, vol. III, *Trattati d'arte*, ed. C. Grayson (Bari: Laterza, 1973), *Della Pittura*, Capitolo XV, 5–22.

> *Che cosa sia disegno*, e come si fanno e si conoscono le buone pitture et a che; e dell'invenzione delle storie. Perché il disegno, padre delle tre arti nostre architettura, scultura e pittura, procedendo dall'intelletto cava di molte cose un giudizio universale simile a una forma overo idea di tutte le cose della natura, *la quale è singolarissima nelle sue misure, di qui è che non solo nei corpi umani e degl'animali, ma nelle piante ancora e nelle fabriche e sculture e pitture*, cognosce la proporzione che ha il tutto con le parti e che hanno le parti fra loro e col tutto insieme; e perché da questa cognizione nasce un certo concetto e giudizio, *che si forma nella mente quella tal cosa che poi espressa con le mani si chiama disegno*, si può conchiudere

che esso disegno altro non sia che una apparente espressione e
dichiarazione del concetto che si ha nell'animo, emo di quello che altri si è
nella mente imaginato e fabricato nell 'idea. E da questo per avventura
nacque *il proverbio de' Greci Dell'ugna un leone, quando quel valente*
uomo, vedendo sculpita in un masso l'ugna sola d'un leone, comprese
con l'intelletto da quella misura e forma le parti di tutto l'animale e dopo il tutto insieme, *come se l'avesse avuto presente e dinanzi*
agl'occhi (italics mine).

62. Vasari, *Vite*-Milanese, in 1568, notes the extension of the agricultural.
63. See Derrida, *Truth in Painting*, 64, on the "seductive" role of ornament:

According to Kant it is possible for the *parergon* (external or separate ornament) to enhance the representation if, and only if, the
parergon has "beautiful form." Otherwise it becomes mere adornment (*Schmuck*) and takes away from the beauty of the object.
Kant's example is the gilded frame that recommends the painting
by "attraction" (*Reiz*). What is bad, external to the pure object of
taste, is thus what seduces us by an attraction; and the example of
what leads astray by its force of attraction is a *color, the gilding,* in
as much as *it is nonform, content, or sensory matter.* The deteriora-
tion of the *parergon,* the perversion, the adornment, is the attraction of sensory matter.

64. *Due dialogi di M. Giovanni Andrea Gilio da Fabriano. Nel primo de;*
quali si ragiona de le parti morali e civili appertenenti a' letterati Cortigiani et
ad ogni Gentilhuomo, e l'utile che i Prencipi cavano dai letterati. Nel secondo si
ragiona degli errori e degli abusi de'Pittori circa l'historie, con molte annotationi
fatte sopra il Giuditio di Michelangelo et altre figure, tanto de la vecchia quanto
de la nova Cappella; et in che modo vogliono essere dipinte le Sacre Imagini ...
All'Illustriss. e Reverendiss. Mons. il Cardinale Farnese, In Camerino, per Antonio Giososo, 1564.
    The second dialogue with notes is partially reprinted in *Scritti d'Arte*
del Cinquecento, ed. Paola Barocchi, 2 vols. (Milan and Naples: Riccardo Ricciardi, n.d), 1:303–25 [hereafter referred to as *Scritti*-Barocchi]. Although
Gilio's criticism was directed primarily at religious paintings, some of his
examples were mythological, i.e., pagan and secular. I will deal separately
with Gilio's critique of painters of the 1540s.
    65. 1527 would be at the beginning of the second Republic. See Ales-
sandro Cecchi, "Il Bronzino, Benedetto Varchi e l'Accademia Fiorentina:

Ritratti di poeti, letterati e personaggi illustri della corte Medicea," *Antichità viva* 30, nos. 1/2 (1991), 17–28; idem, "'Famosi frondi di cui santi honori.' Un sonetto di Varchi e il ritratto di Lorenzo Lenzi dipinto dal Bronzino,"; and Leatrice Mendelsohn, "Restoration and Replication: Ancient Bronze Techniques and the Construction of the Figure in Cinquecento Painting," in C.C. Mattusch, A. Brauer, and S.E. Knudsen, *From the Parts to the Whole: Acta of the 13th International Bronze Congress, Cambridge, Mass. May 29–June 1, 1996, The Journal of Roman Archaeology*, Supplement 39, no. 2 (2002), 273–85.

66. For the most part, these portraits are thought to have been begun and completed before Bronzino's departure from Florence, that is, before 1531. Other portraits of the Academicians, left either unfinished or merely commissioned at the time of his departure, would have been completed shortly after his return. Still others have been dated as late as 1547. Alessandro Cecchi dates the portrait of Lorenzo Lenzi as early as 1527 in Cecchi and Natali, *L'officina della maniera*, 372; later datings are maintained by Maurice Brock, *Bronzino* (Paris: Flammarion, 2002), 108–10, who places it in 1532; and Elizabeth Cropper, "Reading Bronzino's Florentine Portraits (Per una lettura dei ritratti di Bronzino)," in Falciani and Natali, *Bronzino*, 246, who also places this painting *after* Bronzino's return from Pesaro. It should be noted here that Varchi returned to Florence only briefly in 1532, after which he returned to exile in Venice, travelling to Padua, Rome, Bologna, and Ferrara before being pardoned by Cosimo I in 1543. During Varchi's brief stay in 1532, he could have commissioned the other portraits or initiated negotiations to have them painted (or completed) after his or Bronzino's return from Pesaro. It is plausible (although not documented) that the Lenzi portrait was painted as an early prototype for those portraits that followed.

67. For a summary of the question of the dates of Bronzino's stay in Pesaro, see Mendelsohn, "Bronzino in Pesaro," 81–105. Craig H. Smyth, "On Dosso Dossi at Pesaro," in Luisa Ciammitti, S.F. Ostrow, and S. Settis, eds., *Dosso's Fate: Painting and Court Culture in Renaissance Italy* (Los Angeles, CA: The Getty Research Institute for the History of Art and the Humanities: Issues & Debates, 1998), 241–62, gives the probable dates of Bronzino's stay from "after April 2, 1531 until c. April 2, 1532." While Smyth did not believe the artist extended his stay beyond the latter date, he considered the arrival might have been earlier (243). He noted that according to Vasari's *ricordanze*, Bronzino was definitely back in Florence by 20 March 1533; see *Il libro delle ricordanze di Giorgio Vasari*, ed. Alessandro del Vita (Arezzo: R. Istituto d'Archeologia e Storia dell'Arte, 1938), 20. Brock, *Bronzino*, 50, mentions Bronzino as still being in Pesaro during the summer of 1532. Giorgio Spini, *Cosimo I e la indipendenza del' principato*

mediceo (Florence: Vallechi editore, 1980), 6, states (with no documentation) that in 1533 Pontormo convinced Bronzino to return from Urbino to assist him at the Medici Villa. The painting, wherever it was begun, was not, in my view, completed until after Bronzino returned to Florence, and perhaps not immediately. I accept the possibility that the painting was completed as late as 1539/40 for reasons mentioned in the text below. In any event, it could not have been completed before Bronzino left Pesaro in 1533, for reasons given in Mendelsohn, "Bronzino in Pesaro and After." Although Cropper, "Portrait of a Lady," 177–78, based on X-ray and infrared studies outlined by Bambach in *The Drawings of Bronzino*, eds. Carmen C. Bambach, Janet Cox-Rearick, and George R. Goldner, with contributions by Philippe Costamagna, Marzia Faietti, and Elizabeth Pilliod, Exh. New York: Metropolitan Museum of Art (New Haven, CT, and London: Yale University Press, 2010), 47, figs. 8 and 9, believes the painting could *not* have been done in two stages, it is not unthinkable that Bronzino had a cartoon of the *Halberdier* in his possession from the time he painted the cover. It is also possible that the changes Pontormo made to his *Halberdiere*—particularly to the sitter's left hand—were, like those of Bronzino, an attempt to conform to a model hand, perhaps from an antique fragment or from Michelangelo's lost *Hercules*. In both paintings, the third and fourth fingers are touching, while the others are splayed, an idiosyncratic and unnatural formula that appears in Rosso's *Portrait of a Young Man* and other similar works.

68. A technique mastered by Fra Angelico and Botticelli in religious paintings for the Medici. In works such as Botticelli's *Adoration of the Magi*, in which the participants in the ritual resemble members of the Medici family and other Florentine dignitaries, including the self-portrait of the artist, the personifications (or more aptly, substitutions) have provided art historians with an ongoing mission to verify identities. Despite being court portraitist to the Medici, the identifiable personages in Bronzino's *Descent into Limbo*, painted in the 1550s, are the artist's friends, acquaintances, and fellow academicians. Nor are they meant to stand out from the crowd "asking to be adored"; instead, they were often so well absorbed into the crowd that, centuries later, they have become anonymous.

69. We do not know whether the portraits were commissioned by a representative of the group or individually, but the spread of dates suggests the latter.

70. For example, the influential phrase justifying the art of painting by verifying the Renaissance acknowledgement of the Roman use of ancestor portrait busts in funeral processions described by Pliny, with which Alberti opens Book II of *De pictura*: "Painting possesses a truly divine power in that not only does it make the absent present as they say of friendship,

but it also represents the dead to the living many centuries later, so that they are recognized by spectators with pleasure and deep admiration for the artist … Through painting, the faces of the dead go on living for a very long time"; see Alberti, ed. Grayson, *On Painting and On Sculpture, De pictura*, Bk. 2, 61.

71. See Constance M. Furey, *Erasmus, Contarini, and the Religious Republic of Letters* (Cambridge and New York: Cambridge University Press, 2006), 11–13, 20ff.

72. For examples of coded erotic language in the dictionary of Jean Toscan, see Leatrice Mendelsohn, "L'Allegoria di Londra del Bronzino e la retorica del carnevale," in *Kunst des Cinquecento in der Toskana*, Italienische Forschungen, Kunsthistorisches Institut in Florenz, Band 17, ed. M. Cämmerer (Munich: Bruckmann, 1992), 152–67, 157, notes. 29–38, on innuendo and *double entendre* in Bronzino's *Allegory of Love*. Sexual innuendo in particular was made visible in image play as well as word play. Explicit depictions of sexual activity occur in paintings by Salviati, who worked beside Bronzino in Florence in the Palazzo Vecchio and jointly on the tapestries; some drawings parallel the allusions scattered throughout Bronzino's *Capitoli*. See Catherine Monbeig Goguel, "Francesco Salviati et la *Bella Maniera*, quelques points a revoir," in *Francesco Salviati et la Bella Maniera*, eds. Catherine Monbeig Goguel, P. Costamagna, and M. Hochmann (Rome: École Française de Rome, 2001), 20–21, 31–34, notes 54, 55, and 62. It is clear from contemporary poetry that indirect sexual allusion and coded innuendo were a natural part of the literary vocabulary of academicians and artists. For some literary examples by Bronzino, see Parker, *Bronzino*, 29–35. The small number of surviving drawings attributed to Bronzino in comparison to his reputation as a master draftsman makes it impossible to catch all the allusions to his many pictorial subjects that may reflect his written legacy.

73. Since both portraits to be discussed have already received serious scholarly attention, it is not necessary to recapitulate all the basic information presented in numerous articles and exhibition catalogues, most recently, the two major Bronzino shows: at New York's Metropolitan Museum on drawing and in Florence at the Palazzo Strozzi on the paintings.

74. Cropper, in Cecchi and Natali, *L'officina della maniera*, Exhibition Catalog entry 101, 376–77 also remarked on the painting's Michelangelesque. Other scholars have dismissed this connection in order to support different identities for the sitter.

75. See Francesco Caglioti, "Il Perduto 'David Mediceo' di Giovanfrancesco Rustici e il 'David' Pulszky del Louvre," *Prospettiva* 83–84 (July–October 1996), 80–101; and Francesco Cagliotti, *Donatello e I Medici: Storia del David e della Giuditta*, 2 vols. (Florence: Olschki, 2000), 1:262–63. Essays

and a book devoted to Donatello's *David* by Caglioti stress the statue's significance as a Republican symbol, thus complicating the identification of the *Halberdier* as a Medici or Medici supporter.

76. The first to make this assertion was Herbert Keutner, "Zu einigen Bildnissen des frühen Florentiner Manierismus: im Anhang; das Gemälde-Inventar der Familie Riccardi aus dem Jahre 1612," *Mitteilungen des Kunsthistorischen Institutes in Florenz* 8 (1957/1959), 139–54. Janet Cox-Rearick's identification occurs in an expanded catalogue entry published expressly for the 1989 Christie auction of the painting identified as Pontormo's "Portrait of Cosimo de' Medici," no. 6856: *An Important Painting by Pontormo from the Collection of Chauncey D. Stillman* (New York: Christie's, 1989), 26–29. Aware that the costume would not have been typical for the mid-1530s, Cox-Rearick speculated that Cosimo was dressed to resemble his father, the *condottiere* Giovanni delle Bande Nere.

77. Identified as French mid-sixteenth century from Lyons, belonging to the National Gallery of Art, Washington, DC, Widener Collection, no. 1942.9.373. A similar table might well have been seen in the Florentine home of the Panciatichi, who still had residences in Lyon. The sphinx as ornamental furniture decoration originates with the *Sedes Sapientiae* or ancient throne of Wisdom ultimately adapted for the throne of the Virgin Mary. Not just a symbol of the occult and cryptic Greek oracles, the *akroteria*-like figure also functioned as an apotropaic warning against evil. The appearance of this monster in Quattrocento images connected with the Virgin is noted by Andrée Hayum, "The Nuns at S. Apollonia and Castagno's Last Supper," *The Art Bulletin* 88, no. 2 (June 2006), 256n74. In Andrea's *Last Supper* in the convent of St. Apollonia, the sphinxes can signify the Wisdom of the Bible, as well as the opposite, the monstrous; Hayum refers to them as "guardian figures."

78. In a discussion of the dating of the Metropolitan *Gentleman*, Elizabeth Cropper has proposed that Bronzino may have had in mind the carved architectural ornaments of Tasso one of the other court artists to Cosimo de' Medici; see Elizabeth Cropper, "Preparing to Finish: Portraits by Pontormo and Bronzino around 1530," in *Opere e giorni. Studi su mille anni di arte europea dedicati a Max Seidel*, eds. K. Bergdolt and G. Bonsanti (Venice: Marsilio, 2006), 499–501, 503–04, and repr. in Michael Cole, ed., *Sixteenth Century Italian Art* (Malden, MA: Blackwell Publishing, 2006), 177–81. While no comparable carvings have been found in Italian furniture, examples are found in several portraits painted in the North and in printed ornamental frames surrounding book illustrations.

79. In the North, God's presence was demonstrated in a profusion of detail rather than by means of an idealized abstraction; see Svetlana Alpers, *The Art of Describing: Dutch Art in the Seventeenth Century* (Chicago,

IL: University of Chicago Press, 1983), xxiii, 224. Pictorial details found in fifteenth-century Northern paintings appealed to Florentines living and working north of the Alps, for example, the Arnolfini or Portinari, whose patronage of Flemish and Netherlandish painters resulted in the exportation of significant works by Van Eyck, Roger van der Weyden, and Memling into Italy. Francisco de Hollanda's Roman dialogues, purportedly quoting Michelangelo's denigration of Flemish painting because of its banal accumulation of particulars and its sentimentality, have been used as proof of his rejection of detail. The second book of Hollanda's Portuguese treatise, *Da pintura antigua* (Lisbon, c. 1541–48), quotes Michelangelo as having denigrated Northern painters, while Hollanda dichotomized the art of northern and southern Europe in the early modern period (Alpers, *The Art of Describing* (1983), xxiii, 224). Admiration for Northern pictorial techniques, such as the use of oil that enabled the precise imitation of the very smallest details, only partially explains the Italian emulation of a profusion of detail but is an important incentive, since the relationship between material goods and demonic powers is heavily stressed in Reformation treatises.

80. On the Arnolfini chair, see Craig Harbison, "Sexuality and Social Standing in Jan van Eyck's Arnolfini Double Portrait, "*Renaissance Quarterly* 43, no. 2 (Summer 1990), 249–91; and Craig Harbison, *The Mirror of the Artist: Northern Renaissance Art in its Historical Context* (New York: Harry N. Abrams, 1995), illustrations on pp. 12 and 13. It has also been suggested that the chair resembles a birthing chair as well as a princely throne. On the use of a symbolic papal birthing "throne," see Sergio Bertelli, *Il corpo del re: Sacralità del potere nell'Europa medievale e moderna* (Florence: Ponte Alle Grazie, 1990), 147–50, ill. 50, 51. For an example of this type of carved, enthroned Madonna, see Metropolitan Museum of Art, an ivory example from Navarre or Aragon (1200–50), in The Cloisters Collection, Accession Number: 1972.143, on which is carved a devil being stamped out by the Virgin at the bottom left and, partly hidden under the folds of her dress and culminating in a snake-like tail on the right bottom corner of the carving, the apparent "hand" of the devil.

81. See cover design and pp. 4–5 of Aston, *The King's Bedpost*. On the basis of historical data, specifically, the enthronement of Edward VI after the death of his father Henry VIII, the author dates this oil painting 1547.

82. We know Dürer's woodcuts and engravings provided models for compositions and backgrounds in sixteenth-century Italian paintings, not least because of their attention to detail. Dürer's engraved works, such as his *Large Passion* cycle or the *Apocalypse* series, filled a void in Italian painting, supplying the everyday objects and the minutia of nature for backgrounds of interiors and landscapes, the very subjects that, according

to Francisco da Hollanda, Michelangelo purportedly criticized as pandering to women and the ignorant. On Bronzino's use of Dürer prints, see Graham Smith, "Bronzino and Dürer," *The Burlington Magazine* 895 (1977), 709–10.

83. For a different interpretation and revised meaning of this famous passage, see Laura Camille Agoston, "Male/Female, Italy/Flanders, Michelangelo/Vittoria Colonna," *Renaissance Quarterly* 58, no. 4 (2005), 1175–1219. Francisco da Hollanda, from his *Dialoghi di Roma*, ed. Rita Biscetti (Rome: Bagatto Libri, 2003; alternate title *Quadro dilogos de pintura antiga*) (as cited in David Summers, *Michelangelo and the Language of Art* (Princeton, NJ: Princeton University Press, 1982), 285, 332, is represented as denigrating Flemish art.

84. Now in the Vatican Belvedere. Michelangelo was at one time thought to have restored the head. See Michael Collareta, "L'historien et la technique: Sur le rôle de l'orfèvrerie dans les *Vite* de Vasari," in *Histoire de l'histoire de lárt*, ed. Édouard Pommier (Paris: Klincksieck, 1995), 163–76, here 51–55; repr. as "The Historian and the Technique: On the Role of Goldsmithery in Vasari's *Lives*," in *Sixteenth-Century Italian Art*, ed. Michael W. Cole (Malden, MA: Blackwell Publishing, 2006), 291–300. For the meanings that the Egyptian sphinx held in the Renaissance, see Brian Curran, *The Egyptian Renaissance: The Afterlife of Ancient Egypt in Early Modern Italy* (Chicago, IL: University of Chicago Press, 2006), 45, 193–99.

85. Curran, *Egyptian Renaissance*, 197–99.

86. Andreas Alciato, *Emblemata Liber d'A. Alciati* (Augsburg: Augusta, 1534), a date that might possibly provide a terminus post quem for the table grotesque in the Metropolitan Museum painting. There is, of course, a possibility that the same head was available to him in another print. A similar head appears in the decorative base of the Joseph Tapestry series c. 1545, in *Joseph Fleeing Potiphar's Wife*. On this tapestry see, Lucia Meoni's Entry Chapter II.6, p. 124 and plate opposite in *Bronzino, Artist and Poet*. Note the central head in the lower border, as well as the bedpost in the foreground and the fruit transformed into a snake on the left and the head of another hybrid monster on the right in the entablature of the room.

87. This source has also been suggested by Charles Burroughs for Michelangelo's decoration of the façade of the senatorial building on the Campidoglio in Rome. See Burroughs, "Michelangelo at the Campidoglio: Artistic Identity, Patronage, and Manufacture," *Artibus et Historiae* 14, no. 28 (1993); 85–111.

88. Employed as an assistant to Primaticcio between 1537 and 1550, Fantuzzi is documented as having created designs for *grotteschi* to decorate the Sala di Ulisse, no longer extant. See Henri Zerner, *The School of Fontainebleau, graveures*, trans. from French by S. Baron (New York: Harry

Abrams, 1968 17–21 and fig. A.F. 60 (no pagination).

89. This figure appears again in the tapestry borders designed for Cosimo, for example, *Joseph Fleeing Potiphar's Wife*. For the Fontainebleau figures see Zerner, *The School of Fontainebleau*, fig. 13; and Falciani and Natali,
Bronzino, Entry and illustration pages: II.6. p. 124, ill 125; II. 7. p. 124, ill
129 and ill 131.

90. See Jean de Toscan, *Le carnaval du langage: Le lexique érotique des
poètes de l'équivoque de Burchiello a Marino (XVᵉ–XVIIᵉ siècles)*, 4 vols. (Lille:
Reproduction des thèse Université de Lille, 1981), a dictionary of coded
eroticisms in use in Italy at this time. This use of garlands goes back to Raphael's ceiling in the Farnesina and is a staple of sixteenth-century decorative vocabulary, presuming an antique origin.

91. For a possible encounter between Ammannati and Serlio, see Deb-
orah Howard, "Sebastiano Serlio's Venetian Copyrights," *The Burlington
Magazine* 115, no. 895 (1973), 512–16. See also Loredano Olibato, "Con il
Serlio tra i'dilettanti di architettura Veneziana della prima metà del '500:
Il ruolo di Marcantonio Michiel," in J. Guillaume, ed., *Les traités d'architecture de la Renaissance* (Paris: Picard, 1988), 247–54. On Ammannati and
ornament, see *Bartolomeo Ammannati, Scultore e Architetto 1511–1592*, eds.
Niccolò Del Turco Roselli and Federica Salvi (Florence: Alinea editrice,
1995). Relevant photos are on the following pages: 28, una ruota del carro
del Nettuno della fontana, detail; 159, teste caprine, Palazzo Budini Gattai;
244, Peduccio ornato con testa, Palazzo Portinari Salviati, Florence; and
235, Palazzino di Bianca Capello. These would appear to be the type of
drawings and reliefs from which Bronzino drew his *grottesche*.

92. On this artist, see the text and illustrations in Zerner, *The School of
Fontainebleau*, no pagination, Artist DB [Domenico Barbieri's initials, by
which he is known] no. 14, dated 1540–45, text p. 38. The drawing is likely
a study for a wall decoration. Significantly, Domenico Ricoveri del Barbieri was, like Fantuzzi, also a sculptor, primarily working in Troyes.

93. Vitruvius, *The Ten Books of Architecture*, trans M.H. Morgan (New
York: Dover Publications, 1960), Bk. VII, 212.

94. Vitruvius, *The Ten Books of Architecture*, ed. E.H. Warmington, trans.
Frank Granger, 2 vols. (Cambridge, MA: Harvard University Press, 1975),
Bk. VII, C. v., 2:105. In short, the descriptions coincide with our knowledge
of ornamental grotesques and combinations of animal and plant forms
with human elements added to form hybrid monsters such as "slender
stalks with heads of men and of animals attached to half the body" that
covered the walls of the Golden House of Nero, imitated, shortly after
its excavation in Rome, by Raphael with Giovanni del Udine in the Villa
Madama built for Clement VII. Yvonne Elet's forthcoming NYU dissertation on the architecture and decoration of the Villa will shed light on the

significance of this decoration and its diffusion throughout Italy in the Cinquecento.

95. "… nella regola una licenzia che, non essendo di regola, fusse ordinata nella regola e potesse stare senza fare confusione o quastare l'ordine." *Regola* (rule), a term from Vitruvius' *Ten Books on Architecture*, might also be translated as "canon," referring in a more general sense to "tradition." It is unclear whether Bronzino's references to *regola* stem directly from Vitruvius or were derived from Vasari's text. If from the latter, it would date close to Bronzino's relevant *Capitoli*, after 1550. On Vasari's text, see Barocchi, *Vita di Michelangelo*, 5:40, 41, 84, 146, and 147. On Michelangelo's *licenzia*, see Summers, *Michelangelo and the Language of Art*, 453–54, and idem, "Michelangelo on Architecture," *The Art Bulletin* 54 (1972), 146–157.

96. The resemblance to edicts of the Council of Trent on art indicates a return to Augustan imperial attitudes on what makes cities great, showing how the inappropriateness of artistic taste in relation to established rules could leave a permanent stain on the reputation of a governing body. There is also a slight suggestion on the part of Vitruvius of the hubris of the artists for overstepping accepted limits. On the practical side, the displacement of guilt from artist to patron relates to the excessive expenditure (i.e., *luxuria*), also presented as a negative aspect of visual art as well as reflecting on government support for such an "indecorous art."

97. Vasari, *Vite*-B-B, 1:58.

98. Even when the prefaces and additional reportage are attributed to authors other than Vasari, as Charles Hope argued, the concept of freedom as a necessary precondition for the artist is so filtered throughout the text of the *Lives of the Artists* that authorship would not constitute a limiting factor in its usage; see Charles Hope, "'Vite' Vasariane: Un esempio di autore multiplo," in *L'Autore Multiplo*, ed. Anna Santoni (Pisa: Scuola Normale Superiore, 2002), 59–64.

99. We should not forget that a large number of Italian artists were employed in France at Fontainebleau as well as Lyon and Paris.

100. The spelling of the word *licenzia* varies depending on the context. On the Council proceedings, see O'Malley, *Trent*, 244, 281, which presents a day-to-day accounting of the acts of the Council. The author's demurral that it is merely a clear summarizing of events does not do justice to the wealth of material presented in a highly readable manner, useful for every level of scholarship. An earlier usage of the term *licenzia* appears in Alciato's *Emblemata*, which, because of its popularity and numerous subsequent editions, may have reinforced its frequent usage in artistic circles.

101. In their austerity, the architectural background of Bronzino's *letterati* portraits can be considered an elaboration of the background of Botticelli's portraits, such as his *Portrait of Giuliano de' Medici*, National Gal-

lery, Washington, DC, c. 1478/1480, tempera on panel, Samuel H. Kress Collection, inv.1952.5.56.

102. In other of Bronzino's portraits, like those of Salviati, the sculptures take the form of small models or figurines that generally resemble Michelangelesque nudes as interpreted by Cellini. The Triumph shield placed in the vestibule outside the entrance to the Medici chapel includes a figure that reappears as such a figurine in the lower left portion of Bronzino's 1552 painting of the *Resurrection* in SS. Annunziata. On what is either the handle of the shield or the front of a helmet sits a small gilded female nude, seemingly a replica of the minute female situated on the crown of Venus in the London *Allegory*, probably painted about six years earlier. For the *Resurrection*, see Liala Morini, in Falciani and Natali, *Bronzino*, Section VI, Entry 6, 306–07.

103. On Michelangelo's masks, see John T. Paoletti, "Michelangelo's Masks," *The Art Bulletin* 74, no. 3 (1992), 423; Eckhard Leuchner, *Persona, Larva, Maske: Ikonographische Untersuchungen vom 16 bus zum früen 18 Jahrhundert* (Frankfurt-am-Main: Peter Lang, 1994); and Charles Dempsey, "Portraits and Masks in the Art of Lorenzo de' Medici, Botticelli, and Politian's *Stanze per la Giostra*," *Renaissance Quarterly* 52, no. 1 (1999), 1–42.

104. Contrary to the "myth" of Michelangelo perpetuated by Francisco da Hollanda, the sculptor had a history of interest in just those details of Northern art that he supposedly denigrated. Vasari and Condivi corroborate that Michelangelo's first panel painting was a copy of Schongauer's *Temptation of St. Anthony*. According to Ascanio Condivi, *The Life of Michelangelo Buonarroti*, trans. Alice Sedgwich Wohl, ed. Helmut Wohl (Philadelphia: Penn State University Press, 1999), it contained "many strange forms and monstrosities of demons." Condivi remarks that the engraving inspired the young artist to enhance its lifelike details with studies from nature. In painting his *Descent into Limbo*, more visible in a recently completed restoration, Bronzino utilized similar demonic hybrids in the upper regions of the painting, apparently drawn from Dürer's engraving of the same subject.

105. In his *London Allegory* of c. 1546, Bronzino will use the mask-like female figure of Deceit (*Inganno*) (to whom scholars have given several alternate names) as the interlocutor or curtain manager who hides (or perhaps unveils) the *dishonesto rapporto* enacted below by mother and son. The three masks at the foot of Venus, two of which are also eyeless, in light of the interpretation proposed in Mendelsohn, "L'Allegoria di Londra del Bronzino," would epitomize falsehood, theatrical disguise, and in keeping with a carnival spirit, a transgressive form of *imitatio*.

106. An attitude of ease indicating a denial of effort, known as *Sprezzatura*, was intended to hide the very artifice we sense in looking at this

proud young man. See Castiglione, *Il Libro del Cortegiano con una scelta delle Opere Minore di Baldassare Castiglione*, ed. Bruno Maier (Turin: Unione Tipografico-Editrice Torinese, 1973), Il Cortegiano, Bk. 1, Ch. XXVI, pp. 124–25. This can be seen in the X-ray showing the under drawing of the painting. It is noteworthy that special care was given to the fingers. See the X-ray with comments by Carmen Bambach in *The Drawings of Bronzino*, 44, 45.

107. Cropper has identified the sitter as Buonacorsi Pinadori, based on his age and the mention of his name regarding a portrait of him by Vasari, *Vite*-Milanesi, in the "Life of Bronzino," 7:595, listed along with the portraits of Lenzi and Martelli seemingly preceding them, although no dates are given.

108. For an extensive listing of the literary and visual descriptions and depictions of Hercules, see Emma Stafford, *Herakles* (New York: Routledge, 2012). Special attention should be given to pp. 137 and 153 (Heracles in *Aeneid* 8, on Augustus' victories over his enemies in Rome, and Aeneas as a second Heracles) in her chapter on the political Heracles.

109. Emblem 181, 1531; E6r 1534 98. These Emblems can been found on-line at: <http://www.mun.ca/alciato/e181.html>. The Latin proverb beneath the image is given here:

> Arcum laeva tenet, rigidam fert dextera clavam,
> Contegit et Nemees corpora nuda leo.
> Herculis haec igitur facies? Non convenit illud
> Quod vetus, et senio tempora cana gerit.
> Quid quod lingua illi levibus traiecta catenis,
> Queis fissa facile is allicit aure viros?
> Anne quod Alciden lingua, non robore Galli
> Praestantem populis iura dedisse ferunt?
> Cedunt arma togae, et quamvis durissima corda
> Eloquio pollens ad sua vota trahit.

110. See Callahan, "The Erasmus-Hercules Equation," for references to the letters exchanged between Erasmus and his friend: "The adage concludes with Erasmus's assertion that in dealing with the many difficulties of producing his literary works he had been, like Hercules, battling with huge monsters, and that he, too, was born in the fourth quarter of the moon, since by some inexplicable fate he had been plunged into these more than Herculean labors." (Kindle Location 3345).

111. See Stafford, *Herakles*, 23–50, on the twelve labors, the hero, and his monsters. In addition to the popular depictions of the strangling of the Nemean Lion on vase paintings, the reliefs on the metopes from the

Temple of Zeus at Olympia show him resting over the body of the lion with his head in his hand, like an Olympian athlete (boxer), a pose that has been linked to the Belvedere torso and perhaps should also be tied to Dürer's *Melencolia*; see Stafford, *Herakles*, ill. on p. 35. In addition to the seven labors, other feats, including the freeing of Prometheus from his punishment by releasing his bonds from the arch-shaped rock to which he is tied (Pausanias 5.11.6), are illustrated in the emblems; see: Stafford, *Herakles*, 67, 68. The Prometheus scene, painted by Panainos at the base of the statue of Zeus at Olympia, is considered to be an allegory of "Mithradates liberation of the Hellenistic world from the Romans." This subject would have been equally appropriate as a reference to Florence liberated from the Medici and the pope.

112. See Benedetto Varchi, "Lezzione di M. Benedetto Varchi nell' Accademia di Padova sopra un sonetto del Casa e sulla gelosia," in *L'Opere di Benedetto Varchi*, 2 vols. (Trieste: Lloyd Austriaco, 1859), 1:570–82. Martelli would have heard this lecture in Padua at the *Accademia degli Infiammati*, since he was among the founders and remained there until 1542. The academy name itself refers to Hercules' immortalization at his cremation as the flames rose to heaven. A lecture on the same subject, repeated in Florence on Varchi's return in 1543, "Sopra l'Invidia, Lezione Una al molto ilustre e molto reverendo Mons. De'Rossi vescovo di Pavia Signor suo Oservandissimo" (MS Corsiniano, pubblicato per la prima volta dal prof. Luigi Maria Rezzi), appears in *L'Opere di Benedetto Varchi*, 1:585–611. See especially Lohr,"...*e nuovi Omeri, e Plati...*," on the *Accademia degli Infiammati*, 14n68, with additional bibliography.

113. See Leatrice Mendelsohn, "Madonna and Child with St. John in the Uffizi," Cat. Entry. in Falciani and Natali, *Bronzino*, 172. In a paper delivered in 2003 at the meetings of the RSA in Toronto, entitled "Signed in Stone," I proposed that Bronzino's trompe l'oeil signature indicated the artist's desire to identify and compete with the Greek sculptor Lysippos. See also Mendelsohn, "Restoration and Replication," 273–85, on Bronzino and Lysippos, with regard to statues in bronze and Bronzino's nickname. Bronzino's interest in the antique sculptor of bronzes, may explain the artist's predilection for a pose close to the *Lysippan Hercules*. See the Lysippan sarcophagus fragment (Fig. 13).

114. See Mendelsohn, "Restoration and Replication," 172.

115. See Rudolf Wildmoser, "Das Bildnes des Ugolino Martelli von Agnolo Bronzino," in *Jahrbuch der Berliner Museen* 31 (1989), 181–214; Cropper, *Pontormo*, 120n147, 121n154; and Lohr, "...*e nuovi Omeri, e Plati...*," 47, 48–100.

116. Photographs of cleanings and restorations from 1925, 1950, 1951, 1956, 1962, 1987, and 2004 were kindly provided by the courtesy of the

Gemäldegalerie Staatliche Museen zu Berlin–Preußischer Kulturbesitz and the photographers Gustav Schwarz, Dore Barleben in Wiesbaden, Walter Steinkopf, Walter Steinkopf, Walter Steinkopf, Jörg P. Anders, and Jörg P. Anders, respectively.

117. I turned this questionnaire into something of a Rorschach test for art historians, requesting a sampling of opinions on the subject of the carving. Some based their opinion on a first-hand viewing of the painting, others on inadequate photographs. I can report, however, that no two scholars saw the same image. Lohr, "... *e nuovi Omeri, e Plati* ...," 84, end of n. 154: "I should like to see the arm of the infant Hercules wrestling with a snake in the much damaged relief in Ugolino's portrait." This is closest to my view in his suggestion of a hand of Hercules reaching out toward a snake; however, I do not believe it is a hand, because of its crude configuration and its similarity to the Lysippan foot.

118. See Brock, *Bronzino*, 132–33, on Bronzino's carved heads.

119. In the most recent cleaning, the painting has been restored and the carving clarified to show a human hand grasping a snake. I am indebted to Roberto Contini for discussing this painting with me in Berlin.

120. See Paolo Moreno, *Lisippo: L'Arte e La Fortuna* (Rome: Fabbri, 1995), on Lysippos' *Hercules* relief and its numerous copies. Taking a closer look at the painting in photographs before and after the earlier restoration, and subsequently viewing first-hand the newly restored state of the painting as realized by the museum conservator, I revised my original idea as delivered in my talk. Rather than focus on the adage of the Lion's claw as synecdoche, I prefer to view the larger meaning as referring to Hercules, and to emblem no. 181 dealing with speech (or silence) over strength, seen in relation to the Homeric passage referring to the same content on the open page of the book, held by the sitter for the benefit of the audience.

121. I should add that the pose of the first Hercules in the horizontal relief series shares a pose, in the slight twist of the left shoulder, with the alleged wax modello of a youth (considered by some to be a modello for Michelangelo's *Hercules*). Thus it might be possible that Michelangelo too was inspired by the same relief of the *Labors*.

122. A comparable fragment of a frieze, originally installed in the choir and pulpits of the Basilica of San Lorenzo Fuori le Mura in Rome, later transferred to the Palazzo Nuovo, Musei Capitolini, was utilized by other artists for similar purposes. On this fragment, see Curran, *Egyptian Renaissance*, 147, fig. 56. The fact that these frieze fragments were copied by many artists, including Sebastiano del Piombo, suggests that a horizontal series of individual signs in relief was a type of erudite antique reference sought out by painters especially for use in portraits. This use

of antique reliefs containing letters and hieroglyphs strengthens my interpretation of the meaning given to the adage in Bronzino's *Martelli* portrait. I am grateful to Brian Curran, who mentioned the relief in a talk delivered at a Columbia University conference shortly before I was to deliver my RSA paper from which this essay is derived. Dr. Curran generously lent me his slide of the image for my lecture. He also reminded me of the pseudo hieroglyph Bronzino inserted in his *Allegorical Portrait of Andrea Doria* as Neptune. On the Sebastiano hieroglyph, see G. Gorse, "Augustan Mediterranean Iconography and Renaissance Hieroglyphics," in Gowens and Reiss, *Pontificate of Clement VII*, 314–37. The dependence of the pose of Andrea Doria on a classical sarcophagus is not, however, the focus of Gorse's article.

123. Mendelsohn "Restoration and Replication." See Pliny the Elder, *Natural History* (trans. H. Rackham (Cambridge, MA: Harvard University Press, and London: William Heinemann, 1995), vol. IX, bks, XXX111–XXXV, for parallels between Bronzino and the life, subjects, and style of Lysippus, surely familiar to the well-read Bronzino.

124. In Italy, where the tradition was far less common in painting than in sculpture. A version of the Epitaph from Martial—*Ars utinam mores animumque effingere posset! Pulchior in terris nulla tabella foret* (How I wish that … (or) If art could only portray her character and mind, there would be no lovelier painting on earth)—is inscribed behind the profile portrait of Giovanna Tornabuoni (by Ghirlandaio), who is shown bust length, as if a sculpted effigy (Martial, *Epigrammata*, with commentary by D. Calerino and G. Merula, was published in Venice in 1491; see Martial, *Epigrams*, ed. and trans. D.R. Shackleton Bailey, 3 vols. (Cambridge, MA: Harvard University Press, 1993), 3:354). However, the tradition of engraved portraits of the deceased with an epitaph inscribed below on a parapet was far more common among Northern artists such as Dürer and Cranach.

125. William S. Heckscher, "Reflections on Holbein's Portrait of Erasmus at Longford Castle," in *Essays in the History of Art presented to Rudolf Wittkower*, eds. Douglas Fraser, H. Hibbard, and Milton J. Lewine (London: Phaidon Press, 1969), 128–48. See Callahan, *The Verbal & the Visual* (Kindle Edition, 2011-07-25, Kindle locations 668–72). Heckscher notes the unusual position of the book, with the text side of the volume facing the viewer (rather than the closed bound edge) on which is written the book's title, "The Labors of Hercules," in large Roman letters. On the bound side we read next to the name of the author, "Erasmus of Rot" (not fully visible). The painted words connect the Holbein portrait directly to the Hercules adage and Erasmus' commentary.

126. On audience response, see above, n. 35.

127. See above, n. 39, for the citation from Robortellus regarding "au-

dience." The publication of the complete text of Aristotle's *Poetics* in Italian, authored, translated, and commented on by Varchi's Paduan mentor Robertellus, was not issued until 1548, followed shortly by Bernardo Segni's *Retorica e Poetica di Aristotele in volgare* (1549–1550). However, these ideas had already been presented in lectures and had circulated in manuscript form to friends, students, and colleagues outside of Padua. Robertellus' concept of audience in his translation of *Poetics* 1453a5 (1548), 46, would have stimulated Varchi's statements in his *Lezzione* and furthered the increasingly rapid dissemination of the *Poetics* in the second half of the Cinquecento. The translations resulted in the smooth transfer of verbal descriptions from the *Poetics* to painting theory that reshaped the characteristics defining portraiture as it was interpreted by Bronzino.

128. Lohr, "… *e nuovi Omeri, e Plati* …," 32 ff.

129. For example, Varchi's debate with Castelvetro hinged on the desire of Cosimo de' Medici to foster the association between the Tuscan language and Etruscan civilization. On this subject, see Benedetto Varchi, *L'Ercolano*, editio princeps (Florence: Giunti, 1570), on the volgare vs. Castelvetro.

130. On Martelli's biography and political ties, see Wildmoser, "Das Bildnis des Ugolino Martelli von Agnolo Bronzino," and Cropper, "Reading Bronzino's Florentine Portraits," 245–46.

131. On the Italian preference for Erasmus over Luther, see Seidel, "Alcuni Atteggiamenti della cultura Italiana di fronte a Erasmo," in Biondi, *Eresia e Riforma nell' Italia del Cinquecento*, 71–133.

132. The text for 138 reads: "His left hand holds a bow, his right carries a rough club, and the Nemean lion cloaks his naked body. Is this therefore the likeness of Hercules? That he is old and his temples hoary with age suggests otherwise. What of his tongue, pierced with light chains, by which he cleaves the ears of men and draws them to him without difficulty? Don't the Gauls say that with his tongue, not with his might, Alcides excelled in providing nations with laws? Arms yield to the toga, and he who is powerful in speech draws to his wishes even the most resistant hearts." For both illustrations, original text and English translation, see the on-line site: <http://www.mun.ca/alciato/f181.html>.

133. See Mendelsohn, *Paragoni*, 132–37 (Disputà III of Varchi's, *Due Lezzioni*).

134. See Lohr, "… *e nuovi Omeri, e Plati* …," 67–68. This theme supports the idea that the book is, in fact, Virgil's *Aeneid*, in spite of a lack of a title, as described in a letter from Varchi to Martelli, cited in Mendelsohn, *Paragoni*, 30.

135. See full text in Franca Petrucci Nardelli, ed., *Agnolo Bronzino: Rime in burla* (Rome: Istituto della Enciclopedia Italiana, 1988), 'Il Secondo delle

Scuse,' XV, 22, p. 197–98. I am grateful to Victoria Kirkham for helping me refine my translation of this difficult passage. For comments on the *Capitoli*, see Parker, *Bronzino*, 21, 107, 114–24, 209n67, and 217n82.

136. Vitruvius, *Ten Books of Architecture*, 2:5, 103–09.

137. Particularly those of the Northern variety. This opinion is contrary to one expressed by Parker, *Bronzino*, 117–26.

138. Regarding dissimulation and deception, see Harry Berger, Jr., *Fictions of the Pose: Rembrandt against the Italian Renaissance* (Stanford, CA: Stanford University Press, 2000); and idem, *The Absence of Grace: Sprezzatura and Suspicion in Two Renaissance Courtesy Books* (Stanford, CA: Stanford University Press, 2000). The uses of deception and its corollary dissimulation are described in several treatises outlining acceptable behavior for aristocrats and courtiers such as Castiglione's *Il Cortegiano* and Caro's *Galatea*. Both books were influential in artistic circles and contributed to the portrayal of members of society in pose and costume, assuming an attitude of *disinvoltura*. Simoncelli, "Florentine *Fuorusciti*," 300, points out that after the investiture of Cosimo as Florentine Duke in 1537 and despite his initial appearance of leniency toward the anti-Medici exiles, "a cryptic and temporizing form of opposition, a political Nicodemism consisting of allusive gestures and eventually the exploitation of religion, began to develop within Florence." See also Paolo Simoncelli, *Evangelismo italiano del Cinquecento: questione religiosa e nicodemismo politico* (Rome: Istituto storico italiano per l'età moderna e contemporanea, 1979), 330ff, on the religious aspects of the revolt; and Cox-Rearick, "From Bandinelli to Bronzino," on Nicodemism.

139. On Beauty, see the essential bibliography by Elizabeth Cropper in "The Beauty of Women: Problems in the Rhetoric of Renaissance Portraiture," in *Rewriting the Renaissance: The Discourse of Sexual Difference in Early Modern Europe*, eds. M. Ferguson, M. Quilligan, and N. Vickers (Chicago, IL, and London: University of Chicago Press, 1986); and in eadem, "The Place of Beauty in the High Renaissance and its Displacement in the History of Art," in Alvin Vos, *Place and Displacement in the Renaissance*, conference proceedings, Papers from the 25th Annual CEMERS Conference, State University of New York at Binghamton, Center for Medieval and Early Renaissance Studies (Binghamton: SUNY Press, 1995), 159–205, especially in regard to portraiture by Bronzino. For Varchi on *Bellezza* related to portraiture, see also Mendelsohn, *Paragoni*, 128, 129n37, and 275nn132–30, on two poems "In Praise of a Portrait of Giulia Gonzaga," a known sympathizer of the Catholic reform movement; see also the section on Beauty and Pleasure in Varchi's *Lezzioni*.

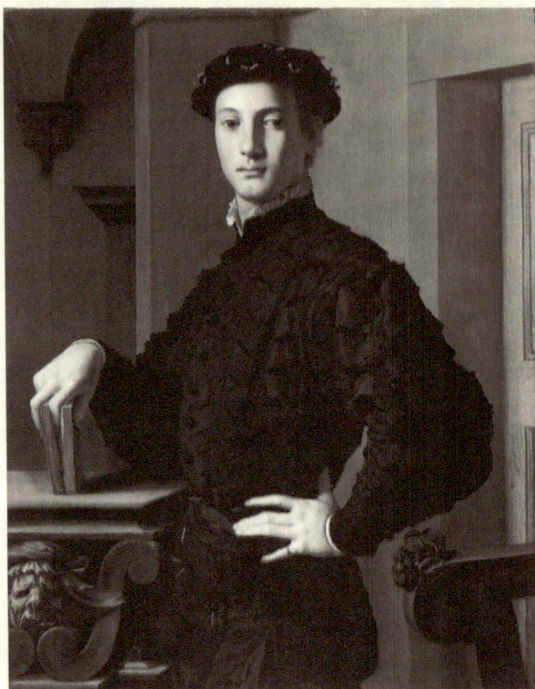

Fig. 1. Agnolo Bronzino, *The Young Man with a Book*, 1530s. Metropolitan Museum of Art, New York. Photo credit: The Metropolitan Museum of Art, NY/Art Resource, NY.

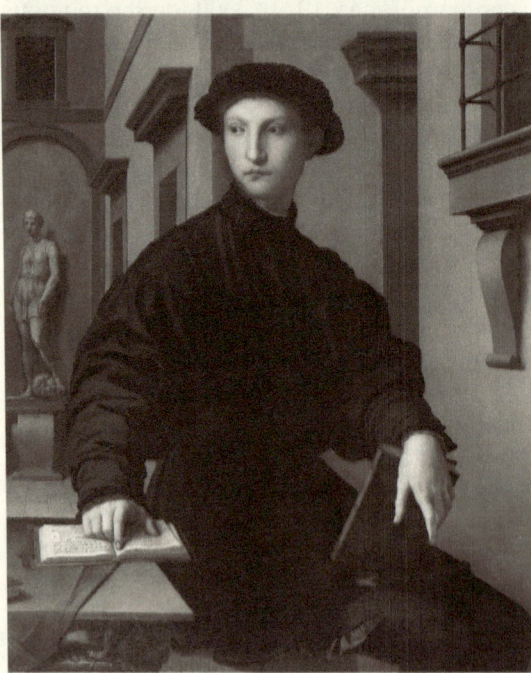

Fig. 2. Agnolo Bronzino, *Portrait of Ugolino Martelli*, Gemäldegalerie Staatliche Museum, Berlin. Photo credit: Gemäldegalerie Staatliche Museum, Berlin/Art Resource, NY.

Fig. 3. Jacopo
Pontormo,
*Cosimo de' Medici
Pater Patriae*,
1519–20. Galleria
degli Uffizi,
Florence. Photo
credit: Scala/Art
Resource, NY.

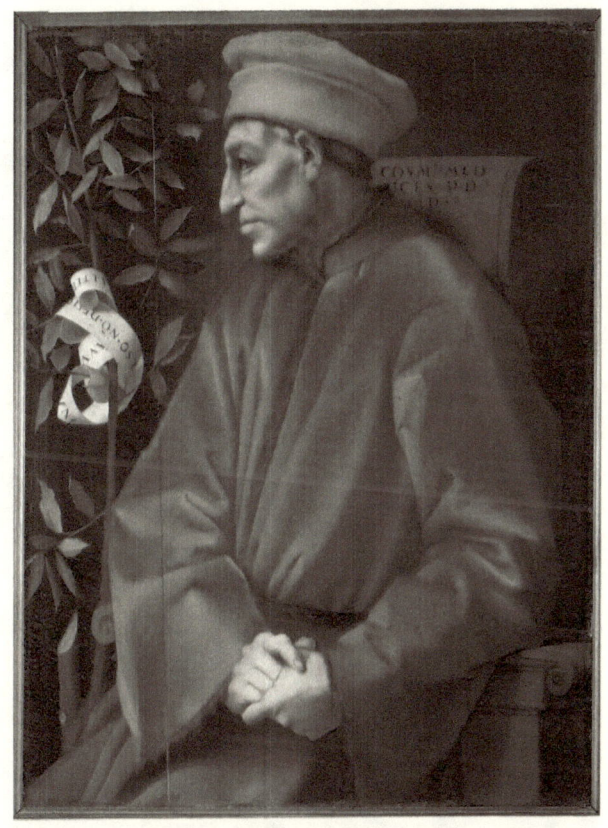

Fig. 4. Andrea Alciato,
Emblem on *Those who
ventured on what is beyond their
powers* (*In eos qui supra vires
quicquam audent*). In *Livret
des emblemes* (Paris: Chrestien
Wechel ed. 1536) <http://
www.emblems.arts.gla.ac.uk/
alciato/emblem>.

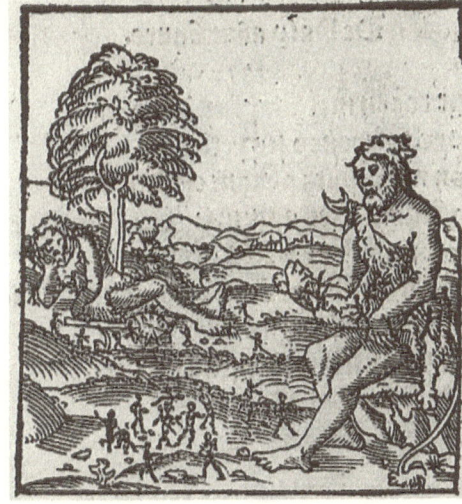

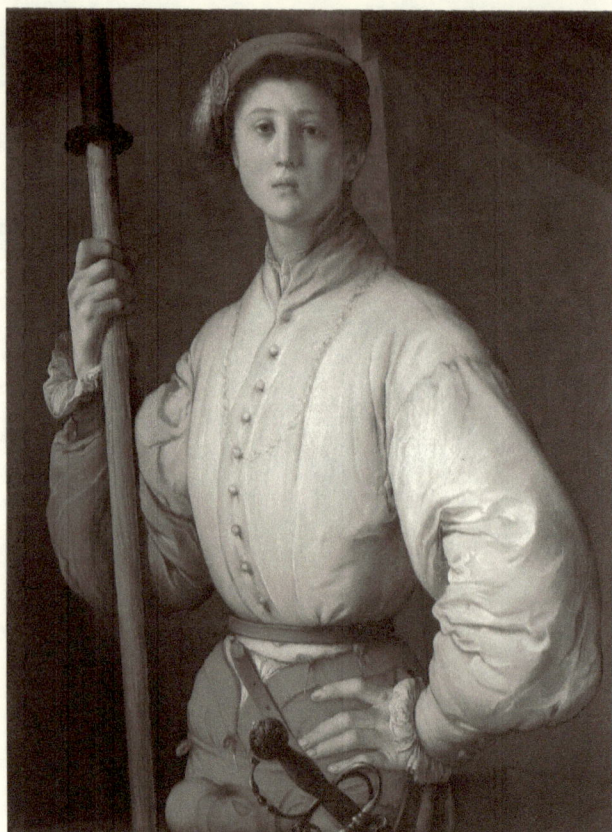

Fig. 5. Jacopo Pontormo, *Portrait of Francesco Guardi* (*Halberdier*), 1529. J.P. Getty Museum, Los Angeles, California. Photo credit: J.P. Getty Museum, Los Angeles, California.

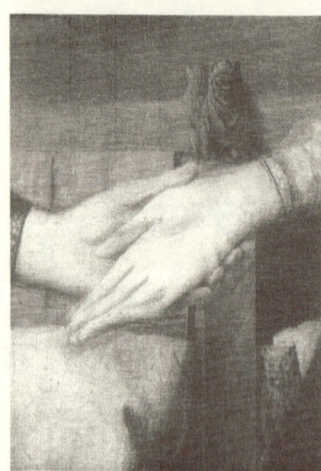

Fig. 6. Jan Van Eyck, *Giovanni Arnolfini and his Betrothed* (det.), 1434. The National Gallery, London. Inventory Number: NG186/ART380412. Photo credit: National Gallery, London/Art Resource, NY.

Fig. 7. Antonio
Fantuzzi, *Ornamental
Design for
Fontainebleau*, n.d.
Photo credit: Henri
Zerner, *The School
of Fontainebleau:
Etchings and
Engravings* (New
York: Abrams, 1977),
n.p.

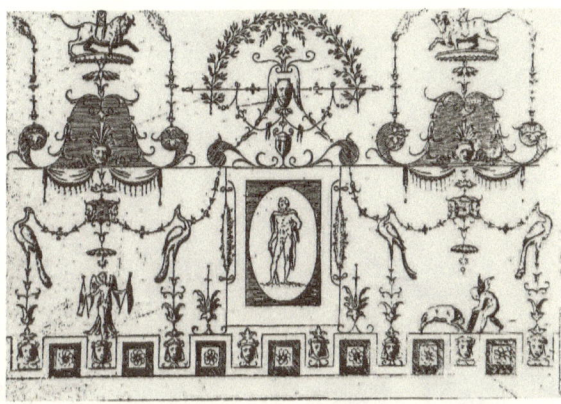

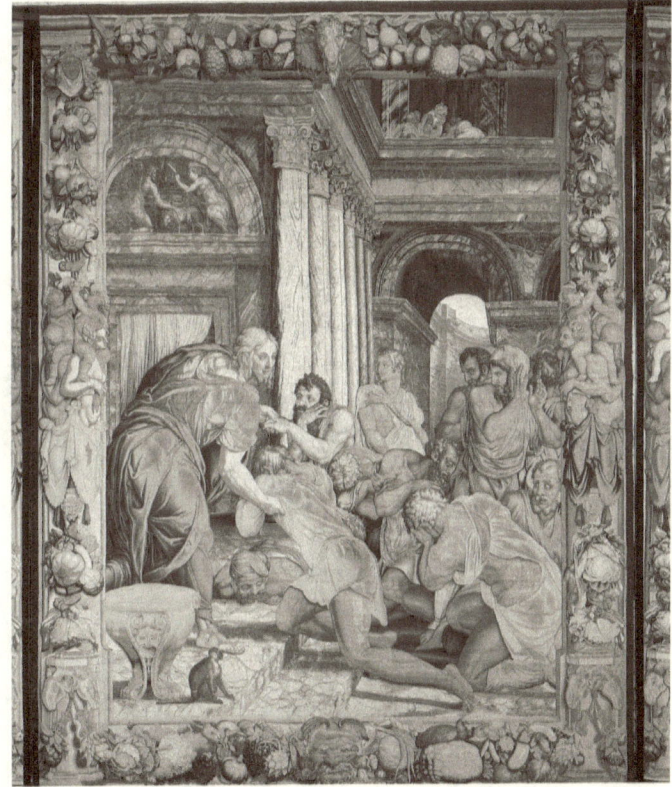

Fig. 8. Agnolo Bronzino with Rafaellino del Colle (or
Alessandro Allori), *The Meeting of Joseph and Jacob in
Egypt*, 1550–53. Detail: *Lower Border*, design by Nicholas
Karcher. Palazzo Vecchio, Florence. Photo credit: Scala/Art
Resource.

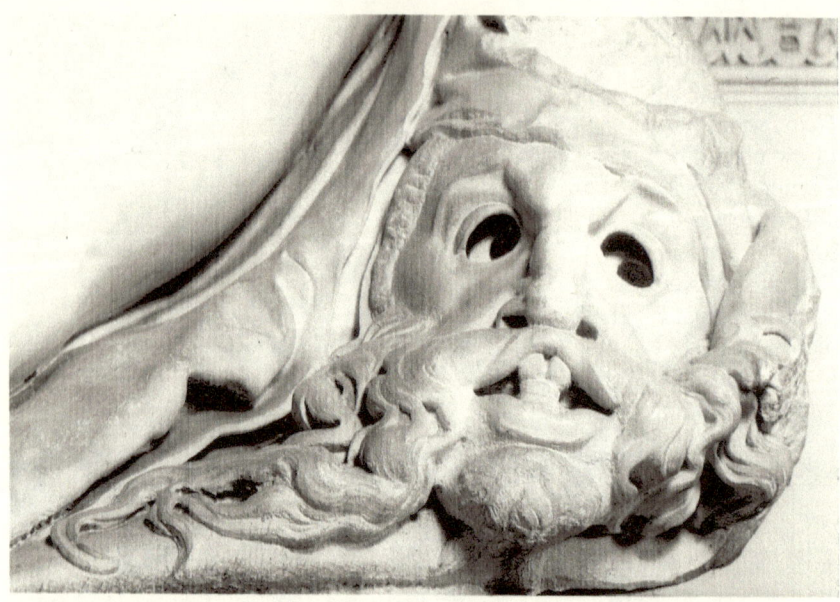

Fig. 9. Michelangelo, *Mask of Night* (det.), 1534, marble. New Sacristy, San Lorenzo, Florence. Photo credit: author.

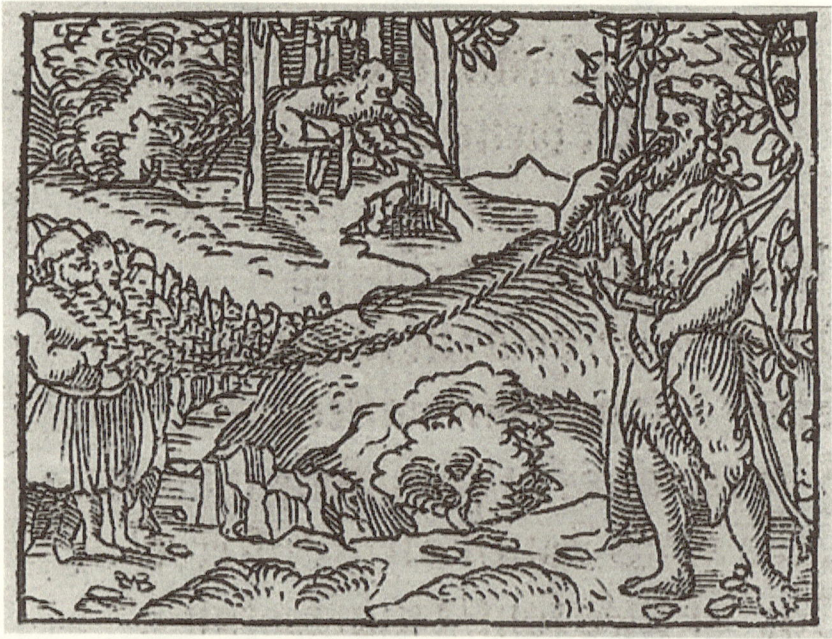

Fig. 10. Andrea Alciato, Emblem on *Eloquence, surpassing strength* (*Eloquentia fortitudine praestantior*). In *Les Emblems* (Paris: Chrestien Wechel ed. 1539) <http://www.emblems.arts.gla.ac.uk/alciato/emblem>.

Fig. 11. Agnolo
Bronzino, *Portrait
of Ugolino Martelli*.
Before first cleaning.
Staatliche Museum,
Berlin. Photo credit:
Courtesy of Dr.
Bernd Lindemann,
Director, Staatliche
Museum, Berlin.

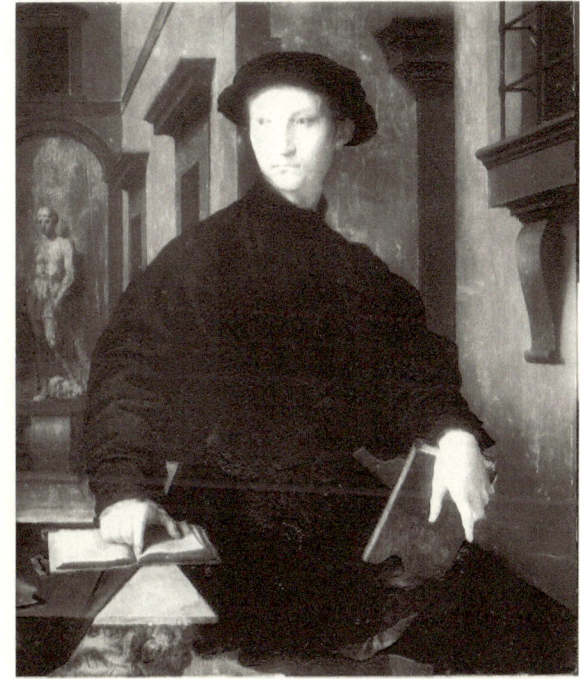

Fig. 11a. Agnolo
Bronzino, *Portrait
of Ugolino Martelli*.
Gemäldegalerie
Staatliche Museen zu
Berlin–Preußischer
Kulturbesitz.
Photo credit:
Gustav Schwarz.
Year: 1925, 338A_
NegNr-1540_1925.
jpg.

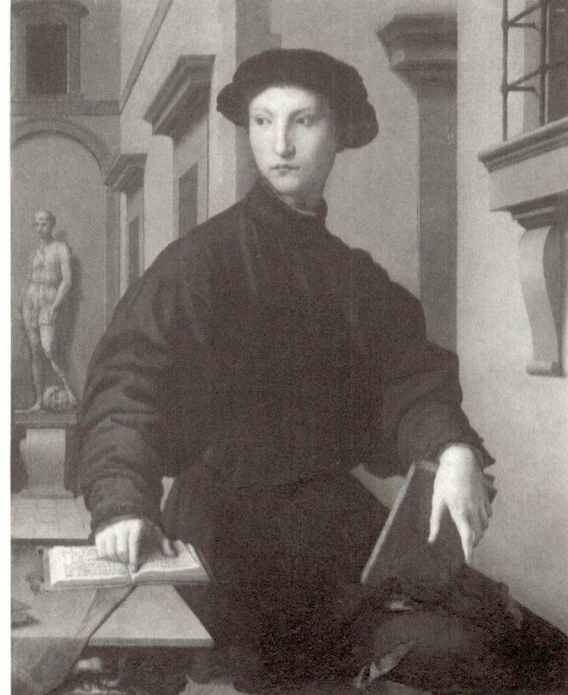

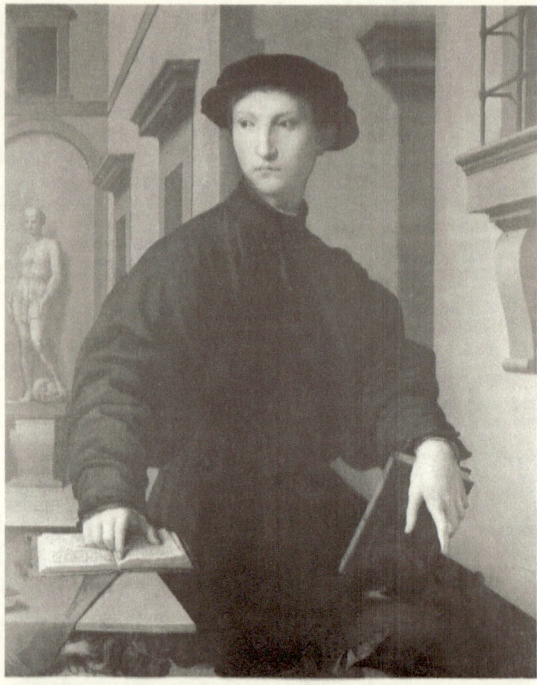

Fig. 11b. Agnolo Bronzino, *Portrait of Ugolino Martelli*. Gemäldegalerie Staatliche Museen zu Berlin–Preußischer Kulturbesitz. Photo credit: Dore Barleben in Wiesbaden. Year: 1950, 338A_Dore Barleben_1950.jpg.

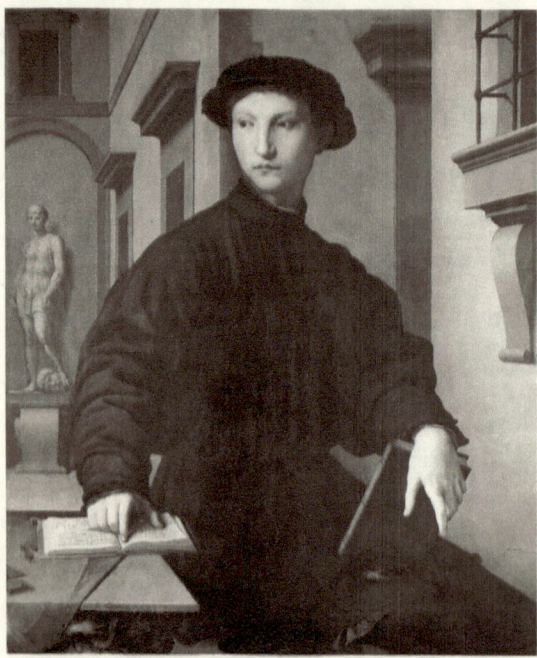

Fig. 11c. Agnolo Bronzino, *Portrait of Ugolino Martelli*. Gemäldegalerie Staatliche Museen zu Berlin–Preußischer Kulturbesitz. Photo credit: Walter Steinkopf. Year: 1951, 338A_ NegNr-151_1951.jpg.

Fig. 11d. Agnolo
Bronzino, *Portrait
of Ugolino Martelli*.
Gemäldegalerie
Staatliche Museen zu
Berlin–Preußischer
Kulturbesitz.
Photo credit:
Walter Steinkopf.
Year: 1956, 338A_
NegNr-1403_1956.jpg.

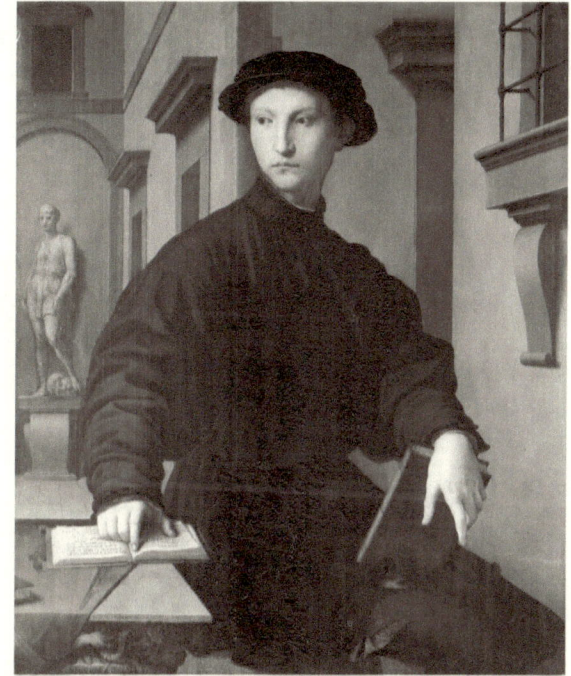

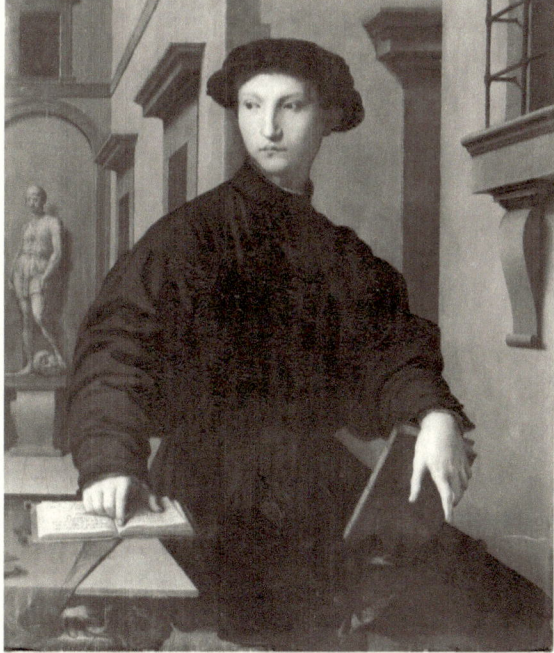

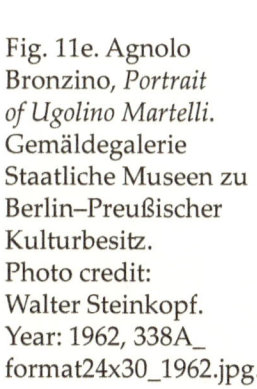

Fig. 11e. Agnolo
Bronzino, *Portrait
of Ugolino Martelli*.
Gemäldegalerie
Staatliche Museen zu
Berlin–Preußischer
Kulturbesitz.
Photo credit:
Walter Steinkopf.
Year: 1962, 338A_
format24x30_1962.jpg.

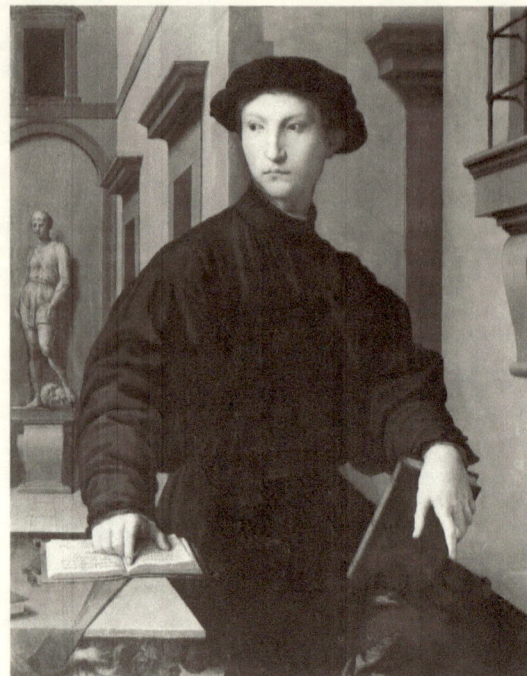

Fig. 11f. Agnolo
Bronzino, *Portrait
of Ugolino Martelli*.
Gemäldegalerie
Staatliche Museen zu
Berlin–Preußischer
Kulturbesitz. Photo
credit: Jörg P. Anders.
Year: 1987, 338A_
NegNr-14829_1987.jpg.

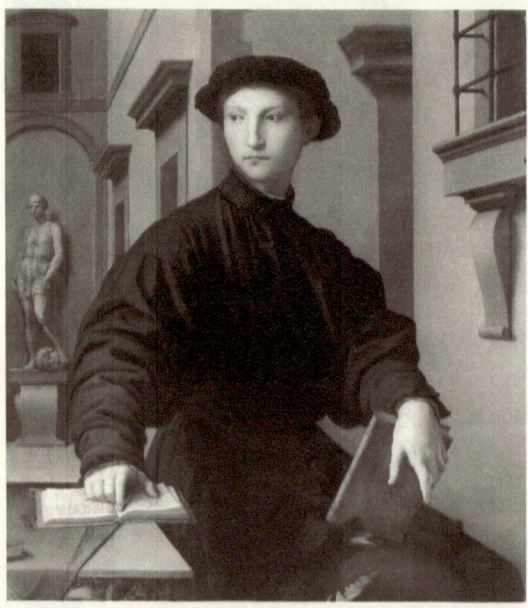

Fig. 11g. Agnolo
Bronzino, *Portrait
of Ugolino Martelli*.
Gemäldegalerie
Staatliche Museen zu
Berlin–Preußischer
Kulturbesitz. Photo
credit: Jörg P. Anders.
Year: 2004, 338A_
NegNr-19252_2004.jpg.

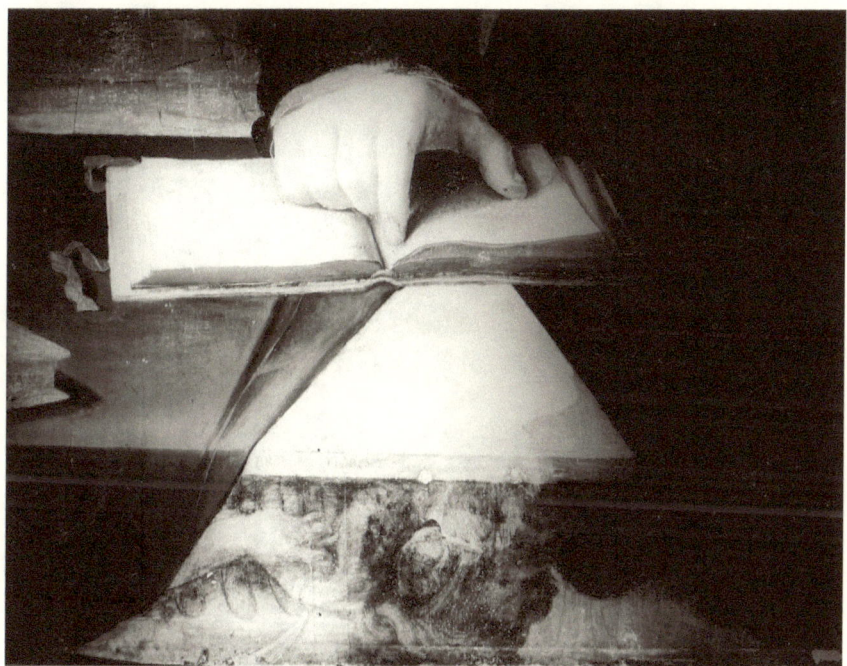

Fig. 12. Agnolo Bronzino, *Portrait of Ugolino Martelli* (det.). Table with carving. Before first cleaning. Staatliche Museum, Berlin. Photo credit: Courtesy of Dr. Bernd Lindemann, Director, Staatliche Museum, Berlin.

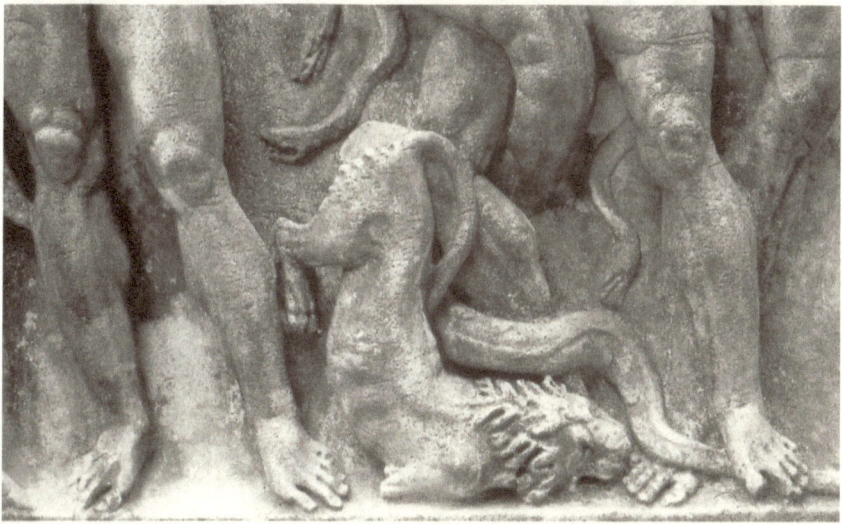

Fig. 13. Sarcophagus: after Lysippus, *Labors of Hercules* (det.), n.d. Boboli Gardens, Florence. Photo credit: author.

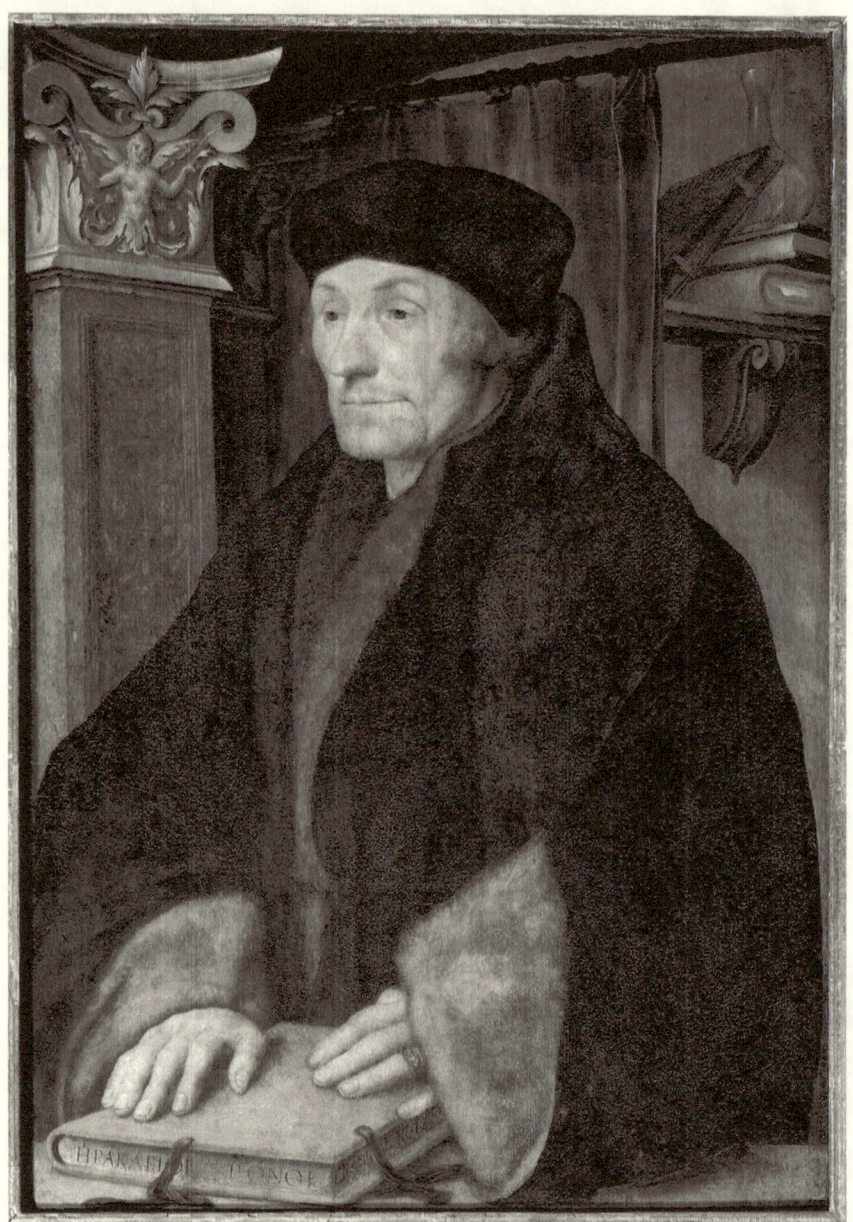

Fig. 14. Hans Holbein the Younger, *Portrait of Erasmus*, 1523. National Gallery, London. Photo credit: National Gallery, London/ Scala/Art Resource, NY.

Bronzino's *Pygmalion and Galatea*: The Metamorphosis of a Muse[1]

Liana De Girolami Cheney

Venite, o Muse e conducete Pane,
che, non ci terreno a cintola le mane.
Bronzino, *In Lode della Galea*, Capitolo Secondo (1555)[2]

This chapter examines the complex history and symbolism of Agnolo di Cosimo or Bronzino's (1503–72) *Pygmalion and Galatea* of 1530, now in the Galleria degli Uffizi in Florence (Fig. 1). In the *Vita* of *Jacopo Pontormo* (1494–1557), Vasari recalls how Pontormo,

> At the time of the siege of Florence, executed a portrait of Francesco Guardi in the costume of a soldier, which was a very beautiful work; and how afterwards as the cover of this picture, [his pupil, Agnolo di Cosimo di Mariano, nick-named] Bronzino [because of his dark complexion] paint-ed Pygmalion praying to Venus that his statue, receiving breath, might spring to life and become, as it did—according to the fables of the poets–flesh and blood.[3]

This chapter considers two significant statements from Vasari's writing: (1) The interconnection between two images painted by two different artists—Pontormo's portrait of a solider and Bronzino's mythological tale; and (2) whether the mythological scene was painted after the portrait in order to cover its image.

The purpose of a portrait cover, like a painted reverse side, is to provide a moral allegory to the image, as in Ridolfo Ghirlandaio's (1483–1561) *Portrait of a Woman* of 1510 at the Uffizi, whose cover bears an enigmatic motto from Publius Maro Virgil (70 BCE–19 BCE) and in Lucius Annaeus Seneca (45 BCE–54 CE), "Sua Cuique Persona" ("To Each His Own Mask").[4] Or the paintings of Bronzino and Pontormo that were superimposed on each other as one panel sliding into another with hinges to hide or reveal the portrait. Because of the difference in the physical size of these two paintings, it is not possible to figure out how they were connected; perhaps they were even placed back to back or next to each other in the form of a diptych.

Bronzino's *Pygmalion and Galatea* of 1530 is painted with oil on panel and covered Pontormo's *Portrait of Francesco Guardi*, also called the *Halberdier* of 1529 and also an oil painting on panel, but now transferred to canvas, presently located at the J. Paul Getty Museum in Los Angeles (Fig. 2). The survival history of these two painting is intriguing. First, they were part of the Medici collection at the Uffizi. Then, in 1612, they were still in Florence since they are recorded in the Riccaridi's family inventory. And in 1644, the paintings are listed in the inventory of the Barberini collection in Rome. But during World War II, they were confiscated by Hitler and moved to Linz to be housed in the new Führer Museum. During 1984–88, the Siviero's Recuperation Program discovered them, and in 1988, the painting of Bronzino's *Pygmalion and Galatea* moved to the State of Florence. But the whereabouts of Pontormo's *Portrait of Francesco Guardi* was not known until 1989, when it is purchased by the Getty Museum at a Christie's sale in London.[5]

A drawing at the Gabinetto Disegni e Stampe degli Uffizi (6701 F.r., Fig. 3) of Pontormo's *Portrait of Francesco Guardi* reveals the compositional changes undertaken by Pontormo in the final painting.[6] The turning of the body creates a 3/4-view portrait, and the background depicts the city wall or bastion, colored in dark green. At the age of sixteen, the young Guardi, as his name indicates, "guards" the city and his lands at the La Piazzuola, near San Miniato, during the Florentine siege, where heavy artillery threaten the walls of San Miniato. Guardi is depicted elegantly dressed as a soldier, holding a long lance, with short hair, and wearing a red *berrette*.[7] The medallion in the *berrette* depicts Hercules and Antenus, alluding to the triumph of Florence, as Hercules, symbol of Florence and virtue, raises the defeated Antaeus, symbol of vice, from the ground. Pontormo is inspired by Antonio Pollaiolo's *Hercules and Antaeus* of 1490, at the Galleria degli Uffizi in Florence.

According to Alessandro Cecchi, Francesco Guardi was born on 29 April 1514 in the Borgo La Croce. During his lifetime, he received numerous civil appointments, including membership in the Council of the Dugento. Through his family's patrimony, Guardi owned several land-holdings, such as il "Palagietto" in via Ghibellina, l'Orto alla "Matonaia," and "La Piazzuola" near San Miniato (later transformed by Michelangelo as the Piazzale Michelangelo). With the sack of Rome in 1527, the Medici family was cast out from Florence, and a Republic was established. In 1530, the imperial Germanic troops of Charles V besieged Florence, nullified the republic, and established a duchy with the return of the Medici.[8] In 1556, recalling this ordeal, Vasari depicts a panoramic view of the Florentine blockade in the Palazzo Vecchio.

In Pontormo's painting, Guardi is placed in front the walls of San Miniato, thus protecting his family lands during the Florentine siege and defending the Republic. The elegant and beautiful portrayal of this figure alludes to two aspects of guarding: one is civic, denoted by the soldier's attire, and the other is angelic, revealed by the expression and beauty of the figure.[9] After the fall of the Republic, this type of portrait alluding to the "bella gioventù" ready to die to defend the liberty of the city[10] was compromising. Concealing the painting with a cover rather than destroying it would be simpler and safer for the patron. As Vasari notes, Bronzino painted the portrait cover after the siege of 1530. However, Bronzino translates Pontormo's visual civic sentiment in the cover painting *Pygmalion and Galatea* by rendering in the background a gloomy landscape with icy and blue tonalities attesting to the Germanic devastation in Florence. Thus, in view of the civic connection between the painting and its cover, or the portrait and its mythological curtain, it is intriguing to understand its signification as well as the underlying moral intention or other didactic message revealed in the painting.

In *Pygmalion and Galatea*, Bronzino invents an imagery that, although appropriating stylistically from his masters such as Michelangelo and Pontormo, reveals his own artistic conceit—a dressed supplicant male and a nude standing female. Thematically, Bronzino fuses the classical literary with the medieval legendary tradition. He is inspired, in particular, by Ovid's *Metamorphoses* (X 238–97). The Roman lyrical and mythic poet Publius Ovidius Naso (43

BCE–17/18 CE) describes Pygmalion's love story as an imaginative impulse to mold a love object to one's own desire.

The sculptor Pygmalion, disgusted by the wanton behavior of the women of Cyprus, had sworn never to marry. He pours his longing for a purer beauty into carving an ivory statue of a woman. Pygmalion's creation assumes a form so lovely and lifelike that he promptly falls in love with her (*ars adeo latet arte sua*). On the Feast of Venus, the Goddess of Love, he clothes the statue, lays her on feather pillows; brings her shells, pebbles, birds, flowers, and amber; and caresses her with such passion that he is a afraid he might bruise her limbs. Venus hears his prayers and takes pity on him. The ivory softens and grows warm, veins throbs at his kiss, and the statue's eyes open.[11]

The Pygmalion legend also fits neatly into Bronzino's understanding of artistic creativity as dependent on past art, since this saga is associated with a long tradition of images. The legend, originally based on Ovid's *Metamorphoses*, is elaborated in the Middle Ages in Guilluame de Lorris and Jean de Meun's *Le Roman de la Rose* and subsequently in *Ovid moralise*, works which were frequently illustrated with woodcuts and miniatures, such as *Pygmalion and Galatea*, a miniature of 1370 at the Pierpont Morgan Library in New York, and Christine de Pizan's (1364–1430) *Pygmalion and Galatea* in *Cent hystories de troyes* of 1480, a woodcut in the Bibliothèque nationale de France in Paris.[12] Unlike Pizan, and like the artist of the *Le Roman de la Rose*, Bronzino focuses on Pygmalion as supplicant and sculptor, as tools of the trades are found all around the foreground of the painting.

In *Pygmalion and Galatea*, perhaps as *burla* (scoff), Bronzino parallels the creative instruments of art (chisel, hammer, pointers) employed by Pygmalion in carving the sculptural figure of Galatea, to cover up Pontormo's depicted destructive instruments of war (halberd and sword) held by the guard. Bronzino's stylistical appropriations extend to the simple attire of the sculptor, Pygmalion: in particular, the boots of a sculptor, recalling Raphael's portrait of Michelangelo as Heraclitus of 1510, in the School of Athens in the Stanza della Segnatura at the Vatican. Bronzino also refers to compositions of his master Pontormo, such as the supplicant pose of Pygmalion from Pontormo's *Study of a Kneeling Nude in Profile with*

Supplicant Hands of 1514, a black pencil drawing at the Gabinetto Disegni e Stampe degli Uffizi in Florence (Inv no. 6744, Fig. 4)[13] for San Francis of the Pala Pucci of 1518 in San Michele Visdomini in Florence, and Pontormo's semi-kneeling figure supporting Christ's dead body in the *Deposition* of 1525 in the Capponi Chapel of Santa Felicita in Florence. Furthermore, for the figure and stance of Galatea's *figure serpentinata*, Bronzino is also indebted to his teacher, as seen in Pontormo's sepia drawing of *Venus and Cupid* of 1515 in the Gabinetto Disegni e Stampe degli Uffizi (Fig. 5).[14] Compositionally, both Pontormo and Bronzino are indebted to Michelangelo's *David* of 1501–04, at the Accademia Gallery in Florence (compare Fig. 6, flipped image, with Figs. 1 and 5).

By using elongated figures, *figura serpentinata*, sinuous rhythms, and unreal color schemes, forms evolved from reality but were transformed into fantasy.[15] The translation into an unreal space with no perspectival structure enhanced the ambiguity of that reality. Bronzino's *Pygmalion and Galatea* clearly embodies the Mannerist aesthetic ideals expounded by Benedetto Varchi in the *Due Lezzioni* or *Paragone* of 1547.[16]

In the *Due Lezzioni* of 1547, Benedetto Varchi defined the intention of artistic creation of Mannerist artists as "an artificial imitation of nature."[17] In Bronzino's *Pygmalion and Galatea*, the *paragoni* are complex, varying from physical quests to metaphysical quests. The natural or physical quest refers to the artist's desire to imitate nature or to observe reality and transform it into an imaginary realm. Another aspect of the *paragone* is a rivalry quest among the arts, in particular here, the superiority of the art of painting versus the art of sculpture.

Bronzino's visual response to Varchi's question is intriguing and invested with meaning. Perhaps Bronzino's response to this debate is visually depicting two painted images of sculpture: a sculptor (Pygmalion) and a sculpture (Galatea), showing the superiority of painting. Or, perhaps Bronzino painted a sculptor (Pygmalion) pleading to a painted sculpture (Galatea as the reverse figure of Michelangelo's *David*) in order to end this artistic debate, since both painting and sculpture may borrow and benefit from each other's artistic merits.[18] With this in mind, he explores another *paragone*, which is the visualization of the various sculptural forms and techniques of ceramics, carving, and casting—a *paragone* of the art of sculpture depicted in painting. In addition to the carved statue of Galatea (in ivory or marble), Bronzino portrays a sacrificial altar made of *pietra serena* (Florentine natural material) and containing relief carvings such as the figures of Mars and Venus, the sculptural ornaments of bucrania, and the male and female herms holding an epitaph. Above it, a large bull burns, surrounded by huge flaming fire, a possible allusion to casting bronze. The sparks of the blaze scatter down the altar. The painted image of the bull is of bronze coloration (an allusion to Bronzino's name). Framing the sacrificial altar, on the left, is a wooden stool holding the sculptor's instruments and measuring tools, suggesting wood carving. On the right, a garden ceramic vase, decorated with grotesque masks and classical ornaments, contains a fire poker. The various techniques in ceramics, wheel throwing, slap, and pinching are incorporated in the image of this large vessel. In portraying the various sculptural techniques, Bronzino is emphasizing the validity of the various methods employed by artists to compose art—whether a sculptor with a chisel or a painter with a brush, the artistic conception (conceit) is its superiority and not its technical execution.

The metaphysical *paragone* alludes to the signification of spiritual evocation or artistic inspiration, which I refer to as *furor artisticus*, and natural *furor*, which is the sacrificial fire to a deity.[19] In the Cinquecento, the *furor* notion is imbedded in the Renaissance Neoplatonic concept of *furor poeticus* or poetic inspiration, which derives from the writings of philosopher and physician Marsilio Ficino (1433–99). Ficino explains in his Orphic writings that there are four forms of inspiration or *furor*: divine, prophetic, amorous, and poetic.[20] Considering Ficino's philosophical influence in the arts I would like to coin the artistic inspirational fire as a particular type of *furor*, a *furor artisticus*, a unique artistic frenzy of visual artists.[21] This artistic inspiration is based fundamentally on the Italian Renaissance tradition, which considers creativity to be a faculty present in all human activity.[22] In his writings, Giorgio Vasari also explains this magical intellectual passion: "Thus [creativity must be activated] when the intellect (*l'ingegno*) wants to work, and when the fire of inspiration is kindled (*il furore è acceso*), because it is then that one sees excellent and divine results, and marvelous conceptions (*concetti meravigliosi*)."[23]

These notions about artistic creativity combined with the conception of poetic inspiration relate to yield yet another central idea, *ut pictura poesis* ("as is painting, so is poetry").[24] Bronzino, as painter as well as poet, is aware of these and other similar types of *paragoni* as he embraces Horace's motto.[25] The idea of *ut pictura poesis* captures the complementary nature of poetry or writing with painting, equating the inspiration of the poet and writer with the imagination of the painter.[26] Derived from Horace, the phrase is frequently employed by artists and theoreticians of the sixteenth century (Cinquecento), including the Florentine Leonardo da Vinci (1452–1509), the Venetian Ludovico Dolce (1508–68), the Milanese Gian Paolo Lomazzo (1538–92), and the Florentine Giorgio Vasari (1511–74).[27] In his writings, Vasari relates the concept of *furor poeticus* to the creation of visual arts and says: "Many painters ... achieve in the first design of their work, as though guided by a sort of inspirational fire, something of the good and a certain measure of boldness, but afterwards, in finishing it, the boldness vanishes."[28]

Mannerist painters, in particular Bronzino, strove to invent an image that evoked poetical inspiration and found as an artistic vehicle the desire to create a beautiful image. Thus the aim was to create beauty by surpassing nature, arousing a spiritual emotion, thus creating an aesthetic ideal. With the Neoplatonic doctrine in mind—"beauty consists of a certain charm" as something spiritual that transcends sensual experience and that makes us long for the origin of what we perceive—the Mannerist painters, such as Pontormo and Bronzino, emphasize the ideal beauty in the mind of the artist rather than the reproduction of beauty discovered in nature.[29]

The Mannerist moral quest for aesthetic gave great importance to invention. Michelangelo's conception of love and beauty is reflected in his Rime 41: "Love seizes me and beauty keeps me bound."[30] The sixteenth-century sculptor finds that love is the wish to find the origin of its source—the essence of beauty—because the image is in the artist's mind, which will be eventually carved in marble—observed in Bronzino's *Pygmalion and Galatea*. Vasari, too, made beauty one of the critical components of art in the Preface to the *Vite* (1550–68).[31]

The eclecticism of Bronzino's style is further revealed when comparing *Pygmalion and Galatea*'s foreground composition with

Andrea del Sarto's (1486–1530) *Annunciation* of 1512 at the Galleria Palatina in Florence. For example, in an open courtyard, two figures frame an altar. In Sarto's painting, Mary and the Angel surround the tabernacle; in Bronzino's imagery, it is Galatea and Pygmalion who frame an ancient sacrificial altar. However, he might also have considered the genre scene of Lucas van Leyden's (1494–33) copper engraving of the *Milkmaid* of 1510, at the Rijksmuseum in Amsterdam, for the compositional arrangement of representing male and female framing a bull in a landscape. Familiarity with and borrowing from German prints was commonly done by Cinquecento artists, in particular, Pontormo's inspiration from German prints (engravings and woodcuts) on the *Passion of Christ* by Albrecht Dürer, Hans Baldung Grien, and Lucas van Leyden.[32]

Ingeniously, Bronzino fuses religious and pagan compositions to depict his ancient tale. Although there is a general consensus about the stylistic and historical connections of the depiction of Bronzino's painting, still there is a room for further analysis on its symbolism.

The fusion between his artistic and mental *furors* (painter and poet) makes of Bronzino a musing muse. Not only are his paintings ingeniously conceived but also he composes images with complex conceits (*concetti*),[33] thus inviting the viewer to musing as well, cogitating and meditating, sometimes humorously or sardonically, on the artistic conceit. Masterfully, he assimilates his teachers' composition and renders them into a new embellished visual vocabulary. He also addresses the parallelism of transformation and appropriation of literary sources, the ancient philosophical writings such as Horace's *ut pictura poesis* and Ovid's *Metamorphoses* in his painting *Pygmalion and Galatea*, as well as in his related literary expression. For example, the parallelism of transformation is observed between Venus' creation and divine intervention in making the ideal (Beauty) into the real (Galatea) as the sculptor Pygmalion transforms and creates a sculptural figure from a mass of stone. Ovid's *Metamorphoses* are paralleled with the representation of a material form, although an idealized image, as an expression of a spiritual sentiment—love. The transmutation is from physical matter to form; creation of form to ideal; expression of the ideal to sentiment; and sentiment of love into the aesthetic of beauty.

Furthermore, Bronzino utilizes the amorous tale of Pygmalion and Galatea to focus on the theme of artistic creativity, and perhaps more characteristically, to reveal the very anxiety associated with artistic inspiration, that *furor artisticus* and *furor poeticus* evoke the creative act. The poetic imagination of his creation and the manner in which he embodies them in his visual imagery created a work of art, which contained beauty of form and color as well as—a Mannerist conceit.

On a symbolic level, Pontormo's portrait alludes to the art of war, through the depiction of a soldier in arms who guards the city walls. The red coloration of his *berrette* and codpiece reflects the violent struggle of Hercules and Antenus in the *berrette*'s medallion[34] or the passion for freedom, civic patriotism, and youth's *furor*. Francesco Guardi was, after all, only sixteen years old when he became a solider. Pontormo's symbolic "external fire" is internalized in Bronzino's portrait cover, e.g., in the depiction of a love tale between Pygmalion and Galatea and Mars and Venus (relief in the altar's base) as well as the sacrificial fire of Apis, the sacred bull.

In the sixteenth century, the importance of the study of human nature extended to the study of the elements—fire, water, air, and earth—in association with cosmological implications or astrological signs. Treatises on alchemy emphasized the interaction and transformation of natural elements—for example, *Aura consurgens*, an early sixteenth-century text, notes that "the fire gives form and makes everything perfect, as it is written":

> He blows into his face the real of life … the fire makes subtle all earthly things that serve matter … Nothing that is heavy can be made light without help of the lighting thing. And the light things cannot be pressed down without the presence of the having thing. [Then] make the body spiritual and what is fixed makes volatile.[35]

Furthermore, astrological texts connected human behavior with the zodiacal signs and constellations, for example, spring and Mars are connected with the element of fire. Individuals born in the spring, under the sign of Mars, ruled by Aries, are empowered with the element of fire, which provides them with passion, vitality, and intense energy. The attributes of Mars are the lance and instruments of warfare, as well as banners of victory for having triumph in battle.[36] Perhaps Pontormo envisioned Francesco Guardi as an image of Mars, the Roman God of War, while Bronzino's cover painting relates to Venus, the Goddess of Love, an antidote to Mars and war. The planet Venus rules the house of Taurus, whose attribute is the bull, a symbol of earth and fertility, providing a person with vigor, strength, and natural energy or rebirth.[37] The connection between Mars and Venus is depicted in the altar's relief alluding to parallel connections and transformation; as Venus transformed the fury of Mars into love, so has Pygmalion transformed the amorphous stone into a figure, Galatea. The inscription on the altar "Heu Vicit Venus" ("Alas Venus has won!") affirms Venus' victory.

But adroitly and amusingly, Bronzino presents another possible allusion to his painting: the relief depicts Mars embracing Venus while she gazes at the held apple of discord, recalling the Judgment of Paris. In the celestial Mount Olympus, Venus' participations and cunning actions in the selection of the fairest are revealed on earth—with devastating consequences caused by her vain judgment on beauty, love, and pride, which, in turn, transform into abandonment, desolation, and war, namely, the Trojan War. With Bronzino's version in mind, one could interpret the Latin message as "Alas Venus is conquered!" Then, does Mars hold Venus for love or for restraint? Thus, does the meaning here imply that Mars conquers Venus as well? Or that war has ruled over love? Have Pygmalion's vigorous and persistent pleas to Venus succeeded? His marble statue is now transformed into a human form, Galatea.

Another puzzling interpretation surfaces when considering the legendary dual role of Mars as a Roman god of War and as a guardian of Agriculture.[38] According to Roman tradition, having Mars as a patron god, a Roman man served the state in two capacities: as a soldier and as a farmer. Perhaps, Pontormo's covered portrait symbolizes the duality of the public and private function of a Florentine man: in time of war, he publicly acts as a soldier, attending to military affairs; while in times of peace, he engages as a citizen in caring for the land and his private daily activities. Bronzino's Pygmalion represents the second role of a Florentine man: a sculptor working in his open studio, carving beautiful statues.

Furthermore, Bronzino's composition also presents a paradox. It is divided into two rectangles comprised of a foreground and background. In the foreground there is an ambitious interpretation of the Ovidean tale with human figures, while in the background there is a vast landscape. The desolated and icy landscape alludes to the mandate of the Medici to the Florentines to burn their lands in order to prevent the siege.[39] However, the luminous horizon suggests a sunset of a vernal season, which alludes to a transformation from bareness to fullness. With the suspension of war, the burnt Florentine land will be fertile again, as seen in the growing plants depicted in the painting, which allude to the forthcoming of spring.

Perhaps the *clavis interpretandi* to Bronzino's painting is the depiction of the bull. According to antiquity, the cult of the bull considers the animal to have two natures because of its fertilizing powers: earthly and celestial.[40] Thus, the symbolism of the bull has an ambiguous nature. It carries a complex symbolism of fertility as a primordial creature—horn, sky, water, lightening, and rain. At times, the bull embodies the masculine procreative power, the solar generative force, strength or warriors, royalty, and the Sky Gods. But the bull may also represent the earth and the humid and seminal power of rain, so it becomes associated with lunar Great Mother, the feminine generative force of nature. The bull contains feminine and masculine reproductive forces associating at the natural level with the gender identity of Venus and Mars and their respective humors: cold and wet for the female, and hot and dry for the male.[41] And at the mythical level, the bull (Taurus) is the astral sign for both gods, Venus and Mars.

According to the ancient historians, Herodotus' (484 BCE–425 BCE) *Histories* (3.28) and Plutarch's (46–120) *Lives* (Isis and Osiris 359b; 362c-d), Apis or the bull is one of the most revered animals in Egypt. Apis as a sacred bull is the result of a virgin birth: his mother, the cow, conceived him when a ray of generative light from the moon fell on her.[42] In ancient religions, the bull or Taurus is associated with the rites of Venus as well as with the cult of Mars, *Mars Grabovius*, where common offerings to these divinities were to sacrifice a bull.[43]

In the sixteenth century, artists and humanists consulted and composed allegorical, emblematic, and mythological texts as sources for their visual conceits.⁴⁴ With a moral overtone, these manuals contain verbal and visual representations of virtues, vices, passions, and temperaments.⁴⁵ The fascination with Egyptian hieroglyphs and their legends was kindled by humanist writings such as Pierio Valeriano's (1477–1558) *Hieroglyphica* (Venice, 1556), where in Book Three he analyzes the various aspects and symbolisms of the bull according to the Egyptians.⁴⁶ The Florentine physician and humanist Paulo Giovio (1483–1552) also composed a book with *imprese* or devises, *Dialogo delle imprese*,⁴⁷ where he designs an *impresa* of a sacrificed bull for the brothers Prospero and Fabritio Colonnesi. The *pictura* (image) depicts Apis standing among the flames of a classical altar, ornamented with bucrania and festoons. An elaborate ribbon encircles the scene with the motto: "Ingegnio Explerior Funera Digna Meo" ("I suffer ruin worthy of my own invention"), while a long descriptive text explains the meaning of the image (Fig. 7).⁴⁸

Artists also integrated the mythographic imagery in papal and noble palaces. Bernardino Pinturicchio (1454–1513), for example, depicted a fresco cycle with a *Procession of Apis* of 1492, in the Sala dei Santi at the Vatican, for Alexander Borgia, Pope Alexander VI.⁴⁹ Apis is visualized as *Pacis cultori* (Cultivator of Peace) and as a symbol of the "peaceful arts" because of his Egyptian association with the celestial realm, divinity (Isis and Osiris), and the natural realm of agriculture and cultivation. In this scene, the burning altar is behind the bull.

Bronzino assimilates the humanist and the artistic conventions in placing a sacred bull on an altar, as a sacrificial offering, but he enhances the imagery and signification with his own renditions (compare Figs. 1 and 7). In the center of the composition, he depicts a fanciful classical altar, where a large burning fire envelops part of the body of Apis. The sacred bull decorated with a band and Isis medal below his horns attests to the authenticity of his divinity. Pygmalion offers to the Olympian gods, Mars and Venus, his highest donation, knowing that the bull (Apis, Taurus) is their sacred animal. Bronzino also portrays a parallel between Apis' magical firing powers, Venus and Mars' amorous passion, and Pygmalion's artistic desire. As the sacrificial offer is burning (the bull), Pygmalion supplicates for his artistic form (Galatea) to be transformed into a natural figure. While pleading for divine intervention, Pygmalion does not realize the magical process of transformation that is occurring as the bull gazes at the generative power of Galatea, infusing her with *furor* or animated powers of life and transforming her from an inanimate object, a statue, into a human form. Thus, the divine's creative power converts the artist's creation of a statue into a natural form. Here is a *paragone* of magic and nature.

The separation from the natural realm depicted in the background of the painting in the form of a landscape with a sunset is contrasted in the foreground with the artist's realm of fantasy. With this conceit, Bronzino composes his own museum for viewers to learn about his art. Inanimate forms metamorphoze into symbolic forms with cultural and didactic meanings, as burning desires and passion can be purified. Artistic language transforms into paintings or sculptures, where the laws of one or the other can merge as the artist composes a three-dimensional structure, a statue, into a two-dimensional design, a relief or a painting. The magic of art rests with the viewer, whose perception embodies a painting or a sculpture with enchanting powers. With *Pygmalion and Galatea*, Bronzino creates more than a portrait cover for the painting of his master; he transforms the art of war depicted in Pontormo's *Portrait of Francesco Guardi* into the art of love, a tale about magic and fantasy.

NOTES

1. A shorter version of this chapter was presented as "Bronzino's *Pygmalion and Galatea*," at the International Congress of Mediterranean Studies Association, in Budapest, Hungary, 24–29 May 2003, and published as Liana De Girolami Cheney and Sonia Michelotti Bonetti, "Bronzino's *Pygmalion and Galatea*: l'antica bella maniera," in *Discovery Journal* (2006), 5–10.

2. See *Agnolo Bronzino. Rima in burla*, ed. Franca Petrucci Nardelli (Rome: Istituto della Enciclopedia Italiana, 1988), 84; and Deborah Parker, *Bronzino: Renaissance Painter as Poet* (Cambridge: Cambridge University Press, 2000), passim, for a discussion on Bronzino's burlesque and lyric poetry. His burlesque poems are confusing and obscene, while the sonnets are rhetorical in the Petrarchan mode.

3. See Giorgio Vasari, *Le vite de' più eccellenti pittori, e architettori*, ed. Gaetano Milanesi, 9 vols. (Florence: Sansoni, 1970–74, hereafter noted as Vasari-Milanesi), 6:275. Before returning to the Galleria degli Uffizi after WWII, the painting was recorded in the Galleria Barberini in Rome. See

Edi Baccheschi, ed., *L'Opera completa del Bronzino. Introdotta da scritti del pittore e coordinata* (Milan: Rizzoli, 1973), 87, Entry 11.

4. See Virgil, *Aeneid* X, 467. See also Seneca, *De beneficiis*, II, 17, and Quintilian, *Istitutiones*, v, 12, cited in Alessandro Cecchi, et al., *L'officina della maniera* (Florence: Marsilio, 1997), 123. See Maurice Brock, *Bronzino* (Paris: Flammarion, 2002), 67–69, discussion on Ghirlandaio's portrait and cover.

5. For Pontormo's painting, the Getty Museum paid more than thirty-two million dollars.

6. Curiously, in the nineteenth century, the *Halberdier* was attributed to Bronzino. See Charles McCorquodale, *Bronzino* (New York: Harper and Row, Publishers, 1981), 27; Elizabeth Pilliod, "The Life of Bronzino," in Carmen C. Bambach, Janet Cox-Rearick, and George R. Goldner, *The Drawings of Bronzino* (New Haven, CT, and London: Yale University Press, 2010), 3–9, in particular, 5, questions the soldier identity as Francesco Guardi. Other scholars disagree; see Elizabeth Cropper, "Entry on Pontormo's Portrait of Francesco Guardi," in Cecchi, et al., *L'officina della maniera*, 376; Elizabeth Cropper, "Pygmalion and Galatea," in Carlo Falciani and Antonio Natali, eds., *Bronzino: Artist and Poet at the Court of the Medici* (Florence: Mandragora, 2010), 76–78; and Maurice Brock, *Bronzino* (Paris: Flammarion, 2002), 52–58.

7. See Cropper, "Entry on Pontormo's Portrait of Francesco Guardi," 376; and Maurizia Tzartes, *Il "ghiribizzoso" Pontormo* (Florence: Polistampa, 2008), 140–42.

8. See André Chastel, *The Sack of Rome, 1527*, trans. Beth Archer (Princeton, NJ: Princeton University Press, 1983), passim; and Judith Hook, *The Sack of Rome, 1527* (New York: Macmillan, 1972; repr. Ann Arbor: The University of Michigan Press, 2008), passim.

9. See Philippe Costamagna, *Pontormo* (Paris: Gallimard, 1994), 233–36; Cropper, "Entry on Pontormo's Portrait of Francesco Guardi," 376; and Luciano Berti, *Pontormo e il suo tempo* (Florence: Banca Toscana, 1993), 152–57.

10. See Brock, *Bronzino*, 54.

11. See *The Metamorphoses of Ovid*, ed. Allen Mandelbaum (New York: Harcourt Brace, 1995), Section X 238–97. There are several interpretations of the Greek meaning of Galatea, "she who is milk-white," as well as the mythological legends associated with the name, e.g., Galatea was a woman who prayed for her daughter, Leucippus, to be transformed into a son. See Antoninus Liberalis, *Metamophoses*, 17, derived from Nicander of Colophon's *Heteroeumena* ("*Methamorphoses*," now lost), second century BCE. And Galatea is a sea-nymph in another Ovidean myth. See Ovid, *Metamorphoses, Acis and Galatea*, XII, 750–68.

12. See Barbara Eschenburg, *Pygamlions Werkstatt* (Cologne: Lenbach-haus München, 2001), 13–54, for a discussion on the history of Pygmalion and art.

13. See Tzartes, *Il "ghiribizzoso" Pontormo*, 49.

14. See Berti, *Pontormo*, 276.

15. For a discussion on the Mannerist style, consult Craig H. Smyth, *Mannerism and Maniera* (New York: Locust Vallery, 1962), passim; John Shearman, *Mannerism* (Baltimore, MD: Penguin Books, 1967), passim; Sydney Freedberg, *Painting in Italy, 1500–1600* (Baltimore, MD: Penguin Books, 1971), passim; David Summer, "Maniera and Movement: The *Figura Serpentinata*," *Art Quarterly* 35 (1972), 209–311; and Liana De Girolami Cheney, *Readings in Mannerism* (London and New York: Peter Lang, 2005), passim.

16. See Leatrice Mendelsohn, *Paragoni: Benedetto Varchi's Due Lezzioni and Cinquecento Art Theory* (Ann Arbor, MI: UMI Research Press, 1982), 109–42. Benedetto Varchi (1503–65) was a Florentine historian, poet, and philologist. The book of the *Due Lezzioni* is based on Varchi's lectures delivered before the *Accademia Fiorentina* in 1547 and published in 1549 by the Florentine press Ap. L. Torrentino. See also Simonetta La Barbera Bellia, *Il paragone delle arti: nella teoria artistica del Cinquecento* (Rome: Cafaro, 1997; digitized by Ann Arbor: The University of Michigan Press, 2009), passim.

17. See Mendelsohn, *Paragoni*, 9 and 113.

18. Pontormo as well is considering the collaborative aspects of the paragone between drawing and sculpture as an important artistic tool. For example, in the drawing of *Venus and Cupid*, he reveals an appropriation from sculpture, Michelangelo's *David* of 1504, Accademia Gallery, Florence.

19. See Michael J. Allen, *The Platonism of Marsilio Ficino* (Los Angeles: University of California Press, 1984), 41–67, for a reference to the four types of *divinus furor* in Ficino's writings, in particular, in his *Commentary on Plato's Symposium* (7:14): "The four divine furors are first poetical, then mythical, third prophetic and amorous fourth" ("Quatuor ergo divini furoris sunt speties. Primus quidem poeticus furor, alter mysterialis, tertius vaticinium, amatorious affectus est quartus"). See also Paul Oskar Kristeller, ed., *The Letters of Marsilio Ficino*, 3 vols. (New York: Ginko Press, 1985), 1:14–20; and Marsilio Ficino's letter to Perregrino Agli on *De divino furore*.

20. See Jayne Sears, "Ficino and the Platonism of the English Renaissance," *Comparative Literature* 4 (Summer 1952), 214–38; Michael J.B. Allen, *Marsilio Ficino and the Phaedran Charioteer* (Los Angeles: University of California Press, 1984), 339–439; and Allen, *The Platonism of Marsilio Ficino*, 41–67.

21. André Chastel, *Marsile Ficin et L'Art* (Geneva: Droz, 1975), 129–33, chapter on "Furor divinus: L'inspiration."

22. See *The Letters of Marsilio Ficino*, Preface by Paul Oskar Kristeller, trans. and ed. from Latin by members of the Language Department of the School of Economic Science in London (no names), 3 vols. (New York: Gingko Press, 1985), vol. 1, Letter 7, Marsilio Ficino to Peregrino Agli, *On Divine Frenzy*, 14–20 (no date, probably between 1457 and 1476); Marsilio Ficino, *Meditations on the Soul: Selected Letters of Marsilio Ficino*, ed. and trans. Clement Salaman (Rochester, VT: Inner Traditions International, 1996), 64–70, on divine frenzy; Thomas Moore, *The Planets Within* (Hudson, NY: Lindisfarne Press, 1990), 41 and 86–87; and D.P. Walker, *Spiritual and Demonic Magic: From Ficino to Campanella* (University Park: Pennsylvania State University Press, 2000), 3–11.

23. See the comparative study of Rosana Bettarini and Paola Barocchi on the 1550 and 1568 editions of Giorgio Vasari, *Le vite de' più eccellenti architetti, pittori, et scultori* (Florence: Sansoni, 1971–86), 6 vols. (hereafter referred as Bettarini-Barocchi). For this passage, see Bettarini-Barocchi, 3:62. "Attesoché l'ingegno vuol essere affaticato quando l'intelleto ha voglia di operare, e che il furore è acceso, perché allora si vede uscirne parti eccellenti e divini, e concetti meravigliosi."

24. Michael J.B. Allen, *Marsilio Ficino and the Phaedran Charioteer* (Los Angeles: University of California Press, 1981), 339–439; and Chastel, *Marsile Ficin et L'Art*, 81–89.

25 See Allen, *Marsilio Ficino and the Phaedran Charioteer*, 339–439; and Chastel, *Marsile Ficin et L'Art*, 81–89.

26. See *Horace: Epistles Book II and Arts Poetica*, trans. H. Rushton Fairclough (Cambridge, MA: Harvard University Press [Loeb Classical Library, No. 194], 1929 revised), *Ars Poetica*, lines 10–11: "Pictoribus atque poetis quidlibet audendi semper fuit aequa potestas" ("But painters and poets have always shared the right to dare anything"), and lines 38–39: "Sumite materiam uestris qui scribitis, aequam uiribus et uerstate diu quid ferre recusent" ("You who write choose a subject that's matched by your powers").

27. The phrase originates from Horace's *Arts poetica* (line 361), first century BCE. For further study, see *Horace on Poetry: The Ars Poetica*, ed. C.O. Brink (Cambridge: Cambridge University Press, 1971), passim. But in the Renaissance, Cristoforo Landino (1424–98) popularized Horace's phrase in his edition of *Horatius cum quattuor commentariis* (Venice, 1498), citing Horace's passage: *ut pictura poesis erit.i. non erit dissimilis/poetica ars picturae*. See Jean H. Hagstrum, *Sister Arts: The Tradition of Literary Pictorialism and the English Poetry from Dryden to Gray* (Chicago, IL: University of Chicago Press, 1958), 59. See also K. Borinski, *Die Antike in Poetik und*

Kunsttheorie von Ausgang des klassichen Altertums bis auf Goethe und Wilhelm von Humboldt, 2 vols. (Leipzig: K.F. Koehler, 1914–24), 1:30, 97, 175, 183, and 238; 2:106, in particular, 125–27, on the history of the dispute about *ut pictura poesis*; Mario Praz, *Mnemosyne: The Parallel Between Literature and the Visual Arts* (Princeton, NJ: Princeton University Press, 1967), 2–28; Mendelsohn, *Paragoni: Benedetto Varchi Due Lezzioni*, 109–42, where Varchi notes in the third disputation: "Onde, se bene i poeti et i pittori imitano, non imitano però, ne le medesime cose, nei medesimi modi. Imitando quelli colle parole, e questi co' colori; il perché pare che sia tanta differenza fra la poesia e la pittura, quanta è fra l'anima e'l corpo. Bene è vero che, come i poeti discrivono ancora il di fuori, così i pittori mostrano quanto più possono il di dentro, cioè gli affetti" (Thus, if poets and painters imitate, they do not imitate the same things [or] in the same manner. [Poets] imitate with words, and [painters] with colors; so there seems to be such a great difference between poetry and painting, like between the soul and the body. Of course, it is true that poets describe the exterior [of a person] while painters show as much as they can the interior [of a person], that is emotions). See John R. Spencer, "*Ut Rhetorica Pictura*: A Study in Quattrocento Theory of Painting," *Journal of the Warburg and Courtauld Institutes* 20 (1957), 26–44; Anthony Blunt, *Artistic Theory in Italy* (Oxford: Oxford University Press, 1968), 52; Rensselaer Lee, *Ut Pictura Poesis: Humanist Theory of Painting* (New York: W.W. Norton and Company, Inc., 1967), 1n2; *Ludovico Dolce's Dialogo della Pittura* (1557), trans. M. Roskill (New York: New York University Press, 1968), 97 and 239; and Gian Paolo Lomazzo's *Trattato dell' arte della pittura, scultura et architettura* (1584), which summarizes Leonardo's and Dolce's conceptions of the relationships between poetry and painting. See also Giovanni Battista Armenini, *De' veri precetti della pittura* (Ravenna, 1587), ed. Marina Gorreri (Turin: Einaudi, 1988), 23, who comments on this fashion: "Per cio si chiama la pittura, Poetica che tace, et la Poetica, Pittura che parla, et questa l'anima dover esser, et quella il corpo, dissimile pero quin questo si tengono, perche, l'una imita con i colori, l'altra con le parole. Ma certamente che qui quanto all'inventione predetta et quin quanto alla Verita sono d'una stessa proprietà et d'uno effetto medesimo" (For this reason painting is called muted Poetry, and Poetry Painting that speaks, and one is the soul, and the other the body, different, but they relate to each other because one imitates with colors and the other with words. Of course, there is invention that rules and in there is truth [that governs], but both have the same property and the same effect). Torquato Tasso refers as well to the poet as a *pittore parlante* (speaking painter) in *Discorsi dell'arte poetica e del poema eroico* (1587, new Italian edition eds. Giovanni Gheradini and Angelo Fabroni [Charleston, SC: Nabu Press, 2012]).

28. See Vasari-Milanesi, 5:260; and Liana De Girolami Cheney, *The Homes of Giorgio Vasari* (London and New York: Peter Lang, 2006), 94 and 97.

29. See Marsilio Ficino, *Symposium*, I. 3, in *Opera* (Basel, 1561). For an understanding of Mannerist art theory, see: Chastel, *Marsile Ficin et L'Art*, 81–90, on "Le Beau: L'Universelle Volupte et la Lumiere"; Laura Vestra, "Love and Beauty in Ficino and Plotinus," in Konrad Eisenbichler and Olga Zorzi Pugliese, eds., *Ficino and Renaissance Neoplatonism* (Toronto: Dovehouse Editions, 1986), 79–85; D. Summers, *The Judgment of Sense* (New York: Cambridge University Press, 1987), passim; and for a study on the impact of Marsilio Ficino's Neoplatonism and Renaissance art, see Liana De Girolami Cheney, *Botticelli's Neoplatonic Images* (Potomac, MD: Scripta Humanistica, 1993), passim.

30. See Moshe Barasch, *Theories of Art* (New York: New York University Press, 1986), 190–99, for a discussion of Michelangelo's concept of beauty in relation to Neoplatonism.

31. See Vasari-Milanesi, 4:5–7.

32. See Berti, *Pontormo*, 204, on Pontormo and Lucas van Leyden; Tzartes, *Il "ghiribizzoso" Pontormo*, 87–93; Elizabeth Pilliod, *Pontormo, Bronzino, Allori: A Genealogy of Florentine Art* (New Haven, CT, and London: Yale University Press, 2001), 65, on Pontormo and Hans Baldgun Grien; and David Landau and Peter Parshall, *The Renaissance Print, 1470–1550* (New Haven, CT, and London: Yale University Press, 1994), passim. Also, Bronzino is inspired by Albrecht Dürer's prints and his followers, e.g., Bronzino's relief composition of Mars and Venus in the sacrificial altar resembles Dürer's *Adam and Eve* of 1504 as well as Jacopo de Barbi's *Mars and Venus* of 1509.

33. See Marco Collareta, "Painting and its Sisters: Bronzino and the Art System," in Carlo Falciani and Antonio Natali, eds., *Bronzino: Artist and Poet at the Court of the Medici* (Florence: Mandragora, 2010), 195–201.

34. With the depiction of this imagery, Pontormo is referring to Antonio Pollaiuolo's painting of *Hercules and Antaeus* of 1478 at the Galleria degli Uffizi, and his sculpture of 1475 at the Museo Nazionale del Bargello in Florence. Here too, Pontormo alludes to a *paragone* between painting and sculpture.

35. Quoted in Alexander Roob, *The Hermetic Museum: Alchemy and Mysticism* (Cologne: Taschen, 1997), 363.

36. See Solange de Mailly Nesle, *Astrology: History, Symbols and Signs* (Rochester, VT: Inner Traditions International, 1981), 130–31.

37. See Nesle, *Astrology: History, Symbols and Signs*, 134–35; and Cristoforo de Predis' *The Planet Venus* in *De Sphaera* of 1470, a Latin manuscript, Folio 209, verso 9, in the Biblioteca Estense, Modena, and *The Planet Mars*, Folio. This illuminated manuscript on parchment is regarded as the most

beautiful astrological book of the Italian Renaissance, produced in the Milanese court of the Sforza by Leonardo Dati.

38. See Mary Beard, ed., *Religions of Rome: A History* (Cambridge: Cambridge University Press, 1998), 47–48.

39. See Berti, *Pontormo*, 167, for a discussion of the siege.

40. See Jean Chevalier and Alain Gheerbrant, *A Dictionary of Symbols* (London: Blackwell, 1994), 131.

41. See Thomas Moore, *The Planets Within: The Astrological Psychology of Marsilio Ficino* (New York: Lindisfarne Press, 1990), 142–46, on Venus' humors, and 185–88, on Mar's humors; see also Zirka S. Filipczak, *Hot Dry Men and Cold Wet Women: The Theory of Humors in Western European Art: 1575–1700* (New York: The American Federation of Arts, 1997), 8–9.

42. See J.C. Cooper, *Symbolic and Mythological Animals* (London: The Aquarian Press, 1992), 43.

43. See Beard, ed., *Religions of Rome*, 153. For example, for a Roman altar with a relief of a sacrificial bull, see http://www.crystalinks.com/RomeReligionSacrifice.jpg.

44. The most important of these are Francesco Colonna's *Hypnertomachia Poliphili* (Venice, 1499); Horapollo's *Hieroglyphica* (Venice, 1505); Andrea Alciato's *Emblemata* (Basel, 1529) and the Lyon editions of 1531, 1546, 1546 and 1549 and Venice 1551; Lelio Gregorio Giraldi's *De Deis Gentium* (Paris, 1548); Natale Conti's *Mythologiae* (Paris, 1551/58); Pierio Valeriano's *Hieroglyphica* (Venice, 1556); Paolo Giovio's *Dialogo dell'Imprese Militari et Amorose* (Venice, 1556); and Vincenzo Cartari's *Imagini delli Dei de gl' Antichi* (Venice, 1556–57). See also Mario Praz, *Studies in Seventeenth Century Imagery*, 3 vols. (London and Rome: Phaidon, 1941, 1947 and 1964), Introduction; and Jean Seznec, *The Survival of the Pagan Gods* (New York: Harper and Row Publishers, 1961), 279–327.

45. See Claudia Cieri Via, *Le Favole Antique: Produzione e Committenza a Roma nel Cinquecento* (Rome: Bagatto Libri, 1996), 25–30; Praz, *Studies in Seventeenth Century Imagery*, 2:5, 36 and 139; George Boas' translation of *The Hieroglyphics of Horapollo*, Bollingen Series, 23 (New York: Pantheon, 1950, based on the 1505 version published by Aldus Manutius in Venice); and Daniel Russell, "Alciati's Emblems in Renaissance France," *Renaissance Quarterly* 34 (1981), 549. Russell defines the importance of Alciato's book in Cinquecento art and literature: "[It] served as a manual to train readers in a particular approach to artistic artifacts. It taught them to participate actively in the moralizing of visual art, and it showed them how to fragment texts—mainly poetic or dramatic texts; it would appear—into short passages that they could summarize into titular paroemia."

46. Valeriano's tome is influenced by Horapollo's *Hieroglyphica* (Venice: Aldus Manutius, 1505).

47. See Paolo Giovio, *Dialogo dell'Imprese Militari et Amorose* (1555), eds. L. Domenichi and G. Simeoini (Lyon: Guglielmo Rovillio, 1574). See also T.C. Zimmerman, *Paolo Giovio: The Historian and the Crisis of Sixteen-Century Italy* (Princeton, NJ: Princeton University Press, 1995).

48. See Giovio, *Dialogo dell'imprese*, lines 0064–0085:

Alle nominate due imprese non cedeuano punto
ne di bellezza, ne di proprietà di significato, quelle
de' due fratelli cugini Colonnesi, Prospero e Fabritio, i
quali in diuersi tempi portarono diuerse inuentioni
seco[n]do le fantasie loro, parte militari, e parte amorose.
Perche ciascun di loro, infino all'estrema vecchiezza
non si vergognò mai d'essere innamorato, massima—
mente Prospero; il quale hauendo posto il pensiero in
vna nobilissima do[n]na, della quale per coprire il fauore
ch'egli n'haueua, e mostrar l'honestà, s'assicurò di me—
nar seco per compagno vn famigliar suo caualier di
bassa lega, il che fu molto incautamente fatto; percioche
la donna sua (come generalmente quasi tutte le donne
sono) vaga di cose nuoue, s'innamorò del compagno
talmente, che lo fece degno dell'amor suo; di che au—
uedutosi Prospero, e sentendone dispiacere infinito, si
mise per impresa il Toro di Perillo; che fu il primo
à prouare quella gran pena del fuoco, acceso sotto 'l
ventre del Toro, nel quale egli fu posto dentro, per
capriccio del Tiranno Falari, onde usciua lamento di
voce humana; e miserabil mugito. E ciò fece Prospero
per inferire, ch'egli medesimo era stato cagione del
mal suo: e 'l motto era tale.

Another interesting emblem is illustrated in Joachim Camerarius, *Symbolorum and Emblematum* (1534–98), ed. Ludwig Camerarius, et al., 3 vols. (Leipzig: Voegelinianis, 1604), vol. 1, Emblem 24 with the Virgilian motto, *In utrumque paratus* ("Prepared for either alternative" or "Prepared for both alternatives" or "Ready for both"). The *pictura* (image) illustrates a bull working in the field and looking at a classical altar with a burning fire at top. The motto and image allude at possible alternatives that confronts the bull: to work in the fields or be sacrificed or both. In Pinturicchio's *Procession of Apis*, the sacrificial altar is included in the scene but placed behind the bull.

49. See Brian Curran, *The Egyptian Renaissance: The Afterlife of Ancient Egypt in Early Modern Italy* (Chicago, IL: University of Chicago Press, 2007), 107–20.

Fig. 1. Agnolo Bronzino, *Pygmalion and Galatea*, 1530. Galleria degli Uffizi, Florence. Photo credit: Scala/Ministero per i Beni e le Attività culturali/Art Resource, NY.

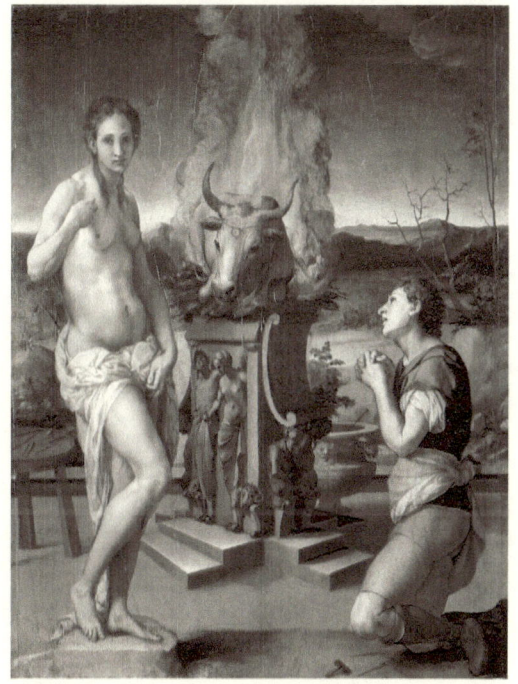

Fig. 2. Jacopo Pontormo, *Portrait of Francesco Guardi* (*Halberdier*), 1529. J.P. Getty Museum, Los Angeles, California. Photo credit: Alinari/Art Resource, NY.

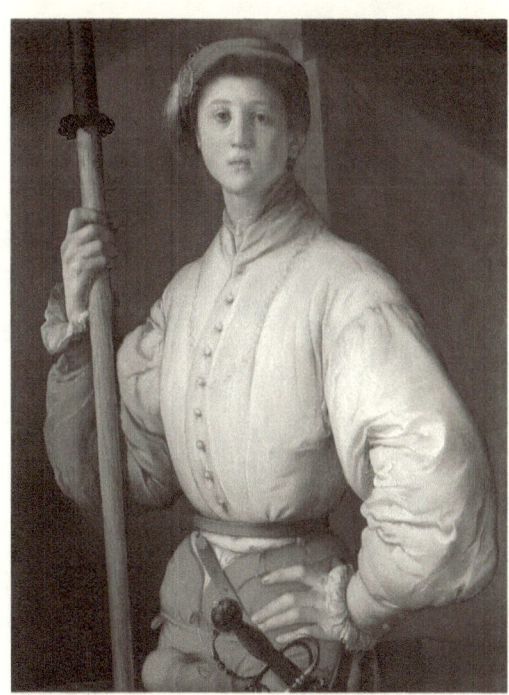

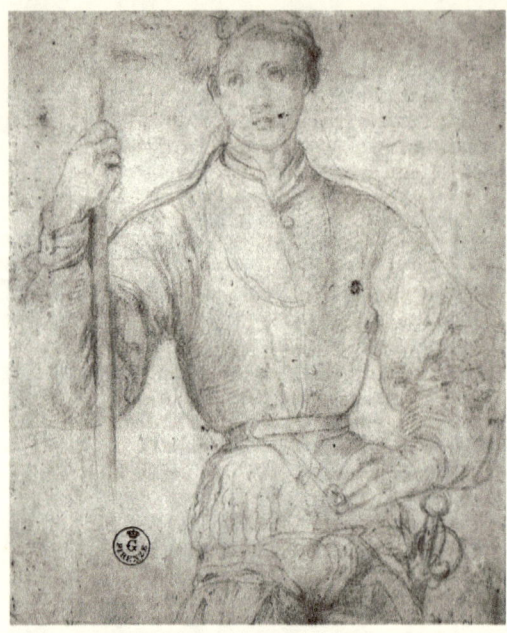

Fig. 3. Jacopo Pontormo, *Portrait of Francesco Guardi* (*Halberdier*), c. 1529, drawing. Gabinetto Disegni e Stampe degli Uffizi, Florence (Inv. No. 6701F.r.). Photo credit: Gabinetto Disegni e Stampe degli Uffizi, Florence.

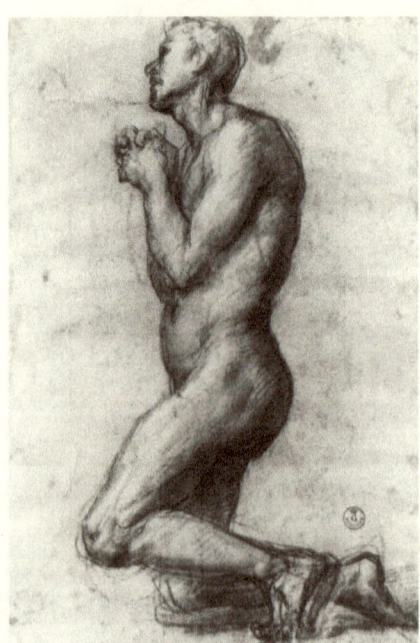

Fig. 4. Jacopo Pontormo, *Study of a Kneeling Nude in Profile with Supplicant Hands*, 1529, drawing. Gabinetto Disegni e Stampe degli Uffizi, Florence (Inv. No. 6744). Photo credit: Gabinetto Disegni e Stampe degli Uffizi, Florence.

Fig. 5. Jacopo Pontormo, *Venus and Cupid*, 1515, drawing. Gabinetto Disegni e Stampe degli Uffizi, Florence (Inv. No. 6744). Photo credit: Gabinetto Disegni e Stampe degli Uffizi, Florence.

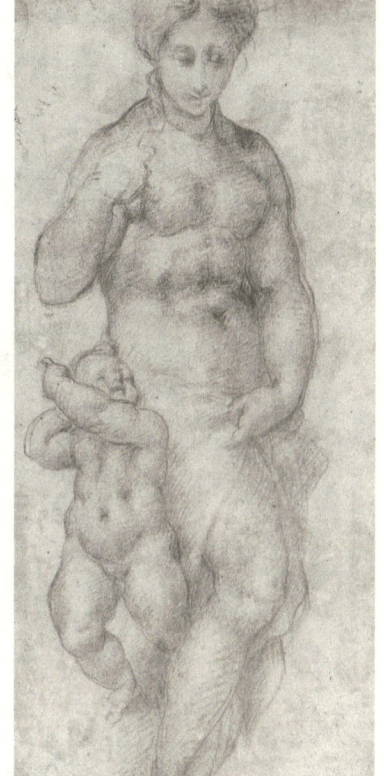

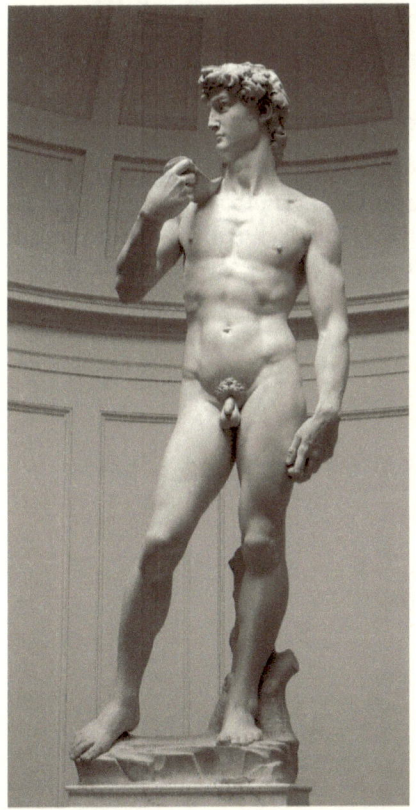

Fig. 6. Michelangelo, *David*, 1501–04 (flipped image). Accademia Gallery, Florence. Photo credit: Scala/Art Resource, NY.

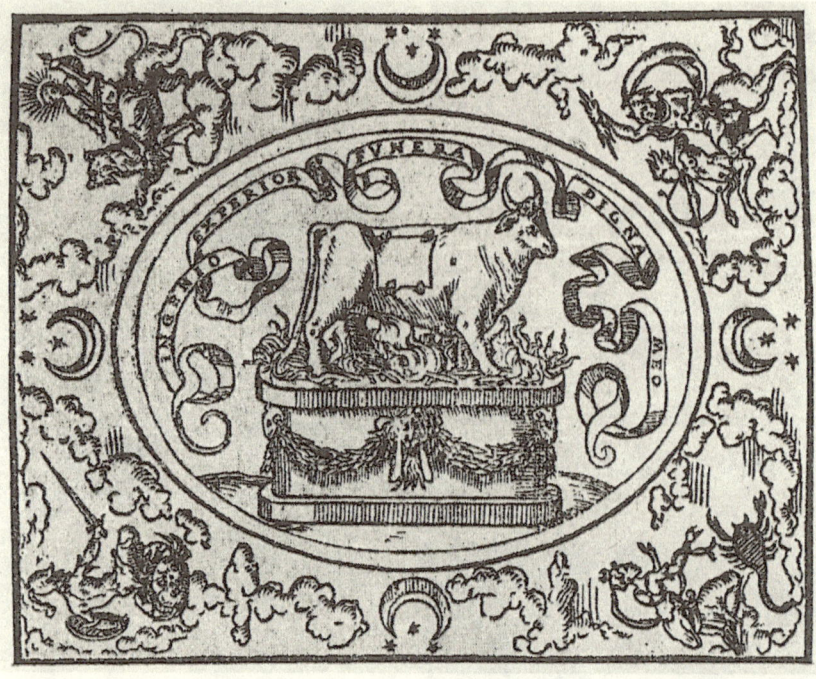

Fig. 7. Paolo Giovio, *Impresa for the Colonnesi Brothers*, in *Dialogo delle Imprese*, c. 1555–59, reprinted in Jacopo Gelli, *Divisi, Motti e Imprese Di Famiglie e Personaggi Italiani* (Milan: Ulrico Hoepli, 1976), 272. Photo credit: Jacopo Gelli, *Divisi, Motti e Imprese Di Famiglie e Personaggi Italiani* (Milan Ulrico Hoepli, 1976), 272.

Bronzino's *Triumph of Felicity*: A Wheel of Good Fortune[1]

Liana De Girolami Cheney

Ma perché, Polimnia, mi frughi? E taci,
Erato, perché, dimmi? Io mi vi scuso,
Non so dire e tacere, e poi le paci
Cercare, e non le discordie, so uso.
Bronzino, *Delle scuse*[2]

In the 1568 edition of the *Vite*, in the section *On the Accademici del Disegno*, Giorgio Vasari (1511–74) praises his fellow artist Agnolo di Cosimo di Mariano (1503–72), known as Bronzino.[3]

> Agnolo Bronzino is a Florentine painter, truly most rare and worthy of all praise. He has been and still is the most gentle and very courteous friend, agreeable in his conversation and in all his affairs, and much honored; and as loving and liberal with this possessions as a noble craftsman, such as he is could well be. He has been peaceful by nature, and has never done any injury to any man and he has always loved all able men in this profession.

Vasari continues: "For Francesco de' Medici, Bronzino painted in a few months, after the nuptial with Queen Joanna of Austria, a small picture with little figures, which has no equal, and it may be said that it is truly a miniature."[4] This painting is Bronzino's *Triumph of Felicity* or *Allegory of Felicity* (also referred to as the *Allegory of Happiness* and the *Allegory of Public Felicity*). The painting, signed as *Bronz.Fac*, is composed in oil-on-copper, measuring 40 x 30 cm, and is presently on view at the Galleria degli Uffizi (Fig. 1).

In *Il principe dello studiolo*, Luciano Berti establishes 1567 as the date for completion of the painting.[5] Other scholars—Arthur McComb,[6] Charles McCorquodale,[7] Edi Baccheschi,[8] Janet Cox-Rearick,[9] recently Claudio Strinati,[10] and, in particular, Maurice Brock[11]—discuss the stylistic merit of the painting, while Robert Gaston[12] and, in particular, Graham Smith[13] decode the symbolism of the painting. Continuing on with their iconographical interpretation, this essay illuminates the Mannerist emblematic tradition of Good Fortune. With Time, the vigilance of Justice and Prudence protects Felicity against the arbitrary forces of Chance (*Occasio*), Ignorance, Deceit (Anger), Folly (Adulation), and Fraud (Envy).

Summarizing the iconographic interpretation of Smith, the conceit for Bronzino's *Triumph of Felicity* derives as well from a passage on the *Triumph of Felicity* in Cosimo Bartoli's *Trionfo della felicità* in the third book of *Ragionamenti accademici ... sopra alculi loughi difficili di Dante. Con alcune inventioni e significanti* (Venice, 1567). The passage reads: "The four cardinal virtues are seated with *Felicitas* ... with their counterpart."[14] Another significant literary source for Bronzino's imagery is Paolo Giovio's books on imprese, *Sentiose Imprese* of 1562 and *Dialogo dell' imprese militari et amorose* of 1555, where the virtues of Prudence and Virtue are associated with good government.[15]

In brief, Smith's identification of Bronzino's figures in the *Triumph of Felicity*, which he calls the *Allegory of Happiness*, is as follows.[16] In the center of the composition is frontally enthroned Felicity or *Felicitas publica*, who holds a cornucopia and a caduceus.[17] Above her, two winged figures honor her: Fame by blowing a trumpet, and Virtue by crowning her. Framing Felicity are the standing cardinal virtues: Prudence with a Janus head and holding a terrestrial globe, while naked Justice holds a sword and places the scales on a cubical platform. Behind Prudence, a figure running away is identified as Blind Envy or Envy, while behind Justice a falling-down figure is identified as Injustice or Fury. The identification of the foreground figures is less clear.

In front of Justice kneels Fortune or *Occasio* (Chance) with her forelocked hairdo and resting her hands on a wheel. In front of Prudence kneels an old man holding a celestial globe, perhaps Time or Kronos. At the feet of Felicity, three disturbing figures reflect aspects of adversity as Folly, Envy, and Deceit. Folly is identified as the gnome and wears a jester's cap and an anklet of bells, and holds a short club. Across from Folly is Deceit holding an iron grapple and observing a fragmented snake. The foreshortened figure in the foreground between Time and Fortune holds a curved razor. This nude figure is identified as the god Kairos, the Greek equivalent of *Occasio*. Another figure whose *clavis interpretandi* is unclearly decoded is Cupid. The standing figure of Cupid points an arrow toward Felicity's breast. For Smith, Bronzino's inclusion of Cupid reveals the association of Felicity with Venus, the Goddess of Love.[18]

Focusing on the personification of Prudence with the Janus head, Smith views the portrait of the past as a portrait of Duke Cosimo I de' Medici. Thus, for Smith, Bronzino's painting has civic connotations: it is a political allegory of Duke Cosimo I's accomplished welfare, "Felicitas publica florentiae or Felicitas publica florentina,"[19] since Prudence and Fate are the principal ingredients for a ruler's continuous and successful reign.[20] However, if the focus is on the figure of Cupid, another level of meaning is implied. The connection between Cupid and Venus reveals the theme of *Venus felix* and *Fecuditas* as depicted in Roman medals with these themes. Furthermore, in connecting these symbols of love and fecundity with the commission of the painting (it was commissioned for the marriage of Francesco de' Medici with Joanna of Austria), then, Smith concludes, the painting has sensual and erotic connotations. In sum, for Smith, the painting symbolizes Medicean personal and public happiness because of the marital and political bond between Francesco and Joanna.

The Cinquecento manner of composing images for a program, as a compendium of visual iconography, derives from and parallels the literary practices and conceptions of humanists[21] such as Annibale Caro (1507–66)[22] and Paolo Giovio (1483–1552)[23] and emblematists such as Andrea Alciato (1492–1550), Vincenzo Cartari (1531–69), and Pierio Valeriano (1477–1558).[24] The emblematic and mythological manuals then available were Andrea Alciato's *Emblemata* (Lyon, 1531, 1541, and Venice 1546), Pierio Valeriano's *Hieroglyphica* (Basel, 1521–56), Boccaccio's *Geneologia de gli Dei* (1360, printed in Venice 1547), Francesco Colonna's *Hypnerotomachia Poliphili* (Venice, 1499), Natale Conti's *Mythologiae* (Venice, 1557), Giglio Gregorio Giraldi's *De deis gentium* (Basel, 1548), and Vincenzo Cartari's *Imagini delli Dei de gl' Antichi* (Venice, 1556). These were compilations of medieval mythographies, hieroglyphs, and numismatic sources. These manuals served as commonplace books for Cinquecento humanists and artists—a kind of figurative encyclopedia or "dictionary-album" for easy consultation when time was lacking to read the primary texts in their entirety. Since these manuals had become well known to Cinquecento artists and literati, humanists borrowed or copied information directly from them without feeling any need to credit their sources. Throughout the Renaissance, secular paintings were habitually painted according to the instructions of such humanists who assembled, assimilated, and adapted subjects from classical mythology into complex and allusive schemes.

Viewing a similarity between painting and poetry, Roman humanist Annibale Caro[25] considered the writings of emblematists such as Alciato's *Emblemata* (Venice, 1546) and Cartari's *Imagini delli Dei de gl' Antichi* (Venice, 1556) to be outstanding iconographical manuals for artists and humanists and so praises them for their significance.[26] In the prefaces of the *Vite*, Vasari likewise emphasized that an allegory or personification must assimilate, visually and verbally, its ancient sources,[27] e.g., "L'invenzione fa metter insieme in istoria le figure" ("Invention joins together history and imagery or invention joins imagery in history").[28] Such emblematic sources provided Bronzino, Vasari, and Mannerist painters with an extensive repertoire of images that they collected and employed in the iconography of their commissions.[29]

Under the influence of the humanists and emblematists, Bronzino, a poet as well,[30] also assimilates the connection between the pictorial and symbolic world, manifesting in his painting that "the universe is a forest of symbols, a projection of things that are visible in the natural realm [which] are the mirror of those things which are invisible since they are in the heavenly realm, and all the world's objects have a signification."[31] Incorporated in the Cinquecento's visual theory is a Neoplatonic view concerning the meaning of an idea or conceit (*concetto*), expounded by Marsilio Ficino (1433–99) in *De vita coelitus comparanda* (Florence, 1484) and *Teologia Platonica* (Florence, 1469–74).[32] In these texts, Ficino discussed the use and the magic potency of images by deliberating on the virtue of imagery, what power pertains to the figure in the sky and on earth, which of the heavenly configurations are impressed on images by the ancients, and how the images are employed in antiquity.[33] Correspondingly, the symbol, emblem, or image embodies the humanistic and Neoplatonic traditions, along with the emblematic, in its effort to unveil a *clavis interpretandi* in a mysterious story filled with hieroglyphs and enigmatic actions with a secret purpose. Thus, the symbol or image requires a decoding of the riddles at many levels in order to achieve an understanding of the meaning of the story. For the viewer, then, the imagery reveals magical sensations.

Bronzino's painting reveals two significant concerns in Mannerist art: love for the creation of beauty, and fascination for symbolic ambiguity—thus, the creation of a cunning undecipherable *concetto*. Bronzino's *Triumph of Felicity* embodies these Mannerist conceits.

In the *Due Lezzioni* of 1547, the humanist, Benedetto Varchi (1503–65) defines the intention of artistic creations by Mannerist artists as "an artificial imitation of nature."[34] Mannerist painters strove to create an image of beauty by surpassing nature, arousing a spiritual emotion, thus creating an aesthetic ideal. Also Vasari, like Varchi, makes beauty one of the critical components of art in the Third Preface of the *Vite*.[35] Varchi's approach to the concept of beauty reveals aspects of Renaissance Neoplatonism. With the Neoplatonic doctrine in mind, "beauty consists of a certain charm" as something spiritual that transcends sensual experience and that makes us long for the origin of what we perceive.[36] The Mannerist painters emphasized the ideal beauty in the mind of the artist rather than the reproduction of beauty discovered in nature. The Mannerist moral quest for aesthetic gives great importance to *invenzione* (invention). Bronzino invents with his mind and transforms his creations with brushes in an *istoria* as the *Triumph of Felicity*.

Furthermore, the impact of classical mythology and emblematic mythography provides a visual reference to classical antiquity at two levels. One level focuses on the visual appropriation or *all'antica* assimilation of forms. For example, by using elongated figures, *figura serpentinata*, sinuous rhythms, and unreal color schemes, forms evolve from reality but are transformed into fantasy. The translation into an unreal space with no perspectival structure enhances the ambiguity of that reality. And the second level, by composing imagery with many strata of symbolism, is at times overt and other times covert. Bronzino's *Triumph of Felicity* clearly embodies the Mannerist aesthetic ideals expounded by Benedetto Varchi in the *Due Lezzioni* or *Paragone* of 1547.[37]

In considering the Cinquecento's emblematic, mythographic, philosophical, and visual sources, other interpretations are here suggested.[38] In the *Triumph of Felicity*, Bronzino teases the viewer with positive and negative iconographical imagery. Virtues are counterpointed with vices. These virtues and vices are embellished with attributes, which are not always clearly recognizable. The intellectual and visual tension is part of the Maniera conceit as well as Bronzino's astute jocular interplay between the visual imagery and its meaning. This intellectual playfulness is also found in his poetry.[39]

In the center of Bronzino's composition, winged Honor crowns Felicity with laurel, while winged Fame announces the event by blowing on two trumpets. Alciato's well-known emblem on Honor or Fame relates to the Mannerist composition (Fig. 2).[40] Enthroned as a prophetess, Felicity (*Felicità humana or Felicità publica; Bonus Eventus*) gazes at Honor while holding a cornucopia and raising a Mercurial caduceus.[41] The image was earlier depicted in Vasari's *Felicità publica* in the Chamber of Fortune in his house at Arezzo in 1548 (compare Figs. 1 and 3).[42] Vasari's personification of Felicity is seated on a wheel, holding a caduceus and a cornucopia. Both attributes symbolize the elements needed for happiness: the caduceus is a symbol of peace and industry, and the cornucopia contains the products of hard work. Laurel leaves decorate her tresses, alluding to her peaceful and triumphant state. Probably, the sources for both Maniera painters were the imagery of Giraldi's *Felicità*[44] and Cartari's *Felicity* (*Felicità humana* or *Bonus Eventus*; compare Figs. 1, 3, and 4)[43] and the descriptions of Valeriano's *Felicità*. Valeriano commented: "when [in an image] with a caduceus, a cornucopia is added felicity is implied ("ma se al Caduceo s'aggiunge il Cornucopia è segno di felicità")[45] For the emblematists as well as for Vasari and Bronzino, Felicity was a personification of happiness, since she "symbolized a fortunate event and the happy issue of an enterprise."[46]

A suggestive speculation is to imagine Bronzino visiting Vasari's house at Arezzo where he admired the iconographical programs in the Chamber of Fame, with the depiction of trumpeting Fame in the ceiling, and in the Chamber of Fortune, with the personifications of Fortune, Virtue, and Envy in the *palco* and Justice, Felicity, and Prudence on the walls. We can imagine the artists engaging in a dialogue about artistic imagery, art theory, and sources for their inventions. Unfortunately, at this time, there are no records that indicate such a visit. However, visually one observes likenesses, which derive from looking at similar artistic sources. Furthermore, as indicated in his *Vite,* Vasari greatly admired his fellow artist. By coincidence, Bronzino's mirror with the personification of Prudence is presently displayed in the Aretine house.[47] This mirror-picture is encased in an elaborate carved wooden frame. Ser Carlo Gherardi of Pistoia (1502–80), friend and patron of Bronzino, commissioned the mirror in 1567. Vasari notes that in 1546, Gherardi moved from Pistoia to Florence to continue his notary practice. On the recommendation of Vasari, Gherardi was appointed by Duke Cosimo I de' Medici as Cancelliere dell'Opera del Duomo in 1560.

In Bronzino's painting, Felicity is framed by two personifications of the cardinal virtues of Prudence and Justice. Standing on her right, clothed Prudence with a Janus head holds a terrestrial globe, while nude Justice rests on her sword and places the scales on a cubical platform. Smith identifies the portrait of the male counterpart of Prudence's Janus head as a portrait of Cosimo I de' Medici.[48] With this reference in mind, one also notices that the female portrayal of the Janus head resembles Eleonora de Toledo's Cosimo I's wife—the parents of Francis I de' Medici, patron of the painting.

In the Chamber of Fortune, Vasari too depicts the personification of Prudence with a Janus head; while seated, she holds the key of the Janus Temple.[49] Although no snake is visible (one of the attributes of Prudence that is missing), she carries a cornucopia, which coils around her shoulder like a snake. At Prudence's feet, a globe is barely visible. Bronzino's Prudence embraces a terrestrial globe; one of her arms is decorated with a coiled snake. For both painters, Prudence with her Janus head has a dual signification as *Prudenza* and *Providenza,* to foresee and to provide ("prevedere e provedere") for the future, having experienced the past. A familiar emblematic reference is Alciato's Janus head in Emblem 16 on *Prudentes. Problema* (The Wise—A Problem, Fig. 5).[50] With this emphasis, Bronzino's Prudence alludes to the wise actions and civic vision in creating a favorable terrestrial atmosphere for the Medici family and Florence by Duke Cosimo I de' Medici and Eleonora of Toledo.[51]

In Bronzino's painting, behind Prudence, a figure running away is identified as Blind Envy or Envy,[52] but the figure lacks the traditional attributes of the personification of Envy, such as an old, ugly, and haggard woman, crowned with snakes and with sagging breasts. The blindfolded figure likely is a personification of Ignorance, based upon its germane attributes of a blindfold, donkey's ears, and rushing and running without direction.[53] The blindfold on the figure alludes to two types of sightlessness: the lack of physical perception and the lack of metaphysical perception. The deficiency of these faculties is encountered in the personification of Ignorance contrasting with Prudence's judgment and wisdom. Without a direction, Ignorance hastily trudges into a foliaged area. This action counterpoints with the steady stance of Prudence. The blindfolded figure, Ignorance, is nude, contrasting with the clothed figure of Prudence, whose open eyes gaze at Felicity. Ignorance raises her hand, coiled with her hair, in search of boundaries, while Prudence's hands firmly embrace the terrestrial globe. In her left hand, a serpent coils as a decorative bracelet. This attribute reveals the biblical motto in Matthew 10:16: "Estote ergo prudentes sicut serpents et simplices sicut columbae" ("Therefore be as prudent as snakes and as innocents as doves").

Virtuous Prudence resides between two vices: blindfolded Ignorance and Folly. Prudence steadily steps on the nude body of Folly. This personification is identified as a reclining nude, a gnome wearing a fool's cap with bells, like a court jester. An anklet of bells is visible on an exposed leg. He holds a rudimentary flute, which appears to be also a fool's staff. The flute is a symbol of Adulation or praised flattery.[54] Repugnant Folly, with a smirking expression, demonstrates poor judgment as he intensely gazes at the personification of Fortune, unwisely hoping for good luck or a good opportunity.

Accompanying Felicity, Bronzino portrays another cardinal virtue: the personification of Justice. This imagery draws a parallel with Cartari's text: "una vergine nuda a sedere sopra un sasso quadro, e teneva con l'una mano una bilancia, & con l'altra una spade nuda" ("a nude female figure seated on a square stone, holding a balance with one hand, and a sword with another").[55] Bronzino's unusual brilliant gaze depicted in Prudence's eyes might relate to Cartari's description of Justice: "con occhi accutissimi vista: onde Platone disse, che la Giustizia vede tutto, e che gli antichi sacerdoti fu chiamata vendicattrice di tutte le cose" ("eyes with a very keen sense of sight: as Plato noted that Justice sees everything, and the ancient priests called her avenger of all things").[56]

Like Prudence, Justice is also accompanied by two vices: Injustice and Deceit. Behind the beautiful sculptural figure of Justice, the personification of Injustice or Fury (Anger) is depicted as a screaming, falling-down figure that grabs a broken sword. Imitating the stepping gesture of Prudence, Justice also stands on the figure of Deceit. This nude, unkempt figure, while crouching, clutches an iron grapple. Malevolently, she stares at the personification of Fortune. An overt product of her wickedness is a snake in fragments portrayed next to her iron device. Deceit's disheveled hair and emaciated look advocates for this being the personification of Envy. The depiction of the segmented snake alludes to another negative attribute of Envy as well.

In the foreground of the painting, Folly and Deceit (Envy) anxiously wait for Fortune's wheel to turn. Between them, a foreshortened nude figure holds a broken, curved razor or curved sword. This reclining *serpentinata* figure is identified as the ancient god Kairos, the Greek deity equivalent to *Occasio* (Fig. 6). Mark R. Freier comments on Kairos' actions alluding to *carpe diem* and recurrence.[57] For Poseidippos, Kairos (in the Greek verse "I am ever running") is *aeì trochào*, which literally means "I always rotate,"[58] thus connecting Kairos' function of gyration to a Wheel of Fortune. Unfortunately, his actions allude to a negative aspect of Fortune, which is *Occasio* or Chance.[59]

At the feet of the virtuous Felicity, Bronzino depicts the three vices Folly, *Occasio*, and Deceit (Envy). Crowned and enthroned, Felicity triumphantly conquers the corrupted dispositions and actions of these vices. Assisting Felicity in her success are not only the impartment of Prudence's wisdom and Justice's veracity but also the positive interferences of Fortune and Time. These two later personifications are respectively depicted in front of Justice and Prudence and in front of Felicity.

Bronzino's exquisite headdress decorations of the personifications allude to several levels of physical and metaphysical signification. Winged Honor wears a headdress of precious jewels—pearls, rubies, and emeralds. Felicity is crowned with a variety of spring flowers, alluding to the season of rebirth, life rejuvenation, and fertility; as well, she wears clothing in spring colors such as pink and blue. Prudence is covered with a prophetic veil, referring to her earthly and celestial powers.[60] Justice's golden headband contains in its apex a triangular diamond.[61] This crystal refracts light, like her shining eyes, and implies her extraordinary powers for revealing truth. The color of the sash, which hides her nature and reveals the contour of her breasts, is green, a symbol for the season of spring as well the theological virtue of Hope.[62] In contrast to the above personifications, winged Fame (above Justice), Fortune (in front of Justice), and Time (in front of Prudence) are not crowned.

The personification of Fortune is depicted with her attributes as a symbol of good Fortune, with a forelocked hairdo and resting her hands on a wheel. In a state of tranquility, as she tilts her wheel not cranking her rotation, she gazes at Prudence. This peaceful stance is paralleled by the equanimity of Justice, whose scales are resting on a plinth, as no judgment is imparted. The personification of Time or Kronos is depicted as a nude old man, partially bald, holding a celestial globe.[63] He points to Felicity, showing in the band of the zodiac the signs of Aries and Taurus, announcing the season of spring. Prudence's terrestrial globe and Time's celestial globe are counterpoints of the natural and spiritual realms in life.

With the collaboration of Prudence, Justice, Good Fortune, and Time, Felicity triumphs over the adversities and vicissitudes of life portrayed in the personifications of Ignorance, Folly, Deceit (Anger), Envy, and *Occasio*. Thus is created a realm of beauty, love, and peace; a utopia for the new Medicean household and the marital and political union between Francesco and Joanna.[64]

In observing Bronzino's compositional construction of the

painting, several geometric configurations are implied, such as a square, a circle, and a diamond. The square format is composed by the inclusion of two realms: one is spiritual, composed by two cardinal virtues Prudence and Justice; and the second is natural, composed by Time and Fortune. These two realms frame or enclose what Cartari calls *Felicità humana*.[65] This three-dimensional square or cubical format is a traditional symbol of stability or firm foundation, as seen in the square platform where enthroned *Felicity* rules, thus communicating the harmonious creativity of nature.[66] In ancient times, Plato associated the cube with the element of earth or nature.[67] In the Cinquecento, this concept persisted: in Emblem 99 (Fig. 7), *Ars naturam adiuvans* ("Art Helps Nature"), for example, Alciato's *pictura* depicts Mercury with a helmet and a caduceus. He rests on a cube-shaped pedestal. In front of him, Fortuna precariously stands on a sphere holding a windblown sail. The emblem's epigram reads: "Art (Mercury) is made to counter the power of nature (Fortuna); but when Fortuna is bad, it often requires the help of art; therefore, eager youths learn the good arts, which have within themselves the advantages of an assured fate."[68]

Years later, Cartari would appropriate Alciatio's emblem, thus continuing the debate between the symbolism of the cube (terrestrial or finite)—in placing Mercury's attributes of caduceus, cornucopia, and winged helmet on a plinth—and the sphere (celestial or infinite)—in depicting Fortune standing on a globe (compare Figs. 7 and 8).[69]

Thus, Bronzino, with the cubical construction, creates an allusion to a terrestrial existence for good fortune to reign on earth thanks to the influence of Justice, Prudence, and, in particular, *Felicità humana* and *Felicità publica*. Thus, the association with Medicean symbolism could both be at a civic (political) and a personal (marital) level.

The second geometrical configuration is a circle. The circular format includes all the major figures, starting the rotation from the foreground with Fortune and across to Time and moving toward Prudence, *Felicity*, and Justice. With the circular motion, all the personifications exist in the same realm, the realm of the heaven or, in Renaissance Neoplatonic terms, the realm where the individual strives for divine perfection with the assistance of virtues or good elements. The circle is associated with the gyratory symbol of the wheel or the cyclical movement of life. Bronzino alludes to this element of rotating by depicting Fortuna with a wheel, one of her attributes, thereby also implying the positive and negative vicissitudes of life. The positive is indicated with the presence of the personifications of Time, Kronos, Prudence, and Felicity (Spring), whereas the negative is indicated with the personifications of *Occasio*, Chance, and Bad Fortune.

The Goddess Fortuna is traditionally depicted standing on a sphere or on a wheel.[70] In ancient times, the poet and astronomer Aratus, in *Phaenomena* (227, 309), commented on the eternal motion of the celestial spheres in the shape of a rotary wheel.[71] Anacreon (580–495 BCE) was negative when he noted that the inconstancy of Fortuna makes "human life rolls along, shifting like the spoke of a wagon,"[72] as depicted in the tenth card of the Major Arcana in the tarot deck. The same pessimistic allusion was projected during the Middle Ages, when, in *The Consolation of Philosophy*, Boethius commented on "how Fortuna is ever most friendly and alluring to those whom she strives to deceive, until she overwhelms them with grief beyond bearing, by deserting them when least expected."[73] In the *Burana Codex* of 773, Carmina Burana (before 1250) alludes to the turning of a wheel of fortune where figures are labeled "Regno, Regnavi, Sum sine regno, Regnabo" ("I reign, I reigned, My reign is finished, I shall reign").[74] In Burana, Fortuna's actions are connected with power and governance.[75] In the Cinquecento, allusions to the benevolent or malevolent actions of Fortuna contained political implications and were visualized and described in the emblematic texts of Alciato and Cartari and, in particular, in Niccolò Machiavelli's *Prince* of 1532. Machiavelli strongly alluded to the power of Fortuna in a governmental enterprise.[76]

Considering the whole composition, another interpretation on the meaning of the implied circularity is suggested, namely, the symbolism of the wheel. This symbol is associated with the personification of Fortuna (I use the term *Fortuna* as derived from *Vortumna*, a Roman Goddess, "she who revolves the year"). Traditionally, the allegory of Fortuna is associated with multiple meanings, most commonly with the symbolism of terrestrial and celestial time. When the association is celestial, Fortuna connects with the heavenly spheres and the cosmic movement of the universe—for example, Bronzino's depictions of Prudence holding a terrestrial globe and Time embracing a celestial globe. When the association is terrestrial, Fortuna connects with the earthly realm in two ways: publicly, as part of human civic endeavors; and privately, as part of individual feelings, in particular love, as interpreted in the emblematic imagery of Alciato and Cartari.

During 1544 and 1555, Bronzino completed several paintings with the theme of love and including as protagonists Venus and her son Cupid or Eros, e.g., *The Allegory of Love* (*Allegory of Lust* or *Venus and Cupid*) of 1544–45, at the National Gallery in London (Fig. 9),[77] *Venus, Cupid, Two Amorini and Jealously* of 1550s, at the Szémüvészeti Múzeum in Budapest (Fig. 10),[78] and *Venus and Cupid with Satyr* of 1555, at the Galleria Colonna in Rome (Fig. 11).[79] Unlike these paintings on the theme of love, where Cupid's bow is present and winged Cupid or Venus holds or points with an arrow, the young Cupid of *Felicity* does not carry a bow; he just points to his mother or to her breast.[80] Perhaps, Bronzino's Felicity embodies the good nature of Fortune by Cupid's gesture, thus making a poetic allusion to Dante's *Paradiso*, Canto 17, lines 25–7, where he associates the arrow with Fortune.[81] His knowledge of Dante is not only literary; he also honors the Florentine poet in a painting, *Allegorical Portrait of Dante* of 1530, now at the National Gallery of Art, Washington, DC.

The association of Fortuna with love is rare, but Bronzino was likely aware of similar texts and allusions, such as Boccaccio's *De casibus virorum illustrium* (1355–60), where Fortuna is associated with love: Lady Fortune spins her wheel, alluding to the vicissitudes of love;[82] also Cartari's text on Fortuna as symbol of love, according to ancient Greek geographer Pausanias (110–80).[83] In *Periegesis Helliados* (*Descriptions of Greece* or *Guide to Greece*), Pausanias describes a statue of Fortune in Egira, region of Achaea in West Greece.[84] The ancient image depicts on one side a seated figure of Fortune holding a cornucopia (Fig. 12) and on the other the god Cupid. Cupid carries a bow as sign of love. In this instance, Bronzino is connecting Fortuna with the *Felicity* of the Medicean wedding event. However, the unknown complexities of a marital relationship may be overcome with the assistance of Prudence, Fairness (Justice), and Love.

Bronzino's third geometrical composition is in the shape of a diamond or rhomboid, which is centric in the paintings, the focal point of the theme, the personification of Felicity and her victory. Cupid pointing with an arrow to Felicity's large diamond brooch, surrounded by four pearls, further emphasizes the diamond design as well as its symbolism in the painting. Two realms are considered in the construction of the diamond shape: the physical and metaphysical. The physical realm refers to the natural attributes of the gem—hardness, brightness, and beauty. The Medici family were great admirers of this gem, not only employing the diamond for their *impresa* (Fig. 13)[85] but also collecting other precious and rare stones, which would come to be housed in the Palazzo Vecchio. In 1570, Francesco de' Medici commissioned Vasari to construct and decorate a *studiolo* or *tesoretto* for his gem collection.[86] The metaphysical realm alludes to the axial immutability of the diamond shape as a symbol of perfection and equanimity.[87] For the Medici, the *diamante* was a symbol of divine love as decoded in a pun *di-o* (God) and *amante* (loving). Felicity wears the beautiful gem, revealing her association with the Medici as well as to express her beauty and triumph over the vicissitudes of life. Bronzino's geometrical constructions of a square, a circle, and a diamond in the painting refer to the terrestrial and celestial levels as well as to allusions of moral qualities such as truth, wisdom, and goodness or beauty revealed in the *Triumph of Felicity*.

Bronzino's *Triumph of Felicity* embodies the humanistic and Neoplatonic traditions. Also, filled with symbols and enigmatic actions, it embodies the emblematic as well. According to Adolf Katzenellenbogen's *Allegories of the Virtues and Vices in Medieval Art*, allegorical representations combine interweaving thoughts of mental images with actual forms and convey a spiritual message.[88] This is Bronzino's *invenzione* (invention). Bronzino's *Triumph of Felicity* is a transmutation from physical matter (paint) to form (painting); a creation of form (invention) to ideal (conceit); and an expression of the ideal to sentiment and the sentiment of love into the aesthetic of beauty (art).

For artists and humanists, familiarity with the language and imagery of the allegorical, emblematic, hieroglyphic, and visual traditions prompted Mannerist artists such as Bronzino to create a new vocabulary in art—an encyclopedia of images and symbols. This visual dictionary demonstrates the assimilation of the emblematic tradition in Italian paintings of the sixteenth century as a didactic method of moralizing on past and present events.

In the *Triumph of Felicity*, Bronzino reveals at the abstract level the success of art over nature and the ability of art to advocate for and portray notions of beauty, love, and truth in nature. At the practical level, the art of painting depicts such metaphysical notions with the visual elements and the principles of design. Although Bronzino constructed a complex geometrical composition with a square, a circle, and a diamond and composed sculptural figures *all'antica*, the overall compositional imagery evokes the fusion of the visual bond between a three-dimensional construct on a two-dimensional surface. The *Triumph of Felicity* is also a pictorial triumph, painting over sculpture. Thus, it constitutes Bronzino's poetical and visual response to Varchi's *Due Lezzioni*.

NOTES

1. This essay benefits from the generous comments of Professor Jan L. de Jong, Institute for the History of Art and Architecture, Groningen University, The Netherlands. A version of this essay was presented as "Bronzino's *Allegory of Happiness*," at the annual conference of Renaissance Society of America in Chicago, IL, on 5 April 2008.

2. See Edi Baccheschi, ed., *L'Opera completa del Bronzino. Introdotta da scritti del pittore e coordinata* (Milan: Rizzoli, 1973), 8, citing Bronzino's poem. This early completed study and catalogue of the works and writings of Bronzino is often ignored by scholars.

3. For the most recent enterprise on the evaluation of both Vasari's *Vite* with commentaries and note, see Giorgio Vasari, *Le vite de' più eccellenti pittori, scultori, e architettori nelle redazioni del 1550 e 1568*, eds. Rosanna Bettarini and Paola Barocchi, 10 vols. (Florence: Sansoni and S.P.E.S., 1966–97); hereafter cited as Bettarini-Barocchi, *Le vite*.

4. See Bettarini-Barocchi, *Le vite*, 6:231–39. See also Gaetano Milanesi, ed., *Le vite de' più eccellenti Pittori, Scultori, et Architettori*, 9 vols. (Florence: Sansoni 1858–78 edition, reissued in 1970–74), 7:604, on Vasari referring to the Bronzino's painting: "Ed a detto signor principe, ha dipindo sono, sono pochi mesi un quadretto di piccolo figure, che non ha pari, e is può dire che sia di minio, veramente"; hereafter cited as Vasari-Milanesi, *Le vite*.

5. See Luciano Berti, *Il principe dello studiolo* (Florence: Edam, 1967), 282.

6. See Arthur McComb, *Agnolo Bronzino His Life and Works* (Cambridge, MA: Harvard University Press, 1928), 32.

7. See Charles McCorquodale, *Bronzino* (New York: Harper and Row, Publishers, 1981), 149.

8. See Baccheschi, *L'Opera completa del Bronzino*, 105.

9.See Janet Cox-Rearick, *Bronzino's Chapel of Eleonora in the Palazzo Vecchio* (Berkeley: University of California Press, 1993), passim; and Janet Cox-Rearick, "Art at the Court of Duke Cosimo I de' Medici (1537–1574)," in *The Medici, Michelangelo and the Art of Late Renaissance Florence*, Exhibition Catalogue, ed. Alan P. Darr et al. (New Haven, CT: Yale University Press, 2002), 35–35 and 153–54.

10. See Claudio Strinati, *Bronzino* (Rome: Viviani Editore, 2010), 191–92, restating Brock's iconographical discussion.

11. See Maurice Brock, *Bronzino* (Paris: Flammarion, 2002), 236–37.

12. See Robert W. Gaston, "Love's Sweet Poison: A New Reading of Bronzino's London *Allegory*," in *I Tatti Studies: Essays in the Renaissance* 4 (1991), 249–88; and Robert W. Gaston, "Towards a Postmodernist Bronzino," in *Agnolo Bronzino: Medici Court Artist in Context*, ed. Andrea M. Gáldy (Newcastle upon Tyne: Cambridge Scholars Publishing, 2013), 107–28.

13. See Graham Smith, "Bronzino's *Allegory of Happiness*," *The Art Bulletin* 66, no. 3 (September 1984), 390–99.

14. See Cosimo Bartoli, *Trionfo della felicità*, in the third book of *Ragionamenti accademici ... sopra alculi loughi difficili di Dante. Con alcune inventioni e significanti* (Venice, 1567), 48b–54a; and P.T. Baxter, "Catalogue Entry 33," in L. Corti, et al., *Giorgio Vasari: Principi, letterati e artisti nelle carte di Giorgio Vasari* (Florence: Edam, 1981), 137–38. Likely Bartoli was influenced by Vincenzo Cartari's *Imagini delli Dei de gl' Antichi* (Venice, 1556), and his citations and imagery of *Felicità humana* and *Felicitas publica* derive from Giglio Gregorio Giraldi's *De deis gentium* (Basel, 1548), Syn. I, 51:

Felicitas, ... etiam antiquis dea exiftimata cf. Plin Libro 35 ... Vidimus & ipfi in nomifmatibus antiquis Felicitatis effigiem, & praecipuè in Iuliae Mammaeae Aug. in cuius tergo foemina erat, in folio fedens, dextera caduceum, finifra grande cornucopiae tenens, cum hac infcriptione, **Felicitas Publica** ... Scribit Dion libro Hift. 44 C. Caefari dictatori fenatum concefsiffe, ut fenatum nouum conftruerer, quamuis curia Hoftilia in flaurata fuiffer, & cius uice Felicitatis templum, quod etiam Lepidus magifter equittum fecit. Cebes uero Thebanus in Tabula hoc modo defcrifit: In emineti quopiam arcis ueftibolo Felicitatem in folio federe, liberali ornatu[ait] comptam, fed non accurate, & florentifsimo ferto coronatam.

See Catherina Volpi, ed., *Le immagini degli Dei di Vincenzo Cartari* (Rome: De Luca, 1996), 543. This edition is significant because Volpi cites the actual sources for Cartari's imagery, such as Hesiod, Pausanias, Lucian, Cicero, Ovid, Virgin, Dante, and Giraldi, and illustrates the text with Roman numismatic examples, including emblematic images from the texts of Alciato and Giraldi; hieroglyphs from Valeriano's compendium and Colonna's book; and Cinquecento paintings and prints.

15. See Smith, "Bronzino's *Allegory of Happiness*," 396n39.

16. See Smith, "Bronzino's *Allegory of Happiness*," 390.

17. See Smith, "Bronzino's *Allegory of Happiness*," 391, focusing on Roman coins, in particular, Denarius of Julia Mamaea; and *Felicitas Publica*, cited in Cartari, *Imagini*, 255. A copy of the coin is at the British Museum in London.

18. See Smith, "Bronzino's *Allegory of Happiness*," 398.

19. See Smith, "Bronzino's *Allegory of Happiness*," 394.

20. See Smith, "Bronzino's *Allegory of Happiness*," 394.

21. See Jean Seznec, *The Survival of the Pagan Gods* (New York: Harper and Row, Publishers, 1961), 296, 279–323, for a study of the manuals available in the Cinquecento and for a specific account of the sources that Cartari drew upon in his book, particularly Pausanias, Apuleius, Macrobius, and Martianus Capella. See also Arthur Henkel and Albrecht Schone, *Emblemata: Handbuch zur Sinnibildkunst des XVI. und XVII. Jahrhunderts* (Stuttgart: J.B. Metzler, 1967); and Mario Praz, *Studies in Seventeenth Century Imagery*, 2nd edn. (Rome: Edizioni di Storia e letteratura, 1964). In particular, see Barbara Carman Garner, "Francis Bacon, Natalis Comes and the Mythological Tradition," *Journal of the Warburg and Courtauld Institutes* 33 (1970), 264–91, for the correct dating on the publication of this mythographic manuscript, not in 1551 but later, in 1567, in Venice.

22. Annibale Caro, *Lettere Familiari*, ed. Aulo Greco (Florence: Sansoni, 1957–61), passim.

23. For example, Paolo Giovio's *Dialogo delle imprese militare et amorose* (Lyon 1559); and Borghini's *Discorsi* (Venice, 1556). See R.A. Scorza, "Vincenzo Borghi and Invenzione: The Florentine Apparato of 1565," *Journal of the Warburg and Courtauld Institutes* 44 (1981), 57–75; and T.C.P. Zimmerman, *Paolo Giovio: The Historian and the Crisis of Sixteenth-Century Italy* (Princeton, NJ: Princeton University Press, 1995), passim.

24. Acquainted with the Medici family, in particular with Pope Leo X and Pope Clement VII, Valeriano became the private tutor of Alessandro de' Medici and Ippolito de' Medici, as well as of Vasari. After the redis-

covery of Horapollo's *Hieroglyphica*, Valeriano composed the first Renaissance dictionary of symbols, *Hieroglyphica sive de sacris Aegyptiorum literis commentarii*, published in Latin in 1521–51 in Basel, later translated into French in 1576 and into Italian in 1602.

25. Ernest Gombrich, *The Heritage of Apelles* (Ithaca, NY: Cornell University Press, 1976), 124–25, for Caro's letter from Rome to Vasari in Florence, 10 May 1548.

26. In *Survival of the Pagan Gods*, Seznec notes how Vincenzo Cartari's *Imagini delli Dei de gl' Antichi* (Venice, 1556) was read and used by Annibale Caro and Giorgio Vasari (Paris: Flammation, 1980, 2nd edn.), 256–62. See also Clare Robertson, "Annibale Caro as Iconographer: Sources and Method," *Journal of the Warburg and Courtauld Institutes* 45 (1982), 160–81; and Clare Robertson, *Il Grande Cardinale* (New Haven, CT: Yale University Press, 1992), 218, where she explains how Caro, one of the first iconographer advisors in the Cinquecento, discusses the possibilities offered by emblematic books such as Cartari's *Imagini*,

27. See Bettarini-Barocchi, *Le vite*, First Preface, 1:7–16, and 179–227, for Giovambatista Adriani's letter to Vasari on Ancient Art, 8 September 1576. This letter was included only in the 1568 edition of the *Vite*. See Liana De Girolami Cheney, *Giorgio Vasari's The Prefaces: Art and Theory* (London and New York: Peter Lang Publishers, 2012), 21–66, for an English translation of the letter; and Julia Haig Gaisser, *Pierio Valeriano on the Ill Fortune of Learned Men* (Ann Arbor: University of Michigan Press, 1999), 17–18, on Valeriano's contact with Vasari.

28. See Bettarini-Barocchi, *Le vite*, 1:30, "Invention combines history with images." See Vasari-Milanesi, *Le vite*, 2:93–107, for Vasari's explanation of *invenzione* (invention), *imitazione* (imitation), and *concetti* (conceit). See André Chastel, *Marsile Ficin et L'Art* (Geneva: Droz, 1975), 141–62, on the meaning of ambiguities and allegories.

29. See, for example, Vasari's imagery in the decoration of Palazzo Vecchio in Florence. See Vasari-Milanesi, *Le vite*, 8:1–22; J. Draper, *Vasari's Decorations in the Palazzo Vecchio: The Ragionamenti* (Diss., University of North Carolina, 1973); and Elizabeth MacGrath, "'Il Senso Nostro.' The Medici Allegory Applied to Vasari's Mythological Frescoes in the Palazzo Vecchio," in *Giorgio Vasari tra decorazione e storiografia artistica*, ed. G.C. Garfagnini (Florence: Olschki, 1985), 117–34.

30. See Deborah Parker, *Bronzino: Renaissance Painter as Poet* (Cambridge: Cambridge University Press, 2000), passim; Albertina Furno, *La vita e le rime di Angiolo Bronzino* (Pistoia: Kessinger Publishing 1902, reissued 2009); and Baccheschi, *L'Opera completa del Bronzino*, 6, citing the printed editions of Bronzino's poetry, and 8–11, citing some of the sonnets.

31. See Ernest Gombrich, "'Icones Symbolicae': Philosophies of Sym-

bolism and their Bearing on Art," in his *Symbolic Images: Studies in the Art of the Renaissance* (London: Phaidon, 1979), 172.

32. See Carol V. Kaske and John R. Clark, ed. and trans., *Marsilio Ficino: Three Books on Life: A Critical Edition and Translation and Notes* (Binghamton, NY: Medieval and Renaissance Texts and Studies, 1989), passim; and Enrico Vitale, ed., *Marsilio Ficino: Teologia Platonica* (Milan: Bompiani, 2011), 249, on the creation of art reflecting divine wisdom.

33. See also Richard H. Wilkinson, *Symbol and Magic in Spiritual Art* (London: Thames and Hudson, 1994), 16–26; D.P. Walker, *Spiritual and Demonic Magic: From Ficino to Campanella* (Philadelphia: The Pennsylvania University Press, 2000), 7–10, on Ficino's theory of sensation; and Wallis Budge, *Magia egizie* (Rome: Newton, 1980), 14–27.

34. See Leatrice Mendelsohn, *Parogoni: Benedetto Varchi Due Lezzioni and Cinquecento Art Theory* (Ann Arbor, MI: UMI Research Press, 1982), 9 and 113; and Vitale, ed., *Marsilio Ficino: Teologia Platonica*, 247, on art imitating nature. I am classifying and defining Mannerism and Maniera style according to Craig Hugh Smyth, *Mannerism and Maniera* (Vienna: IRSA, 1992), passim; see also Liana De Girolami Cheney, ed., *Readings in Italian Mannerism* (London: Peter Lang, 1996, revised 2005), Introduction, 9–34; and Sydney Freedberg, *Painting in Italy, 1500–1600* (Baltimore, MD: Penguin Books, Pelican History of Art, 1971), 255–95, for an analysis of the Maniera style.

35. See Bettarini-Barocchi, *Le vite*, Preface Two, 3:5, and Preface Three, 4:7–9.

Ma perchè più chiaro ancor si conosca la qualità del miglioramento che ci hanno fatto i predetti artefici, non sarà certo fuori di proposito dichiarare, in poche parole, i cinque aggiunti che io nominai … La maniera venne poi la più bella, dall'aver messo in, uso il frequ'ente ritrarre le cose più belle, e da quel più bello, o mani o teste o corpi o gambe aggiugnerle insieme e fare una figura di tutte quelle bellezze che più si poteva; e metterla, in uso in ogni opera per tutte le figure, che per questo si dice esser bella maniera.

(But to the end that the nature of the improvement brought about by the aforesaid artists may be even more clearly understood, it will certainly not be out of place to explain in a few words the five additions that I have named … Manner (style) then attained to the greatest beauty from the practice which arose of constantly copying the most beautiful objects, and jointing together these most beautiful things, hands, heads, bodies, and legs, so as to make a figure of the greatest possible beauty. This practice was carried out in every work for all figures for all the works executed is what is called beautiful manner [style]).

36. See Marsilio Ficino, *Symposium*, I. 3 in *Opera* (Basel, 1561). See also Vitale, ed., *Marsilio Ficino: Teologia Platonica*, xxxi–xliii, on Ficino and Platonism, and 957–61, on beauty and goodness; Chastel, *Marsile Ficin et L'Art*, 6–85, on beauty and the beautiful; and A.E. Denham, ed., *Plato on Art and Beauty* (New York: Palgrave Macmillan, 2012), 181.

37. For a reprint of Bronzino's letter and its translation, see Appendix 1 in "Il Bronzino: A Short Biography" in this volume. See Baccheschi, *L'Opera completa del Bronzino*, "Letter from Bronzino to Varchi," 6–7, in Italian. For an English translation, see McCorquodale, *Bronzino*, Appendix II, "Bronzino's Answer to Benedetto Varchi," on the superiority of painting over sculpture, 161–63. In his unfinished letter, Bronzino speaks in favor of painting as superior because this art best imitates Nature, in a single view creates beauty, and withstands the effects of time, i.e., "painting is enjoyable for a longer time"; in McCorquodale, *Bronzino*, 161. See also Alessandro Cecchi, "Il Bronzino, Benedetto Varchi e l'Accademia Fiorentina: ritratti di poeti letterati e personaggi illustri della corte medicea," *Antichità viva* 30, nos. 1–2 (1991), 17–28.

38. Some of Smith's identifications of Bronzino's imagery, although most helpful and convincing, rely on Cesare Ripa's *Iconologia* (Rome, 1603). See Cesare Ripa, *Iconologia* (Rome: Giovanni Gigliotti, 1593), published without images; and Cesare Ripa, *Iconologia* (Rome: Lepido Facii, 1603), published with 400 images. The images and text of Alciato, Cartari, and Vasari anticipate Cesare Ripa's *Iconologia*. See Liana De Girolami Cheney, "Giorgio Vasari's and Cesare Ripa's *Iconologia*: The Chamber of Fortune's Allegories of Virtues in the Casa Vasari," in *Exploration in Renaissance Culture* (Summer 2008), 35–45, for a discussion on Vasari as precursor of Ripa's *figurazioni* (visual images), e.g., the personification of Felicity.

39. See Parker, *Bronzino: Renaissance Painter as Poet*, passim.

40. See Andrea Alciato, *Emblemata: Diverse Imprese* (Lyon: Macé Bonhomme for Guillaume Ruille, 1551), 130, Emblem on Honor or Fame. The motto says, "Immortality won through literary pursuits" or "Man gains immortality through literary pursuits" ("Ex literarum studiis immortalitatem acuiri," "Che per li studi di lettere l'huomo si fa immortale"). The *pictura* depicts:

> Triton, Neptune's trumpeter, whose tail shows him as a sea-monster, his face as a god of the sea, is surrounded by an encircling snake, which bites on its own tail, gripped fast in its mouth. Fame follows after men of outstanding intellect and their noble achievements, and bids them be read throughout the world.

The meaning of the emblem is that the conch/trumpet represents fame, encircled by a serpent, which is a symbol of eternity. For the image, see <http://www.emblems.arts.gla.ac.uk/alciato/emblem>.

41. The seated composition of Bronzino's Felicity resembles Michelangelo's *Prophet Isaiah* of 1508–12, in the Sistine Ceiling at the Vatican. Not only was Bronzino visually influenced by Michelangelo but he also symbolically appropriated the prophetic allusion to the virtue of Felicity as an image of a predictive positive outcome for the Medici family, in particular, for Francesco de' Medici's marriage to Joanna of Austria.

42. Vasari described this image as "Felicità ... una donna vestita, con un corno di novitia nella sisnistra, et un caduceo di mercurio nella destra" ("Felicity ... a dressed woman, holding a horn of plenty with her left hand and a Mercury's caduceus with her right"). See Alessandro del Vita, *Lo Zibaldone di Giorgio Vasari* (Rome: R. Istituto Archeologico e Storia dell'Arte, 1938), 9, citing Vasari.

43. See Vincenzo Cartari, *Imagini delli Dei de gl' Antichi*, ed. Marco Bussagli (Genoa: Nuova Stile Regina, 1987), 255, for a description: "Dea Felicità ... con il Caduceo and il Corno di Dovitia in mano quello significante la virtù, questo le richezze, necessarie e l'una, è l'altra all Felicità humana" ("Goddess of Felicity ... with the caduceus and holding the horn of plenty, the former signifying virtue, the latter richness, both necessary for human felicity"). He elaborates, "una donna sopra un bello seggio, che tiene nella destra il caduceo, & hà nella sinistra un corno di dovitia. Si può dire che quello significhi la virtù, questo le richezze come che, ne la virtù da se, ne le richezze per loro medesime possono fare qui l'huomo felice" ("a woman in a beautiful chair, holding on her right hand a caduceus and a horn of plenty on her left hand. It is said that the former signifies virtue, the latter richness, however, virtue alone or richness by itself cannot make a happy man").

44. See n. 14 above.

45. See Giovanni Pierio Valeriano, *I Ieroglifici overo Commentarii delle occulte significationi degl'Egittij & Altre Nationi* (Venice: Gio Battista Combi, 1627), Bk. V, 201.

46. See Guy de Tervarent, "Veritas and Justitia Triumphant," *Journal of the Warburg and Courtauld Institutes* 7 (1944), 95–101, esp. 95; and James Hall, *Dictionary of Subjects and Symbols in Art* (New York: Harper and Row, 1974), 86.

47. See Brock, *Bronzino*, 237 and 234, for the image; and, in particular, Alessandro Cecchi, "La 'Prudenza' del Bronzino per Ser Carolo Gherardi," *Antichità viva* 26 (1987), 19–21, on the mirror-picture.

48. See Smith, "Bronzino's *Allegory of Happiness*," 394.

49. See Liana De Girolami Cheney, "Giorgio Vasari's *Allegory of Pru-*

dence: Mirroring Alciato and Valeriano's Emblems," *Emblem Studies* 7 (2009), 26–37.

50. See Alciato, *Diverse imprese*, 20, Emblem 16. The subject is on *Prudentia* (Wisdom). "About the same gain, and what it signifies" ("Da capo quel, ch'apportiene"). The subscription explains the image: "Two-headed Janus, you know about what has already happened and what is yet to come, you see the jeering faces behind just as you see them in front. Why do they represent you with so many eyes, why with so many faces? Is it because this form tells us that you were a man of circumspection?" For the image, see <http://www.emblems.arts.gla.ac.uk/alciato/emblem>. See also R. Bacou and C. Monbeig-Goguel, "Giorgio Vasari' *Prudenza*," *Reveu de l'Art* (1968), 88–92.

51. See Carlo Falciani and Antonio Natali, *Bronzino, pittore e poeta alla corte dei Medici* (Florence: Mandragora, 2010), passim; and Brock, *Bronzino*, 182–211.

52. See Smith, "Bronzino's *Allegory of Happiness*," 393n22.

53. See Cartari, *Imagini*, 243.

54. See Valeriano, *Ieroglifici*, Bk. VII, 84; and Horapollo, *Hieroglyphica*, 482.

55. See Cartari, *Imagini*, 242.

56. See Cartari, *Imagini*, 242.

57. See Mark R. Freier, *Time Measured by Kairos and Kronos* (2006), no pagination, <http://www.whatifenterprises.com/whatif/whatiskairos.pdf>.

58. See Freier, *Time Measured by Kairos and Kronos*, for an explanation on how the ancient poet and astronomer Aratus' *Phaenomena* (227, 309) employed the same verb, *aeì trochào*, to determine the eternal movements of the celestial spheres.

59. See Cartari, *Imagini*, 528–32, for a reference to Giraldi's description in *De Deis*, Syn. XVI, 629, and, in particular, to Alciato's Emblem "In Ocassionem" ("Chance" or "Opportunity") in *Emblematum liber* (Augsburg, 1534). Alciato's text says:

> This image is the work of Lysippus, whose home was Sicyon.—Who are you?—I am the moment of seized opportunity that governs all.—Why do you stand on points?—I am always guided.—Why do you have winged sandals on your feet?—The fickle breeze bears me in all directions.—Tell us, what is the reason for the sharp razor in your right hand?—This sign indicates that I am keener than any cutting edge.—Why is there a lock of hair on your brow?—So that I may be seized as I run towards you.—But come, tell us now, why ever is the back of your head bald?—So

that if any person once lets me depart on my winged feet, I may not thereafter be caught by having my hair seized. It was for your sake, stranger that the craftsman produced me with such art, and, so that I should warn all, it is an open portico that holds me.

For the citation, see <http://www.emblems.arts.gla.ac.uk/alciato>.

60. See Antionette Clark Wire, *The Corinthian Women Prophets: A Reconstruction Through Paul's Rhetoric* (Minneapolis, MN: Fortress Press, 1995), 220.

61. See Helmut Nickel, "Two Falcon Devices of the Strozzi: An Attempt at Interpretation," *Metropolitan Museum Journal* vol. 9 (1974), 229–32; Hall, *Subject and Symbols in Art*, 264; and Guy de Tervarent, *Attributs et symbols dans l'art profane, 1450–1600* (Geneva: Droz, 1959), 147, for an interpretation of the Medici *impresa*. The shape of a triangular diamond is employed in the Medici devices. From the time of Cosimo de' Medici, his son Piero de' Medici, and his grandson, Lorenzo de' Medici, their heraldic *impresa* evolved from the depiction of three encircled rings with a pyramidal-diamond atop, to a falcon holding a ring in a claw, to the inclusion of three ostriches colored feathers. The motto of Medici's *impresa* "Semper" ("Forever") states: "Sempre fa-lcon Di (o) amante" or "Deo amante" ("Do all for the love of God" or Through God's love), sounding like "Falcone e diamate" ("Falcon and diamond"). Lorenzo de' Medici adopted his father's device with three ostrich feathers in white, green, and red colors, which refer respectively to the theological virtues of Faith, Hope, and Charity as well as the symbolism of eternity, loyalty, and union. See also Horapollo's *Hieroglyphica*, ed. Jesus María González de Zárate (Madrid: AKAL, 1991), 83–84, for Horapollo's commentary on the hieroglyph of the falcon as a symbol of divinity, dignity, excellence, and victory, and 409, for the ostrich's plumes as a symbol of Justice; see also Valeriano, *Ieroglifici*, Bk. XXI, Section III, on Justice and plumes, and Bk. XXV, Section II, on falcon and plumes.

62. See J.C. Cooper, *An Illustrated Encyclopaedia of Traditional Symbols* (London: Thames and Hudson, 1978), 40.

63. Perhaps Bronzino is visually recalling the theme of time in Vasari's Sala degli Elementi of 1560s at the Palazzo Vecchio. See Carlo Francini, ed., *Palazzo Vecchio: Officina di opera e di ingegno* (Florence: Silvana, 2006), 236–37.

64. See Smith, "Bronzino's *Allegory of Happiness*," 397; and Brock, *Bronzino*, 327.

65. See Cartari, *Imagini*, 255. In 1603, Cavalier d'Arpino appropriates Cartari's design of *Felicità humana* for a frontal view of the emblem *Bonus Eventus* as a *figurazione* in Cesare Ripa's illustrated *Iconologia* (New York: Garland Publications, 1970 edition), 155.

66. See Hans Biedermann, *A Dictionary of Symbols* (New York: Meridian Books, 1992), 85.

67. See Biedermann, *Dictionary of Symbols*, 86.

68. See Alciato, *Emblemata* (Venice: Aldus, 1546), Emblem 99; and see Cartari, *Imagini*, 360, Fig. 104, for Alciato's emblem and commentary.

69. See Cartari, *Imagini*, 533. See Jean Chevalier and Alain Gheerbrant, *A Dictionary of Symbols* (London: Blackwell, 1994), 268, on the symbolism of the cure, and 901, on the symbolism of the sphere.

70. See Cartari, *Imagini*, 511–44, for a discussion on Fortuna in all her negative and positive aspects and interpretations.

71. See Freier, *Time Measured by Kairos and Kronos*.

72. See Biedermann, *Dictionary of Symbols*, 380.

73. See Freier, *Time Measured by Kairos and Kronos*, with his citation on Boethius, *The Consolation of Philosophy*, trans. W.V. Cooper (London: J.M. Dent, 1902), n.p.: "Are you trying to stay the force of her turning wheel? Ah! dull-witted mortal, if Fortune begin to stay still, she is no longer Fortune."

74. See Freier, *Time Measured by Kairos and Kronos*, for excerpts from the poems on *Fortuna Imperatrix Mundi* ("Fortune, Empress of the World") and *Fortune Plango Vulnera* ("I Bemoan the Wounds of Fortune").

> Sors immanis/et inanis,/rota tu volubilis,/status malus,/
> vana salus/semper/dissolubilis, obumbrata et velata/
> michi quoque niteris;/nunc/per ludum//dorsum nudum/
> fero tui sceleris.
> ⋯⋯⋯
> Fortune rota volvitur;/descendo minoratus;/alter in altum tollitur;/
> nimis exaltatus/rex sedet in vertice/caveat ruinam!/Nam sub axe legimus/
> Hecubam reginam.

> (Fate—monstrous/and empty,/you whirling wheel,/you are malevolent,/
> well-being is vain/and always fades to nothing,/shadowed/and veiled/
> you plague me too;/now through the game/I bring my bare back/
> to your villainy.
> ⋯⋯⋯
> The wheel of Fortune turns;/I go down, demeaned;/another is raised up;/
> far too high up/sits the king at the summit -/let him fear ruin!/
> for under the axis is written/Queen Hecuba).

75. See Freier, *Time Measured by Kairos and Kronos*, also commenting on Albius Tibullus (55–19 BCE), who describes Fortune with a wheel, "Versatur celeri Fors levis orbe rotate," in *Elegies* I, 5, 70.

76. See Hanna Fenichel Pitkin, *Fortune is a Woman* (Chicago, IL: Uni-

versity of Chicago Press, 1987), 138–69; and Harvey C. Mansfield, *Machiavelli Virtue* (Chicago, IL: University of Chicago Press, 1996), 47–52, 129–30, and 189–90.

77. See Leatrice Mendelsohn, "L'Allegoria di Londra del Bronzino e la retorica di carnevale," in *Kunst des Cinquecento in der Toskana*, ed. Monika Cämmerer (Munich: Bruckmann, 1992), 152–67; and Brock, *Bronzino*, 214–31, for a most recent interpretation.

78. See Brock, *Bronzino*, 231–34, for a most recent analysis.

79. See Brock, *Bronzino*, 231–34, for a most recent analysis.

80. The erotic playfulness between Cupid and Venus found in the love theme paintings is not depicted in the *Triumph of Felicity*. In the London *Venus*, Cupid wears a bow and Venus points to Cupid with an arrow; in the Budapest Venus, Cupid points the arrow upward while crowning Venus with his bow, and Venus erotically points the arrow to herself; and in the Rome Venus, Cupid points the arrow upward, while Venus holds his bow and points one of his darts at herself.

81. "Touching my future destiny have heard/Words grievous, though I feel me on all sides/Well squared to fortune's blows. Therefore my will/Were satisfied to know the lot awaits me;/To arrow, seen beforehand, slacks his flight."

82. See Virginia Brown, trans. of 1347 edition of Giovanni Boccaccio's *Famous Women* (Cambridge, MA: Harvard University Press, 2001), Section on Lady Luck (Change); and Vittorio Zaccharia, "La fortuna del 'De Mulieribus claris' del Boccaccio nel secolo XV: Giovanni Sabbadino degli Arienti, Jacopo Filippo Foresti e le lore biografie femminili (1490–1497)," in F. Mazzoni, ed., *Il Boccaccio nelle culture e letterature nazionali* (Florence: Olschki, 1978), 519–45.

83. See Cartari, *Imagini*, 535, citing Pausanias, and 537, for the image.

84. See Pausanias, *Periegesis Helliados*, Bk. VII, 26:8.

85. See n. 61 above.

86. See Berti, *Il principe dello studiolo*, 257–316, registry of the collection; and Valentina Continelli, *Guardaroba di cose rare et preciose: Lo studiolo di Francesco I de'Medici, Arte, Storia e Significati* (Lugano: Agorà Publishing, 2007), 17–43, including the most complete bibliography on the subject.

87. See Chevalier and Gheerbrant, *A Dictionary of Symbols*, 290–91.

88. See Adolf Katzenellenbogen, *Allegories of the Virtues and Vices in Medieval Art* (New York: W.W. Norton & Company, Inc. 1964), Introduction.

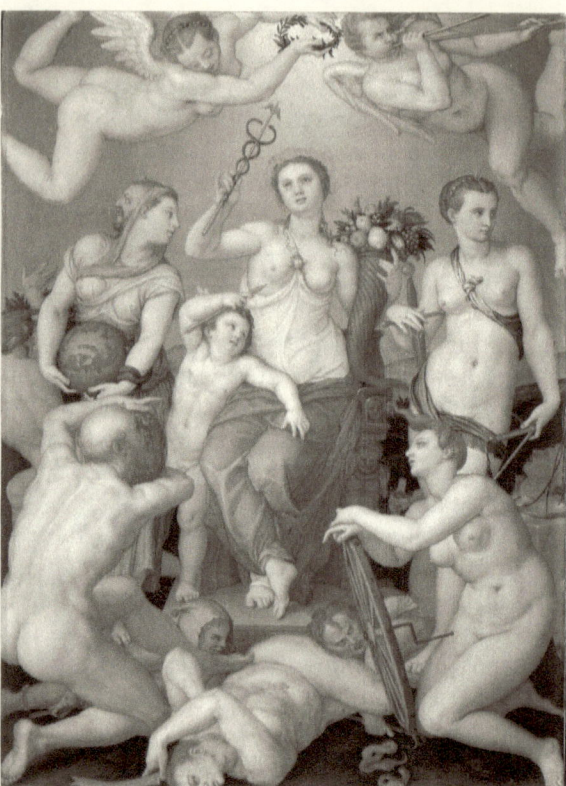

Fig. 1. Agnolo
Bronzino, *Triumph
of Felicity* (*Allegory
of Felicity*),1567.
Galleria degli Uffizi,
Florence. Photo
credit: Scala/Art
Resource, NY.

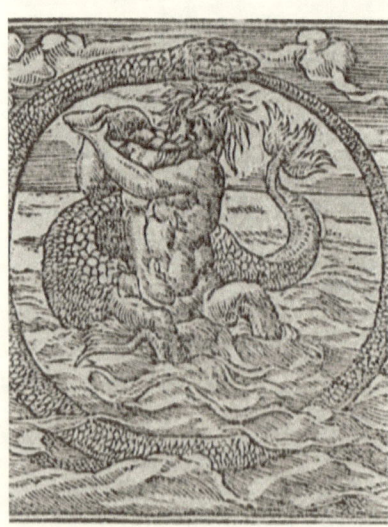

Fig. 2. Andrea Alciato, Emblem on
Fame or *Honor*. In *Emblemata* (Lyon,
1551). <http://www.emblems.arts.
gla.ac.uk/alciato/emblem>.

Fig. 3. Giorgio Vasari, *Felicità Publica* or *Bonus Eventus*, 1548. Chamber of Fortune, Casa Vasari, Arezzo. Photo credit: author.

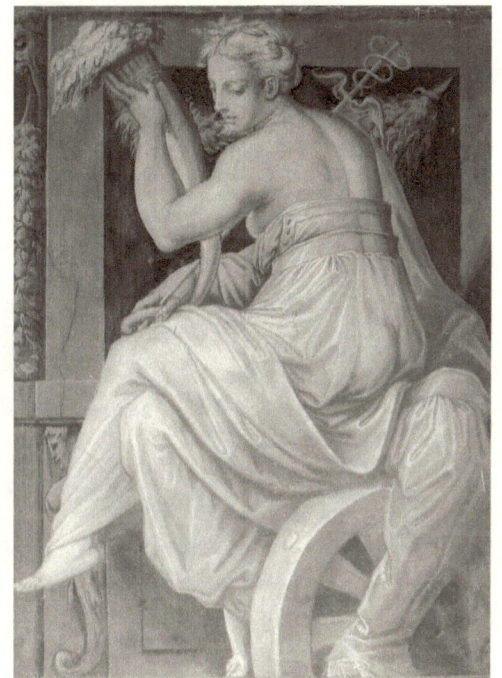

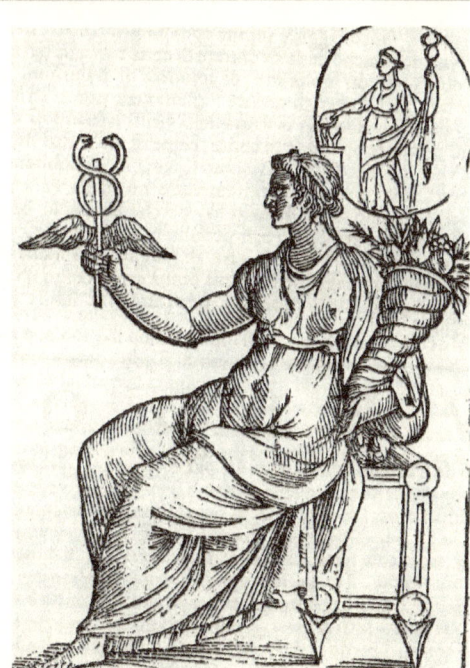

Fig. 4. Vincenzo Cartari, *Felicità humana* or *Bonus Eventus*. In *Imagini delli Dei de gl' Antichi* (Venice, 1556). Photo credit: author.

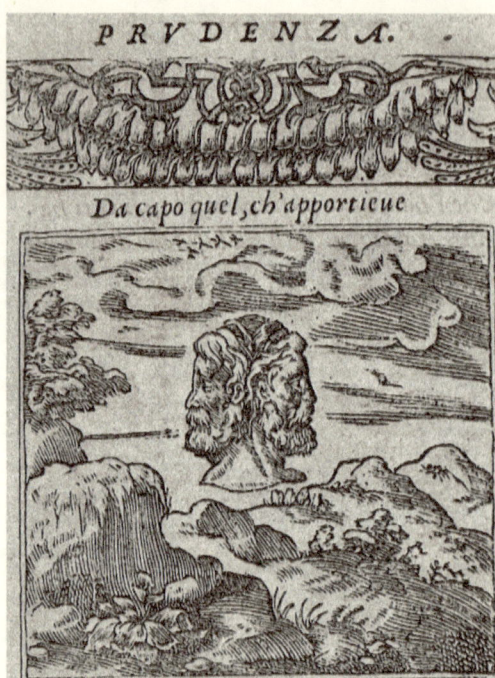

Fig. 5. Andrea Alciato, Emblem on *Prudentes*. *Problema*. In *Emblemata* (Lyon: Macé Bonhomme for Guillaume Rouille 1551) <http://www.emblems.arts. gla.ac.uk/alciato/emblem>.

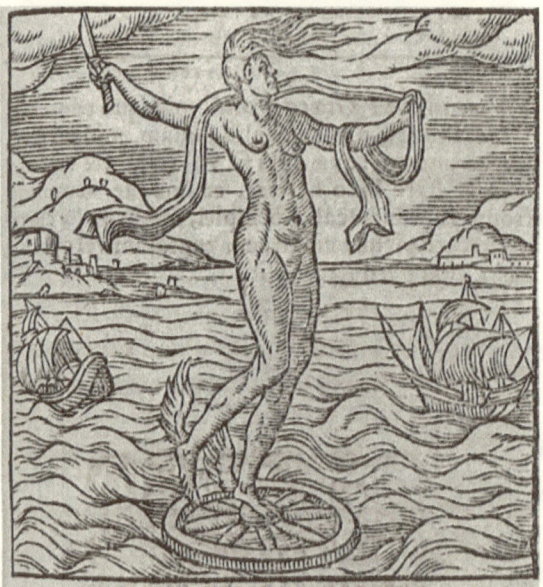

Fig. 6. Andrea Alciato, Emblem on *Occasio* (Kairos). In *Emblemata* (Lyon: Macé Bonhomme for Guillaume Rouille 1551) <http:// www.emblems.arts. gla.ac.uk/alciato/emblem>.

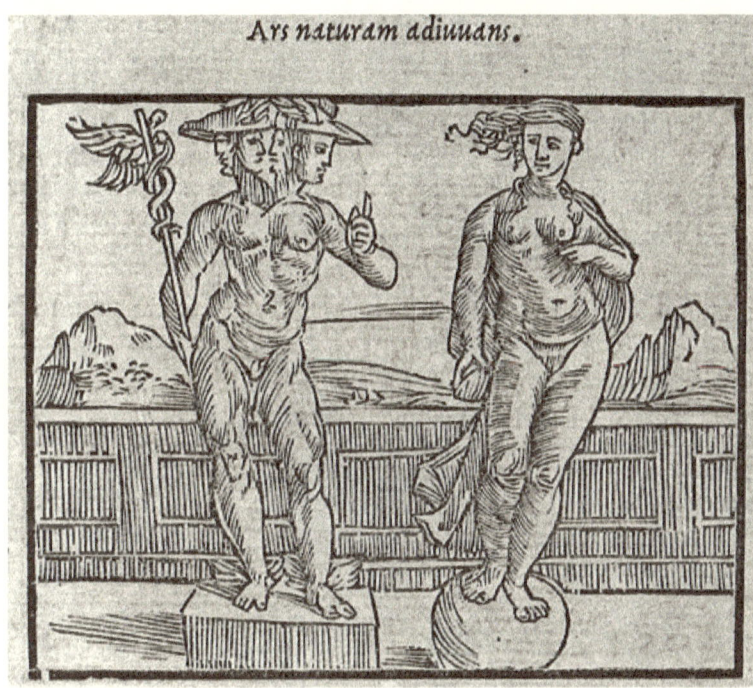

Fig. 7. Andrea Alciato, Emblem on *Ars naturam adiuvans*. In *Emblemata* (Lyon: Macé Bonhomme for Guillaume Rouille 1551) <http://www.emblems.arts.gla.ac.uk/alciato/emblem>.

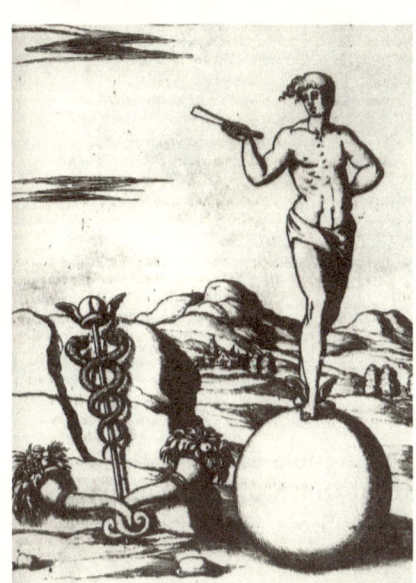

Fig. 8 Vincenzo Cartari, *Fortuna* (*Fortune*). In *Imagini delli Dei de gl' Antichi* (Venice: Evangelista Deuchino, 1556). Photo credit: author.

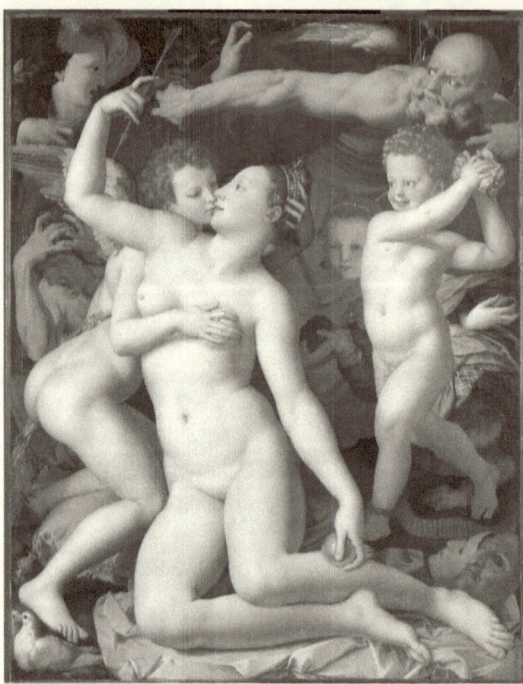

Fig. 9. Agnolo Bronzino, *Allegory of Venus and Cupid* (*Allegory of Love*), 1544–45. National Gallery, London, Great Britain. Photo credit: National Gallery, London/Art Resource, NY.

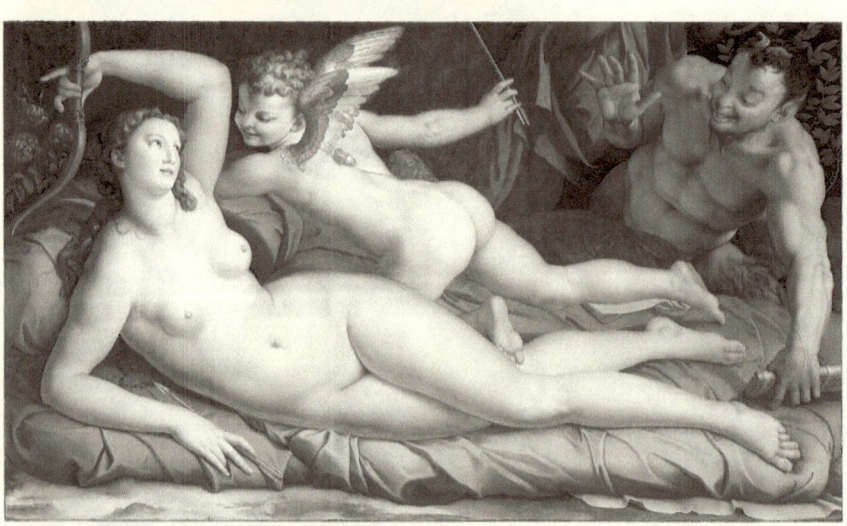

Fig. 10. Agnolo Bronzino, *Venus, Cupid, Two Amorini and Jealousy*, 1550s. Szémüvészeti Múzeum, Budapest. Photo credit: The Museum of Fine Arts Budapest/Scala/Art Resource, NY.

Fig. 11. Agnolo
Bronzino, *Venus
and Cupid and
Satyr*, 1555.
Galleria Colonna,
Rome. Photo
credit: Alinari/Art
Resource, NY.

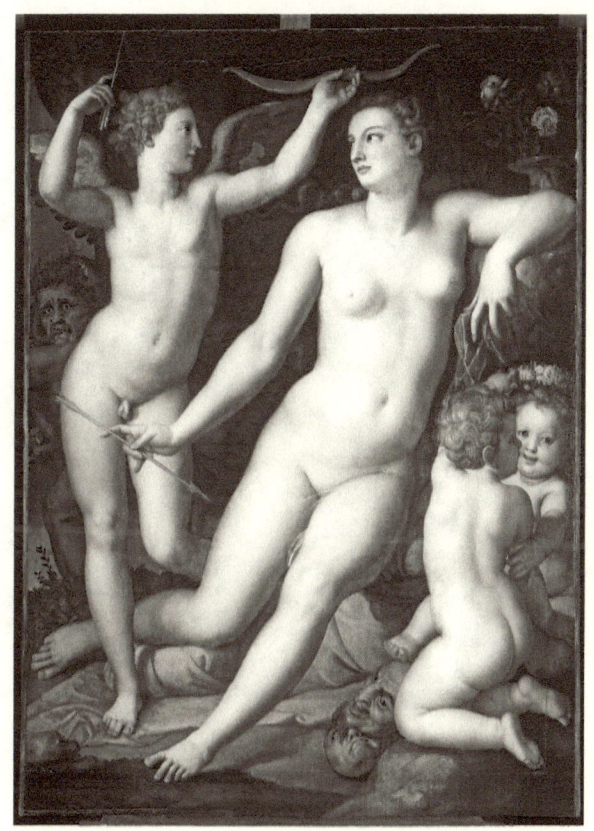

Fig. 12. Vincenzo
Cartari, *Cupid and
Fortune* (det.). In
*Imagini delli Dei de
gl' Antichi* (Venice:
Evangelista
Deuchino, 1556).
Photo credit:
author.

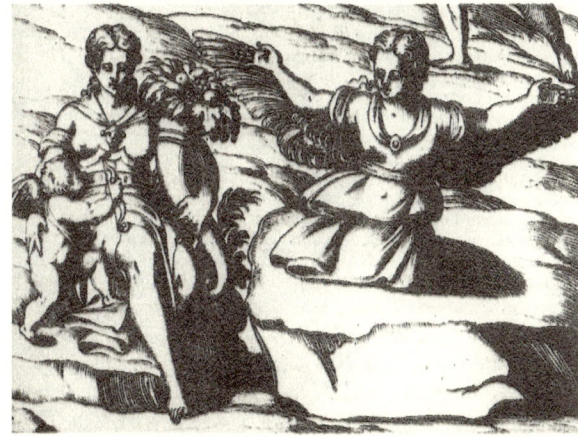

Fig. 13. Paolo Giovio, Medici Impresa *Semper*. In *Ragionamento dell'impese* (Rome, 1555), from Jacopo Gelli, *Divise, Motti e Imprese* (Turin: Ulrico Hoepli, 1976), 438. Photo credit: author.

Bibliography

Consulted Archival and Manuscripts Source

Archivio di Stato di Firenze, Raccolta Sebregondi, pezzo n° 4000.
Archivio di Stato di Firenze, Carte Ceramelli Papiani, pezzo n° 3570.
Archivio di Stato di Firenze, Decime Granducali, pezzi n° 2997, n° 3020, n° 3024, n° 3119, n° 3234.
Archivio di Stato di Firenze, Ufficiali poi Magistrato della Grascia, pezzi n° 192 e 193, bobine 8 e 9.
Biblioteca Nazionale Centrale di Firenze, Repertorio Gargani, pezzo n° 1469, "Panciatichi."
Biblioteca Nazionale Centrale di Firenze, Fondo Magliabechiano, classe XXV, n° 401.
Biblioteca Nazionale Centrale di Firenze, Fondo Magliabechiano, classe VII, n° 263.
Biblioteca Nazionale Centrale di Firenze, Fondo Magliabechiano, classe VII, n° 115.

Selected Bibliography

Acidini Luchinat, Cristina, et al. *The Medici, Michelangelo and the Art of Late Renaissance Florence*. Exhibition Catalogue. New Haven, CT, and London: Yale University Press, 2002.

Agosti, Giovanni, and Vincenzo Farinella. *Michelangelo e L'Arte Classica*. Exhibition Catalogue. Florence: Cantini, 1987.

Agoston, Laura Camille. "Male/Female, Italy/Flanders, Michelangelo/Vittoria Colonna." *Renaissance Quarterly* 58, no. 4 (2005), 1175–1219.

Alberti, Leon Battista. *On Painting and On Sculpture: The Latin Texts of De pictura and De statua*. Ed. Cecil Grayson. London: Phaidon Press Ltd., 1972.

———. *On the Art of Building in Ten Books* [*De re aedificatoria*]. Trans. Joseph Rykwert, Neil Leach, and Robert Tavernor. Cambridge, MA, and London: MIT Press, 1988.

Alciato, Andrea. *Emblemata: Diverse Imprese*. Lyon: Macé Bonhomme for Guillaume Ruille, 1551.

_____, ed. *Emblematum liber d'A. Alciati*. Augsburg, 1531 and 1550.

Alighieri, Dante. *Commedia-Inferno*. Ed. Anna Maria Chiavacci Leonardi. Milan: Mondadori, 1991.

Allen, Michael J.B. *Marsilio Ficino and the Phaedran Charioteer*. Los Angeles: University of California Press, 1981.

_____. *The Platonism of Marsilio Ficino*. Los Angeles: University of California Press, 1984.

Allen, P.S. *Opus Epistolarum: Des Erasmi Roterodami*. 12 vols. Oxford: Clarendon Press, 1906–58. 5:534–36, no.1488.

Aloia, Elena. *I Panciatichi degli Uffizi, Tesi di Laurea, Facoltà di Lettere e Filosofia, Corso di Laurea Specialità in Storia dell'Arte*. Perugia: University of Perugia, 2008–09.

Alpers, Svetlana. *The Art of Describing: Dutch Art in the Seventeenth Century*. Chicago, IL: University of Chicago Press, 1983.

Ames-Lewis, Francis. "Early Medicean Devices." *Journal of the Warburg and Courtauld Institutes* 42 (1979), 122–43.

Anderson, Ruth Matilda. *Hispanic Costume*. New York: Hispanic Society of America, 1979.

Andreoni, Annalisa. "La *Lezzione seconda* sulla grammatica di Benedetto Varchi." *Nuova Rivista di Letturatura Italiana* 6, nos. 1–2 (2003), 137–68.

Aristotle. *Retorica e Poetica di Aristotele in volgare*. Trans. and commentary by Bernardo Segni. Florence, 1549.

Armenini, Giovanni Battista. *De' veri precetti della pittura* (Ravenna, 1587). Ed. Marina Goreri. Turin: Einaudi, 1988.

Aston, Margaret. *The King's Bedpost: Reformation and Iconography in a Tudor Group Portrait*, Cambridge: Cambridge University Press, 1993.

Baader, Hannah. "Anonym: *Sua Cuique Persona*: Maske, Rolle, Porträt (ca. 1520)." In *Porträt. Herausgegeben von Rudolf Preimesberger*. Eds. Rudolf Preimesberger, H. Baader, and N. Suthor. Berlin: Reimer, 1999. 239–46.

Baccheschi, Edi, ed. *L'opera completa del Bronzino. Introdotta da scritti del pittore e coordinata*. Milan: Rizzoli, 1973.

Baia, Anna. *Leonora di Toledo, Duchessa di Firenze e Siena*. Todi: Z. Foglietti, 1907.

Bambach, Carmen C., Janet Cox-Rearick, and George R. Goldner, eds. With contributions by Philippe Costamagna, Marzia Faietti, and Elizabeth Pilliod, *The Drawings of Bronzino*. New Haven, CT: Yale University Press, 2010.

Barasch, Moshe. *Theories of Art*. New York: New York University Press, 1986.

Barilli, Renato. *Maniera moderna e manierismo*. Milan: Feltrinelli Editore, 2004.

Barker, William Watson. *The Adages of Erasmus*. Toronto: University of Toronto Press, 2005, 2010, and 2012.

Barocchi, Paola, ed. *Giorgio Vasari, La Vita di Michelangelo*. 5 vols. Milan: Riccardo Ricciardi, 1962.

_____. *Trattati d'Arte del Cinquecento, fra manierismo e controriforma*. 3 vols. Bari: Laterza, 1960–62.

Barolsky, Paul. *Infinite Jest: Wit and Humor in Italian Renaissance Art*. Columbia: University of Missouri Press, 1990.

Barucco, Pierre. *Le maniérisme italien*. Paris: Presses Universitares de France, 1981.

Battiferri, Laura. *Laura Battiferra and her Literary Circle: An Anthology: A Bilingual Edition*. Ed. and trans. Victoria Kirkham. Chicago, IL: University of Chicago Press, 2006.

_____. *Il primo libro dell'opere toscane*. Ed. Enrico Maria Guidi. Urbino: Accademia Raffaello, 2000.

_____. *I sette salmi*. Ed. Enrico Maria Guidi. Urbino: Accademia Raffaello, 2005.

Baxandall, Michael. *Giotto and the Orators: Humanist Observers of Painting in Italy and the Discovery of Pictorial Composition*. Oxford: Oxford University Press, 1971.

Beard, Mary, ed. *Religions of Rome: A History*. Cambridge: Cambridge University Press, 1998.

Bellia, Simonetta La Barbera. *Il paragone delle arti: nella teoria artistica del Cinquecento*. Rome: Cafaro, 1997; digitized by Ann Arbor: The University of Michigan Press, 2009.

Berti, Luciano. *Pontormo e il suo tempo*. Florence: Banca Toscana, 1993.

_____. *Il principe dello studiolo*. Florence: Edam, 1967.

Betts, John T. *A Glance at the Italian Inquisition: A Sketch of Pietro Carnesecchi: His Trial Before the Court of the Papal Inquisition and His Martyrdom In 1566*.Whitefish, MT: Kessinger Publishing, 2010.

Becherucci, Luisa. *Manieristi toscani*. Bergamo: Istituto italiano d'arti grafiche, 1944.

Bellosi, Luciano. "Il ritratto fiorentino del Cinquecento." In *Firenze e la Toscana dei Medici nell'Europa del Cinquecento. Il primato del disegno*. Florence: Centro di edizioni, 1980. 39–46.

Berger, Jr., Harry. *The Absence of Grace: Sprezzatura and Suspicion in two Renaissance courtesy books*. Stanford, CA: Stanford University Press, 2000.

_____. *Fictions of the Pose: Rembrandt against the Italian Renaissance*. Stanford, CA: Stanford University Press, 2000.

Bertelli, Sergio. *Il corpo del re: Sacralità del potere nell'Europa medievale e moderna*. Florence: Ponte Alle Grazie, 1990.

Bertoli, Gustavo. "Luterani e anabattisti processati a Firenze nel 1552." *Archivio Storico Italiano* 154, no. 3 (1996), 59–122.

Biedermann, Hans. *A Dictionary of Symbols*. New York: Meridian Books, 1992.

530   Bibliography

Biondi, Albano. "La Giustificazione della Simulazione nel Cinquecento." In idem, *Eresia e Riforma nell' Italia del Cinquecento, Miscellanea I.* DeKalb: Northern Illinois University Press, Chicago: The Newberry Library, and Florence: Sansoni, 1974. 7–68.

Blumenberg, Hans. *Schiffbruch mit Zuschauer. Paradigma einer Daseinsmetapher.* 1979; Frankfurt am Main: Suhrkamp Verlag, 1997.

Blunt, Anthony. *Artistic Theory in Italy.* Oxford: Oxford University Press, 1968.

Bacou, R., and C. Monbeig-Goguel. "Giorgio Vasari: *Prudenza.*" *Revue de l'Art* (1968), 88–92.

Boccaccio, Giovanni. *Famous Women.* Trans. Virginia Brown. Cambridge, MA: Harvard University Press, 2001.

Bodart, Diane. "Bodart on Spanish Portraiture." Review of Joanna Woodall, *Anthonis Mor: Art and Authority,* 2007, and Laura R. Bass, *The Drama of the Portrait: Theater and Visual Culture in Early Modern Spain,* 2008. *The Art Bulletin* 94, no. 2 (June 2012), 301–05.

Borghini, Raffaello. *Il Riposo.* 1584; Milan: Edizioni Labor, 1967 (facsimile reprint).

_____. *Il Riposo.* 1584; Milan: Società Tipografica de'Classici Italiani, 1807.

Borinski, K. *Die Antike in Poetik und Kunsttheorie von Ausgang des klassichen Altertums bis auf Goethe und Wilhelm von Humboldt.* 2 vols. Leipzig: K.F. Koehler, 1914–24.

Bosch, Lynette M.F. *Art, Liturgy and Legend in Renaissance Toledo.* University Park: Pennsylvania State University Press, 2000.

_____. "Bronzino's London Allegory: Love versus Time." *Source: Notes in the History of Art* 9, no. 2 (Winter 1990), 30–35.

Brendel, Otto J. *Prolegomena to the Study of Roman Art.* Foreword by Jerome J. Pollitt. New Haven, CT: Yale University Press, 1979.

Brock, Maurice. *Bronzino.* Paris: Flammarion, 2002.

Bronzino, Agnolo. *Agnolo Bronzino. Rime in burla.* Ed. Franca Petrucci Nardelli. Rome: Istituto della Enciclopedia Italiana, 1988.

Brown, Clifford M., ed. *Engraved Gems: Survivals and Revivals.* Washington: National Gallery of Art, 1997.

Budge, Wallis. *Magia egizie.* Rome: Newton, 1980.

Burroughs, Charles. "Michelangelo at the Campidoglio: Artistic Identity, Patronage, and Manufacture." *Artibus et Historiae* 14, no. 28 (1993), 85–111.

Cagliotti, Francesco. *Donatello e I Medici: Storia del David e della Giuditta,* 2 vols. Florence: Olschiki, 2000.

_____. Il Perduto 'David Mediceo' di Giovanfrancesco Rustici e il 'David' Pulszky del Louvre." *Prospettiva* 83–84 (July–Oct. 1996), 80–101.

Callahan, Virginia W. "The Erasmus-Alciati Friendship." In *Acta Conventus Neo-Latini Lovaniensis.* Munich: Fink, 1973. 133–41.

_____. "The Erasmus-Hercules Equation in the Emblems of Alciati." In *The Verbal and the Visual: Essays in Honor of William Sebastian Heckscher*. Eds. Karl-Ludwig Selig and Elizabeth Sears. Studies in Art & History. New York: Italica Press, 1990. 41–58. Kindle Edition. (Kindle Location 3345).

_____. "The Mirror of Princes: Erasmian Echoes in Alciati's liber Emblematum." In *Acta Conventus Neo-Latini Amstelodamensis*. Munich: Fink, 1979. 183–96.

Campbell, Malcolm. "Il ritratto del Duca Alessandro de'Medici di Giorgio Vasari: contesto e significato." In *Giorgio Vasari tra decorazione ambientale e storiografia artistica*. Ed. G.C. Garfagnini. Florence: Olschki, 1985. 339–61.

Campione, Francesco Paolo. *La regola del Capriccio. Alle origini di una idea estetica*. Palermo, Centro Internazionale di Studi di Estetica, 2011.

Caponetto, Salvatore. *La riforma protestante nell'Italia del Cinquecento*. Turin: Claudiana, 1997.

Caro, Annibale. *Lettere Familiari*. Ed. Aulo Greco. Florence: Sansoni, 1957–61.

Carocci, Guido. *I dintorni di Firenze*. Florence: Galletti & Cocci, 1906–07.

Cartari, Vincenzo. *Imagini delli Dei de gl' Antichi*. Ed. Marco Bussagli. Genoa: Nuova Stile Regina, 1987.

Castiglione. *Il Cortegiano*. Trans. C. Singleton. Garden City, NY: Doubleday, 1959.

_____. *Il Libro del Cortegiano con una scelta delle Opere Minore di Baldassare Castiglione*. Ed. Bruno Maier. Turin: Unione Tipografico-Editrice Torinese, 1973.

Cecchi, Alessandro. *Agnolo Bronzino*. Florence: Scala, 1996.

_____. "Il Bronzino, Benedetto Varchi e l'Accademia Fiorentina: Ritratti di poeti, letterati e personaggi illustri della corte Medicea." *Antichità viva*, 30, nos. 1, 2 (1991), 17- 28.

_____. "Entry 18: Pietro Candido, Ritratto di Giuliano de' Medici, duca di Nemours, 1586." In *Pieter de Witte, Pietro Candido: un pittore del Cinquecento tra Volterra e Monaco*. Eds. Mariagiulia Burresi and Alessandro Cecchi. Exhibition Catalogue, Volterra, Palazzo dei Priori, 31 May–Nov. 9, 2009. Milan: Cinisello Balsamo, 2009. 130.

_____. "Il Maggiordomo Ducale Pierfrancesco Riccio e Gli Artisti Della Corte Medicea." *Mitteilungen des Kunsthistorischen Institutes in Florenz* 42, no. 1 (1998), 115–43.

_____. "Pratica fierezza e terribilità nelle grottesche di Marco da Faenza in Palazzo Vecchio a Firenze." *Paragone* (1977), 25–28.

_____. "La 'Prudenza' del Bronzino per Ser Carolo Gherardi." *Antichità viva* 26 (1987). 19–21.

Cecchi, Alessandro, and Antonio Natali, eds. *L'officina della maniera: varietà e fierezza nell'arte fiorentina del Cinquecento fra le due repubbliche (1494–1530)*. Florence: Giunta, and Venice: Marsilio, 1996.

Cesariano, Cesare, ed. *Di Lucio Vitruvio Pollione De architectura libri dece traducti de latino in vulgare, affigurati, commentati*. (Como: Gotardus de Ponte, 1521.), Bks. 2–4, trans. in Italian by Alessandro Rovetta. Milan: V&P Università, 2002.

Chastel, André. "L'Art de la Signature." *Revue de l'Art* 26 (1974), 8–14.

_____. *Marsile Ficin et L'Art*. Geneva: Droz, 1975.

_____. *The Sack of Rome, 1527*. Trans. Beth Archer. Princeton, NJ: Princeton University Press, 1983.

Cheney, Liana De Girolami. *Botticelli's Neoplatonic Images*. Potomac, MD: Scripta Humanistica, 1993.

_____. "Giorgio Vasari's *Allegory of Prudence*: Mirroring Alciato and Valeriano's Emblems." *Emblem Studies* 7 (2009), 26–37.

_____. "Giorgio Vasari's and Cesare Ripa's *Iconologia*: The Chamber of Fortune's Allegories of Virtues in the Casa Vasari." *Exploration in Renaissance Culture* (Summer 2008), 35–45.

_____. *Giorgio Vasari's Prefaces: Art & Theory*. Foreword by Wolfram Prinz. New York and London: Peter Lang, 2012.

_____. *The Homes of Giorgio Vasari*. New York/London: Peter Lang, 2006.

_____. ed. *Readings in Italian Mannerism*. Foreword by Craig Hugh Smyth. New York and London: Peter Lang, 1997; revised edn. 2005.

Cheney, Liana De Girolami, and Sonia Michelotti Bonetti. "Bronzino's *Pygmalion and Galatea: l' antica bella maniera*" *Discoveries* 24, no. 1 (August 2007). Posted on 15 September 2011 by anydam <http://www.scrc.us.com/discoveries/bronzinos-pygmalion-and-galatea-1%e2%80%99-antica-bella-maniera/pdf>.

Chevalier, Jean, and Alain Gheerbrant. *A Dictionary of Symbols*. London: Blackwell, 1994.

Christiansen, Keith, and Stefan Weppelmann, eds. *The Renaissance Portrait from Donatello to Bellini*. Exhibition Catalogue. New York: The Metropolitan Museum of Art, 2011. Distributed by Yale University Press, New Haven, CT, and London.

Cicero, Marcus Tullius. *De Oratore*. Trans. E.W. Sutton and H. Rackham. 2 vols. Cambridge, MA: Harvard University Press, 1960.

Civai, Alessandra. *Dipinti e Sculture in Casa Martelli. Storia di una collezione patrizia fiorentina dal Quattrocento all'Ottocento*. Florence: Opus Libri, 1990.

_____. "Il Gabinetto di Belle Arti in Palazzo Martelli a Firenze." *Proporzioni* n.s. 1 2000 (2001), 216–40.

Clapp, Frederick Mortimer. *Les dessins de Pontormo: catalogue raisonné précédé d'une étude critique*. Paris: Universitè de Paris, 1914.

Cochrane, Eric. *Florence in the Forgotten Centuries 1527–1800: A History of Florence and the Florentines in the Age of the Grand Dukes*. London and Chicago, IL: University of Chicago Press, 1973.

Cole, Michael, ed. *Sixteenth Century Italian Art*. Malden, MA: Blackwell Publishing, 2006.

Collareta, Marco. "L'historien et la technique: Sur le rôle de l'orfèvrerie dans les *Vite* de Vasari." In *Histoire de l'histoire de lárt*. Ed. Édouard Pommier. Paris: Klincksieck, 1995. 163–76. Repr. as "The Historian and the Technique: On the Role of Goldsmithery in Vasari's *Lives*." In *Sixteenth-Century Italian Art*. Ed. Michael W. Cole. Malden, MA: Blackwell Publishing, 2006. 291–300.

_____. "Michelangelo e le statue antiche: un probabile intervento di restauro." *Prospettiva* 43 (1985), 51–55.

Conti, Giusto de. *La bella mano: Di Giusto de' Conti romano senatore e una raccolta delle rime antiche di diversi Toscani*. Florence: J. Guiducci e Santi Franchi, 1715; and Verona: Giannalberto Tumermani, 1732.

Continelli, Valentina. *Guardaroba di cose rare et preciose: Lo studiolo di Francesco I de'Medici, Arte, Storia e Significat*. Lugano: Agorà Publishing, 2007.

Cooper, J.C. *An Illustrated Encyclopaedia of Traditional Symbols*. London: Thames and Hudson, 1978.

_____. *Symbolic and Mythological Animals*. London: The Aquarian Press, 1992.

Corti, Laura. *Vasari, catalogo completo*. Florence: Cantini Editore, 1989.

_____. et al. *Vasari: Principi, letterati e artisti nelle carte di Giorgio Vasari*. Florence: Edam, 1981.

Costamagna, Philippe. "De la *fiorentinità* des portraits de Pontormo et de Bronzino." *Paragone* 62 (2005), 50–75.

_____. "De l'idéal de beauté aux problèmes d'attribution. Vingt ans de recherche sur le portrait florentin au XVIe siècle." *Studiolo. Revue de l'histoire de l'art de l'Académie de France à Rome* 1 (2002), 193–220.

_____. "Nouvelles considérations sur un 'Portrait d'homme' de Pontormo." *Paragone* 59 (2005), 65–72.

_____. *Pontormo, catalogue raisonné de l'oeuvre peint*. Paris: Gallimard, 1994.

_____. "Portraits of Florentine Exiles." In *Raphael, Cellini and A Renaissance Banker: The Patronage of Bindo Altoviti*, Exhibition Catalogue. Eds. A. Chong, D. Pegazzano, and D. Zikos. Boston: Isabella Stewart Museum of Art, 2003. 329–32.

_____. "Seconda Parte–Les Portraits." *Antichità Viva* 27, no. 1 (1988), 23–30.

Costamagna, Philippe, and Carlo Falciani. "Le Christ en Croix d'Agnolo Bronzino peint pour Bartolomeo Panciatichi." *Revue de l'Art* 168, no. 2 (2010), 45–52.

Cox-Rearick, Janet. "Art at the Court of Duke Cosimo I de' Medici (1537–

1574)." In *The Medici, Michelangelo and the Art of Late Renaissance Florence* Ed. Alan P. Darr, et al. New Haven, CT: Yale University Press, 2002. 35–35 and 153–54.

_____. *Bronzino's Chapel of Eleonora in the Palazzo Vecchio.* Berkeley: University of California Press, 1993.

_____. "Bronzino's Crossing of the Red Sea and Moses Appointing Joshua: Prolegomena to the Chapel of Eleonora di Toledo." *The Art Bulletin* 69 (1987), 45–67.

_____. "Bronzino's *Young Woman with Her Little Boy*." *Studies in the History of Art* 12 (1982), 67–79.

_____. *La Collection de François I^ier^.* Antwerp: Fonds Mercator Paribas, 1995.

_____. "Les Dessins de Bronzino pour la Chapelle d' Eleonora au Palazzo Vecchio." *Revue de l'Art* 14 (1971), 7–22.

_____. *Dynasty and Destiny in Medici Art: Pontormo, Leo X and the Two Cosimos.* Princeton, NJ: Princeton University Press, 1984.

_____. "From Bandinelli to Bronzino." *The Burlington Magazine* 129 (1987), 155–62.

_____. "From Bandinelli to Bronzino: The Genesis of the *Lamentation* for the Chapel of Eleonora di Toledo." *Mitteilungen des Kunsthistorischen Institutes in Florenz* 33 (1989), 37–84.

_____. *An Important Painting by Pontormo from the Collection of Chauncey D.*
_____. *lman.* New York: Christie's, 1989.

_____. "Power-Dressing at the Courts of Cosimo de' Medici and François I: The 'moda alla spagnola' of Spanish Consorts Eléonore d'Autriche and Eleonora di Toledo." *Artibus et Historiae* 30, no. 60 (2009), 39–69.

Cox-Rearick, Janet, and Mary Westerman Bulgarella. "Public and Private Portraits of Cosimo de' Medici and Eleonora di Toledo: Bronzino's Paintings of His Ducal Patrons in Ottawa and Turin." *Artibus et Historiae* 25, no. 49 (2004), 101–59.

Cropper, Elizabeth. "The Beauty of Women: Problems in the Rhetoric of Renaissance Portraiture." In *Rewriting the Renaissance: The Discourse of Sexual Difference in Early Modern Europe.* Eds. M. Ferguson, M. Quilligan, and N. Vickers. Chicago, IL, and London: University of Chicago Press, 1986. 175–90.

_____. "The Place of Beauty in the High Renaissance and its Displacement in the History of Art." In Alvin Vos, *Place and Displacement in the Renaissance,* Conference Publication (Binghamton, NY: Medieval & Renaissance Texts & Studies, 1995). 159–205.

_____. *Pontormo: Portrait of a Halberdier.* Los Angeles, CA: Getty Museum, 1997.

_____. "Portrait of a Lady (La Monaca)," Entry 39, and "Portrait Cover with Mask and Grotesques," Cat. Entry 36. In *Virtue and Beauty, Leon-*

ardo's Ginevra de'Benci and Renaissance Portraits of Women. Princeton, NJ: Princeton University Press, 2001.

_____. "Preparing to Finish. Portraits by Pontormo and Bronzino around 1530." In *Opere e giorni. Studi su mille anni di arte europea dedicati a Max Seidel*. Eds. K. Bergdolt and G. Bonsanti. Venice: Marsilio, 2001. 499–504. Repr. in *Sixteenth-Century Italian Art*. Ed. Michael Cole (Malden, MA: Blackwell, 2006), 177–81.

_____. "Prolegomena to a New Interpretation of Bronzino's Florentine Portraits." In *Renaissance Studies in Honor of Craig Hugh Smyth*. Eds. Andrew Morrough, Fiorella Gioffredi Superbi, et al. 2 vols. Florence: Villa I Tatti, The Harvard University Center for Italian Renaissance Studies, 1985. 1:149–60.

_____. "Pygmalion and Galatea." In *Bronzino: Artist and Poet at the Court of the Medici*. Eds. Carlo Falciani and Antonio Natali. Florence: Mandragora, 2010. 76–78.

_____. "Reading Bronzino's Florentine Portraits (Per una lettura dei ritratti di Bronzino)." In *Bronzino: Painter and Poet at the Court of the Medici*. Eds. Carlo Falciani and Antonio Natali. Florence: Mandragora, 2010. 245–55.

Curran, Brian. *The Egyptian Renaissance: The Afterlife of Ancient Egypt in Early Modern Italy*. Chicago, IL: The University of Chicago Press, 2007.

Daniel, Ladislav. *The Florentine: Art from the Time of the Medici Grand Dukes*. Prague: Národní Galerie v Praze, 2002.

Danti, Vicenzo. *Il primo libro del trattato delle perfette proporzioni*. Florence: Giunti, 1567.

Del Turco Rosselli, Niccolò, and Federica Salvi, eds. *Bartolomeo Ammannati, Scultore e Architetto 1511–1592*. Florence: Alinea editrice, 1995.

De Luca, Francesca. "Bronzino in Florentine Dynastic Collections: *diligenza* and *prestezza*." In *Bronzino: Artist and Poet at the Court of the Medici*. Eds. Carlo Falciani and Antonio Natali. Florence: Mandragora, 2010. 339–44.

Deleuze, Gilles. *The Fold: Leibniz and the Baroque*. Trans. Tom Conley. Minneapolis: University of Minnesota Press, 1993.

Denham, A.E., ed. *Plato on Art and Beauty*. New York: Palgrave Macmillan, 2012.

Dempsey, Charles. "The Greek Style and the Prehistory of Neoclassicism." In Elizabeth Cropper, *Pietro Testa, 1612–1650: Prints and Drawings*. Philadelphia: Philadelphia Museum of Art, 1988. xxxvii–lxv.

_____. "Portraits and Masks in the Art of Lorenzo de'Medici, Botticelli, and Politian's *Stanze per la Giostra*." *Renaissance Quarterly* 52 (1999), 1–42.

Derrida, Jacques. *The Truth in Painting*. Trans. Geoff Bennington and I.

McLeod. Chicago, IL: University of Chicago Press, 1987. Originally published as *La Vérité en Peinture*, Paris: Flammarion, 1978.

Dolce's Dialogo della Pittura (1557). Trans. M. Roskill. New York: New York University Press, 1968.

Draper, J. *Vasari's Decorations in the Palazzo Vecchio: The Ragionamenti*. Diss., University of North Carolina, 1973.

Eisenbichler, Konrad. "Bronzino's Portrait of Guidobaldo II della Rovere." In *Desire and Discipline in the Premodern West*. Eds. Jacqueline Murray and Konrad Eisenbichler. Toronto: Toronto University Press, 1966. 21–33.

_____, ed. *The Cultural Politics of Duke Cosimo I de' Medici*. Aldershot: Ashgate, 2001.

_____, ed. *The Cultural World of Eleonora di Toledo, Duchess of Florence Siena*. Aldershot: Ashgate, 2004.

Eisenbichler, Konrad, and Olga Zorzi Puglies, eds. *Ficino and Renaissance Neoplatonism*. Toronto: Dovehouse Editions, 1986.

Edelstein, Bruce L. "Bronzino in the Service of Eleonora di Toledo and Cosimo I de' Medici: Conjugal Patronage and the Painter Courtier." In *Beyond Isabella: Secular Women Patrons of Art in Renaissance Italy*. Eds. Sheryl E. Reiss and David G. Wilkins. Kirksville, MO: Truman State University Press, 2001. 225–62.

_____. *The Early Patronage of Eleonora di Toledo: The Camera Verde and its Dependencies in the Palazzo Vecchio*. Ph.D. diss., Harvard University, 1995.

_____. "*Nobildonne napoletane e committenza: Eleonora d'Aragona ed Eleonora di Toledo a confronto*." *Quaderni Storici* 104 (2000), 295–329.

_____. "Observations on the Genesis and Function of Bronzino's Frankfurt *Modello* for the Vault Decoration in the Chapel of Eleonora." In *Coming About: A Festschrift for John Shearman*. Eds. Lars R. Jones and Louisa C. Matthew. Cambridge, MA: Harvard University Art Museums, 2001. 157–63.

Emiliani, Andrea. *Il Bronzino*. Busto Arsizio: Bramante Editrice, 1960.

_____. *Bronzino*. Milan: Fabbri, 1966.

Erasmus, Desiderius. *The Adages of Erasmus*. Ed. William Barker. Toronto: University of Toronto Press, 2001.

_____. *Adagia: Sei saggi politici in forma di proverbi*. Ed. Silvana Seidel Menchi. Turin: Einaudi, 1980 (1st edition Basel: Froben, 1517).

_____. *The Collected Works of Erasmus, Adages II vii I to III iii 100*, vol. 34. Ed. R.A.B. Mynors. Toronto: University of Toronto Press, 1992.

_____. "Copia: Foundations of the Abundant Style (*De duplici copia verborum ac rerum commentarii duo*)." *Collected Works of Erasmus*, vol. 24. Ed. Craig R. Thompson. Toronto: University of Toronto Press, 1978.

_____. *Opera Omnia, IV/3*. Ed. Clarence H. Miller. 3 vols. Amsterdam: North Holland, 1979 (first ed. Paris: before 1511).

Eschenburg, Barbara. *Pygamlions Werkstatt*. Cologne: Lenbachhaus München, 2001.

Falciani, Carlo. "Il Bronzino e i Panciatichi." In *Bronzino. Pittore e poeta alla corte dei Medici*. Eds. Antonio Natali and Carlo Falciani. Exhibition, Florence, Palazzo Strozzi, 24 September 2010–23 January 2011. Florence, Mandragora, 2010. 153–65.

_____. "Della pittura sacra, ma anche di 'fianchi, stomachi." In *Bronzino. Pittore e poeta alla corte dei Medici*. Eds. Antonio Natali and Carlo Falciani. Exhibition, Florence, Palazzo Strozzi, 24 September 2010–23 January 2011. Florence, Mandragora, 2010. 277–95.

Falciani, Carlo, and Antonio Natali, eds. *Bronzino: Artist and Poet at the Court of the Medici*. Florence: Mandragora, 2010.

Ficino. Marsilio. *Meditations on the Soul: Selected Letters of Marsilio Ficino*. Ed. and trans. Clement Salaman. Rochester, VT: Inner Traditions International, 1996.

Filipczak, Zirka S. *Hot Dry Men and Cold Wet Women: The Theory of Humors in Western European Art: 1575–1700*. New York: The American Federation of Arts, 1997.

Firenzuola, Agnolo. *Dialogo delle Bellezze delle donne*. Venice, 1552.

Firpo, Massimo. "Bronzino and the Medici." In *Bronzino: Artist and Poet at the Court of the Medici*. Eds. Carlo Falciani and Antonio Natali. Florence: Mandragora, 2010. 91–99.

_____. *Gli affreschi di Pontormo a San Lorenzo. Eresia, politica e cultura nella Firenze di Cosimo I*. Turin: Giulio Einaudi Editore, 1997.

Fragnito, Gigliola. "Un Pratese alla corte di Cosimo I." *Archivio Storico Pratese* 62 (1986), 31–83.

Freedberg, David. "Warburg's Masks: A Study in Idolatry." In *Anthropologies of Art*. Proceedings of the Clark Conference on Anthropologies of Art, April 25–26, at the Sterling and Francine Clark Art Institute. Ed. Mariët Westermann. Dalton, MA: Studley Press, 2005. 3–25.

Freedberg, Sidney J. *Painting in Italy 1500–1600*. Baltimore, MD: Penguin Books, Pelican History of Art, 1971.

Freier, Mark R. *Time Measured by Kairos and Kronos*. 2006. N.P. <http://www.whatifenterprises.com/whatif/whatiskairos.pdf>.

Frick, Carole Collier. *Dressing Renaissance Florence: Families, Fortunes, and Fine Clothing*. Baltimore: Johns Hopkins University Press, 2002.

Foster, Leonard. *The Icy Fire: Five Studies in European Petrarchism*. Cambridge: Cambridge University Press, 1969.

Francini, Carlo, ed. *Palazzo Vecchio: Officina di opera e di ingegno*. Florence: Silvana, 2006.

Furey, Constance M. *Erasmus, Contarini, and the Religious Republic of Letters*. Cambridge: Cambridge University Press, 2006.

Furno, Albertina. *La vita e le rime di Angiolo Bronzino*. Pistoia: Kessinger Publishing 1902; reissued 2009.

Gaisser, Julia Haig. *Pierio Valeriano on the Ill Fortune of Learned Men*. Ann Arbor: University of Michigan Press, 1999.

Gáldy, Andrea. "Tuscan Concerns and Spanish Heritage in the Decoration of Duchess Eleonora's Apartment in the Palazzo Vecchio." *Renaissance Studies* 20, no. 3 (June 2006), 293–319.

_____. *Agnolo Bronzino: Medici Court Artist in Context*. Newcastle-upon-Tyne: Cambridge Scholars Publishing, 2013.

Gáldy, Andrea M., and Robert G. La France. "Golden Chambers for Eleonora of Toledo: Duchess and Collector in Palazzo Vecchio." In *Women Patrons and Collectors*. Eds. Susan Bracken and Adriana Turpin. Newcastle upon Tyne: Cambridge Scholars Publishing, 2012. 1–34.

Garner, Barbara Carman. "Francis Bacon, Natalis Comes and the Mythological Tradition." *Journal of the Warburg and Courtauld Institutes* 33 (1970), 264–91.

Gaston, Robert W. "Eleonora di Toledo's Chapel: Lineage, Salvation and the War Against the Turks." In *The Cultural World of Eleonora di Toledo: Duchess of Florence and Siena*. Ed. Konrad Eisenbichler. Aldershot: Ashgate, 2004. 157–81.

_____. "Love's Sweet Poison: A New Reading of Bronzino's London *Allegory*." *I Tatti Studies* 4 (1991), 247–88.

_____. "Towards a Postmodernist Bronzino." In *Agnolo Bronzino: Medici Court Artist in Context*. Ed. Andrea M. Gáldy. Newcastle upon Tyne: Cambridge Scholars Publishing, 2013. 107–28.

Geremicca, Antonio. *Agnolo Bronzino: "La dotta penna al pennel dotto pari."* Rome: Universitalia, 2013.

Gilbert, Creighton. *Michelangelo: On and Off the Sistine Ceiling. Selected Essays*. New York: Braziller, 1994.

Giambullari, Pierfrancesco. *Apparato et feste nelle nozze dello illvstrissimo signor duca di Firenze, & della duchessa sua consorte, con le sue stanze, madriali, comedia & intermedij in quelle recitati*. Florence, 1539.

Ginzburg, Carlo. *I Costituti di Don Pietro Manelfi*. DeKalb: Northern Illinois University Press, 1970.

Giordano, Michael. "The *Blason anatomique* and Related Fields: Emblematics, Nominalism, Mannerism, and Descriptive Anatomy as Illustrated by Maurice Scève's *Blason de la gorge*." In *An Interregnum of the Sign: The Emblematic Age in France: Essays in Honor of Daniel Russell*. Ed. David Graham. Glasgow: University of Glasgow, 2001. 121–48.

Giovio, Paolo. *Dialogo dell'Imprese Militari et Amorose* (1554). Eds. L. Domenichi and G. Simeoini. Lyon: Guglielmo Rovillio, 1574.

Goldschmidt, Fritz. *Pontormo, Rosso und Bronzino*. Diss., Leipzig University, 1911.

Gombrich, Ernst H. "Icones Symbolicae." In *Symbolic Images: Studies in the Art of the Renaissance II*. 2nd edn. New York: E.P. Dutton, 1978. 132–34.
_____. *The Heritage of Apelles*. New York: Cornell University Press, 1976.

Gowens, Kenneth, and Sheryl Reiss, eds. *The Pontificate of Clement VII: History, Politics, Culture*. Aldershot: Ashgate, 2005.

Green, Henry. *Andrea Alciati and His Books of Emblems: A Biographical and Bibliographical Study*. London: Trübner, 1872. Repr. New York: B. Franklin, n.d.

_____. *Andreae Alciati Emblematum fontes quatuor*. Manchester: Holbein Society 4 [reprints of Augsburg 1531, Paris 1534, and Venice 1546].

Greenblatt, Stephen. *The Swerve: How the World Became Modern*. New York: Norton, 2011.

Grendler, Paul F. *Critics of the Italian World, 1530–1560: Anton Francesco Doni, Nicolò Franco and Ortensio Lando*. Madison: University of Wisconsin Press, 1960.

Hale, J.R. *Florence and the Medici: The Pattern of Control*. London: Thames and Hudson, 1977.

Hall, James. *Dictionary of Subjects and Symbols in Art*. New York: Harper and Row, 1974.

Hall, Marcia B. *Color and Meaning: Practice and Theory in Renaissance Painting*. Cambridge: Cambridge University Press, 1992.

Hagstrum, Jean H. *Sister Arts: The Tradition of Literary Pictorialism and the English Poetry from Dryden to Gray*. Chicago, IL: Chicago University Press, 1958.

Harbison, Craig. *The Mirror of the Artist: Northern Renaissance Art in its Historical Context*. New York: Harry N. Abrams, 1995.

_____. "Sexuality and Social Standing in Jan van Eyck's Arnolfini Double Portrait." *Renaissance Quarterly* 43, no. 2 (Summer 1990), 249–91.

Hayum, Andrée. "The Nuns at S. Apollonia and Castagno's Last Supper." *The Art Bulletin* 88, no. 2 (June 2006), 256–62.

Heckscher, William S. "Reflections on Holbein's Portrait of Erasmus at Longford Castle." In *Essays in the History of Art presented to Rudolf Wittkower*. Eds. Douglas Fraser, H. Hibbard, and Milton J. Lewine. London: Phaidon Press. 2nd impression, 1969. 128–48.

Henkel, Arthur, and Albrecht Schone. *Emblemata: Handbuch zur Sinnibildkunst des XVI. und XVII. Jahrhunderts*. Stuttgart: J.B. Metzler, 1967.

The Hieroglyphics of Horapollo. Trans. George Boas. Bollingen Series, 23. New York: Pantheon, 1950.

Hirschboeck, Martin. *Florentinische Palastkapellen unter der ersten Medici-Herzögen (1537–1609)*. Verborgene Orte frommer Selbstdarstellung und konfessioneller Identität, I Mandorli Bd. 12. Berlin and Munich: Deutscher Kunstverlag, 2011.

Holbrook, Richard Thayer. *Portraits of Dante: From Giotto to Raffael*. London: Medici Society, 1911.

Holian, Heather L. Sale. "Family Jewels: The Gendered Marking of Medici Women in Court Portraits of the Late Renaissance." *Mediterranean Studies Journal* 17 (2008), 148–82.

Hollanda, Francesco de (as Holanda). *Dialoghi di Roma* (alternate title *quatro dilogos de pintura antiga*). Ed. Rita Biscetti. Rome: Bagatto Libri, 1993.

_____. *Da pintura antigua*. Lisbon, c. 1541–48.

_____. *I trattati d'arte*. Ed. Grazia Modroni. Livorno: Sillabe, 2003.

Hook, Judith. *The Sack of Rome, 1527*. New York: Macmillan, 1972. Repr. Ann Arbor: University of Michigan Press, 2008.

Horace. *Epistles Book II and Arts poetica*. Trans. H. Rushton Fairclough. Cambridge, MA: Harvard University Press [Loeb Classical Library, No. 194], 1929 revised.

Horace on Poetry: The Ars Poetica. Ed. C.O. Brink. Cambridge: Cambridge University Press, 1971.

Horapollo. *Hieroglyphica*. Ed. Jesus María González de Zárate. Madrid: AKAL, 1991.

Howard, Deborah. "Sebastiano Serlio's Venetian Copyrights." *The Burlington Magazine* 115, no. 895 (1973), 512–16.

The Illustrations from the Works of Andreas Vesalius of Brussels. Ed. and trans., J.B. de C.M. Saunders and Charles D. O'Malley. New York: The World Publishing Company, 1950.

Janson, H.W. "The *Image Made by Chance* in Renaissance Thought." In *De Artibus opuscula XL: Essays in Honor of Erwin Panofsky*. Ed. Millard Meiss. New York: New York University Press, 1961. 254–55.

_____. "The Right Arm of Michelangelo's *Moses*." In *Festschrift Ulrich Middeldorf*. Eds. Antje Kosegarten and Peter Tigler. Berlin: de Gruyter, 1968. 241–47.

Joannides, Paul. "Michelangelo's Lost Hercules." *The Burlington Magazine* 119, no. 893 (1977), 550–55.

_____. "A Supplement to Michelangelo's Lost Hercules." *The Burlington Magazine*, 123 (1981), 20–23.

Joost-Gaugier, Christiane L. "A Rediscovered Series of Uomini Famosi from Quattrocento Venice." *The Art Bulletin* 58, no. 2 (June 1976), 184–95.

Kaske, Carol V., and John R. Clark, eds. and trans. *Marsilio Ficino: Three Books on Life: A Critical Edition and Translation and Notes*. Binghamton, NY: Medieval and Renaissance Texts and Studies, 1989.

Katzenellenbogen, Adolf. *Allegories of the Virtues and Vices in Medieval Art*. New York: W.W. Norton & Company, Inc., 1964.

Kay, Sarah. "Original Skin: Flaying, Reading, and Thinking in the Legend of Saint Bartholomew and Other Works." *Journal of Medieval and Early Modern Studies* 36, no. 1 (Winter 2006), 35–74.

Kent, Dale. "Women in Renaissance Florence." In *Virtue and Beauty: Leonardo's Ginevra de' Benci and Renaissance Portraits of Women*. Ed. David Alan Brown, et al. Washington: National Gallery of Art, and Princeton, NJ: Princeton University, 2001. 25–47.

Kirkham, Victoria. "Dante's Phantom, Petrarch's Specter: Bronzino's Portrait of the Poet Laura Battiferra." In *Visibile parlare: Dante and the Art of the Italian Renaissance. Lectura Dantis*. Ed. Deborah Parker. Special issue of *Lectura Dantis* 22–23 (1998), 63–139.

_____. "Laura Battiferri degli Ammannati's 'First Book' of Poetry: A Renaissance Holograph Comes out of Hiding." *Rinascimento* 36 (1996), 351–91.

Klapisch-Zuber, Christiane. *Women, Family, and Ritual in Renaissance Italy*. Trans. Lydia Cochrane. Chicago, IL: University of Chicago Press, 1985.

Kliemann, Julian. *Gesta Dipinta: The Heroic Fresco: Ancestral Fresco Cycles in Italian Patrician Residences from the 1400s to the 1600s*. Rome: Silvana, 1993.

_____. "Il pensiero di Paolo Giovio nelle pitture eseguite sulle sue 'invenzione.'" In *Paolo Giovio: Il Rinascimento e la memoria*. Conference Proceedings. Como: Societa Storica Comense, 1985. 197–23.

Krautheimer, Richard. "Alberti and Vitruvius." In *Studies in Early Christian, Medieval and Renaissance Art*. New York: New York University Press, 1969. 323–32.

Krinsky, Carol Herselle. "Cesare cesariano and the como vitruvius edition of 1521." Ph.D. diss., New York University, 1965.

_____. *Vitruvius Pollio. Cesare Cesariano 1475–1543*. Munich: Fink, 1969. Offprint.

Landau, David, and Peter Parshall. *The Renaissance Print, 1470–1550*. London: Yale University Press, 1994.

Kristeller, Paul Oskar, ed. and trans. *The Letters of Marsilio Ficino*. 3 vols. New York: Ginko Press, 1985.

Landini, Roberta Orsi. *Moda a Firenze 1540–1580: Cosimo I de' Medici's Style*. Florence: Mauro Paglia Editore, 2011.

Landini, Roberta Orsi, and Bruna Niccoli. *Moda a Firenze 1540–1580: Lo stile di Eleonora di Toledo e la sua influenza*. Florence: Pagaliai Polistampa, 2005.

Langdon, Gabrielle. *Medici Women: Portraits of Power, Love and Betrayal from the Court of Duke Cosimo I*. Toronto: University of Toronto Press, 2006.

Langedijk, Karla. *The Portraits of the Medici: 15th–18th Centuries*. Vol. 1. Florence: Studio per edizioni Scelte, 1981.

Laurenza, Domenico. *Art and Anatomy in Renaissance Italy: Images from a Scientific Revolution*. New York: The Metropolitan Museum of Art, 2012.

_____. *De figura umana: Fisiognomica, anatomia e arte in Leonardo*. Florence: Olschki, 2001.

Lee, Rensselaer. *Ut Pictura Poesis: Humanist Theory of Painting*. New York: W.W. Norton and Company, Inc., 1967.

Leuchner, Eckhard. *Persona, Larva, Maske: Ikonographische Untersuchungen vom 16 bus zum früen 18 Jahrhundert*. Frankfurt-am-Main: Peter Lang, 1997.

Lévi-Strauss, Claude. *Anthropologie structurale*. Paris: Plon, 1958.

Lewis, Douglas. "Bernardo o Antonio Rossellino, David di Casa Martelli [D 55] 1460–1468 ca." In *Donatello e i Suoi, Scultura fiorentina nel primo Rinascimento*. Eds. Alan Phipps Darr and Giorgio Bonsanti. Detroit, MI: Detroit Institute of Arts. Founders Society, and Milan: Arnoldo Mondadori Editori, 1986. Cat. Entry 92, 232–33.

Liska, James J. *The Semiotic of Myth*. Bloomington: Indiana University Press, 1989.

Lohr, Wolf-Dieter. "... e nuovi Omeri, e Plati ... Painted Characters in Portraits by Andrea del Sarto and Agnolo Bronzino." In *Poetry on Art: Renaissance to Romanticism*. Ed. Thomas Frangenberg. Donington: Shaun Tyas, 2003. 48–100. (personal typescript w. pagination: 1–43)

Lucian. "Essays in Portraiture." In *Ikones*. Trans. A.M. Harmon. 8 vols. London: William Heinemann Ltd., 1913.

_____. *Heracles: An Introduction*. Trans. A.M. Harmon. 8 vols. London: William Heinemann Ltd., 1929: 4: 62–67.

Lucrezio. *De rerum natura*. Ed. A. Schiesaro. Turin: Einaudi, 2003.

Liles, J.N. *The Art and Craft of Natural Dyeing: Traditional Recipes for Modern Use*. Knoxville: University of Tennessee Press, 2006.

MacGrath, Elizabeth. "'Il Senso Nostro.' The Medici Allegory Applied to Vasari's Mythological Frescoes in the Palazzo Vecchio." In *Giorgio Vasari tra decorazione e storiografia artistica*. Ed. G.C. Garfagnini. Florence: Olschki, 1985. 117–34.

Malaguzzi, Silvia. "Un amore senza fine." *Arte e Dossier* 17, no. 180 (July-August 2002), 33–37.

Mansfield, Harvey C. *Machiavelli Virtue*. Chicago, IL: University of Chicago Press, 1996.

Marot, Clément. Œuvres *complètes*. 2 vols. Ed. François Rigolot. Paris: G.F. Flammarion, 2009.

Martial [Marcus Valerius Martialis]. *Epigrams*. Ed. and trans. D.R. Shackleton Bailey. 3 vols. Cambridge, MA: Harvard University Press, 1993.

Martin, John Jeffries. "Renovatio and Reform in Early Modern Italy." In *Heresy, Culture, and Religion in Early Modern Italy: Contexts and Con-*

testations. Eds. Ronald K. Delph, M.M. Fontaine, and J.J. Martin. Sixteenth Century Essays & Studies, 76. Kirksville, MO: Truman State University Press, 2006. 1–18.

Matucci, Benedetta. "'Ornamentation symbolique': una rilettura del cenotafio Soderini di Benedetto da Rovezzano." *Artista. Critica dell'arte in Toscana* (2007), 74–109.

McComb, Arthur K. *Agnolo Bronzino: His Life and Works.* Cambridge, MA: Harvard University Press, 1928.

McCorquodale, Charles. *Bronzino.* New York: Harper & Row, 1981 (repr. 2005).

Mendelsohn, Leatrice. "L'Allegoria di Londra del Bronzino e la retorica del carnevale." In *Kunst des Cinquecento in der Toskana*, Italienische Forschungen, Kunsthistorisches Institut in Florenz, Band 17. Ed. M. Cämmerer. Munich: Bruckmann, 1992. 152–67.

_____. "Boccaccio, Betussi e Michelangelo: Ritratti delle donne illustri come 'Vite Parallele.'" In *Letteratura Italiana e Arti Figurative [Atti del XII Congresso, AISLII, Toronto, Ontario, May 1985].* Ed. A. Franceschetti. Florence: Olschki, 1988. 323–34.

_____. "Bronzino in Pesaro and After: The Impact of Raphael and Raphaelism on Bronzino's Florentine Manner." In *The Translation of Raphael's Roman Style*, ed. Henk Van Veen. Conference Proceedings from The Translation of Raphael's Roman Style in Groningen, The Netherlands, November 2002. Leuven: Peeters, 2007. 81–105.

_____. "Emblemi, Epigrammi e Statue: L'immagine di Eros Nella Pittura Del Cinquecento e La Diffusione Della Cultura Greca Nel Italia Del Nord." In *Storia della lingua e storia dell'arte in Italia: Dissimmetrie e intersezioni.* Atti del Terzo Convegno ASLI, Associazione per la storia della lingua italiana Roma, 30–31 maggio 2002. Eds. Vittorio Casale and Paolo D'Achille. Florence: F. Cesati, 2004: 125–97.

_____. "Der Florentiner Kreis—Michelangelos Sonett an Vittoria Colonna, Varchis *Lezzioni* und Bilder der Reformation (Catholic reform)." In *Vittoria Colonna, Dichterin und Muse Michelangelos.* Exhibition Kunsthistorisches Museum, Vienna, 1997. Catalogue. Ed. Sylvia Ferino-Pagden. Vienna: Skira, 1997. 265–73.

_____. "Madonna and Child with St. John in the Uffizi." Cat.Entry, in Falciani and Natali, *Bronzino: Painter and Poet at the Court of the Medici.* Florence: Mandragora, 2010.

_____. *Paragoni: Benedetto Varchi and Cinquecento Art Theory.* Ann Arbor, MI: UMI Research Press, 1982.

_____. "Restoration and Replication: Ancient Bronze Techniques and the Construction of the Figure in Cinquecento Painting." In C.C. Mattusch, A. Brauer, and S.E. Knudsen, *From the Parts to the Whole, Acta of the 13th International Bronze Congress, Cambridge Mass. May 29–June 1, 1996. The Journal of Roman Archaeology,* Supplement 39, no. 2 (2002), 273–85.

———. "Simultaneität und der *paragone*: Die Rechtfertigung der Kunst im Augedes Betrachters." Trans. from English by Hella Preimesberger. In *Im Agon der Künste. Paragonales Denken, ästhetische Praxis und die Diversität der Sinne,* Acts of the Conference, Berlin, 19–22 February 2001 at the Frei Universität. Ed. Ulrike Mueller Hofstede, Hannah Baader, Kristine Patz, and Nicola Suthor. Berlin: Fink, 2007. 294–335.

———. "The Sum of the Parts: Recycling Antiquities in the *Maniera* Workshops of Salviati and his Colleagues." *Atti del Convegno: Salviati ou 'La Bella Maniera,'* Academie de France a Rome, American Academy in Rome and l'École Française, 6 March 1998. Special issue of *Melanges de l'École Française* (2002), 107–48.

The Metamorphoses of Ovid. Ed. Allen Mandelbaum. New York: Harcourt Brace, 1995.

Miedema, Hessel. "The Term Emblema in Alciati." *Journal of the Warburg and Courtauld Institutes* 31 (1966), 234–44.

Miller, Clyde Lee. *Reading Cusanus: Metaphor and Dialectic in a Conjectural Universe.* Washington, DC: Catholic University Press, 2003.

Minor, Andrew Collier, and Bonner Mitchell. *Renaissance Entertainment: Festivities for the Marriage of Cosimo I. Duke of Florence, in 1539. An edition of the music, poetry, comedy, and descriptive account, with commentary by Andrew C. Minor and Bonner Mitchell.* Columbia: University of Missouri Press, 1968.

Monbeig Goguel, Catherine. "Francesco Salviati et la *Bella Maniera,* quelques points a revoir." In *Francesco Salviati et la Bella Maniera.* Eds. Catherine Monbeig Goguel, P. Costamagna, and M. Hochmann. Rome: École Française de Rome, 2001. 15–68.

Moore, Thomas. *The Planets Within: The Astrological Psychology of Marsilio Ficino.* New York: Lindisfarne Press, 1990.

Moreno, Paolo. *Genio Differente, alla scoperta della maniera antica.* Milan: Mondadori Electa, 2002.

———. *Lisippo: L'Arte e La Fortuna.* Rome: Fabbri, 1995.

Müller-Hofstadter, Ulrike. "Benedetto Varchi: 'principium factivum.' Der Anfang des Porträts und die Seele des Künstlers (1546)." In *Porträt. Geschichte der klassischen Bildgattungen in Quellentexten und Kommentaren.* Eds. Rudolf Preimesberger, Hannah Baader, and Nicola Suthor. 2 vols. Berlin: Georg Muller, 1999. 254–59.

———. "Grazia." In *Lexikon für Kunstwissenschaft.* Ed. Ulrich Pfisterer. Stuttgart and Weimar: Reclam Verlag, 2003. 132–36.

Murray, Jacqueline, ed. *Marriage in Premodern Europe: Italy and Beyond.* Toronto: CRRS, 2012.

Murry, Gregory William. *Monarchy and Sacral Politics in Duke Cosimo de' Medici's Florence*. Cambridge, MA: Harvard University Press, 2014.

Musacchio, Jacqueline Marie. "Imaginative Conceptions in Renaissance Italy." In *Picturing Women in Renaissance and Baroque Italy*. Eds. Geraldine A. Johnson and Sara F. Matthews Grieco. Cambridge: Cambridge University Press, 1997. 42–60.

Musée des Beaux-Arts. Nice. Le Bronzino. La Crucifixion. Exhibition Catalogue. Curator, Anne D'Evroye-Stiltz. Nice: Musée des Beaux-Arts Publication, 2011.

Najemy, John M. *A History of Florence 1200–1575*. Malden, MA: Blackwell, 2006.

Napolitano, Nocturno. *Opera nova amorosa de Nocturno Napolitano*. Milan: Jo. Jacobo et fratelli da Legnano, 1518.

Natali, Antonio. "I duchi e l'eucarestia. La cappella d'Eleonora di Toledo." In *Bronzino. Pittore e poeta alla corte dei Medici*. Eds. Antonio Natali and Carlo Falciani. Exhibition, Florence, Palazzo Strozzi, 24 September 2010–23 January 2011. Florence, Mandragora, 2010. 101–13.

Nesle, Solange de Mailly. *Astrology: History, Symbols and Signs*. Rochester, VT: Inner Traditions International, 1981.

Newman, Harold. *An Illustrated Dictionary of Jewelry*. London: Thames and Hudson, 1981.

Nickel, Helmut. "Two Falcon Devices of the Strozzi: An Attempt at Interpretation." *Metropolitan Museum Journal* 9 (1974), 229–32.

O'Malley, John W. *Religious Culture in the Sixteenth Century: Preaching, Rhetoric, Spirituality and Reform*. Varorium Collected Studies Series: CS404. Burlington, VT: Ashgate, 1993.

———. *Trent: What Happened at the Council*. London: The Belknap Press of Harvard University Press, 2013.

Onians, John. *Bearers of Meaning: The Classical Orders in Antiquity, the Middle Ages, and the Renaissance*. Princeton, NJ: Princeton University Press, 1988.

Pagel, Walter. "The Prime Matter of Paracelsus." *Ambix: The Journal of the Society for the Study of Alchemy and Early Chemistry* 9, no. 3 (1961), 117–35.

Paoletti, John T. "Michelangelo's Masks." *The Art Bulletin* 74, no. 3 (September 1992), 423–40.

Paolucci, Antonio. *Bronzino*. Florence: Giunti, 2002.

Patrick, J. Max, R.O. Evans, and J.W. Wallace, eds. *Attic & Baroque Prose Style: Essays by Morris W. Croll*. Princeton, NJ: Princeton University Press, 1969.

Payne, Alina A. *The Architectural Treatise in the Italian Renaissance: Architectural Invention, Ornament and Literary Culture*. Cambridge: Cambridge University Press, 1999.

_____. "Reclining Bodies: Figural Ornament in Renaissance Architecture." In *Body and Building: Essays on the Changing Relation of Body and Architecture*. Eds. George Dodds and R. Tavernor. Cambridge, MA: MIT Press, 2002. 94–113. Repr. in Michael W. Cole, *Sixteenth Century Italian Art*. Malden, MA: Blackwell Publishing Ltd., 2006.

Parker, Deborah. *Bronzino: Renaissance Painter as Poet*. Cambridge: Cambridge University Press, 2000.

Passerini, Luigi. *Genealogia e storia della famiglia Panciatichi*. Florence: Coi tipi di M. Cellini e C. alla Galileiana, 1858.

Pastoureau, Michel. *Traité de l'héraldique*. Paris: Picard, 1993.

Pelikan, Jaroslav. *Imago Dei: The Byzantine Apologia for Icons*. The A.W. Mellon Lectures in the Fine Arts, 1987, The National Gallery of Art, Washington, DC. Princeton NJ: Princeton University Press, 1990.

Petrarca, Francesco. *Petrarch's Lyric Poems: The Rime Sparse and Other Lyrics*. Trans. and ed. Robert M. Durling. Cambridge, MA: Harvard University Press, 1976.

Pilliod, Elizabeth. "Cosimo and the Arts." In *Florence*. Ed. Francis Ames-Lewis. Cambridge: Cambridge University Press, 2012. 330–73.

_____. "The Life of Bronzino." In *The Drawings of Bronzino*. Eds. Carmen C. Bambach, Janet Cox-Rearick, and George R. Goldner. New Haven, CT, and London: Yale University Press, 2010. 3–9.

_____. *Pontormo, Bronzino, Allori: A Genealogy of Florentine Art*. New Haven, CT, and London: Yale University Press, 2001.

Phillips, Claude. "An Unknown Bronzino." *The Burlington Magazine* 26 (1914–15), 3–4.

Pinelli, Antonio. *La bella maniera, Artisti del Cinquecento tra regola e licenza*. Turin: Giulio Einaudi editore, 1993.

Piovan, Francesco. "Gli studi padovani di Bartolomeo Panciatichi." *Quaderni per la storia dell'Università di Padova* 20, no, 11 (1987), 119–22.

Pitkin, Hanna Fenichel. *Fortune is a Woman*. Chicago, IL: The University of Chicago Press, 1987.

Plazzota, Carol. "Bronzino's Laura." *Burlington Magazine* 140 (April 1998), 251–63.

Pliny the Elder. *Natural History*, Eng. trans. by H. Rackham. Vol. IX, Bks. XXXIII–XXXV. Cambridge, MA: Harvard University Press, and London: William Heinemann, 1995.

Poggetto, P. Dal. "La diffusione del verbo raffaellesco: La Villa Imperiale; l'attività del Raffaellino del Colle." In *Pesaro nell'età dei Della Rovere*. Ed. Gido Arbizzoni, Antonio Brancati, and Maria Rosaria Valazzi. 3 vols. Venice: Marsilio, 1997–2001. 3:203–46.

Poliziano, Angelo. *Poesie italiane di messer Angelo Poliziano*. Milan: G. Silvestri, 1825.

Pope-Hennessy, Sir John. *The Portrait in the Renaissance*. Bollingen Series 30, Lecture 12, The National Gallery of Art, Washington, DC. Princeton, NJ: Princeton University Press, 1979.

Possevino, Antonio. *Tractatio de Poësi et Pictura ethnica, humana et fabulosa collata cum vera, honesta et sacra*. Lugduni: Apud Ioannem Pillehotte, 1595.

Praz, Mario. *Mnemosyne: The Parallel Between Literature and the Visual Arts*. Princeton, NJ: Princeton University Press, 1967.

_____. *Studies in Seventeenth Century Imagery*. 3 vols. London and Rome: Phaidon, 1941, 1947, and 1964.

Preimesberger, Rudolf. "'*The Face that is known draws the eyes of all spectators* ...' Leon Battista Alberti on the Impact of the Face in a Painting." In *The Renaissance Portrait from Donatello to Bellini*. Eds. Keith Christiansen and Stefan Weppelmann. Exhibition Catalogue. New York: The Metropolitan Museum of Art, 2011. 77–84.

Preimesberger, Rudolf, H. Baader, and N. Suthor, eds. *Porträt. Geschichte der klassischen Bildgattungen in Quellentexten und Kommentaren*. 2 vols. Berlin: Reimer, 1999.

Procaccioli, Paolo. "Cinquecento capriccioso e irregolare. Dei lettori di Luciano e di Erasmo; di Aretino e Doni; di altri peregrini ingegno." In *Cinquecento capriccioso e irregolare. Eresie letterarie nell'Italia del classicismo*. Eds. Paolo Procaccioli and Romano Angelo. Manziana (Rome): Vecchiarelli, 1999. 5–30.

Prosperi, Valentina. *Di soavi licor gli orli del vaso. La fortuna di Lucrezio dall'Umanesimo sino alla Controriforma*. Turin: Aragno Editore, 2004.

The Pythagorean Sourcebook and Library. Trans. Kenneth Sylvan Guthrie. Ed. And intro. David Fideler. Grand Rapids, MI: Phanes Press, 1988.

Quintilian. The *'Institutio Oratoria' of Quintilian*. Latin and English trans. By H.E. Butler. Cambridge, MA: Harvard University Press, 1922. Repr. 1966. Vol. III, Bks. VII–IX.

Richelson, Paul William. *Studies in the Personal Imagery of Cosimo I de' Medici, Duke of Florence*. New York: Garland Dissertation Publishing, 1978.

Ripa, Cesare. *Iconologia*. Rome: Giovanni Gigliotti, 1593.

_____. *Iconologia*. Rome: Lepido Facii, 1603.

Robertson, Claire. "Annibale Caro as Iconographer Sources and Method." *Journal of the Warburg and Courtauld Institutes* 45 (1982), 160–81.

_____. *Il Grande Cardinale*. New Haven, CT: Yale University Press, 1992.

Robortelli, Francisci. *Utinensis in librum Aristotelis De arte poetica explicationes*. Basel: n.p., 1555.

Roob, Alexander. *The Hermetic Museum: Alchemy and Mysticism* Cologne: Taschen, 1997.

Rosetti, Gioanventura. *Notandissimi secreti de l'arte profumatoria: per far ogli, acque, paste, balle, moscardini, vccelletti, paternostri, e tutta l'arte intiera,*

548   Bibliography

come si ricerca, cosi nella città di Napoli del Reame, come in Roma, e quini in la città di Vinegia nuouamente ristampati. Venice, 1560.

Rosselli Dell Turco, Niccolò, and F. Salvi, eds. *Bartolomeo Ammannati, scultore e architetto, 1511–1592.* Florence: Alinea editrice, 1995.

Rossi, Massimiliano. "Artisti e discorsi sull'arte nei *Marmi.*" In *I Marmi di Anton Francesco Doni: la storia, i generi e le arti.* Ed. Giovanna Rizzarelli. Mangiar libri e inghiottire scritture. Florence: Olschki, 2012. 311–29.

_____. "… quella naturalità e fiorentinità (per dir così), Bronzino: lingua, carne e pittura." In *Bronzino. Pittore e poeta alla corte dei Medici.* Eds. Antonio Natali and Carlo Falciani. Exhibition, Florence, Palazzo Strozzi, 24 September 2010–23 January 2011. Florence, Mandragora, 2010. 177–93.

Rubin, Patricia. "Contemplating Fragments of Ancient Marbles: Sitters and Statues in Sixteenth-Century Portraits." *La Revue d'histoire de l'art de l'Académie de France à Rome: Studiolo* 4 (2006), 17–39.

Ruvoldt, Maria. "Michelangelo's Slaves and the Gift of Liberty." In *Renaissance Quarterly* 65, no. 4 (2012), 1029–59.

Sangiorgio, F., ed. *Documenti Urbinati, Inventari del Palazzo Ducale (1582–1631)* Urbino: Accademia Raffaello, 1976.

Sassoferrato, Olympo de. *Parthenia. Pegasea. Olimpia. Nova Phenice. Gloria d'amore. Linguaccio Aurora. Ardelia.* Venice, 1538–39.

Saulnier, V.-L. *Maurice Scève,* 2 vols. Paris: Klincksieck, 1948.

Saunders, Alison. *The Sixteenth-Century Blason Poétique.* Berne: Peter Lang, 1981.

Sawday, Jonathan. *The Body Emblazoned: Dissection and the Human Body in Renaissance Culture.* London and New York: Routledge, 1995.

Schulze, Hans. *Die Werke Angelo Bronzinos.* Strassburg: Heitz, 1911.

Scorza, R.A. "Vincenzo Borghi and Invenzione: The Florentine Apparato of 1565." *Journal of the Warburg and Courtauld Institutes* 44 (1981), 57–75.

Sears, Jayne. "Ficino and the Platonism of the English Renaissance." *Comparative Literature* 4 (Summer 1952), 214–38.

Seidel, Silvana Menchi. "Alcuni Atteggiamenti della cultura Italiana di fronte a Erasmo." In *Eresia e Riforma nell' Italia del Cinquecento, Miscellanea I.* DeKalb: Northern Illinois University Press, Chicago: The Newberry Library, and Florence: Sansoni, 1974. 71–133.

_____. *Erasmo in Italia, 1520–1580.* Turin: Bollati Boringhieri, 1987.

Seznec, Jean. *The Survival of the Pagan Gods.* New York: Harper and Row Publishers, 1961.

Sframeli, Maria. *I gioielli dei Medici dal vero e in ritratto.* Livorno: Sillabe, 2003.

Shearman, John. *Mannerism.* Baltimore: Penguin Books, 1967.

Simmons, Lawrence. "The Monument to Ornament: Michelangelo's Moses." *Interstices: A Journal of Architecture and Related Arts*. Sydney, Australia: University of Technology (UTS), n.d. <http://www.interstices. auckland.ac.nz/i4/thehtml/papers/simmons/main.htm>.

Simoncelli, Paolo. *Evangelismo italiano del Cinquecento: questione religiosa e nicodemismo politico*. Rome: Istituto storico italiano per l'èra moderna e contemporanea, 1979.

_____. *La Lingua di Adamo:Guillaume Postel, tra accademici e fuorosciti fiorentini*. Florence: Olschki, 1934.

_____. "Florentine *Fuorusciti* at the Time of Bindo Altoviti." In *Raphael, Cellini and a Florentine Banker, The Patronage of Bindo Altoviti*. Eds. A. Chong, D. Pegazzano, and D. Zikos. Exhibition Catalogue for Boston, Isabella Stewart Museum of Art. Milan: Mondadori Electra, 2003. 285–328.

_____. "Republicani fiorentini in esilio nuove testimonianze (1538–1541)." In *Renaissance Studies in Honor of Craig Hugh Smyth*. Ed. Andrew Morrogh, 2 vols. Florence: Giunti Barbera, 1985. 1:217–29.

_____. "The Turbulent Life of the Florentine Community in Venice." In *Heresy. Culture and Religion in Early Modern Italy: Context and Contestations*. Ed. Ronald K. Delph, M.M. Fontaine, and J.J. Martin. Sixteenth Century Essays & Studies Series, 76, 113–33. Kirksville, MO: Truman State University Press, 2006.

Spencer, John R. "*Ut Rhetorica Pictura*: A Study in Quattrocento Theory of Painting." *Journal of the Warburg and Courtauld Institutes* 20 (1957), 26–44.

Smyth, Carolyn. "An Instance of Feminine Patronage." In *Women and Art in Early Modern Europe. Patrons, Collectors, and Connoisseurs*. Ed. Cynthia Lawrence. University Park: Pennsylvania State University Press, 1997.

Smith, Graham. "Bronzino and Dürer." *The Burlington Magazine* 895 (1977), 709–10.

_____. "Bronzino's *Allegory of Happiness*." *The Art Bulletin*, 66, no. 3 (September 1984), 390–99.

_____. "Bronzino's Holy Family in Vienna: A Note on the Identity of Its Patron." *Source: Notes in the History of Art* 2, no. 1 (1982), 21–25.

_____. "Bronzino's *Portrait of Laura Battiferri*." *Source: Notes in the History of Art* 15, no. 4 (1996), 30–38.

Smyth, Craig H. *Bronzino as Draughtsman; An Introduction, with Notes on his Portraiture and Tapestries,* Locust Valle, NY: J.J. Augustin, 1971.

_____. *Mannerism and Maniera*. Locust Valley, NY: J.J. Augustin 1962, 2nd ed. Vienna: IRSA, 1992.

_____. "On Dosso Dossi at Pesaro." In *Dosso's Fate: Painting and Court Culture in Renaissance Italy*. Eds. Luisa Ciammitti, S.F. Ostrow, and S. Settis, 241–62. Los Angeles: The Getty Research Institute for the History of Art and the Humanities: Issues & Debates, 1998.

Sohm, Philip. *Style in the Art Theory of Early Modern Italy*. New York, Cambridge University Press, 2001.

Spini, Giorgio. *Cosimo I e la indipendenza del' principato mediceo*. Florence: Vallechi editore, 1980.

Stafford, Emma. *Herakles*. New York: Routledge, 2012.

Strehlke, Carl Brandon. *Pontormo, Bronzino, and the Medici: the transformation of the Renaissance portrait in Florence*; with essays by Elizabeth Cropper [et al.] Philadelphia: Philadelphia Museum of Art in association with Pennsylvania State University Press, 2004.

Strinati Claudio. *Bronzino*. Rome: Viviani Editore, 2010.

Summers, David. *The Judgment of Sense*. New York: Cambridge University Press, 1987.

_____. "Maniera and Movement: The *Figura Serpentinata*." *Art Quarterly* 35 (1972), 209–311.

_____. *Michelangelo and the Language of Art*. Princeton, NJ: Princeton University Press, 1982.

_____. "Michelangelo on Architecture." *The Art Bulletin* 54 (1972), 146–57.

Syson, Luke, and D. Thornton. *Objects of Virtue: Art in Renaissance Italy*. Exhibition Catalogue, J. Paul Getty Museum. Los Angeles, CA: Getty Publications, 2001.

Tanturli, Giuliano. "Formazione d'un codice e d'un canzoniere: "Delle Rime del Bronzino pittore libro primo." *Studi di filologia italiana* 62 (2004), 195–224.

Tervarent, Guy de. *Attributs et symbols dans l'art profane, 1450–1600*. Geneva: Droz, 1959.

_____. "Veritas and Justitia Triumphant." *Journal of the Warburg and Courtauld Institutes* 7 (1944), 95–101.

Thoenes, Christof, ed. *Sebastiano Serlio, Architettura civile, Libri settimo e ottavo nei manoscritti di Monaco e Vienna*. Milan: Il Polifilo, 1994.

Tillander, Herbert. *Diamond Cuts in Historic Jewellery 1381–1910*. London: Art Books International, 1995.

Tinti, Mario. "Agnolo Bronzino pittore 'platonico.'" *Dedalo*, I. n.p, 1920–21. 1–14.

_____. ed. *Bronzino*. Florence: Fratelli Alinari, 1927.

Toscan, Jean de. *Le carnaval du langage, Le lexique erotique des Poètes de l'équivoque de Burchiello a Marino (XVᵉ–XVIIᵉ siècles)*. 4 vols. Lille: Reproduction des thèse Université de Lille, 1981.

Tzartes, Maurizia Tzartes. *Bronzino*. Milano: Rizzoli Skira, 2003.

_____. *Il "ghiribizzoso" Pontormo*. Florence: Polistampa, 2008.

Varchi, Benedetto. *Due Lezzioni*. Florence: Ap. L. Torrentino. 1549.

_____. *L'Ercolano*. editio princeps, Florence: Giunti, 1570.

_____. *L'Ercolano Dialogo Di Benedetto Varchi: Dove Si Ragiona Delle Lingue in Paticolare Della Toscana Fiorentina, con la Correzione di Lodovico Castelvetro Girolamo Muzio, note di G. Bottari e G.A.Volpi.* Ed. rivedata e illustrata da Pietro dal Rio. Florence: L'Agenzia Libraria, 1846, facsimile of original MS 1 July 1914. Repr. n.d.c. 2012.

_____. "Lezzioni della maggioranza delle arti." In Paola Barocchi, *Trattati d'Arte del Cinquecento, fra manierismo e contrariforma.* 3 vols. Bari: Laterza, 1960–62. 1:3–82.

_____. "Lezzione di M. Benedetto Varchi nell'Accademia di Padova sopra un sonetto del Casa e sulla gelosia." In *L'Opere di Benedetto Varchi*. 2 vols. Trieste: Lloyd Austriaco, 1858–59. 2:570–82.

_____. *La prima parte delle Lezzioni di M. Benedetto Varchi, nella quale si tratta della Natura, Della Generazione del corpo humano e de' mostri: lette da lui publicamente nella Academia Fiorentina.* Florence, 1560.

_____. "Sopra l'Invidia. Lezione una al molto illustre e molto reverendo Mons. De' Rossi vescovo di Pavia Signor suo Oservandissimo" (MS Corsiniano, publicato per la prima volta dal prof. Luigi Maria Rezzi). In *L'Opere di Benedetto Varchi*. 2 vols. Trieste: Lloyd Austriaco, 1858–59. 2:582–85.

Vasari, Giorgio. *Le Vite* ... Ed. Gaetano Milanese. 9 vols. Florence 1878. Repr. Florence: Sansoni, 1970–74.

_____. *Le Vite de' più eccellenti Pittori Scultori e Architettori nelle redazioni del 1550 e 1568.* Ed. Rosanna Bettarini and Paola Barocchi. Florence: Sansoni. 1966–87.

_____. *Le Vite de'più eccellenti Pittori Scultori e Architettori, scritta da M. Giorgio Vasari, pittore et architetto aretino, con i ritratti loro et con l'aggiunta dei viti de' vivi & dei morti dallánno 1550, infino al 1567.* 2 vols. in 3. Florence: Giunti, 1568.

Valeriano, Giovanni Pierio. *I Ieroglifici overo Commentarii delle occulte significationi degl'Egittij, & Altre Nationi.* Venice: Gio Battista Combi, 1627.

Vesalius, Andreas. *De humani corporis fabrica.* Basel, 1555.

_____. *The Epitome of Andreas Vesalius.* Trans. L.R. Lind, with anatomical notes by C.W. Asling and foreword by Logan Clendening. New York: Macmillan, 1949.

_____. *On the Fabric of the Human Body: An Annotated Translation of the 1543 and 1555 Editions of Andreas Vesalius' De Humani Corporis Fabrica.* Ed. and trans. Daniel Garrison and Malcolm Hast. Historical Introduction by Vivian Nutton. <http://vesalius.northwestern.edu>.

Via, Claudia Cieri. *Le Favole Antique: Produzione e Committenza a Roma nel Cinquecento.* Rome: Bagatto Libri, 1996.

Vita, Alessandro del., ed. *Il libro delle ricordanze di Giorgio Vasari.* Arezzo: R. Istituto di Archeologia e Storia dell'Arte, 1938.

_____, ed. *Lo Zibaldone di Giorgio Vasari*. Rome: Arezzo: Zelli, 1938.

Vitale, Enrico, ed. *Marsilio Ficino: Teologia Platonica*. Milan: Bompiani, 2011.

Vitruvius. *The Ten Books of Architecture*. Ed. E.H. Warmington. Trans. Frank Granger. 2 vols. Cambridge, MA: Harvard University Press, 1975.

_____. *The Ten Books of Architecture*. Trans. M.H. Morgan. New York: Dover Publications, 1960.

Volpi, Catherina, ed. *Le immagini degli dèi di Vincenzo Cartari*. Rome: De Luca, 1996.

Voragine, Jacobus de. *The Golden Legend: Readings on the Saints*. 2 vols. Trans. William Granger Ryan. Princeton, NJ: Princeton University Press, 1993.

Vos, Alvin, ed. *Place and Displacement in the Renaissance*. Conference Procedings, Papers from the 25th Annual CEMERS Conference, State University of New York at Binghamton. Binghamton, NY: Center for Medieval and Early Renaissance Studies, 1995.

Walker, D.P. *Spiritual and Demonic Magic: From Ficino to Campanella*. University Park: Pennsylvania State University Press, 2000.

Warburg, Aby. *The Renewal of Pagan Antiquity: Contributions to the Cultural History of the European Renaissance*. Los Angeles, CA: The Getty Research Institute, 1999.

Ward, Michael. "Benedetto Varchi and the Social Dimension of Language." *Italica* 68, no. 2 (1991), 176–94.

Watt, Mary A. "*Veni, sponsa*: Love and Politics at the Wedding of Eleonora di Toledo." In *The Cultural World of Eleanora di Toledo, Duchess of Florence and Siena*. Ed. Konrad Eisenbichler. Burlington, VT: Ashgate, 2004. 28–39.

Watson, Rowan. "Book of Hours (The Eleanor of Toledo Hours), Use of Rome, in Latin." In *Western Illuminated Manuscripts*. 2 vols. London: V & A Publishing, 2011. 2:851–57.

_____. "Manual of Dynastic History or Devotional Aid? Eleanor of Toledo's Book of Hours." In *Excavating the Medieval Image: Manuscripts, Artists, Audiences: Essays in Honor of Sandra Hindman*. Eds. David S. Areford and Nina A. Rowe. Aldershot: Ashgate, 2004. 179–95.

Wildmoser, Rudolf. "Das Bildnis des Ugolino Martelli von Agnolo Bronzino." *Jahrbuch der Berliner Museen* 31 (1989), 181–214.

Wilkinson, Richard H. *Symbol and Magic in Spiritual Art*. London: Thames and Hudson, 1994.

Wire, Antionette Clark. *The Corinthian Women Prophets: A Reconstruction Through Paul's Rhetoric*. Minneapolis: Fortress Press, 1995.

Wohl, Helmut. *The Aesthetics of Italian Renaissance Art: A Reconsideration of Style*. New York and Cambridge: Cambridge University Press, 1999.

Zaccaria, Vittorio. "La fortuna del 'De Mulieribus claris' del Boccaccio nel secolo XV: Giovanni Sabbadino degli Arienti, Jacopo Filippo Foresti e le lore biografie femminili (1490–1497)." In *Il Boccaccio nelle culture e letterature nazionali*. Ed. F. Mazzoni. Florence: Olschki, 1978. 519–45.

Zanrè, Domenico. *Cultural Non-Conformity in Early Modern Florence*. Burlington, VT: Ashgate, 2004.

_____. "Ritual and Parody in Mid-Cinquecento Florence: Cosimo de' Medici and the Accademia del Piano." In *The Cultural Politics of Duke Cosimo I de' Medici*. Ed. Konrad Eisenbichler. Burlington, VT: Ashgate, 2001. 189–204.

Zerner, Henri. *The School of Fontainebleau, graveures*. Trans. from French by S. Baron. New York: Harry Abrams, 1969.

Zimmerman, T.C. *Paolo Giovio: The Historian and the Crisis of Sixteen-Century Italy*. Princeton, NJ: Princeton University Press, 1995.

Contributors

Elena Aloia, from Perugia, Umbria, Italy, received her classical training in History of Art and Sciences at the Università degli Studi di Perugia and received her degree in 2006. Her thesis focused on a discovered and restored fourteenth-century fresco of the Umbrian school, located in her great-grandfather's home in Perugia. In 2010, she obtained an M.A. in Art History with honors. Professor Antonio Natali, Director of the Uffizi Gallery in Florence, directed her thesis on *I Panciatichi*. She is presently an official tour guide for the Umbria Region and is collaborating with private companies that manage museums and exhibitions in this area. Her interests are in pursuing further studies on the cultural aspects of Perugia and collections of Italian Renaissance art.

Donna A. Bilak has a Master's degree in History from York University and holds a Ph.D. from the Bard Graduate Center: Decorative Arts, Design History, and Material Culture in New York City. She is presently the Edelstein Postdoctoral Fellow at the Chemical Heritage Foundation in Philadelphia (2013–14). Prior to graduate school, she was a jewelry designer and wax-model maker in Toronto's jewelry industry. Dr. Bilak's research interests encompass early modern history of science and alchemy, emblem culture, and nineteenth-century jewelry history and technology.

Lynette M. F. Bosch is a professor of Art History at State University of New York College (SUNY) at Geneseo. She has a Ph.D. from Princeton University. Her books include: *Art, Liturgy and Legend in Renaissance Toledo*, which was awarded the ASHAS Eleanor Tufts

Prize (2001); *Cuban-American Art in Miami*; and *Ernesto Barreda: Contemporary Chilean Painter*. She has published articles on Michelangelo, Bronzino, Bomarzo, and Spanish illuminated manuscripts. She has forthcoming *Life Streams: The Cuban and American Art of Alberto Rey* and is working on a book-length study of Mannerism.

Liana De Girolami Cheney (Editor), presently Investigadora de Historia del Arte, SIELAE, Universidad de Coruña, Spain. Dr. Cheney received her B.S./B.A. in Psychology and Philosophy from the University of Miami, Florida, her M.A. in History of Art and Aesthetics from the University of Miami, Florida, and her Ph.D. in Italian Renaissance and Baroque from Boston University in Massachussetts. Dr. Cheney is a Renaissance and Mannerist scholar, author, and co-author of numerous articles and books, including: *Botticelli's Neoplatonic Images*; *Neoplatonism and the Arts*; *Neoplatonic Aesthetics in Literature, Music and the Visual Arts*; *The Paintings of the Casa Vasari*; *Readings in Italian Mannerism*; *The Homes of Giorgio Vasari* (English and Italian); *Self-Portraits of Women Painters* (SECAC Scholarship Award 2005); *Giorgio Vasari's Teachers: Sacred and Profane Love*; *Giuseppe Arcimboldo: The Magic Paintings* (French and German); *Giorgio Vasari's Life and Lives: The First Art Historian by Einar Rud*; *Giorgio Vasari: pennello, pluma e ardore*; *Giorgio Vasari's Prefaces: Art and Theory*; *Giorgio Vasari's Artistic and Emblematic Manifestations*; and *Giorgio Vasari in Context*. Her forthcoming book is on *Readings in Italian Mannerism II: Architecture and Sculpture*.

Michael J. Giordano is a professor of French and director of the Ph.D. program in modern languages in the Department of Classical and Modern Languages, Literatures, and Cultures, Wayne State University, Detroit. His fields of specialization are French Renaissance and Baroque Literature and Culture and the European emblem. He is the author of *The Art of Meditation and the French Renaissance Love Lyric: The Poetics of Introspection in Maurice Scève's 'Délie object de plus haulte vertu' (1544)* (2010). His most recent article is "Sexualité cosmique et apocalypse du sujet amoureux," in *Maurice Scève ou l'emblème de la perfection enchevêtrée*, ed. Bruno Roger-Vasselin (2012). In press is "Une comparaison entre *Le Moyen de parvenir* de Béroalde de Verville et *Tristram Shandy* de Laurence Sterne," and a recent grant has accelerated progress on a book titled *The French Anatomical Blazon and Its Cultural Correlates: Italian Models, Emblematics, Descriptive Anatomy, Mannerism, and Nominalism.* He is a member of the International Advisory Board of the Society for Emblem Studies.

Thomas MacPherson received a B.A. from the State University of New York College (SUNY)–Oswego in 1973 and an M.F.A. from the University of South Carolina in 1976. His work has been exhibited in solo and juried-group national and international exhibitions in galleries and museums in the United States and abroad. He has been a professor of Studio Art at the SUNY at Geneseo since 1985 and attained the rank of professor in 2003. In the summer of 2007, he received a Mid-Career Summer Research Fellowship to study egg tempera painting in Italy.

Leatrice Mendelsohn received her A.B. in Art History from Vassar College and an M.A. and Ph.D. in Art History from the Institute of Fine Arts of New York University. She taught Renaissance art at graduate and undergraduate level in the United State, Canada, and Italy. She received numerous prestigious scholarships and awards, from the Samuel Kress Foundation, the Gladys Kreibel Delmas Foundation, the Folger Shakespeare Library, and the National Endowment for the Humanities at the Villa I Tatti, among others. A Mannerist scholar, her numerous publications focus on the art and theory of Agnolo Bronzino, Francesco Salviati, Michelangelo, and Giorgio Vasari. Her seminal work on Benedetto Varchi's *Due Lezzione* remains an invaluable study on Cinquecento art theory. Her current project is a study of the *paragone* and the ideal woman in early twentieth-century France.

Massimiliano Rossi graduated with honors in the Department of Modern Letters at the University of Pisa in 1988 and obtained a Ph.D. from the Scuola Normale Superiore of Pisa in 1992. He has received several scholarships: Art History and Modern Letters from the Scuola Normale Superiore of Pisa in 1981; Fondazione Bernard Berenson of Villa I Tatti, The Harvard University Center for Italian Renaissance Studies of Florence in 1992; and J. Paul Getty Postdoctoral Fellowship in the History of Art and the Humanities in 1996. He was a research associate at Villa I Tatti (1998–2003) and taught history of art criticism at University of Florence (2008–13). Since 1998, he has been an associate professor of "Museologia e storia della critica d'arte" at the University of Salento in Lecce, and since July 2003 he has been full professor in the Faculty of "Beni Culturali" (Cultural Heritage) of the University of Salento where he still teaches Art Criticism and The Art of Collecting. He has contributed essays for several exhibition catalogues, among them *Un'altra bellezza. Francesco Furini* (Florence, 2007–08), *Firenze 1640* (Florence, 2008–09); *Galileo e le Arti* (Pisa 2010–11); and *Agnolo Bronzino* (Florence, 2010–11).

Index